The post-2015 Sustainable Development Agenda focuses on a more effective design, financing and management of infrastructure within a multi-level world, where local institutions interact with global financial markets. This volume provides an excellent basis for additional research and policy making.

Ehtisham Ahmad, *London School of Economics*

This splendid collection of essays describes and assesses both the basic principles of the decentralized provision of infrastructure and offers several illuminating case studies. It's an essential work on this issue.

Wallace E. Oates, *Distinguished University Professor, Emeritus, University of Maryland*

In a more complex and interlinked world, coordination problems among countries and among governments in federations become increasingly difficult. These difficulties become especially pronounced in building infrastructures. This book makes a much welcome and useful contribution to this important issue.

Vito Tanzi, *former Director of Fiscal Affairs Department, IMF*

This book represents a very timely and useful contribution to the decentralization and infrastructure literatures. With its focus on sustainable growth and improved equity the book provides practical and very useful recommendations to national and sub-national policy makers.

Teresa Ter-Minassian, *former Director of Fiscal Affairs Department, IMF*

Local infrastructure is a crucial input into economic development in poorer countries. In this valuable collection, a distinguished team of experts and practitioners offer lessons and insights from recent practice.

Daniel Treisman, *Professor of Political Science, UCLA*

Decentralization and Infrastructure in the Global Economy

The subnational dimension of infrastructure has emerged as one of the greatest challenges in contemporary public finance policy and management. Ensuring the efficient provision of infrastructure represents a challenge for all countries irrespective of their level of centralization or decentralization. This book proposes an innovative approach for the strengthening of decentralized public investment and infrastructure management.

Decentralization and Infrastructure in the Global Economy: From Gaps to Solutions covers the most important aspects of infrastructure investment in a decentralized setting. It discusses infrastructure gaps and the quality of subnational spending; how functional responsibilities, financing, and equalization can be designed; sector-specific arrangements in high expenditure areas, such as health education, and roads; key steps of the public investment cycle and management; and analyzes the political economy and corruption challenges that typically accompany decentralized infrastructure projects.

This book challenges some of the well-accepted principles of intergovernmental fiscal relations and will be useful to researchers and practitioners of public finance policy and management.

Jonas Frank is Senior Public Sector Management Specialist, Governance Global Practice, World Bank, Washington, DC.

Jorge Martínez-Vázquez is Regents Professor of Economics and Director of the International Center for Public Policy, Andrew Young School of Policy Studies, Georgia State University in Atlanta.

Routledge studies in the modern world economy

1 **Interest Rates and Budget Deficits**
A study of the advanced economies
Kanhaya L. Gupta and Bakhtiar Moazzami

2 **World Trade after the Uruguay Round**
Prospects and policy options for the twenty-first century
Edited by Harald Sander and András Inotai

3 **The Flow Analysis of Labour Markets**
Edited by Ronald Schettkat

4 **Inflation and Unemployment**
Contributions to a new macroeconomic approach
Edited by Alvaro Cencini and Mauro Baranzini

5 **Macroeconomic Dimensions of Public Finance**
Essays in honour of Vito Tanzi
Edited by Mario I. Blejer and Teresa M. Ter-Minassian

6 **Fiscal Policy and Economic Reforms**
Essays in honour of Vito Tanzi
Edited by Mario I. Blejer and Teresa M. Ter-Minassian

7 **Competition Policy in the Global Economy**
Modalities for co-operation
Edited by Leonard Waverman, William S. Comanor and Akira Goto

8 **Working in the Macro Economy**
A study of the US labor market
Martin F. J. Prachowny

9 **How Does Privatization Work?**
Edited by Anthony Bennett

10 **The Economics and Politics of International Trade**
Freedom and trade: volume II
Edited by Gary Cook

11 **The Legal and Moral Aspects of International Trade**
Freedom and trade: volume III
Edited by Asif Qureshi, Hillel Steiner and Geraint Parry

12 **Capital Markets and Corporate Governance in Japan, Germany and the United States**
Organizational response to market inefficiencies
Helmut M. Dietl

13 **Competition and Trade Policies**
Coherence or conflict
Edited by Einar Hope

14 **Rice**
The primary commodity
A. J. H. Latham

15 **Trade, Theory and Econometrics**
Essays in honour of John S. Chipman
Edited by James C. Moore, Raymond Riezman and James R. Melvin

16 **Who Benefits from Privatisation?**
Edited by Moazzem Hossain and Justin Malbon

17 **Towards a Fair Global Labour Market**
Avoiding the new slave trade
Ozay Mehmet, Errol Mendes and Robert Sinding

18 **Models of Futures Markets**
Edited by Barry Goss

19 **Venture Capital Investment**
An agency analysis of UK practice
Gavin C. Reid

20 **Macroeconomic Forecasting**
A sociological appraisal
Robert Evans

21 **Multimedia and Regional Economic Restructuring**
Edited by Hans-Joachim Braczyk, Gerhard Fuchs and Hans-Georg Wolf

22 **The New Industrial Geography**
Regions, regulation and institutions
Edited by Trevor J. Barnes and Meric S. Gertler

23 **The Employment Impact of Innovation**
Evidence and policy
Edited by Marco Vivarelli and Mario Pianta

24 **International Health Care Reform**
A legal, economic and political analysis
Colleen Flood

25 **Competition Policy Analysis**
Edited by Einar Hope

26 **Culture and Enterprise**
The development, representation and morality of business
Don Lavoie and Emily Chamlee-Wright

27 **Global Financial Crises and Reforms**
Cases and caveats
B. N. Ghosh

28 **Geography of Production and Economic Integration**
Miroslav N. Jovanović

29 **Technology, Trade and Growth in OECD Countries**
Does specialisation matter?
Valentina Meliciani

30 **Post-Industrial Labour Markets**
Profiles of North America and Scandinavia
Edited by Thomas P. Boje and Bengt Furaker

31 **Capital Flows without Crisis**
Reconciling capital mobility and economic stability
Edited by Dipak Dasgupta, Marc Uzan and Dominic Wilson

32 International Trade and National Welfare
Murray C. Kemp

33 Global Trading Systems at Crossroads
A post-Seattle perspective
Dilip K. Das

34 The Economics and Management of Technological Diversification
Edited by John Cantwell, Alfonso Gambardella and Ove Granstrand

35 Before and Beyond EMU
Historical lessons and future prospects
Edited by Patrick Crowley

36 Fiscal Decentralization
Ehtisham Ahmad and Vito Tanzi

37 Regionalisation of Globalised Innovation
Locations for advanced industrial development and disparities in participation
Edited by Ulrich Hilpert

38 Gold and the Modern World Economy
Edited by MoonJoong Tcha

39 Global Economic Institutions
Willem Molle

40 Global Governance and Financial Crises
Edited by Meghnad Desai and Yahia Said

41 Linking Local and Global Economies
The ties that bind
Edited by Carlo Pietrobelli and Arni Sverrisson

42 Tax Systems and Tax Reforms in Europe
Edited by Luigi Bernardi and Paola Profeta

43 Trade Liberalization and APEC
Edited by Jiro Okamoto

44 Fiscal Deficits in the Pacific Region
Edited by Akira Kohsaka

45 Financial Globalization and the Emerging Market Economies
Dilip K. Das

46 International Labor Mobility
Unemployment and increasing returns to scale
Bharati Basu

47 Good Governance in the Era of Global Neoliberalism
Conflict and depolitization in Latin America, Eastern Europe, Asia and Africa
Edited by Jolle Demmers, Alex E. Fernández Jilberto and Barbara Hogenboom

48 The International Trade System
Alice Landau

49 International Perspectives on Temporary Work and Workers
Edited by John Burgess and Julia Connell

50 Working Time and Workers' Preferences in Industrialized Countries
Finding the balance
Edited by Jon C. Messenger

68 **Globalization and Regional Integration**
The origins, development and impact of the single European aviation market
Alan Dobson

69 **Russia Moves into the Global Economy**
Breaking out
John M. Letiche

70 **The European Economy in an American Mirror**
Barry Eichengreen, Michael Landesmann and Dieter Stiefel

71 **Working Time Around the World**
Trends in working hours, laws, and policies in a global comparative perspective
Jon C. Messenger, Sangheon Lee and Deidre McCann

72 **International Water Treaties**
Negotiation and cooperation along transboundary rivers
Shlomi Dinar

73 **Economic Integration in the Americas**
Edited by Joseph A. McKinney and H. Stephen Gardner

74 **Expanding Frontiers of Global Trade Rules**
The political economy dynamics of the international trading system
Nitya Nanda

75 **The Macroeconomics of Global Imbalances**
European and Asian perspectives
Edited by Marc Uzan

76 **China and Asia**
Economic and financial interactions
Edited by Yin-Wong Cheung and Kar-Yiu Wong

77 **Regional Inequality in China**
Trends, explanations and policy responses
Edited by Shenggen Fan, Ravi Kanbur and Xiaobo Zhang

78 **Governing Rapid Growth in China**
Equity and institutions
Edited by Ravi Kanbur and Xiaobo Zhang

79 **The Indonesian Labour Market**
Shafiq Dhanani, Iyanatul Islam and Anis Chowdhury

80 **Cost-Benefit Analysis in Multi-level Government in Europe and the USA**
The case of EU cohesion policy and of US federal investment policies
Alessandro Ferrara

81 **The Economic Geography of Air Transportation**
Space, time, and the freedom of the sky
John Bowen

82 **Cartelization, Antitrust and Globalization in the US and Europe**
Mark LeClair

83 **The Political Economy of Integration**
Jeffrey Cason

84 **Critical Issues in Air Transport Economics and Business**
Rosario Macario and Eddy Van de Voorde

85 **Financial Liberalisation and Economic Performance**
Luiz Fernando de Paula

86 **A General Theory of Institutional Change**
Shiping Tang

87 **The Dynamics of Asian Financial Integration**
Edited by Michael Devereux, Philip Lane, Park Cyn-young and Wei Shang-jin

88 **Innovative Fiscal Policy and Economic Development in Transition Economies**
Aleksandr Gevorkyan

89 **Foreign Direct Investments in Asia**
Edited by Chalongphob Sussangkarn, Yung Chul Park and Sung Jin Kang

90 **Time Zones, Communications Networks, and International Trade**
Toru Kikuchi

91 **Miraculous Growth and Stagnation in Post-War Japan**
Edited by Koichi Hamada, Keijiro Otsuka, Gustav Ranis, and Ken Togo

92 **Multilateralism and Regionalism in Global Economic Governance**
Trade, investment and finance
Edited by Junji Nakagawa

93 **Economic Growth and Income Inequality in China, India and Singapore**
Trends and policy implications
Pundarik Mukhopadhaya, G. Shantakumar and Bhanoji Rao

94 **Foreign Direct Investment in China**
Spillover effects on domestic enterprises
Deng Ziliang

95 **Enterprise Forms and Economic Efficiency**
Capitalist, cooperative and government firms
Kazuhiko Mikami

96 **Diversity and Transformations of Asian Capitalisms**
Edited by Robert Boyer, Hiroyasu Uemura and Akinori Isogai

97 **Knowledge Transfer in the Automobile Industry**
Global-local production networks
Dessy Irawati

98 **Exchange Rates and Foreign Direct Investment in Emerging Asia**
Selected issues and policy options
Ramkishen S. Rajan

99 **Singapore, the Energy Economy**
From the first refinery to the end of cheap oil, 1960–2010
Ng Weng Hoong

100 **China-India Economics**
Challenges, competition & collaboration
Amitendu Palit

101 **Case Studies on Chinese Enterprises**
Edited by Donglin Xia

102 **Argentina's Economic Growth and Recovery**
Michael Cohen

103 **The Korean Labour Market After the 1997 Economic Crisis**
Edited by Joonmo Cho, Richard B. Freeman, Jaeho Keum and Sunwoong Kim

104 **China and India**
The quest for energy resources in the 21st century
Zhao Hong

105 **Beyond the Global Crisis**
Structural adjustments and regional integration in Europe and Latin America
Edited by Lionello Punzo, Carmen Aparecida Feio and Martin Putchet Anyui

106 **The Global Economic Crisis in Latin America**
Impacts and responses
Edited by Michael Cohen

107 **The Processes and Practices of Fair Trade**
Trust, ethics and governance
Edited by Brigitte Granville and Janet Dine

108 **Regional Development through Ecological Business**
Unique cases in Japanese rural regions
Makoto Hirano

109 **Aging and Economic Growth Potentials in the Pacific Region**
Edited by Akira Kohsaka

110 **Crises of Global Economy and the Future of Capitalism**
An insight into the Marx's crisis theory
Edited by Kiichiro Yagi, Nobuharu Yokokawa, Shinjiro Hagiwara and Gary A. Dymski

111 **The Financial History of the Bank for International Settlements**
Kazuhiko Yago

112 **Freight Transport and the Modern Economy**
Michel Savy and June Burnham

113 **Thoughts on Economic Development in China**
Edited by Ma Ying and Hans-Michael Trautwein

114 **China's Ethnic Minorities**
Social and economic indicators
Rongxing Guo

115 **Globalization, Outsourcing and Labour Development in ASEAN**
Shandre Thangavelu and Aekapol Chongvilaivan

116 **The Role of Informal Economies in the Post-Soviet World**
The end of transition?
Colin C. Williams, John Round and Peter Rodgers

117 **Demystifying the Chinese Economy Miracle**
The rise and future of relational capitalism
Yongqin Wang

118 Globalism and Regional Economy
Edited by Susumu Egashira

119 Russia's Changing Economic and Political Regimes
The Putin years and afterwards
Andrey Makarychev and André Mommen

120 Innovation and Regional Development in China
Edited by Ingo Liefner and Yehua Dennis Wei

121 International Trade Negotiations and Domestic Politics
The intermestic politics of trade liberalization
Edited by Oluf Langhelle

122 Emerging Knowledge Economies in Asia
Current trends in ASEAN 5
Edited by Dessy Irawati and Roel Rutten

123 The Internationalization of the Renminbi
International Monetary Institute, Renmin University of China

124 Financial Globalization and Regionalism in East Asia
Edited by Takuji Kinkyo, Yoichi Matsubayashi and Shigeyuki Hamori

125 Successful Business Dealings and Management with China Oil, Gas and Chemical Giants
EurIng. Henry K. H. Wang

126 State Building and Development
Edited by Keijiro Otsuka and Takashi Shiraishi

127 International Economic Development
Leading issues and challenges
Edited by Fu Lai Tony Yu, Wai Kee Yuen and Diana S. Kwan

128 Innovation, Globalization and Firm Dynamics
Lessons for enterprise policy
Edited by Anna Ferragina, Erol Taymoz and Kamil Yilmaz

129 International Remittance Payments and the Global Economy
Bharati Basu with James T. Bang

130 The Open Society and its Enemies in East Asia
The relevance of the Popperian framework
Edited by Gregory C. G. Moore

131 The Economics of Knowledge Generation and Distribution
The role of interactions in the system dynamics of innovation and growth
Edited by Pier Paolo Patrucco

132 Japan's Aid
Lessons for economic growth, development and political economy
Edward M. Feasel

133 The Geographical Transformation of China
Edited by Michael Dunford and Weidong Lui

134 The Economics of Cooperative Education
A practitioners' guide to the theoretical framework and empirical assessment of cooperative education
Yasushi Tanaka

135 Comparing Post War Japanese and Finnish Economies and Societies
Edited by Yasushi Tanaka, Toshiaki Tamaki, Jari Ojala and Jari Eloranta

136 Measuring National Income in the Centrally Planned Economies
Why the west underestimated the transition to capitalism
William Jefferies

137 Crises in Europe in the Transatlantic Context
Economic and political appraisals
Edited by Bruno Dallago and John McGowan

138 The International Monetary System, Energy and Sustainable Development
Edited by Sung Jin Kang and Yung Chul Park

139 Capitalism and the World Economy
The light and shadow of globalization
Edited by Toshiaki Hirai

140 Irish Economic Development
High-performing EU state or serial under-achiever?
Eoin O'Leary

141 Banking on Equality
Women, work and employment in the banking sector in India
Supriti Bezbaruah

142 Poverty, Inequality and Growth in Developing Countries
Theoretical and empirical approaches
Edited by Atsushi Maki

143 Decentralization and Infrastructure in the Global Economy
From gaps to solutions
Edited by Jonas Frank and Jorge Martínez-Vázquez

144 The Global Commercial Aviation Industry
Edited by Sören Eriksson and Harm-jan Steenhuis

Decentralization and Infrastructure in the Global Economy

From gaps to solutions

Edited by
Jonas Frank and
Jorge Martínez-Vázquez

Routledge
Taylor & Francis Group
LONDON AND NEW YORK

First published 2016 by Routledge

2 Park Square, Milton Park, Abingdon, Oxfordshire OX14 4RN
52 Vanderbilt Avenue, New York, NY 10017

Routledge is an imprint of the Taylor & Francis Group, an informa business

First issued in paperback 2020

British Library Cataloguing in Publication Data
A catalogue record for this book is available from the British Library

Library of Congress Cataloging in Publication Data
Frank, Jonas.
Decentralization and infrastructure in the global economy : from gaps to solutions / Jonas Frank, Jorge Martínez-Vázquez.
pages cm
Includes bibliographical references and index.
1. Infrastructure (Economics) 2. Public investments. 3. Decentralization in government. 4. Intergovernmental fiscal relations. I. Martinez-Vazquez, Jorge. II. Title.
HC79.C3F73 2015
336–dc23 2015003520

ISBN: 978-1-138-90920-5 (hbk)
ISBN: 978-0-367-66876-1 (pbk)

Typeset in Times New Roman
by Wearset Ltd, Boldon, Tyne and Wear

Disclaimer

The findings, interpretations, and conclusions expressed in this work do not necessarily reflect the views of The World Bank, its Board of Executive Directors, or the governments they represent. The World Bank does not guarantee the accuracy of the data included in this work. The boundaries, colors, denominations, and other information shown on any map in this work do not imply any judgment on the part of The World Bank concerning the legal status of any territory or the endorsement or acceptance of such boundaries.

Contents

Boxes

Figures

Maps

Tables

Contributors

Luis Alberto Andrés is Lead Economist in the Water Global Practice at the World Bank. Earlier, he held positions in the Sustainable Development Department for the Latin America and the Caribbean, and the South Asia Regions. His work at the World Bank involves both analytical and advisory services, with a focus on infrastructure, mainly in water and energy sectors, impact evaluations, private sector participation, regulation, and empirical microeconomics. He worked with numerous Latin American and South Asian governments on infrastructure and impact evaluation. Before joining the World Bank, he was the Chief of Staff for the Secretary of Fiscal and Social Equity for the Government of Argentina and held other positions in the Chief of Cabinet of Ministries and the Ministry of Economy. He holds a Ph.D. in Economics from the University of Chicago and has authored a book published on the impact of private sector participation in infrastructure, chapters in several books, monographs, and articles on development policy issues.

Roy Bahl is an expert in public finance. He has extensive experience consulting on state and local government issues with public and private agencies, including Standard & Poor's Corp., several city and state governments, and federal agencies. Bahl headed the staffs of the Ohio and Georgia Tax Commissions. He has served on the editorial boards of the *National Tax Journal*, *The Journal of Public Budgeting and Finance*, and *Growth and Change*. He is the author of the book *Fiscal Policy in China* and, with Johannes Linn, of *Urban Public Finance in Developing Countries*. He served as Principal Economic Advisor to IBM's Worldwide Tax Practice. Roy Bahl has consulted on fiscal matters with governments in developing and transition economies all over the world, as well as with the International Monetary Fund, the Asian Development Bank, the US Agency for International Development, the United Nations, and the World Bank. Roy Bahl is the author of numerous books, monographs, and scholarly papers in the area of urban/regional economics, public finance, and economic development. He came to Georgia State University from Syracuse University, where he was the director of the Metropolitan Studies Program and Maxwell Professor of Political Economy.

Dan Biller is Sector Manager of the Economics Unit in the Multilateral Investment Guarantee Agency (MIGA), the political risk insurance and credit enhancement arm of the World Bank Group. He oversees MIGA's country and project risk assessment as well as analysis of development impact and leads the development of MIGA's research agenda. Prior to joining MIGA in 2013, Dan Biller was the Sustainable Development Lead Economist for the World Bank's South Asia Region, Lead Economist for the East Asia and Pacific Region, and Environment and Natural Resources Program Leader at the World Bank Institute. He was also a senior economist at the Organisation for Economic Co-operation and Development, and has taught at universities and worked with private sector and governments on infrastructure and mining/hydrocarbon regulatory issues while he was on the staff of the Getulio Vargas Foundation in Brazil. Dan Biller received his Ph.D. and Master's degree in economics from the University of Illinois at Urbana-Champaign and a bachelor's degree in economics with a minor in geophysics from the University of Kansas. He has published extensively on topics such as economic development, natural resource and environmental economics, sustainable consumption, urban/rural linkages, infrastructure, climate change, and social development issues.

Richard M. Bird is Professor Emeritus of Economics, Rotman School of Management and Adjunct Professor and Senior Fellow of the Institute for Municipal Governance and Finance, Munk School of Global Affairs, University of Toronto. He is also Distinguished Visiting Professor, Andrew Young School of Public Policy at Georgia State University in Atlanta, and Adjunct Professor of the Australian School of Taxation and Business Law of the University of New South Wales, Australia. He has served with the Fiscal Affairs Department of the IMF, and has been a visiting professor in the United States, the Netherlands, Australia, Japan, and India as well as a frequent consultant to the World Bank and other national and international organizations. He has published extensively on tax and public finance issues, with special emphasis on the fiscal problems of developing and transitional countries, and is currently Chair of the Central Advisory Group of the new International Centre for Tax and Development at the Institute for Development Studies in the UK.

Claire Charbit is the Deputy Head of Division of the OECD's Regional Development Policy Division within the Public Governance and Territorial Development Directorate. Claire Charbit has developed and led the OECD's work program on intergovernmental relations, and their impact on regional development policies. She has contributed to several horizontal reports on related topics and territorial reviews and has, on a regular basis, participated in expert meetings on both national and international level. She also pioneered the OECD's work on intergovernmental contracts, the use of performance indicators in regional politics, and has developed what has become a standard methodology for analyzing multi-level governance—thereby informing studies on water governance, fiscal decentralization, and public investment.

Claire Charbit holds a Ph.D. in Economics, specializing in institutional economics. Before joining the OECD, she was an associate professor of innovation, networks, and institutional economics at École Nationale Supérieure des Télécommunications in Paris.

Bernard Dafflon has been Professor of Public Finance at the University of Fribourg since 1987. Previously he was Chief Economist at the Department of Institutions and Decentralization of the canton Fribourg (1977–1990). He has also served as external consultant for the Council of Europe (1994–2006); the World Bank (since 1999); the Agence Française de Développement (AFD), Paris (since 2008); the Swiss Development and Cooperation Agency, Bern (since 2008); the Forum of Federation (since 2010); and several Swiss cantons and local authorities. He has published extensively on fiscal federalism and decentralization, local public finance, equalization, deficit and debt limit, and on the amalgamation of local government; taxation; and the user-pays principle in drinkable water, wastewater, and solid waste recycling and treatment.

Luiz de Mello has been Deputy Chief of Staff of the Secretary-General of the OECD since 2011. Previous to his current position, Luiz de Mello acted as Economic Counselor to the Chief Economist of the OECD. In that role, he advised and supported the Chief Economist and contributed to the OECD involvement in the G20 process. Luiz de Mello joined the Economics Department of the OECD in 2003, working initially in multilateral surveillance activities related to the OECD Economic Outlook. He then worked as Head of Desk responsible for bilateral surveillance activities with Brazil, Chile, and subsequently Indonesia. In that position, he contributed to enhancing relations with partner countries, including through the publication of Economic Surveys and the first OECD Economic Assessment of Indonesia. Prior to joining the OECD, Luiz de Mello worked in the Fiscal Affairs Department of the International Monetary Fund, where he was involved in different projects in the areas of public finances, as well as program monitoring and country surveillance, with an emphasis on emerging-market and transition economies in Asia, Latin America, and Eastern Europe.

Robert D. Ebel is a Senior Economist with Local Government Innovation and Development (LGID, Budapest) and an Adjunct Professor at the Central European University. For the period 2006–2009 he served as Deputy Chief Financial Officer for Revenue Analysis and Chief Economist for the Washington, DC government. Prior to joining the Office of the Chief Financial Officer, he was a Senior Fellow at joint Urban Institute/Brookings Institution Tax Policy Center (TPC) and Lead Economist for the World Bank Institute's (WBI) Capacity Building programs on Public Finance, Intergovernmental Relations, and Local Financial Management. While at WBI he served as the World Bank's technical representative to the Sudan Peace Consultations (2002–2005), and was for the African Union a technical resource person at the Inter-Sudanese Peace Consultations on Darfur (2006). At the World Bank he directed, managed, and wrote technical reports on intergovernmental fiscal relations for a wide range of countries, including Hungary, Egypt, Iraq, Jordan, Pakistan, Palestine (West Bank-Gaza Strip), Nepal, Sierra Leone, South Sudan, Sudan, and Yemen. Robert is also the recipient of several awards, including membership in the United States National Academy of Public Administration and, as a member of a team, the World Bank President's Award for Excellence.

Simon D. Ellis is Lead Transport Specialist in the Transport and Information Technology Global Practice of the World Bank, with a focus on Eastern Europe and the Central Asia Region where he is working on Romania, Ukraine, Belarus, and Moldova. Before taking this position he has worked in countries in the South Asia Region and countries in the East Asia Region including a four-year field assignment as the Transport Sector Coordinator in Vietnam. He has operational experience of projects in rural transport, highways, inland waterways, and port development, and experience of working with both national and local government. Simon D. Ellis has also worked on a number of analytical pieces including transport sector Public Expenditure Reviews, program financing for rural roads, multi-modal transport development, and country transport strategies. Prior to joining the World Bank in 2002, Simon worked at the Transport Research Laboratory (TRL) where he worked on consultancy and research assignments primarily related to rural transport but also in roads appraisal, efficiency of vehicle operations, and transport planning in developing and emerging economies. While at TRL, he also spent time working on UK transport issues, particularly in intelligent transport systems. Simon has a B.A. in Economics and Ph.D. in Transport Economics where his thesis was on the provision of rural transport services.

Jonas Frank is Co-Lead of the World Bank's Decentralization and Subnational Finance Thematic Group which has about 300 members. At the Governance Global Practice he works on public finance with a focus on fiscal decentralization and public investment. In his capacity as Senior Public Sector Specialist in the Latin America region he primarily dealt with intergovernmental relations and institutional reform across a wide range of countries. He also led the Bank's Country Office in Ecuador where he engaged in economic and social development. He holds a Doctorate in Economics and Social Sciences earned at University of Potsdam (Germany).

William Fox has held appointments as a visiting scholar for the Federal Reserve Bank of Kansas City, as a visiting professor at the University of Hawaii, and as Distinguished Fulbright Chair for American Studies at the University of Frankfurt, Germany. In addition, William Fox has served as a consultant on finance, taxation, and economic development in a number of states and developing countries. William Fox is a member of the American Economics Association and a past president of the National Tax Association.

Cathérine Gamper is currently an economist at the OECD's Public Governance and Territorial Development Directorate. She is responsible for projects concerned with multi-level governance, subnational public investment, and decentralization, looking specifically at coordination mechanisms across levels of government and related subnational capacity issues. Prior to her engagement with the OECD she worked for four years at the World Bank, where she contributed to the Policy Research Report on *Localizing Development* and to Bank operations on decentralization, community-driven development, and disaster risk management, with a focus on results-based monitoring and impact evaluation. The countries she worked on specifically include Morocco, Benin, Burkina Faso, and Bangladesh. Before joining the World Bank, Cathérine Gamper worked as an assistant professor of public finance at the University of Innsbruck, where she obtained her Ph.D. in Political Economy. She has been a member of the strategy board of alpS, a research institute working, among others, on the socio-economic dimensions of disaster risk management.

Alec Gershberg's work focuses on accountability, school governance, education finance, institutional arrangements for public service provision, and intergovernmental relations, both in the developing world and in the United States. He has conducted extensive research on Latin America—particularly Mexico, Nicaragua, and Ecuador—focusing on the devolution of power to schools, communities, and governments. More recently, he has done research in these areas in Egypt, Romania, and sub-Saharan Africa. Alec Gershberg has frequently served as a consultant to the World Bank, the Inter-American Development Bank, USAID, and the Urban Institute. In 2004–2005, he worked full-time at the World Bank as a senior education economist. His current research interests include immigrant students in public schools in New York and California. Alec Gershberg is lead author of the book *Beyond "Bilingual" Education: New Immigrants and Public School Policies in California*. As a research associate of the National Bureau of Economic Research, he has argued for increased competition (particularly through reduced negotiated bidding) in the municipal bond market.

Jorge Martínez-Vázquez is Regents Professor of Economics and Director of the International Center for Public Policy, Andrew Young School, Georgia State University. He has published over 20 books and numerous articles in academic journals, such as *Econometrica*, the *Journal of Political Economy*, the *Journal of Public Economics*, and the *Review of Economics and Statistics*. He serves on several editorial boards and has directed multiple fiscal reform projects, having worked in over 70 countries. He has consulted with the World Bank, the IMF, the ADB, the UNDP, the IADB, and numerous country governments. He was inducted into the Russian Academy of Natural Sciences in 1997, and in 2006 he was made an Honorary Professor of China Public Finance and Public Policy Academy, Beijing. In 2011 he was awarded an honorary doctorate from the University of Vigo in Spain, and in 2012 he delivered the Raja Chelliah lecture at NIPFP in New Delhi.

Aurelio Menendez is Practice Manager in the Transport and Information Technology Global Practice at the World Bank. Earlier, he was Transport Sector Manager at the Sustainable Development Department in the Latin-America and Caribbean (LAC) Region. Aurelio Mendendez has directed the World Bank transport strategy in the region and managed the World Bank team responsible for over 40 projects and a wide range of technical assistance initiatives across the Latin America and Caribbean countries. Before taking this position, he was the Transport Sector Leader at the East-Asia and Pacific (EAP) Region of the World Bank since January 2005, and a senior transport economist at the LAC Region since 1999. Aurelio Menendez holds a Ph.D. in Urban and Regional Planning from the Massachusetts Institute of Technology in Cambridge, Massachusetts, and a Masters in Urban Planning from the University of Pennsylvania, in Philadelphia, Pennsylvania, and a Civil Engineering Degree and Doctorate from the Polytechnic University in Madrid, Spain.

Matthew Murray holds a joint appointment with the Center for Business and Economic Research (CBER) and the Department of Economics at The University of Tennessee, Knoxville. He is Associate Director of CBER, Director of the Howard H. Baker Jr. Center for Public Policy, the Ball Corporation Professor of Business in the College of Business Administration, and Program Director for the Public Administration Major in Economics. He served as Department Head of Economics from 1997 to 2002 and Director of Graduate Studies from 2002 to 2007. His research interests include state and local tax policy, education finance, tax compliance, and regional economic development. Matthew. Murray is a member of the National Tax Association and the American Economics Association. He has worked closely with state and local governments on a wide range of public policy issues including economic development incentives, economic/fiscal impact analysis, tax policy analysis, education finance reform, and transportation infrastructure finance.

Leonardo G. Romeo is President of Local Development International (LDI) l.l.c , an international development consulting firm providing policy and technical advisory services to developing countries in support of decentralization reforms, good local governance, and local development planning and management. In 2007 he retired as Principal Technical Adviser for Local Development Planning with the United Nations Capital Development Fund (UNCDF), after a career of 30 years dedicated to building local/municipal governments' capacity and designing, managing and evaluating urban and rural infrastructure projects in developing countries. His research, teaching, and consulting work covers public sector decentralization reforms, local government planning/budgeting processes, and investment projects planning and analysis in developing economies. Leonardo G. Romeo holds a Dott.Arch. degree in Urban and Regional Planning (University of Venice, Italy) and an M.Sc.in Civil Engineering (Columbia University, New York, USA).

Jordan Schwartz is the World Bank's Head of the Global Infrastructure Facility. He has spent over 20 years working in the field of economic development, primarily in infrastructure regulation, planning, and finance, including public-private partnerships.

Anwar Shah (Ph.D. Economics) is Director of the Centre for Public Economics, Chengdu/Wenjiang, China and also serves as an advisor/consultant to the World Bank and the Asian Development Bank. He directed the World Bank Institute's Governance Program from 2004 to 2009. He has previously served the Ministry of Finance, Government of Canada, the Government of Alberta, the US Agency for International Development, and the UN Intergovernmental Panel on Climate Change (as a lead author). He has published more than two dozen books and numerous articles in leading economic journals on governance, public management reforms, budget reform, federalism, local governance, fiscal reforms, and global climate change issues. His recent books include *Fiscal Federalism* (with Robin Boadway), *The Practice of Fiscal Federalism: Comparative Perspectives*, *Fiscal Incentives for Investment and Innovation*, and *Local Governance in Developing Countries and Performance Accountability and Combating Corruption.*

Paul Smoke, Professor of Public Finance and Planning and Director of International Programs at the University of New York, teaches courses on public finance, development planning, governance, and development assistance in developing countries. His research and policy interests include urban and regional development and the political economy of fiscal reform and public sector decentralization. He previously taught in the International Development Program and chaired the Master in City Planning Program at MIT, and he worked as a resident policy advisor with the Harvard Institute for International Development in Kenya and Indonesia. Paul Smoke is a visiting scholar with the Fiscal Affairs Department of the International Monetary Fund and is an affiliated scholar with the Center on International Development and Governance at the Urban Institute. His research and policy work has covered several regions and multiple countries, including Cambodia, Uganda, South Africa, Vietnam, India, Ethiopia, Palestine, Yemen, Brazil, Nepal, Egypt, and the USA. He has worked with various international organizations.

Douglas Sutherland is a senior economist in the public economics division of the OECD's economics department. Douglas Sutherland joined the economics department in 1998, initially working on bilateral economic surveillance and contributing to the publication of Economic Surveys of the Russian Federation. He then worked on a wide range of topics, including examining the design sub-central government fiscal rules, sustainable development, and public sector efficiency. More recently he has led projects on infrastructure investment, counter-cyclical economic policy, fiscal consolidation, and debt and macroeconomic stability. Prior to joining the OECD he worked as a research fellow at the University of Birmingham on a project examining economic transformation in Russia's regions.

Andrey Timofeev is a research associate with the International Center for Public Policy and a research assistant professor at the Department of Economics, both at the Andrew Young School of Policy Studies, Georgia State University. In this capacity, he has contributed to numerous reports on intergovernmental fiscal relations, tax policy, and budget transparency. In particular, he has been engaged in the development of a system of (World-Bank funded) performance-based infrastructure grants to the Gram Panchayats in West Bengal, India and assessment of capital grants in Latvia, Macedonia, and Namibia. From 1999 to 2000, he served as an advisor to Russian regions' governments under a USAID Fiscal Reform Project in the Russian Federation through Georgia State University. He holds a B.S. in Mathematics from Novosibirsk State University (Russia) and a Ph.D. in Economics from Charles University (Czech Republic).

François Vaillancourt holds a Ph.D. from Queen's University at Kingston, Ontario, is a fellow at the CIRANO research center, and Emeritus Professor in Economics at the Université de Montréal. He has published extensively in public economics, particularly on fiscal federalism and tax compliance, and on economics of language issues. He has been a Fulbright Scholar and a visiting scholar in various institutions including the Institute for Policy Analysis in Toronto, the Andrew Young School of Policy Studies in Atlanta, and the École Normale Supérieure in Paris. He has done consulting work for various Canadian and international bodies and worked in 22 countries, mainly in Africa, on various intergovernmental and local finance issues.

Lorena Viñuela is a Public Sector Specialist in the Governance Global Practice of the World Bank, where she works on issues related to intergovernmental relations, decentralization, and institution building in Africa, East Asia and the Pacific, and Latin America. Prior to joining the World Bank, she worked at the Maxwell School of Public Affairs of Syracuse University, the Inter-American Development Bank, and EuropeAid. Her research relates to the political economy of public policy reform, fiscal policy, public investment, intergovernmental relations, and party politics in developing countries.

Ha T. T. Vu is a Public Financial Management Advisor at the Fiscal Affairs Department of the International Monetary Fund (IMF). Prior to joining the IMF she was a member of the Public Sector Governance unit at the World Bank as a specialist on public investment management, medium-term expenditure frameworks, and fiscal decentralization. She holds a Ph.D. in Public Policy from the George Mason University (Virginia, United States). She has contributed to the *Oxford Handbook on State and Local Government Finance in the United States*, edited by John Petersen and Robert Ebel, and a paper for the Board of the IMF entitled "Toward More Efficient Public Investment" covering 25 countries in the world (2015).

Preface

This book is in honor of Dana Robin Weist (1961–2010). Dana was a leading expert in public finance and fiscal decentralization. She graduated from the University of Delaware with a B.A. in Economics in 1982 and from Syracuse University with a Ph.D. in Public Finance in 1990. At the World Bank, as an economist and sector manager for the Economic Policy and Debt Department, she worked on fiscal and governance issues in East Asia, Latin America and the Europe and Central Asia regions. In her career, she received more than 15 honors and awards for her outstanding work in economics and public finance. Dana was a kind person and a wonderful professional who touched the lives of many people including those that so generously have contributed to this volume.

The papers in this volume are the fruit of two conferences held in honor of Dana Robin Weist. The first Conference was held in Stone Mountain, Atlanta, during September 25–27, 2012. The second Conference was held at the World Bank in Washington DC during February 13–14, 2013.

As editors we would like to recognize the contributions of many colleagues and friends who have embraced this endeavor and contributed to celebrate Dana's life and achievements.

We would like to acknowledge the support from the family of Dana Robin Weist, particularly Dana's brother, Mark Weist, for his heartening dedication throughout the different stages of this effort.

We also very much appreciate the encouragement for this venture received from Roy Bahl, Kai Kaiser, Jennie Litvack, Paul Smoke and Deborah Wetzel. Their guidance and support have been pivotal in the conceptualization of the two conferences and this publication.

The entire work has benefited greatly from a valuable partnership between Georgia State University and the World Bank. At Georgia State University we express gratitude to the International Center for Public Policy and the Andrew Young School of Policy Studies for their generous patronage. Paul Benson, Shereen Bhan, Arienne Wyatt Gladney and Hiram Seraphin provided excellent logistical assistance.

At the World Bank, we have received dedicated support and generous endowments by the Governance Global Practice as well as the Macroeconomics and Fiscal Management Global Practice. We appreciate the guidance provided by

James Brumby, Otaviano Canuto, Sudarshan Gooptu, Nick Manning, and Linda van Gelder.

Our particular appreciation is to the authors who have contributed voluntarily to this volume. We have valued tremendously the enriching dialogue with: Luis Andrés, Roy Bahl, Dan Biller, Richard Bird, Claire Charbit, Bernard Dafflon, Luiz de Mello, Robert D. Ebel, Simon D. Ellis, William F. Fox, Cathérine Gamper, Alec Gershberg, Aurelio Menendez, Matthew Murray, Leonardo Romeo, Jordan Schwartz, Anwar Shah, Paul Smoke, Douglas Sutherland, Andrey Timofeev, François Vaillancourt, Lorena Viñuela, and Ha T.T. Vu.

Several colleagues have contributed through peer reviews and substantive commentary to individual chapters. These include Giorgio Brosio, Luis Crouch, Kent Eaton, Tim Goodspeed, Mihaly Kopanyi, Abha Prasad, Mark Rider, Paul Bernd Spahn, Michel Welmond, and Christine Wong. Our acknowledgment also goes to Marianne Fay, Alan Gelb, Vikram Nehru, and Christine Wallich for supporting the second Conference. Elin Bergman, Patricia Ravelomanantsoa, Mayya Revzina, and Grace Verances have provided assistance at several stages of the process.

We finally would like to thank Routledge for endorsing and buttressing this book project. The enthusiasm, advice, and assistance by Penny Harper, Emily Kindleysides, Ashleigh Phillips, and Lisa Thomson were of great help during the production process and in finalizing the volume.

Jonas Frank and Jorge Martínez-Vázquez

1 Decentralization and infrastructure

From gaps to solutions

Jonas Frank and Jorge Martínez-Vázquez

Introduction and motivation

The subnational dimension of infrastructure emerges as one of the key dimensions for improved public investment. Whether a country is centralized or decentralized, whether it relies on delegated authorities or autonomous subnational governments, it has to face the question of multi-level coordination and provision of infrastructure. Given the localized nature of most infrastructures, the territorial dimension cannot be obviated. Any country that wishes to improve service delivery, increase competitiveness, as well as foster growth through investment in infrastructure faces the intergovernmental coordination challenge.

The approaches which countries have used to tackle this multi-level challenge vary widely. Some countries execute up to 90 percent of their public investment through subnational level governments, while others not nearly 10 percent. But this share of expenditures is not always a good indicator of the decision-making authority of subnational governments in the selection, prioritization, funding, and execution of infrastructure projects. The several stages and decision-making steps which need to be coordinated across levels typically give rise to a complex web of accountability over final results. Not surprisingly, outcomes have been mixed and vary widely from country to country and from region to region in the same country. The greatest challenge is that inefficiencies in management and execution can be pervasive across the different subnational units ultimately translating into poor service delivery and wasted resources.

The main objective for the collection of original essays in this book is to advance our understanding of the interplay between decentralization and infrastructure. This fundamental issue is approached from multiple perspectives and in an interdisciplinary fashion. The chapters in this book are intended to cover the most important aspects of infrastructure investment in a decentralized setting. They discuss the nature of the infrastructure gaps and the quality of subnational spending; inquire how functional responsibilities, finance, and equalization can be best designed; discuss issues related to infrastructure and service delivery in different areas of the public sector; drill-down to key steps of the public investment cycle and management aspects; and also analyze political economy and corruption challenges. The essays offer academic rigor but also attempt to inform the policy debate with the aim of improving the outcomes of decentralized investment spending. Far from representing a closed set of final recommendations, the chapters highlight diverse views and avenues for improving public investment in decentralized settings, keeping in mind that ultimately what will work needs to be "country and place specific."

Against this backdrop, three global challenges have motivated this book:

i Coordination matters: The volatile macro environment which prevails internationally underscores now more than ever the need to coordinate public investment and infrastructure provisions across levels of government. While responses to the 2007/2008 crisis have varied and involved different strategies regarding capital spending, countries will continue to rely on subnational levels of government to provide a substantial part of their infrastructure needs. National growth inherently relies on regional growth, and due to its localized nature, public investment can be a critical ingredient to achieve this goal. However, decisions to spend, and decisions to finance, are often not taken on the same level of government. Poor coordination within decentralized systems of government can prevent countries from achieving their goals.

ii Equity matters: Infrastructure gaps are still significant, and vary substantially across subnational units. While starting points are much different, particularly across OECD and non-OECD countries, in many cases there are notable advances in reducing gaps. But progress has not been even. Country-wide statistics based on national averages can be misleading and hide deep disparities. Gaps can be particularly large across subnational jurisdictions (horizontal gaps); these gaps are increasingly structured along urban-rural lines, particularly in the developing world. This represents a major impediment to improving access to public services on an equitable basis, and for reducing poverty. Due to the shifting nature of gaps and the localized nature of infrastructure itself—often spanning across several jurisdictions—finding responsible agents to address these disparities constitutes a serious challenge.

iii Efficiency matters: Many countries have already "invested" much in decentralization as well as subnational infrastructure provision in the last two decades, but the results are mixed. Efficiency cannot easily materialize in environments where responsibilities over the investment cycle or service delivery are unclear; or where public investment is carried out bypassing critical decision steps. The pressure to demonstrate results is increasing on behalf of citizens, but cannot be adequately addressed without looking deeper into institutional design issues. The challenge here lies in identifying the responsible levels of government for planning, financing, and executing investment, and ultimately delivering services with some standard of equity.

The responses to these three challenges are necessarily complex as evidenced by the efforts under way in many countries, and they require careful examination. This is what the following 13 chapters in this book attempt to do. Before turning to the discussion of these sections, we take a closer look at the main institutional aspects of decentralized infrastructure and public investment. As will become clear in the next section, decentralized infrastructure is quickly emerging as one of the greatest challenges in contemporary public finance policy and management.

The complexity of the institutional dimensions of decentralized infrastructure and public investment

Infrastructure provision entails the construction, operation, and maintenance of the long-lived physical assets required to deliver specific public services. There are different ways to classify types of infrastructure. A useful approach is to divide infrastructure into "network infrastructure," such as roads, streets, bridges, electricity, and water; and "point infrastructure," such as hospitals and school buildings, which is more common to the social sectors. The latter often require further inputs—such as teachers and health personnel—in order to provide full service delivery to citizens.

While practices vary, the investment cycle for infrastructure encompasses the following key steps.[1] Planning and project appraisal constitute the initial steps; this is followed by project selection and a decision to provide the necessary budgetary resources. Implementation entails procurement as well as contract management to account for changes during execution, before facilities can be operated and services delivered eventually. Ex-post evaluation of completed projects is usually the final step in the building process. After that come operation and more importantly maintenance. Each of these steps can be decentralized, or performed in a shared fashion across levels of government. Regulation of the service including setting standards, can also be decentralized or shared among levels of government.

As a multi-sector, cross-cutting, and multi-level process, decentralized public investment typically involves a high number of actors and agents.

- At both subnational and national levels, it involves Ministries or Secretaries of Finance, planning entities, sector ministries, and service delivery units.
- In some settings, community associations play a large role, particularly in post-conflict countries with limited state presence.
- Infrastructure is also provided by public enterprises.
- With diverging models and approaches, public investment can involve private agents (Public-Private-Partnerships—or PPP as one form);[2] but not all governments handle private involvement under a unified project cycle, which creates a separate, often complex layer in decision-making and management.
- In aid-dependent countries, international development agencies can also play a major role.

The relationships among these players can be complex, and therefore also poorly defined in law and/or practice. From a territorial point of view it is noteworthy that some investments are carried out in single-purpose districts, which may or not coincide with territorial jurisdictions of (general) subnational governments. In addition, further complexity can be introduced through sub-tiers within the main levels, while having only some of them playing a role in infrastructure.

In this myriad of organizational possibilities for the provision of infrastructure in intergovernmental arrangements, three main models have emerged:

- Some countries provide a leading role to sector agencies, which at the national or subnational levels oversee or perform directly critical steps in the project cycle, such as performing planning functions and setting standards for project appraisal; some of these tasks can be centralized with subnational governments having to follow them, independently of the level of central co-financing. Spain provides an example for this approach.
- Another group of countries emphasize the role of ministries of finance or planning as leading agencies, whether at the central or subnational levels. In federal systems such as the US and Canada federal governments have limited powers to regulate in many areas, so it is left to subnational governments to act with wide margins of autonomy. In other countries, subnational governments are required to follow the standards set by central government entities. The sector agencies keep only a marginal role in this model. South Korea is an example of this model.
- In another group of countries, particularly in the developing world, a community management model is applied. In these arrangements, planning and project selection is done from the bottom up, with marginal participation of subnational governments, if they are present at all. Particularly in post-conflict situations, limited state presence at any level of government requires different approaches. Indonesia and Cambodia are examples for this model.

In practice, the degree of formality with which these models are applied varies widely, particularly in developing countries with emerging intergovernmental frameworks. Often, the role of subnational governments can remain under-regulated giving rise to widely discretionary environments.

But regardless of the main model used a common trait is that decentralized infrastructure provision requires coordination among levels of government. Service standards or procurement rules tend to be shared to some extent; and even in the most decentralized countries, subnational governments are often required to adopt central regulations and standards. This is even more true for infrastructure which generates positive externalities or spillover effects to other jurisdictions, since it usually requires coordinated planning and central co-financing.

As an outcome of the above complexity of the institutional dimensions, the traditional labels that are used to characterize the degrees of subnational autonomy are not easily applicable to infrastructure provision. Even if formally labeled "autonomous," "delegated," or "deconcentrated," public investment more often than not requires joint decisions, which cannot be easily coordinated. This is so independently of unitary or federal countries, or the specific decentralization model at hand. Given the usually high level of co-financing, subnational governments in practice are often subject to standards of quality, quantity, and access established by higher levels of government. Upper level authorities often also exercise monitoring and evaluation functions.

A discussion of the contributions

The individual contributions to this volume fall naturally in five main sections:

Part I Measuring infrastructure gaps: quantity and quality perspectives

How large are infrastructure gaps?: Access to infrastructure services is very disparate across the world regions. Irrespective of possible differences across the sectors, South Asia and Sub-Saharan Africa (SSA) have the largest infrastructure gaps compared to other regions of the world. By comparison, most of the OECD countries have already well-developed infrastructure and are able to focus on quality considerations. The measurement of infrastructure gaps is the main theme of **Chapter 2** by **Luis Alberto Andrés, Dan Biller,** and **Jordan Schwartz** entitled **"The Infrastructure Gap and Decentralization."**

Recognizing the different starting points in the stock of infrastructure is critical to assess improvements and progress. Another dimension is the quality of infrastructure. Deficiencies tend to be large in this dimension and even in the most advanced countries, quality challenges remain or are reappearing. Figure 1.1 tracks countries with regards to (i) their overall level of public investment spending in GDP terms,[3] and (ii) their different levels of progress in quality as assessed by surveys.[4] As is apparent, countries experience not only advances but also backward steps—and these have occurred also in the OECD countries. In turn, some countries in the developing world have taken respectable leaps forward. But again, it is important to recognize the different starting points with regards to the stock and also quality of infrastructure.

The subnational dimension comes into play once country-level data are disaggregated across the different territorial units. As documented in Chapter 2, differences in access to services can be particularly heterogeneous among subnational units. Using district level data for the entire South Asia Region, Andrés, Biller, and Schwartz ranked districts by quintiles on access to electricity, gas, improved water, improved sanitation, and telecommunications. In India, some of the best indicators of access to improved water sources can be found in districts located in the north and northwest of the country, while some of the worst indicators are in districts in the northeast and west as well as in the southwest coast. To complicate matters, districts with "good" access to one infrastructure service do not have necessarily "good" access to other types of infrastructure services. For example, districts in Kerala fare well with regards to improved sanitation, but have among the worst indicators for access to improved water sources (Andrés *et al.*, 2014).

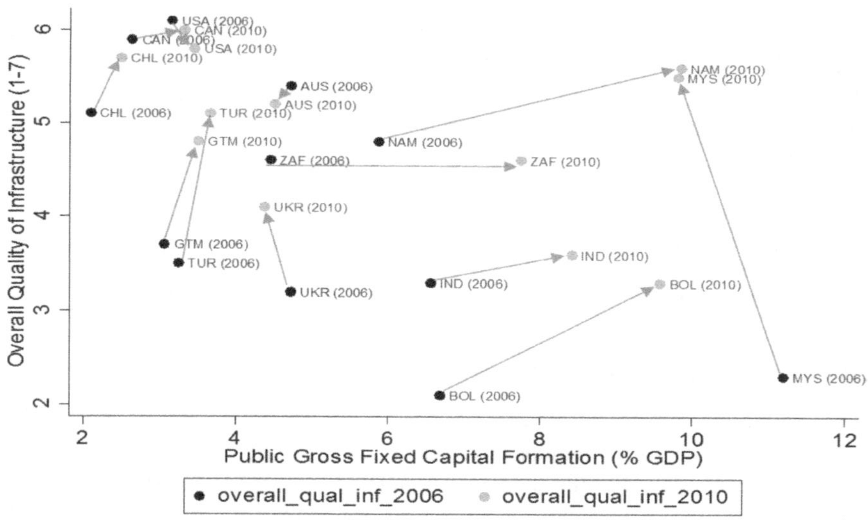

Figure 1.1 Progress in quality of infrastructure and public investment spending (2002–2010) (source: Authors, based on information from World Economic Forum (2006 and 2010) and IMF-WEO (2002–2010)).

The overarching trend that shapes the development of infrastructure gaps is urbanization. While the urbanization process is less pronounced in some regions like South Asia and Sub-Saharan Africa, it implies that the demand for services is and will be even more territorially uneven—and shifting across the different subnational units. This creates the need to target infrastructure even more precisely to particular geographical areas and the needs of citizens.[5] Addressing these challenges is also critical to achieving some of the 2015 Millennium Development Goals (MDGs). This is necessarily so given the link between reducing poverty and infrastructure coverage. At the same time, given shifting population density and the limited capacity to estimate future demand, the risk of over- or under-supply of infrastructure is equally large, and can easily lead to wasteful spending.

In the process of urbanization, achieving efficiency is challenging also from another point of view. Urban areas can benefit from economies of scale—implying diminishing unit costs—in many services (water; health above the primary level); but it is also true that the large, growing urban areas often do not integrate sufficiently well in a horizontal sense to reap these benefits even further. On the other hand, some services are only demanded in urban areas (urban transport and mass transit). In rural areas the situation tends to be quite different: the cost for delivering services and infrastructure increases often considerably due to geographic reasons and distance; while some infrastructure can be delivered without significant economies of scale (school buildings, as relevant for primary education), this is not equally true for water systems, or health services particularly when considering increasing levels of care.

This has also implications for fiscal equalization. The urban-rural dynamics imply that costs and needs for the provision of infrastructure are changing, along with fiscal capacity. This might require different approaches as to how equity should or could be achieved, a topic to which we will return to further below.

How have subnational governments responded in addressing the infrastructure gaps?: The two fundamental questions which need to be answered in first place are: Who is and will be responsible for addressing infrastructure gaps? And who will be responsible for paying the cost? Answering these questions is paramount as the current demand for infrastructure is estimated at approximately US$0.8–0.9 trillion of annual infrastructure investments in the developing world; by 2020 this figure inflates to US$1.8–2.3 trillion per year. This equates to roughly an increase in annual infrastructure investment from 3 percent of developing world GDP to 6–8 percent of GDP.[6] In principle, in a decentralized system such costs need to be distributed among the different levels of government. How that is actually done remains the one critical question in addressing infrastructure gaps.

Finding satisfying answers to these questions is not very straightforward. Countries involve subnational governments to varying degrees. Figure 1.2 highlights the level of decentralization of public investment. While one can conclude that by and large, the share of subnational governments in total capital expenditures of a country is typically twice their share in total recurrent expenditures (Martínez-Vázquez and Timofeev, 2012), there is wide variation among countries in their level of decentralized investment spending. This ranges from less than 10 percent to up to 90 percent of the total.[7] But again this is not a full indicator of subnational autonomy—as decision-making power usually varies, among others, due to the high levels of joint infrastructure management.

These aggregate numbers also hide other important facts. There are large up-and-down-swings and volatility in the level of decentralized investment spending. Countries usually register considerable changes in spending both in GDP terms as well as in the overall share of decentralized public investment, both across years and within years. This is due to a mix of factors:

- Public investment is an important fiscal adjustment variable. It is often the first expenditure item to be cut down or to be increased—for both practical and political reasons.
- Given the often considerable shares of co-financing, which can be allocated competitively, funding for public investment is by nature subject to a high level of unpredictability.
- Subnational governments themselves may have different preferences and needs. This is the original idea of decentralized government—and given the relative degree of flexibility in the nature of resources often being used, it facilitates the definition of own priorities.
- More recently however it has become evident that spending levels and speed of execution of investment can be induced and incentivized from higher

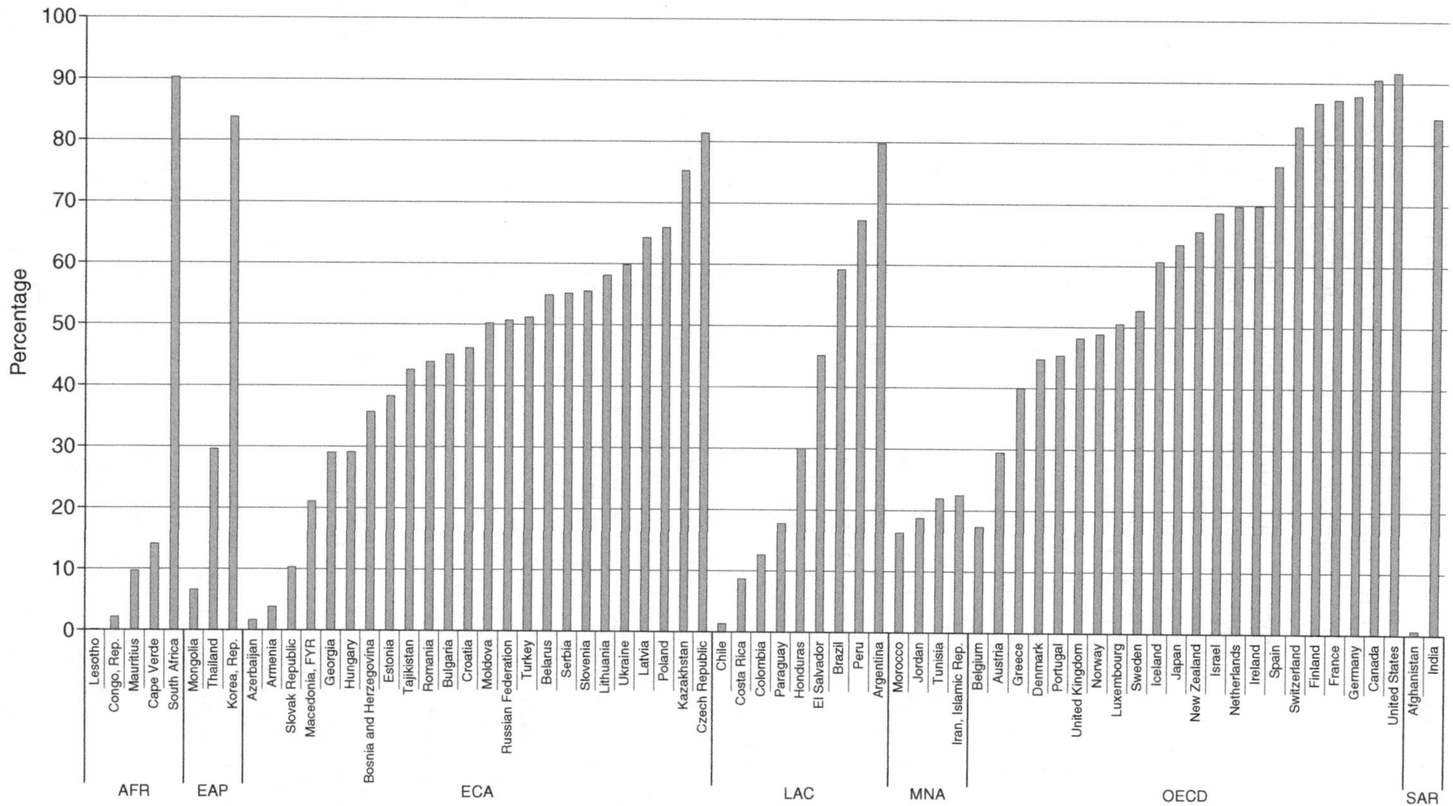

Figure 1.2 Subnational government share of public investment, 2010 (source: Lorena Viñuela, Chapter 3 in this volume).

levels of government, including the center. Such changes were particularly pronounced in the years following the economic crisis ensuing 2007/2008. Countries such as South Korea or the Czech Republic have responded with stimulus packages executed through subnational governments, and have increased the level of expenditures considerably.[8] About three-quarters of the investment package announced by Korea and Spain was to be delivered by the subnational jurisdictions (Allain-Dupreé, 2011). Other countries, in turn, have done significant adjustment efforts and cut back expenditures, among them some hard-hit countries in Eastern Europe (Armenia, Estonia), and a series of OECD countries (Switzerland, Austria).[9]

- Countries employ different strategies as to what extent the risk of macroeconomic volatility is shared among levels of government; this determines the degree of predictability and stability with which transfers are being transferred. At the same time this can result in procyclical spending patterns, only to be affected later by adjustments if transfer amounts fall back under predicted levels; fiscal responsibility rules can also play a role in explaining these trends.
- Finally, natural resource rich countries can experience substantial changes in the level of public investment, as demonstrated by Peru's commodity boom and the involvement of subnational governments. But if stop-and-go implementation of infrastructure works is the result, the impact on expenditure efficiency becomes problematic.

Given these context factors, subnational governments have to maneuver through a series of obstacles to achieve quality spending. On what factors then, does success in raising the quality of spending depend? As highlighted in **Chapter 3** by **Lorena Viñuela** entitled **"Trends and Quality of Decentralized Public Investment,"** a critical factor are subnational own revenue efforts, both related to the decentralization of tax administration and tax autonomy. This does not come as a surprise since a key tenet of own revenue decentralization is that it creates an accountability nexus and induces more fiscally responsible expenditure decisions. Viñuela also finds that reducing opportunities for corruption and enhancing transparency reduces opportunities of wasteful spending.

But achieving quality of spending also requires an understanding of the specific challenges related to the assignment of responsibilities, funding, and equalization, topics to which we now turn.

Part II Fundamentals in flux: functions, finance, and equalization for decentralized public investment

The shifting nature in the assignment of responsibilities: The decentralization of infrastructure challenges some of the well-accepted principles of intergovernmental fiscal relations. This holds true for both revenue assignments and the assignment of functional responsibilities.

The assignment of responsibilities over infrastructure represents a triple challenge: it requires not only defining (i) who is responsible for the "end-service" to citizens (health, education, transport, etc.); but also defining (ii) responsibilities over the project and investment cycle (appraisal; project selection; budgeting; procurement; ex-post evaluation, among others); and (iii) regulation as a cross-cutting task. Each of these three different responsibilities can be centralized, decentralized, or shared among levels of government. This does represent not only a major alignment and accountability issue, but also, for practical matters, a significant sequencing challenge during a process of aligning responsibilities.

- i **Responsibility for "end-services."** In principle which level of government is assigned responsibility for infrastructure provision depends on which level is assigned "end-responsibility" for the service in question. But there are important differences: some of the "network infrastructure," such as roads, streets, bridges, can itself constitute an end-service; this is different from "point infrastructure," such as hospitals and school buildings, which require further inputs—such as teachers and health personnel—in order to provide full service delivery to citizens.
- ii **Responsibilities over the project cycle.** These responsibilities primarily refer to planning, appraisal, selection, budgeting and financing, implementation, adjustment during execution, and ex-post evaluation. As projects move along the project cycle, different entities need to be responsible for these tasks. It is particularly noteworthy that given the changing ownership over physical assets (PPP arrangements, or through decentralization) those responsibilities are required to shift, so change is desirable and required to some extent.
- iii **Regulation.** This entails responsibility for policy, standards, and oversight. Regulation is also necessary for the setting of user costs, access prices, or final prices, depending on whether the network provider is vertically integrated and competition is feasible. Given the importance of pricing to investment decisions, the credibility and consistency of the regulatory framework are important determinants of infrastructure investment, among others for PPP schemes.[10]

Given the changing nature of some of these responsibilities, these dynamics can lead to a "hollowing out" of "end-service" responsibilities, impacting negatively on accountability and transparency. The competition aspect in the provision of some infrastructure does reinforce this trend. Recognizing the need for flexibility is highlighted by **Roy Bahl** and **Richard M. Bird** in **Chapter 4** entitled **"Principles and Practice."** According to authors, responsibilities need to be clearly defined and monitored, although this represents, as can be expected, a major operational and practical challenge.

<u>Challenges in the financing of decentralized infrastructure:</u> Given the changing nature of responsibilities, the next immediate question is how to finance

infrastructure. Financial options for decentralized infrastructure can be, among others: (i) local taxes; (ii) intergovernmental grants and transfers; (iii) user charges;[11] and (iv) debt. Private-sector co-financing (concessions, PPPs) is an additional modality. As is underscored by **Luiz de Mello** and **Douglas Sutherland** in **Chapter 5** entitled **"Financing Infrastructure,"** the choice of financing instrument depends on:

- the nature of the investment (size, revenue-generating capacity, potential for competition);
- the modality of service delivery (pure government provision, concession, PPP);
- the budgetary capacity of the jurisdiction (breadth and depth of own taxes, intergovernmental transfer arrangements, borrowing constraints); and,
- the technical capacity of the jurisdiction to design and negotiate contracts with private-sector providers.

In principle, infrastructure finance faces the same dilemma of vertical fiscal gaps as is the case for "common" subnational service delivery: subnational governments tend to have lower revenue mobilization capacity than the central government. Higher levels of administration therefore participate in the financing of subnational provision through transfers and grants, even when investments are carried out entirely by subnational jurisdictions. More emphasis is generally put on debt financing, required to finance costly investment projects which generate future benefits to the population and yield a revenue stream that can be used to service the debt.[12]

These particular financing sources and the array of possible arrangements give rise to at least four specific issues and challenges.

i **Assignment challenges.** Finance sources need to be flexible to adjust to the regulatory and assignment challenge: given that responsibilities are often "in flux," so does—or should be—the financing. This is more challenging with regards to multi-year budget commitments.

ii **Transaction cost challenges.** (a) Grants may be complex to administer and involve transaction costs (matching grants; co-financing). Matching requirements are typically used to reveal the policy preferences of the recipient, and for effective co-funding and risk sharing. The conditionality in capital grants typically focuses on assuring certain conditions ex ante, such as verifying technical feasibility, impact analyses, cost-benefit assessments, or the capacity to administer the project. And the allocation of such grants requires priority setting through cooperative arrangements. However surveillance and cooperative pacts often remain a central responsibility, especially in the developing world. (b) Coordinating such co-financing effectively is a serious challenge because these institutions typically compete with each other; they could "crowd out" secured funding (jeopardizing "additionality" of spending by subnational governments); favor "bankable" assets with immediate and higher returns (thus "betting on the same horse"); and they impose conditions that may interfere with the political priority setting of local authorities.

iii **Efficiency challenges.** (a) Revenue earmarking—often used for roads as well as social expenditures—often complicates expenditure management and discourages efforts to improve the cost-effectiveness of government expenditures, because policymakers are unable to reallocate scarce budgetary resources to cost-effective activities. They may result in excessive funding in some places, and in too limited funding in others. (b) There are potential efficiency losses associated with the different treatment of operating and capital cost needs of subnational governments: a separated treatment can lead to deferred maintenance; or local managers might try to save on operating costs by not performing (or deferring) maintenance at the proper time without perceiving, or trying to shift to another level of government, the incurred capital costs of this strategy.

iv **Fiscal responsibility and contingent liability challenges.** (a) Sunk costs associated with "poor" infrastructure projects are often too high to be fully financed by subnational budgets, whose revenue mobilization and borrowing capacity is lower than that of higher levels of administration. This may constitute an enforcement problem of fiscal responsibility rules, independently of whether they are based on administrative controls or market mechanisms. (b) PPPs are usually too complex to be administered by subnational governments, particularly given that sub-central governments effectively are not often providers of last resort for very visible public goods. Therefore, mechanisms to minimize the potential for opportunistic behavior from both parties and costly renegotiation need to be considered, notwithstanding the need for flexibility.

As is underscored by de Mello and Sutherland, these challenges require constant adjustment, tailoring to specific projects, and localities. But given that infrastructure has an important temporal dimension it is critical that capital financing be timed and provided in the "right" way if the "right" projects are to be carried out in the "right" places.

<u>Addressing horizontal inequities:</u> With infrastructure gaps shifting among urban and rural areas in quickening pace, the need for "place-based" responses to the service delivery challenge are increasing. Socio-economic dynamics of urbanization also imply changing fiscal capacity, costs, and needs among the jurisdictions of a country, so horizontal disparities and hence the need for equalization is increasing. Therefore equity concerns regarding the geographical distribution of capital infrastructure are paramount. Ideally, financing instruments would create the incentives for place-based responses but they would also take into account either existing disparities in capital stock, which are unrelated to the own decisions of the subnational government, or significant disparities in financing capacity or expenditure needs.

To the extent that the main objective of intergovernmental grants, and more in particular equalization transfers, is to ensure the adequate financing of decentralized functions in an equitable manner, it is clear that this adequacy should be assessed in terms of the entire expenditure needs which include capital infrastructure. However, this broad consensus in the theory and practice of fiscal federalism has been, as of yet, mainly focused on the recurrent expenditures needed to finance those public services. As highlighted by **Jorge Martínez-Vázquez** and **Andrey Timofeev** in **Chapter 6** entitled **"Capital Infrastructure and Equity Objectives in Decentralized Systems,"** once taking into account the infrastructure dimension, the criteria for equalization become more complex:

- The potential use of user charges (which typically cannot be recognized in fiscal capacity equalization), and access to debt financing (for which high income territories have more access) can create "new sources" of inequities.
- Differences in access to borrowing sources and the costs of borrowing create inter-temporal issues that can be challenging to address explicitly and correctly in the context of general equalization grants (traditionally focused on recurrent expenditure needs and financing means).
- Cost- and time-overruns have a direct budgetary impact. Cost-drivers, which in the case of infrastructure can be considerable and highlight transparency problems, can accentuate lack of transparency and perverse incentives if they are used as a base for cost equalization. But, of course, not all cost overruns are planned or intentional, and therefore there is no straightforward way in limiting these contradictory effects.

Given these factors, placing the different subnational units on equal footing through fiscal equalization does not work uniformly well in all sectors. Perhaps not unsurprisingly, most countries have faced limitations in crafting responses to the equalization challenge regarding infrastructure, or if there have been responses, they have been developed on parallel tracks with other objectives which may not necessarily go hand in hand with the objective of equalization:

- The so-called Social Investment Funds are often caught between competing objectives: compensating for needs across sectors or across jurisdictions.
- National co-financing is often driven on an ad-hoc basis, particularly under competitive schemes.
- The new wave of performance-based transfers, adopted widely in developing countries, can exacerbate horizontal inequities.
- Compensating objectives of capital transfers remain often diffuse; earmarking is difficult to enforce in practice, so the equalizing effect is uncertain.

Such responses naturally will have to vary according to the level of decentralization of investment spending. In turn, in some deconcentrated or delegation models, equalization has to come—in theory at least—more from centrally steered programs; municipalities in Chile for instance merely spend about 4 percent of the total, but a much larger share is executed centrally via deconcentrated regional governments. In countries with a high involvement of subnational governments on infrastructure spending—for instance France (about 87 percent), South Korea (84 percent), Spain (about 75 percent), or Peru (67 percent)—equalization is likely more effective and achieved through transfer schemes, oftentimes between autonomous agents.

Ensuring equalization for investment expenditures in many cases therefore will remain a challenge—although countries are applying different models which can be taken as references to guide the design and implementation of policy. The need for mixed and flexible approaches also is underscored by the fact that there are important differences across sectors, their resourcing needs, and the role different forms of financing play in the pricing of services, if any, and in the modality of service delivery.

Part III Sectoral perspectives

Point versus network infrastructure: As mentioned above, it is useful to divide infrastructure into "network infrastructure," such as roads, streets, bridges, electricity, and water; and "point infrastructure," such as hospitals and school buildings, which is more common to the social sectors. The latter often require further inputs—such as teachers and health personnel—in order to provide full service delivery to citizens.

There are noteworthy differences across these two types of infrastructure. For "point infrastructure," in particular, the locational decisions are paramount: Where should a service facility be built, and then also maintained and operated? And who decides the location? While "network infrastructure" cannot obviously ignore such decisions, and the consequences of poorly connected physical assets can be more visible and lead to undesirable effects.

The complexity of locational decisions can be illustrated in the health sector. Health can be categorized as a "point infrastructure" service. As emphasized by **Bernard Dafflon** and **François Vaillancourt** in **Chapter 7** entitled **"Investing in Health Infrastructure: How Decentralization Matters,"** the key questions with regards to a locational decision are the following. To begin with, there needs to be clarity on who decides which health and hospital services are attributed to primary, secondary, and tertiary health centers. Subsequently, the decisions are: First, how is vertical coordination secured? Second, appropriate distances to service centers must be set in order to optimize the network. Third, are private clinics and hospitals considered part of the health network, under what conditions?

In addition, most "point infrastructure" requires connectivity to certain types of "network infrastructure" such as roads, electricity, and water supply. It is clear that such basic connectivity needs to exist: the utility of a hospital without road access is extremely limited. In "point infrastructure" services in particular, such as education and health facilities, there is a requirement of other inputs to deliver the full service, such as personnel (teachers or health workers) and supplies and materials (books or medicines), which complicates management and decision-making in several dimensions. The perennial questions also include whether responsibilities for infrastructure and operation and maintenance be assigned to the same level or different levels; and the implications of those decisions for optimal input combination and cost minimization in service delivery.

Multiple agents: To make matters more complex, the organizational logic of each sector also differs and has implications, particular in defining responsible agents. In education the provision of the different levels of service—that is, compulsory versus higher education—is usually carried out by separate agents in different locations; in turn, in the health sector different levels of service are provided by the same agent such as local health centers; similar arrangements can be applied in the road sector, given that there are often similar providers for primary and secondary roads.

These different agents again can have their own priorities, not only for asset creation but also with regards to combining necessary inputs and current expenditures. This is underscored by **Alec Gershberg** in **Chapter 8** entitled **"Educational Infrastructure, School Construction, and Decentralization in Developing Countries: Key Issues for an Understudied Area."** Often these decisions can be politically driven and, for example, "attractive" infrastructure be created without the necessary teacher allocations or the means (or incentives) to maintain the newly built infrastructure.

Coordination and competition: From the above it is clear that infrastructure implies and requires a complex web of vertical and horizontal coordination. Spatial horizontal coordination is needed between service jurisdictions that deliver the same baskets of services. Vertical coordination is needed not only from the territorial point of view, but also for the assignment of particular service attributes to each governmental layer.

Competition aspects can make coordination challenging, but it is important to bear in mind that competition may be desirable and actually warranted in some sectors; its effectiveness ultimately may depend on the organizational model adopted in a particular country for service delivery. Particularly in the health sector, public service providers are more often in competition with private providers than is the case for roads or even education. There is not only competition between private and public hospitals/clinics in a given territory/jurisdiction but also potential competition across jurisdictions between public hospitals.

The role of the financing levers: Given the complexities mentioned above it would seem reasonable to leverage financing instruments to induce coordination, and also to clarify expenditure responsibilities. This possibility is more straightforward in the road sector, as underscored by **Simon D. Ellis** and **Aurelio Menendez** in **Chapter 9** entitled **"Rural Roads: The Challenge of Decentralized Implementation."** Earmarked grants for maintenance can be used to maintain levels of funding for this critical management responsibility, and in addition this can be done with the objective of equalizing maintenance needs. Similar approaches can be used in the other sectors.

However, the extension of this operation principle may not be universal. For example its application to the health sectors is not as straightforward. Independent from the level of health service (primary, secondary health, among others), provision calls for differentiated and nuanced approaches to financing infrastructure: on the one hand, there are the objectives of universal access, emergency services, and hospital network ("collective health"), and, on the other hand, there are individual curative services ("private health"). Clearly, these services require different types of funding, which can have far-reaching consequences over health services as a whole.

The challenge of shifting responsibilities: All sectors in turn seem to be based on shifting responsibilities during the investment cycle. Planning for a new facility may be initiated by a local group of potential users, by a local politician or central deconcentrated administrator, and then be formally accepted by the sector agency, ministry, or subnational government. In general, it is not always the case that the entity that plans, appraises, and provides the budget, is also the one that implements or later also operates the facility. Often, there is necessary handover of assets as construction is completed and operation starts. Indeed, changing ownership of infrastructure over time is often explicitly required, particularly under private sector financial arrangements.

Similarly, some sectors may see different agents taking a leadership role in different steps in the project cycle. Subnational governments are then only one among the many different entities potentially involved: community-based organizations, NGOs, and social funds, all can play a role. In weak capacity environments, delegation to contract management agencies can also play a role. In addition, making use of some parallel and asymmetric application of organizational models can ensure some level of efficiency for decentralized infrastructure. Such approaches seem to be relevant for most sectors, particularly when capacities are uneven across the different territorial units.

Part IV Investing into the invisible: management and coordination of decentralized public investment

The investment cycle: From the above it implies that one needs to drill down into the investment cycle to understand the incentives at play, as projects move along the different stages. This is highlighted by **William F. Fox** and **Matthew Murray** in **Chapter 10** entitled **"The Challenge of Operating and Maintaining Infrastructure,"** who provide substantial evidence for these incentive dilemmas.

Planning and appraisal. Credible ex-ante appraisal can be limited in local planning processes because local politicians have little incentive to adopt an exercise that may constrain their autonomy in political decision-making. So, even if a local infrastructure project is selected through a participatory process, it may not be informed by evidence from even basic project appraisal. Local planning may, therefore, lead to capital development programs that are exclusively driven by the resources available and the urgency to spend on popular projects with widespread benefits. There is however a necessary differentiation: risks of costly technical "errors"—some of which can be intentional or strategic—can theoretically be more limited for "off-the-shelf" projects (e.g., education, health care, administrative and other building facilities) that rely on standard designs, but in turn may become exceedingly high for certain projects (e.g., irrigation schemes, water supply systems, flood control, and hydraulic structures) with site-specific design considerations and engineering.

i **Selection, budgeting and financing.** Where funding possibilities are limited, and local authorities operate under strong incentives to distribute resources widely for immediate political gains, there can be a trend towards fragmentation of local investment programs and a bias in favor of small, quick, and simple projects, with little connection to a well-grounded local development agenda. On the other hand, the prospects of undertaking larger infrastructure projects through co-financing with central agencies are limited by the reluctance of local politicians to lose control of the project, and, as outlined above, weak incentives for inter-agency coordination.

ii **Implementing local infrastructure.** Procurement is the most critical step during implementation. A common and major problem is insufficient national attention to developing appropriate local authority procurement systems and capacity. Standard legal provisions and guidelines often largely reproduce at the local level the requirements of the central procurement process. This approach can lead to an abuse of exceptions and imply fiduciary risks, which can be widespread without effective enforcement mechanisms and sanctions. The approach can also create incentives to artificially break projects into several contracts of smaller value and thereby work around the standard low thresholds beyond which competitive bidding is mandatory.[13] With limited incentives to supervise and monitor execution, and breaking larger projects into tranches extending implementation over multiple years, this can lead to delays that increase costs and reduce benefits.

iii **Operation and maintenance.** Despite the convincing arguments for making greater use of maintenance funding and joint budget decisions, there are several challenges which explain the often lower than optimal level of maintenance.

- First of all, there could be lack of clarity over the asset ownership, particularly in a decentralized setting. Consequently there can be confusion over which level of government is responsible for its maintenance.
- Furthermore, O&M are both substitutes (in financing and political decisions) and complements (in a technological dimension). In particular, greater capital investments require greater operations and maintenance; also altering the type of investment, such as using more expensive cement rather than asphalt roads, can sometimes reduce the necessary maintenance—that is, they are not simply components of a fixed proportions production function.
- In a decentralized setting, in particular, there could be preference variation, along with limited user support and demand. Preference variation will

surface if asset management responsibilities are unbundled; in addition, in some localities, there may simply not be sufficient user demand and willingness to pay to support the required operations and maintenance.

- In some services there could be lack of an effective signaling device for the level of use of some assets (urban streets, for instance) and hence lack of ability to assess their deterioration. This dilemma is even more pronounced for under-ground assets like water pipes, among others.
- Finally, rent extraction for political and personal gain may accrue from the diversion of operations and maintenance expenditures to other uses. Politically, decentralized governments may play the strategy of implementing low maintenance in the hope that the central government will intervene and replace the capital infrastructure. There may also be waste and inefficiencies through the contracting process.

iv **Ex-post evaluation.** There is a general paucity of systematic ex-post evaluations in most settings. This can be explained by the lack of interest for being self-evaluated on performance and by the fact that given the long life of many infrastructure projects it may be far from clear who needs to be held accountable. But it is also the case, however, that mapping out accountability over results and outcomes is often cumbersome, particularly given the multi-year nature of projects where shifting responsibilities and accountabilities are more acute.

As a result of all the above, it is not surprising that there is often an "optimism bias" in investment projects: costs are estimated low to fit into local budgets, but projects once implemented, turn out to be much more expensive. This requires an upfront recognition of this bias and a systemic approach to undercut those incentives. Some countries, for example South Korea, have demonstrated impressively the possibility to change behavior by signaling agents ex ante that projects with cost and time overruns above a certain threshold will be re-appraised at a later stage. Such approaches, however, are not too often applied at the subnational or intergovernmental level. As a first step, this would require increased effort to monitor progress and all stages of the investment cycle. But as discussed by **Ha T.T. Vu** and **Robert D. Ebel** in **Chapter 11** entitled **"Multi-Tier Monitoring of Infrastructure: Top Down and Bottom Up,"** organizing such a cross-cutting function is complex by itself, and in an intergovernmental setting it is even more challenging because of the high levels of co-financing, which itself raises questions over responsibilities and accountability.

Coordination: Coordination issues therefore seem to be emblematic for decentralized public investment, in both vertical and horizontal dimensions. Vertical coordination includes infrastructure decisions, financing, implementation, and other aspects of management across levels. Horizontal interaction, among subnational governments, is required when there are positive or negative external spillovers; when scale for infrastructure projects goes beyond administrative boundaries; and when policymakers seek to realize potential complementarities across sectors. As highlighted by **Claire Charbit** and **Cathérine Gamper** in **Chapter 12** entitled **"Coordination of Infrastructure Investment across Levels of Government,"** political economy constraints often lie at the heart of coordination failures, and these can be further driven by information asymmetries; uneven institutional capacities; and limited subnational autonomy over resources and infrastructure policy—which is, in fact, a prerequisite to be able to coordinate in the first place. It seems highly worthwhile to further invest into these invisible, often neglected, but at the end critical aspects of infrastructure management.

Part V The political economy and corruption challenges

Political economy: As a process which establishes localized benefits, decentralized infrastructure provision is particularly exposed to political economy incentives. It is not clear that all of these interests would support efficient provision of infrastructure; nor do these interests provide any guarantee that management and decisions on infrastructure provision are actually being decentralized. This is highlighted by **Leonardo Romeo** and **Paul Smoke** in **Chapter 13** entitled **"The Political Economy of Local Infrastructure Planning."** These authors conclude that local politicians may overlook the identification of larger, more complex projects that support a strategic development vision for the locality and the wider region. But addressing these shortcomings would require greater efforts over a multi-year horizon to build institutional partnerships and mobilize additional resources. If such conditions are absent or weak, infrastructure planning then is reduced to the preparation of "free-standing" local capital programs that have little connection to upstream strategic plans or to downstream work-programs of the local administration's departments.

Corruption: These sets of incentives will vary according to the country context and its governance. In "limited access" political systems prevailing in less developed countries funds for public investment are necessary to extend patronage networks and effect the intra-elite distribution of rents, which in turn may be essential for managing the risk of violent conflicts between elite factions and maintaining the stability of the political system (North *et al.*, 2006). This makes it particularly challenging to define a "dividing line" between transparency and corruption.

Indeed, as concluded by **Anwar Shah** in **Chapter 14** entitled **"Decentralized Provision of Public Infrastructure and Corruption,"** opportunities for corruption can be identified in nearly all sectors of service delivery and infrastructure provision (Table 1.1). While corruption is country- and locality-specific, it can range from petty, administrative, or bureaucratic corruption to grand corruption, to state or regulatory capture and influence peddling, and to patronage and paternalism.

The decentralized provision of infrastructure holds the promise of curtailing corruption provided there is no elite capture, that there are strong institutions of

Table 1.1 Vulnerability to corruption in the provision of infrastructure in various sectors

Water and Sanitation	Land acquisition, selection of contractors, bid rigging, compromising quality, bribes for connections, meter tampering, conflict of interest with officials involved in private provision, collusion with companies offering bottled water or tanker provision.
Roads	Land acquisition, rehabilitation, selection of contractors, false procurement and maintenance expenditures, quality of construction.
Electricity	Public utilities: Land acquisition, rights of way, rehabilitation, equipment purchase and repair markups, patronage appointments, defective meters, meter tampering, theft of electricity by tapping distribution lines with side payments, connections delays, false billing, response to non-payment of bills, false subsidy payments. Private utilities: Selection, regulatory regime, price hikes, blind eye to capital deterioration.
Hospitals	Ghost hospitals, false procurement and construction.
Schools	Ghost schools, false procurement and corruption.

Source: Adapted from Anwar Shah, Chapter 14 in this volume.

accountability in governance, a results-based governance culture, and an educated and empowered citizenry. These ideal conditions are present only to varying degrees in most countries. This means that there is a need to tailor institutional design for integrity to specific country and locality conditions in order to increase transparency, which has been identified as a key factor for improving the quality of infrastructure spending.

From gaps to solutions: policy options and the way forward

Understanding how subnational governments can move from "infrastructure gaps to solutions" is the key motivation of this book. Given their "proximity to the gaps," they are often best suited in detecting them in the first place and in crafting the most adequate solutions. However, as has been underscored throughout the contributions contained in this volume, the role of subnational governments varies considerably depending on country, sector, and even local, settings.

Decentralized infrastructure and the intergovernmental strategy

While overall country strategies for decentralization are often difficult to design and implement, it is also true that policy advice for intergovernmental relations has been consolidating significantly in recent years and there is now a useful and robust catalogue of "best practices" available. Three principles which have been emerging as nearly universally applicable are immediately relevant for the infrastructure challenge—gradualism, flexibility, and asymmetry—but they need to be enhanced and amended sensibly so that the particular relevant infrastructure issues can be addressed.

i Gradualism: tailored as a quick gain strategy. A key principle for implementing decentralization is that it should proceed gradually and step by step, among others to cater to uneven capacities. Infrastructure however might require a different approach through a "quick gain" strategy. The rationale is to set a precedent for reform, creating self-sustained dynamics. This can be done by selecting individual sectors, or individual steps in the project cycle. For instance, roads can be a priority sector given that contracts can be based on more easily identifiable outputs. Likewise, procurement can provide for quick gains in efficiency as well as transparency as it is an area easily vulnerable to corruption. Irrespective of the particular entry point selected, a quick gain approach needs to create a winning coalition in a path of successful rounds of bargaining, leading eventually to more efficient management.

ii Flexibility: tailored to sectors and projects. It has long been recognized that decentralization needs to be flexible, adapting to the institutional, political, as well as social context of a country. Infrastructure decentralization might follow primarily a sector-approach, tailored to individual projects. As a cross-cutting, multi-agency, and multi-level process, there is otherwise the high risk that efforts for improved infrastructure management will fail due to "lack of traction" and "lack of demand for reform." This can be the case in a "territorial" approach which aims at transferring power in several sectors to individual subnational governments.

iii Asymmetry: tailored to gaps. Given uneven capacities and demand for decentralization, power and resources are in most cases managed asymmetrically across the different jurisdictions, reflecting different depth and scope of decentralization. For infrastructure, the urban-rural divide is particularly relevant. It would be useful to tailor differentiated responses, one the one hand, to the large urban and metropolitan governments, and, on the other, to smaller rural governments, perhaps complemented by even an additional differentiated approach for some of the emerging intermediate cities and secondary towns.

It is clear that this type of strategy will not be free of tensions, and significant trade-offs will need to be negotiated. This can and should be done within the several policy domains that follow below.

Specific policy options

There are five specific policy areas which merit further attention: (i) responsibilities in end-services, the investment cycle, and regulation; (ii) setting incentives for the whole investment cycle; (iii) increasing capacities; (iv) enhancement of horizontal equity; and (v) strengthening coordination.

Getting a hold on shifting responsibilities

In an intergovernmental setting, all starts and ends with defining appropriate expenditure responsibilities. This should encompass the three types of responsibilities relevant for infrastructure: (a) the "end-service" to citizens (health, education, transport, and so forth); (b) responsibilities over specific steps in the investment cycle; and (c) regulation as a cross-cutting task.

a **Defining end-level services.** The importance of defining "end-services" cannot be sufficiently underscored. This has been a perennial challenge for any intergovernmental system. But there are several aspects which are relevant for infrastructure:

- **Unbundling.** It is useful to unbundle infrastructure services so that those sub-functions not characterized by clear advantages of centralization might be assigned to subnational governments. Costs could be reduced by disaggregating infrastructure expenditures into components, and making assignments on the basis of comparative advantage. For example, while perhaps technical specifications required to ensure water quality might be a matter of national concern, the construction of major water supply and sewage lines (like interurban highways) may best be handled at the regional level, and local distribution lines might be the responsibility of local governments.
- **If a service has been assigned to subnational governments, limit interference from upper level governments that may increase costs.** Interference by higher level governments, for example by imposing mandates, should be limited to concerns about externalities, and perhaps the regular monitoring of maintenance.
- **Use advantages of all levels of government for a vertical assignment.** The intermediate (or regional) tier is often given less emphasis for service delivery in decentralized systems. A regional level can have genuine advantages, particularly for the assignment of overarching functions. This could integrate more effectively externalities and address economies of scale.

b **Defining responsibilities over the steps in the investment cycle.** It seems necessary to define responsibilities for individual steps, in order to tackle the origin of the "hollowing out" of responsibilities. As pointed out above, procurement seems, by and large, the most effective way in reducing corruption opportunities. A differentiated approach by which non-standard bidding procedures are centralized can avoid situations where corruption is facilitated by weak capacity often prevailing at local levels. Another area is operations and maintenance: it would be useful to explore different organizational models, including private, public, and community-based operations and maintenance.

c **Defining responsibilities for regulation.** Given that traction for reform is not uniformly strong across all sectors, regulation may need to prioritize a sector-approach. Regulation aspects should be clearly spelled out so that the route for a project through the individual approval steps is straightforward. Some countries have advanced with simplification, creating thresholds by size of projects (monetary values), or for individual type of projects (module projects), which then may or not require special treatment. Such approaches should be further explored, without creating loopholes in transparency.

Provided there is no elite capture and there are credible regulatory agencies, unbundling infrastructure services for market competition should be considered. By isolating the natural monopoly segments of the sector, one can examine a range of market alternatives for unbundling the rest of infrastructure provision. This includes regulatory framework that encourages: (i) competition for substitutes; (ii) competition for infrastructure markets; (iii) competition for the right to supply the entire market through leases and concessions; (iv) privatization of some monopolies to reap efficiency gains. It is clear that such approaches can be more effective in urban areas, as compared to many rural areas where competition may simply be absent.

Set incentives outright for the whole public investment cycle

Public investment needs to be treated systematically, as weaknesses in one step of the investment cycle may undermine capacity in another step. The following are useful guidelines:

- **Selecting strategic entry points based on the investment portfolio.** If there are a particularly high number of new investment projects (particularly frequent in natural resource countries), it makes sense to focus on transparent management of the appraisal stages; in turn, if most projects are already at the construction stage, it might be more effective to focus attention on implementation. In general, it seems efforts at ex-post evaluation are the weakest chain in the project cycle, and there is no straightforward way to address this challenge.
- **It will be useful to signal to actors in an ex-ante fashion that their behavior has consequences ex-post.** Allowing and encouraging conscious and technically well-founded project redefinitions by setting thresholds for cost- and time-overruns can signal to actors that effective planning and appraisal are necessary. This will help to weed out "poor" projects in the initial steps before they get funded and gain further political support. South Korea has implemented such proceeding with great success.
- **Creating pressure from the private sector.** Initiatives like the Construction Transparency Initiative (CoST)[14] involve private sector companies to reveal information about contracts. In settings where the public sector is reluctant to cooperate, this can create the relevant incentives from one "receiving end."
- **Strengthen demand from end-users.** Given overall limited possibilities to get traction for reform in processes which span several agencies and several

layers of government, it seems key to strengthen the demand from end-users of public services or infrastructure works. Modern information technology (reporting through cell phones, websites) can help create immediate "transmission belts" to implementing agencies to report on delays or poor delivery of services.

Enhance institutional capacities

Infrastructure provision is a cross-cutting process requiring specialized capacity. Such capacity can be limited either at individual levels of government, or across the different subnational units. Here again there are useful guidelines that can be followed:

- **Create specialized capacities for public investment—but of an intergovernmental nature.** Institutional capacities today—whether in financial management, human resources, or procurement—increasingly require shared approaches which go beyond individual levels of government. Procurement systems, monitoring arrangements, and ex-post reviews, can be done as shared undertaking between levels of government. Further rolling out financial management systems, and building them as "main systems" capturing information on procurement and public investment across several levels of government, can contribute to reducing transaction costs while increasing transparency.
- **There is room for creating special-purpose districts or bodies** (e.g., for river basin management, mass transit, irrigation, conservation, sewerage, solid waste management, water supply, and other utilities). This could be tailored to serving local needs better than through a central provider—but gauged against the risk of creating coordination challenges.
- **Create support mechanisms for increased capacity.** Capacity creation can only be place-specific. Subnational governments should not perceive implementation monitoring as a sanction, particularly if low capacity is the underlying cause. Technical support should be dispatched if delays in implementation become apparent; systematic implementation monitoring precisely can flag problematic sectors or subnational governments. A mix between top-down learning, and horizontal, peer-to-peer learning within a community of practitioners can be useful approaches applicable in a wide range of contexts.

Enhance equity

Disparities in the stock of capital infrastructure have a direct impact on the equal opportunity in access to basic services and can be damaging to the efficient allocation of productive resources in the economy by generating unwarranted migration. However, the different objectives pursued by intergovernmental policies can significantly condition the appropriate interventions to address those disparities. For example, capital transfers policies can be designed to address differences in access to public services, or longer-term regional disparities in economic development, or the presence of significant externalities across jurisdictions. In this sense, an equitable distribution of infrastructure at the subnational level needs to be interpreted in the light of all other government policy objectives, and therefore not all disparities in the spatial distribution of the stock of infrastructure need to be addressed from a balanced view of the equity objective. But it is clear, that from an equity perspective infrastructure spending in general does not deserve any special attention or priority separate from the ultimate provision of public services—which requires capital infrastructure as inputs.

From a policy viewpoint, the relevant question is on the most appropriate form of intervention. In particular, should disparities be addressed with conditional capital grants, be incorporated into a general-purpose equalization grant, or through credit facilitation policies? The right answer is likely to depend on the type of infrastructure and may also vary with specific circumstances, such as subnational capacity and credit availability.

- In the case of infrastructure for social services, such as health and education, the different needs may be incorporated into recurrent equalization grants because of the large presence of operation and maintenance costs.
- In the case of infrastructure that is largely fee recoverable, such as in the case of utilities, credit facilitating policies may be the most adequate.
- For network infrastructure that is largely non-fee recoverable, such as no-toll roads, a conditional grant may be most appropriate.

Strengthening coordination: from signaling to contracting

Coordination is key for making infrastructure provision efficient, equitable, and sustainable. It is required vertically (across tiers of government) and horizontally (across jurisdictions and agents). Importantly, it is not a substitute for a proper definition of responsibilities. Coordination can entail a range of possibilities. Countries and subnational governments should exploit the full range of options.

i Signalling is the weakest form of coordination; this is done, for instance, through earmarking of funds. In practice it is difficult to track the use of funding; and to enforce signaling.
ii Conditionalities can be attached to certain services or projects (for instance, coverage and quality targets; operational efficiency targets).
iii Contracts among levels of government—as used in OECD countries—are typically used for multi-sector outcomes in a variety of services. In the case of partnerships it is needed to make both common objectives and each party's commitments clear.

Risks entailed in coordination need to be mitigated. It is important to ensure that they do not simply add to administrative burdens by creating structures that parallel existing administrative processes. For example, conditionality is frequently seen by subnational and central authorities alike as increasing the administrative burden without increasing impact of public investment projects.

Concluding remarks

Subnational governments around the world play a fundamental and increasing role in the provision of infrastructure. This appears to be a trend which is unlikely to change in the foreseeable horizon. And yet, ensuring provision of infrastructure through subnational governments represents formidable challenges.

This book volume provides clear evidence that these multiple challenges are not easy to be reconciled. Making trade-offs between different approaches need to be recognized openly and upfront. Nevertheless, there are many positive examples around the world where infrastructure managed in a decentralized fashion has been improving, and it is worthwhile investing future efforts and further research and data on their factors of success. Likewise, it is worth continuing with efforts to address the knowledge gaps which are identified in this book and that are only now beginning to emerge.

The essays in this volume make innovative contributions to the different aspects of decentralized infrastructure provision while providing guidance for improved design with the objective to improve the efficiency and equity of public capital infrastructure around the world. For sure this will not be the last word on the challenges of infrastructure provision in decentralized settings but it is our hope that the volume will help advance the debate.

Notes

1 Public investment is defined as gross public fixed capital formation (IMF's World Economic Outlook; WEO). Public gross fixed capital formation is referred to the general government sector, excluding public corporations. For the analysis of subnational public investment, such a definition is not without shortcomings since, for example, critical infrastructure such as water or electricity is often provided by public enterprises managed or regulated by subnational governments.

2 There are a number of different delivery modes involving the public or private sector to differing degrees. These include public ownership and procurement, which has often characterized the water supply and road networks; concessions and public-private partnerships (PPPs), which are increasingly involving the private sector in the delivery of infrastructure; and fully privately owned companies, which has often been the case in the energy sector.

3 The figure compares the averages of years 2002–2006, which represent the pre-crisis years; and the averages of years 2007–2010, which reflect post-crisis responses.

4 The infrastructure quality is ranked from 1 to 7: "extremely underdeveloped" as 1 and "extensive efficient" by international standards as 7 according to the Global Competitiveness Report 2010–2011 of the World Economic Forum (WEF 2010). These are survey results based on the question: "How would you assess general infrastructure (e.g., transport, telephony, energy) in your country?" The survey is administered to citizens and businesses.

5 Based on these findings, the emerging wisdom from a policy perspective is to provide a package of basic services independent of the location of citizens, and facilitate

connectivity among rural and urban areas to allow for and facilitate migration. For the rural areas—which is where the poor are mostly concentrated—this should encompass social services, education, health, water, and social assistance where appropriate. Road and other transport and communication are also needed to better link urban and rural areas.

6 Data from Andrés *et al.* (Chapter 2 in this volume). Also see Bhattacharya *et al.* (2012); Fay *et al.* (2011); Estache (2010); and the MDB Working Group on Infrastructure (2011).

7 In 2010, a group of countries spent between 80 and 90 percent of total public investment through subnational governments. These include India, South Africa, Czech Republic, Argentina, and a series of OECD countries, including the United States, Canada, and Germany. Among the more "centralized" countries—spending less than 20 percent of total public investment sub-nationally—are some countries in Africa (Congo, Cape Verde); Eastern Europe (Slovak Republic, Macedonia), and in the Middle East and North Africa (Morocco, Jordan, Tunisia).

8 Stimulus packages accounted for 4 percent of GDP or more in some OECD countries (Australia, Canada, Korea, United States), with a strong focus on public investment, including labor-intensive infrastructure in sectors such as transport and urban utilities and on subnational levels of administration for the implementation of investment programs.

9 This crisis-driven expansion in investment is nevertheless losing impetus as support packages are unwound in some countries and as a result of ongoing fiscal consolidation in several OECD countries (Blöchliger *et al.*, 2010; OECD, 2012).

10 Some countries like Brazil have decentralized this regulatory function to the states; while in other cases, such as Peru, this remains centralized, despite the fact that about two-thirds of public investment in this country is executed by subnational governments.

11 De Melo and Sutherland (Chapter 5 in this volume) underscore that the scope for user charges depends more broadly on the pricing regime for infrastructure projects and on the willingness/ability to pay of local residents as well as the capacity to collect fees for infrastructure use. User charges are attractive as they can provide more than simply a source of revenue. By putting a price on service provision, user charges can influence demand, which is particularly attractive for congestible public goods. Pricing can help internalize environmental and other externalities. The externalities can be significant for some types of infrastructure typically provided by subnational governments, such as water supply and wastewater. In practice, however, pricing infrastructure and associated services often fails to cover operating costs, let alone capital and external costs. Full-cost recovery remains rare, especially in developing countries.

12 Borrowing costs tend to be higher for subnational governments than the central government. Subnational governments, especially in developing countries and emerging-market economies, often face restrictions on borrowing in the form of outright bans (such as on foreign borrowing, for example), administrative restrictions (such as central government approval) and/or prudential regulations (such as limits based on debt service capacity and debt ceilings).

13 This has been well documented in many cases and most recently on an insightful report on local government procurement in Bangladesh. See Abrams *et al.* (2010).

14 Further information is available at www.constructiontransparency.org.

Bibliography

Abrams J., B., Hafiz and H. Sung Kim (2010): *Review of Procurement Practice in the Bangladesh Local Government Support Programme—Learning and Innovation Component*. United Nations Capital Development Fund, New York.

ACCA (2012): *Taking Stock of PPP and PFI Around the World*. The Association of Chartered Accountants, London.

Allain-Dupré, D. (2011): "Multi-level Governance of Public Investment: Lessons from the Crisis," OECD Regional Development Working Papers, 2011/05, OECD Publishing, Paris.

Alm, James (2010): "Municipal Financing of Urban Infrastructure: Knowns and Unknowns," Working Paper 19, Wolfensohn Center for Development, The Brookings Institution, Washington, DC.

Andrés, L., D. Biller, and M. Herrera Dappe (2014): *Infrastructure Gap in South Asia: Infrastructure Needs, Prioritization, and Financing*. The World Bank, Washington, DC.

Annez, Patricia Clarke (2007). "Urban Infrastructure Finance from Private Operators: What Have We Learned from Recent Experience?" in George Peterson and Patricia Clarke Annez (eds.) *Financing Cities*. The World Bank and Sage Publications, Washington, DC, pp. 307–338.

Bahl, Roy, Johannes Linn, and Deborah Wetzel (eds.) (2013): *Financing Metropolitan Governments in Developing Countries*. Lincoln Institute of Land Policy, Cambridge.

Bardhan, Pranab and Dilip Mookherjee (2006): "Decentralisation and Accountability in Infrastructure Delivery in Developing Countries," *Economic Journal*, 116 (508): 101–127.

Bhattacharya A., M. Romani, and N. Stern (2012): "Infrastructure for Development: Meeting the Challenge," London School of Economics and G-24 Policy Paper, June 2012.

Blöchliger, Hansjörg *et al.* (2010): "Sub-central Governments and the Economic Crisis: Impact and Policy Responses," OECD Economics Department Working Papers No. 752, Paris.

Briceño-Garmendia, Cecilia, Antonio Estache, and Nemat Shafik (2004): "Infrastructure Services in Developing Countries: Access, Quality, Costs and Policy Reform." Policy Research Working Paper Series 3468, World Bank, Washington, DC.

Calderón, C. and L. Servén (2004): "The Effects of Infrastructure Development on Growth and Income Distribution," Policy Research Working Paper No. 3400, World Bank, Washington, DC.

Charbit, C. (2011): "Governance of Public Policies in Decentralised Contexts: The Multi-level Approach," OECD Regional Development Working Papers, 2011/04, OECD Publishing, Paris.

CoST (2013): Construction Sector Transparency Initiative, Briefing Notes, accessible at: www.constructiontransparency.org.

De Mello, Luiz (2012): "Fiscal Decentralisation and Public Investment: The Experience of Latin America," in Giorgio Brosio and Juan Pablo Jimenez (eds.) *Decentralization and Reform in Latin America: Improving Intergovernmental Relations*. Edward Elgar, Northampton, MA.

Eaton, Kent, Kai Kaiser, and Paul Smoke (2011): *The Political Economy of Decentralization: Implications for Aid Effectiveness.* World Bank, Washington, DC.

Estache, Antonio (2006): "Infrastructure: A Survey of Recent and Upcoming Issues," World Bank, April.

Estache, Antonio (2010): "Infrastructure Finance in Developing Countries: An Overview," *EIB Papers*, 15(2): 61–88.

Estache, Antonio and Marianne Fay (2007): "Current Debates on Infrastructure Policy." Paper prepared for the Growth Commission (www.growthcommission.org).

Estache, A. and S. Sinha (1995): "Does Decentralization Increase Spending on Infrastructure?," Policy Research Working Paper, No. 1457, World Bank, Washington, DC.

Faguet, J.-P. (2004): "The Effects of Decentralisation on Public Investment: Evidence and Four Lessons from Bolivia and Colombia," Working Paper, No. 62, Crisis States Research Centre, LSE, London.

Faguet, Jean-Paul (2005): "The Effects of Decentralisation on Public Investment: Evidence and Four Lessons from Bolivia and Colombia," Crisis States Research Centre Working Papers Series 1, 62.

Fay, M. M. Toman, D. Benitez, and D. Csordas (2011): "Infrastructure and Sustainable Development," in S. Fardoust, Yongbeom Kim, and Claudia Paz Sepúlveda (eds.) *Postcrisis Growth and Development: A Development Agenda for the G20*. World Bank, Washington, DC.

Frank, Jonas (2013): "Public Investment Management in Latin America and the Caribbean: Institutions under Evolution," in The World Bank, *Investing to Invest, Building the Foundation for Effective Public Investment Management*. World Bank, Washington, DC.

Guerra-Garcia, Gustavo and Frank, Jonas (2013): "Peru Revamps Its Public Investment System. Country Case Study," in The World Bank, *Investing to Invest, Building the Foundation for Effective Public Investment Management*. World Bank, Washington, DC.

Gutman, J. (1999): "Decentralizing Roads: Matching Accountability, Resources, and Technical Expertise," in S.J. Burki, G. Perry, and W. Dillinger (eds.) *Beyond the Center: Decentralizing the State, Latin American and Caribbean Studies*, Viewpoints No. 19636. World Bank, Washington, DC, pp. 87–105.

Herrero-Alcalde, Ana, Jorge Martínez-Vázquez, and Encarnacion Murillo-Garcia (2011): "The Challenge of Designing Capital Equalization Transfers: An Application to Spanish Regions," *Publius: The Journal of Federalism*, 42(2): 260–288.

High Powered Expert Committee for Estimating the Investment Requirements for Urban Infrastructure Services (2011): *Report on Indian Urban Infrastructure and Services*. Ministry of Urban Development, Government of India, Delhi.

Hulbert, Claudia (2012): "Public Investment Across Levels of Government: The Case of Galicia, Spain," OECD 28th Territorial Development Policy Committee.

Hulten, C.R. and R.M. Schwab (1997): "A Fiscal Federalism Approach to Infrastructure Policy," *Regional Science and Urban Economics*, 27: 139–159.

Humplick, F. and A. Estache (1995): "Does Decentralization Improve Infrastructure Performance?" in A. Estache (ed.) *Decentralizing Infrastructure: Advantages and Limitations*, World Bank Discussion Paper Series, No. 290. World Bank, Washington, DC.

IMF (2013): World Economic Outlook (WEO) database, accessible at www.imf.org/external/pubs/ft/weo/2013/01/weodata/index.aspx.

Kaganova, Olga (2011): "Guidebook on Capital Investment Planning for Local Governments," Urban Development Series, Knowledge Papers, World Bank, Washington, DC.

Kappeler, A. and T. Välilä (2008): "Fiscal Federalism and the Composition of Public Investment in Europe," *European Journal of Political Economy*, 24: 562–570.

Kappeler, Andreas, Albert Solé-Ollé, Andreas Stephan, and Timo Välilä (2012): "Does Fiscal Decentralization Foster Regional Investment in Productive Infrastructure?" KTH/CESIS Working Paper Series in Economics and Institutions of Innovation No. 273, April.

Kehew, Robert, Matsukawa, Tomoko, and Petersen, John (2005): *Local Financing for Sub-sovereign Infrastructure in Developing Countries*. World Bank, Washington, DC.

Kim, Jay-Hyung (2013): "Public Investment Management in South Korea," in The World Bank, *Investing to Invest: Building the Foundation for Effective Public Investment Management*. World Bank, Washington, DC.

Lucioni, L. (2009): "La Provisión de Infraestructura en América Latina: Tendencias, Inversiones y Financiamiento," *Macroeconomía del Desarrollo*, No. 72, CEPAL, Santiago.

Martínez-Vázquez, Jorge and Andrey Timofeev (2012): "Propensity to Invest and the Additionality of Capital Transfers: A Country Panel Perspective," Working Paper 12–16,

International Studies Program, Andrew Young School of Policy Studies, Georgia State University.

MDB (Multilateral Development Banks) Working Group on Infrastructure (2011): "Infrastructure Action Plan."

Mizell, L. and D. Allain-Dupré (2013): "Creating Conditions for Effective Public Investment: Sub-National Capacities in a Multi-Level Governance Context," OECD Regional Development Working Papers, No. 2013/04, OECD Publishing.

North D., J. Wallis, S. Webb, and B. Weingast (2006): "Limited Access Orders in the Developing World: A New Approach to the Problems of Development," Policy Research Working Paper 4359, World Bank, Washington, DC.

OECD (2007): *Linking Regions and Central Governments: Contracts for Regional Development*. OECD, Paris.

OECD (2008): *Public-Private Partnerships: In Pursuit of Risk Sharing and Value for Money*. OECD, Paris.

OECD (2010): *Managing Water for All, An OECD Perspective on Pricing and Financing*. OECD, Paris.

OECD (2011): *OECD Regional Outlook*. OECD, Paris.

OECD (2012): *Mobilising Investments for Urban Sustainability, Job Creation and Resilient Growth*, Issues Paper for the OECD Roundtable for Mayors and Ministers, Chicago.

OECD (2013): *Investing Together: Working Effectively Across Levels of Government*. OECD, Paris.

Oyewole, Olugbenga E. and Volker Treichel (2012): "Public Investment Management in Lagos State, Nigeria," in The World Bank, *Investing to Invest: Building the Foundation for Effective Public Investment Management*, World Bank, Washington, DC.

Pagano, Michael (2011): *Funding and Investing in Infrastructure*, Urban Institute, Washington, DC.

Peterson, George E. and Elisa Muzzini (2005): "Decentralizing Basic Infrastructure Services," in Roland White and Paul Smoke (eds.) *East Asia Decentralizes: Making Local Government Work*. World Bank, Washington, DC, pp. 209–236.

Rajaram, A., K. Kaiser, T.M. Le, J.-H. Kim, and J. Frank (2014): *The Power of Public Investment Management. Transforming Resources Into Assets for Growth*, World Bank, Washington, DC.

Rao, M. Govinda and Richard M. Bird (2011): "Coping with Change: The Need to Restructure Urban Governance and Finance in India," IMFG Papers on Municipal Finance and Governance No. 4, Toronto.

Sutherland, D., S. Araújo, B. Égert, and T. Kozluk (2011): "Public Policies and Investment in Network Infrastructure," *OECD Economic Studies*, 2011: 161–183.

Van Ryneveld, Philip (2007): "Fiscal Decentralization and Financing of Urban Infrastructure in South Africa," in George Peterson and Patricia Clarke Annez (eds.) *Financing Cities*. World Bank and Sage Publications, Washington, DC, pp. 183–204.

WEF (2006): *The Global Competitiveness Report 2006–2007*, World Economic Forum.

WEF (2010): *The Global Competitiveness Report 2010–2011*, World Economic Forum.

World Bank (2009): *Colombia Decentralization: Options and Incentives for Efficiency*, Report No. 39832-CO. World Bank, Washington, DC.

World Bank (2013): *Investing to Invest*, World Bank, Washington, DC.

Part I

Measuring infrastructure gaps

Quantity and quality perspectives

2 The infrastructure gap and decentralization

Luis Alberto Andrés, Dan Biller, and Jordan Schwartz[1]

Introduction

The lack of infrastructure services often referred as the infrastructure gap is felt throughout the economy and society at large. The infrastructure gap acts as a bottleneck to economic sectors, directly curtailing the growth potential. It also impacts negatively the opportunities to improve health, education, and other social sectors that can be just as, or even more, important to current welfare improvement, poverty alleviation, and future economic growth. The infrastructure gap often disproportionally affects the poor more than the rich not only at the population level but also at different jurisdictions within a country. Even if the rich also suffer with the infrastructure gap, rich people, districts, and countries are also more able to implement coping mechanisms.

The policy discussion on filling the infrastructure gap takes several forms. One of them is the need to complement access to infrastructure with policies to incentivize the use of services, or make its potential benefits more obvious or attainable. In this sense, policy makers would focus on subsidizing (implicitly or explicitly and with sunset clauses) the infrastructures that provide the greatest public benefit (public good) in contrast to those that provide large private benefits. This should be true across infrastructure sectors as well as within sectors. However, evidence shows the need to think through the location of the infrastructure facilities, their maintenance, and campaigns to promote their use. Another form is about who should be financing this gap. Given the magnitude of this funding requirement, it is not feasible to expect governments to fund the gap only with public resources. However, this situation can be seen as an opportunity to rethink and improve the infrastructure service provision approach currently in place, which refers to the organizational form that defines and structures the roles of the public and private sectors.

While the above statements are often true, the real story lies in the heterogeneity of infrastructure service provision. The nexus of the infrastructure gap and decentralization is both diverse and complex. For example, connective infrastructure such as interstate transport and telecommunication may have a higher direct impact on economic growth by facilitating agglomerations. They could thus be the focus of central service provision. At least in the short term and in countries where economic sectors are not highly dependent in water as an input, water and sanitation provision may have a higher impact on welfare; thereby being the focus of local service provision. At a higher conceptual level, the nexus of the infrastructure gap and decentralization is guided by the economic dimension of individual infrastructures, technologies available for service delivery, and political economy realities. For instance, the economic dimension of an infrastructure subsector in terms of service delivery could fall into four broad categories, namely economies of scale, network effects, cross jurisdiction externalities, and allocative efficiency. These categories may hint at the jurisdiction in which the service should be provided thus indicating where the infrastructure gap should be addressed. However, available technologies may result in a diverse response to addressing service provision, and political realities may add an extra layer of complexity. Power distribution may serve as a good example. There are compelling economic reasons to have power distributed via a grid (e.g., economies of scale, less air pollution when compared with certain alternatives). Yet, technologies are available to supply single households with power at different need levels (e.g., generators) and adequately taking into account environmental considerations (e.g., solar panels). Political realities may however push for solutions that require central or regional power distribution. Ultimately, this array of factors influencing infrastructure service provision also generates a diverse response to the infrastructure gap. Pre-established formulas are thus difficult to come by, and policy makers are left primarily with some guiding principles to be adjusted to specific realities.

This chapter provides this higher conceptual discussion of the nexus of the infrastructure gap and decentralization. It starts by detailing the definition of the infrastructure gap and the methodologies to calculate it. It provides some global trends for developing countries in terms of the gap and briefly discusses financing possibilities for developing countries to address the gap. The chapter then turns to the discussion of the link between the infrastructure gap and decentralization, providing a typology of infrastructure subsectors and possible jurisdiction of service provision. It briefly discusses the potential for raising local finances for provision and the relationship between poverty and provision. The chapter concludes with some broad policy lessons.

Infrastructure gap: What is it? How to measure it?

In order to assess the infrastructure gap, a country's level of infrastructure provision needs first to be evaluated. This includes a diagnosis of coverage, quality, and efficiency of infrastructure services, and investments in infrastructure. It involves gathering existing data on access rates to the various infrastructure services. To the extent possible, the quality of service provision should also be appraised. In order to gage the realism of infrastructure service targets, a review of the historic level of investment in infrastructure through creation of a time-series on actual public and private investment is also essential. In its simplest form, the actual gap is thus the difference between targets and baseline over a time period in which the gap is aimed to be filled.

There are many ways of estimating the investment needed in physical infrastructure. The actual amount depends on targets, and each target may be priced in a variety of ways. Different sectors inevitably require different methodological approaches. These include:

- ***Costing set targets.*** This approach estimates the physical needs as the difference between the baseline and the aimed targets. These targets may be defined as universal service access, the Millennium Development Goals (MDGs), or can be assessed using any type of benchmarking exercise. This compares normalized infrastructure performance indicators across countries or areas with similar characteristics (usually socio-economic variables). It can also be compared to predetermined standards defined as optimal. The choice of benchmark can affect the results significantly, and the targets do not usually have clear theoretical foundations. The benchmarking can be done through a simple comparison with peers. For example, what would it cost South Asia to reach the infrastructure density of a region deemed as an appropriate comparator or target? An even simpler approach is to benchmark countries in terms of how much the region spends on infrastructure with respect to historical investment levels. Once these values are estimated, the analysis should assess the unit cost per physical unit needed, and once aggregated these figures will result in the total investment needed for filling the gap.
- ***Estimates based on sectoral analysis.*** The best approach may be to rely on micro-sectoral analysis. This effort should build estimates based on sector data and sector specialists' views. Although the approach varied across sectors, this may be summarized as follows. In the case of transport, the estimate would be based on planned expenditures by responsible agencies and operators, adjustments based on experts' opinions of what could be postponed and what must be done within the next five years. In the case of water and sanitation, estimates will be based on various approximations of the cost of achieving coverage targets under the MDGs. Finally, in the case of the power sector, the figures would be largely based on experts' opinions about what is the minimum requirement to preserve the integrity of the systems (lower case scenario) or the investments needed to provide high quality reliability of service (higher case scenario). Sectoral estimates can, at times, be no more than "wish lists" and can benefit from benchmarking. It is useful, therefore, to pull them together and compare them with what peer countries are doing through various kinds of benchmarking exercises. It is also interesting to price socially desirable targets, such as universal coverage, and compare the estimated costs with the sectoral scheme. These various comparisons provide a "reality check" and allow for a more robust set of estimates.
- ***Macro-econometric models.*** More sophisticated approaches rely on either macro-econometric models, or micro-engineering economic models. For the macro-econometric models, there are several ways of looking at what might be needed. One could look at the infrastructure coverage needed to achieve a particular growth objective, assuming given levels of other inputs.

An approximation can be obtained using econometric models based on cross-country panel data to estimate the relationship between infrastructure stocks, social and economic variables including GDP and population. Using GDP and population projections, the model allows estimating the future infrastructure investment needs. Maintenance costs are estimated as predetermined percentages of the total investments. The model predicts infrastructure needs at the aggregate (regional) level, but it is weak to estimate at the country level due to its high level of aggregation, limited explanatory factors, and lack of location specific analysis.[2]

Current global trends of the infrastructure gap

The demand for infrastructure, whether it is from private or commercial users, is not static but is dynamic evolving with country conditions. A notable feature of infrastructure is its relationship with growth. The relationship is not unidirectional as infrastructure investments create and perpetuate growth, which in turn changes the type of infrastructure demanded as society becomes more prosperous and as the economy's structure alters. The demand for infrastructure has been growing in the world in general and Asia in particular. Two decades ago, the South Asia region (SAR) and the East Asia and the Pacific region (EAP) had similar urbanization rates at 25 percent and 29 percent respectively and were close in terms of infrastructure service provision. Since 1990 SAR has enjoyed the second highest economic growth in the world behind only EAP (see Table 2.1). During the 1990s decade, growth in SAR averaged over 5 percent, while between 2000 and 2011, it averaged almost 6.7 percent. While economic growth has been accompanied by rapid urbanization in EAP (49 percent urbanization rate in 2011), SAR remains the least urbanized region in the world (31 percent), well below the world urbanization rate (52 percent). The economic growth that the region has been experiencing is both influenced and influences the region's demand for infrastructure. For example, forecasts indicate that India will have more cars than the United States by 2050.

Access to infrastructure services significantly varies across regions. While SAR's economic growth is second only to EAP, SAR and Sub-Saharan Africa (SSA) have similar access to infrastructure services, ultimately translating in a large infrastructure gap when compared with other regions of the world (see Table 2.1):

1 Power: SSA, with 31 percent of its population having access to electricity, is followed by SAR where only 61 percent of the population enjoys the benefits of electricity access. This remarkably contrasts with the rest of the regions where more than 90 percent of the population has access to power services. According to businesses in South Asia, infrastructure is a major or severe hindrance to their growth, and electricity is the largest problem.
2 Improved sanitation: Access is quite low with only 31 and 38 percent of SSA and SAR's population having access, which is close to half the world

average of 63 percent population access. Open defecation seems to be one of the most salient issues facing SAR, with 700 million people (i.e., 43 percent of the population) relying on it in 2010. This ranks South Asia as the region with the highest incidence of open defecation in the world.

3 Improved water: This indicator is the only indicator where South Asia is about even with the rest of the world and EAP, averaging 90 percent population access. Yet the quality and quantity of improved water may be in question. Most of the access to water is through public stands; only 22 percent of the population has access to piped water and 24/7 water supply is a rare exception in South Asian cities.

4 Communications: SAR lags significantly behind both EAP and Latin America and the Caribbean region (LAC) when it comes to connectivity, being at times similar to SSA. Communication among people who are not in close proximity is inefficient. In terms of telecom access, measured as fixed and mobile lines per 100 people, SAR and SSA rank at the bottom (72 and 54) with less than half the access found in EAP and LAC (105 and 125). This situation becomes even more dramatic when we add urbanization to the picture, with only 31 and 36 percent of the population in SAR and SSA respectively, living in urban areas.

5 Transport: The transport infrastructure in SAR is not the exception when it comes to poor access, though this problem seems more pervasive throughout the developing world. Using total road network per 1,000 people as an indicator, SAR has 2.7km, which is close to EAP (2.5km), SSA (2.5km), and MNA (2.8km), but is well below the World average (4.7km), ECA (8km), and North America (24km). Furthermore, the transport infrastructure suffers from serious shortcomings such as lack of intraregional connectivity between the national road networks, unrealized potential for rail and inland water freight transport, and inadequate road and rail connectivity of ports with hinterlands. These limitations turn transport infrastructure into a hindrance for regional and international trade, as investment climate surveys indicate.

The fight to alleviate absolute poverty in the last 20 years has had a marked effect on increasing access to basic infrastructure services; however outcomes have neither been uniform across countries nor across infrastructure sectors. Nearly two billion people have gained access to improved water supplies over the last two decades, largely due to the MDGs (UN, 2011). However, networked electricity remains well below demand especially in Africa where an additional 7,000MW of new power generation capacity is required yearly, but less than 20 percent of this figure is currently being installed (Foster and Briceño-Garmendia, 2011).

The heterogeneity on access to infrastructure services is not just among countries, but also among districts within countries. For instance, using district level data from the entire SAR region, districts were ranked by quintiles on access to electricity, gas, improved water, improved sanitation, and telecoms respectively. In India, some of the best performing districts in terms of access to improved water sources are in the north and northwest of the country, while some of the worst performing districts are in the northeast and west as well as in the southwest coast (see Box 2.1). An interesting example of the heterogeneity on access to improved sanitation is found on the Indian side of the border with Pakistan, where some of the best performing districts in the country are next to some of the worst performing districts. Furthermore, districts that perform well on access to one infrastructure service don't necessarily perform well on access to another infrastructure service. For example, districts in Kerala are high performers in access to improved sanitation, but are among the worst performers on access to improved water sources (Andrés *et al.*, 2013).

Table 2.1, therefore, provides a snapshot of the access deficit in 2011, but this deficit has risen and will continue to rise in the coming years. To meet the current demand for infrastructure approximately US$0.8–0.9 trillion worth of annual infrastructure investments are required in the developing world. By 2020 this figure inflates to US$1.8–2.3 trillion per year. This equates to roughly an increase in annual infrastructure investment from 3 percent of developing world GDP to 6–8 percent of GDP.[3] Climate change has created an additional financial burden on the public provision of infrastructure as US$200–300 billion of the aggregate US$1.8–2.3 trillion figure cited above is needed to retrofit existing infrastructure assets. These estimates are more closely related to the costing the targets approach.

Bearing this in mind, Figure 2.1 below quantifies investment needs by sector, by region and by phase of project development (preparation or construction)

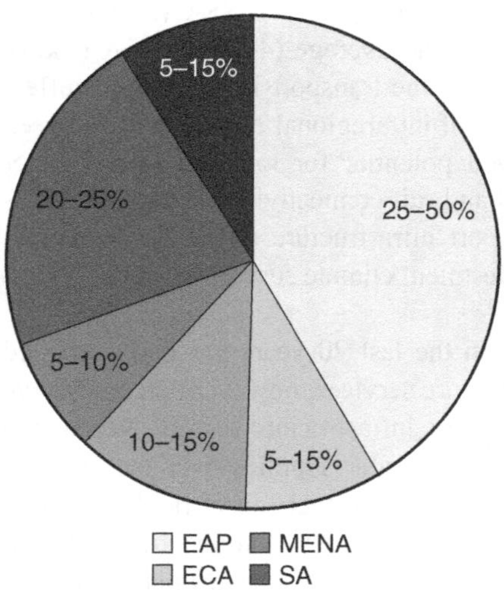

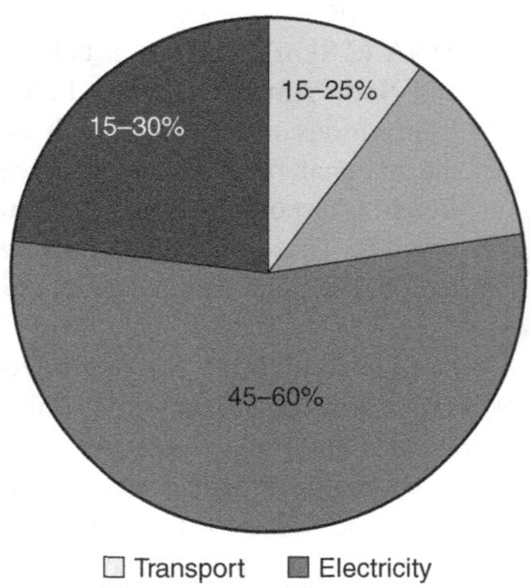

Figure 2.1 Annual infrastructure spending requirements in the developing world (US$1.9–2.5tr).

Notes
US$ trillion per year (2013 real prices), capital investments only (excl. operation and maintenance costs). Estimated annual infrastructure spending need for 2020 calculated by taking the Fay *et al.* (2010) figures with an extension by Bhattacharya *et al.* (2012).

Box 2.1 Districts in poor states that perform better than districts in rich states in India

Bihar is the poorest state in India while Maharashtra is one of the richest. Yet, several districts in Bihar are performing better than several districts in Maharashtra. It is not surprising that Maharashtra has significantly more coverage in tap water and access to electricity than Bihar; but Bihar has higher access to improved water services (95 percent vs. 79 percent) than Maharashtra. Moreover, the top 25 percent of the districts in Bihar, in terms of overall access to infrastructure services, over-perform half of the districts in Maharashtra in access to improved sanitation, gas, and telecom; sectors that are more capital than natural resource intensive. The map below presents bad districts in rich states and good districts in poor states, and shows that the case of Bihar and Maharashtra is not isolated. In the map, districts in the bottom quartile of the GDP per capita distribution have their boundaries drawn in dark gray, while those in the top quartile have their boundaries drawn in light gray. The districts among the top performers (i.e., top two quartiles) on infrastructure access, but located on states in the bottom quartile of the GDP per capita distribution, are shaded in light gray. Similarly, those districts among the bottom performers (i.e., bottom two quartiles) on infrastructure access, but located on states in the top quartile of the GDP per capita distribution are shaded in dark grey. As it can be seen from the map, there are 67 districts ranked among the top 50 percent of districts in terms of access to infrastructure services, which are located in poor states (those on the first quartile of GDP per capita distribution). Similarly, there are 16 districts among the bottom 25 percent of the districts in terms of access, which are in rich states (those on the fourth quartile of the GDP per capita distribution).

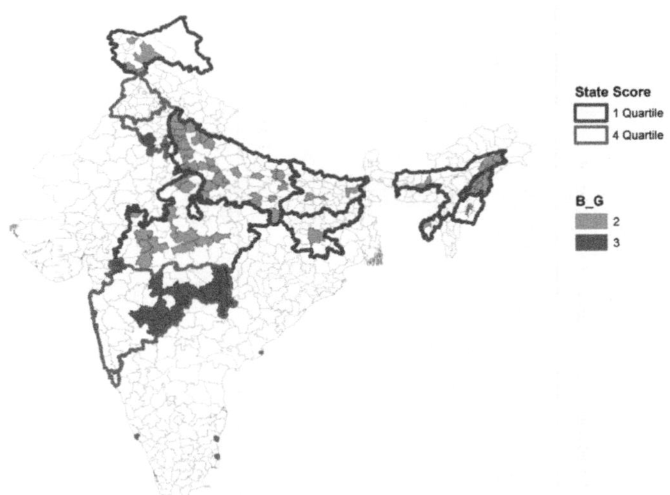

Map 2.1 Districts in poor states that perform better than districts in rich states in India.

Source: Andrés *et al.* (2013).

Table 2.1 Access to infrastructure services by region

	Avg GDP growth (2000–2011)	*Urbanization rate (2011)*	*Telecom access (per 100 people) (2011)*	*Electricity access (% of pop.) (2009)*	*Access to improved sanitation (% of pop.) (2010)*	*Access to improved water (% of pop.) (2010)*
EAP	8.9	49	105	91	66	90
ECA	5.1	65	157	100	84	96
LAC	3.6	79	125	93	79	94
MNA	4.3	59	105	90	88	89
SAR	6.7	31	72	62	38	90
SSA	4.6	36	54	31	31	61
World	2.7	52	103	79	63	88

Source: Andrés *et al.* (2013).

highlighting that bridging the gap between estimated needs and the current level of investments in infrastructure is a significant challenge in all regions. Reinvigorating the supply of infrastructure requires supplementing traditional sources of finance with new sources of equity and debt finance, pairing existing instruments with innovative techniques to lower the cost of sovereign borrowing, and promoting institutional performance to improve market and project environments.

Decentralization and the infrastructure gap

Decentralization means to distribute the administrative powers or functions of a central authority over a less concentrated area. As stated by the *World Development Report* (World Bank, 2004: 29):

> Decentralization can be a powerful tool for moving decision making closer to those affected by it. Doing so can strengthen the links and accountability between policymakers and citizens—local governments are potentially more accountable to local demands. It can also strengthen them between policymakers and providers—local governments are potentially more able to monitor providers. But local governments should not be romanticized. Like national governments they are vulnerable to capture—and this might be easier for local elites on a local scale.

Ultimately, decentralization is a tool for improving service delivery to the smallest units of society—households and individuals. If it worked well, decentralization would mean diminishing the infrastructure gap. Yet, as stated above it cannot be viewed as a silver bullet. There are several conditions and characteristics of infrastructure services that need to be considered when analyzing the nexus of decentralization and the infrastructure gap.

The degree of decision-making at the local level determines the type of administrative decentralization. For example, deconcentration refers to the process of dispersing responsibility of the central government to its regional offices—often a mere shift of responsibilities from the capital offices to the regional ones. Delegation, however, enables local governments to perform on behalf of the central government, sharing decision-making and administration responsibilities. However, the most complete form of decentralization is devolution which transfers authority for decision-making, finance, and management to local government. Local governments elect their own mayors, raise their own revenues, and have independent investment powers.

Each type of infrastructure investment has its own specific characteristics that directly or indirectly impact the desirability and type of decentralization at all stages of the process including design, finance, construction, operation, and maintenance. Two roads with the same physical characteristics, built in very different environments will result in different growth impacts, amongst others. Given that variations of decentralization differ in response to a multitude of factors, it is challenging to generalize and recommend the best fit without taking a country and sector specific approach. Decentralization for infrastructure depends on the nature of the investment, the reason it is being provided, how it is being financed, and where is located.

In this vein, Table 2.2 outlines which sectors would benefit from decentralization and the challenges they face. It serves only as a general guide for considering decentralization phases and highlights the myriad of variations existent by sector, geographic location, and country. In theory, local residents should finance the cost of infrastructure projects (through user fees and taxation) but regional and national governments should assume financial responsibility for the spillover benefits; however, in some sectors, it is not always easy to differentiate. There are two important strategies or institutional arrangements which can render the assignment of responsibilities more complex: (i) horizontal cooperation, when two or more subnational governments cooperate in joint delivery of infrastructure services so there are higher economies of scale; and (ii) vertical cooperation, when this assistance occurs between a regional and local government, for instance.

Frequently, when infrastructure services are unbundled as in Table 2.2, at least two aspects become apparent: (i) the diversity of potentially adequate provision in a given subsector; and (ii) those subsectors that require special attention at a given level of jurisdiction. Power generation offers an interesting example. All jurisdictions are potentially involved in power generation—from central authorities (private or public) to households. Technology is readily available at different private and public costs (via for example air pollution). The quality of generation (e.g., individual solar panels, diesel generators, etc.) and usage (lighting, appliances, etc.) varies greatly. Yet, there are some noticeable advantages in having a central or regional generation due to economies of scale, mitigating public bads like air pollution, among others, which doesn't necessarily mean that all households in a country should be connected to the power grid. The power sector alone sheds light on the heterogeneous nature of decentralization and the importance of collaboration between the central and local governments in identifying and serving the interest of their constituents.

The experience on decentralization and infrastructure service delivery is mixed. The varying impacts of decentralization point to its underlying essence which is highly contingent on the type of infrastructure and the existing institutional, political, and economic environment in a given country. It is also a dynamic process, which takes time to be fully integrated in any given society. There are, however, several features that characterize successful decentralization: (i) the local decision process is fully democratic, transparent, and inclusive of the beneficiaries; (ii) the cost of local decisions are fully borne by the local government; and (iii) the benefits don't spill over jurisdictional boundaries. When these criteria are met, decentralization is promising.

A key issue that often occurs is a mismatch between responsibilities in terms of infrastructure service delivery and the ability to execute the responsibilities. This mismatch is often financial/fiscal in nature, namely local authorities are not financially capable of delivering or at least regulating the delivery of a particular infrastructure service. Financial/fiscal decentralization is multifaceted, including: (i) self-financing or cost recovery through user charges; (ii) co-financing arrangements in which respective users contribute to infrastructure services through monetary or labor contributions; (iii) raising local revenues through property or sales taxes; (iv) transferring tax revenues from the central government to local governments, amongst others.

Even if funding were available, capacity for implementation at lower tiers of government or communities is often lacking. While with adequate funding this issue could be surpassed over time, a lag between decentralization and filling the infrastructure gap should be expected. In addition, while decentralization often follows a constitutional legal process, the actual application of laws varies widely. Equally important is the lack of clarity in the laws. Some infrastructure services could be tagged to local jurisdictions, but status-quo or even different legal interpretations may prevent or slow decentralization. Decisions from courts at times to the highest levels are needed to provide the necessary clarity. Finally, there are infrastructure services where unregulated decentralization may not be desirable. This is true especially for those services with large cross-jurisdiction externalities. For example, what would be the incentives for a municipality in upper watersheds to avoid contaminating waters (e.g., via sewage treatment) for the use of a municipality downstream? Yet, piped water distribution is often though not always considered a local service.

The key to decentralization is flexibility in accommodating a wide range of local conditions. Sometimes this is achieved through decentralized public, or centralized public means, but what really determines the right fit is accounting for the heterogeneity of local needs, potential for quality, efficient and cheap service provision, and the existence of market failures (e.g., public bads, externalities) associated with the provision. Through this decentralization lens, the results then depend on three primary factors: (i) the weight ascribed to various criteria; (ii) the nature of infrastructure; and (iii) the economic, political, and environmental characteristics of the respective country, region, and infrastructure via available technologies. In the end assigning responsibility is always also a political decision, and driven by political economy factors.

Decentralization and filling the infrastructure gap: what policy tools, where does the money come from, how are investments made?

A detailed discussion on decentralization policy tools, financing to fill the infrastructure gap, and the consequences of infrastructure expenditures (e.g., impact on economic growth, poverty alleviation, etc.) is beyond the scope of this chapter. It includes traditional public finance instruments such as central/local taxes and subsidies, central to local cash transfer schemes, local to local payments (e.g., payments for ecological services), pooling resources in metro or user association arrangements, privatization and public-private partnerships (PPPs) at all jurisdiction levels, community driven development schemes, and

Table 2.2 Economic logic underpinning decentralization in the infrastructure sectors

Infrastructure sector		*Level of jurisdiction*	*Economic determinants*	*Institutional arrangements*
WATER	Catchment (often the case for groundwater as well)	Central or Regional	Cross-jurisdiction externalities or open access issues *Central and regional governments or water user associations should regulate (i.e., catchment, groundwater and watershed management to ensure equitable distribution across jurisdictional boundaries)*	*State or Regional Water utility; responsible line ministry; national/regional water agencies, user associations*
	Distribution	Local*	Allocative efficiency, economies of scale	*Local sector entities*
SANITATION	On-site and off-site	Local*	Cross-jurisdiction externalities; allocative efficiency	*Local sector entities, private household level solutions*
SEWAGE TREATMENT	On-site and off-site (depends on collection)	Local*	Cross-jurisdiction externalities and addressing local public bads	*Local sector entities, private household level solutions*
FLOOD CONTROL	Catchment Urban	Central, Regional, Local*	Cross-jurisdiction externalities and addressing local public bads	*National/regional water agencies* *Local authorities*

POWER	Generation	Central, Regional, Local*	Economies of scale and cross-jurisdiction externalities	Para-statal, State Company, National Agency, Local communities; individual user
	Transmission	Central, Regional	Economies of scale and cross-jurisdiction externalities	Para-statal, State Company or National Agency
	Distribution	Local	Economies of scale; allocative efficiency	Private or public entity
ROADS	Highways	Central, Regional	Economies of scale; club good issues** (i.e., congestion)	National Highway Administrators
	Rural roads	Local*	Club good issues,** allocative efficiency	State or local government/ communities
SOLID WASTE	Collection	Local	Allocative efficiency	Local government
	Disposal	Regional	Cross-jurisdiction externalities; economics of scale	Metro agencies, Local government associations
ICT	Landlines	Central, Regional	Economies of scale; network externalities	Regulated private sector
	Mobile	Central, Regional	Economies of scale; network externalities	Regulated private sector

Notes
* While operation and implementation should be local, the central and regional governments could play an important role in regulation.
** Club goods present excludability but non-rivalry in consumption.

household private investments, among others. There are several financing possibilities and the impacts of infrastructure investments in the economy are far and wide. Nonetheless, this chapter wouldn't be complete without at least a brief analysis of some main current issues in addition to those covered above.

The 2008 global economic crisis heightened a reality that existed for much of the past 30 years in most developing countries perhaps with the exception of China, Vietnam, and a few others. Access to easy sources of financing either from government budgets or access to capital markets is limited across the developing world. This translates both into a lack of new infrastructure investments as well as accentuated depreciation of existing infrastructure stocks. As Figure 2.2 indicates, government budgets remain the lion share of infrastructure investments. Even if 2008 numbers may have been spurred by Keynesian policies to counteract the economic downfall, and even if fiscal space is becoming a severe issue in several countries, governments are likely to remain the main

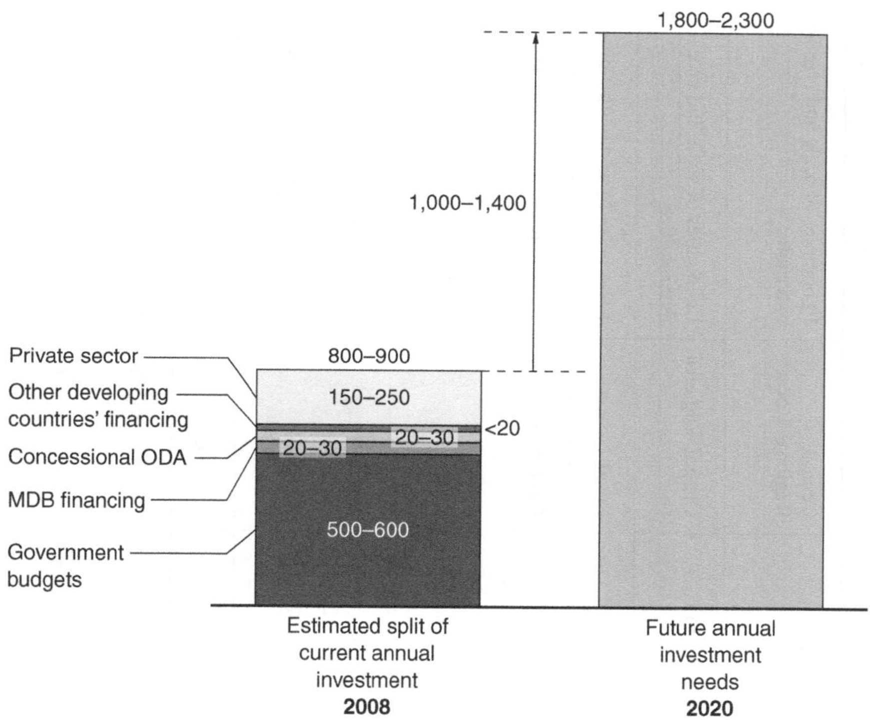

Figure 2.2 Annual infrastructure spending by sources (real US$bn, 2008) (source: Split of current sources of finance is a G-24 own assessment based on various estimates including Estache, 2010; Macquarie Bank, 2009; MDB Working Group on Infrastructure, 2011).

Note
Split by sources of finance are approximate ranges only and don't add to exactly to the totals given for that reason.

source of infrastructure spending. The increasing constraints in government spending around the world highlight the importance of policy instruments to improve the efficiency of infrastructure service delivery. Yet, it also indicates the importance of private sector participation in filling the infrastructure gap at different jurisdictions in the future. Only 20 MICs have the ability to access capital markets at the national level, while an additional 20 have limited access to volatile and costly short-maturity loans. MDB instruments, such as the suite of guarantee instruments, can be used to lower borrowing costs for those MICs able to access international debt markets and to mitigate country level risk that might otherwise dissuade international investors. The rest of the MICs, as well as most provincial and local governments in all MICs, have little or no market access severely constraining the provision of subnational, publically funded infrastructure unless funding is sought from official development assistance (PPIAF, 2013).

Private sector investments, both debt and equity, have the potential to reduce the financing shortfall, but substantial barriers remain. Recent experience with private investment shows that investments pool within sectors that can be readily commercialized and in countries that offer minimal risk.[4] The reasoning for this is intuitive: projects must generate an adequate and reliable financial return that can be ring-fenced by the investor and risks must be carefully defined, allocated, and as far as possible mitigated. According to PwC (2011)'s latest survey on infrastructure, poor capacity including urban infrastructure planning, transaction capacity, lack of political and public support, poorly defined and unstructured procurement processes have contributed to the slow development of private sector financing.

Decentralization and infrastructure: can finances be raised locally?

Infrastructure investments are illiquid and require substantial upfront capital contributions. Local governments often lack the user base and, therefore, revenue streams to finance large-scale urban infrastructure. Therefore, matching the financial requirements of a given infrastructure project with the political mandate to deliver the service is a complicated matter for many local authorities.

As urbanization and fiscal decentralization shift more responsibilities to local authorities, the importance of intergovernmental fiscal transfers increases. However, recent experience shows that fiscal subsidies have not grown together with the increased responsibility vested in local authorities and for many cities in the developing world revenues from basic service provision fail to recover costs, because the payment capacities of consumers are severely constrained.

Similar to cost recovery, the mobilization of tax revenues faces political and economic challenges. On one hand the tax base may be insufficient to mobilize the financing necessary, or, even if it is sufficient, political opposition to the proposed increase may prevent local governments from pursuing the initiative. In addition, non-payment of traditional local taxes such as property tax is usually high due to lack of capacity to collect, corruption, and political will to curb the lack of compliance. As a result city governments have attempted to shift to market borrowing. However, the ability of local governments in the developing world to borrow directly on national or international capital markets at an attractive price is limited. In many low income countries, local capital markets tend to be illiquid and shallow. With limited secondary market activity and a limited range of short-term instruments which are generally not suitable for infrastructure investment, as a consequence, domestic funding is limited and very costly.

Without domestic credit markets, and often lacking the transparency needed in municipal bond markets, many city governments in developing countries cannot access long-term credit. Creditworthiness is not only limited to local governments; it also extends to their utility companies. For instance, in Kenya the Water Services Regulatory Board calculated and published utility shadow credit ratings for 43 water service providers in 2011 and found only 13 providers to have investment grade ratings. In addition, lack of policy and regulatory support from the central government and lack of capacity of the local government to handle the borrowing in a responsible way further constrain credit to local governments in many developing countries.

Local governments need to navigate a challenging financial landscape to secure the resources needed to provide their beneficiaries with basic infrastructure services. Decentralization has vested many subnational authorities in the developing world with increased fiscal, political, and administrative autonomy allowing regional and local authorities to respond directly and independently to the infrastructure services provision. However, the assumption that input costs can be recovered from user fees, or some form of beneficiary taxation, does not hold for many cities in the developing world as the payment capacities of consumers are severely constrained.

Decentralization and infrastructure: Who benefits from infrastructure investments?

It is often said that infrastructure investments are regressive in income and that the poor are disproportionately affected by the lack of infrastructure services and the infrastructure gap. This intuitively makes sense. On the governance side, elite capture is a common problem from community driven development interventions all the way to lobbying for public funding at the highest levels of government. Moreover, the rich are more equipped to find private solutions to the infrastructure gap due to better education, greater disposable income, and access to information and better technology.

Yet, as the discussion above indicates, there are nuances that can be found at district levels. Decentralization also allows us to delve into the question of infrastructure service availability relative to poverty in some detail. While the above intuition is likely correct, even in a region with one of the largest infrastructure gaps such as South Asia the picture that emerges is also heterogeneous.[5] For instance in Sri Lanka access to key infrastructures like power, and water and sanitation (W&S) seems quite inclusive. District level analysis (where data is available) yields very low access Gini coefficients adjusted by the household distribution Gini coefficients[6] for Power, and W&S services (0.04, 0.01, and 0.01 respectively).[7] Access is widely spread, and quality of these services in the country is generally good. At least for some basic infrastructure, Sri Lankan services are generally not regressive in income.[8] Map 2.1 provides an illustration for the country as a whole.[9]

The same however could not be stated for India. District level analysis yields much higher Gini coefficients for Power, and W&S services (0.15, 0.06, and 0.29 respectively) than in Sri Lanka. There is also evidence that the quality of these services in the country is generally poor. Even with LPG subsidies in India, the Gini coefficient is similar to Sri Lanka (0.35 versus 0.33 respectively), implying that richer households capture a large share of the subsidy, while poorer households largely rely on fuel wood and animal waste for cooking. Yet, access to phones is widespread given the popularity of mobiles (Gini of 0.20). As Map 2.2 below illustrates, the leading regions of India have lower relative poverty and are better served in terms of infrastructure than the rest of the country, which is intuitively expected.[10]

Decentralization and infrastructure: policy lessons

Investment in infrastructure has proven to be indispensable in triggering and sustaining economic growth. But often times, infrastructure investments have also proven to be ineffective to the intended beneficiaries, when designed, allocated, or managed poorly. Some countries provide expensive infrastructure for the few and inadequate infrastructure for the poor, who also pay a disproportionate amount of their income for lower quality service. The overarching reason for this is explained by wrong incentives at various decision-making levels prompted by rent seeking behavior, policy failures, and complexities associated with addressing market failures. What type of infrastructure gets built, where, how, when, and how it is maintained directly depends on the level of government responsible for these decisions and whether or not they contribute to economic development and poverty reduction goals.

The previous sections offer a glimpse of the global trends in infrastructure gaps, the need for new and innovative financing mechanisms, and the role that decentralization plays in improving allocative efficiency and local participation in solving local problems. Unfortunately, there is no straightforward answer to which level is responsible for the gap; but this chapter attempted to propose an economic logic for underpinning decentralization in the infrastructure sectors.

While it is very difficult to provide blanket recommendations on decentralizing the various sectors and respective subcomponents of infrastructure services, we do offer a modest set of guidelines to direct policy makers in their decision to decentralize or not:

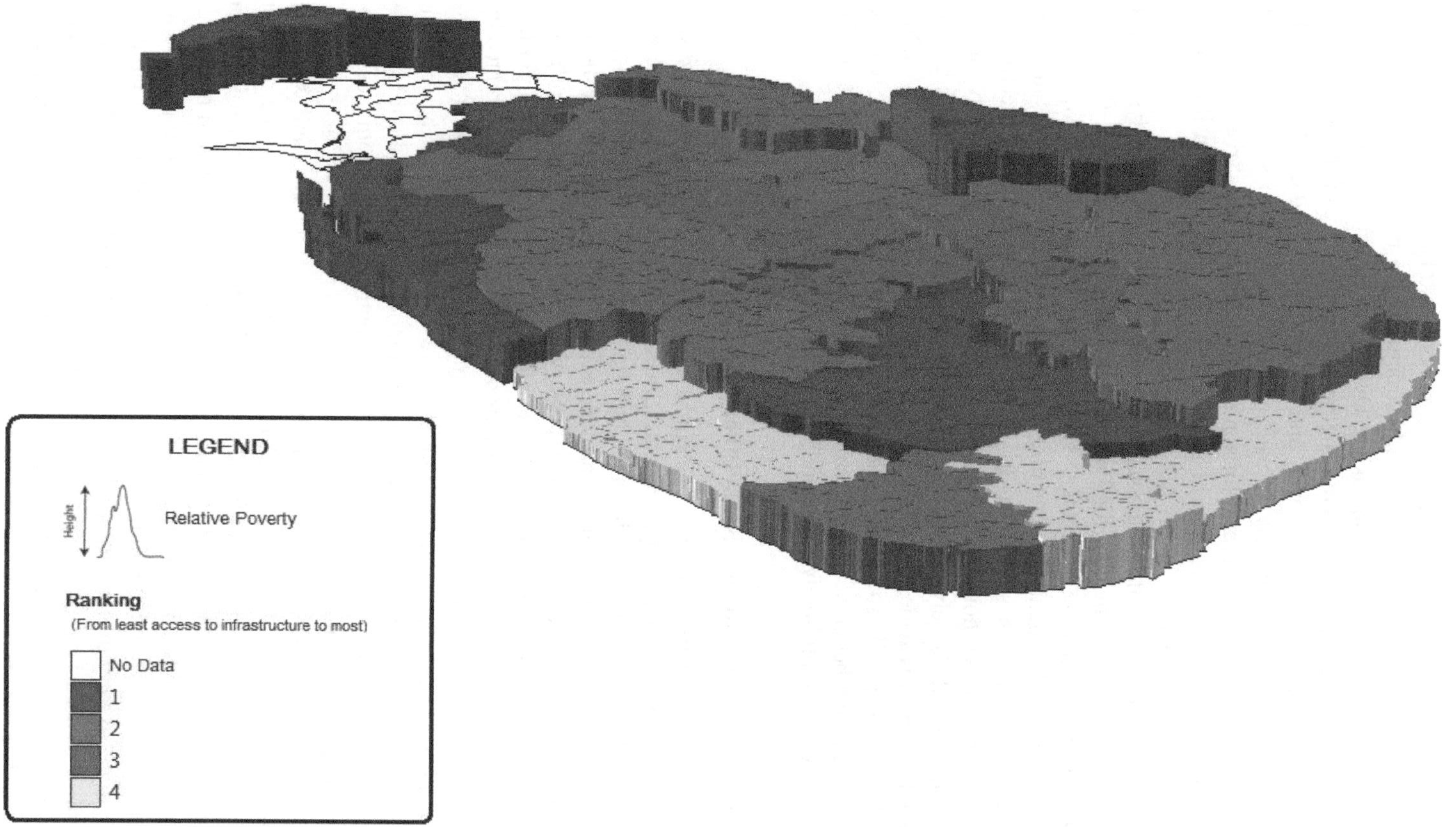

Map 2.1 Relative poverty and access to selected infrastructure services in Sri Lanka (source: Andrés *et al.* 2013).

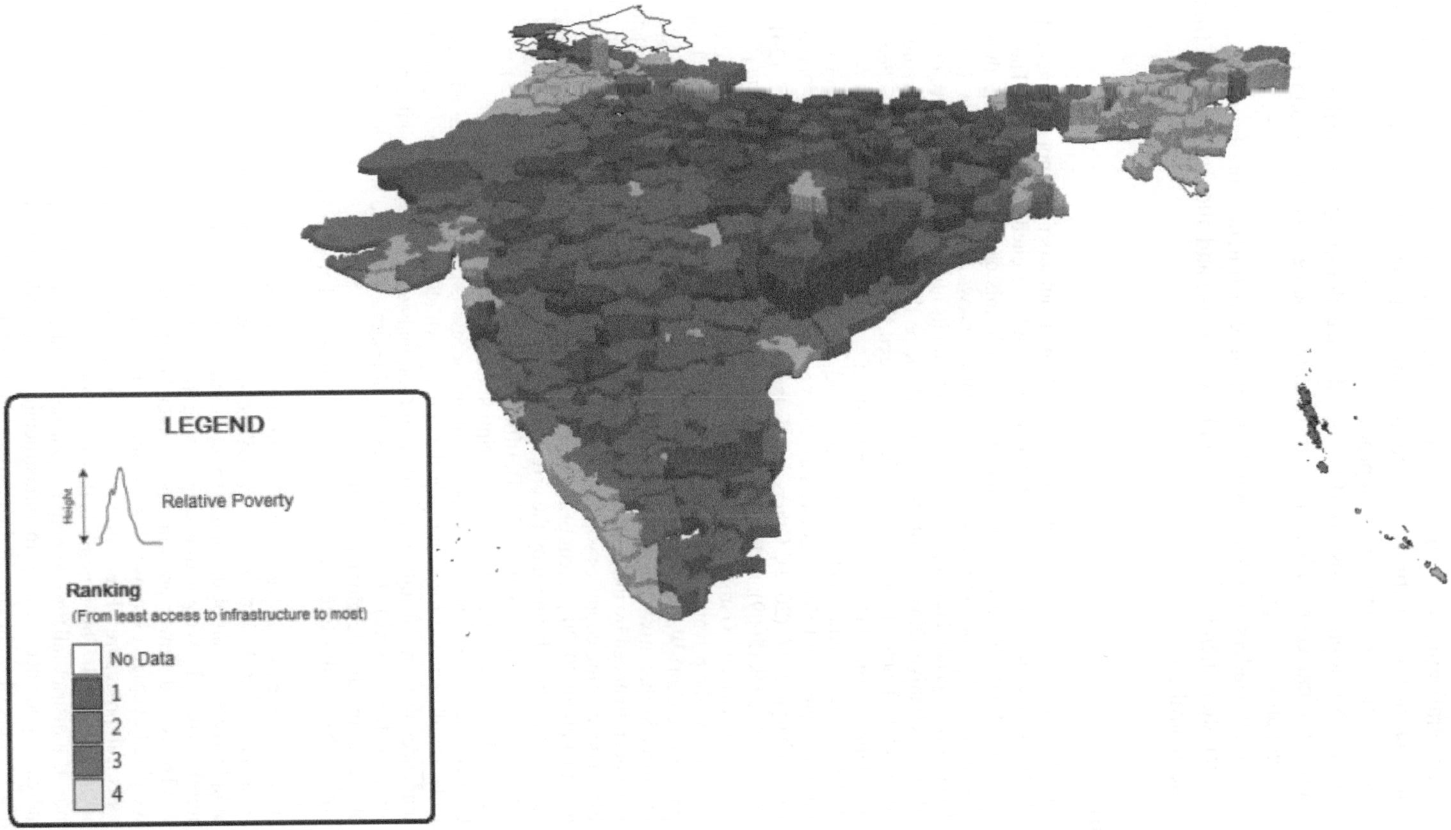

Map 2.2 Relative poverty and access to selected infrastructure services in India (source: Andrés *et al.* 2013).

1 Decentralization is intrinsically neither good nor bad for infrastructure; its impact depends entirely on the incentives facing the various decision-makers in the decentralization process;
2 Decentralization is most fruitful when the decision-makers bear the financial and political cost with respect to design, finance, operation, and maintenance; and
3 Political leaders are accountable to their constituents for the manner in which they spend tax revenues and how they use and allocate transfers from the central government.

Notes

1 The World Bank, Washington, DC, USA. Senior authorship is not assigned. The chapter carries the names of the authors and should be cited accordingly. The findings, interpretations, and conclusions expressed in this chapter are entirely those of the authors. They do not necessarily represent the views of the International Bank for Reconstruction and Development/World Bank and its affiliated organizations, or those of the Executive Directors of the World Bank or the governments they represent. Research assistance from Georgeta Dragoiu, Jared Haddon, Juan Agustin Echenique, and Ashma Basnyat is gratefully acknowledged.
2 The relevant literature includes: Calderón and Servén (2004); Chatterton and Puerto (2005); Estache and Yepes (2004); Fay and Yepes (2003); and World Bank (2006).
3 Bhattacharya *et al.* (2012). Others are: Estache and Fay (2010); Fay *et al.* (2011); Macquarie Bank (2009); and the MDB Working Group on Infrastructure (2011).
4 Foster and Briceño-Garmendia (2011) estimated the following shares of financial contribution by the private sector in Africa: ICT (81 percent); Power (10 percent); Transport (13 percent) Water, Sanitation, and Sewerage (45 percent). For MICs, the share of power in that mix is much higher whereas only a tiny share of water investments have been financed by the private sector. Between 2007 and 2009, 49.6 percent of all PPI in developing countries was in the power sector. Bhattacharya *et al.* (2012) estimates that about 20–30 percent of total current annual infrastructure spending in developing countries is financed by the private sector.
5 This is based on Andrés *et al.* (2013), Biller (2012) and Biller and Nabi (2013).
6 See Andrés *et al.* (2013) for more description on this methodology.
7 Gini coefficient for gas is 0.33 and for phone access is 0.03. The former reflects the wide use of firewood for cooking in the country, which may have severe health consequences in terms of indoor air pollution (not analyzed in this study but a possible topic for future work). The latter is less troublesome given the wide use of mobile phones as in other developing countries.
8 For the basic infrastructure, there is little correlation between services and poverty rate.
9 Height represents relative poverty (number of poor individuals in each district/total headcount of each district). For the colors, three scores were constructed. Score I: Simple average (sum of the points for each indicator divided by the number of indicators); Score II: Weighted average using predetermined weights to capture that WATSAN and Power are important direct benefits to households; and Score III: Weighted average using weights obtained from a Principal Component Analysis—a statistical procedure. They all yield similar results. Each district is then ranked between 1 and 4. This ranking is dependent on the quartile the aggregate scores fall into. If a district falls in the bottom quartile it ranks 1 (dark gray in the map) which indicates poor accessibility to infrastructure while a district that scores in the top quartile ranks 4 (light gray in the map) and indicates highest accessibility.

10 With the exception of water, there is a strong negative correlation between access to basic infrastructure services (power and sanitation) and poverty rates. In Map 2.2 this is depicted by the lagging states located mainly in the northeast portion of the country. The exception is the area northeast of Bangladesh, bordering Bhutan, China, and Myanmar. The high score on infrastructure services is driven by power (the area has a high hydropower potential) and sanitation.

References

Andrés, A., D. Biller, and M. Herrera Dappe (2014). "Infrastructure Gap in South Asia: Infrastructure Needs, Prioritization, and Financing," Policy Research Working Paper No. 7032, World Bank, Washington, DC, September.

Bhattacharya, A., M. Romani, and N. Stern (2012). "Infrastructure for Development: Meeting the Challenge," London School of Economics and G-24 Policy Paper, June 2012.

Biller, D. (2012). "The Role of Infrastructure in Securing Economic Growth and Transition to Middle Income Country in Sri Lanka: A Synthesis Paper," in Sri Lanka Economic Research Conference (SLERC).

Biller, D. and I. Nabi (2013). "Investing in Infrastructure: Harnessing Its Potential for Growth in Sri Lanka, Directions in Development—Infrastructure," World Bank, Washington, DC.

Biller, D., L. Andrés, and M. Herrera Dappe (2014). "Infrastructure Gap in South Asia: Inequality of Access to Infrastructure Services," Policy Research Working Paper No. 7033, World Bank, Washington, DC, September.

Calderón, C. and L. Servén (2004). "The Effects of Infrastructure Development on Growth and Income Distribution," Policy Research Working Paper No. 3400, World Bank, Washington, DC.

Chatterton, I. and O.S. Puerto (2005). "Estimation of the Investment Needs in the South Asia Region," World Bank, Washington, DC.

Estache, A. and M. Fay (2010). "Current Debates on Infrastructure Policy." In M. Spence and D. Leipzoger (eds.), *Globalization and Growth Implications for a Post-Crisis World* (pp. 151–193). World Bank, Washington, DC.

Estache, A. and T. Yepes (2004). "Assessing Africa's Investment Needs," World Bank, Washington, DC.

Fay, M. and T. Yepes (2003). "Investing in Infrastructure: What Is Needed from 2000–2010," Policy Research Working Paper No. 3102, World Bank, Washington, DC.

Fay, M., M. Toman, D. Benitez, and D. Csordas (2011). "Infrastructure and Sustainable Development." In: S. Fardoust, Yongbeom Kim, and Claudia Paz Sepúlveda (eds.) *Postcrisis Growth and Development: A Development Agenda for the G20*, World Bank, Washington, DC.

Foster, V. and C. Briceño-Garmendia (2010). "Africa's Infrastructure: A Time for Transformation," World Bank, Washington, DC.

Macquarie Bank (2009). *Annual Report.*

MDB Working Group on Infrastructure (2011). "Infrastructure Action Plan."

Public-Private Infrastructure Advisory Facility (PPIAF) (2013). "Public-Private Infrastructure Advisory Facility Database." World Bank, Washington, DC. http://ppi.worldbank.org/index.aspx.

PWC Infrastructure Survey (2011).

United Nations (2011). *The Millennium Development Goals Report 2011.* UN Statistics division

World Bank (2004). *World Development Report 2004: Making Services Work for Poor People.* World Bank, Washington, DC.

3 Trends and quality of decentralized public investment

Lorena Viñuela

Introduction

Around the world state and local governments have an important and growing role in the provision of public infrastructure services. Subnational governments presently account for an average of 63 percent of public fixed capital formation in OECD countries and of approximately 40 percent in developing countries. However, to date, the subnational dimension of public investment has been largely overlooked and it is not as well documented as other aspects of service delivery.

In order to contribute to a better understanding of public investment and capital formation in multi-tiered governments, this chapter reviews the relevant literature and empirically examines possible determinants of the quality of infrastructure and quantity of public investment, with particular attention to the effect of the overall level of fiscal decentralization. The following questions are explored using cross-sectional and time series analysis: (i) Has decentralization led to an increase or decrease of public investment?; (ii) Are more decentralized countries better off in terms of stock and quality of infrastructure?; and (iii) What are the factors that shape the distribution of public investment across levels of government? In addition, through two short cases I further analyze the impact of decentralization on the allocative efficiency of public investment and whether it is helping to better identify and meet infrastructure needs.

The results support the expectation that fiscal decentralization is associated with lower amounts of fixed capital formation and better quality of public infrastructure. Estimates are provided for two different country samples, one including OECD members and the other comprising 58 developing countries. Comparing the two groups shows that the effects of decentralization are greater in developed countries. This suggests than the positive impact of decentralization is contingent on the efficiency of public investment management and overall level of institutional quality. The lower levels of public investment may be reflective of efficiency gains, but they also raise concerns about potentially insufficient access to financing and steady funding sources for subnational governments. Lower investment rates can also be symptomatic of the fact that states and municipalities may be prioritizing other types of social investments over infrastructure.

Developing countries are investing more in public infrastructure and are doing so in a more decentralized manner than in the previous decade. After a sharp decline in the mid-1980s, the average public gross fixed capital formation increased approximately 2 percentage points of GDP between 2001 and 2010. During that period, subnational governments contributed approximately two-fifths of new public capital. Developing countries are also adding public fixed capital at a faster pace than developed countries. In the 2000s, low and middle income countries created on average 3.7 percentage points of GDP more of public infrastructure than high income countries.

Levels of capital formation have remained relatively low in OECD countries, possibly indicating that most of their infrastructure needs have already been met. Nonetheless, the volume of resources dedicated to capital projects and the share of public investment carried out by the second and third tiers of government are significantly higher than that of developing countries. Subnational governments in industrialized countries spend on average 9 percentage points of total public expenditure more than the rest of the world and are on average responsible for 25 percentage points more of the total public fixed capital formation. In the developed world, most local infrastructure services—local and regional roads, urban transit, water and sanitation, and others—are fully decentralized[1] and subnational governments are increasingly participating in the implementation of bigger infrastructure projects.

Decentralization is in general expected to have positive effects on public performance and the efficiency of spending, including public investment. Ostensibly, it should facilitate the participation of citizens in decisions regarding public goods and services made available to them, allow governments to better accommodate local preferences and needs, and even generate production efficiencies. In order to achieve such benefits, responsibilities and resources need to be given to the level of government that is better able to perform a given activity, while accountability mechanisms must be put in place to prevent the capture of public resources by local elites and avoid other governance risks.

On the other hand, producing and maintaining infrastructure is a complex task and requires a long term planning horizon, sustained commitments for maintenance and operation, the mobilization of sizable financial resources, and the coordinated action of actors across different levels of government. If institutions are weak or incentives misaligned, decentralization may exacerbate coordination failures and discourage fiscal discipline and the prioritization in public investment. Poor vertical and horizontal coordination may lead to the under- or over-supply of infrastructure, overlooking potential economies of scales in the production of infrastructure, and preventing the full internalization of costs and benefits from projects that have spillovers to other regions.

At the same time, devolving infrastructure services also involves distinctive technical and assignment issues. In order to be an effective policy, it needs to be accompanied by sustained investments in capacity and the establishment of systems to manage the life cycle of capital projects at the local level. In many developing countries, subnational governments may not be as well positioned to manage multi-year investments as central agencies. Additional difficulties may arise from the heterogeneity of local and regional governments, which typically vary significantly in terms of population, revenue base, and administrative capacity. Concurrently, subnational governments are subject to regulations passed by the central government on infrastructure provision, which may restrict their ability to accommodate for the local preferences.

In terms of financing, subnational governments generally face additional challenges in accessing resources and managing revenue volatility. The design of the intergovernmental fiscal framework affects the spending choices of lower tiers and how much they can effectively dedicate to capital investment. For example, matching capital grants have the potential of creating incentives to expand public investment, but other earmarked or general grants may result in less than proportional additions to capital spending because resources are fungible. Importantly, revenue-sharing and transfers schemes determine how much of the volatility in government revenue would be transmitted to lower tiers.

In particular, the predictability of transfers and revenue sources are important factors affecting the decisions of regional and local governments. Because public investment is a discretionary form of spending, it is more sensitive to cuts than recurrent expenditure, such as wages and social services to which cuts would generate more concentrated opposition. Revenue volatility will also affect sustainability of capital spending and the proper maintenance of the existing capital.

Considering these factors, the chapter proceeds as follows. The next section presents observed changes in capital formation and trends in fiscal decentralization in OECD and developing countries. The following section reviews the theory of assignment concerning infrastructure services and earlier empirical analyses of the impact of decentralization on public investment levels. That section also states the relevant hypotheses concerning the relationship between decentralization and infrastructure outcomes. The next section tests several hypotheses using a cross-country panel data. There also the results from the statistical analysis are presented. In the following section, the cases of Argentina and Mexico analyze more closely changes in the allocative efficiency of public investment as a result of decentralization reforms. The last section presents the main findings and policy implications.

What do we know about public investment in decentralized settings?

In this section the stylized facts of public investment in relation with the overall level of fiscal decentralization are discussed. Despite the many gaps in the available data and the limitations in the measurement of both public investment and fiscal decentralization, it is still possible to describe the major trends in these areas and identify the most salient issues for how they relate to each other.

Definitions, data sources, and limitations

Before turning to the data, it is important to introduce some of the main concepts used in the chapter. There is a key distinction between the level of public investment and the stock of fixed capital. On the one hand, *public investment* or capital spending is a flow measure and refers to the outlays made by various levels of government with the aim of adding to their capital. In contrast, *gross public fixed capital formation* measures increases in the stock of capital.[2] This concept refers to addition of capital assets minus depreciation of the existing assets in a given period.

There are no consistent estimates on capital outlays that can be used to compare countries. However, both the IMF's World Economic Outlook database and the World Development Indicators offer yearly data on fixed capital formation, total and for the public sector. In this chapter, this measure is used as a proxy for the flow of resources. An important caveat is that the gap between capital flows and actual fixed capital formation would be determined by the efficiency with which resources are managed. This gap is likely to be bigger for developing countries (Chakraborty and Dabla-Norris 2009; Pritchett 2000). Countries with more efficient public investment management systems would see greater increases in the overall stock of infrastructure for the same amount of capital expenditures than countries with poor systems.[3]

On the other hand, the *stock of public fixed capital* and the *quality of public infrastructure* of a given country are a function of past and cumulative investments in infrastructure and the adequate maintenance of existing assets and as such they are outcome measures. The quality of infrastructure not only reflects the fact that there is sufficient infrastructure, but also provides information about its condition and attributes.

There are several possible proxies for the stock and quality of the public infrastructure. Using indicators of coverage of various services—such as the percentage of paved road, road density, access to water and sanitation, and other similar ones—can provide an overview of how countries and localities compare to each other in terms of capital endowments. Moreover, there are several indicators from perception surveys that rate on a Likert scale satisfaction with the quality of infrastructure including, for example, measures for overall quality of infrastructure, quality of ports, and quality of logistic and trade infrastructure, such as those provided in the World Economic Forum's *Global Competitive Report.* These scores are based on the responses to the Executive Opinion Survey that polls 94 top level managers in each country from a sample of domestic and international (public and private) companies. While this data is considered fairly reliable, comparability over time is limited due to changes in the country coverage and the structure of the survey in 2006 (Munck 2009).[4] The data should also be considered with caution as it captures the perceptions of a subset of the population and, like other perception data, may be influenced by prevailing or past conditions and events that unduly affect respondents' views. Note also that these measures are not necessarily capturing the spatial distribution of the existing infrastructure, and that it is likely to be giving a greater weight to urban centers or areas where the polled companies are located.

The measurement of the level of decentralization and how it changes over time is equally problematic. It is common practice in the literature to use data from the International Monetary Fund's Government Finance Statistics (GFS). The most commonly used indicator to measure fiscal decentralization is the *subnational share of public expenditures*. This measure provides information on the relative position of local governments within the public sector and how it changes over time. However, there is widespread consensus on the fact that this measure only offers very partial information on the level of decentralization and effective subnational autonomy, which by definition are multifaceted phenomena.

Several potential problems arise from the GFS dataset that may affect the validity of an analysis using such an indicator. First, the measure does not provide information on what proportion of transfers from national governments to subnational entities are conditional or already earmarked for a specific sector. Second, the indicator does not provide a measure of the level of autonomy that subnational governments have to determine and raise their revenue base (Ebel and Yilmaz 2002). Such data is available for selected OECD countries and years, but it is yet to be compiled for rest of the world. Third, the data does not provide information on state-owned enterprises, for example in telecommunications or energy sectors, which could be responsible for substantial shares of public investment at the national and subnational level.

To have a fuller picture of fiscal decentralization, it is necessary to consider not only the percentage of subnational expenditure that is locally controlled (Eaton and Schroeder 2010), but also whether subnational governments have the ability to decide the bases and rates of local taxes and to borrow from markets (Ebel and Yilmaz 2002). It is also important to consider how the measures of fiscal decentralization intersect with the political and administrative dimensions of devolution (Rodden 2004).

The same problems affect the proxy used to assess the vertical distribution of capital expenditure that is also drawn from GFS. The *subnational share of net fixed public capital formation* is calculated as the percentage of net capital formation reported by subnational governments relative to the total for all levels of government combined. According to the GFS 2001's definition, "net acquisition of nonfinancial assets equals gross fixed capital formation less consumption of fixed capital plus changes in inventories and transactions in other nonfinancial assets."

Yet, despite the conceptual limitations of the GFS and potential problems related to the quality of the primary information collected, this dataset is the only one available that can be used to compare, albeit imperfectly, developed and developing countries and assess change over time. Considering these caveats, some of the most relevant trends across regions are presented below.

Trends in capital formation and fiscal decentralization

The relationship between decentralization and infrastructure service provision is complex. Both sets of variables are correlated with the overall level of institutional and economic development. Developed countries are on average more decentralized than the rest of the world. At the same time, these countries have both a greater stock of fixed capital and exhibit greater quality of infrastructure. To set the background for a closer examination of this relationship, a number of indicators and trends are summarized in this section.

Fiscal decentralization

The trend towards greater decentralization has continued across the world, although at a slower pace than in previous decades. In all regions the average subnational expenditure and revenue shares corresponding to subnational governments have increased since the 1980s. The only exception is the Middle East that has the lowest levels of fiscal decentralization. Table 3.1 describes the relative position of subnational governments grouped by regions. In most developing countries, subnational expenditures have grown faster than revenues leading to greater vertical imbalances across tiers of governments. The comparison shows that OECD countries exhibit the highest levels of decentralization. East Europe and Central Asia and Latin America and the Caribbean follow. Nonetheless, these estimates hide considerable intra-region variation.

There are substantive and statistically significant differences between industrialized and developing countries in the various dimensions of fiscal decentralization and decentralized infrastructure provision. On average, subnational share of revenue is 8.5 percentage points higher for OECD members than for the rest of the world. Also, OECD countries observe a subnational share of expenditure that is 9.3 higher than others. The disparity is even more accentuated in terms of the share of net fixed capital formation accounted for by subnational governments. In OECD countries that share is on average 64 percent, which is 25.5 higher than for other countries. Nonetheless, infrastructure additions represent a greater portion of subnational expenditure in developing countries.

Stock and quality of infrastructure

There are also considerable disparities between OECD countries and the rest of the world in all the indicators related to the existing stock of infrastructure and its quality. Table 3.2 summarizes various indicators of access to infrastructure services including water and sanitation, road density and pavement, electricity, and telecommunication across regions. Developing countries display consistently lower coverage for the various infrastructure services. Nonetheless, Latin America, East Europe and Central Asia, and the Middle East stand out for having relatively high percentages of the population with access to electricity, water, and sanitation.

Table 3.1 Decentralization indicators by region, 2001–2010

	AFR	*EAP*	*ECA*	*LAC*	*MNA*	*SAR*	*OECD*	*Non-OECD*	*Diff. OECD/Non-OECD*
Subnational share of revenue (% of total revenue)	14.1	33.7	22.6	23.8	8.2	30.1	30.7	22.2	8.5***
Subnational own source revenue (% of subnational expenditure)	44.4	71.4	62.1	63.7	80.2	67.9	62.4	60.2	2.2
Subnational share of expenditure (% of total expenditure)	23.9	19.0	19.7	19.1	4.5	24.6	28.5	19.2	9.3***
Subnational share of capital Formation (% of total cap. form.)	28.4	35.0	43.1	34.9	18.9	47.3	63.9	38.4	25.5***
Subnational capital formation (% of subnational expenditure)	23.0	37.2	20.9	27.4	35.0	21.2	8.1	23.8	–15.7***

Source: IMF's Government Finance Statistics 2012 and World Bank Indicators 2012.

Notes

*** Significant at the 0.01 level (2-tailed).

Table 3.2 Decentralization and infrastructure indicators by region, 2001–2010

	AFR	*EAP*	*ECA*	*LAC*	*MNA*	*SAR*	*OECD*	*Non-OECD*	*Diff. OECD/Non-OECD*
Overall quality of infrastructure (1=low, 7=high)	3.1	4.8	3.5	3.3	4.4	2.9	5.6	3.6	2.0***
Quality of port infrastructure, WEF (1=low, 7=high)	3.7	4.3	3.6	3.7	4.4	3.5	5.4	3.8	1.6***
Quality of trade and transport infrastructure (1=low, 7=high)	2.1	2.7	2.5	2.4	2.6	2.1	3.8	2.4	1.4***
Access to electricity (% of population)	32.6	71.6	N/A	88.4	94.5	50.9	99.7	66.0	33.7***
Improved sanitation facilities (% of population with access)	33.0	66.2	91.8	79.1	83.7	50.7	99.9	64.9	35.0***
Improved water source (% of population with access)	66.3	80.5	94.8	90.9	88.1	82.5	99.9	81.9	18.0***
Road density (km of road per 100 sq. km of land area)	25.1	106.1	80.7	50.5	70.5	52.1	268.1	64.4	203.7***
Roads, paved (% of total roads)	32.5	64.7	72.7	31.3	70.5	53.4	81.0	54.5	26.5***
Fixed broadband Internet subscribers (per 100 people)	0.2	4.6	5.9	3.9	1.5	0.4	17.1	2.8	14.3***
Telephone lines (per 100 people)	3.0	15.8	26.4	21.5	14.8	4.3	53.9	14.6	39.3***

Source: World Economic Forum 2012 and World Bank Indicators 2012.

Notes
*** Significant at the 0.01 level (2-tailed).

In general, the overall quality of infrastructure is positively associated with the level of income. OECD and high income countries have an average score close to the maximum, but the mean for developing countries is approximately half of that. East Asia and the Pacific and the Middle East and North Africa also have relatively high average scores with 4.8 and 4.4 respectively. OECD members and other high income countries (including several resource-rich Middle Eastern countries) appear to be converging. Low and middle income countries have also observed improvements and the gap between these two groups is slowly closing.

Public capital formation

OECD countries compare favorably to the rest of the world in terms of stock and quality of infrastructure as well as in the level of fiscal decentralization. On the other hand, developing countries are adding capital assets to their inventories at a higher rate. After a sharp decline in the 1980s, levels of overall gross public fixed capital formation have stabilized or increased in most regions (see Figure 3.1). Conversely, the OECD and East Asian Pacific regions have observed a decrease of 14 percent in their average capital formation when compared to 1990s levels.

The recovery of public investment has been especially marked in the Middle East and North Africa. As prices of energy commodities, which are the mainstay

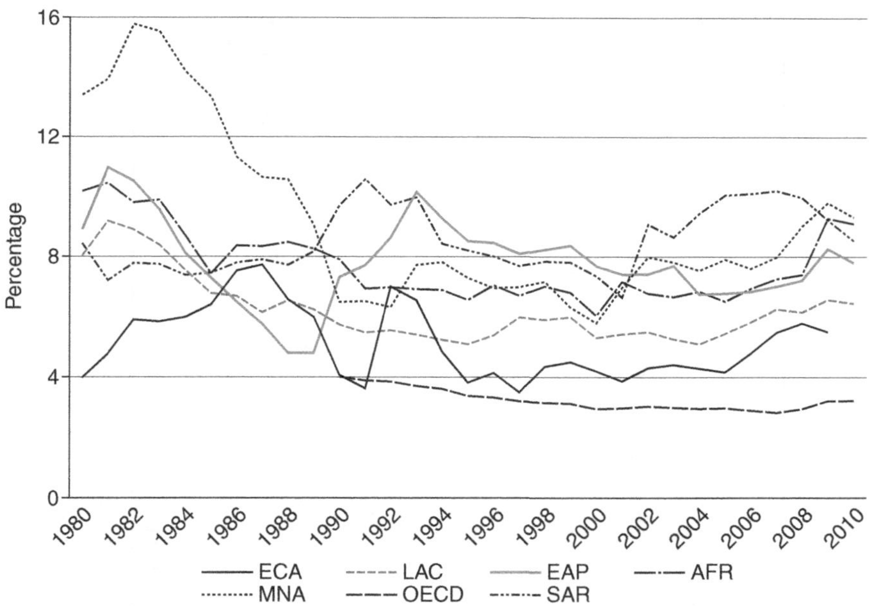

Figure 3.1 Average gross public fixed capital formation by region (percentage of GDP), 1980–2010 (source: IMF World Economic Outlook Database 2012).

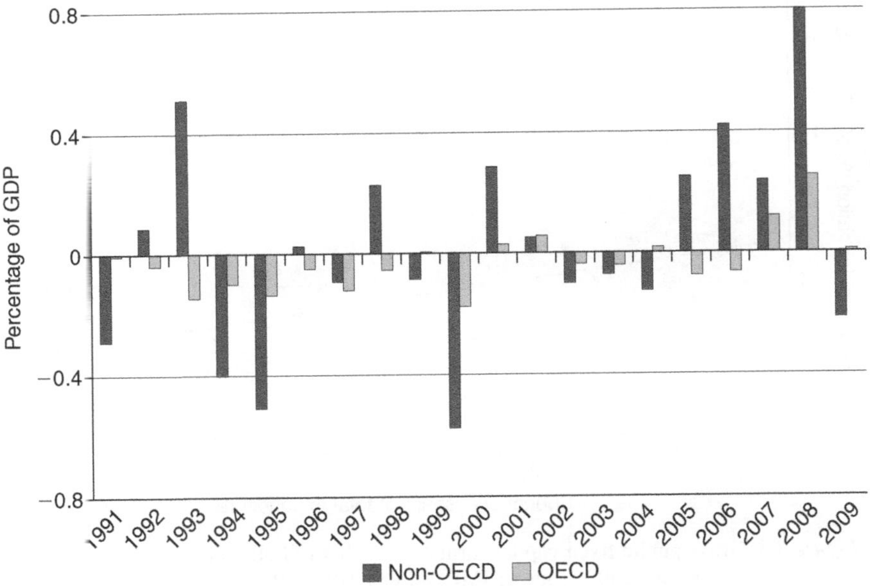

Figure 3.2 Average gross public fixed capital formation yearly change (percentage of GDP), 1990–2010 (source: IMF World Economic Outlook Database 2012).

of their economy, started increasing again in the 2000s, the average level of gross public fixed capital formation rose by 13 percent as compared to the previous decade. As well, Africa saw capital formation increase by 19 percent during the same period, while East Europe Central Asia and Latin America experienced positive but smaller changes, with 7 and 4 percent increases respectively.

Although developing countries are creating more fixed capital as a share of GDP, their investments tend to be more volatile than those of developed countries. The average year-to-year change, as shown by Figure 3.2, is considerably higher for non-OECD countries. High volatility can be particularly disruptive for public investment portfolios as public officials are not able to forecast revenues and make decisions on multi-year projects. The degree to which this aggregate volatility is transmitted to subnational government is, however, a function of the design of the intergovernmental fiscal framework.

Diverging trends?

A closer examination of the data shows that the relationship between decentralization and the quantity and quality of public investment may be going in different directions for OECD and the rest of the world. Using a cross-section of observations, Figure 3.3 and Figure 3.4 display the results across these two groups of countries.

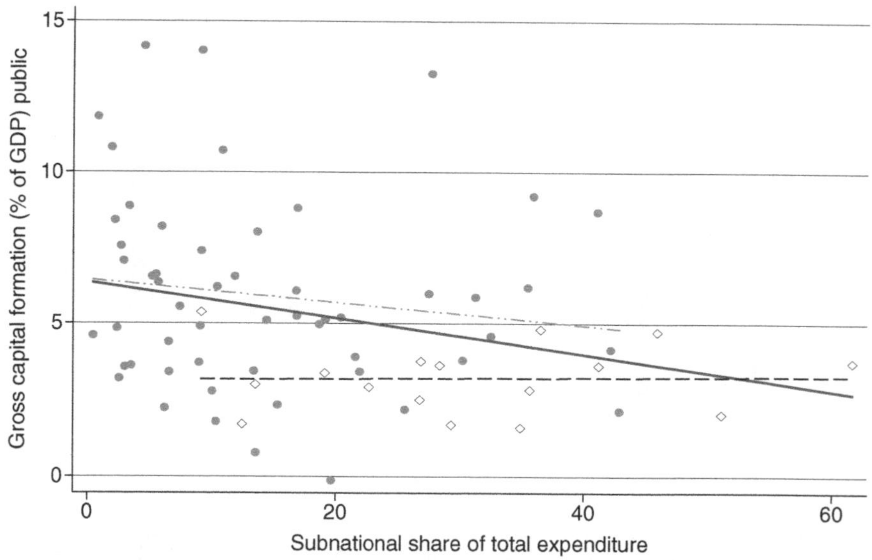

Figure 3.3 Gross public fixed capital formation as % of GDP and subnational expenditure share, 2009 (source: IMF WEO 2012; WB Decentralization Indicators 2012).

Notes
Diamonds represent OECD countries, grey dots represent developing countries. The dash (– – –) line is the fitted line for OECD countries and the dash dot (–··–··–) line is the fitted line for developing countries.

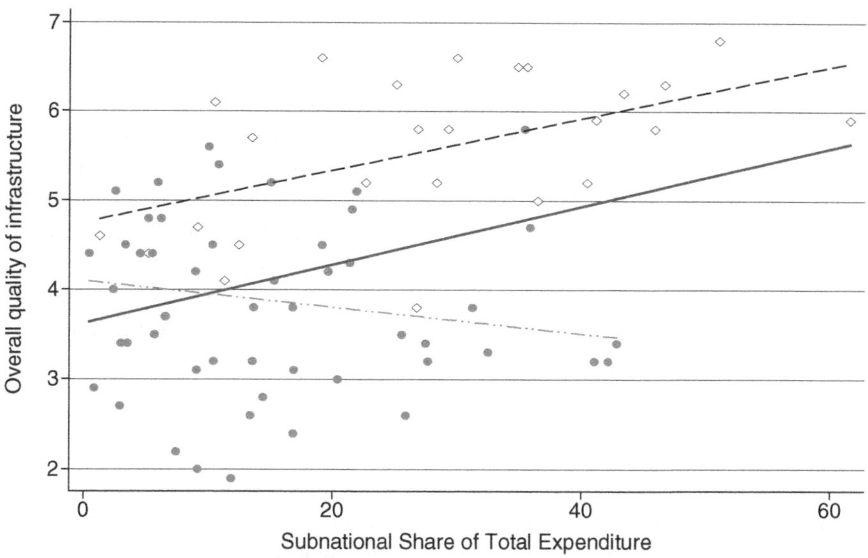

Figure 3.4 Quality of infrastructure and subnational expenditure share, 2009 (source: WEF 2012; WB Decentralization Indicators 2012).

When the data for all countries is considered together, it is possible to observe a negative relationship between fiscal decentralization and the quantity of gross formation of public assets (see Figure 3.3). Similarly, the data shows a positive relationship between the degree of fiscal decentralization and the quality of infrastructure (see Figure 3.4). Nevertheless, in the first case, OECD countries fall below the fitted line, whereas in the second they fall north of the predicted value for countries with the same degree of fiscal decentralization. It is to be expected they would have a lower ratio of fixed capital formation to GDP than developing countries facing significant infrastructure gaps.

Greater decentralization is positively associated with better outcomes in terms of quality infrastructure in OECD countries. However, the sign of the relation between capital expenditure and the level of decentralization turns negative for developing countries. The same difference is observed when comparing the relationship between the level of gross public capital formation and fiscal decentralization.

This divergence may suggest that the effect of decentralization on the quantity and quality of public investment is contingent on the overall quality of institutions. Institutional capacity and the degree to which local governments are accountable to citizens affect their ability to use resources and their incentives to respond to local preferences and address infrastructure gaps. On the other hand, if accountability and institutional capacity are weak, decentralization can lead to an erosion of infrastructure stocks.

Nevertheless, when using the subnational share of net capital formation as the independent variable, a positive relationship is observed between the degree of decentralization in capital investment and the quality of infrastructure for both country groups—OECD and non-OECD. An important caveat is that there are fewer observations available for that variable and countries that report data for subnational governments are likely to be the ones that have a longer tradition of decentralization and more established institutions at the subnational level.

Insights from the literature and relevant hypotheses

To help us interpret the emerging data, this section turns to the literature on decentralization. Although the empirical research examining the effect of decentralization on infrastructure spending and quality is relatively limited, it offers some relevant insights that are here discussed and tested in the following section.

A central tenet of the first generation of federalism literature is that decentralization should contribute to reducing aggregate public spending and taming fiscal pressure. Brennan and Buchanan developed a hypothesis, known in the literature as the "Leviathan hypothesis," that states that the "[t]otal government intrusion into the economy should be smaller, ceteris paribus, the greater the extent to which taxes and expenditures are decentralized…" (1980: 15). The central mechanism through which the reduction of government size is achieved according to this theory is the competition among subnational governments that offer different fiscal packages to citizens.[5] Importantly, this theory assumes that individuals are highly mobile across jurisdictions. Following the logic of the "Leviathan hypothesis," decentralization may be expected to reduce all forms of spending, including capital spending.

Estache and Sinha (1995) compare data from a small sample of OECD and developing countries to examine how decentralization affects spending in infrastructure. Contrary to the Leviathan hypothesis, they conclude that decentralization tends to increase both total and subnational spending on public infrastructure. According to these authors the elasticity of infrastructure spending is similar across developed and developing countries. The explanation offered in the paper for the increase in capital spending is that subnational governments' preferences on quality and quantity of infrastructure are different from those of the central government. In other words, local governments are thought to put a greater weight in capital spending. It is important to note that the number of developing countries included in that sample is fairly limited in comparison with the ones included in this chapter. Kappeler and Välilä (2008) find similar results using a sample of European countries.

A fundamental argument in favor of decentralizing infrastructure is that moving decision-making and implementation closer to clients yields efficiency gains. These gains can come from two sources. First, production efficiency implies that local entities can build and operate a certain type of infrastructure less expensively. Cost savings may derive from cheaper local building materials, less expensive local labor, more efficient project design, fewer layers of bureaucratic oversight, and lower corruption, among other sources (Peterson and Muzzini 2005). Sustainability is an important aspect of production efficiency. Second, allocative efficiency implies that locally identified investment priorities would better reflect citizens' preferences than those determined by the central government. And, citizens would value each unit of infrastructure spending more highly.

Yet there is little agreement on whether these benefits have materialized, as shown by two studies including the work of Asthana (2003) on water provision in India and Faguet's (2004, 2008) on per capita infrastructure spending in Bolivia and Colombia that offer opposite conclusions. On the one hand, using state level data, Asthana (2003) finds that state and local public investment in the water sector is less efficient and has higher costs per unit of output. On the other hand, Faguet (2008) compares the impact of decentralization on municipalities' uses of public resources, the distribution of resources across space, local government responsiveness, and poverty-orientation. The author reports that devolving responsibilities to local governments reduces public investment levels and shifts resources to social and human capital spending. Nonetheless, Faguet finds evidence that operating costs remain steady and that decentralization leads to more responsive and better spatially distributed investments.

How subnational governments make decisions over capital allocation and administer infrastructure has only also been thinly studied. The limited literature on the subject highlights that greater fiscal autonomy, in particular on the revenue side, fosters competition among localities to attract citizens and investors. Inter-jurisdictional competition may have positive effects on the responsiveness of local governments to infrastructure needs and may even lead to an oversupply of fixed capital assets, especially if actions to improve existing infrastructure are not properly coordinated across levels of government (Keen and Marchand 1997). Yet, if the competition for private capital leads to lowering tax rates and revenues, there could be an underinvestment in infrastructure (Sinn 2003). As well, in a similar manner to national level public investment, capital spending by subnational governments is expected to be affected by year-to-year variation in their fiscal balance and access to financing and their ability to take new debt.

The existing literature also warns about the highly procyclical character of subnational public investment and about potential disproportional cuts during fiscal downturns. The more dependent subnational governments are on capital grants from the central government, the more volatile their capital expenditure envelope will be. Holtz-Eaking and Schwartz (1995) report that in the United States local capital investment allocations are affected by revenue changes and, in turn, this leads to procyclical spending. In Spain, Costas-Pérez *et al.* (2011) document a disproportional fall of investment at the subnational level as a result of fiscal adjustment.

Decentralization may not only change the level of investment at the subnational level, but also change the composition of the investment portfolio. Kappeler and Välilä (2008) report that, in EU members, decentralization has increased infrastructure investments in schools and hospitals. As well, there may even be an inverse relationship between infrastructure gaps and subnational allocations to capital projects. Cai and Treisman (2005) argue that regions that are unattractive to investors because of the low quality of their infrastructure would not be able to compensate for its initial disadvantage. As a result, they are more likely to use public resources for other goals that offer greater short term benefits.

From the review of the literature, it is possible to extract several testable hypotheses about the relationship between fiscal decentralization and public investment. They are synthesized in Table 3.3. Four sets of factors are expected to influence public investment in three areas, including: (i) the overall quality of infrastructure; (ii) aggregate quantity of public fixed capital formation; and (iii) how much of those additions are accounted for by subnational governments.

The first hypothesis is that greater subnational fiscal autonomy is expected to increase the efficiency of capital spending, as well as positively impact the quality of created fixed capital assets as a result of informational advantages and greater direct accountability enjoyed by regional and local governments. Larger subnational shares of expenditure and own revenue should in general be accompanied with more decentralized capital spending.

The second group of variables refers to the magnitude of the demand for infrastructure services in a given country. The underlying hypothesis is that the bigger the gap between the stock of present capital and unmet needs is, the larger public investment would be, other things equal. Countries experiencing rapid urbanization would more likely have greater demands for transport, electricity, sanitation, and infrastructure for the new dwellers of large urban centers and the

Table 3.3 Summary of hypotheses

	Overall quality of infrastructure	*Aggregate quantity public investment*	*Subnational share of public investment*
Fiscal Decentralization	+	–	+
Revenue	+	–	+
Expenditure	+	–	+
Vertical Imbalance	–	+	–
Demand for Infrastructure	–	+	+
Infrastructure Gaps	–	+	+
Per Capita Income Growth	+	+	+
Urbanization	–	+	+
Population Density	–	+	+
Economic Context	+	+	+
Per Capita Income	+	+	+
Fiscal Space (Balance, Debt)	+	+	+
Volatility of Capital Spending	–	–	–
Quality of Institutions	+	–	+
Control of Corruption	+	–	+
Voice and Accountability	+	–	+
Government Effectiveness	+	–	+

Source: Author's compilation.

settlements and secondary cities that surround them. Similarly, more densely populated countries would need larger investments than those which are not. On the other hand, developing countries with large infrastructure gaps may resort to decentralization of public investment as a policy to tackle the challenge of increasing access to various services. Additionally, as the measure infrastructure quality is reflective of how much infrastructure services are already available, it is expected that it would be inversely associated with the demand for public investment.

A third hypothesis is that better economic conditions would allow for higher rates of public investments as they would make capital spending more affordable. The better the fiscal position of a country is, the greater the room it would have to invest without compromising fiscal sustainability. Higher income would also increase the likelihood that investments are more consistent over time and, consequently, the quality of infrastructure should be greater. Additionally, the reviewed data showed that developed countries are more decentralized.

Fourth, the literature suggests that outcomes may be contingent not only on the level of economic development, but also on the overall level of institutional capacity and degree of accountability. Decentralization can shift resources from needed infrastructure investments to recurrent spending or lead to waste if local governments are "too susceptible to elite capture, and too lacking in technical, human and financial resources, to produce a range of public services that are varied, efficient and responsive to local demand" (Faguet 2012: 1116).

Empirical cross-sectional analysis

In this section, I test the validity of the hypotheses just discussed. Before turning to the analysis, the data, estimation methodology (pooled time series cross-section analysis), and the model specification are presented. Then, I discuss the results linking them to the hypotheses.

Data

In the previous section, the main definitions and limitations considered have been presented. The (unbalanced) panel comprises yearly observations from 1990 to 2010 for 87 countries, with a total of approximately 1,540 data points. Each observation represents the aggregate national measure. The main sources of data used are the World Bank Decentralization Indicators based on the International Monetary Fund's Government Finance Statistics (GFS), the IMF's World Economic Outlook (WEO) databases, the World Bank Development Indicators, and the World Economic Forum. The unit of analysis used is "country-year" within the framework of a multivariate analysis. A detailed description of the variables, their summary statistics, and the sample are available in Tables 3.7–3.10 in the Annex.

Estimation methodology and model specification

Taking the data's limitations discussed earlier in the chapter into consideration, the analysis uses pooled time series cross-sectional (TSCS) estimation to overcome the degree of freedom problem created by the limited number of countries and years examined and to have greater variability in the dependent and independent variables. A feasible generalized least squares regression is used to correct for potential heteroschesdastic and autocorrelated errors across time and across countries. Using this technique to estimate the effects of decentralization on gross fixed capital formation as a ratio of GDP, the score for quality of infrastructure, and the subnational share of fixed capital formation are regressed on the indicators of decentralization and the variables best capturing each of the hypotheses discussed in the previous section.

The following multiple regression model is used:

$$Y_{it} = \beta_0 + \sum_{k=1}^{k} \beta_k X_{kit} + e_{it}$$

Where $i = 1,2,\ldots;$ N refers to a cross-sectional unit; $t = 1,2,\ldots;$ T refers to a time period and $k = 1,2,\ldots;$ K refers to each specific explanatory variable. Y_{it} and x_{it} refer respectively to dependent and independent variables for unit i and time t; and e_{it} is a random error and β_0 and β_k refer, respectively, to the intercept and the slope parameters. Therefore, a complete model of public investment is given by:

$$Y_{it} = \beta_0 + \beta_1 \text{ Fiscal Decentralization}_{kit} + \beta_2 \text{ Stock of Infrastructure}_{kit} + \beta_3 \text{ Economic Conditions}_{it} + \beta_4 \text{ Quality of Institutions}_{kit} + \varepsilon_{kit}$$

First, in order to address the possibility that fiscal decentralization is endogenous, and following the literature on the subject (Arzaghi and Henderson 2005; Panizza 1999), the model uses geographical area of countries as a control for fiscal decentralization. As Enikolopov and Zhuravskaya (2007: 2283) explain, "[t]he intuition behind this instrument is that, ceteris paribus, costs of centralized governance increase with geographical size of the country which leads to higher economic decentralization in countries with larger area." While geographical area can be endogenous in the long run, it is possible to assume that of the size of countries is exogenous when only analyzing the last three decades.

Partial models are used to test the explanatory power of different independent variables identified by the literature as relevant and presented in the earlier section. Some of the variables used to test the various hypotheses include urban population growth (to proxy for the demand for investment in infrastructure), GDP per capita (to proxy for the purchasing power), cash balance and the ratio of debt to GDP of the central government (to proxy fiscal space), ratio of government consumption to GDP (to proxy for the size of government), road density per sq. km. and access to improved sanitation (to proxy infrastructure stock), and the population density (to consider density effects).

Results

This section discusses the results from the econometric analysis. Regressions are run for the complete set of countries, on the one hand, and separately for the OECD and developing countries, on the other hand. The results should be interpreted with caution as some of the predictions in the literature hinge on assumptions whose relevance cannot be examined with the available data.

Public investment quantity

The results give support to the hypothesis that decentralization lowers the quantity of public investment. Table 3.4 displays the results of FGLS regressions for gross public fixed capital formation as a share of GDP. The estimates for subnational revenue and subnational expenditure shares are negative. All else equal, a 10 percentage point increase in the share of revenue implemented by the subnational level is associated with a decrease of $^1/_5$ percentage point in fixed capital formation ratio to GDP. The coefficient for developing countries is the same. For OECD countries, while the coefficient is smaller, the effect of expenditure decentralization is similar with a negative coefficient of 0.02.

While the rate of urbanization, a proxy for the demand for infrastructure, has a positive coefficient, a higher share of urban dwellers appears to negatively affect the aggregate level of capital formation. A percentage point of urban population growth is associated with a 0.1 percentage point decrease in public fixed capital formation, all else equal. The coefficient for OECD countries is 0.3, but it is not statistically significant for the developing country sample.

Population density, which is a measure of potential for economies of scale, does not appear to have a meaningful influence on either aggregate public fixed capital formation or the quality of infrastructure. In contrast, total population and the land area of a country have substantive and statistically significant effects, but the sign of their coefficients go in different directions. A 1 percentage increase in the number of inhabitants will lead to a decrease of 0.6 percentage points in gross public fixed capital formation as a share of GDP, whereas a 1 percentage increase in the total population will increase in the quality of infrastructure. But, a 1 percentage point increase in the surface area of a country in square kilometers will lead to an increase in capital formation of 0.7 percentage points of GDP, while the same percentage increase will lead to a decrease of 0.1 points in the overall quality of infrastructure.

Economic development positively affects the ratio of gross public fixed capital formation to GDP positively, with 1 percent increase in per capita GDP leading to a 0.5 rise in that measure. The estimate is also statistically significant for developing countries and the OECD run separately. These results are consistent with the assumed positive relationship between overall level of development and the affordability of capital spending.

Higher levels of government debt, or lower fiscal space, reduce aggregate public investment. A 1 percentage point increase in the ratio of government debt to GDP will lead to a decrease of 0.3 percentage points of public fixed capital formation to GDP. Besides, for each additional percentage point of cash deficit to GDP, or the revenue minus expense and the acquisition of nonfinancial assets, there will be a decrease of 0.04 in public fixed capital formation. However, for the sample of developing countries the coefficient is not statistically significant. These results are consistent with the idea that countries with greater fiscal space would be able to invest in capital stocks and maintain them more sustainably.

Finally, greater government effectiveness would seem to reduce aggregate fixed capital formation but increase the quality of infrastructure. A point increase in the average score for government effectiveness would lead to a 0.8 decrease in capital formation. The coefficient is higher for the developing country sample, supporting the hypothesized association between low capacity and larger public investment allocations.

Quality of infrastructure

The results are also consistent with the hypothesis that greater decentralization would contribute to improving the quality of infrastructure services. As shown in Table 3.5, an increase of 10 percentage points in the subnational share of revenue will lead to 0.1 points in the overall score for quality of infrastructure, which given that the score goes from 1 to 7 means a sizable change. The coefficient for OECD countries is higher, 0.2. Nevertheless, when the same model is used with the data corresponding to non-OECD countries, the coefficient becomes insignificant. This may be a result of the lower quality of governance and institutions observed in developing countries.

The percentage of urban population is positively associated with the overall quality of infrastructure, both for OECD and non-OECD countries. The effect is small, nonetheless—a 10 percentage point increase in the share of the population living in urban centers will result in an increase of 0.1 points in the quality score.

Similarly, the results also show that 1 percent change in GDP per capita would increase the quality by 0.7 percent, giving support to the proposition that the quality of overall infrastructure is positively associated with economic development. It is important to underscore that the coefficients for subnational expenditure are different for developed and developing countries.

Concurrently, 1 average point higher in control of corruption and government effectiveness would translate into a 0.3 and 1 point higher score for quality of infrastructure, respectively. However, the accountability and voice estimate goes in the opposite direction for both dependent variables. Greater accountability appears to be associated with larger shares of fixed capital formation and also with better quality. An increase of 1 average point of this estimate would be accompanied with a drop of 0.8 percentage points in fixed capital formation as share of GDP and of 0.6 points in the score of quality of public infrastructure, respectively.

Determinants of the subnational share of fixed capital formation

As expected, the share of public fixed capital formation accounted for regional and local governments is largely shaped by the level of fiscal decentralization as shown in Table 3.6. Increases in the percentage of revenue or expenditure that subnational governments carry on generate similar increases in their share of capital formation. In the subsample of OECD, the share of urban population and population density further add 0.01 and 0.6, respectively. Additionally, a percentage increase in the total population increases the subnational governments' share of capital formation by 6.5.

Decentralization of public investment appears to be positively impacted by GDP per capita. For every percentage increase in GDP per capita there would be an additional 3.1 percentage points to the subnational share of fixed capital formation. Similarly, countries would have on average a subnational share that is 5.5 higher for every point added to the estimate of control of corruption. Lastly, greater indebtedness, on the other hand, reduces the subnational share by 0.2 percentage points of total fixed capital formation.

A closer look at allocative efficiency in public investment: the cases of Argentina and Mexico

Decentralized management of capital expenditures is expected to increase allocative efficiency as local officials are better placed to identify citizens' priorities and preferences. Local officials have more direct access to better and more up-to-date information about the evolving needs of their jurisdiction than central

Table 3.4 Multivariate regression analysis of gross public fixed capital formation (% of GDP)

	All									*Non-OECD countries*		*OECD countries*	
	1	*2*	*3*	*4*	*5*	*6*	*7*	*8*	*9*	*10*	*11*	*12*	*13*
Constant	4.1 (0.2)***	4.4 (0.2)***	3.8 (0.2)***	4.0 (0.1)***	7.5 (0.6)***	9.0 (0.5)***	5.0 (0.1)***	8.6 (1.2)***	8.2 (1.2)***	7.8 (2.5)***	9.0 (2.4)***	0.2 (2.2)	2.5 (2.0)
SN revenue share	–0.01 (0.0)***							–0.02 (0.0)***		–0.02 (0.01)**			
SN own revenue share of expenditure		–0.01 (0.0)***											
SN expenditure share			–0.01 (0.0)***						–0.01 (0.01)**		–0.003 (0.0)		–0.02 (0.0)***
SN cap. formation share				0.004 (0.0)***									
Access to sanitation (%)					0.0 (0.0)								
Road density					–0.0 (0.0)**								
Urbanization growth					0.4 (0.1)***			–0.1 (0.0)***	–0.1 (0.01)***	–0.1 (0.0)***	–0.1 (0.0)***	–0.01 (0.0)	–0.03 (0.0)***
Urban population (% of total)					–0.1 (0.0)***								
Population density					0.0 (0.0)**			0.0 (0.0)***	0.0 (0.0)***	0.0 (0.0)	0.0 (0.0)	0.01 (0.0)***	0.0 (0.0)***
LN GDP per capita						–0.5 (0.1)***		0.3 (0.1)***	0.3 (0.1)**	0.5 (0.2)***	0.5 (0.2)**	0.6 (0.2)***	0.4 (0.2)**
GDP per capita growth						0.01 (0.0)							
Cash surplus/deficit						–0.03 (0.0)**		–0.04 (0.0)***	–0.03 (0.01)***	0.02 (0.02)	0.03 (0.0)*	–0.1 (0.0)*	–0.04 (0.0)***
Central government debt (% GDP)						–0.01 (0.0)**							
Control of corruption							0.01 (0.2)						
Voice and accountability							–0.6 (0.2)***	–0.8 (0.2)***	–0.7 (0.2)***	–1.1 (0.3)***	–1.0 (0.3)***	–0.4 (0.2)*	–0.1 (0.2)
Government effectiveness							–0.3 (0.2)**	0.04 (0.2)***	–0.01 (0.2)	0.03 (0.3)	0.1 (0.3)	0.1 (0.2)	0.07 (0.1)
LN population total								–0.6 (0.1)***	–0.6 (0.1)***	–0.3 (0.3)	–0.4 (0.3)	–0.8 (0.1)***	–0.6 (0.1)***
LN surface area (sq. km.)								0.7 (0.1)***	0.7 (0.1)***	0.4 (0.3)	0.5 (0.3)	0.9 (0.1)***	0.7 (0.1)***
N	882	753	890	452	425	802	1,848	453	490	311	324	142	166
N groups	67	70	69	60	87	81	159	58	63	44	47	14	16
Wald χ^2	8	7.1	2.8	0.2	113.7	129.7	104.1	224.8	151.5	158.1	116.9	114.5	87.8
Prob>$\chi 2$	0	0	0.1	0.6	0	0	0	0	0	0	0	0	0

Notes

*** Significant at the 0.01 level (2-tailed).

** Significant at the 0.05 level (2-tailed).

* Significant at the 0.10 level (2-tailed).

Table 3.5 Multivariate regression analysis of overall quality of infrastructure

	All										*Non-OECD countries*		*OECD countries*	
	1	*2*	*3*	*4*	*5*	*6*	*7*	*8*	*9*	*10*	*11*	*12*	*13*	*14*
Constant	6.5 (0.8)***	6.0 (0.8)***	4.3 (0.9)***	3.0 (1.3)**	3.9 (0.1)***	0.1 (0.2)	−2.1 (0.5)***	3.8 (0.0)***	1.8 (0.6)***	0.5 (0.5)	1.7 (1.1)	1.7 (1.0)*	4.8 (1.2)***	2.8 (1.4)**
SN revenue Share	0.02 (0.0)***								0.01 (0.0)*		−0.0001 (0.0)		0.02 (0.0)***	
SN own revenue share of expenditure		0.004 (0.0)**												
SN expenditure share			0.01 (0.0)**							0.003 (0.0)***		−0.004 (0.0)		0.01 (0.0)***
SN cap. formation share				0.002 (0.0)***										
Gross public fixed capital formation (% of GDP)					−0.01 (0.01)*									
Access to sanitation (%)						0.02 (0.0)***								
Road density						0.002 (0.0)***								
Urbanization growth						0.2 (0.0)***			0.0 (0.0)	0.01 (0.0)***	0.02 (0.0)***	0.02 (0.0)***	0.01 (0.0)	0.02 (0.0)***
Urban population (% of total)						0.03 (0.0)***								
Population density						0.0 (0.0)			−0.0 (0.0)**	−0.0 (0.0)***	0.0 (0.0)	0.0 (0.0)	−0.0 (0.0)***	−0.0 (0.0)***
LN GDP per capita							0.7 (0.1)***		0.2 (0.1)***	0.2 (0.1)***	0.2 (0.1)*	0.2 (0.1)**	−0.04 (0.1)	−0.1 (0.1)
GDP per capita growth							−0.01 (0.0)**		−0.0 (0.0)	0.0 (0.0)	0.0 (0.0)	0.0 (0.0)	0.0 (0.0)	0.0 (0.0)
Cash surplus/deficit							0.03 (0.0)***		−0.01 (0.0)***	−0.02 (0.0)***	−0.02 (0.0)*	−0.02 (0.0)**	−0.0 (0.0)	−0.01 (0.0)
Central government debt (% GDP)							0.01 (0.0)***		0.0 (0.0)	0.0 (0.0)	−0.0 (0.0)	−0.0 (0.0)	−0.0 (0.0)	−0.0 (0.0)
Control of corruption								0.4 (0.1)***	0.3 (0.1)***	0.3 (0.1)***	−0.3 (0.2)	−0.2 (0.2)	0.3 (0.1)***	0.3 (0.1)**
Voice and accountability								−0.2 (0.1)***	−0.6 (0.1)***	−0.7 (0.1)***	−0.6 (0.1)***	−0.7 (0.1)***	−0.2 (0.2)***	0.03 (0.2)
Government effectiveness								0.9 (0.1)***	1.0 (0.1)***	1.0 (0.1)***	1.2 (0.2)***	1.3 (0.2)***	0.6 (0.1)	0.5 (0.1)***
LN population total	−0.04)	−0.04 (0.1)	0.1 (0.1)*	0.3 (0.1)***					0.1 (0.0)*	0.2 (0.0)***	0.1 (0.1)	0.1 (0.1)	0.1 (0.1)***	0.2 (0.1)***
LN surface area (sq. km.)	−0.2 (0.1)***	−0.1 (0.1)*	−0.2 (0.1)***	−0.3 (0.1)***					−0.10 (0.0)***	−0.2 (0.0)***	−0.2 (0.1)***	−0.2 (0.1)***	−0.2 (0.0)***	−0.2 (0.1)***
N	464	447	508	424	896	430	455	1028	304	268	128	135	176	205
N groups	63	67	69	65	115	86	64	132	44	45	23	25	21	24
Wald χ^2	7.4	17	13.1	11.9	3.5	2,057.8	290.8	2,463.7	1,370.6	2,084.7	193.5	549.9	281.8	149.9
Prob>χ^2	0	0	0	0	0.1	0	0	0	0	0	0	0	0	0

Notes

*** Significant at the 0.01 level (2-tailed).

** Significant at the 0.05 level (2-tailed). * Significant at the 0.10 level (2-tailed).

Table 3.6 Multivariate regression analysis of subnational share of net fixed capital formation (% of total)

	All									*Non-OECD countries*		*OECD countries*	
	1	*2*	*3*	*4*	*5*	*6*	*7*	*8*	*9*	*10*	*11*	*12*	*13*
Constant	7.1 (1.2)***	53.1 (3.6)***	14.3 (1.4)***	53.5 (2.1)***	21.3 (12.1)*	8.9 (11.3)	29.5 (1.2)***	−72.3 (15.3)***	−72.3 (15.3)***	−20.0 (46.0)	−80.2 (23.4)***	0.2 (2.2)	−22.2 (39.2)
Decentralization										0.7 (0.2)***			
SN revenue share	1.6 (0.1)***							0.7 (0.1)***				−0.0001 (0.0)	
SN own revenue share of expenditure		−0.1 (0.1)											
SN expenditure share			1.5 (0.1)***						0.7 (0.1)***		0.8 (0.2)***	−0.01 (0.0)	0.5 (0.2)***
Gross public fixed capital formation (% of GDP)				−1.8 (0.3)***									
Access to sanitation (%)					−0.1 (0.1)								
Road density					0.02 (0.0)								
Urbanization growth					1.8 (1.6)								
Urban population (% of total)					0.5 (0.1)***			−0.2 (0.1)*	−0.2 (0.1)*	−0.3 (0.3)	−0.1 (0.2)	0.01 (0.0)***	−0.5 (0.3)*
Population density					−0.04 (0.0)***			−0.01 (0.0)	−0.01 (0.0)	0.0 (0.0)	−0.1 (0.0)***	0.6 (0.2)***	−0.0 (0.0)
LN GDP per capita						6.2 (1.2)***		3.1 (1.6)*	3.1 (1.6)*	1.5 (3.9)	0.8 (2.3)	−0.1 (0.0)***	2.0 (3.7)***
GDP per capita growth						−0.1 (0.2)							
Cash surplus/deficit						−0.2 (0.2)							
Central government debt (% GDP)						−0.2 (0.1)***		−0.1 (0.03)***	−0.1 (0.0)***	−0.2 (0.1)***	−0.04 (0.0)	−0.4 (0.2)*	−0.2 (0.1)***
Control of corruption							−8.9 (2.4)***	5.2 (1.6)***	5.2 (1.6)***	3.6 (2.8)	0.4 (2.8)	0.1 (0.2)	1.4 (2.8)
Voice and accountability							1.4 (1.9)						
Government effectiveness							25.5 (2.4)***						
LN population total								6.6 (1.1)***	6.5 (1.1)***	4.0 (1.8)**	11.5 (1.5)***	−0.8 (0.1)***	5.3 (1.7)***
LN surface area (sq. km.)								−0.8 (1.1)	−0.8 (1.1)	0.7 (1.7)***	−6.2 (1.5)***	0.9 (0.1)***	0.8 (1.9)
N	536	457	603	452	257	359	528	322	322	156	132	142	190
N groups	68	62	73	60	55	47	73	47	47	20	24	14	23
Wald χ^2	1,554.1	1.7	732.2	37.5	43.6	32.5	303.9	666.3	666.3	305.8	566.2	114.5	188.3
Prob>χ^2	0	0.2	0	0	0	0	0	0	0	0	0	0	0

Notes
*** Significant at the 0.01 level (2-tailed).
** Significant at the 0.05 level (2-tailed).
* Significant at the 0.10 level (2-tailed).

bureaucracies. In some cases, citizens may have the channels to influence local decision-making more directly, for example through voice mechanisms such as participatory budgeting. If informational gains were to be realized, capital spending is expected to be more responsive to infrastructure gaps than before the implementation of decentralization reforms. In other words, larger infrastructure needs should be accompanied by higher levels of spending, and vice versa. Thus, devolution of fiscal and administrative functions should contribute to correct existing distortions in capital spending and horizontal disparities in access to infrastructure services across jurisdictions.

Whether decentralization has had an impact on the horizontal distribution of capital spending is a critical question that remains unaddressed. Understanding if decentralization changes the distribution of capital spending across subnational units and whether it helps to close horizontal gaps requires analyzing data at the subnational level. Given that information on outcomes and allocations by jurisdictions is not available for cross-sectional analysis, I examine the issue through two brief country cases.

In this section, the experiences of Argentina and Mexico, two large federal countries, are used to illustrate how decentralization may lead to dissimilar outcomes as a result of different intergovernmental fiscal framework design choices. Both countries have devolved sizable shares of fiscal resources to subnational governments since the mid-1980s, in particular to second tier governments (see Figure 3.5 and Figure 3.7). More recently, in 2007, Mexico introduced a new change in the equalization formula. At the same time, in both cases, levels of capital formation have continued to rise since 1995 and much of the increase is accounted for subnational levels (see Figure 3.6 and Figure 3.8).

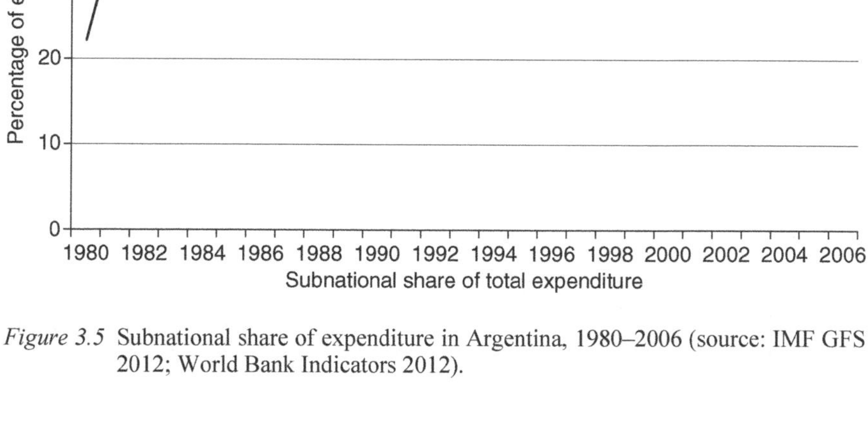

Figure 3.5 Subnational share of expenditure in Argentina, 1980–2006 (source: IMF GFS 2012; World Bank Indicators 2012).

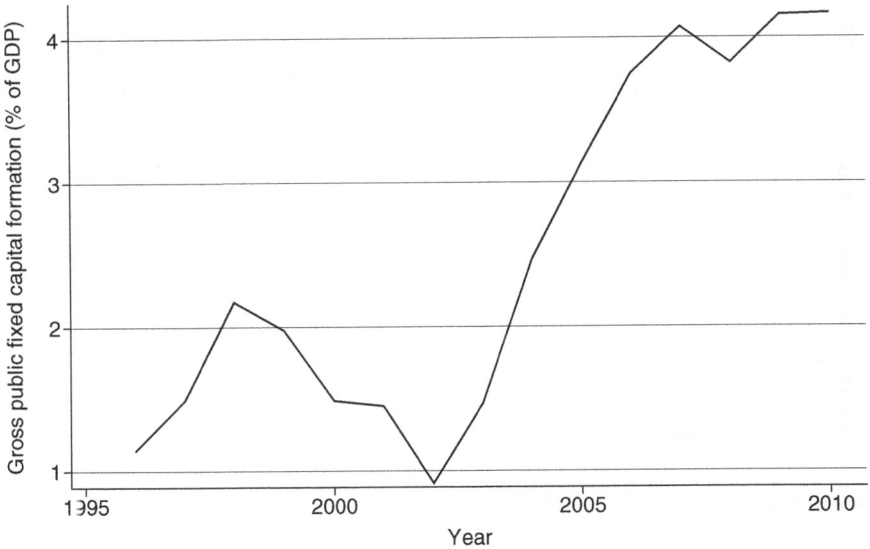

Figure 3.6 Gross public fixed capital formation in Argentina, 1995–2010 (source: IMF WEO 2012).

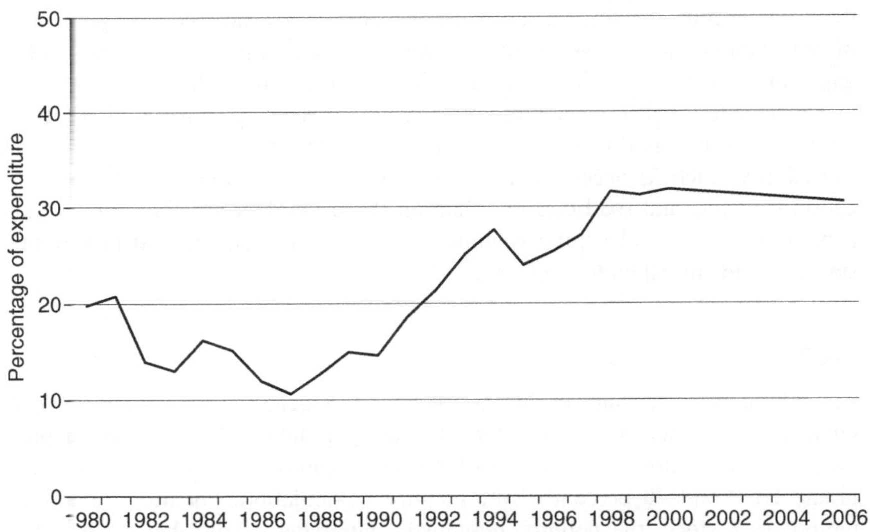

Figure 3.7 Subnational share of expenditure in Mexico, 1980–2006 (source: IMF GFS 2012; World Bank Indicators 2012).

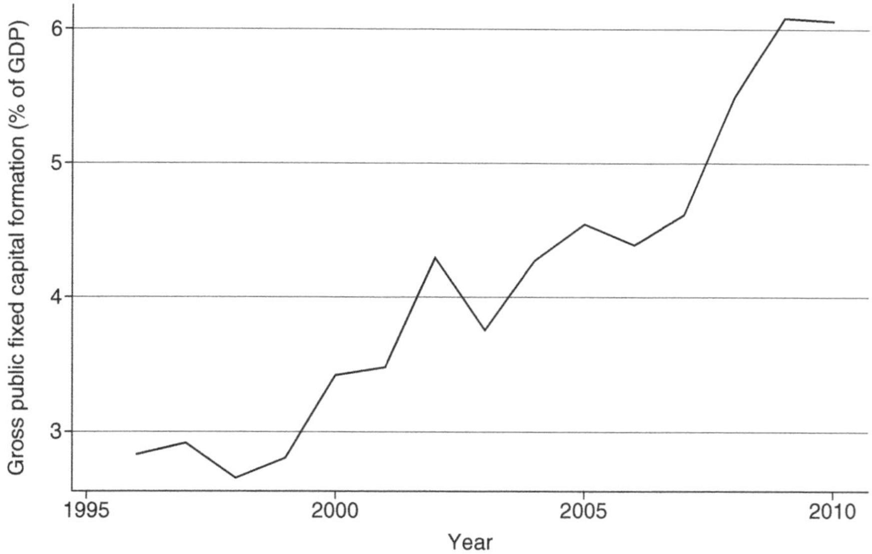

Figure 3.8 Gross public fixed capital formation in Mexico, 1995–2010 (source: IMF WEO 2012).

In each case, the before and after distribution of public investment across subnational units is compared. Also, how well the resulting distribution responds to the needs or infrastructure gaps of various localities is examined. The percentage of households with access to running water is used to proxy the infrastructure gap. This indicator was chosen because it is available for each of the cases at the province/state level in census reports. Access to running water is also a fairly reliable indicator as it is highly correlated with other measures of infrastructure availability, such as access to improved sanitation, coverage of telecommunication services, and road density. Data on the dependent variable, public fixed capital formation and capital spending, were drawn from official government statistics and annual budget reports.

Argentina

As with many other countries in Latin America, Argentina is characterized by an unequal distribution of economic wealth and population. The four major provinces—Buenos Aires, Santa Fe, Córdoba, and Mendoza—account for 78 percent of the GDP and 70 percent of the country's population. For most of its contemporary history, the country remained centralized despite having a federal system. The frequent democratic breakdowns sustained and reinforced centralization. The national government directly provided most services, even most of basic and secondary education and basic health until the early 1980s.

But after re-democratization in 1983, provincial governments and municipalities have consistently expanded their responsibilities over service delivery and resources, and they currently control almost half of government expenditure and revenue. The original *coparticipation* formula adopted in 1988 included various indicators of expenditure needs to determine the distribution of a common pool of tax revenue. However, later revisions and introduction of new taxes have eroded the system and transfers are no longer necessarily aligned with needs in all cases; a considerable share of the common resource pool is now being distributed on an ad hoc basis.

The process of decentralization accelerated in the late 1980s. In 1992, the subnational share of expenditure stabilized at 45 percent through the "second" *coparticipation* agreement between the national government and the provinces. This agreement limited the percentage of federal revenue to be shared with provinces and it was part of a macroeconomic stabilization package. In exchange for such reduction, the provincial governments were guaranteed a minimum revenue floor. In years of economic growth, this arrangement favored the federal government, but in years of recession the revenue floor provided provinces with secured minimum amount of resources. This provision made fiscal adjustment more difficult during the 2001–2002 crisis.

The rapid move toward fiscal decentralization was reflected in the distribution of capital spending across levels of government. Subnational governments came to total 80 percent of gross fixed capital formation in 1992, a level that has remained stable, with the exception of 2001 when 90 percent was reached. Provinces currently account for more than two-thirds of that share and the rest is the responsibility of municipalities. Concomitantly, the absolute volume invested in fixed assets has more than doubled since 1993. Provinces and municipalities contributed 70 percent of the increase (see Figure 3.9). Despite the acute nature of the 2001 fiscal crisis, public investment returned to previous levels by 2003–2004 and has continued to grow since. National investments have also risen, but these remain highly concentrated in Buenos Aires (see Figure 3.10).

Despite the risks to macroeconomic stability that the existing intergovernmental system entail, the guaranteed threshold prevented a bigger drop at the subnational level of capital spending during the 2001 crisis. Since 1992, most provinces increased public fixed capital formation per capita, but the biggest gains were observed in Salta, Santa Cruz, and Rio Negro provinces, which have benefited from growing mineral royalties (see Figure 3.11). Only one province, Tucúman, has seen a decline in the per capita capital formation. In the short term, moving away from a pegged currency in 2002 created additional fiscal space for provinces as inflation reduced the share of the budget needed to pay wages and other current expenditures. Figure 3.12 shows that spending per capita varies considerably across provinces.

The stock and quality of infrastructure in Argentina lags behind the country's level of economic development and remains very unequally distributed. This is the legacy of centralization and decades of underinvestment and poor maintenance of existing assets. Although the range has narrowed since decentralization

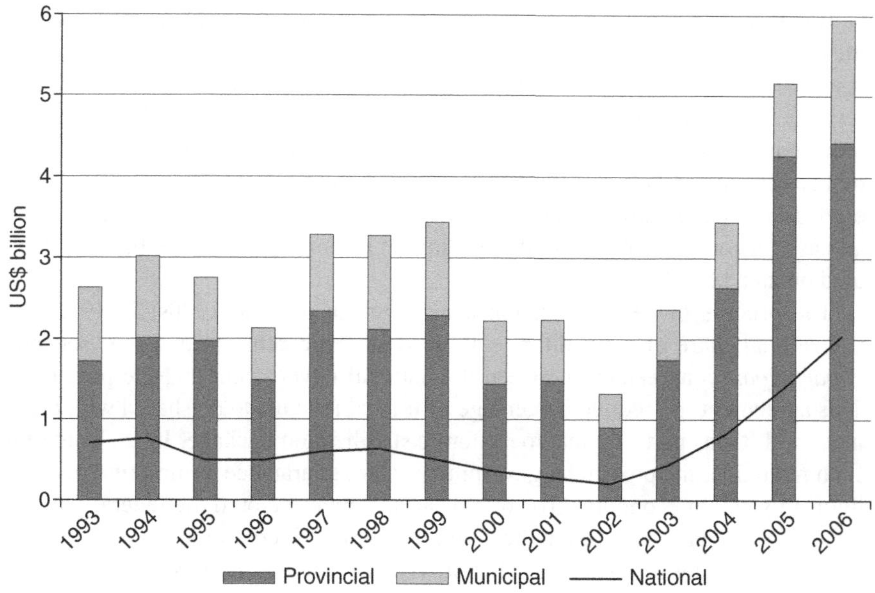

Figure 3.9 Gross public fixed capital formation (1993 constant prices), 1993–2006 (source: INDEC 2012).

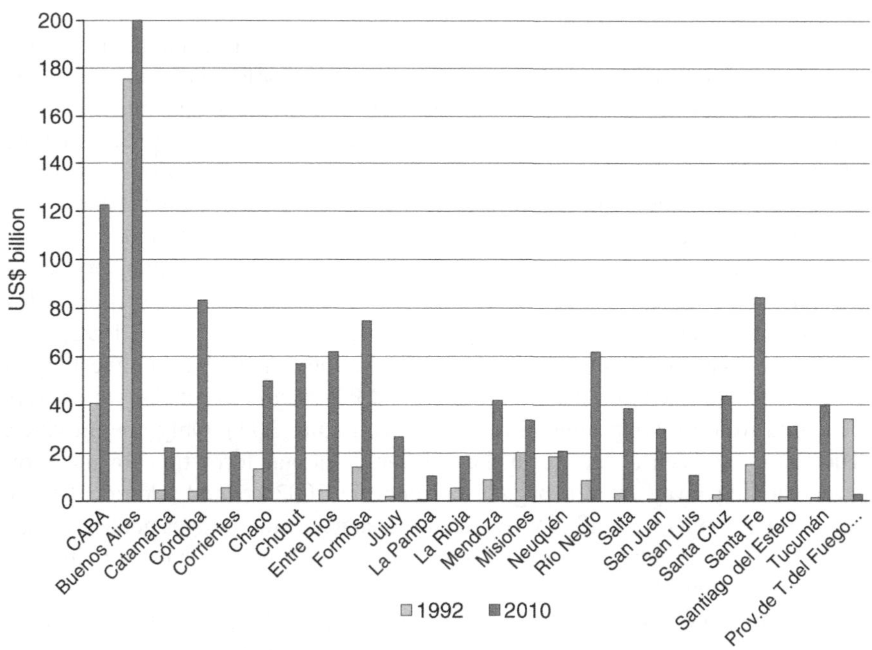

Figure 3.10 National government gross public fixed capital formation by province (1993 constant prices), 1992 and 2010 (source: INDEC 2012).

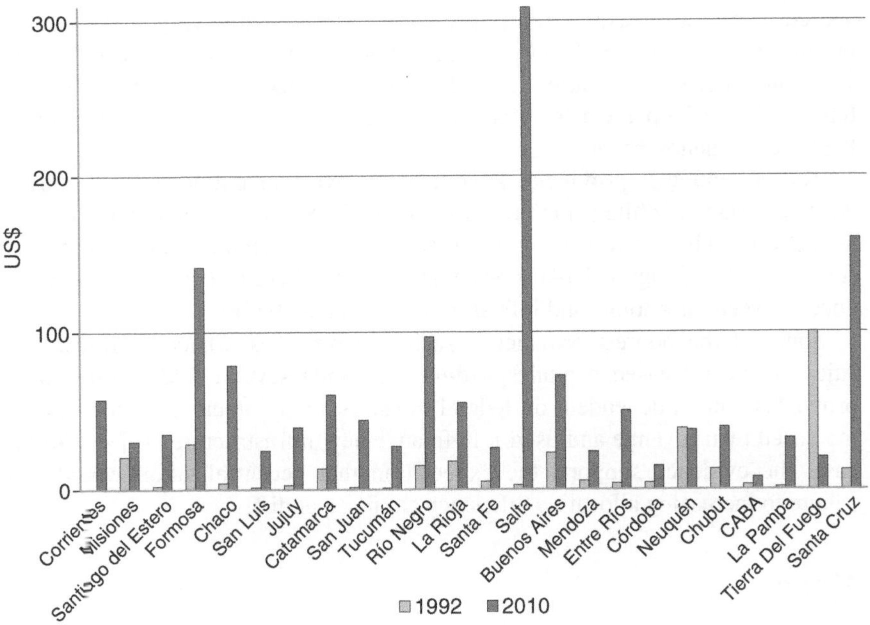

Figure 5.11 Gross public fixed capital formation per capita (1993 constant-ordered by poverty rate), 1992 and 2010 (source: INDEC 2012).

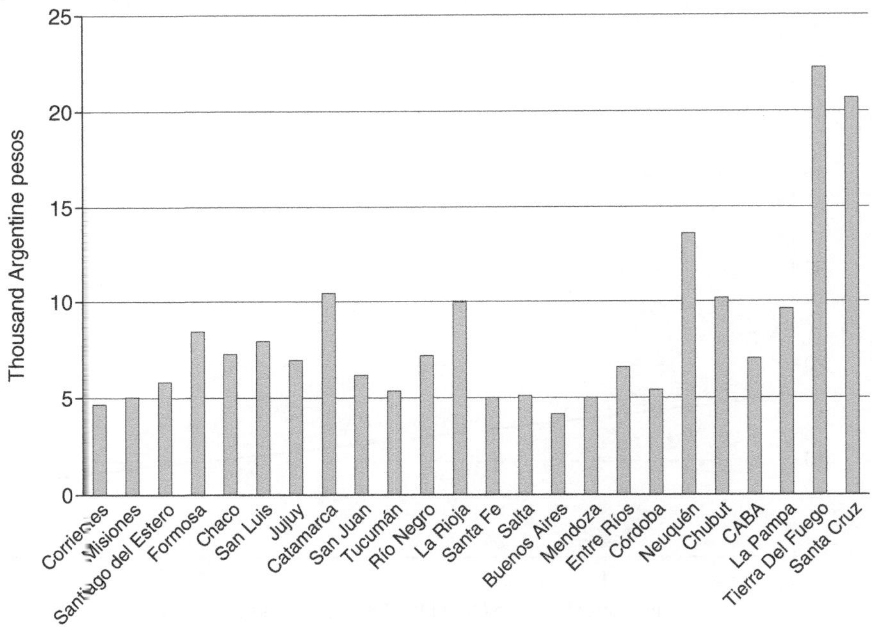

Figure 5.12 Total provincial expenditures per capita in Argentina (ordered by poverty rates), 2010 (source: INDEC 2012).

started, outcome measures for infrastructure services still vary widely across provinces. For example, the percentage of households without access to running water and improved sanitation is close to 25 percent for Chaco, Formosa, or Santiago and over 28 percent for Misiones, while only half of a percentage point in the City of Buenos Aires.

The amount that provincial governments invest in public infrastructure is equally variable. While some provinces invest US$8 per capita, others go as far as US$310. However, leaving outliers aside, a before-and-after comparison (Figure 3.13 and Figure 3.14) shows that presently there is a greater correspondence between allocations and infrastructure gaps than before.

Some of the poorest provinces—such as Corrientes, Chaco, Formosa, and Jujuy—have increased capital spending per capita several fold. While poorer provinces remain dependent on federal transfers, many others have successfully increased own revenue and used it to finance new infrastructure projects. In this case, the evidence supports the expectation that decentralization would contribute to increasing allocative efficiency capital spending.

Mexico

Mexico started devolving functions and resources to states only in the early 1990s with the transfer of primary education responsibilities and, later, of health services. The country has not gone as far in implementing decentralization as other federations in the region. States and municipalities are responsible for

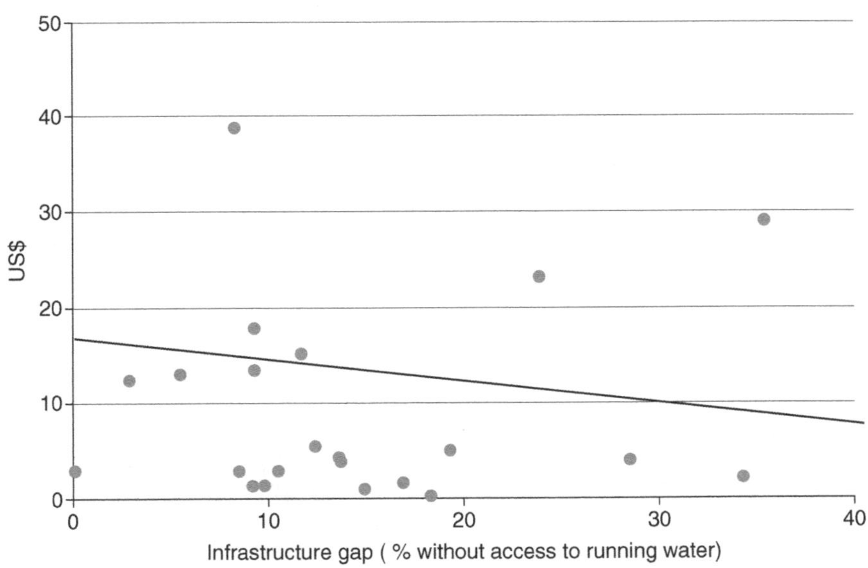

Figure 3.13 Capital expenditure per capita and infrastructure needs by province, 1992 (source: INDEC 2012).

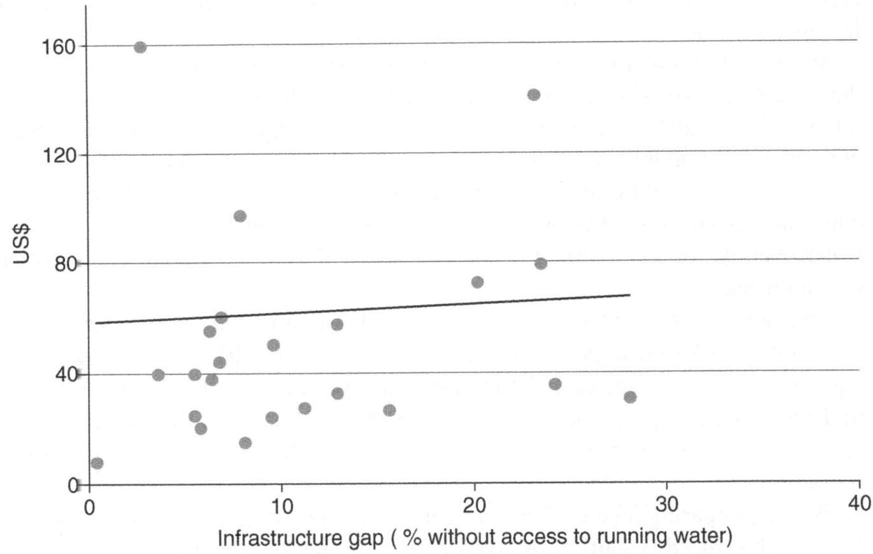

Figure 3.14 Capital expenditure per capita and infrastructure needs by province, 2010 (source: INDEC 2012).

approximately 30 percent of public expenditures and little over 20 percent of public fixed capital formation is done at the subnational level.

Mexico is marked by a very uneven distribution in economic development and population. Of its 112 million inhabitants, almost 20 percent are concentrated in the Federal District's metropolitan area. The level of dependence from federal transfers varies considerably as well. While some states finance up to 90 percent of their budget with transfers, as in the case of Coahuila, others are largely reliant on their own revenues as in the case of Nuevo Leon, with transfers representing only 22 percent of their expenditure.

Mexico's intergovernmental transfer system prior to 2007 distributed half of the revenue derived from several "assignable" taxes—including excise and vehicle taxes—according to their origin and the rest according to population. The federal government was in charge of setting the tax rate and base and collecting the revenue. Subnational governments had little influence over what revenue would be mobilized. Because these taxes correlate with economic activity and local revenue, there was little room for equalization or to incentivize own revenue mobilization within the transfer system. In parallel, there were numerous earmarked transfers for specific purposes that were given to states and municipalities, including capital grants.

The formulae were updated to promote a more equitable distribution of federal transfers according to expenditure needs. In the current system, per capita unconditional grants are calculated on the basis of per capita GDP growth and revenue effort. Conditional grants are primarily used for cost reimbursements, particularly of teacher salaries. The new formula guarantees states transfers at no less than 2007 levels.

With the introduction of the revised transfer system, the amount of resources that states receive without earmarking went from 204 billion Mexican pesos in 2006 to 239 in 2010. The new system favors poorer regions and provides states with greater autonomy and discretion over spending choices. Yet in many cases, states and municipalities continue to be overwhelmed with not fully funded mandates and spend most of their resources on the education and health wage bills. Consequently, non-earmarked resources are mainly used to cover recurrent expenditures.

The nominal amount of state fixed capital formation has also risen, going from 4 billion Mexican pesos in 2003 to 205 billion in 2011. These figures are equivalent to an average of 405 Mexican pesos per capita or US$37 in 2003 and to 1,969 Mexican pesos per capita or US$151 in 2010 (see Figure 3.15). The federal government continues to be responsible for the majority of fixed capital formation.

When comparing levels of investment before and after the formula reform, it appears that the distribution of fixed capital formation per capita has become more scattered. While the average level of investment in 2003 was considerably lower, states were much closer to each other than they are currently (see Figure 3.16). There also seems to be little correspondence between the per capita capital formation and poverty levels.

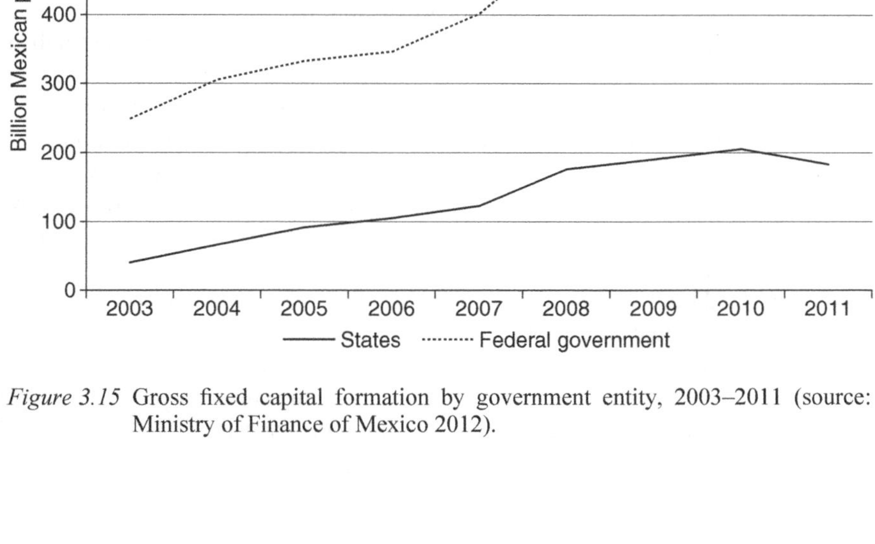

Figure 3.15 Gross fixed capital formation by government entity, 2003–2011 (source: Ministry of Finance of Mexico 2012).

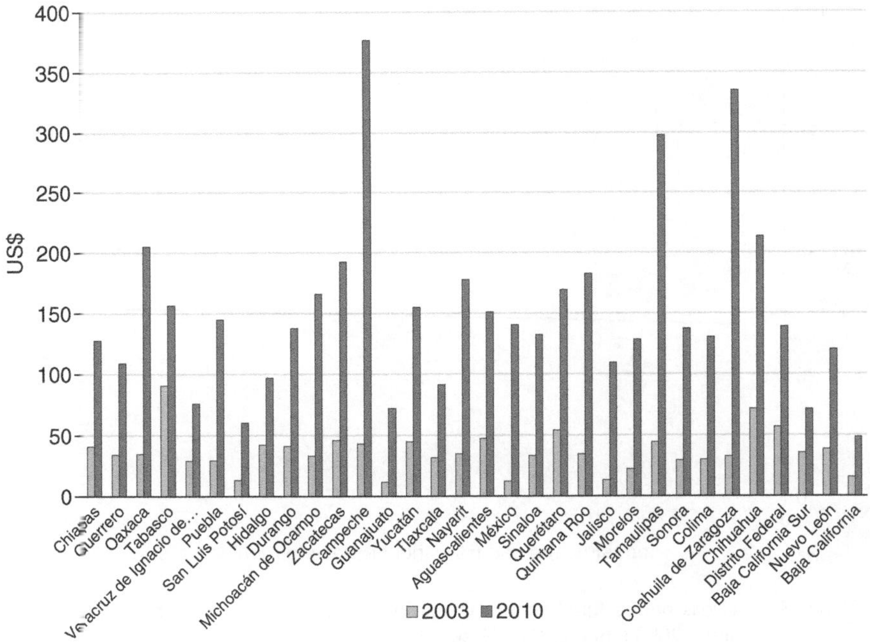

Figure 3.16 Gross public fixed capital formation per capita (by poverty level), 2003 and 2010 (source: INEGI 2012).

As well, investment per capita has become less aligned with infrastructure gaps than before the change of allocation formula (see Figure 3.17 and Figure 3.18). For example, in Chiapas and Guerrero more than a quarter of households do not have access to running water or sewage. Though these states have more than double increased fixed capital formation, yet their per capita investment are about half of that of Yucatan or Colima, where the coverage is almost complete. In this case, it appears that decentralization may have contributed to worsen the correspondence between needs and investment levels.

The two cases illustrate that although decentralization can help address horizontal disparities in infrastructure endowments, the outcome ultimately depends on the features of the intergovernmental fiscal framework and the incentives it creates. While in Argentina greater local autonomy in expenditure management contributed to increasing public investment and better aligning spending levels with needs, in the case of Mexico decentralization has led to a slower growth of subnational capital spending and a lower allocative efficiency. Differences in own revenues and access to financing are some of the main drivers behind this. In the case of Argentina, provinces have a minimum of resources that are guaranteed every year. This, to some extent, shields them from the overall volatility in federal revenue. At the same time, Argentina enjoys greater autonomy regarding public salaries.

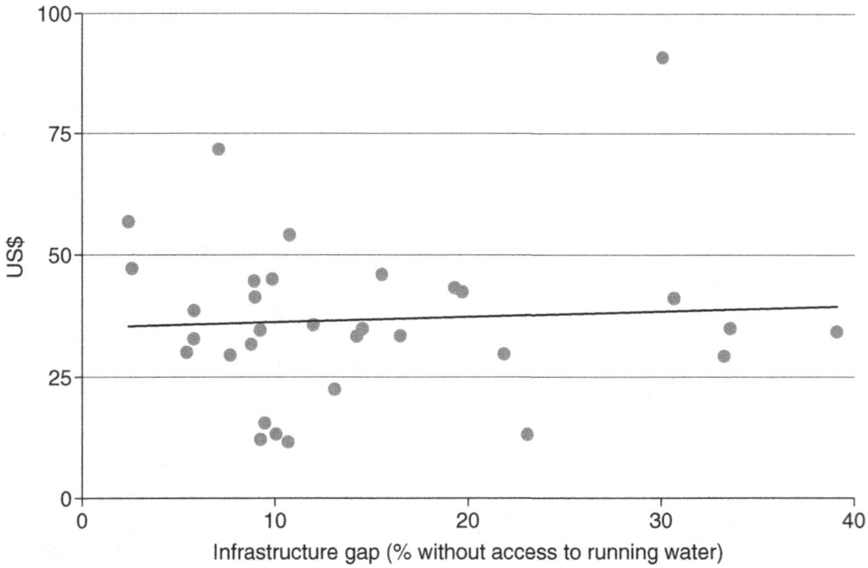

Figure 3.17 Gross public fixed capital formation per capita and infrastructure needs by state, 2003 (source: INEGI 2012).

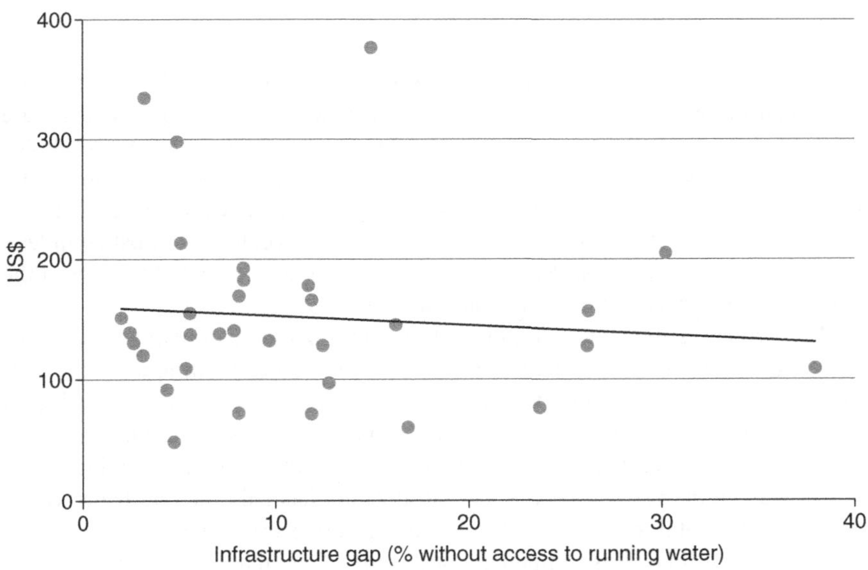

Figure 3.18 Gross public fixed capital formation per capita and infrastructure needs by state, 2010 (source: INEGI 2012).

Conclusions

The relationship between decentralization and outcomes in infrastructure services remain largely understudied, in particular in the context of developing countries. Having reviewed the existing evidence, this chapter highlights the pressing need for expanding data collection efforts and refining definitions around public investment at the national and subnational levels. Many of the predictions found in the literature and the assumptions that these hinge on cannot be tested with the available data. In a large number of countries not even the most basic monitoring or analysis on public investment portfolios is possible. Consequently, there is an important agenda for development partners, and the developing countries implementing decentralization reforms they assist, to improve the quality and coverage of data.

The existing evidence suggests that decentralization leads to lower aggregate levels of fixed capital formation. This may be reflective of efficiency gains, but it also raises concerns about potentially insufficient access to financing and steady funding sources for subnational governments. Lower investment rates can also be symptomatic of the fact that states and municipalities may be prioritizing other types of social investments over infrastructure. The results from the econometric analysis should be interpreted with caution as the available indicators only offer very imperfect approximations to the variables needed to more adequately analyze the impact of decentralization on public investment efficiency. On the other hand, with the necessary caveats in mind, the two cases discussed in the previous section show that, under certain conditions, decentralization can lead to a better horizontal allocation of capital spending and favor lagging regions.

Future research and policy work on decentralized infrastructure provision should consider several issues. The review of the literature and the analysis of the cases also point to the need of paying greater attention to better aligning the incentives provided by the intergovernmental fiscal system for subnational levels to respond to infrastructure needs. It is not uncommon for countries in which subnational governments heavily rely on vertical transfers to end up with uneven, excessively fragmented, or misaligned levels of capital spending.

The design of transfer and revenue-sharing systems should also pay closer attention to providing mechanisms for vertical coordination and promoting inter-jurisdictional cooperation. Both matching grants and technical assistance may be attractive tools to ensure that regional infrastructure is not neglected. Improving the ability for collective action among subnational governments would also be important in helping them to access financing and get better bids. States, and especially municipalities, can greatly benefit from pooling together risks and resources. Vertical coordination is as important as the horizontal one. Infrastructure provision implies the joint production of assets and the management of networks that require coordinated actions by various levels of government. Many countries are creating institutions to facilitate dialogue and decision-making across levels of government and using regional development strategies and contracts to implement joint agreements.

Similarly, central government may assist state and local governments to access financing by facilitating borrowing, providing subsidized loans, acting as guarantors in loans to subnationals, or temporarily relaxing fiscal rules. Yet there are important lessons to be learned from Latin America and Southern Europe on the danger of excessive subnational borrowing and its implication for fiscal stability.

Greater predictability and transparency of vertical transfers is a critical ingredient for better public investment management. As well, measures that delink annual revenues from spending are a necessary ingredient for medium term predictability in infrastructure envelopes. Increasing the revenue base of subnational governments and incentivizing them to raise their own revenues can help to stabilize and smooth capital spending over time.

Another dimension of infrastructure provision in multi-tiered governments that is often overlooked is the quality of public investment management systems. Central governments, and development partners, can support and encourage subnational units to strengthen public investment management systems and "invest to invest" by establishing a more systematic preparation, appraisal, selection, and implementation of infrastructure investment projects.

To end, there is also great potential to mobilize demand side governance around public investment at the subnational level by helping improve the capacity of civil society and oversight institutions to act collectively and demand that public resources are invested in the assets that generate greater public benefits. Capital expenditure tracking surveys could be used to monitor financing flows to actual contracts and physical works and leverage citizen control over local government officials.

Annex: Variable definitions and summary statistics

Table 3.7 Dependent and independent variables definitions

Variable	*Description*
Gross fixed capital formation, public (% of GDP).	*Source*: International Monetary Fund WEO Database.
Subnational expenditure share	Percentage of total expenditures by subnational governments, measured as the sum of local and state total expenditures minus state to local grants, divided by the sum of local, state, and national expenditures. Scale 0 to 100. *Source*: Decentralization Indicators Database 2012, by the World Bank, based on IMF's Government Finance Statistics.
Subnational net fixed capital formation share	Percentage of total net fixed capital formation accounted for by subnational governments, measured as the sum of local and state divided by the sum of local, state, and national net fixed capital formation. Scale 0 to 100. *Source*: Decentralization Indicators Database 2012, by the World Bank, based on IMF's Government Finance Statistics.
Subnational own source revenue as a share of subnational expenditure	Percentage of expenditures financed with subnational governments' own source revenue, measured as the sum of local and state revenues minus grants received from other levels of government, divided by the total subnational expenditures.
Subnational revenue share	Percentage of total revenues accounted for by subnational governments, measured as the sum of local and state total revenues minus grants from state to local government, divided by the sum of local, state, and national revenues. Scale 0 to 100. *Source*: Decentralization Indicators Database, by the World Bank 2012, based on IMF's Government Finance Statistics.
Subnational tax effort	Percentage of tax revenues collected by subnational governments, measured as the sum of local and state tax revenues, divided by the sum of local, state, and national tax revenues. Scale 0 to 100. *Source*: Decentralization Indicators Database 2012, by the World Bank, based on IMF's Government Finance Statistics.
GNI per capita	Data in constant 2000 dollars. *Source:* World Development Indicators 2012, by the World Bank.
Population	Total population. *Source:* World Development Indicators 2012, by the World Bank.
Surface area	Data in squared kilometers. *Source:* World Development Indicators 2012, by the World Bank.
Federation	1 if Federal Country, 0 if otherwise. Scale from 0 to 1. *Source*: Political Decentralization Indicators Database.

Source: IMF GFS 2012; IMF WEO 2012; World Bank Indicators 2012.

Table 3.8 Correlation coefficients, world

	Gen. gov. final cons. expenditure (% of GDP)	*Overall quality of infrastructure*	*Gross public fixed cap. form. (% of GDP)*	*SN revenue share*	*SN own source revenue share of expenditure*	*SN expenditure share*	*SN capital expenditure share*
Overall quality of infrastructure	0.19***						
Gross public fixed capital formation (% of GDP)	0.13***	–0.14***					
SN share of revenue (% of total rev.)	0.10***	0.31***	–0.08**				
SN own source rev. (% of SN exp.)	–0.08**	0.23***	–0.11***	0.28***			
SN share of expenditure	0.10***	0.32***	–0.11***	0.96***	0.20***		
SN share of cap. expenditure	0.15***	0.41***	–0.12***	0.32**	0.15***	0.32***	
GNI per capita (US$ constant 2000)	0.26***	0.48***	–0.07***	0.24***	0.10***	0.20***	0.23***
LN surface area (sq. km.)	–0.14***	–0.20***	–0.09***	0.45***	0.20***	0.41***	0.11***
High income	0.23***	0.44***	–0.09***	0.21***	0.04***	0.14***	0.22***
OECD	0.22***	0.34***	–0.11***	0.30***	0.04***	0.27***	0.22***

Source: IMF GFS 2012; IMF WEO 2012; World Bank Indicators 2012.

Notes

*** Significant at the 0.01 level (2-tailed).

** Significant at the 0.05 level (2-tailed).

* Significant at the 0.10 level (2-tailed).

Table 3.9 Number of observations and averages by country, 1990–2009

Variable	*1990–1999*			*2000–2009*		
	Obs	*Mean*	*St. Dev.*	*Obs*	*Mean*	*St. Dev.*
Africa						
Overall quality of infrastructure (1=low, 7=high)	—	—	—	195	3.1	1.1
Public investment (% of GDP)	404	7.0	7.4	543	8.3	22.7
SN share of revenue (% of total revenue)	20	18.8	15.2	33	13.7	15.7
SN own source revenue (% of SN expenditure)	22	43.6	18.1	66	43.8	25.7
SN share of expenditure (% of total expenditure)	20	15.6	12.8	39	25.4	33.9
SN share of capital expenditure (% of total cap. exp.)	2	68.2	4.1	31	27.5	35.5
SN capital expenditure (% of SN expenditure)	2	9.2	1.8	63	22.6	17.9
East Asia Pacific						
Overall quality of infrastructure (1=low, 7=high)	—	—	—	106	4.8	6.3
Public investment (% of GDP)	104	8.5	6.6	171	7.3	5.1
SN share of revenue (% of total revenue)	33	16.5	10.5	23	31.8	22.0
SN own source revenue (% of SN expenditure)	21	55.8	27.2	19	70.3	14.0
SN share of expenditure (% of total expenditure)	34	15.9	12.1	19	18.6	12.2
SN share of capital expenditure (% of total cap. exp.)	0			15	33.8	31.9
SN capital expenditure (% of SN expediture)	0			24	39.3	25.0
Europe and Central Asia						
Overall quality of infrastructure (1=low, 7=high)	—	—	—	204	3.5	0.9
Public investment (% of GDP)	162	4.6	4.5	323	4.9	3.4
SN share of revenue (% of total revenue)	98	21.9	8.2	212	22.8	9.1
SN own source revenue (% of SN expenditure)	86	68.3	23.8	177	63.3	17.7
SN share of expenditure (% of total expenditure)	98	18.6	8.0	224	19.9	9.4
SN share of capital expenditure (% of total cap. exp.)	10	34.8	25.1	182	43.2	21.1
SN capital expenditure (% of SN expenditure)	6	27.9	17.0	199	20.8	14.2

continued

Table 3.9 Continued

Variable	*1990–1999*			*2000–2009*		
	Obs	*Mean*	*St. Dev.*	*Obs*	*Mean*	*St. Dev.*
Latin America and the Caribbean						
Overall quality of infrastructure (1=low, 7=high)	—	—	—	197	3.3	0.9
Public investment (% of GDP)	271	5.5	3.3	333	5.7	3.4
SN share of revenue (% of total revenue)	67	21.2	15.0	78	24.4	21.5
SN own source revenue (% of SN expenditure)	45	65.7	23.8	70	64.3	21.5
SN share of expenditure (% of total expenditure)	68	17.6	13.0	84	19.4	20.5
SN share of capital expenditure (% of total cap. exp.)	5	.	641.2	70	35.1	24.5
SN capital expenditure (% of SN expenditure)	5	38.8	7.6	76	27.6	22.2
Middle East and North Africa						
Overall quality of infrastructure (1=low, 7=high)	—	—	—	83	4.4	0.9
Public investment (% of GDP)	144	7.0	2.9	199	7.9	5.6
SN share of revenue (% of total revenue)	0			21	8.2	1.9
SN own source revenue (% of SN expenditure)	0			10	80.2	5.5
SN share of expenditure (% of total expenditure)	0			24	4.5	1.7
SN share of capital expenditure (% of total cap. exp.)	0			18	18.6	8.6
SN capital expenditure (% of SN expenditure)	0			5	35.0	19.7

OECD						
Overall quality of infrastructure (1=low, 7=high)	—	—	—	223	5.6	0.9
Public investment (% of GDP)	118	3.5	1.6	176	3.0	1.2
SN share of revenue (% of total revenue)	175	32.4	13.5	228	30.7	15.5
SN own source revenue (% of SN expenditure)	173	66.7	21.3	221	62.6	19.6
SN share of expenditure (% of total expenditure)	193	28.6	14.1	265	28.6	14.9
SN share of capital expenditure (% of total cap. exp.)	36	61.7	24.6	202	63.9	24.6
SN capital expenditure (% of SN expenditure)	50	6.2	7.4	239	8.0	8.1
South Asia						
Overall quality of infrastructure (1=low, 7=high)	—	—	—	40	2.9	0.7
Public investment (% of GDP)	63	8.9	5.3	90	8.9	8.0
SN share of revenue (% of total revenue)	9	47.0	1.3	14	31.3	23.5
SN own source revenue (% of SN expenditure)	9	63.1	3.1	9	67.1	8.7
SN share of expenditure (% of total expenditure)	9	38.3	0.7	14	25.6	19.4
SN share of capital expenditure (% of total cap. exp.)	0			12	47.3	40.6
SN capital expenditure (% of SN expenditure)	0			9	21.2	10.5

Source: IMF GFS 2012; IMF WEO 2012; World Bank Indicators 2012.

Table 3.10 Public investment and decentralization indicators by country, 2009 (or latest available year)

	Overall quality of infrastructure (1 = low, 7 = high)	*Access to electricity (% of population)*	*Improved sanitation facilities (% of population with access)*	*Improved water source (% of population with access)*	*Road density (km of road per 100 sq. km.)*	*Fuel exports (% of merchandise exports)*	*Gen. gov. final consumption expenditure (% of GDP)*	*Public invesmtent (% of GDP)*	*SN share of revenue (% of total revenue)*	*SN own source revenue (% of SN expenditure)*	*SN share of expenditure (% of total expenditure)*	*SN share of capital expenditure (% of total cap. exp.)*	*SN capital expenditure (% of SN expediture)*
Cape Verde			60.0	87.0	33.0		25.7	14.0	12.7	56.2	9.2	14.1	62.1
Congo, Rep.		37.1	18.0	71.0	5.0		12.2	10.8	1.6	59.1	1.9	2.1	31.5
Ethiopia	3.2	17.0	20.0	44.0	4.0	0.0	8.2	17.6		23.9			29.3
Kenya	3.2	16.1	31.0	58.0	11.0	4.2	15.8	3.8		95.3			39.4
Lesotho	2.9	16.0	26.0	78.0	20.0		39.8	11.8	2.5	44.6	0.8	0.1	1.9
Mauritius	4.4	99.4	89.0	99.0	101.0	0.0	14.1	6.6	5.7	25.9	5.5	9.7	18.4
South Africa	4.7	75.0	79.0	91.0	30.0	11.1	21.1	9.2	40.7	29.1	35.9	90.2	12.0
Swaziland			57.0	68.0	21.0		14.7	8.4	2.2	94.8	2.2		
Uganda	2.9	9.0	34.0	71.0	29.0	1.4	11.6	5.4		4.6			5.0
Zambia	2.9	18.8	48.0	61.0	12.0	0.9	13.1	3.4		84.6			0.6
Zimbabwe	3.2	41.5	39.0	80.0	25.0	0.9	13.3	0.8	14.7		13.6		
China	4.0	99.4	63.0	90.0	40.0	1.7	13.4	22.9	67.5	79.9			7.9
Fiji			83.0	98.0	19.0	0.2		2.9		88.8			
Indonesia	3.1	64.5	54.0	81.0	25.0	28.4	9.6	4.9	10.9	37.7	9.1		
Korea, Rep.	5.8		100.0	98.0	105.0	6.4	16.0	6.2	40.4	58.0	35.5	83.8	46.1
Malaysia	5.4	99.4	96.0	100.0	30.0	14.8	14.1	10.7	11.4	98.8	10.8		
Mongolia	1.9	67.0	51.0	82.0	3.0		14.7	6.5	12.9	88.6	11.9	6.6	12.1
Thailand	4.8	99.3	96.0	96.0	35.0	5.2	13.4	6.5	15.0	65.4	5.2	29.6	40.6
Albania	3.1		94.0	95.0	63.0	11.6	8.8	8.8	20.8	3.5	16.9		
Armenia	3.5		90.0	98.0	26.0	0.1	13.3	6.3	6.8	49.9	5.7	3.8	17.9
Azerbaijan	4.5		82.0	80.0	61.0	92.9	13.8	8.9	2.2	30.8	3.4	1.7	21.7
Belarus			93.0	100.0	46.0	37.3	16.9	3.8	31.7	84.1	30.2	54.9	18.8
Bosnia and Herz	2.0		95.0	99.0	43.0	13.1	21.4	7.4	11.3		9.2	35.7	20.3
Bulgaria	2.8		100.0	100.0	36.0	12.6	16.3	5.1	16.7	37.8	14.4	45.1	36.6
Croatia	4.5		99.0	99.0	52.0	12.9	21.5	1.8	12.3	98.7	10.4	46.2	19.9
Czech Republic	4.5		98.0	100.0	166.0	3.6	21.7	5.1	25.2	68.5	19.2	81.4	26.9
Estonia	5.1		95.0	98.0	129.0	16.2	22.0	3.4	23.0	63.5	21.9	38.2	11.3
Georgia	3.8		95.0	98.0	29.0	5.0	24.5	8.0	19.6	39.3	13.7	29.0	37.8
Hungary	4.3		100.0	100.0	212.0	2.5	22.7		22.0	34.6	21.4	29.1	4.1
Kazakhstan	3.8		97.0	95.0	4.0	70.6	11.7	5.9	43.0	61.5	31.3	75.3	52.6
Kyrgyz Republic	2.8		93.0	90.0	17.0	6.2	18.4	5.0		56.6			9.7

Latvia	4.2		78.0	99.0	107.0	3.1	19.0	[illegible]	23.4	73.1	19.7	61.2	33.3
Lithuania	4.9		86.0	92.0	125.0	21.4	21.9	3.9	26.9	39.3	21.6	58.1	10.0
Macedonia, FYR	3.2		88.0	100.0	54.0	1.1	19.1	6.2	12.5	49.1	10.5	21.1	26.0
Moldova			85.0	96.0	38.0	0.4	22.1	5.0	23.2	50.6	18.7	50.2	13.2
Poland	2.6				123.0	3.0	18.4		30.6	49.3	25.9	66.0	17.8
Romania	2.4				83.0	5.9	15.2	5.2	23.6	26.7	16.9	43.9	21.8
Russian Fed.	3.3		71.0	97.0	6.0	66.7	21.0	4.6	48.8	97.6	32.5	50.7	17.3
Serbia	2.6		92.0	99.0	50.0		20.2	3.4	15.5	79.7	13.4	55.1	28.7
Slovak Republic	4.1		100.0	100.0	89.0	4.5	20.1	2.3	18.2	61.0	15.3	10.3	6.9
Slovenia	5.2		100.0	99.0	192.0	3.3	20.3		19.5	70.9	15.1	55.5	30.9
Tajikistan	3.2		94.0	64.0	19.0		28.3	13.3		72.1	27.7	42.6	98.4
Turkey	4.2		90.0	99.0	46.0	4.0	14.7	3.7	11.7	54.4	9.0	51.2	28.9
Ukraine	3.5		94.0	98.0	28.0	5.2	20.1	2.2	28.7	53.5	25.6	59.8	4.5
Argentina	3.2	97.2	90.0	97.0	8.0	10.3	15.2	4.2	44.3	87.9	42.2	79.8	12.9
Brazil	3.4	98.3	78.0	97.0	21.0	9.0	21.2	2.1	45.6	76.1	42.9	59.2	9.5
Chile	5.6	98.5	96.0	96.0	10.0	0.8	12.6	2.8	11.7	70.5	10.0	1.4	1.1
Colombia	3.4	93.6	77.0	92.0	15.0	50.7	15.8	6.0	30.1	69.9	27.5	12.6	4.3
Costa Rica	3.4	99.3	95.0	97.0	76.0	0.6	16.8	3.6	6.7	99.0	3.5	8.7	24.8
Dominican Rep.	3.4	95.9	83.0	86.0	26.0	0.2	7.8	3.6	0.9	36.9	3.0		
Ecuador	3.1	92.2	92.0	94.0	17.0	49.8	12.3	12.1	18.3				
El Salvador	4.8	86.4	87.0	87.0	48.0	2.8	10.6	2.2	10.1	72.8	6.3	45.2	48.6
Guatemala	4.3	80.5	78.0	92.0	13.0	4.1	10.2	3.8		60.3			
Honduras	3.7	70.3	77.0	87.0	12.0	4.3	18.5	3.4	10.4	70.7	6.6	30.0	79.8
Jamaica	4.4	92.0	80.0	93.0	201.0	17.2	15.4	4.6		80.7	0.5		
Mexico	3.8		84.0	95.0	19.0	13.5	12.0	6.1	36.7	79.4	16.8		
Nicaragua	2.7	72.1	52.0	85.0	17.0	0.9	10.8	7.1	8.8	45.3	2.9		
Panama	4.0	88.1	69.0	93.0	19.0	0.9	10.8	4.8	2.5		2.4		
Paraguay	2.2	96.7	70.0	86.0	8.0	0.0	11.8	5.5	8.8	67.9	7.5	17.8	36.4
Peru	3.0	85.7	70.0	85.0	10.0	10.3	10.3	5.2	29.4	23.7	20.4	67.3	77.0
Trinidad and T.	4.4	99.0	92.0	94.0	162.0	79.0		14.2		96.9	4.6		
Iran		98.4	100.0	96.0	11.0			7.6	6.9		2.7	22.5	
Jordan	5.2	99.9	98.0	97.0	9.0	0.6	21.9	8.2	7.7		6.0	18.7	63.3
Morocco	3.7	97.0	70.0	82.0	13.0	2.3	18.2	4.4	10.1	80.7	6.5	16.3	29.1
Tunisia	5.1	99.5	85.0	94.0	12.0	13.6	16.2	3.2		86.0	2.6	22.0	8.4
Australia	5.0		100.0	100.0	11.0	32.0	17.6	4.8	38.9	59.0	36.6		
Austria	6.6		100.0	100.0	127.0	3.5	19.8		30.4	69.1	30.0	29.5	

continued

Table 3.10 Continued

	Overall quality of infrastructure (1 = low, 7 = high)	*Access to electricity (% of population)*	*Improved sanitation facilities (% of population with access)*	*Improved water source (% of population with access)*	*Road density (km of road per 100 sq. km.)*	*Fuel exports (% of merchandise exports)*	*Gen. gov. final consumption expenditure (% of GDP)*	*Public invesmtent (% of GDP)*	*SN share of revenue (% of total revenue)*	*SN own source revenue (% of SN expenditure)*	*SN share of expenditure (% of total expenditure)*	*SN share of capital expenditure (% of total cap. exp.)*	*SN capital expenditure (% of SN expediture)*
Belgium	5.8		100.0	100.0	504.0	7.0	24.5	1.7	30.7	39.6	29.3	17.3	0.0
Canada	5.9		100.0	100.0	14.0	25.0	22.1	3.7	61.9	68.9	61.6	90.6	9.0
Denmark	6.3		100.0	100.0	170.0	7.5	29.8		48.3	43.0	46.7	44.8	0.8
Finland	6.5		100.0	100.0	23.0	6.6	25.1	2.8	36.7	70.3	35.7	86.7	2.1
France	6.6		100.0	100.0	173.0	3.6	24.8	3.4		28.9	19.2	87.2	4.9
Germany	6.5		100.0	100.0	180.0	2.1	20.0	1.6	35.0	83.1	34.9	87.9	0.4
Greece	4.4		98.0	100.0	89.0	9.5	20.4		8.1	39.4	5.2	40.0	13.7
Iceland	6.3		100.0	100.0	13.0	1.0	26.5		29.9	89.0	25.1	60.7	6.5
Ireland	4.1		99.0	100.0	137.0	0.7	19.9				11.4	69.8	27.8
Israel	4.5	99.7	100.0	100.0	83.0	0.0	24.0	1.7	14.1	65.1	12.5	68.7	3.1
Italy	3.8			100.0	162.0	3.6	21.4	2.5	29.5	49.5	26.8		3.5
Japan	5.8		100.0	100.0	320.0	1.8	19.9	4.7	58.5	56.8	45.9	63.5	1.8
Luxembourg	6.1		100.0	100.0	202.0	1.3	16.9		12.1	61.8	10.5	50.5	19.9
Malta	4.6		100.0	100.0	968.0	1.6	21.2		1.7	24.9	1.3		15.3
Netherlands	5.8		100.0	100.0	329.0	8.2	28.7	3.8	29.2	29.7	26.9	69.8	4.3
New Zealand	4.7			100.0	35.0	5.1	20.3	5.4	10.0	90.7	9.2	65.7	23.4
Norway	5.2		100.0	100.0	29.0	63.0	22.5	3.6	22.5	58.0	28.4	48.9	5.4
Portugal	5.7		100.0	99.0	90.0	4.9	22.1	3.0		95.7	13.6	45.4	5.7
Spain	5.2		100.0	100.0	132.0	4.4	21.3		47.0	55.2	40.5	76.3	9.5
Sweden	6.2		100.0	100.0	129.0	6.1	27.7		43.7	79.4	43.4	52.7	2.5
Switzerland	6.8		100.0	100.0	173.0	2.8	11.6	2.0	51.3	80.5	51.1	82.8	1.0
United Kingdom	5.2		100.0	100.0	172.0	11.2	23.5	2.9	28.0	30.3	22.7	48.2	5.9
United States	5.9		100.0	99.0	67.0	5.8	17.6	3.6	53.3	78.7	41.2	91.7	5.2
Afghanistan		15.6	37.0	50.0	6.0		10.1	22.9	0.8		0.4	0.7	
India	3.2	66.3	33.0	91.0	125.0	13.4	12.0	8.7	49.5	58.7	41.1	84.2	25.1

Source: IMF GFS 2012; IMF WEO 2012; World Bank Indicators 2012.

Notes

1 And in some cases, they have been privatized.
2 Fixed assets are tangible or intangible assets produced as outputs from production processes that are used repeatedly, or continuously, for more than one year. Gross fixed capital formation, as defined in the 2008 System of National Accounts, is measured "by the total value of a producer's acquisitions, less disposals, of fixed assets during the accounting period plus certain specified expenditure on services that adds to the value of nonproduced assets." Public gross fixed capital formation is calculated by subtracting from the overall measure the share accounted for by the private sector. This definition excludes consumer durable goods and small and inexpensive tools that perform simple operations and the services they generate following the "so called" asset boundary. (For more information see http://unstats.un.org/unsd/nationalaccount/docs/SNA2008.pdf.)
3 An efficient public management system is one that translates one unit of spending into an equivalent unit of economically and socially productive capital stock.
4 See more details of Gerardo Munck's commentary on WEF data at www.iadb.org/datagov.
5 The relationship between fiscal decentralization and public spending has spurred numerous empirical analyses, but to date there no consensus on what the outcome is.

References

Arzaghi Mohammad and J. Vernon Henderson. 2005. "Why Countries Are Fiscally Decentralizing," *Journal of Public Economics* 89(7): 1157–1189, July.

Asthana, Anand. N. 2003. "Decentralisation and Supply Efficiency: The Case of Rural Water Supply in Central India," *Journal of Development Studies* 39(4): 148–159.

Brennan, Geoffrey and James M. Buchanan. 1980. *The Power to Tax: Analytical Foundations of a Fiscal Constitution.* Cambridge: Cambridge University Press.

Cai, Hongbin and Daniel Treisman. 2005. "Does Competition for Capital Discipline Governments? Decentralization, Globalization, and Public Policy," *American Economic Review* 95(3): 817–830.

Chakraborty, Shanka and Era Dabla-Norris. 2009. "The Quality of Public Investment," IMF Working Paper WP/09/154.

Costas-Pérez, Elena, Albert Solé-Ollé, and Pilar Sorribas-Navarro. 2011. "Corruption Scandals, Press Reporting, and Accountability. Evidence from Spanish Mayors," Working Paper 2011/9, Institut d'Economia de Barcelona, Barcelona.

de Mello, Luiz. 2012. "Fiscal Decentralization and Public Investment." In: Giorgio Brosio and Juan Pablo Jiménez, eds. *Decentralization and Reform in Latin America: Improving Intergovernmental Relations.* London: Edward Elgar.

Eaton, Kent and Larry Schroeder. 2010. "Measuring Decentralization." In: E. Connerley, K. Eaton, and P. Smoke, eds. *Making Decentralization Work: Democracy, Development, and Security.* Boulder, CO: Lynne Rienner Publishers, pp. 167–190.

Ebel, Robert D. and Serdar Yilmaz. 2002. "On the Measurement and Impact of Fiscal Decentralization," Policy Research Working Paper Series 2809, World Bank, Washington DC.

Ebel, Robert and Serdar Yilmaz. 2003. "On the Measurement and Impact of Fiscal Decentralization." In: Jorge Martínez-Vásquez and James Alm, eds. *Public Finance in Developing and Transitional Countries: Essays in Honor of Richard Bird.* Cheltenham, UK: Edward Elgar.

Enikolopov, Ruben and Ekaterina Zhuravskaya. 2007. "Decentralization and Political Institutions," *Journal of Public Economics* 91(0): 2261–2290.

Estache, Antonio and S. Sinha. 1995. "Does Decentralization Increase Spending on Infrastructure?" Policy Research Working Paper 1457, World Bank, Washington, DC.

Faguet, Jean-Paul. 2004. "The Effects of Decentralisation on Public Investment: Evidence and Four Lessons from Bolivia and Colombia," Working Paper 62, Crisis States Research Centre, LSE, London.

Faguet, Jean-Paul. 2008. "Decentralisation's Effects on Public Investment: Evidence and Policy Lessons from Bolivia and Colombia," *Journal of Development Studies* 44(8): 1100–1121.

Faguet, Jean-Paul. 2012. *Decentralization and Popular Democracy: Governance from Below in Bolivia.* Ann Arbor: University of Michigan Press.

Holtz-Eakin, Douglas and Amy Ellen Schwartz. 1995. "Infrastructure in a Structural Model of Economic Growth," *Regional Science and Urban Economics* 25(2): 131–151.

Kappeler, Andreas, and Timo Välilä. "Fiscal Federalism and the Composition of Public Investment in Europe," *European Journal of Political Economy* 24(3): 562–570.

Keen, Michael and M. Marchand. 1997. "Fiscal Competition and the Pattern of Public Spending," *Journal of Public Economics* 66(1): 33–53.

Munck, Gerardo. 2000. "Description of Indicators," Inter-American Development Bank's DataGob database. www.iadb.org/datagob/index.html, accessed 11/15/09.

Panizza, Ugo. 1999. "On the Determinants of Fiscal Centralization: Theory and Evidence," *Journal of Public Economics* 74: 97–139.

Peterson, George E. and Elisa Muzzini. 2005. "Decentralizing Basic Infrastructure Services." In: *East Asia Decentralizes: Making Local Government Work.* World Bank: Washington, DC.

Pritchett, Lant. 2000. "The Tyranny of Concepts: CUDIE (Cumulated, Depreciated, Investment Effort) Is Not Capital," *Journal of Economic Growth* 5(4): 361–384.

Rodden, Jonathan. 2004. "Comparative Federalism and Decentralization: On Meaning and Measurement," *Comparative Politics* 36(4): 481–500.

Sinn, Hans-Werner. 2003. *The New Systems Competition.* Oxford: Oxford University Press.

Part II

Fundamentals in flux

Functions, finance, and equalization for decentralized public investment

4 Principles and practice

Roy Bahl and Richard M. Bird[1]

Introduction

The theory of expenditure assignment tells us that, under the right circumstances, certain services, including the infrastructure needed to provide them, can be more efficiently provided by subnational governments. At least in industrial countries, infrastructure investment is decentralized to a significant extent (Estache and Sinha 1995). In OECD countries, even such big projects as ports and airports are often locally managed and funded (Bel and Fageda 2009). In the European Union, for example, the share of subnational investment in economic infrastructure is 60–70 percent in the older member states and 40 percent in the new member states; subnational shares in social investments (e.g., in schools and hospitals) are even higher (Kappeler *et al.* 2012).

In low and middle income countries, economic theory provides less guidance to best practice. This is mostly because the assumptions beneath the decentralization model do not fit the developing country setting as well. The result is a great deal of variation in the extent to which responsibility for infrastructure service delivery is assigned to local governments (Alm 2010). In the countries included in Table 4.1, for instance, the equivalent of a large share of subnational own revenue is devoted to infrastructure. In fact, the amount spent on infrastructure by subnational governments in Peru is greater than the amount they raise from own sources.

Even in countries in which subnational governments are important investors in infrastructure, however, it is by no means obvious whether expenditures on infrastructure have been over-assigned or under-assigned to such governments, or whether the right expenditures have been devolved.[2] The open question is whether a change in governance arrangements (or in the incentives to policy-makers that lie beneath these governance arrangements) would lead to an improvement in the delivery of infrastructure services.[3] The institutional arrangements in question include not only the structure of subnational governments but the nature of political representation, spending and revenue mobilization powers, borrowing restrictions and practices, the degree of autonomy in management, the design and implementation of intergovernmental transfer systems, and the accountability of governments at all levels to those for whom they presumably speak.

Table 4.1 Public investment and decentralization in Latin America

Country	*General government investment (% GDP)*	*Subnational government investment (% GDP)*	*Subnational as share of total (%)*	*General government taxes (% GDP)*	*Subnational own revenues (% GDP)*	*Subnational as share of total (%)*
Argentina	1.3	1.1	84.6	30.8	5.6	18.2
Colombia	1.9	1.3	68.4	15.9	2.9	18.2
Chile	1.4	0.2	14.3	19.6	1.5	7.6
Peru	2.4	1.2	50.0	17.4	0.8	5.0

Sources and notes: Investment (average acquisition of fixed capital on accrual basis; data for 1995–2006) from de Mello (2012); revenue (for 2008 only) from Gomez Sabaini and Jimenez (2012).

This chapter is a review of the theoretical and practical issues surrounding the decentralization of responsibility for infrastructure to local governments. The focus is on local governments rather than provincial or state level governments in federations, and on structural issues rather than day-to-day management issues. Management issues are important, of course, but may contribute little to productive infrastructure investment if the structure of local governance and finance is flawed. In the second section of this chapter, we define how we understand "decentralization" and "infrastructure," discuss the normative principles that guide the assignment of responsibility for delivering infrastructure services, and note how the practice observed in most countries deviates from what theory appears to suggest. The next section of the chapter then considers a number of ways in which theory and practice might be better reconciled, emphasizing in particular the need to consider the broader governance context of each country. The following section considers more briefly two special "asymmetrical" issues of importance in many developing countries: infrastructure provision in metropolitan and remote rural areas and regional equity. The final section concludes with a summary of the policy directions suggested by this review.

Infrastructure and expenditure assignment

Though "infrastructure" is a term commonly used in the development economics literature, it is not always defined, and in fact can take on different meanings. The term "public infrastructure investment" for instance is sometimes used to denote government investment, even though it also includes investment by publicly owned companies such as utilities. As a rule, however, such corporate investment is recorded as government (rather than corporate) investment only if the revenues of such firms cover less than half their production costs: that is, the source of funding, not the formal ownership, determines how investment is classified (Alegre *et al.* 2008). More importantly for the present argument, "infrastructure investment" itself is sometimes used broadly to include not only physical capital formation but also expenditure considered to increase human capital formation, for example, on education. Even excluding such expenditure, it is often useful to think of government capital formation as falling into several distinct categories. Alegre *et al.* (2008), for example, distinguish four such categories in terms of the functions served by such investment: (1) Redistribution (housing, recreation, social protection); (2) Public Goods (defense, environment, order and safety, general public services); (3) Hospitals and Schools (health and education); and what they call simply (4) Infrastructure, that is traditional public works projects, of which by far the most important example in quantitative terms in most countries is transport. As they argue (Alegre *et al.* 2008, 26–27):

> This type of government investment has the most direct economic impact by reducing firms' production and transaction costs. The economic impact of government investment in health and education sectors is more long-term and less direct in character, as it facilitates the building up and maintenance

> of the economy's stock of human capital. Investment in public goods affects the economy's allocative efficiency indirectly through framework conditions for productive activity. Finally, redistribution affects the economy's income distribution rather than allocative or productive efficiency per se.

Although one may quibble with some of these statements, this classification is nonetheless useful in that it distinguishes clearly between investments that have direct and indirect effects on the level and nature of economic activity. It also makes it clear that the most relevant government investment from this perspective usually takes the form of "network" investment (e.g., transportation and communication) rather than "point" investment (e.g., hospitals, administrative buildings), even though the former is also geographically specific in its location and the latter may often also be part of a network from some perspectives (e.g., primary health centers feeding into hospitals or elementary schools into secondary schools).

For the most part, the focus in this chapter is on the narrower definition of infrastructure investment as the construction, operation, and maintenance of the long-lived physical assets required to deliver such specific public services as land transportation (highways, roads, streets, bridges, and ancillary services such as street lighting, street cleaning, signage, etc.), potable water (supply, distribution), wastewater management (sewerage, disposal), and solid waste collection and disposal (including hazardous waste).[4] Much of the discussion—for example, with respect to public-private partnerships—may also apply to other "utility" services such as electric power generation and distribution, natural gas distribution, airports and airways, ports and navigation control systems, railroads and public transit systems, irrigation, and telecommunications, as well as to the other types of investment mentioned by Alegre *et al.* (2008). For the most part in this chapter, however, we focus on the simplest, most basic, and arguably most important infrastructure investments usually assigned to decentralized governments—roads, water and sewerage, and solid waste disposal.[5] Since infrastructure investments are, by definition, both located in a particular physical location and within the jurisdiction of one or more specific political jurisdictions, even with this restricted set of activities much the same wide range of factors must be considered as with a broader definition.

Fiscal decentralization also requires definition. In this chapter, we interpret decentralization to mean the devolution of explicit authority and responsibility for a specific activity to a specific unit of government. Even this definition is both too broad and too narrow for our purposes, however. It is too broad in the sense that the "assignment" of a particular discretionary power to a level of government is almost never simply an issue of drawing lines between broad classes of activity such as "water and sewers" and "education" and assigning each exclusively to one level of government. As discussed below, each activity or function can be and usually is "unbundled" in a number of ways. At the same time, defining decentralization as simply equivalent to devolution is also too narrow because it excludes much of the important infrastructure investment undertaken by decentralized governments engaged in delivering delegated services such as health and education. Although our principal focus here is on the provision of physical infrastructure (including O&M) by subnational governments to whom the task of ensuring that the associated services are provided, inevitably some of the specific instances to which we refer and some of the arguments we make will stretch these boundaries to varying extents.

The basic rule of expenditure assignment: efficiency

The basic rule of efficient expenditure assignment is to devolve each function to the lowest level of government consistent with its efficient performance. This idea is expressed in the "decentralization theorem" (Oates 1972). So long as there are local variations in tastes and costs, there are potential efficiency gains from assigning responsibility for public sector activities to the lowest level of government possible. Under such an arrangement, local decision-makers will act on behalf of voters to decide what services are provided, to whom, and in what quantity and quality. The apt phase is that "people get what they want" under a decentralized system with the result that overall public welfare is enhanced. A well-known example of this principle is the rule of "subsidiarity" in the European Union.[6]

For some expenditure functions, however, assignment to the lowest level of government does not lead to a welfare gain. The two primary reasons why a public function would not pass the decentralization test are the presence of externalities and economies of scale. Although there are other ways to deal with such problems (such as intergovernmental transfers and private contracting), either might cause one to favor more centralized infrastructure spending, especially because many infrastructure projects are expensive, capital intensive, and are characterized by spillover effects. Nonetheless, as Table 4.1 illustrates, in at least some developing countries a large proportion of capital expenditures are made by subnational governments. One explanation might be the importance placed on satisfying local preferences. Another explanation might be that fiscal centralization is not the only way to deal with economies of scale and spillover effects or such other commonly cited pro-centralization factors as corruption and administrative capacity. Yet another explanation might be that there are overwhelming political economy considerations (e.g., regional equity concerns) for decentralizing more infrastructure investment than is strictly warranted by the conventional fiscal federalism literature.

One way around the assignment problems that arise when externalities or economies of scale are present is unbundling. This involves breaking the delivery of a function down into its subcomponents so that the most appropriate assignment can be made to local governments. For example, expenditures can be disaggregated to sectors (e.g., education, health), services (e.g., primary curative care, primary education), or activities (e.g., policy and standards, planning, asset creation, operation, and maintenance and operation). The World Bank (2007) has proposed unbundling service responsibilities for rural local governments in India by cross-classifying activities against sectors and services. The result of such an approach is to provide clarity in expenditure assignment, but also to provide constituents with a more clear idea of who to hold accountable for what service.

Boadway and Shah (2009) take a similar approach. In their schema—outlined in Table 4.2—only water, sewer, refuse, and fire protection are assigned to local governments, with local control over such local infrastructure (roads, water, sewage, irrigation) likely to be "…more cost-effective as well as more suited to the needs of the users" (147). In addition, although their enthusiasm for public enterprises in general is restrained, Boadway and Shah (2009) recognize that local control over public enterprises providing local utility and transportation services is also sensible, provided users are also local (148).

Even in principle, however, matters are complicated for two reasons. First, as already mentioned, there are often shared responsibilities for some services between different levels of government (national, state, and local). As Table 4.2 shows, in the Boadway–Shah presentation such sharing is deemed appropriate not only with respect to police, highways, parks and recreation, education, health, and social welfare but also even broader policy areas such as fiscal policy, regulation, and natural resources as well as, interestingly, direct foreign investment. Second, since "responsibility" may be thought of in several different ways—(Level 1) responsibility for policy, standards, and oversight, (Level 2) responsibility for provision (financing) and administration, and (Level 3) responsibility for production and administration—to some extent the shared responsibility among levels of government may be divided along these lines. With respect to primary and secondary education, for example, it is not uncommon for a national Ministry of Education to be responsible for determining national standards to be met by schools, teachers, and students, while regional (state) governments have the primary responsibility for financing education, and local (municipal) governments (or special school authorities) are in charge of delivering education. In Chile, for instance, although municipal governments deliver both basic health services and primary and secondary education these services are largely financed by the national government, which is also responsible for ensuring that minimum national standards are met in all municipalities.

Applying this line of thinking to the "project cycle" commonly associated with infrastructure investment, one might end up placing the "policy" responsibility for ensuring that appropriate technical standards are met with one level of government, the primary regulatory (and likely some financing) responsibility with another, and the responsibility for actually delivering such services with a third. In the case of water, sewer, and refuse collection, for example, one level of government might have responsibility for project design and management of water quality and waste disposal projects, another level of government with making provision for adequate water quality and quantity as well as environmentally sound wastewater and disposal services, and a third with operating the delivery system including waste collection and disposal, and maintenance of the water-sewer infrastructure. In their attempt to develop a general framework, Boadway and Shah (2009) argue the assignment of water, sewer, refuse, and fire protection entirely to local governments (the lowest level) but suggest that responsibility for policy and service delivery for other expenditure functions should be divided among governments as illustrated in Table 4.2.[7]

Table 4.2 The traditional theory of infrastructure expenditure assignment: an illustration

Function	*Policy, standards, oversight*	*Provision, administration*	*Production, distribution*	*Comments*
Water, sewer, refuse, fire protection	L	L	L,P	Primarily local benefits
Police	S,L	S,L	S,L	Primarily local benefits
Parks and recreation	N,S,L	N,S,L	N,S,L	Benefits and costs vary in scope
Highways, roads	N,S,L	N,S,L	S,L,P	Benefits and costs vary in scope
Education, health, social welfare	N,S,L	S,L	S,L,P	Transfers in kind
Natural resources	N	N,S,L	N,S,L,P	Promotes regional equity, common market
Fiscal policy	N	N,S,L	N,S,L,P	Coordination possible
Regulation	N	N,S,L	N,S,L,P	Internal common market
Foreign direct investment	N,L	L	P	Local infrastructure critical

Source: Extracted (including comments) from Boadway and Shah (2009, 134–135).

Notes

N=national government, S=state (provincial, regional) government, L=local government, P=private or non-governmental.

In practice, the unbundling of expenditure responsibility differs from country to country. Expenditure unbundling is common, but not a foolproof solution to the assignment problem. Most countries provide a central and a local government list of service responsibilities, sometimes in great detail. However, there often is a concurrent list that makes matters murky. The result can be great confusion about who is responsible for what, and much overlap. For example, rural local governments' welfare programs in Karnataka state in India are overlapped by eight central government programs and 47 state government programs (Rao *et al.* 2004).

Three aspects of this brief summary of the traditional approach deserve close attention in the present context. First, the argument for local control depends not only on beneficiaries being local, as emphasized in Table 4.2, but also on local control being more likely to meet local needs and, ideally, on local users being able and willing to pay the costs. Only when local governance institutions ensure in an accountable way that those who benefit and pay are also those who decide what is done should all aspects of infrastructure decisions be assigned to local governments. Strictly earmarked user charge financing (including an appropriate intertemporal dimension) meets this standard but general fund financing, even if entirely local, will do so only when governance institutions are both strong and fully accountable. Many developing countries do not have such institutions—or perhaps, in some cases, may have conflicting local institutions (e.g., traditional, appointed, and elected officials)—so even when all benefits of public sector activity are realized (and even paid for) locally, it is not always as clear as the conventional approach suggests that all aspects of the provision of such services are necessarily best provided locally.

Second, with respect to the important "shared" infrastructure responsibilities mentioned in Table 4.2, the appropriate local component depends on clearly understanding who benefits, how much, and when—and again it is critical to tie together the financing and expenditure sides of the infrastructure budget (including O&M). Not only does this require careful consideration of "spillovers" or "externalities" (network, interurban, etc.) but it is also critical that there be adequate horizontal and vertical coordination, cooperation, and burden sharing between affected jurisdictions. Similar concerns often arise even with critical aspects of such "local" activities as water, sewers, and refuse disposal as well as such "point" investments as new schools or health centers. Few developing countries are likely to satisfy these conditions, so again the guidance provided by theory may not always be as clear as the traditional literature suggests.

Infrastructure projects can never all be lumped in one group and treated symmetrically and in the same way. Even with respect to economic infrastructure, for instance, big projects such as intercity highways are quite different from small ones such as village to market roads not only in scale and complexity of design (as well as the need to fit the project within a national perspective) but also in financing, execution, and operation (maintenance). Small "purely local" projects of whatever character can and should be left primarily to local decision-makers both to decide and to fund (including funding from general transfers and borrowing). The latitude for error (e.g., corruption) may be greater with such small projects but the consequences of such errors are (and should be) largely borne by those who make them. Much the same may often be true with respect to "point" projects such as the design and location of a particular health center or school. Mistakes can and will be made; but so long as those who make them bear the costs they have a strong incentive to get it right. Large network projects, on the other hand, both because of their broader externality effects and because of the sheer magnitude of their technical and financial demands usually require both support and guidance either from higher levels of government or perhaps from cooperating jurisdictions at the same level (although the appropriate design of such intergovernmental agreements is beyond the scope of this chapter).

Third, even with respect to purely local infrastructure, localities require an ample tax base and/or ample access to capital markets to be able to access the lump sums needed to undertake most infrastructure projects. By definition, infrastructure has an important temporal dimension and it is critical that capital financing be timed and provided in the "right" way if the right projects are to be carried out in the right places—even when in principle it should be solely local governments that decide what is right, albeit perhaps subject to "standards" of quality, quantity, and access established by higher levels of government and presumably subject also to some monitoring and evaluation by them. Once again, few developing countries seem to provide a promising environment for the effective implementation of such ideas.

The solution of the assignment problem with respect to infrastructure decentralization suggested in the traditional literature is thus simple in principle but considerably more complex if examined in detail. The simple principle is what is sometimes called subsidiarity. Decentralized provision of the infrastructure needed to fulfill local expenditure responsibilities should clearly be the responsibility of local governments. In some instances, restructuring subnational government borders or reassigning functions to different levels of subnational government may be essential to achieving efficient decentralization. In other instances, the most efficient way to proceed may be establishing some sort of "special district," although, as noted below, the effective governance and operation of such special-purpose governmental units can turn out to be surprisingly difficult to resolve (Berry 2009). An additional complication arises because in principle since capital assets provide services over their sometimes long lives the most efficient and equitable way to finance such infrastructure is often through borrowing. However, since in most developing countries local borrowing is subject to various regulatory and quantitative restraints in practice, especially when combined with the less developed capital markets in most countries, much local infrastructure ends up being financed by capital grants (or subsidized loans) from higher levels of government or even foreign donors.

More broadly, one cannot consider decentralization and infrastructure in isolation from the critical issues raised in the "second-generation" fiscal federalism literature with respect to decentralized governance in general (Oates 2005; Weingast 2009). As this literature shows, local responsibility and accountability is crucial in any decentralization program if it is to be incentive-compatible. Without good local governance in a good intergovernmental system, local provision of infrastructure is likely to be far from the theoretical ideal. The appropriate long-term solution is not, however, to shift responsibility to levels of government that are unlikely to deliver anything better—and may even from the perspective of local consumers do worse—but to improve local governance institutions by establishing workable and meaningful local accountability by fiscally responsible governments. To do this, local governments need to have control over adequate resources for which they are fully accountable to those who provide them, whether local citizens through user charges and local taxes (including those servicing capital debts) or higher levels of government that provide grants or subsidized loans or private financial institutions that provide infrastructure loans. Even if decentralization is perfectly designed, some failures—breakdowns of service delivery, payment arrears, even extreme insolvency—are likely to occur in some places, so that there is always a need not only for the central government to maintain a sound macroeconomic framework (e.g., with respect to subnational borrowing) but also to develop and, if necessary, implement, the equivalent of a "bankruptcy" takeover of failed local governments.

The requisite balance between assigning expenditure responsibilities to a decentralized governance institution that is just large enough to encompass the immediately relevant externalities while at the same time taking adequately into account the interests of all those affected (e.g., those in the areas where the refuse is dumped, buried, or burned) rather than just the interests of such specific groups as shareholders or public sector workers is not easy to attain. Finding an expenditure delivery arrangement that passes this test becomes even more difficult when it becomes necessary to align "who pays" with "who benefits."

Two other factors drive a wedge between the theory of assigning infrastructure responsibility, and the practice. One is the inherent complication of the matter. Imagine trying to unbundle education expenditures into the various activities, and then developing an operating definition of an activity such as "standard setting." And then there are requirements that the benefit zone for certain infrastructure services be defined. Finally, there is politics. Unbundling may be a good idea for finding the right level of government to deliver a service, but elected politicians may be loath to give up control and may impose new mandates in the name of more efficient infrastructure service delivery.

From principle to practice

The traditional assignment of expenditure responsibility suggests that much of the spending on infrastructure will be made by local governments. About 1 billion people lack clean water and perhaps 3 billion lack access to adequate sanitation facilities. The annual infrastructure expenditures required to meet simply this one essentially local need have been estimated at 2.0 percent of GDP in Sub-Saharan Africa and 1.7 percent in South Asia, with about 40 percent of these amounts required for new investment and the balance for operation and maintenance (Estache 2010). In practice, as Table 4.1 suggests for some Latin

American countries, total local expenditures on all infrastructure have sometimes been less than these levels, and the share financed from "own" revenues is smaller. It is not surprising that in practice new investments made in even the most local of infrastructure in poor countries are largely financed by foreign aid and capital transfers. Indeed, in many cases local "ability to pay" is so low that even recurrent O&M expenditures, when made at all, are sometimes financed from such outside sources.[8]

A major obstacle in the way of assigning more responsibility for infrastructure to local governments is that most local governments in developing countries lack the financial, managerial, and technical ability to do the job. Two paths to solution seem possible: Kick it all upstairs to a higher level government, or work away at the long, grinding process of building up local governance structures and managerial capacity. Since it is always quicker and easier to give money and to outsource tasks (e.g., via public-private partnerships—PPP—of various sorts) than to build up the institutional structure needed to enable local people to do the job themselves, the short horizons under which aid agencies and national governments operate ensure that they usually choose the easy way. In Bangladesh, for example, the national Local Engineering Department essentially centralized local investment. By following this path, however, although probably improving the technical efficiency of projects and although usually enthusiastically supported by local governments glad to be freed of the need to tax their own people, local autonomy was significantly undermined. The result is that (1) local people have little or no ownership in the asset, so they tend to run it down rather than maintain it properly, that (2) they still lack most of the capacities needed to do it right anyway, that (3) the asset provided may not be what local people really want, and that (4) the whole cycle is likely to continue as long as outsiders are willing to pay. A similar system of centrally controlled infrastructure investment existed in Indonesia during the 1970–2000 period. However, this was replaced with a decentralized system in 2000 and the responsibility for choosing and implementing infrastructure projects began to shift to elected local governments.

Preferences

Preferences for capital projects will vary across regions within a country because of differences in the economic base, differences in the existing quality of infrastructure services, and differences related to urban population densities. The idea that local familiarity and information can lead to better project selection and implementation is both generally accepted and supported by some country studies (e.g., Fiszbein 1997; Faguet 2004). The demand for local control of infrastructure spending is high because the benefits are more readily identified by voters than is the case for many government outlays: neighborhood residents are more likely to get excited about better water supply or a new street lighting system than they are about an increase in public employee wages, the preparation of a new master plan, or improved tax administration services. This kind of anecdotal reasoning leads some to the conclusion that decentralized infrastructure responsibility should improve allocative (economic) efficiency, by attuning provision more closely to local preferences. One example is some recent research showing that giving responsibility for water supply to local governments rather than public enterprises increased the quality of the output in Colombia (Bird 2012).

Other evidence suggests that local control may also lead to increased overall levels of infrastructure spending (Estache and Sinha 1995; Boadway and Shah 2009). A recent careful econometric study in Europe, for example, found that decentralizing revenue authority to subnational governments definitely increased their investment in economic infrastructure, without reducing their "social" investment (Kappeler *et al.* 2012). Although the political attraction of investing in highly visible public works is obvious, and the economic outcomes of such projects may also be positive, legitimate questions may still be raised about the relative effectiveness of such programs in terms of poverty alleviation compared to, say, conditional cash transfers (McCord 2012). Even in this respect, however, some evidence suggests that appropriately locating such "geographic capital" (Jalan and Ravallion 2002) may have significant impacts on improving the access of the poor to markets, work, and improved welfare (Majumder 2012). As Fiszbein (1997) noted some years ago, for example, poor people in an isolated mountain village may quite rationally choose to employ increased resources in improving market roads rather than primary education or whatever planners in the capital city may think is best for them.

But are such potential efficiency gains from decentralization always or even often captured? There are a number of reasons why they may not be, starting with the possibility that the local population may not have a vote which allows them to express preferences (and they also may not have a creditable exit threat), as in the cases of China, Vietnam, or Nepal. In China, for example, subnational governments have considerable discretion in making infrastructure decisions, but their political leaders are appointed and are accountable upward. Infrastructure accomplishments have been remarkable in China, but it is not clear how much of this is driven by local preferences (Dollar and Hofman 2008). Bird *et al.* (2011) discuss a study of some 500 villages which indicates that relatively little attention was paid to local preferences in making decisions about local expenditures in China.

Even if there is local voting, decision making about public spending may have been captured by powerful interest groups within the community, such as local politicians or community organizations, or by central ministries.[9] The process of selecting and designing capital projects may not be weighted in favor of the preferences of the local population (Peterson and Muzzini 2005), and the procurement process may be corrupt and inefficient. Government structure itself may be an impediment in cases in which the large size of provinces and cities make the benefit flow from capital investments all but invisible to individual households.

Some of these obstacles to capturing the potential efficiency gains from fiscal decentralization can be overcome or at least ameliorated. One way is to provide for sub-municipalities within large urban areas and to give them some degree of decision-making power and budget. This will allow for implementation of small-scale projects at the neighborhood level, and might provide a stronger voice for neighborhood populations in the selection and design of larger capital projects. Examples of this are the barangay governments in metropolitan Manila and the extensive use of locally based benefit funding of investment projects in some Colombian cities (Bird 2012).

Another way to do a better job of capturing the benefits of decentralized infrastructure spending is to monitor client satisfaction with infrastructure services. The use of surveys to gain some information on citizen perceptions about the quality of services delivered can be an important input to identifying new infrastructure needs and maintenance needs. While this is often done in the case of recurrent expenditures with household surveys and report cards, it is less often done with respect to infrastructure (Peterson and Muzzini 2005).

Technical efficiency

Welfare gains from the decentralization of responsibility for infrastructure services can also result when services are produced at lower cost. One important way to lower costs is to deliver services more efficiently. A recent study in Ontario, Canada, for example, reports that 20 percent of treated water is "lost" in the distribution system before it reaches consumers (Herstein 2012). Such leakages through technical failures (as well as simple theft) are often much larger in developing countries and might be lowered when providers are more directly responsible and responsive to consumers, although there seems to be a paucity of empirical evidence bearing on this point. One must also consider the technology used to produce and, especially, maintain, services; for instance, in rural areas pumps that can be repaired locally may be preferable to more modern equipment that requires more expert servicing just as schools that can be built with local labor and materials may be cheaper to construct and maintain than those that meet the latest specifications sent from the experts in the capital. On the other hand, sometimes many infrastructure inputs may be more efficiently "outsourced" to central (or private) design, production, and procurement, provided adequate attention is paid to local conditions and preferences.

Some of these points may be illustrated by an interesting recent project in Ahmedabad, India, to improve public transit by building a new Ahmedabad Bus Rapid Transit Service (ABRTS). This project seems to be surprisingly successful in its first years (National Institute of Urban Affairs 2011) for a number of reasons. First, its designers paid close attention to experience elsewhere with similar projects, both successful (e.g., Bogotá) and unsuccessful (e.g., Delhi). Second, in both the design and the implementation phases, extensive efforts were made to consult not only with customers (actual and prospective) but with such "stakeholders" as competitive modes of transport. As a result, substantial efforts were made to turn competing into complementary (feeder) modes. Moreover, close attention was paid to the specific urban context in which the system was to operate, by establishing routes that would reduce congestion, and minimizing conflict about religious sites. In addition, an extensive "pilot" operation was carried out to test the system, and this led to significant improvements. For example, the initial trial buses had metal seats which (unsurprisingly in the Indian context) turned out to be too hot for comfort and were therefore replaced by others before the system was finally launched. Involving local people is important in all stages of the project cycle, not just by securing their agreement and approval but by actively involving them in identifying and initiating projects (what most needs to be done, and where), in project design (exactly where, and in what way), and even to some extent execution and operation (including, perhaps, using local labor where feasible) as well as in continually monitoring and evaluating services.

For capital intensive services, the presence of economies of scale rules out some functions for decentralized assignment, such as railways and national trunk roads. The cost of delivery by small area governments would be prohibitive for such services. But for most capital projects, the right level to assign expenditure responsibility and the extent to which local governments are "right-sized" with respect to taking advantage of economies of scale (and scope) remains an open question (Fox and Gurley 2006).

Also debatable is the extent to which local governments take advantage of economies of scale.[10] The empirical evidence is, at best, mixed. Byrnes and Dollery (2002), for example, reviewed research on economies of scale in the UK and the US and concluded that only 8 percent of the studies found evidence of economies of scale in local government, 29 percent found evidence of U-shaped cost curves, 39 percent found no statistical relationship between per capita expenditure and population size, and 24 percent found evidence of diseconomies of scale. Studies that analyzed specific services (e.g., fire, housing) also showed mixed results. On the whole there is not strong evidence of economies of scale with respect to most services once municipalities are much larger than 20,000–40,000 or so in population.[11] This does not mean that there are not size effects or that per capita expenditures do not fall as the scale of local government operations increases. More likely it reflects the difficulty of separating the pure effects of scale on government costs from the effects of everything else.

Economies of scale depend on the service in question and the units of measurement—such as the jurisdiction size or the size of the facility. Hirsch (1959), for example, estimated cost functions for police services, fire services, refuse collection, water, sewage, and education and found that expenditures per capita declined with the quantity provided for water and sewage (perhaps unsurprisingly, given the very heavy infrastructure component of such services)—but that there was no similar decline for other urban services generally provided by local governments in the US. For some services, expenditures per capita actually rose as output expanded, indicating that there were diseconomies of scale. Other studies that have estimated cost functions have similarly found economies of scale for hard services such as water, sewers, and transportation but generally not for such soft services as police, refuse collection, recreation, or planning

(Bird and Slack 1993). Hard services are capital intensive, so large government units can more readily make the substantial capital investments needed to extend the water distribution system or build a least unit cost size sewage treatment plant (Bahl and Linn 1992). Other services, such as policing, are highly labor intensive and hence unlikely to show significant economies of scale. Presumably much the same can be said with respect to other labor intensive services like social services, education, and to some extent even health.

Recent studies in both Canada and Finland, for example, have found little evidence of economies of scale in large municipalities. Found (2012) analyzed economies of scale for fire and police in 445 municipalities in Ontario, Canada from 2005 to 2008. He found that fire services exhibited U-shaped costs with a cost-minimizing population of approximately 20,000 residents. Police services also exhibited U-shaped costs with a cost-minimizing population of about 45,000 residents. In Finland, Moisio *et al.* (2010) reported on a number of studies of the effects of municipal mergers on per capita expenditures and found the results to be mixed, with the biggest cities showing relatively low cost efficiency with respect to basic welfare services. Other studies in Finland that focused on specific municipal services (health centers and schooling) found the optimal size of the municipality to be somewhere between 20,000 and 40,000 people (Moisio *et al.* 2010).

As important as economies of scale (and scope) are economies of density (Bel forthcoming). For example, a recent study of annexation that analyzed 952 US cities (with at least 10,000 people) that annexed other municipalities between 1992 and 2002 found efficiencies from increasing land area but only if the annexation was accompanied by higher densities (Edwards and Xiao 2009). If densities are lower following annexation, per capita expenditures may increase or decrease depending on the relationship of the change in land area to changes in density. The authors found that service delivery and administrative efficiencies are achieved with high density developments but compromised with low density developments that are spread out and more costly to serve.

The question of economies of scale aside, there is some support for the argument that decentralization can lead to more cost effective outcomes for capital projects. It can be argued that the cost of production is cheaper using local labor and materials, and avoiding the bureaucratic costs of managing a project from the center. There is some evidence to support this argument, though the results are far from conclusive (Peterson and Muzzini 2005). But this cost advantage does not hold in all countries. For example, The World Bank (2009b) reports that subnational government spending for roads in Colombia is expensive and wasteful. However, as Bird (2012) argues, it appears that this result reflects in part the unclear nature of the initial assignment of functions (which led to continuous disputes about which level of government was responsible for what when it came to roads) and in part the confusing way in which roads were financed. When, as in Colombia, all three levels of government are involved in financing an activity but the two subnational levels receive most of their funding from the national government through several different channels, not only is the "ownership" of (and hence responsibility for) roads further confused, but the diverse and volatile set of funding sources makes it exceptionally difficult either to invest sensibly or to maintain investments properly once made.

Externalities

When the delivery of a service leads to impacts on households that reside outside the boundaries of the jurisdiction, the lower tier governments will underspend (or overspend) because they will only account for local benefits and costs in their budgetary decisions. Because the social costs and benefits due to spillover effects are ignored, society will not achieve as high a level of welfare as would be the case if the service had been assigned to either the regional or even the national level. Such functions are not good candidates for delivery by a subnational government unless the area served can be expanded so that the externalities can be internalized, or, the government can arrange for payment by non-residents that would compensate for the benefits received.

For purposes of working out the assignment of each function to different levels of government, it is necessary to estimate the benefit (cost) zone for each expenditure function. This is mission impossible because nearly all functions delivered by government impose external effects, yet, rational public policy reform requires identification of the degree of the spillover effects and estimation of the costs of internalizing these. The analysis for each function is not likely to result in precise estimates for these benefit zones, but it may often be good enough to guide the expenditure assignment decision for each infrastructure service.

The end result of this exercise will be to assign responsibility for every infrastructure function to either local, provincial, or central government.[12] Sometimes, the external benefit or cost zone is so great that only central government responsibility will do. This will be the case if the service in question is one that benefits or burdens the entire national population (e.g., defense) or one in which there is a strong interest in maintaining national standards (education or the social safety net). In some cases, the external effects are deemed to be small enough to be ignored.

As a rule, however, benefit and cost spillovers related to the provision of infrastructure services generally relate to an area smaller than the entire nation, especially in larger countries. Provincial or state level governments might be the right choice for delivery of functions such as intermunicipal roads and watershed management. Sometimes externalities may be internalized by assigning functions to an even smaller jurisdiction: for example, water supply, mass transit, and urban planning might be best assigned to metropolitan area-wide governments, although such governments all too often do not exist, have the wrong powers assigned, or fail to have the appropriate boundaries (Bahl and Linn 1992).

Various institutional arrangements may be used to address the spillover effects that might come with decentralization. The process should begin with a clear identification of services where government perceives the externalities to be great enough to reject assignment to subnational governments. Doing this homework correctly is not so easy, because of the difficulty of separating true external costs and benefits from the desire of central ministries to continue their control over certain programs.

Second, infrastructure responsibilities might be unbundled into those subcomponents that do not spin off large spillovers and those that do. In China, for example, the central government sets standards for the service, while the subnational governments are given responsibility for design and implementation of the project, and for financing.

Third, central governments might use intergovernmental transfers of various kinds to induce subnational governments to correct for under-spending on services with large externalities. As discussed further below, these usually take the form of conditional grants.

Finally, it might be decided that the lowest levels of government cannot handle the externality (or even the management) issues. In this case, decentralization for certain functions is still possible in the form of special purpose public enterprises that operate on a local basis. In some Indian metropolitan areas, certain local infrastructure services are delivered by single purpose metropolitan special districts, which would seem to address the externalities and economies of scale issues. However, these parastatals are state owned, and so the responsiveness to local preferences is weakened (Mohanty *et al.* 2007). Another option is contracting for services, either to a private firm or to another local government. While arranging some form of contracting between larger and smaller local governments for service delivery is an attractive alternative in principle, in practice it has turned out to be difficult to sustain such arrangements even in such well-governed and homogenous developed countries as Denmark and Finland.[13]

Managing infrastructure

A major consideration as regards production efficiency is maintenance of the infrastructure. A proper schedule of maintenance can markedly enhance the flow of services from capital assets and extend their useful life. But maintenance is problematic under a decentralized system, for three reasons. First, the base of local revenues that can be used to maintain the capital stock is limited. Subnational governments raise only about 2.5 percent of GDP from own sources in developing countries (Table 4.3). Ingram *et al.* (forthcoming) estimate that the required annual maintenance costs for urban infrastructure in developing countries is equivalent to about 2 percent of GDP.[14] Second, there is the question of whether local officials might be more prone to ignore maintenance in favor of more high profile construction of new infrastructure, or in favor of satisfying such other demands as public employee wage increases. There is also the question of whether from their perspective it may not be politically simpler to obtain new capital financing from higher levels of government than to obtain more tax revenue from their constituents. Third, as mentioned earlier with respect to roads

Table 4.3 Fiscal decentralization: international comparisons for the 2000s[a]

Region	*Subnational government expenditures*[a]		*Subnational government taxes*[a]	
	Percent of total government expenditures	*Percent of GDP*	*Percent of total taxes*	*Percent of GDP*
Developing countries	18.8 (16)	5.1 (20)	11.4 (16)	2.3 (20)
Industrial countries	27.8 (26)	13.9 (26)	22.7 (24)	6.4 (25)

Source: IMF (various years) and estimates drawn from case studies.

Notes

Data reported are unweighted averages for the 2000s for years in which data are reported.

a The number in parentheses shows the number of countries included in the comparison.

in Colombia, the ownership of the public asset should be clear, lest there be confusion over which level of government is responsible for its maintenance (World Bank 2009b).

Are there institutional and behavioral arrangements that might overcome some of the production efficiency disadvantages of subnational governments as regards the decentralization of infrastructure services? Four possibilities might be suggested. First, if a service has been assigned to subnational governments, limit interference from upper level governments that may increase costs. Interference by higher level governments, for example by imposing mandates, should be limited to concerns about externalities, and perhaps the regular monitoring of maintenance. Mandates to spend a specified minimum share of the budget on economic development, or a specified maximum share on personnel, reduce local spending flexibility if they are effective, and are not easily enforced in any case. Some countries (e.g., Colombia) commonly earmark significant portions of general intergovernmental transfers to "investment," largely to restrain the feared dissipation of such transfers in current expenditures which all too often appear to line the pockets of local officials and their friends and relatives rather than provide valued services to citizens in general. It is far from clear that such earmarking achieves its objective. Indeed, as noted later, there is both theoretical and empirical support for the contrary view that reducing earmarking is more likely to improve than to distort the allocation of local resources.

Second, in the case of urban governments, expand the tax and user/benefit charge powers of subnational governments. This should involve giving subnational governments access to a larger tax base, and autonomy for using this base. Increased provincial and local revenues would provide a funding base for infrastructure maintenance.

Third, close the "back door" to infrastructure finance that is often provided by higher level governments. In Mexico, for example, as much as 10 percent of intergovernmental transfers to subnational governments are given in the form of ad hoc grants to subnational governments (Bahl and Sethi 2012). This discourages local revenue mobilization and reduces the transparency of the system of intergovernmental transfers.

Fourth, unbundle infrastructure services so that those subfunctions not characterized by clear advantages of centralization might be assigned to subnational governments. Costs could be reduced by disaggregating infrastructure expenditures into components, and making assignments on a basis of comparative advantage. For example, while perhaps technical specifications required to ensure water quality might be a matter of national concern, the construction of major water supply and sewage lines (like interurban highways) may best be handled at the regional level, and local distribution lines might be the responsibility of local governments. As usual, such decentralization is likely to work better the more effort central governments put into establishing good "framework" laws (e.g., on tendering and on intergovernmental agreements), into upgrading local capacity to deal with such issues, and into monitoring and evaluating outcomes. In a sense, the issue here is similar to that raised below with respect to public-private infrastructure projects: in order to reap the full benefits of decentralization, some investment must be made into improving the regulatory framework at the national level and the executive capacity at the local level.

Corruption

A possible cost of fiscal decentralization is that it may lead to a greater rate of corruption. The thinking here is that the "closeness" between elected local politicians and the local political power structure breeds corruption. Both Prud'homme (1995) and Tanzi (1996) have presented this view as one of the dangers of decentralization. There are other reasons why one might expect more corruption in a decentralized fiscal system. One is that the probability of successful stealing is increased by the weakening of central authority and monitoring. Various students of corruption have placed the blame on the greater number of contacts with public officials in developing countries, on lower paid local public officials who have more incentive to steal than higher paid central officials, and on local government voters who have not yet learned to use their power to monitor and discipline their employees. All these problems may perhaps be more serious with respect to infrastructure where there is more latitude for fraud, bribery, embezzlement, and patronage than with respect to other, more "regular" activities of local public officials and politicians. Moreover, local corruption, even if smaller in scale, may be particularly damaging to building "trust" in government owing to the more visible inequalities that may result.

Nonetheless, the case that corruption and decentralization are positively linked might be more impressionistic than real and the empirical evidence is divided on whether corruption costs are greater under a more decentralized system.[15] Perhaps the common perception of high local corruption is unduly influenced by its greater visibility; corruption may be even greater with respect to centralized decisions if they are, as is sometimes true, even less transparent.

We are not aware of comparable recent estimates of the cost of corruption in the infrastructure sector. Such estimates are inherently difficult because data are scarce and because the conceptual model is not easily worked out. In earlier work, however, Tanzi and Davoodi (2000) argued that corruption will lower infrastructure spending (fewer projects will be undertaken) while Mauro (1995) argued that corruption is more likely to raise infrastructure spending (higher unit costs). Whatever the outcome, in the nature of the problem, information is scarce and unreliable, and helpful and feasible solutions short of a fundamental revision of the relationship between state and citizens are not easy to design or implement. Politicians and officials who gain much of their income from exploiting their monopoly power to grant licenses, bestow contracts, or provide services are not likely to give it up easily. Neither regulation nor privatization seems to provide complete answers to controlling the problem.

As Estache (2006) notes, corruption is a symptom of a deeper underlying problem—the lack of political commitment and accountability. For example, Bardhan and Mookherjee (2006) have shown that simply financing local infrastructure through user fees rather than local taxes or intergovernmental transfers will reduce corruption, no matter how poorly local democracy works. As we discuss below, however, almost no infrastructure investment in developing countries is financed this way, and this situation seems unlikely to change soon.

Capacity

Subnational governments in developing countries often do not have the ability to design, build, and operate infrastructure, and are unlikely to even know enough to be able to "outsource" the needed skills efficiently and effectively. Many who write on the possible dangers of decentralization emphasize the poor quality of local administration in most developing countries (Prud'homme, 1995), although the variability even within specific countries makes generalization difficult. On the other hand, there is at least some evidence suggesting that the quality of municipal management of public service delivery has improved in recent years in a number of developing countries (World Bank 2009a).

While there is often good reason for concern about the capacity of subnational governments to deliver services, to a considerable extent countries get the local governments they want and deserve. Subnational politicians and officials, like those at the central government level, respond to the incentives with which they are faced. If those incentives discourage initiative and reward inefficiency and corruption it should not be surprising if local governments turn out to be corrupt and inefficient. Given appropriate incentives (in terms of heightened expectations of improved services from their constituents and access to resources for which they are politically responsible) even very small local governments have sometimes demonstrated significant improvements in administrative capacity within a relatively short time (Fiszbein 1997; Faguet 2004).

As Fiszbein (1997) noted in an early evaluation of decentralization in Colombia, for example, when given the chance to do more when they received more resources after a constitutional revision, some—not all—municipalities took steps to improve their capacities. Some, for example, improved the skills of local officials through competitive hiring, some shared the services of professional staff with neighboring municipalities, and some undertook more training of municipal employees. Some municipalities also improved their capacity to carry out effective infrastructure projects. One, for example, privatized road maintenance; another put private developers in charge of the construction of urban roads; others introduced computers to monitor water and sanitation services, shared equipment with others, and directly attempted to improve their capability of better managing municipal projects. While by no means all did such things, one result of the increased local engagement and "ownership" was that surveys found most respondents trusted the local government more than the national government to deliver the goods and services that they wanted (Fiszbein 1997). Most municipalities concentrated on roads, education, and water works. These priorities may not always have been what the central officials previously in charge of these areas thought was most important, but since these were the needs local people perceived, these were the needs that at least some of the newly empowered and responsive local governments attempted to meet. Although over the succeeding decade of political turmoil and civil strife, much of this initial positive response appears to have faded away, even a decade later surveys continued to show that most Colombians were happier to pay local than national taxes, presumably because they felt they were, so to speak, getting more for their money (Acosta and Bird 2005).

Reconciling theory and practice

Theory tells us that efficient infrastructure is often decentralized infrastructure and that decentralized infrastructure should be efficient. In practice, however, the underlying conditions needed to ensure that either part of this proposition holds are seldom met, and the result is that in too many instances not only is infrastructure not provided efficiently but the perceived failures of decentralized infrastructure lead to "corrective" actions that prevent decentralization itself from realizing its potential advantages. In most cases, the basic answer to these problems is to "decentralize" correctly which means, essentially, that three conditions are satisfied:

- First, public sector functions must be sufficiently unbundled to ensure that they are assigned to the correct levels of government: both who is responsible for what and who is accountable to who for what must be clearly delineated.[16] Clarity in assignment must be matched by *accountability*, in terms of both political democracy and transparency of operation, as well as by *authority* in terms of both the ability to manage expenditures and to determine (within limits) revenues.
- Second, it follows that subnational governments must be adequately accountable in political, administrative, and financial terms both to those

whom they are supposed to serve—their residents—as well as to those above them in the governmental hierarchy who may be responsible for developing policy, regulating how it is carried out, and often financing the activities of such governments. Such "dual accountability" is neither easy to design nor to implement.

- Third, essential to the successful achievement of both the previous conditions is the design and implementation of a sound intergovernmental finance system, one that devolves appropriate revenue-raising powers to subnational governments, makes it possible for them to employ these powers effectively, supplements local finance when appropriate through well-designed transfers, and provides adequate access to private sources of finance, particularly with respect to financing infrastructure investment. We develop some aspects of this third point in the present section.

Improve local governance

The efficiency of decentralized expenditure assignment for infrastructure is enhanced by local financing of these capital projects. If full financing is by transfers from higher level governments and loans from state banks, then local officials will not be fully accountable to the voters for the quality of services delivered.

Subnational governments in developing countries have access to three sources for financing capital expenditures: own source taxes, charges, and other non-tax revenues; intergovernmental transfers; and various types of privatization schemes.[17] In many countries, however, both the structure of these financing instruments and their implementation impede more efficient and equitable outcomes in the delivery of infrastructure services.

Though there is no unified theory of revenue assignment that will allow identification of both the right level of subnational government financing and the right mix of revenue instruments to use (Martínez-Vázquez forthcoming), as Bardhan and Mookherjee (2006) show, if infrastructure investment is financed by user charges, it is efficient. More generally, to the extent that subnational government revenues are raised according to the benefit principle so that at the margin those who benefit from local infrastructure investment are those who finance it, the financing of infrastructure will be efficient. If locally raised taxes will be paid entirely by those who benefit from local services, subnational governments will not overspend because they will not be able to export some or their entire tax burden to other jurisdictions (McLure 1998).

This condition may seem strict, but in fact there are plenty of viable revenue options for covering this amount, including property and non-property taxation, and user and benefit charges (Bahl and Bird 2008). Significant increases in subnational government revenue mobilization through such "good" (local benefit) taxes and charges are feasible in many countries. However, higher level governments in developing countries often are not willing to give up productive revenue sources such as income or general sales taxes to subnational governments.

Already strapped for revenues, they are hesitant to introduce competition for their tax bases, especially in the large urban areas where most taxes are raised, even when those are the subnational governments that both need and could use most effectively additional revenue from such sources. It is also often the case that elected officials in subnational governments are hesitant to push for new taxing powers precisely because it would ultimately force them into a position of greater accountability to their constituents. They are happy to claim increasing shares of national transfers (or foreign aid) rather than have to face their residents with the need to pay higher taxes. All too often, when subnational governments do get the green light on taxation, they are usually both saddled with a limited choice of instruments and in effect encouraged to implement badly structured taxes that have undesirable efficiency effects (Bird 2006; Martínez-Vázquez 2012).

User charges

For utilities in particular, user charges are the obvious and ideal source of finance. [8] Beneficiaries pay, and at full cost recovery, debt service and maintenance can be supported. User-financing of infrastructure ensures that those who benefit are willing to pay for what they receive, which is one of the best ways we know of ensuring that providing a particular service is worth what it costs. However, there are two big problems with advocating user charge financing of infrastructure in developing countries.

One problem commonly perceived is that many people are simply too poor to pay much. Too often this concern has resulted in too low prices that benefit mainly richer consumers. Many governments grant subsidies and hold down tariff rates with the result that much less than full cost recovery—often even less than operating cost recovery—is the rule rather than the exception (Estache 2010). The result is that the bulk of the effective public subsidy is captured by the few and fortunate and the resulting financial stringency ensures that not only do the poor continue to go without access to such essential services as basic water and sewage facilities but that the services that are provided are inadequately maintained, with resultant huge losses in supply. Many schemes to overcome such problems have been put forward over the years but as yet few countries appear to have made a serious attempt to price public services efficiently while taking adequate account (e.g., through "lifeline" or other tariff structures) of the need to provide a basic level of service to those who are unable to bear the full cost.[19]

The second big problem with user charge finance is that no one likes it, especially when paying for what one gets is not now the norm. People who are now receiving (often poor) service do not see why they should have to pay more and are unlikely to believe that they will, someday, receive something better for their money. People who do not now receive services are unlikely to believe that if they agree to pay more than those now getting the service pay they will in fact get some benefits from doing so. Politicians do not want to make current service recipients unhappy by making them pay and cannot easily sell "pay for what you get" to people who have long seen others not paying. While there is some experience that suggests neighborhood groups and small villages can and have sometimes agreed to finance small infrastructure works that will benefit them directly (Bird 1995), there is little or no evidence that anyone has been able to devise and implement a "corrective" user charge structure to rectify the inefficient, inequitable, and ineffective fee structures now found in most developing countries.

Property taxes

The property tax can be an efficient source of revenue for financing infrastructure. In many cases, it finances infrastructure that enhances property values, and its revenue potential is large. Bahl and Martínez-Vázquez (2008) estimate that the property tax yields 2.2 percent of GDP in revenues in industrial countries but only about 0.66 percent in industrial countries. When the family of taxes on real property is considered—transfer taxes and various forms of betterment levies—the revenue potential is even greater, although the economic effects of transfer taxes leave much to be desired. Moreover, the property tax has the virtue of being a levy that higher level governments do not want in their tax structure, either because they recognize the inherent advantage of local governments in administering the tax or because they recognize that the unpopularity of the tax goes well beyond its usually meager revenue yield.

But in fact property taxes do not finance much infrastructure. The political unpopularity of the residential tax often leads to a neutering of the tax base, sometimes by higher level governments who take credit for new exemptions while leaving local governments to deal with covering the revenue costs. Moreover, the administration is often weak and always expensive (Bird and Slack 2004; McCluskey and Franzsen forthcoming).

Subnational governments might also use property-based taxes to recapture the betterment from public investments, and in some cases this has yielded significant amounts of revenue (Alm 2010). In some countries, governments have been aggressive about using value capture methods in connection with infrastructure finance (Colombia) whereas in others (Philippines), it remains a largely unused source. But even in the best of cases, such as Colombia, making a land value recapture scheme successful requires a great deal of technical and political investment (Bird 2012).

Other taxes

Subnational governments in Argentina, Brazil, and Colombia have mobilized significant revenues with subnational government taxes. Argentinean and Colombian subnational governments use a form of turnover tax while Brazil taxes gross receipts from the sale of services. But these taxes are highly distortive and serve as general revenues rather than as earmarked sources of finance for infrastructure. Despite continued calls to modernize these sales taxes, or business taxes, they continue on in their present form. The other option that is often considered is to abolish distortive subnational government taxes. South Africa levied a combination gross receipts and turnover tax, but this was abolished by Parliament in part because of its weak structure and administration. India's octroi, a duty levied on goods entering the city for sale, is still a primary source of revenues for the Mumbai municipal corporation but has been abolished elsewhere in the subcontinent. At least in these cases, the abolished taxes have not been replaced with an equally elastic local revenue source.

Motor vehicle taxes would seem a good candidate for infrastructure finance, particularly for roads and mass transit. All of the possible instruments—licenses, motor fuels, parking fees, and tolls—could be structured as benefit taxes. Certainly the tax base is growing. It is pointed out that for India, the motor vehicle population increased by 100 times between 1951 and 2004 and has increased at an even faster rate in the 2000s (High Powered Expert Committee 2011, 56). On the administration side, the most difficult problem would be to convert the motor fuel tax to a destination basis, but this might be done using distributors' shipment records until collection at the pump became a possibility.

Non-tax revenues

Like motor vehicle taxes, some non-tax revenues might be earmarked for infrastructure finance, even though the link between beneficiaries and burdens might not be so clear. Chinese metropolitan governments have been particularly innovative and have engaged heavily in land sales (long-term leases) as a method of mobilizing resources for infrastructure finances. For all local governments in China, land leases now account for about 30 percent of revenues (Wong forthcoming). Land sales have great advantages, namely the revenue potential and the low political cost (at least in China) of raising money this way. But even in a unique setting like China, there are drawbacks, including the sensitivity of land revenues to the real estate cycle, and the riskiness of land value collateral for loans; the fact that the "easy money" might tempt overspending in local government budgets; the opportunity costs of converting land to urban use might be underestimated; and the fact that government-owned land is an exhaustible resource.

A more difficult arrangement to assess is the earmarking of certain revenues for infrastructure development. An example is Peru where natural resource revenues are distributed on a derivation basis and must be spent for economic development purposes (Canavire-Bacarreza *et al.* 2012; Martínez-Vázquez 2012). On the one hand, the goal of such a program is to replace the lost "heritage" of the region with a new infrastructure. Management issues aside, there is some merit to this justification. On the other hand, this kind of earmarking introduces a function-follows-finance model and provides little incentive for efficient spending.

Even when there is not a separate system of capital transfers, some countries (e.g., Colombia) commonly earmark significant portions of general intergovernmental transfers to "investment," apparently in large part to restrain the feared dissipation of such transfers in current expenditures.[20] It is far from clear that such earmarking achieves its objective. Indeed, some evidence suggests that reducing earmarking is more likely to improve than to distort the allocation of local resources. The theoretical argument is simply the standard decentralization theorem: that allowing funds to be spent according to local tastes yields on the whole superior allocative and distributional results. Empirical evidence in Norway (Borge *et al.* 2012) supports this argument strongly.

Although one may perhaps doubt the relevance of this experience to the many developing countries in which "elite capture" of local governments seems more likely, studies in Bolivia and Colombia (Faguet 2005) also point in this direction. Most interestingly, perhaps, a recent careful study of the European Union (Kappeler *et al.* 2012) finds not only that revenue decentralization tends to increase subnational infrastructure investment. Earmarking local revenues for infrastructure may make sense when there are good benefit (efficiency, equity, and management) reasons for doing so. Small projects with well-defined benefit groups are most likely to meet these conditions. In other cases, however, such earmarking may distort local preferences, exacerbate perverse incentives to build new rather than maintain existing infrastructure, and connect revenue sources with particular expenditures in ways that lack both economic and political logic. And, finally, there is the fungibility problem, i.e., it is not usually possible to separate the expenditure of the earmarked revenues from the expenditure of other revenues.

Intergovernmental transfers

Since subnational governments in most developing countries have very limited own resources and little access to private capital markets, to carry out costly public works as a rule they must rely heavily on grants (or subsidized loans) from higher level governments. Depending on how the transfer system is structured, it may have a direct or an indirect effect on infrastructure finance.

Most countries structure their transfer systems using some combination of three approaches. The first is unconditional grants, which are an indirect way to provide infrastructure finance. These funds can be used for maintenance of the public capital stock and for debt repayment, though the grant funds are not directly tied to either.

In the eyes of lenders, the security associated with unconditional grants as the base for repayment is not strong. Some countries attempt to get around this by making provision for these transfers to cover debt service costs by providing for an intercept arrangement or allowing these transfers to be pledged to repay debt, as has been done in Mexico (Revilla 2012). Although many countries prohibit such arrangements, this approach to, in effect, "earmarking" grants to service the debt on capital projects deserves careful consideration.

A second approach is to make grants to local governments conditional on their expenditure for a particular capital purpose, often with no matching arrangement and in practice often with little supervision, either before or after the money flows. Often these conditional grants are distributed on a formula basis, and in other cases they take the form of cost reimbursements.

Capital grants to support local infrastructure projects, sometimes with a requirement of matching funding from local sources, are not uncommon but again the appropriate design of such transfers is not always easy to determine. A number of questions need to be considered carefully: Is one aim to rectify imbalances in the distribution of existing infrastructure (Ahmad and Searle 2006)? To what extent are such transfers intended to improve economic efficiency—as is presumably the case with respect to most economic infrastructure such as transportation—or be equalizing, e.g., by providing at least a minimum standard of such public services as education and health by providing hospitals and schools in particular areas (Josie *et al.* 2008)? Whatever the intended goal, in allocating such transfers between jurisdictions and in determining the appropriate matching rate, the nature of capital spending requires that concept of fiscal capacity should be expanded to encompass not just tax capacity but also the ability to access credit markets (Herrero-Alcalde *et al.* 2011).

The third channel is more directly tied to infrastructure budgets. This can take the form of a block grant for infrastructure services, on a matching basis. This has been done in India where a large federal grant for urban infrastructure development and slum upgrading is allocated to cities on a matching basis (High Powered Expert Committee 2011). The program was introduced in 2005, and while it has succeeded in focusing increased attention on urban infrastructure issues, implementation progress has been slow (Rao and Bird 2011). South Africa makes use of a more formal municipal infrastructure grant, designed primarily to improve services in poor neighborhoods (van Ryneveld 2007). Brazil is another country where ad hoc grants are made to support specific projects.

If done in conjunction with increased local revenue mobilization and cost recovery levels of user charges, a case can be made that any of these approaches to intergovernmental transfers can lead to a more efficient delivery of infrastructure services by local governments. Still especially conditional grants can be significantly improved in most countries in a number of ways. For example, the terms and conditions of such transfers might require subnational governments to prepare an adequate investment plan and an adequate maintenance plan, as well as an appropriate user charge policy. The governments receiving such transfers should be selected by a systematic process that pays attention both to need and capacity factors and to the economic evaluation (cost-benefit analysis) of the project in question. Adequate technical assistance should be made available to subnational governments to permit them to develop plans, arrange financing, manage construction, and operate the facility (or to contract out its operation) in the most efficient possible fashion. Finally, to ensure accountability as well as good outcomes the execution and operation of the grant-aided work should be monitored and evaluated, with periodic progress reports, field inspections, and formal evaluations of outcomes including consumer surveys.

Of course, achieving all this is a bit of a counsel of perfection in the conditions of many developing countries. Nonetheless, as the early experience with "municipal development funds" (Davey 1988) demonstrated, if such conditions are not satisfied, the results of capital transfers and loans are unlikely to live up to expectations. Subnational infrastructure finance is inevitably greatly dependent on transfers from higher level governments. These transfers may be efficiency enhancing when they take the form of conditional grants designed to correct for under-spending on services characterized by externalities, but few such transfers are to be found in practice in part because the design of a conditional grant for infrastructure involves a great deal of guesswork if (as theory often suggests) one goal is to correct for under-spending as a result of not taking externalities into account. It involves identifying a target for the optimal level of spending for the function that takes account of social as well as local benefits, as well as having some notion of the elasticity of demand for the infrastructure service. Careful targeting along these lines is an essential ingredient of effective subsidy policy in resource-constrained countries but most infrastructure-related transfers, perhaps understandably, take a far more general approach.

Borrowing

Borrowing is not itself a source of revenue but rather an efficient way to arrange payment for the purchase of public assets that have a long life. By matching payment for the infrastructure with the time pattern of consumption of the asset, governments can immediately begin capturing the returns from infrastructure investments while deferring the payments. But in the end, the loans must be repaid, either from the own source revenues of the subnational governments, from user charges, or from intergovernmental transfers. The essential foundation of a sound subnational borrowing program is thus a sound subnational fiscal structure in terms both of access to "own revenues" and a well-designed and stable intergovernmental transfer system. Still, loans are often both essential because they offer subnational governments a way to attract the large amount of funds necessary for financing the construction phase and in principle an economically efficient (and equitable) source of finance because the debt has to be repaid (from current revenues) during the life of the project, that is, while it is providing benefits to local residents.

But borrowing by subnational governments can lead to problems, as students of local public finance have long argued (Prud'homme 1995; Tanzi 1996). The revenue stream of local government revenues may not be large enough to sustain repayment but borrowing may go forward anyway in anticipation of some form of bailout. This well-known moral hazard problem has led to over-borrowing and to some form of bailout of subnational governments in Brazil, Argentina, South Africa, and more recently in China (de Mello 2007; Wong forthcoming). Many countries attempt to control over-borrowing by subnational governments with various forms of fiscal responsibility legislation (Liu and Webb 2011), though these programs have met with varying degrees of success. The problem with bailouts is that subnational governments learn that there is a way around the hard budget constraint, and they may return again to the strategy of overspending on infrastructure. A good borrowing framework can head this off, but it may effectively close the borrowing window for those local governments who have the greatest infrastructure gaps.

Bundling subnational borrowing—for example, by having regional entities borrow for smaller local authorities—may make sense on cost grounds. Similarly, packaging subnational borrowing in some form such as a national infrastructure bank may make sense when financing flows to projects that, although the responsibility of subnational governments, are of national significance, e.g., as part of a national network of roads or electricity distribution. In most cases, however, loans from such public financial institutions are extended on subsidized terms and are in effect a variant form of matching grant. Although hopefully the lessons of unfortunate past experiences with such "soft" funding have been learned, as yet there appears to be no magic institutional way to avoid the hard necessity of first establishing subnational finances on a sound and sustainable basis so that at least some of them—probably the largest and better off—are, when financial markets are sufficiently developed, creditable candidates for private sector financing. When subnational governments are charged with an important role in providing infrastructure, many of them will need both technical and financial support to play that role adequately but it is important to ensure that financial resources do not arrive in ways that distort the incentives facing subnational decision-makers in ways that may damage both the provision of infrastructure and, more broadly, governance at the subnational level.[21]

Public-private partnerships

Much the same can be said with respect to the interest in public-private partnerships (PPP) during the past two decades. During this period, many urged increased private involvement both to increase the efficiency of service provision and provide badly needed resources to support urban infrastructure investment. Klein (2012) argues that both of these justifications need to be qualified. Private sector "resources" would come from user charges, which would also be realized by local governments if levied at cost recovery rates. And, the private sector expertise may be a step up from local government capacity, but would come with a higher cost of financing.

In addition, there are questions about how PPP will deliver services, for example, full privatization with various degrees of regulation, or some form of contracting for operation. The build-operate version is attractive in part precisely because it offers a way to get facilities built without incurring highly visible government debt. It would be fair to say that the high hopes for PPP in the 1990s and early 2000s never materialized. As yet, PPP has added relatively little to urban capital financing in developing countries (Annez 2007; Alm 2010). Moreover, less than 10 percent of the investment has been in the high priority water/sewer sector and an even smaller share in the form of full or partial privatization

(Menard forthcoming). Most PPP has been focused on the energy and telecommunications sectors (Klein 2012). Relatively little has been attracted to the higher priority water and sewer sectors, mostly because of pricing risks. In some instances where private capital has been attracted to these sectors (for example, Bolivia, Venezuela, and Argentina), the projects have failed and in effect a "renationalization" resulted.

Opinions differ sharply with respect to both the merits of PPP arrangements and how best to design and implement them. In a recent assessment of the literature, for example, Merk *et al.* (2012) conclude that a critical feature (if a PPP is to minimize project costs) is that the contract should be "global," that is, that a single contractor is responsible for managing the whole project in order to reap full economies of scale and scope and provide maximum incentives to invest and innovate. In contrast, Siemiatycki and Frieman (2012), considering urban transit projects in which a major issue is how to allocate "ridership (demand) risk" argue that "unbundled" contracts that exclude facility operation are often preferable both because they are likely to attract more competitive bids and to lower the cost of private sector borrowing. The contradictory nature of these recent assessments stress the importance of the specific context and institutional and regulatory settings (e.g., the relative development of financial markets and who sets user charges) as well as the detailed specifics of PPP contracts in determining outcomes.

Even when a transit project is carried out entirely by the public sector, of course, similar regulatory and financial factors are critical. China, for example, has in recent years carried out huge urban infrastructure investments through what may perhaps be thought of as a Chinese variant of PPP, where both parties to the contract are really "public." To illustrate, the extensive Beijing metro system, like many other projects in China, was financed primarily by bank loans to a local investment corporation—the Beijing Infrastructure Investment Corporation—created and controlled by the local government (Su and Zhao 2006). Since the national government strongly encouraged local governments to carry out such investments and banks to finance them in doing so, presumably the banking sector in effect considers such loans to be guaranteed by the state. In addition to this implicit subsidy, loans to local investment corporations have generally received an explicit subsidy in the form of an interest rate about 10 percent less than the normal rate of long-term debt. In reality, however, most local borrowing is directly serviced from local revenues which are in turn highly dependent on revenue from leasing land. Such revenue is highly sensitive both to property values and to the amount of land sold: in 2011, for instance, Beijing's revenue from this source decreased by 36 percent from the 2010 level. Even if one assumes that the whole rapid transit system has been and is optimally designed, constructed, and operated, current plans to expand the metro system further in the next few years and a flat-fare policy that already requires an annual operating subsidy (and will need an even larger one in an expanded system) make it likely that the sustainability of the financing model used to build not only the Beijing metro but also much of the extremely impressive development of urban infrastructure in China in recent years is an example of what Wong (forthcoming) calls "riding the tiger." It may soon require careful reconsideration and in all likelihood substantial adjustment—unless perhaps the urban real estate sector can realistically be expected to continue to boom at pre-2010 rates for the next few decades.

To take a quite different, and perhaps more widely applicable example, Ahmedabad's Bus Rapid Transit System, financed in large part (35 percent) by a national urban development program (the Jawaharlal Nehru National Urban Renewal Mission, JNNURM), in part (15 percent) by the State of Gujarat, with the balance (50 percent) coming from local sources (including a dedicated urban transport fund), was developed and implemented through nine separate PPP arrangements negotiated between the special public corporation (Ahmedabad Janmarg Limited) created for the purpose and various private providers. These arrangements covered everything from the major system investment (bus stations, corridor, flyovers, as well as buses) to housekeeping and parking (National Institute of Urban Affairs 2011). The resulting system has both substantially improved "people transport" in the city and has, like the somewhat similar earlier "Transmilenio" BRTS in Bogotá, won national and international acclaim as a model that seems worthy of emulation elsewhere. Some aspects—notably dedicated funding sources for urban transit systems—have already appeared in several North American cites in recent years: Vancouver, for example, collects a number of fees and taxes that are dedicated to a regional transportation authority, as do Chicago, Los Angeles, and Salt Lake City (Institute of Municipal Finance & Governance 2012).

There are of course risks associated with public-private partnerships. For the private sector, for example, there are risks that the regulatory framework and/or pricing commitments could change and cause delays in the project. Annez (2007) and Ingram *et al.* (forthcoming) argue that the inherent riskiness of urban investments in water and sanitation is the main constraint to increasing the flow of private capital. There is a weak record of full cost recovery, and often an unwillingness of local governments to stand behind the kinds of tariff levels and regulatory arrangements that would be necessary to attract private investors. In many countries there is what Pethe (forthcoming) describes as a "trust deficit" between public and private sectors that has sometimes resulted in episodes like the Bolivian "re-nationalization" mentioned above. For all of these reasons, the World Bank (2009a, 32) points to "few positive results" in efforts to attract private financing of municipal services.

For the public sector, there is the risk that services provided may not be what the public wants. There is also the risk that the private partner will fail, or insist on a recontracting, and the public sector will have to take on the obligation in full. How successful such arrangements are from the perspective of either partner depends very much on the details of exactly how the contractual arrangements are structured and how the risks are shared.[22] Given the weak institutional capacity of subnational governments in many developing countries, it seems unlikely that they will have a strong hand in negotiating such contracts. The Indian High

Powered Expert Committee (2011, 101) puts it well. "Weak governments cannot rely on private agents to overcome their weaknesses nor can they expect to make the best possible bargains for the public they represent."

Two special issues: metropolitan areas and regional equity

In many countries, there are specific problems that call for special consideration, and perhaps for a different approach to infrastructure delivery. We discuss two such problems in this section: (a) how best to organize infrastructure provision in metropolitan areas and in their polar opposite—remote and sparsely populated rural areas—and (b) how to take account of concerns about "regional equity" in the allocation of infrastructure funding and projects.

The need for asymmetry

Some policy-makers in developing countries would argue that in principle political institutions should presumably be structured to treat all citizens as equally as possible: they should be symmetrical. On the other hand, if economic institutions are to produce relatively equal (symmetrical) outcomes they must often be structured asymmetrically: they must recognize explicitly the very different conditions existing in different regions and localities.[23] Big cities—metropolitan areas—are different from other urban areas to call for a different treatment as regards fiscal decentralization. At the other extreme, small, remote municipalities located in sparsely populated regions are also very different from other local governments, and also call for a special set of financing and service delivery arrangements.

Metropolitan areas

The expected rate of migration to urban areas over the next two decades will strain the present network of urban infrastructure and generate new demands that will be difficult to absorb. The number of mega-cities (population greater than ten million) is projected to increase from 19 now to 27 in 2025, when about 10 percent of the world's urban population will reside in these cities. Of the projected 27 mega-cities, 21 will be in less developed countries. By 2025, there will be 48 cities with populations between five and ten million, and three-fourths of these will be in developing countries (United Nations 2008). Ingram *et al.* (forthcoming) estimate that annual urban infrastructure costs will be equivalent to about 3 percent of GDP for new infrastructure and 2 percent for maintenance. The estimates for India are that to meet projected needs, urban infrastructure investments (excluding maintenance expenditures) must increase from current levels of 0.7 percent of GDP to 1.1 percent by 2032 (High Powered Expert Committee 2011). The policy questions that governments in developing countries must answer is which level of government will deliver this infrastructure, with what degree of autonomy, and how will it be financed.

For many (most) large urban areas, heavy infrastructure demands will come from three directions. Natural population growth and new migrants will impose demands for expanding, repairing, and modernizing the capital facilities to accommodate the larger population. Industry, especially the smart growth sectors, will demand an infrastructure that will enable them to be more competitive in the international market place. Transportation and IT support will be featured in their investment wish list. Third, it is expected that there will be about two billion slum dwellers in urban areas by 2050 (United Nations 2008) and services to provide a basic standard of living will be needed.

Efficiency considerations might point toward decentralization in the provision of services in metropolitan areas. Governments in the metropolitan areas have the advantage of knowing the needs and preferences of their population and of their business sector. But the problem is very complicated. Decentralization of expenditure responsibility to metropolitan areas is one thing, but decentralizing to the local governments within the metropolitan area may be quite another. The local units that operate within the metropolitan areas may not be large enough to efficiently deliver the infrastructure services. The underlying problem is the fragmentation of governance within large urban areas (Bahl forthcoming).

Local government structures in metropolitan areas typically emphasize one of three approaches to governance.

- A political fragmentation approach where governance is divided among numerous small municipalities, each operating with some degree of autonomy. This approach features home rule and is the approach taken for example in the Mexico City metropolitan area (two states, a national capital district, and over 50 municipal-type local governments), and the Sao Paulo metropolitan area (39 municipal governments operating with relatively little required coordination.
- A functional fragmentation approach where the municipal government structure is overlaid by some special districts or public enterprises that provide infrastructure services that cover the entire metropolitan area. The emphasis here is on technical efficiency in the delivery of infrastructure services. Such an approach is taken in Mumbai, with state-owned parastatals serving as the metropolitan area enterprises.
- A metropolitan government approach where general services are provided by an area-wide government with little by way of an underlying set of local governments. The emphasis of this approach is on coordination in the delivery of services in the area. This would describe the approach taken in the South African metropolitan cities.

In the case of a politically fragmented government structure, the devolution of responsibility for infrastructure services does not lead to efficient outcomes. With the possible exception of the largest municipality in the area, the jurisdictions are often too small to capture the economies of scale necessary for production efficiency, and management skills might be limited. And, the more fragmented the structure of government, the greater will be the problems with spillover effects from local investments in infrastructure. Finally, local governments in fragmented metropolitan areas are not likely to have broad-based taxing powers that would provide the basis for supporting a large debt issue. If there is to be assignment of responsibilities for infrastructure services to subnational governments in urban areas, and if there are to be broad-based taxes in the system, the better approach would be either metropolitan government or public enterprises whose service district includes the entire metropolitan area. On the other hand, as mentioned earlier, within this general framework there may be ample scope for "neighborhood" (or small municipality) works to be developed (and largely financed) by user-based groups through schemes capturing the value increments generated by such projects.

Remote localities

Rural local governments are a different case, which also may call for a differential treatment. They are small, often remote, and with very limited resources. The literacy rate may be low, financial management capacity of the local governments may be quite limited, and there may be little if any capacity to design or deliver anything beyond the most basic infrastructure project. Own source revenues may be all but non-existent because of the weak tax base, and user charges will be well below cost recovery levels because of the high degree of poverty in the rural area.

China is one of the most rapidly urbanizing countries in the world. Despite the rapid out-migration of recent decades, however, over 600 million people still live in its over 700,000 rural villages, many of which are located in remote and sparsely populated areas. For these villages (and the townships in which they are situated) to become more viable, accountable, and at least moderately effective in providing basic public services, significant efforts and reforms seem needed. Similarly, in India, another huge country with a very large rural population, experience to date suggests that centralized provision of rural services has never worked very well and that, so far at least, more decentralized provision has also not worked very well. While generalizations are dangerous with respect to such matters in either of these huge and heterogeneous countries, it does seem clear that rural service delivery remains a major problem, and a very different problem from the metropolitan problems discussed earlier.

One part of the solution to both problems is similar, however. In metropolitan areas, some kind of region-wide authority is clearly needed to deal properly with area-wide infrastructure problems. In rural areas also, some kind of higher level "regional" authority is also often needed, though not to deal with regional problems of spillovers since there are few such problems in non-contiguous small and geographically separated localities. Rather the need is to provide the technical, administrative, and financial support needed to deal with the problems of providing basic local services in remote, small, and usually very poor communities.[24] For example, small remote communities are unlikely to have an adequate tax base to be economically viable, to have adequate administrative capacity, to finance major capital expenditures, or even to take advantage of economies of scale (Kitchen and Slack 2006). In these circumstances, infrastructure investments required to provide basic local public services must either be provided directly by a higher level government or at least financed (with perhaps some limited in-kind or other local cost-sharing) by such a regional structure, whether a county, a second-tier municipality, or some kind of special district.

Regional equity

Whether the devolution of expenditure responsibility for infrastructure services is efficient is not the only question to be asked. Fiscal disparities among regions in developing countries can be quite large, and the quality of infrastructure usually is most wanting in the poorest places. A national infrastructure decentralization policy will if anything widen fiscal disparities because of the greater revenue mobilization capacity of richer jurisdictions and their superior capacity to deliver services. In addition, as Albalate *et al.* (2012) show in detail for the case of Spain, and as many "provincials" suspect is true with respect to countries everywhere, centralized investment programs (e.g., in network projects) tend to be heavily related to proximity to the political capital. Although infrastructure investment seems to be more an instrument of centralization than of regional redistribution policy, it is nonetheless also commonly a vehicle for "regional policy" in the sense of providing "something for everyone" and perhaps even more for those who have less.

One might take two views about decentralized infrastructure responsibility in this context. One is that the ability to choose capital projects and to deliver them is just as important in small communities as in large urban areas. Devolution can work. There is a good bit of evidence that in some cases small local governments can produce small (local) public works projects at a lower cost and can design them so that the probability of sustainable operations is relatively high.[25] The problem is financing. In this case, decentralization with financing by intergovernmental transfers for smaller projects, and vertical programs for the delivery of larger projects, may be a viable strategy.

On the other hand, much of the evidence on successful devolution of infrastructure is about small, even rural settlements. There are some questions about how much of this success can be transferred to larger settlements or even to the rural sector more broadly. If it cannot, then infrastructure disparities might widen a great deal under devolution. In this case, the right strategy may be an asymmetric system in which the larger urban places have heavy responsibility for delivering and financing their infrastructure, with infrastructure in smaller, less dense, and often poorer localities being delivered primarily by higher level governments.

Conclusions and guidelines for policy

Theory tells us that an appropriately structured fiscal decentralization can lead to a higher quality of infrastructure services than will a fully centralized system. If the assignment of expenditure responsibility is correct and if the capacity to deliver services is in place, consumer-voters will be empowered to express their preferences for infrastructure services, services will be delivered with appropriate technologies and at lower costs, there will be more willingness to pay, and a better record of maintenance of public facilities.

There is plenty of evidence that following the theory can lead to some of these outcomes. But, there is also plenty of evidence that a decentralized infrastructure structure fails the quality test. The problem is that the theory is based on a set of assumptions that may not fit the real world in developing countries, and/or that successful infrastructure decentralization requires supporting governance and finance system changes that most developing countries are not willing (or able) to make. However, from this theory, and from the practice in developing countries, we might draw out some policy rules that could support a successful decentralization of appropriate infrastructure services. Although every country is different, every locality is different, and every infrastructure project is different, there are some general principles about institutional and fiscal practices that can improve both how well decentralized governments carry out infrastructure projects and how well decentralization in general will function. This review of the theory and the practice suggests six policy reform issues that can lead to more success in the delivery of some infrastructure services by local governments.

The first is the need for a comprehensive scope of infrastructure policy reform. Reformers should take a comprehensive view of infrastructure decentralization, and should consider and fit together all the components necessary to make the system work. This is because the argument for local control depends not only on beneficiaries being local, but also on local control being more likely to meet local needs and, ideally, on local users being able and willing to pay the costs. Only when local governance institutions ensure in an accountable way that those who benefit and pay are also those who decide what is done should all aspects of infrastructure decisions be assigned to local governments. A corollary to this is the importance of getting the structure right in order to benefit from management improvements. Improved procurement and financial management systems, and the like, will not achieve their important goals if the responsibility for a capital expenditure is assigned to the wrong level of government.

The second is a clear and appropriate assignment of expenditure responsibility for infrastructure. Public sector functions must be sufficiently unbundled to ensure that they are assigned to the correct levels of government: both who is responsible for what and who is accountable to whom for what must be clearly delineated. While unbundling can be a decided improvement in that it recognizes the comparative advantages of each level of government in infrastructure service delivery, it can lead to complication and confusion, and must be reviewed regularly. Clarity in assignment must be matched by *accountability*, in terms of both political democracy and transparency of operation, as well as by *authority* in terms of both the ability to manage expenditures and to determine (within limits) revenues.

Third, local governments must be adequately accountable in political, administrative, and financial terms both to those whom they are supposed to serve—their residents—as well as to those above them in the governmental hierarchy who may be responsible for developing policy, regulating how it is carried out, and often financing the activities of such governments. Such "dual accountability" is neither easy to design nor to implement, and will require fiscal planners to walk a fine line. On the one hand, unbundling schemes such as allowing higher level governments to set standards and require creditable compliance tests call for an upward accountability by local governments. So do conditional grants. On the other, too much expenditure mandating by higher level governments can take away the local autonomy that is the key advantage of fiscal decentralization of infrastructure. Ultimately, the local governments must be accountable to their voting constituency. Mandates and conditionalities should be held to the test of accommodating externalities.

Fourth, the revenue mobilization efforts of local governments in most developing countries needs to be increased if local governments are to take on more responsibility for delivering infrastructure services. In particular, the larger urban local governments need to be given access to stronger tax bases and encouragement to reform the tax base to which they already have access (namely the property tax). User charges must be ratcheted up significantly so that they approach cost recovery levels. Arguably the major impediments to increased revenue mobilization by local governments is the absence of incentives that are great enough in magnitude to offset the aversion of local politicians to tax increases. Here the reform agenda might include closing off the option of ad hoc capital transfers to cover infrastructure financing by local governments, the provision of incentives for increased local effort, and conditional grants that are designed with a mixture of clearly specified conditions and local matches.

Fifth, borrowing and public private partnerships have great potential as methods of financing capital projects, and in the latter case as a managerial approach to operations. However, governments in developing countries must be more realistic about the prospects of reaching either of these sources for efficiently financing local government infrastructure. Borrowing, even under a reasonable regulatory framework, can be part of the long term infrastructure finance plan for local governments, but only if this is supported by a level of local revenue mobilization and transfers that will make principal and interest repayment, and maintenance, viable. Public-private partnerships are even more problematic for developing countries. For revenue generating projects where the user charge phobia of local governments is not so great (e.g., telecoms, parking garages, etc.), private capital can be drawn. But for the high priority services such as water and sewerage, private investors will probably not buy in until they see a reasonable prospect for cost recovery and for operations that are not hamstrung by the regulatory framework. The High Powered Expert Committee (2011, 101) puts it well, "Weak governments cannot rely on private agents to overcome their weaknesses nor can they expect to make the best possible bargains for the public they represent."

Sixth, there is a strong case for an asymmetric approach to decentralizing infrastructure delivery and finance. The larger urban areas have a greater capacity to plan, deliver, and finance infrastructure services than do smaller and more rural local governments. The regime for infrastructure decentralization should recognize this, perhaps by limiting local government participation until they could grow into the responsibility. Such a guideline will lead to more responsibility for delivering infrastructure in larger urban areas, as well as more responsibility for financing infrastructure with own source revenues. Rural local governments will continue to rely more heavily on vertical programs of higher level governments. This may harm the equalization objectives of government, and it may slow down the capacity development of rural local governments, but it also may increase the productivity of total infrastructure spending.

Notes

1 This chapter has benefited from helpful comments from the editors, Jonas Frank and Jorge Martínez-Vázquez, and our conference discussants, Berndt Spahn and François Vaillancourt, as well as from others at the conference.

2 In the aftermath of the financial crisis, many questions have been raised about the relationship between decentralization and public investment in a time of increasing budgetary pressure. A useful recent survey of this literature may be found in Fernández Llera (2012) but we do not discuss this issue in the present chapter.

3 For example, Afonso *et al.* (2005, 9) argue with respect to Brazil that

> the shortage of investment in infrastructure is even more serious when we consider that an increasing, and already the major part of expenditure on capital formation by public sector authorities has become decentralized.... Institutionally, these regional governments do not have the competence to concede, regulate or carry out functions in the majority of actions and services that are classified as infrastructure related (with the exception of sanitation)...

4 The IMF GFS data that underlie Table 4.1, for example, define capital investment as the acquisition of physical assets with a useful life longer than one year as well as improvements or rehabilitation that extend the life of the asset (Jacobs 2009). However, this definition does not include maintenance expenditure needed to make the asset functional during its life, let alone the operating expenditure needed to actually use the asset. Assigning responsibility for maintenance to one level of government and for maintenance of "new investment" to another as often done creates a serious moral hazard and is almost guaranteed to yield less than optimal results. The line between "maintenance" and "rehabilitation" like that between "operation" and "maintenance" is often hard to draw, but the fact is that not only is both operating and maintenance expenditure (O&M) essential for the delivery of public services but that such expenditure is usually considerably larger over the life of an asset than its initial capital cost (Estache 2010). For the most part, we shall therefore treat O&M directly related to utilizing physical assets as part of "infrastructure investment": a broken water pipe, even if it was acquired yesterday, is not one that is going to deliver the right amount of water in the right quality to the right places.

5 Although, for expositional purposes, we often label decentralized governments "local" there are usually two (regional, local) and sometimes more levels of decentralized government. We discuss later a few aspects of the important distinction, and relations, between different levels of subnational government.

6 For an interesting comparison of the decentralization theorem and the subsidiarity principle, see Breton *et al.* (1998).

7 They of course recognize that in some cases it may be more efficient to contract out many aspects of the construction and management of projects as well as service delivery itself to private providers, although it should be noted that such contracting may increase the regulatory—and perhaps, in some instances, even the financial—burden on the relevant governments.

8 When provincial or state governments are removed from this calculation, the vertical imbalance observed in most countries is larger.

9 Berry (2009) provides a detailed account of the extent to which special-purpose local governments in the US have been "captured" by such groups as developers, other business interests, and public sector workers. The history of municipal infrastructure development around the world is replete with similar stories of elite capture: see, for example, the account in Briggs (1996) of city development in the UK in the nineteenth century, when most infrastructure was financed by (subsidized) private firms.

10 Much of the following discussion is based on Slack and Bird (2012).

11 There are problems with the methodology used to measure cost and output (Byrnes and Dollery 2002). In most studies, expenditures are used as the measure of cost and population is used as the proxy for size or scale. Population may not be the best measure for this purpose. A larger population may mean greater need for expenditures but the characteristics of the population will also influence need. For example, a municipality with a large proportion of elderly will have different expenditure needs than one with a younger population of the same size; an urban population will have different expenditure needs than a rural population. The density and geographic distribution of population may also be an important factor affecting both needs and costs. Furthermore, population does not reflect the non-resident population that visits a local government area and uses services. With respect to the measurement of cost, expenditures are not always the best proxy because they not only include costs but also reflect quality of services and possibly wasteful expenditures. Few studies of economies of scale include service levels.

12 Actually, if such an exercise were done seriously, it would likely end up prescribing a different geographic "benefit" level for every public sector activity and sub-activity—or perhaps even for every geographic locality. As noted earlier, however, such a proliferation of special service districts is seldom a good idea.

13 See the extensive discussion of such problems in, e.g., Kim *et al.* (2010).

14 An earlier study (covering rural and urban areas in developing countries), for the 2005–2010 period, estimated future maintenance needs in developing countries to average about 3.3 to 3.5 percent of GDP (Estache 2006).

15 For reviews of this literature, see Martínez-Vázquez *et al.* (2007) and Boadway and Shah (2009).

16 As mentioned earlier, experience suggests that it is important not to separate responsibilities for building infrastructure from those for operating and maintaining it in order to avoid creating distortionary incentives affecting both current and capital expenditures.

17 Countries may also receive capital transfers from external donors. As Estache (2010) notes, aid-financed infrastructure is especially important in some countries in sub-Saharan Africa. However, we do not consider this source further in this chapter: for a review, see Kharas and Linn (forthcoming).

18 For further discussion of the appropriate role and design of user charges, see, e.g., Bahl and Linn (1992) and Bird (2001).

19 For an early review, see Bird and Miller (1989). Unfortunately, little has changed for the better since this chapter was written.

20 In Colombia, the potentially pernicious effects of such earmarking are perhaps mitigated to some extent by the fact that "investment" is interpreted to include so-called "social investment" in health, education, and so on.
21 For a recent study emphasizing the importance of appropriate incentives, fiscal and otherwise, with respect to establishing and sustaining sound decentralized governance, see Faguet (2011).
22 For detailed exploration of the structuring of PPP arrangements, see Engel *et al.* (2010). For a skeptical view of the range of opportunities to exploit such possibilities, see Menard (forthcoming).
23 A good discussion of the symmetry-asymmetry issue in the South Africa context is in Schroeder (2003).
24 In some instances, the economically most efficient thing to do might be simply to move people to some other area but this is seldom politically possible and, at least in the case of border regions, not even politically desirable.
25 See, for example, the review of the evidence in Peterson and Muzzini (2005).

References

Acosta, Olga Lucia and Richard Bird (2005) "The Dilemma of Decentralization in Colombia," in James Poterba Bird and Joel Slemrod, eds., *Fiscal Reform in Colombia: Problems and Prospects* (Cambridge, MA: MIT Press), 247–286.

Afonso, José Roberto Rodrigues, Erika Amorim Araújo, and Geraldo Biasoto Júnior (2005) "Fiscal Space and Public Sector Investments in Infrastructure: A Brazilian Case-Study," Texto para discussão no. 1141, Prepared for World Bank, Brasilia, December.

Ahmad, Ehtisham and Bob Searle (2006) "On the Implementation of Transfers to Subnational Governments," in E. Ahmad and G. Brosio, eds., *Handbook of Fiscal Federalism* (Cheltenham, UK: Edward Elgar), 381–404.

Albalate, Daniel, Germà Bel, and Xavier Fageda (2012) "Beyond the Efficiency-Equity Dilemma: Centralization as a Determinant of Government Investment in Infrastructure," *Papers in Regional Science*, 91 (3): 599–615.

Alegre, Juan Gonzalez, Andreas Kappeler, Atanas Kolev, and Timo Välilä (2008) "Composition of Government Investment in Europe: Some Forensic Evidence," *EIB Papers*, 13 (1): 22–55.

Alm, James (2010) "Municipal Financing of Urban Infrastructure: Knowns and Unknowns," Working Paper 19, Wolfensohn Center for Development, The Brookings Institution, Washington, DC.

Annez, Patricia Clarke (2007) "Urban Infrastructure Finance from Private Operators: What Have We Learned from Recent Experience?" in George Peterson and Patricia Clarke Annez, eds., *Financing Cities* (Washington: World Bank and Sage Publications), 307–338.

Bahl, Roy (forthcoming) "Financing Service Delivery in Metropolitan Areas," in Roy Bahl, Johannes Linn, and Deborah Wetzel, eds., *Government Finance in Metropolitan Areas in Developing Countries* (Cambridge: Lincoln Institute of Land Policy).

Bahl, Roy and Richard Bird (2008) "Subnational Taxes in Developing Countries: The Way Forward," *Public Budgeting & Finance*, 28 (4): 1–25.

Bahl, Roy and Jorge Martínez-Vázquez (2008) "The Property Tax in Developing Countries: Current Practice and Prospects," in Roy Bahl, Jorge Martínez-Vázquez, and Joan Youngman, eds., *Making the Property Tax Work: Experiences in Developing and Transitional Countries* (Cambridge: Lincoln Institute of Land Policy), 35–57.

Bahl, R.W. and J.F. Linn (1992) *Urban Public Finance in Developing Countries* (New York: Oxford University Press).

Bahl, Roy and Geeta Sethi (2012) "Fiscal Decentralization in Latin America: An Overview," in "Intergovernmental Fiscal Relations in Latin America: The Case of Argentina, Colombia, Mexico and Peru," Public Sector and Governance Unit (LCSPS), Poverty Reduction and Economic Management Unit, Latin America and the Caribbean (World Bank: Washington, DC) (draft version, June).

Bardhan, Pranab and Dilip Mookherjee (2006) "Decentralisation and Accountability in Infrastructure Delivery in Developing Countries," *Economic Journal*, 116 (508): 101–127.

Bel, Germà (forthcoming) "Local Government Size and Efficiency in Capital Intensive Services: What Evidence Is There of Economies of Scale, Density and Scope?" in Santiago Lago-Peñas and Jorge Martínez-Vázquez, eds., *The Challenge of Local Government Size* (Cheltenham, UK: Edward Elgar).

Bel, Germà and Xavier Fageda (2009) "Preventing Competition Because of Solidarity: Rhetoric and Reality of Airport Investments in Spain," *Applied Economics*, 41 (22): 2853–2865.

Berry, Christopher R. (2009) *Imperfect Union: Representation and Taxation in Multilevel Governments* (New York: Cambridge University Press).

Bird, Richard M. (1995) "Financing Local Services: Patterns, Problems, and Possibilities," Major Report 31, Centre for Urban and Community Studies, University of Toronto, February.

Bird, Richard M. (2001) "User Charges in Local Government Finance," in Richard Stren and Maria Emilia Freire, eds., *The Challenge of Urban Government* (Washington, DC: World Bank), 171–182.

Bird, Richard M. (2006) "Local and Regional Revenues: Realities and Prospects," in R.M. Bird and F. Vaillancourt, eds., *Perspectives on Fiscal Federalism.* WBI Learning Resources Series (Washington, DC: World Bank), 177–196.

Bird, Richard M. (2012) "Fiscal Decentralization in Colombia: A Work (Still) in Progress," in Roy Bahl and Geeta Sethi, eds., *Fiscal Federalism in Latin America: Argentina, Colombia, Mexico and Peru* (Washington, DC: World Bank).

Bird, Richard M. and Barbara D. Miller (1989) "Taxation, Pricing and the Poor," in Richard M. Bird and Susan Horton, eds., *Government Policy and the Poor in Developing Countries* (Toronto: University of Toronto Press), 49–80.

Bird, Richard M. and Enid Slack (1993) *Urban Public Finance in Canada*, 2nd edition (Toronto: John Wiley and Sons).

Bird, Richard M. and Enid Slack (2004) *International Handbook of Land and Property Taxation* (Cheltenham, UK and Northampton, MA: Edward Elgar).

Bird, Richard, Loren Brandt, Scott Rozelle, and Linxiu Zhang (2011) "Fiscal Reform and Rural Public Finance in China," in Joyce Yangyn Man and Yu-Hung Hong, eds., *China's Local Public Finance in Transition* (Cambridge, MA: Lincoln Institute for Land Policy), 227–243.

Boadway, Robin W. and Anwar Shah (2009) *Fiscal Federalism* (Cambridge: Cambridge University Press).

Borge, Lars-Erik, Jan K. Brueckner, and Jorn Rattsø (2012) "Partial Fiscal Decentralization and Public-Sector Heterogeneity: Theory and Evidence from Norway," CESifo Working Paper No. 3954, August.

Breton, Albert, Alberto Cassone, and Angela Fraschini (1998) "Decentralization and Subsidiarity: Toward a Theoretical Reconciliation," *University of Pennsylvania Journal of International Economic Law*, 19 (1): 21–51.

Briggs, Asa (1996) *Victorian Cities* (London: Folio Books).

Byrnes, Joel and Brian Dollery (2002) "Do Economies of Scale Exist in Australian Local Government? A Review of the Research Evidence," *Urban Policy and Research*, 20 (4): 391–414.

Canavire-Bacarreza, Gustavo, Jorge Martínez-Vázquez, and Cristian Sepulveda (2012) "Sub-national Revenue Mobilization in Peru," International Center for Public Policy, Andrew Young School of Public Policy, Georgia State University Working Paper 12–09, February.

Davey, Kenneth (1988) "Municipal Development Funds and Intermediaries," WPS 32, World Bank, July.

De Mello, Luiz (2007) "Fiscal Responsibility and Fiscal Adjustment: The Case of Brazilian Local Governments," in George Peterson and Patricia Annez, eds., *Financing Cities* (Washington, DC: World Bank), 40–73.

De Mello, Luiz (2012) "Fiscal Decentralisation and Public Investment: The Experience of Latin America," in Giorgio Brosio and Juan Pablo Jimenez, eds., *Decentralization and Reform in Latin America: Improving Intergovernmental Relations* (Cheltenham, UK: Edward Elgar).

Dollar, David and Bert Hofman (2008) "Intergovernmental Fiscal Reforms toward Realizing a Harmonious Society," in Lou Jiwei and Shuilin Wang, eds., *Public Finance in China: Reform and Growth for a Harmonious Society* (Washington, DC: World Bank), 39–52.

Edwards, M. and Y. Xiao (2009) "Annexation, Local Government Spending, and the Complicating Role of Density," *Urban Affairs Review*, 45 (2): 147–165.

Engel, E., Fischer, R., and Galetovic, A. (2010) "The Economics of Infrastructure Finance: Public Private Partnerships versus Public Provision," Documento de Trabajo Serie Economía No. 276, Centro de Economía Aplicada, Ingeniería Industrial, Universidad de Chile.

Estache, Antonio (2006) "Infrastructure: A Survey of Recent and Upcoming Issues," World Bank, April.

Estache, Antonio (2010) "Infrastructure Finance in Developing Countries: An Overview," *EIB Papers*, 15 (2): 61–88.

Estache, Antonio and S. Sinha (1995) "Does Decentralization Increase Spending on Infrastructure?" World Bank Policy Research Working Paper 1457.

Faguet, Jean-Paul (2004) "Does Decentralization Increase Government Responsiveness to Local Needs? Evidence from Bolivia," *Journal of Public Economics*, 88 (3–4): 867–893.

Faguet, Jean-Paul (2005) "The Effects of Decentralisation on Public Investment: Evidence and Four Lessons from Bolivia and Colombia," Crisis States Research Centre Working Papers Series 1, 62.

Faguet, Jean-Paul (2011) "Decentralization and Governance," Economic Organisation and Public Policy Discussion Paper Series No. 27, Suntory Centre, London School of Economics, June.

Fernández Llera, Roberto (2012) "Descentralización, inversión pública y consolidación fiscal: hacia una nueva geometría del triángulo," Paper prepared for Seminario Tributación y crecimiento con equidad, CEPAL, Santiago, agosto.

Fiszbein, Ariel (1997) "The Emergence of Local Capacity: Lessons from Colombia," *World Development*, 25 (7): 1029–1043.

Found, Adam (2012) "Scale Economies in Fire and Police Services," IMFG Paper in Municipal Finance and Governance, Toronto.

Fox, William F. and Tami Gurley (2006) "Will Consolidation Improve Sub-national Governments?" World Bank Policy Research Working Paper 3913.

Gomez Sabaini, Juan and Juan Pablo Jimenez (2012) "The Financing of Subnational Governments in Latin America," in Giorgio Brosio and Juan Pablo Jimenez, eds., *Decentralization and Reform in Latin America: Improving Intergovernmental Relations* (Cheltenham, UK: Edward Elgar).

Herrero-Alcalde, Ana, Jorge Martínez-Vázquez, and Encarnacion Murillo-Garcia (2011) "The Challenge of Designing Capital Equalization Transfers: An Application to Spanish Regions," *Publius: The Journal of Federalism*, 42 (2): 260–288.

Herstein, Lesley (2012) "Adding Value: Recognizing the Link between Engineers and Municipal Finance and Governance," Presentation at Institute of Municipal Finance and Governance, Munk School of Global Affairs, University of Toronto, May.

High Powered Expert Committee For Estimating the Investment Requirements for Urban Infrastructure Services (2011) *Report on Indian Urban Infrastructure and Services* (Delhi: Ministry of Urban Development, Government of India).

Hirsch, Werner Z. (1959) "Expenditure Implications of Metropolitan Growth and Consolidation," *Review of Economics and Statistics*, 41: 232–241.

Ingram, Gregory, Zhi Liu, and Karin Brandt (forthcoming) "Metropolitan Infrastructure and Capital Finance," in Roy Bahl, Johannes Linn, and Deborah Wetzel, eds., *Government Finance in Metropolitan Areas in Developing Countries* (Cambridge: Lincoln Institute of Land Policy).

Institute on Municipal Finance & Governance (2012) "Moving Our Region: Funding Transportation for our Future," Forum, No. 1 (Toronto).

Jacobs, Divina (2009) "Capital Expenditures and the Budget," published on IMF blog http://blog-pfm.imf.org (Washington, DC: International Monetary Fund).

Jalan, Joytsna and Martin Ravallion (2002) "Geographic Poverty Traps? A Micro Model of Consumption Growth in China," *Journal of Applied Econometrics*, 17 (4): 329–346.

Josie, Jay, Garry MacDonald, and Jeffrey Petchey (2008) "A Dynamic Equalization Model for Economic and Social Capital Grants with a South African Example," *Journal of Development Studies*, 44 (8): 1169–1189.

Kappeler, Andreas, Albert Solé-Ollé, Andreas Stephan, and Timo Välilä (2012) "Does Fiscal Decentralization Foster Regional Investment in Productive Infrastructure?" KTH/CESIS Working Paper Series in Economics and Institutions of Innovation No. 273, April.

Kharas, Homi and Johannes Linn (forthcoming) "External Assistance for Urban Finance Development: Needs, Strategies and Implementation," in Roy Bahl, Johannes Linn, and Deborah Wetzel, eds., *Government Finance in Metropolitan Areas in Developing Countries* (Cambridge: Lincoln Institute of Land Policy).

Kim, Junghun, Jorgen Lotz, and Niels Jorgen Mau, eds. (2010) *General Grants versus Earmarked Grants. Theory and Practice. The Copenhagen Workshop 2009*. Albertslund, Denmark: Published by The Korea Institute of Public Finance and the Danish Ministry of Interior and Health.

Kitchen, Harry and Enid Slack (2006) "Providing Public Services in Remote Areas," in Richard M. Bird and François Vaillancourt, eds., *Perspectives on Fiscal Federalism* (Washington, DC: World Bank), 123–139.

Klein, Michael (2012) "Infrastructure Policy: Basic Design Options," Policy Research Working Paper 6274 (Washington, DC: World Bank).

Liu, Lili and Steven B. Webb (2011) "Laws for Fiscal Responsibility for Subnational Discipline: International Experience," World Bank Policy Research Working Paper 5587.

Majumder, Rajarshi (2012) "Removing Poverty and Inequality in India: The Role of Infrastructure," MRPA Paper No. 40941, Munich Personal RePEc Archive (http://mpra.ub.uni-muenchen.de/40941/).

Martínez-Vázquez, Jorge (2012) "Fiscal Decentralization in Peru: A Perspective on Recent Developments and Future Challenges," in Roy Bahl and Geeta Sethi, eds., *Fiscal Federalism in Latin America: Argentina, Colombia, Mexico and Peru* (Washington, DC: World Bank).

Martínez-Vázquez, Jorge (forthcoming) "Local Non-property Tax Revenues," in Roy Bahl, Johannes Linn, and Deborah Wetzel, eds., *Government Finance in Metropolitan Areas in Developing Countries* (Cambridge: Lincoln Institute of Land Policy).

Martínez-Vázquez, Jorge, Javier Arze del Granado, and Jameson Boex (2007) *Fighting Corruption in the Public Sector* (Amsterdam: Elsevier).

Mauro, Paulo (1995) "Corruption and Growth," *Quarterly Journal of Economics*, 110 (3).

McCluskey, W.J. and Riel Franzsen (forthcoming) "Property Taxes and Land Taxes," in Roy Bahl, Johannes Linn, and Deborah Wetzel, eds., *Government Finance in Metropolitan Areas in Developing Countries* (Cambridge: Lincoln Institute of Land Policy).

McCord, Anna (2012) "The Politics of Social Protection: Why Are Public Works Programmes so Popular with Governments and Donors?" ODI (Overseas Development Institute) Background Note, September.

McLure, Charles E. (1998) "The Revenue Assignment Problem: Ends, Means and Constraints," *Journal of Public Budgeting, Accounting and Financial Management*, 9 (4): 652–683.

Menard, Claude (forthcoming) "Is Public-Private Partnership Obsolete?" in P. De Vries and E. Yehoue, eds., *Assessing the Obstacles and Shortcomings of PPP* (London: Routledge).

Merk, O., S. Saussier, C. Starpoli, E. Slack, and J.H. Kim (2012) "Financing Green Urban Infrastructure," OECD Regional Development Working Papers 2012/10.

Mohanty, P.K., B.M. Misra, Rajan Goyal, and P.D. Jeromi (2007) "Municipal Finance in India: An Assessment," Study No. 28. Development Research Group, Department of Economic Analysis and Policy (Mumbai: Reserve Bank of India).

Moisio, Antti, Heikki A. Loikkanen, and Lasse Oulasvirta (2010) "Public Services at the Local Level—The Finnish Way," Government Institute for Economic Research, Policy Reports 2.

National Institute of Urban Affairs (2011) "Ahmedabad Bus Rapid Transit System (Delhi)" (www.niua.org/projects/tpt/AHMEDABAD%20BRTS.pdf).

Oates, Wallace (1972) *Fiscal Federalism* (New York: Harcourt Brace Jovanovich).

Oates, Wallace (2005) "Toward a Second-Generation Theory of Fiscal Federalism," *International Tax and Public Finance*, 12 (4): 349–373.

Peterson, George E. and Elisa Muzzini (2005) "Decentralizing Basic Infrastructure Services," in Roland White and Paul Smoke, eds., *East Asia Decentralizes: Making Local Government Work* (Washington, DC: World Bank), 209–236.

Pethe, Abhay (forthcoming) "Metropolitan Public Finances: The Case of Mumbai," in Roy Bahl, Johannes Linn, and Deborah Wetzel, eds., *Government Finance in Metropolitan Areas in Developing Countries* (Cambridge: Lincoln Institute of Land Policy).

Prud'homme, Remy (1995) "On the Dangers of Decentralization," *World Bank Research Observer*, 10 (2): 210–226.

Rao, Govinda, Amar Nath, and B.K. Vani (2004) "Fiscal Decentralization in Karnataka," in Geeta Sethi, ed., *Fiscal Decentralization to Rural Governments in India* (New Delhi: Oxford University Press), 43–106.

Rao, M. Govinda and Richard M. Bird (2011) "Coping with Change: The Need to Restructure Urban Governance and Finance in India," IMFG Papers on Municipal Finance and Governance No. 4, Toronto.

Revilla, Ernesto (2012) "Mexico's Fiscal Federalism," in Roy Bahl and Geeta Sethi, eds., "Intergovernmental Fiscal Relations in Latin America: The Case of Argentina, Colombia, Mexico and Peru," Public Sector and Governance Unit (LCSPS), Poverty Reduction and Economic Management Unit, Latin America and the Caribbean (World Bank: Washington, DC) (draft, June), 173–244.

Schroeder, Larry (2003) "Municipal Powers and Functions: The Assignment Question," in Roy Bahl and Paul Smoke, eds., *Restructuring Local Government Finance in Developing Countries* (Northampton, MA: Edward Elgar), 23–70.

Siemiatycki, Matti and Jonathan Friedman (2012) "The Trade-Offs of Transferring Demand Risk on Urban Transit Public-Private Partnerships," *Public Works Management & Policy*, 17: 283–302.

Slack, Enid and Richard Bird (2012) "Merging Municipalities: Is Bigger Better?" in Antti Moisio, ed., *Rethinking Local Government: Essays on Municipal Reform* (Helsinki: Publication 61, Government Institute for Economic Research), 83–130.

Su, Ming and Quanhou Zhao (2006) "The Fiscal Framework and Urban Infrastructure Finance in China," World Bank Policy Research Paper 4051, November.

Tanzi, Vito (1996) "Fiscal Federalism and Decentralization: A Review of Some Efficiency and Macroeconomic Aspects," in M. Bruno and B. Pleskovic, eds., *Annual World Bank Conference on Development Economics* (Washington, DC: World Bank), 295–316.

Tanzi, Vito and Hamid Davoodi (2000) "Corruption, Growth and Public Finances," IMF Working Paper 182.

United Nations (2008) *World Urbanization Prospects: The 2007 Revision*, Economic and Social Affairs (New York: United Nations).

Van Ryneveld, Philip (2007) "Fiscal Decentralization and Financing of Urban Infrastructure in South Africa," in George Peterson and Patricia Clarke Annez, eds., *Financing Cities* (Washington, DC: World Bank and Sage Publications), 183–204.

Weingast, Barry (2009) "Second Generation Fiscal Federalism: The Implications of Fiscal Incentives," *Journal of Urban Economics*, 65 (3): 279–293.

Wong, Christine (forthcoming) "Riding the Tiger: Challenges of China's Municipal Finance in the 21st Century," in Roy Bahl, Johannes Linn, and Deborah Wetzel, eds., *Government Finance in Metropolitan Areas in Developing Countries* (Cambridge: Lincoln Institute of Land Policy).

World Bank (2007) "India: Rural Governments and Service Delivery," Policy Note, Sustainable Development Unit (Washington, DC: World Bank).

World Bank (2009a) *Improving Municipal Management for Cities to Succeed: An IEG Special Study* (Washington, DC: World Bank).

World Bank (2009b) *Colombia Decentralization: Options and Incentives for Efficiency*, Report No. 39832-CO (Washington, DC: World Bank).

5 Financing infrastructure

Luiz de Mello and Douglas Sutherland[1]

Introduction

Global infrastructure investment needs are estimated by the OECD at about 2.5 percent of world GDP per year in the coming 20 years in the areas of electricity transmission and generation, surface transport (roads and rail), telecoms, and water. Estimates could rise to some 3.5 percent of world GDP if additional energy-related investments (such as oil, gas, and coal) are taken into account. In the developing world, rapid urbanization requires increased public investment in water, sanitation, transport, and urban amenities to meet the needs and demands of a growing urban population and to deliver on MDG commitments. Rising incomes in emerging-market economies create demands for addressing deficiencies in provision, upgrading existing infrastructure, and improving access to the underserved population. The need to replace and update ageing infrastructure, and to maintain competitiveness in international markets in an increasingly tight budgetary environment poses challenges for governments in mature economies to provide and finance infrastructure. At the same time, technological change affects the nature of, and scope for, government provision of infrastructure services in developing, emerging-market, and mature economies alike.

The huge resources required to meet infrastructure demands call for combined efforts by the government—including the central and subnational administrations, as well as the public enterprise sector—and private-sector partners. In particular, where infrastructure provision and financing are carried out in a decentralized manner, coordination rises in importance, particularly when resources are limited. Within the government, coordination of infrastructure provision amongst subnational jurisdictions, as well as with national priorities and line ministries, is required to ensure investment is well designed and not wasteful. At the interface with the private sector, governments of all levels need to consider the best arrangements to ensure value for money. In this context, the role of subnational governments needs to be set in a broader context of government intervention.

Governments intervene in infrastructure provision to address market failures that could lead to the under-provision of services, to take into account externalities or public-good features when they are predominant, or to limit the exercise of market power in the case of natural monopolies. This broader context includes decisions on the ownership structure (public or private) of infrastructure, the delivery modalities (pure government provision, public procurement, concessions, PPPs, etc.), the financing options for these different modalities (budget appropriations, user charges), and the regulatory regime for service delivery (market- and/or government-based regulation).

In this chapter, we address general issues related to infrastructure investment but focus on fixed networks, such as water/sanitation, energy, and transport. These networks are interesting, because they require investment that is lumpy and largely irreversible, and therefore costly, which calls for considerable financing for instalment and maintenance. They also account for the bulk of infrastructure development budgets around the world and also often generate a future stream of revenue that accrues to the provider. Moreover, fixed networks concern most of the infrastructure investment already under way around the world and the bulk of demand for future investment. Infrastructure investment in other sectors, including for the provision of social services, such as health care and education, is discussed in Chapters 3 and 13.

This chapter identifies a few general principles that should guide policy-makers' choices for financing infrastructure investment in a decentralized setting. By raising efficiency, there are substantial savings to be made from the choice of appropriate financing, given that the costs of infrastructure investment are substantial. In particular:

- The choice of financing instrument depends on the nature of the investment (size, revenue-generating capacity, potential for competition), the modality of service delivery (pure government provision, procurement, concession, PPP), the budgetary capacity of the jurisdiction (breadth and depth of own taxes, intergovernmental transfer arrangements, borrowing constraints), and the technical capacity of the jurisdiction to design and negotiate contracts with private-sector providers.
- Financing options should maximize the welfare of local residents. Perception of the role of government matters and affects the willingness to pay for services. If local residents believe that provision, especially that financed locally, does not generate benefits that can be internalized by the local community, they are unlikely to be willing to pay for the services associated with the infrastructure.
- Where subnational administrations remain important providers of infrastructure, better coordination mechanisms can help ensure that returns to scale are exploited and inter-jurisdictional spillovers are taken into account, including through decision-making frameworks that bring together subnational and central governments, as well as other stakeholders.
- On the financing side, subnational governments typically need to enhance their capacity to raise own revenue, to make the most of intergovernmental grants and transfers, and to mobilize private-sector funds, including by tapping capital markets, where permitted. They also need to strengthen their

technical capacity to design and implement investment projects, as well as manage increasingly complex, multi-year budgets, especially when there is private-sector involvement.

- To meet the infrastructure investment challenge, making better use of user charges, while dealing with associated affordability and equity drawbacks, can help make sure existing infrastructure that can generate revenue streams is used efficiently and identify where more infrastructure investment is needed, as well as creating more options for private-sector involvement.

The chapter is structured as follows. The next section describes long-term global trends in investment and discusses estimates of future infrastructure investment needs. The following section presents a general framework for government interventions that highlights the specific characteristics of subnational governments. The section after that discusses financing options for subnational governments ranging from budgetary sources (general revenue, intergovernmental grants and transfers, user charges, debt issuance) and private-sector co-financing. The final section concludes.

Trends in infrastructure spending and future needs

General trends and near-term outlook

As noted in Chapter 3, there is a dearth of internationally comparable data and long time-series of government spending on infrastructure development, let alone associated recurrent outlays, such as operations and maintenance. Also, national accounts data on gross fixed capital formation do not usually distinguish between infrastructure and non-infrastructure investment. To the extent that both series move together, trends in infrastructure spending could be gauged, although rather imperfectly, by those in overall gross fixed capital formation, which vary a great deal across countries (Figure 5.1). Investment patterns also differ across countries: typically, investment accounts for a larger share of GDP in fast-growing economies, such as China and India, than in the high-income OECD economies.

Notwithstanding regional differences in infrastructure spending, there has been an increase in government investment, reflecting to a large extent counter-cyclical fiscal support in OECD countries and several emerging-market economies (OECD, 2011c; World Bank, 2012). Stimulus packages accounted for 4 percent of GDP or more in some OECD countries (Australia, Canada, Korea, United States), with a strong focus on public investment, including labor-intensive infrastructure in sectors such as transport and urban utilities and on subnational levels of administration for the implementation of investment programs. About three-quarters of the investment package announced by Korea and Spain was to be delivered by the subnational jurisdictions (OECD, 2011a). This crisis-driven expansion in investment is nevertheless losing impetus as support packages are unwound in some countries and as a result of ongoing fiscal consolidation in several OECD countries (OECD, 2012a).

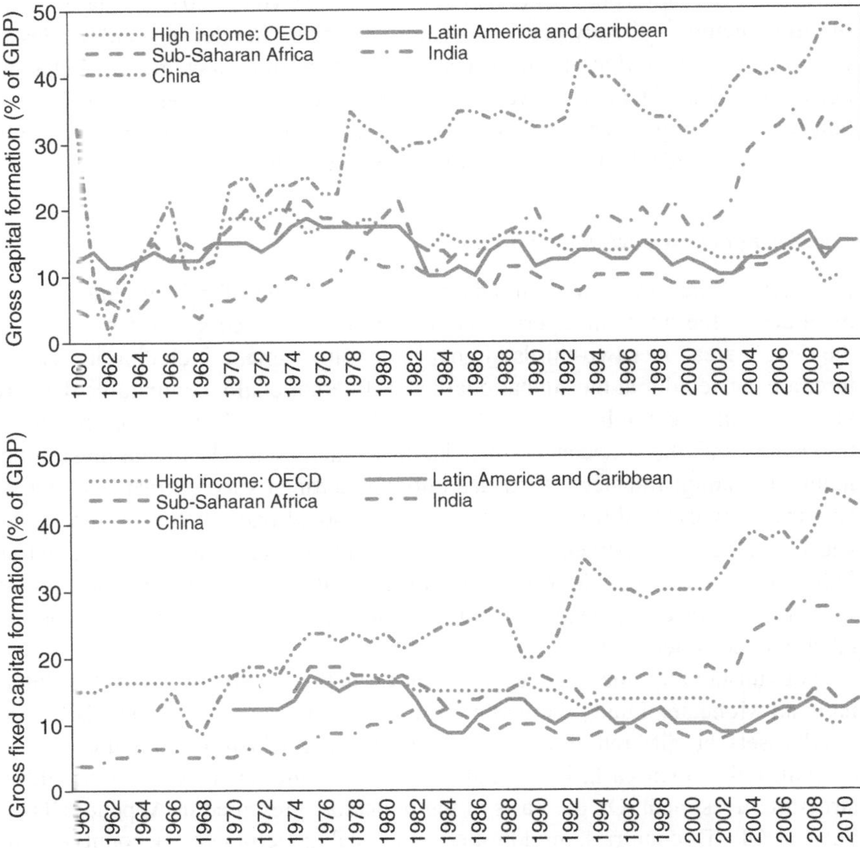

Figure 5.1 Investment trends: international comparisons, 1960–2011 (source: World Bank (*World Development Indicators*)).

Also, there are numerous factors, some of them structural, others stemming from the crisis, which will likely bear down on investment in the coming years. On the demand side, uncertainty about the near-term outlook for the global economy and the poor state of the public finances in many countries will likely constrain investment in the near term. On the supply side, despite historically low interest rates around the world, there is a dearth of financing due to ongoing bank deleveraging and financial sector impairment. At the same time, in some cases strict regulations governing the extent to which institutional investors are able to invest in infrastructure and other long-term projects.

The composition of infrastructure investment between the government and the private sector has also changed over time. Efforts to leverage private-sector financing for investment and privatization, motivated by the potential for enhancing the efficiency of government-owned enterprises through private ownership or management, has led to a decline in the government share of infrastructure investment in many countries (Chan *et al.*, 2009; de Mello, 2012). A large share of infrastructure is already in private hands, especially in telecoms and to a lesser extent power generation and railways. At the same time, technological change, not least in the ICT area, as well as regulatory reform to foster competition in otherwise uncompetitive markets, have altered the scope for government provision and facilitated the involvement of the private sector.

Investment across government layers

It is very difficult to compare trends in the composition of infrastructure investment across the different layers of administration, as discussed in Chapter 2. In the OECD area, over two-thirds of government investment, including infrastructure, are carried out at the subnational level. Internationally comparable data are very difficult to come by, even for very crude measures of infrastructure decentralization and the associated financial flows across levels of administration, including capital transfers. Also, institutional settings vary a great deal across countries, involving different degrees of subnational participation in the design and financing of investment projects. As a result, conventional decentralization indicators, such as the share of subnational capital expenditure in total public investment, can be misleading to the extent that subnational autonomy is not taken into consideration.

Notwithstanding these caveats, the information available from the International Monetary Fund's Government Finance Statistics on the acquisition of fixed assets at different levels of administration, which is computed on an accrual, rather than cash, basis, can be used as a metric for subnational infrastructure investment. On the basis of the indicators presented in Appendix Table 5.2 for OECD countries, middle-tier and local governments account for the lion's share of government investment, at least as far as the ratio of acquisition of fixed assets to GDP is concerned. Of course, there are limitations to GFS data, including the fact that most countries do not report investment spending for the different layers of administration in a systematic manner and that in some cases investment is carried out through extra-budgetary funds that are not consolidated in the fiscal accounts.

Future demand and needs

Current spending levels may not be sufficient to meet future demand for infrastructure development and upgrading. A combination of low levels of investment and poor infrastructure in most developing and emerging-market economies begs the question of how much countries should invest in infrastructure. However, the economic literature is rather limited in this area, reflecting to a large extent data limitations, even in the OECD area. The estimations reported by the OECD suggest that investments to the tune of 2.5 percent of world GDP are needed to improve the world's infrastructure, especially in sectors such as roads, rail, telecoms, electricity (transmission and distribution), and water (OECD, 2007). If electricity generation and other energy-related investments in oil, gas, and coal are taken into account, based on estimates by International Energy Agency (IEA, 2010, 2011), worldwide infrastructure investment needs could rise to 3.5 percent of world GDP per year through to 2030. Given that subnational governments, especially cities and local jurisdictions, account for the lion's share of government investment in mature economies, it is likely that they will remain at the forefront of service delivery in this area in the years to come (OECD, 2012b).

At the same time, competing demands associated not least with population ageing will likely intensify and create additional claims on already stretched government budgets. To illustrate, government spending on health and long-term care alone is likely to increase from the current level of close to 7 percent of GDP in OECD countries to about 10–13 percent of GDP by 2050, and outlays on old-age pensions are set to rise by 3–4 percentage points (OECD, 2007). Governments will find it increasingly difficult to finance future infrastructure investment from traditional sources. This is because the tax base may come under pressure through an ageing workforce, and medium-term fiscal consolidation needs associated with high levels of government indebtedness will constrain the ability of governments to finance investment through debt issuance.

The scope for subnational provision of infrastructure

Against a background of significant demand for infrastructure investment projected over the coming decades, often with the lion's share of responsibility falling to subnational governments, rethinking how best to meet this challenge becomes increasingly important as pressure mounts on both subnational and central government budgets. To address the infrastructure challenge policymakers will need to reassess infrastructure priorities if funding cannot be guaranteed, whether the government remains best suited to take responsibility for provision and whether there are more effective ways to harness the private sector in the provision of infrastructure.

General framework for government intervention[2]

ADDRESSING MARKET FAILURES

Subnational provision of infrastructure needs to be set in a broader context of government intervention to address market failures that could result in the underprovision of infrastructure, when externalities or public-good features are predominant, or to limit the exercise of market power in the case of natural monopolies. The resulting decisions about ownership, delivery modality, and regulation are important factors affecting the supply and demand of infrastructure (Figure 5.2). At the same time, and as discussed in Chapter 4, the assignment of functions across the different layers of government depends on the institutional underpinnings of intergovernmental fiscal relations, which are specific to different countries and set the parameters for subnational government involvement in infrastructure provision and financing.

In general terms, the structure of infrastructure supply depends on the nature of the market failure to be addressed. In particular, in the case of externalities or public-good effects, the private sector would not provide the service, and decentralized government intervention would result in under-provision of the service relative to the social optimum. Under-provision arises because the costs of delivery would be borne by local residents whereas the benefits could accrue at least in part to neighboring jurisdictions. In the case of natural monopolies, the private sector would usually be willing to provide the service, although normally at a level that is below, and a price that is above, the social optimum. Dealing with either type of market failure calls for direct government provision and/or some type of arm's length regulation for private-sector involvement, as well as intergovernmental fiscal arrangements (discussed below) to align the costs and benefits of provision to local tax-payers in the case of decentralized delivery. Due to the often extremely large fixed costs and the irreversibility of investment, investment decisions are also particularly sensitive to the regulatory environment.

When the government is involved in infrastructure provision, investment decision-making should use the standard criterion of setting the level of provision that equates the marginal social benefit to the marginal social cost, which is related to the marginal costs of public funds and production costs. However, due to the characteristics of networks, the marginal benefits of additional investments are often low and declining, but not always, particularly in well-developed networks.

SELECTING APPROPRIATE DELIVERY MODES

There are a number of different delivery modes involving the public or private sector to differing degrees. These include public ownership and procurement, which has often characterized the water supply and road networks; concessions and public-private partnerships (PPPs), which are increasingly involving the private sector in the delivery of infrastructure; and fully privately owned companies, which has often been the case in the energy sector.

An important motivation for greater private sector involvement in infrastructure provision arises from harnessing their financial and technical expertise for investment and their managerial abilities in managing large construction projects and in some cases subsequent operation of the infrastructure.

At one extreme, the private sector will provide and operate the infrastructure themselves, particularly when it is a natural monopoly and user fees are feasible. In this case, the state needs to provide an appropriate regulatory environment (see below). When entry is possible, new infrastructure can be wholly owned and provided by the private sector, such as in the case of electricity generation. When entry is difficult—for example, planning requirements impose important

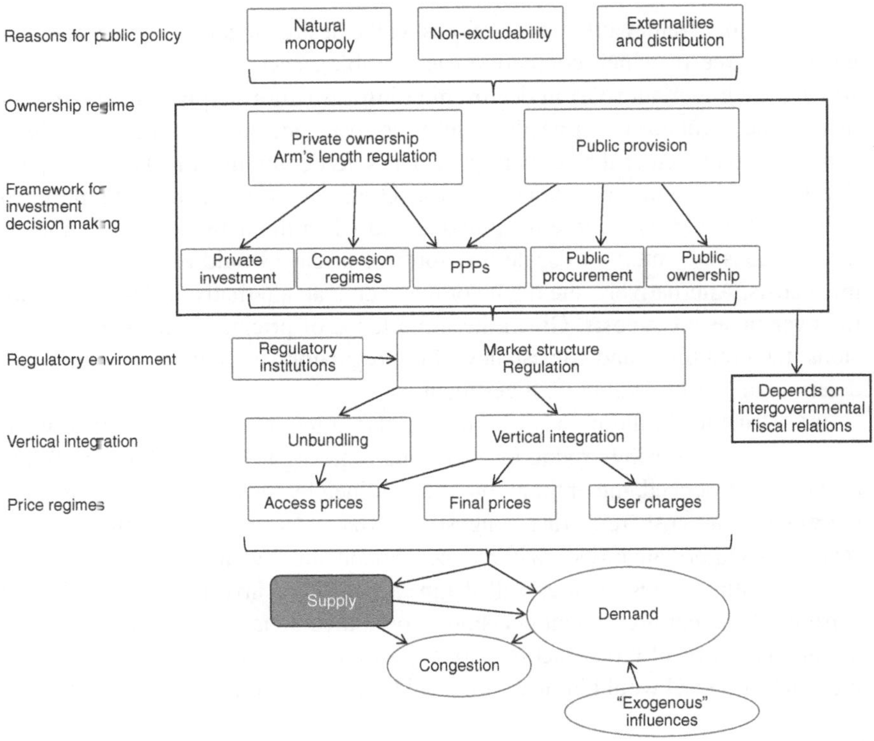

Figure 5.2 Factors affecting investment in infrastructure (source: based on Sutherland *et al.* (2011)).

obstacles or infrastructure already exists—the private sector may be involved through franchises or concessions, largely to operate existing infrastructure, and public-private partnerships (PPPs), to construct and operate new assets.

Franchises or concessions and PPPs occupy a middle ground between public and private provision. In part, this is due to the public good nature of the services, for which the sub-central government is directly accountable to the population, as well as distributional concerns. In this context, the public sector may wish to remain involved in decisions regarding investment, management of infrastructure assets, and provision of services.

At the other end of the spectrum, the public sector will involve the private sector through traditional procurement while retaining ownership of, and managerial responsibility for, the infrastructure asset. This type of arrangement arises when the sub-central government finds it easier to specify the infrastructure asset than the service it wants to provide, which may also be difficult to monitor. In this light, building the local road network may be something easier to specify *ex ante* rather than designing a contact based on local road network availability or usage.

SETTING APPROPRIATE REGULATION

The regulatory framework needs to focus on the desired market structure (reflecting the degree to which competition is possible), access regimes and pricing, which play important roles in determining infrastructure supply and use. In particular, the regulator often needs to set user costs, access prices or final prices, depending on whether the network provider is vertically integrated and competition is feasible. Under certain conditions, setting the price equal to the marginal social cost would be welfare maximizing and when the networks are characterized by constant returns to scale this form of pricing would also cover investment costs. Alternatively, the regulator may adopt an alternative pricing structure to cover investment costs. Given the importance of pricing to investment decisions, the credibility and consistency of the regulatory framework are important determinants of infrastructure investment.

Infrastructure in the network sectors is also often a congestible public good with congestion-raising production costs and reducing individuals' utility. When pricing is introduced, the optimal toll—determined by the difference between the marginal social cost (reflecting congestion costs and wear and tear of the infrastructure) and private costs—will reduce demand and, by enhancing the efficient use of existing infrastructure, will damp the need for investment in additional capacity. Efficient investment decisions would then equate marginal costs to the marginal benefits of infrastructure capacity and quality, which the revenues from the congestion toll would indicate when additional investment is warranted.

Decentralization and government provision of infrastructure: insights from the literature

Although subnational jurisdictions account for the bulk of government investment, the public finance literature is surprisingly limited on the possible effects of fiscal decentralization on infrastructure provision. The Oatesian and Musgravean traditions of fiscal federalism place limited emphasis on the composition of public investment across the different layers of administration. The basic argument is that, as noted above, public investment is best carried out and financed by higher levels of administration because of externality/network effects, which discourage subnational provision and result in a sub-optimal supply of public investment. Economies of scale in production and service delivery are common in fixed networks and also discourage subnational provision, especially by small jurisdictions (de Mello and Lago-Peñas, 2012). Horizontal tax competition, which is likely to arise from the decentralization of revenue sources to lower levels of administration, could result in sub-optimal investment under certain conditions (Hulten and Schwab, 1997).

The empirical literature provides some, albeit limited, validation to the underprovision hypothesis. The cross-country analysis reported by de Mello (2012) suggests that decentralization, measured by the share of subnational revenue in total revenue, encourages aggregate investment (gross fixed capital formation), although it is associated with lower investment at the subnational level (acquisition of fixed assets). In the case of Latin America, greater decentralization is associated not only with lower subnational government investment but also with economy-wide gross fixed capital formation.

By contrast, another strand of literature shows that decentralization could result in over-provision of infrastructure at the subnational level. One argument is that competition among same-level jurisdictions could affect the composition of expenditure, leading subnational governments to over-invest in public goods that would make their jurisdictions attractive to private investment (Keen and Marchand, 1997). Decentralization could therefore be associated with higher levels of subnational spending on infrastructure projects, a result that is validated by the cross-country evidence reported by Estache and Sinha (1995), which suggests that more decentralized countries, especially in the developing world, tend to spend more (total and subnational) on infrastructure projects. More recent evidence reported by Kappeler and Välilä (2008) for European countries also shows that decentralization tilts the composition of public investment towards more productive projects, notably infrastructure, a finding that the authors attribute to increased fiscal competition brought about by decentralization.

Over-provision does not imply that the benefits of infrastructure are shared equally. Bardhan and Mookherjee (2006) find that decentralization of infrastructure does indeed increase the supply of services at the local level, given that local policy-makers are more responsive to local needs than central government officials, but it also leads to over-provision of services to local elites to the detriment of other social groups. As for financing, they find that user charges improves local welfare more than intergovernmental transfers, regardless of the degree of local capture. Evidence for Spain (Esteller and Solé, 2005), Bolivia and Colombia (Faguet, 2004), and Indonesia (Chowdhury *et al.*, 2007) also suggest that decentralization makes investment decisions more responsive to local preferences and needs, which in turn improves the composition of the capital stock among the subnational jurisdictions.

The empirical literature, although limited, provides some evidence on the links between decentralized provision and the quality of infrastructure. For example, Humplick and Estache (1995) estimate the effect of decentralization on the performance of several infrastructure projects, including roads, electricity, and water. Using different measures of decentralization in each sector, the authors find that at least one performance indicator improved in each sector as a result of decentralization, although the correlation between decentralization and performance remains fairly weak in general. However, in some cases, the decentralized provision of infrastructure was subsequently reversed, such as the responsibility for road investment in Bolivia.

All in all, there are theoretical arguments and empirical evidence suggesting a link between decentralized provision, on the one hand, and the level and quality of infrastructure, on the other. The cross-country empirical literature nevertheless does not provide conclusive evidence, suggesting that there is much scope for future research in this area and that country-specific circumstances and characteristics need to be taken into account.

Financing options for subnational governments

To each delivery mode identified in Figure 5.2 corresponds different financing options, which need to be tailored to the needs and capacity of subnational governments, the scope and modalities for private-sector involvement, and the institutional settings for intergovernmental fiscal relations. By and large, and as discussed in Chapter 4, financial options can be of two types: (i) budget appropriations (general revenue, debt, intergovernmental grants and transfers, user charges), and (ii) private-sector co-financing (concessions, PPPs). Of course, these options are not mutually exclusive; for example, to the extent that public funding is required for projects involving private-sector co-financing, a claim is placed on budget appropriations.

The choice of financing options is not without consequences for the delivery of infrastructure services. They depend on the budgetary and administrative capacity of the subnational jurisdictions, the institutional framework for intergovernmental fiscal relations, the mechanisms for oversight of government operations, and the incentives for risk management and private sector involvement (Table 5.1). These issues will be discussed in greater detail below.

The way public infrastructure is financed can also affect its benefits. Funding infrastructure spending by taxes could promote growth if the marginal productivity gains arising from the tax-financed investment exceed the adverse impact of higher taxes. Debt financing could also be desirable to the extent that the investments it finances create a future stream of earnings to the government that meets debt service requirements. In the case of PPPs, efficiency gains can be generated if market risk is shared appropriately between the government and the private-sector partner.

Budgetary appropriations: general revenue, debt, intergovernmental grants and transfers, user charges

The sunk costs associated with public investment are often too high to be fully financed by subnational budgets, whose revenue mobilization and borrowing capacity is lower than that of higher levels of administration. Higher levels of administration therefore participate in the financing of subnational provision through transfers and grants, even when investments are carried out entirely by subnational jurisdictions. The scope for user charges depends more broadly on the pricing regime for infrastructure projects and on the willingness/ability to pay of local residents as well as the capacity to collect fees for infrastructure use.

GENERAL REVENUE

Subnational governments tend to have lower revenue mobilization capacity than the central government, which limits their ability to finance costly investments in fixed networks out of their general budgets. On the basis of conventional public finance principles, the tax bases that can efficiently be assigned to

Table 5.1 Characteristics of financing modalities: a summary

	Budget appropriations				*Private-sector co-financing (procurement, concessions, PPPs)*
	General revenue	*Debt*	*Intergovernmental grants and transfers*	*User charges*	
Subnational budgetary and administrative capacity	Conditional on the revenue mobilization capacity of subnational governments	Conditional on the rules governing subnational financial management and borrowing	Constrained by subnational administrative capacity (conditional and matching grants may be cumbersome)	Constrained by willingness/ability to pay	Constrained by subnational administrative capacity
Intergovernmental fiscal relations	Depends on the assignment of tax bases to subnational governments and their policymaking autonomy	Subnational borrowing is often subject to administrative and/or prudential controls imposed by the center	Depends on the design of grants and transfer system	Often under the purview of subnational governments	Subnational governments often have their own legal framework for partnerships
Scope for private-sector involvement	No scope	No or limited scope	In principle no scope, unless specified by recipient jurisdiction	Depends on ownership structure of project	Scope depends on ownership structure and risk-sharing between government and private-sector partner
Oversight	Local legislature; local capture problems	Local legislature, central or middle-tier government and markets; local capture problems	Local and higher-level legislature; local capture problem	Local legislature and market; could reduce risk of local capture	Local and higher-level legislature; market oversight is strengthened if project is carried out by listed public enterprise
Incentives for risk management and potential for enhancing competition	Depends on oversight mechanisms and accountability of local policymakers	Low, depends on oversight mechanisms, including markets, and accountability of local policymakers; specific-purpose bonds could provide stronger incentives	Low to medium, depends on the design of grants, incentive to inflate costs of projects; matching grants could provide stronger incentives	Medium to high, could provide stronger incentives due to greater transparency and inter-jurisdictional comparability	Medium to high, depends on capacity to ensure appropriate risk-sharing between government and private-sector partner

Source: Authors' elaboration.

subnational governments, such as property, are narrower than those that are typically assigned to the central government, such as personal and corporate income. Arrangements differ considerably across countries, and in many cases, the central and the subnational governments also share the revenue of some taxes, including those on income and consumption, which may enhance subnational revenue.

Subnational governments also often rely on the earmarking of the revenue from own or shared taxes to finance public investment. Revenue earmarking ensures that funds are allocated to activities—including operations and maintenance—that might otherwise be undersupplied once investments come to fruition. However, revenue earmarking complicates expenditure management and discourages efforts to improve the cost-effectiveness of government expenditures, because policymakers are unable to reallocate scarce budgetary resources to cost-effective activities. This practice is widespread in Latin America, and much less prevalent in OECD countries, although provisions vary considerably across (de Mello, 2012). For example, in OECD countries, motor vehicle taxes or fuel duties are sometimes earmarked for road investment.

Financing of investment projects through revenue earmarking is subject to the same oversight procedures as the general budget, which is carried out by subnational legislatures (and in some cases by the central government). Some countries also condition the creation of expenditure mandates to the availability of financing, which encourages a discussion during the budget process on the costs and benefits of investments and the trade-offs that may exist among different interventions.

A final potential source of government funding comes from improvement levies. In this case, the government can levy a charge on those benefiting from infrastructure provision to defray investment costs. In OECD countries, (local) governments frequently charge improvement levies to real estate developers to cover the expenses of extending infrastructure to the new developments. More contentiously and thereby less frequent, existing inhabitants or businesses can face an additional levy for improvements of or new additions to infrastructure.

DEBT

Debt financing is often used in the case of costly investment projects, often with long maturities, that cannot be financed by the general budget and which generate future benefits to the population and yield a stream of revenue that can be used to service the debt. However, when subnational governments can borrow directly from capital markets, particularly when they have limited revenue raising capacity, such borrowing may be perceived as implicitly guaranteed by central government. As a result, subnational governments can take on too much borrowing, thereby forcing the central government to bail them out. Against the backdrop of a possible breakdown in fiscal responsibility, subnational governments, especially in developing countries and emerging-market economies, often face restrictions on borrowing in the form of outright bans (such as on foreign borrowing, for example), administrative restrictions (such as central government approval) and/or prudential regulations (such as limits based on debt service capacity and debt ceilings). Arrangements vary considerably across countries. For example, borrowing is allowed in most European countries subject to a golden rule; that is, long-term borrowing is allowed to finance capital expenditure only. More flexible arrangements involve prudential requirements based on debt service parameters (de Mello, 2010), whereas in Latin America subnational borrowing is severely constrained (Martínez-Vázquez, 2010).

Governments often set up financial institutions, such as investment banks, to provide dedicated financing for investment, in particular infrastructure development projects. The logic of setting up such banks is that the private financial sector may be unable (due to financial shallowness) or unwilling (due to some market failure) to provide long-term financing for large infrastructure development projects. In addition to well-known governance challenges associated with the management of public financial institutions, risks include the possibility that an active government involvement in long-term investment financing may actually inhibit the development of private-sector financing, rather than overcoming obstacles to infrastructure development.

Decisions on whether or not to finance infrastructure projects through the issuance of debt, where permitted, are guided by the usual financial parameters, although borrowing costs tend to be higher for subnational governments than the central government (de Mello, 2001). In this case, on-lending by higher levels of administration would provide less onerous financing for subnational provision. Debt financing also depends on the depth of national capital markets and the tax regime for investment in subnational securities (in some countries, including the United States, investment in local government bonds is exempted from income tax).

In the case of debt financing, oversight is often extended to subnational legislatures and other agencies responsible for ensuring compliance with administrative and/or prudential regulations on subnational borrowing. In some cases, market mechanisms may also exert pressures for enhanced fiscal discipline at the subnational level.

INTERGOVERNMENTAL GRANTS AND TRANSFERS

There is considerable variation across countries on the types of grants from higher levels of administration used to finance infrastructure projects. Intergovernmental grants and transfers can help overcome subnational government revenue shortfalls, allowing them to take on major infrastructure projects. However, in the absence of coordination mechanisms, investment decisions may fail to take into account the consequences for other subnational jurisdictions possibly leading to under-provision. Similarly local investment decisions can be at variance with national priorities. In response to these problems, central governments can attempt to influence infrastructure provision by making grants conditional.

Block grants allow the recipient jurisdiction greater managerial autonomy than do conditional or matching grants, which require financial counterparts and/or impose constraints on the use of funds by the recipient jurisdiction. In many respects, co-financing by different levels of government is similar to conditional or matching grants. Conditionality is often introduced in intergovernmental transfer systems to deal with externalities in subnational provision, although in practice the design of conditional grants is complicated by the fact that externalities are not directly observable. These grants may also be complex to administer. In turn, matching grants are used in some cases to ensure financing for recurrent spending associated with operations and maintenance once infrastructure projects come on stream.

While recognizing that different grants serve different purposes, there is a trend towards increased flexibility in the grant system around the world. For example, conditional and matching grants are hardly used at all in Latin America, where revenue earmarking is more widespread, as discussed above, and are being replaced by block grants in most European countries. Experience within the OECD also demonstrates that sectoral or functional earmarking can be relaxed without risking under-provision of infrastructure, particularly when local residents hold subnational governments accountable for infrastructure investment. Heightened demands for local self-governance are also resulting in the replacement of conditional grants by block grants. However, this is not always the case and in reaction to failures at the subnational level, further conditioning by central governments is a possible response.

As in the case of the creation of dedicated financial institutions (discussed above), governments often establish development funds to channel—essentially subsidized loans and/or grants—to finance infrastructure development in lagging regions. Resources often come from the budgetary sources, including through the earmarking of specific revenues, but the existence of such mechanisms poses challenges because funds are seldom disbursed in a transparent, contestable manner. It is also difficult to assess the cost-effectiveness of these dedicated support mechanisms and the role they play in regional development.

While the management of intergovernmental grants and transfers is subject to conventional budgetary oversight, the wedge that they drive between the costs and benefits of subnational delivery is known to create perverse incentives for decentralized fiscal policymaking. This is especially of "common pool" problems, which encourage the recipient jurisdiction to overspend due to an underestimation of provision costs (de Mello, 2000).

USER CHARGES

When infrastructure is not financed from taxation (either wholly or in part) user charges represent the other principal source of funding. In OECD countries, user charges are most commonly levied for transport services, water supply and wastewater treatment, and waste. User charges can account for a substantial source of subnational government revenue, although considerable heterogeneity exists across countries partly depending on whether the public or private sector provides these services. When the public sector is the provider, revenue to all levels of government from user charges are around 2.5 percent of GDP on average for the OECD. In federal countries the subnational government share is around three-quarters while in unitary countries this drops to around one-half.

User charges are attractive as they can provide more than simply a source of revenue. By putting a price on service provision, user charges can influence demand, which is particularly useful for congestible public goods. As discussed above, the price signal needed to address congestion will reveal where new infrastructure is needed and provide funding. However, the use of road and congestion pricing varies enormously across countries despite substantial costs associated with congestion. Within Europe, estimated costs of congestion of around 2 percent of GDP are not uncommon, but relatively few countries have explicit congestion charging schemes (Kozluk, 2010).[3]

Another attraction is that pricing can help internalize environmental and other externalities. The externalities can be significant for some types of infrastructure typically provided by subnational governments, such as water supply and wastewater. In practice, pricing infrastructure and associated services often fails to cover operating costs, yet alone capital and external costs. In the water sector, charging for wastewater treatment has increasingly been levied separately as costs have risen due to tightening environmental standards. But for water supply, while tariffs account for the lion's share of operating costs, full-cost recovery remains rare. Differences in water price levels are considerable, with price levels lower and the gap to full-cost recovery often larger in countries where water is scarce (OECD, 2010b).

Regardless of the financing arrangements for investment projects, attention is typically placed on the capital expenditure per se, and the recurrent costs of operations and maintenance are often neglected.[4] This is often related to politicians preferring to support new, highly visible projects at the expense of the upkeep of existing infrastructure assets (Romp and De Haan, 2007).

A major drawback with user charges centers on their interaction with affordability and the distribution of income. This is because user charges, especially for essential services, can account for noticeable shares of household disposable income, creating a financial burden that can fall disproportionately on the poor, as discussed in Chapter 7. As a result, pricing mechanisms may introduce some cross-subsidization, as in the case of increasing block tariffs for water supply, or in other cases, revenues from user charges can be used (at least in part) to finance (preferably means tested) transfers to poorer households that would facilitate access to services while addressing equity considerations.

A second complication arises in whether or not local governments possess the administrative capacity to implement user charges. Investments in collection, monitoring, and pricing technology can represent a sizeable financial burden which, combined with difficulties in setting prices effectively, may limit the potential gains from introducing user charges. However, to some extent, technological change has transformed the landscape in recent years in areas such as transport, allowing subnational governments to introduce quite complex pricing mechanisms in both OECD countries and emerging-market economies. In this light, some of the barriers to implementing user charges may be falling, but they will still represent an important obstacle in many cases.

Private-sector involvement

FINANCING MODALITIES: CONCESSIONS, PPPS

No single model of private-sector involvement in infrastructure investment has emerged across countries. However, over time OECD countries have generally moved away from investment by public enterprises and towards public procurement, concessions, and more recently PPPs. This is also the case beyond the OECD area, including many countries in Latin America. One factor influencing the particular choice of procurement versus concessions and PPPs is whether the infrastructure assets raise revenue. When it is possible to raise revenue, a wider range of financing options are available, which would otherwise be largely limited to traditional public procurement.

In the different models involving the private sector, tendering introduces competition either for the public procurement contract or *ex ante* for the market (Demsetz, 1968). In this context, the subnational government's capacity to manage the tendering process effectively determines whether potential benefits are harnessed. For example, the upfront contracting costs for PPPs are typically substantially greater than traditional procurement, making PPPs less attractive for subnational governments with limited experience and lacking the technical skills to negotiate effectively with the private sector. In this context, enhancing subnational governments' capacity to negotiate complex deals and select the most efficient bidder acquires some importance (World Bank, 2012).

With different models of private-sector involvement available, subnational governments need to guard against choices that may be convenient in the short term but may turn out to be costly later on. For example, interest in PPPs can arise to overcome budgetary constraints, which may be imposed by fiscal rules, or in an attempt to disguise pressure on the public finances. A proper and transparent assessment of the expected long-term impact on public finances and accounting for associated contingent liabilities for the different possible models would help ensure that the most appropriate choice is made (OECD, 2008).

Additional consequences of short-termism may also arise for other reasons. Due to the electoral cycle, the relatively short period officials may be in office—when measured in comparison with the life of an investment project—can introduce uncertainty about the subnational government's commitment to the project in the future. In other cases, dependence on transfer arrangements, which underpin subnational government involvement, may also raise concern about project sustainability. In such cases, the increased uncertainty would induce the private sector to demand a higher rate of return on their investment, which could make the investment unattractive.

In contrast to public procurement, concessions and PPPs involve private-sector co-financing, with the choice between them largely determined by the risk characteristics of the project. There are many overlapping issues as contracts for concessions and PPPs are unavoidably incomplete and long-term in nature, requiring ongoing monitoring and control during the life of the project (Araújo and Sutherland, 2010; also discussed in Chapter 9). First, contract design needs to ensure an appropriate and effective transfer of risks and responsibilities to the private sector. A second area of overlap is mitigating investment hold-up throughout the life of the contract. Third, lengthier contractual relationships require scope for flexibility, as output specifications and service standards can become obsolete during the life of the contract. Finally, since governments are effectively the provider of last resort for often very visible public goods, mechanisms to minimize the potential for opportunistic behavior from both parties and costly renegotiation need to be considered, notwithstanding the need for flexibility.

Concessions require the private sector to bear significant demand risk. The concessionaire operates and finances the maintenance of the asset but is generally not involved in its construction though may be responsible for maintenance, as discussed in Chapter 8. Usually the underlying infrastructure asset remains public property. For the private sector, user charges constitute the bulk of revenues and many concession contracts do not envisage any payment from the government and sometimes involve a payment to the government for the concession. This implies that the level of demand risk transferred to the private sector is relatively large.

A PPP contract, by transferring both construction and the operation of the infrastructure asset, including its maintenance, implies greater and sometimes longer private-sector participation compared to traditional procurement or a concession. Due to the infrastructure being new, the private sector may be reluctant to bear the demand risk without some co-financing or guarantees from government (Andres and Guasch, 2008).

PPPs potentially bring a number of advantages. Requiring outside financing entails greater project scrutiny and a better evaluation of the potential risks as well as better monitoring of the private contractor. Second, PPPs, by bundling the construction and the operation phases, create incentives for the private contractor to internalize operational and maintenance costs during the construction phase (Hart, 2003). The private partner will seek to identify the design and construction options that can potentially minimize the costs of construction and provide better service quality throughout the life of the project.[5]

But PPPs are not always easy to get right. The OECD Principles for Private Sector Participation in Infrastructure adopted in 2007 offer a checklist of policy issues to consider when setting up PPPs, including an assessment of the relative long-term costs and benefits and availability of finance, taking into account the pricing of risks transferred to the private operators and prudent fiscal treatment of risks remaining in the public domain; an enabling policy framework for investment; and the capacities at all levels of government to implement projects.

The experience of OECD countries shows that PPPs can obscure real spending and make government actions un-transparent, using off-budget financing, which can be potentially risky for fiscal management and sustainability.

SUPPLY-SIDE CONSIDERATIONS

In most countries, bank loans have traditionally been the most important private source of financing for infrastructure investment. However, deleveraging by banks after the crisis and new banking regulations are taking their toll on the ability of banks to provide credit for infrastructure development. The OECD estimates that the global volume of new project finance, about US$65 billion, was one-third lower in the first quarter of 2012 than in the previous year. In European countries, the fall in the number of announced deals was felt in both large transport infrastructure projects and also in the education sector, where deals are typically much smaller. To some extent, the fall in new project financing may be a temporary response to the ongoing crisis, but how much and how fast project financing recovers remains an open question.

Institutional investors, such as pension funds, insurance companies, and mutual funds, are another important source of private-sector financing for infrastructure. These investors currently hold over US$70 trillion in assets under management in OECD countries alone and, if emerging-market economies are taken into account, including their Sovereign Wealth Funds (with over US$4 trillion in assets), the potential pool of financing for infrastructure investment is considerably larger (OECD, 2010a). Pension funds alone have assets under management to the tune of US$29 trillion and annual inflows of about US$850 billion in OECD countries. However, the OECD estimates that less than 1 percent of the pension funds' investment portfolios is allocated directly to infrastructure projects.

Given their volume of assets under management, and the relatively low share of their investments in infrastructure, institutional investors are the main potential sources of financing for long-term infrastructure investment. However, there are limitations to the ability of institutional investors to redirect their asset portfolios to infrastructure projects, including not least regulatory restrictions on portfolio allocation and risk management considerations related to the tenor and currency composition of investment portfolios. Policy reforms to improve the regulatory framework for institutional investors, for instance by removing investment regulatory barriers and helping investors address long-term risks, would contribute to facilitating investment by institutional investors.[6]

Of course, not all countries have access to private-sector funds and capital markets to raise the necessary financing for infrastructure. In that case, foreign assistance constitutes an obvious instrument. However, the OECD estimates that the share of Overseas Development Finance (ODF) in total infrastructure investment is rather modest (OECD, 2011b) and, in a challenging budgetary environment in many donor countries, it is likely that ODF will come under pressure, stressing the need to harness private sources of finance even in countries that currently rely heavily on foreign assistance. Setting up an appropriate framework for private sector involvement, including capacity building, is therefore critical in those countries, and recent OECD estimates suggest that about one-fifth of ODF for infrastructure in Africa is allocated to setting up and/or improving these framework conditions.

Horizontal arrangements: dealing with scale effects in subnational provision

Although the disincentives for provision arising from scale effects and inter-jurisdictional externalities are conventionally dealt with through conditionality in the intergovernmental grants and transfer systems, there are alternative, more horizontal mechanisms to deal with these challenges. This is the case of the inter-municipal consortia that are currently in place in many countries and allow neighboring local governments to set up—most often on a voluntary basis—single- or multiple-purpose agencies and/or local enterprises to provide local services to residents of different jurisdictions.[7]

Such horizontal arrangements are widespread in Europe, especially for the provision of transport, urban waste management, water supply, fire fighting, and hospital administration by local governments, and arrangements vary considerably across countries (Hulst and van Montfort, 2007). Norway also has an interesting experience with joint ownership of power plants, which allows neighboring jurisdictions to cut costs in providing energy services. In Latin America, the Brazilian experience with inter-municipal consortia in the area of hospital administration is rather rare in the region. These horizontal arrangements are important tools for local governments to improve the cost-effectiveness of provision while satisfying demands for local autonomy.

It is true that such benefits could also potentially arise from the consolidation of local governments into larger units through mergers and amalgamations, for example, but international experience shows that in many cases there is considerable political and public opinion resistance to consolidation (Martínez-Vázquez and Gómez, 2008). In addition, the benefits of proximity between the government and the citizenry, which has much scope for making the government more responsive to local preferences and needs and for strengthening social control over government operations, would also likely be lost through consolidations. Weighing the benefits and costs of alternative governance arrangements is of course an empirical question, but institutional arrangements change only slowly and the structure of local governments, while far from immutable, is not often amenable to experimentation.[8]

Conclusions

The need for infrastructure building, replacement, and updating is large worldwide. In the areas of electricity, telecoms, and water alone, investment requirements are estimated by the OECD at about 2.5 percent of world GDP per year through to 2030. To foot the bill, governments will need to mobilize budgetary resources while at the same time delivering medium-term fiscal consolidation to restore the sustainability of public finances in many OECD countries. Demands associated with health and long-term care in ageing OECD societies and for enhanced social protection in many developing and emerging-market economies will also put an increasingly heavy burden on government budgets.

Middle-tier and local administrations will bear the brunt of the pressures associated with growing demands for infrastructure. Subnational governments already carry out, and sometimes finance, the bulk of government investment—about two-thirds on average in the OECD area—a ratio that is unlikely to change in the years to come. To better prepare subnational governments for the challenge ahead, this chapter provided a general discussion on the factors affecting investment in infrastructure (with emphasis on fixed networks) that could serve as a framework for subnational intervention. The specific characteristics of the different financing modalities applicable to subnational governments were presented to highlight the challenges that are specific to subnational governments.

The central argument presented above is that, on the financing side, subnational governments will need to enhance their capacity to raise own revenue, to make the most of intergovernmental grants and transfers, and to mobilize private-sector funds, including by tapping capital markets, where permitted. In order to exploit fully the various financing options, subnational governments in many countries will need to strengthen their technical capacity to design and implement investment projects, as well as manage increasingly complex, multi-year budgets, especially when there is private sector involvement.

Making better use of user charges while addressing associated affordability and equity challenges can help ensure existing infrastructure is used efficiently and identify where more infrastructure investment is needed. User charges also generally offer more options for private-sector involvement; in particular, different types of concessions, franchise arrangements, and public-private partnerships for revenue-generating infrastructure services are amenable to private-sector co-financing. However, these forms of financing are not always suitable and the authorities need to assess the high upfront transaction costs that are typically incurred, and how risk is best allocated between the government and the private sector.

Where subnational administrations are important providers of infrastructure, better coordination mechanisms can help ensure that returns to scale are exploited and inter-jurisdictional spillovers are taken into account. In this context, decision-making frameworks that bring together subnational and central governments as well as other stakeholders could help increase the efficiency of investment.

Finally, in some cases, governments may need to rethink the boundaries of the state. Advances in technology, contracting, and regulation allow infrastructure, such as telecoms and much of energy, which was often provided by government, to migrate to the private sector. Setting the appropriate regulatory framework will be important for encouraging investment in these cases.

Table 5.2 Public investment across levels of government: OECD countries

Acquisition of fixed capital in percent of GDP, accrual basis, averages since 1995

	General government		*Different layers of government*					
			Central		*Middle-tier*		*Local*	
	Investment	*Total outlays*	*Investment*	*Total outlays*	*Investment*	*Total outlays*	*Investment*	*Total outlays*
Chile	1.4	20.5	1.2	20.5	–	–	0.2	2.6
Italy	0.6	47.8	–0.2	39.0	–	–	0.8	15.0
Japan	1.1	37.8	–	–	–	–	–	–
Spain	1.9	38.6	0.4	27.3	0.8	13.6	0.7	6.1
France	0.7	52.6	0.1	45.5	–	–	0.6	10.4
Mexico[1]	–	–	0.5	15.9	–	7.0	–	1.4
United Kingdom	0.5	42.0	0.0	38.9	–	–	0.5	12.1
Australia	0.6	34.5	0.1	25.3	0.4	13.9	0.2	2.3
Germany	–0.1	46.5	0.0	30.9	0.0	13.1	–0.1	7.2
Switzerland[1]	2.2	37.4	0.1	20.1	1.1	14.6	1.0	9.6
United States	1.2	36.3	0.1	21.0	–	–	–	–
Canada[1]	2.3	40.7	0.3	18.7	1.0	21.4	1.0	7.4

Source: International Monetary Fund (*Government Finance Statistics*).

Note
1 Cash basis.

Notes

1 This chapter was prepared for the workshop on "Infrastructure and Decentralization: A Memorial Conference in Honour of Dana Weist," organized by the International Centre for Public Policy, Andrew Young School, Georgia State University, and the World Bank, which took place in Atlanta, GA, on September 25–27, 2011. We are indebted to workshop participants, in particular Giorgio Brosio, Kent Eaton, Jonas Frank, Jorge Martínez-Vásquez, Paul Bernd Spahn, as well as Teresa Ter-Minassian, for helpful comments and discussions. The opinions expressed and arguments employed herein do not necessarily reflect the official views of the OECD or of the governments of its member countries.
2 This section draws on Sutherland *et al.* (2011).
3 The costs of congestions arise due to a number of factors. Businesses costs rise due to the extra time needed for travel and the greater unreliability of travel time. Individuals are not productive in traffic jams and with the prospect of spending considerable time commuting they may limit their geographical area of job search. The combination of these factors is likely to lower welfare and reduce long-term growth.
4 For example, Peru attempted to decentralize much of its road network to provincial and municipal governments but failed to provide financing for the associated recurrent expenditures, which resulted in a widespread deterioration of the network and ultimately recentralization. In Brazil, federal assistance is now provided to those states that have accepted to take on responsibility for maintaining federal roads in their jurisdictions.
5 By combining private sector innovation and financing as well as the sharing of risks in innovative ways, PPPs can represent value for money for the public sector and a fair deal for the private sector. The OECD estimates that there are about US$0.8 trillion worth of projects in operation under PPP arrangements in OECD countries.
6 It is in this context that the OECD launched in 2007 the OECD Principles for Private Sector Participation in Infrastructure.
7 The empirical evidence reported by de Mello and Lago-Peñas (2012) for Brazil and Spain suggest that the presence of economies of scale in service delivery provides incentives for subnational governments to provide services jointly.
8 For some recent empirical evidence on the benefits and costs of consolidation, see Steiner (2003) for Germany, Sorensen (2006) and Dafflon and Ruegg (2001) for Switzerland.

References

Andres, L. and J.L. Guasch (2008), "Negotiating and Renegotiating PPPs and Concessions," in G. Schwartz, A. Corbacho, and K. Funke (eds.), *Public Investment and Public-Private Partnership: Addressing Infrastructure Challenges and Managing Fiscal Risks*, International Monetary Fund, Washington, DC.

Araújo, S. and D. Sutherland (2010), "Public-private Partnerships and Investment in Infrastructure," *OECD Economics Department Working Papers*, No. 803, OECD, Paris.

Bardhan, P. and D. Mookherjee (2006), "Decentralisation and Accountability in Infrastructure Delivery in Developing Countries," *Economic Journal*, Vol. 116, pp. 101–117.

Chan, C., D. Forwood, H. Roper, and C. Sayers (2009), "Public Infrastructure Financing: An International Perspective," *Productivity Commission Staff Working Paper*, Canberra.

Chowdhury, S., F. Yamauchi, and R. Dewina (2007), "Governance Decentralisation and Infrastructure Provision in Indonesia," *JBIC Institute Working Paper*, No. 25, Japan Bank for International Cooperation, Tokyo.

Dafflon, B. and J. Ruegg (2001), *Réorganiser les communes, créer l'agglomération*, University of Fribourg, Switzerland.

de Mello, L. (2000), "Fiscal Decentralisation and Intergovernmental Fiscal Relations: A Cross-Country Analysis," *World Development*, Vol. 28, pp. 365–380.

de Mello, L. (2001), "Fiscal Decentralisation and Borrowing Costs: The Case of Local Governments," *Public Finance Review*, Vol. 29, pp. 108–138.

de Mello, L. (2010), "Europe," in *The State of Local Government Finances: Are We Ready to Face the Demand?*, Second Global Report on Decentralisation and Local Democracy, United Cities and Local Governments, Barcelona, pp. 149–188.

de Mello, L. (2012), "Fiscal Decentralisation and Public Investment: The Experience of Latin America," in G. Brosio and J.P. Jiménez (eds.), *Decentralisation and Reform: Improving Intergovernmental Relations*, Edward Elgar, Cheltenham.

de Mello, L. and S. Lago-Peñas (2012), "Local Government Cooperation for Joint Provision: The Experiences of Brazil and Spain with Inter-Municipal Consortia," *Working Paper*, No. 1218, Andrew Young School of Policy Studies, Georgia State University, Atlanta, GA.

Demsetz, H. (1968), "Why Regulate Utilities," *Journal of Law and Economics*, Vol. 11, pp. 55–65.

Estache, A. and S. Sinha (1995), "Does Decentralization Increase Spending on Infrastructure?," *Policy Research Working Paper*, No. 1457, World Bank, Washington, DC.

Esteller, A. and A. Solé (2005), "Does Decentralization Improve the Efficiency in the Allocation of Public Investment? Evidence from Spain," *Working Paper*, No. 2005/5, Institut d'Economia de Barcelona.

Faguet, J.-P. (2004), "The Effects of Decentralisation on Public Investment: Evidence and Four Lessons from Bolivia and Colombia," *Working Paper*, No. 62, Crisis States Research Centre, LSE, London.

Hart, C. (2003), "Incomplete Contracts and Public Ownership: Remarks and an Application to Public-Private Partnerships," *Economic Journal*, Vol. 119, pp. 69–76.

Hulst, R. and A. van Montfort (2007), "Inter-municipal Cooperation: A Widespread Phenomenon", in R. Hulst and A. van Montfort (eds.), *Inter-municipal Cooperation in Europe*, Springer, Dordrecht, pp. 1–21.

Hulten, C.R. and R.M. Schwab (1997), "A Fiscal Federalism Approach to Infrastructure Policy," *Regional Science and Urban Economics*, Vol. 27, pp. 139–159.

Humplick, F. and A. Estache (1995), "Does Decentralization Improve Infrastructure Performance?," in A. Estache (ed.), *Decentralizing Infrastructure: Advantages and Limitations*, World Bank Discussion Paper Series, No. 290, World Bank, Washington, DC.

International Energy Agency (IEA) (2010), *World Energy Outlook*, IEA, Paris.

International Energy Agency (IEA) (2011), "Energy for All: Financing Access for the Poor," *World Energy Outlook*, IEA, Paris.

Kappeler, A. and T. Välilä (2008), "Fiscal Federalism and the Composition of Public Investment in Europe," *European Journal of Political Economy*, Vol. 24, pp. 562–570.

Keen, M. and M. Marchand (1997), "Fiscal Competition and the Pattern of Public Spending," *Journal of Public Economics*, Vol. 66, pp. 33–53.

Kozluk, T. (2010), "How the Transport System Can Contribute to Better Economic and Environmental Outcomes in the Netherlands," *OECD Economics Department Working Paper*, No. 804, OECD, Paris.

Martínez-Vázquez, J. (2010), "Latin America," in *The State of Local Government Finances: Are We Ready to Face the Demand?*, Second Global Report on Decentralisation and Local Democracy, United Cities and Local Governments, Barcelona, pp. 189–230.

Martínez-Vázquez, J. and J. Gómez (2008), "El Tamaño Importa: La Estructura Vertical de Gobierno y La Gestión del Gasto Público Local," Working Paper, No. 2008/05, CAF.

OECD (2007), *Infrastructure to 2030: Mapping Policy for Electricity, Water and Transport*, OECD, Paris.

OECD (2008), *Public-Private Partnerships: In Pursuit of Risk Sharing and Value for Money*, OECD, Paris.

OECD (2010a), "Pension Funds Investment in Infrastructure: A Survey," in *International Futures Programme, Project on Strategic Transport Infrastructure to 2030*, OECD, Paris.

OECD (2010b), *Managing Water for All, An OECD Perspective on Pricing and Financing*, OECD, Paris.

OECD (2011a), OECD *Regional Outlook*, OECD, Paris.

OECD (2011b), *Mapping Support for Africa's Infrastructure Investment*, OECD, Paris.

OECD (2011c), *Making the Most of Public Investment in a Tight Fiscal Environment*, OECD, Paris.

Romp, W. and J. De Haan (2007), "Public Capital and Economic Growth: A Critical Survey," *Perpektiven der Wirtschaftspolitik*, Vol. 8, No. S1, pp. 6–52.

Sorensen, R. (2006), "Local Government Consolidations: The Impact of Political Transaction Costs," *Public Choice*, Vol. 127, pp. 75–95.

Steiner, R. (2003), "The Causes, Spread and Effects of Intermunicipal Cooperation and Municipal Mergers in Switzerland," *Public Management Review*, Vol. 5, pp. 551–571.

Sutherland, D., S. Araújo, B. Égert, and T. Kozluk (2011), "Public Policies and Investment in Network Infrastructure," *OECD Economic Studies*, pp. 161–183.

World Bank (2012), *Investing to Invest*, World Bank, Washington, DC.

6 Capital infrastructure and equity objectives in decentralized systems

Jorge Martínez-Vázquez and Andrey Timofeev

Introduction: issues and motivation

Equity concerns about decentralization are particularly acute in the case of capital infrastructure services. This is because the share of subnational governments in total capital expenditures of a country is typically twice their share in total recurrent expenditures (Martínez-Vázquez and Timofeev, 2012). This is true for developing and developed countries. While on average the subnational share of capital expenditures is 60 percent, the share of subnational governments in recurrent expenditures is 30 percent (Figure 6.1). In addition to the potential disparities in the quantity and quality of public services offered to residents, to the extent that the availability of public infrastructure determines the attractiveness of a locality for doing business, unless properly addressed, fiscal disparities in the stock of infrastructure can feed back through different levels of private investments into economic disparities, creating a vicious circle for less endowed subnational jurisdictions. For that reason central governments might desire to implement even higher degrees of equalization for productive economic infrastructure than for social infrastructure.[1]

To the extent that the main objective of intergovernmental grants, and more in particular equalization transfers, is to ensure the "adequate" financing of decentralized functions, it is easy to argue convincingly that this adequacy should be assessed in terms of the entire expenditure needs, including capital infrastructure. Generally, in most decentralized systems the need to provide equal financing abilities, taking into account the different fiscal capacities of subnational units, to provide a standard basket of public services is not questioned. However, this broad consensus in the theory and practice of fiscal federalism has been focused on the recurrent expenditures needed to finance those public services. Nevertheless, it is pretty immediate that most of these services cannot be adequately provided without the existence of the complementary infrastructure inputs (e.g., recurrent expenditures for teacher salaries, textbooks, etc. need to be complemented by school buildings to deliver education services.).

While the system of grants should balance available resources with the entirety of capital and non-capital costs in the provision of subnational services, it is a separate and unresolved question in the intergovernmental grants literature

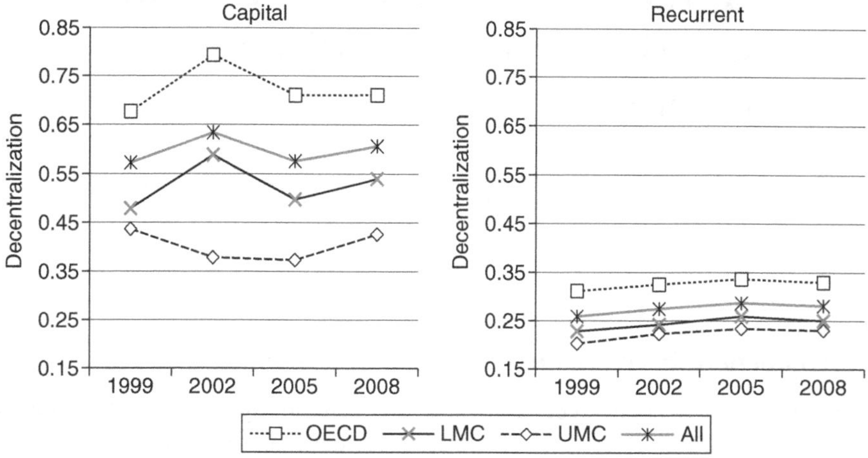

Figure 6.1 Decentralization of recurrent and capital expenditures, 1997–2008 (source: author's computations based on Martínez-Vázquez and Timofeev, 2012).

Note
The sample includes 39 countries, out of which 6 are lower-middle-income, 10 upper-middle-income, 2 non-OECD high-income, and 21 OECD countries.

whether capital financing needs should be arranged separately in an earmarked manner. On average, explicit capital grants account for only about one-third of net subnational investments and this share ranges from less than one-fifth in lower-middle counties to over a half in OECD countries (Figure 6.2). In particular, in the transitional countries capital grants have played a smaller role in the financing of local infrastructure than own current and capital revenues of local governments (the latter often from the sale of assets), and borrowing; in particular, borrowing has been more prevalent in Central Europe (Swianiewicz, 2004).

Conceptually, there are potential efficiency losses associated with the different treatment of operating and capital cost needs of subnational governments; for example, it can lead to deferred maintenance. The practice of budget unity and integrity allows for establishing the optimal level of activities needed to maintain or replace public infrastructure assets according to their originally contemplated serviceability. In particular, proper maintenance can avoid the capital costs of replacement for the optimal period of time. On the other hand, under separation of capital budgets and funding, local managers might try to save on operating costs by not performing (or deferring) maintenance at the proper time without perceiving, or trying to shift to another level of government, the incurred capital costs of this strategy. Furthermore, depending on the practices of upper-level governments, in some countries, proper maintenance of capital infrastructure may reduce the chances of receiving funds for capital rehabilitation, as the practice of allocation of grants may be based on the physical shape of assets.[2]

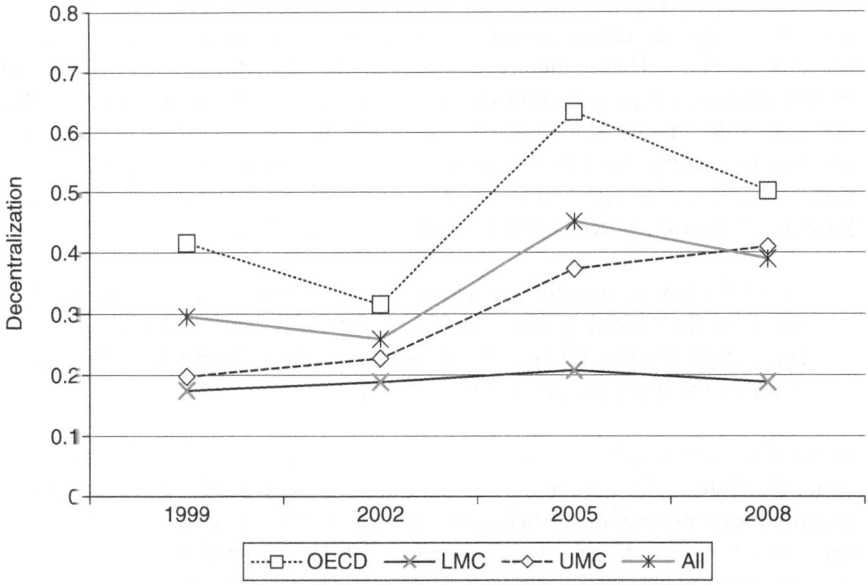

Figure 5.2 Capital grants as a share of subnational capital investments, 1997–2008 (source: author's computations based on Martínez-Vázquez and Timofeev, 2012).

Note
The sample includes 33 countries, out of which 1 is low-income, 7 are lower-middle-income, 7 upper-middle-income, 2 non-OECD high-income, and 16 OECD countries.

When higher-level governments build local infrastructure rather than providing capital grants to local government, this can aggravate rather than help the fiscal conditions of the "lucky" recipient. The separation of decisions among different levels of government for building infrastructure and for operating it has been traditionally interpreted as a main cause of the poor physical shape of assets in the Soviet Union (Wallich, 1994). For a more recent example, in Germany, the states (*Länder*) prescribe hospital capacity levels and finance investment expenditures but do not assume the operating costs or cover any potential hospital losses. As a result, the state politicians have an incentive to overbuild hospital capacity and claim political credit for employment creation while settling local governments with the bill for operating costs, which over the years can be a multifold of the construction costs (Wurzel, 1999). Thus, the central government intervention does not only create the agency problem but also removes the life-time costing of facilities from making investment decisions. There are of course many cases of centrally driven—or foreign donor driven—infrastructure investments in developing countries that have been abandoned because of subnational governments' inability to operate and maintain them on a sustainable basis.

On the other hand, political economy considerations might require going beyond accounting for capital expenditure needs in determining the total amount of equalization transfers by also specifically earmarking some part of these transfers for capital investment purposes. As underinvestment is essentially a form of dissaving, the same moral hazards can be present here as in the case of subnational borrowing.[3] That is the capital costs can be shifted to the successive governments or even next generations of local residents, which violates the so-called "Golden Rule." Thus, Ahmad and Searle (2006, p. 389) argue that in many low- and middle-income countries "scarcity of financial resources and popular pressure to use them for immediate current spending may leave little for capital formation." Similarly, according to Boothe (2007, p. 192),

> one of the key reasons for advocating a move to accrual accounting has been the view that during periods of deficit reduction, governments using cash accounting simply replace fiscal deficits with infrastructure deficits by ignoring the depreciation of public capital.

In addition, Moak and Hillhouse (1975) among many others suggest that, when under fiscal strain, local governments tend to postpone capital projects rather than expenditures for operating agencies. Similar evidence from surveys of coping strategies of US cities was reported by Pagano (1993). Earmarking of some part of intergovernmental grants for capital investments can mitigate these risks.

There may also be other significant practical matters that may require a separate treatment of capital infrastructure needs. For example, as we discuss in more length in the next section, addressing disparities in capital infrastructure can require considering differences in access to borrowing sources and the costs of borrowing; these considerations bring inter-temporal issues that can be hard to address explicitly and correctly in the context of general equalization grants (traditionally focused on recurrent expenditure needs).

All in all, in this chapter we argue that disparities in the availability of and need for capital infrastructure matter for fiscal equity. However, we believe that a proper discussion of this topic should be framed in terms of the incidence of outputs and outcomes of public services produced with this infrastructure. Infrastructure alone cannot be assigned any policy priority independent of programs and services that utilize these capital assets. Once we place this discussion in the framework of access to and quality of public services, we then move to the question of the best form of policy intervention, which can be specific to capital inputs. Thus, we consider both pros and cons of addressing infrastructure disparities in an earmarked fashion—in the line of conditional capital grants still used in many countries—as opposed to incorporating capital infrastructure disparities into a general-purpose equalization grant—which is not explicitly done in many countries. The rest of this chapter is organized as follows. In the next section we make a normative case for addressing infrastructure needs in intergovernmental arrangements. Then, we examine how and to what extent those capital disparities are addressed in practice using three country cases (Peru, Russia, and Spain). Next, we discuss some policy implications. We conclude with a summary of the issues and final comments.

The normative case for addressing disparities in capital infrastructure needs

The general case for addressing disparities in capital infrastructure needs can be built around three different dimensions having to do respectively with:

- i disparities in infrastructure costs;
- ii disparities in borrowing costs;
- iii (historical) disparities in capital endowments.

Furthermore, the treatment of these disparities in infrastructure costs and endowments will also vary depending on the balance of competing government objectives, including economic efficiency (efficient taxation and geographic mobility and location of factors of production), internalization of externality spillovers, national solidarity, and merit goods.

In this section, we apply these policy objectives (efficiency, internalizing externalities, etc.) to the discussion of separate aspects of infrastructure disparities (disparities in endowments, construction costs, and borrowing costs).

To facilitate the extraction of policy implications of the normative discussions in this section, we will conclude this chapter by introducing a two-dimensional matrix summarizing the main points along policy objectives in columns and the aspects of infrastructure disparities in rows.

However, in order to make the discussions easier to follow and lay the foundation for the policy implications, immediately below we start by providing more details on the reasoning and justification behind each of the aforementioned policy objectives.

Understanding the implications of policy objectives for capital infrastructure

Pursuing efficiency: trends in tax assignment and revenue sharing. Even in the most decentralized countries, local jurisdictions cannot operate like sovereign states because they are constrained by national legislation, which among other things, limits taxing and borrowing powers of local governments. As economic development has made economic activities increasingly footless, there has been a trend toward centralizing the taxation of activities at the national level in order to reduce (tax) distortions to the decision of business location. Even in the taxation of consumption, the trend over the last decades has been the substitution of the national VAT for local sales taxes. As a result, throughout the world the bulk of revenue-raising powers has been concentrated at the national level. To accommodate the mismatch between revenue sources and spending obligations, central governments have been providing grants to subnational governments. The sharing of revenue from national taxes with subnational governments thus has become a common remedy for vertical imbalances, where revenue sources available to subnational governments as a group do not correspond to their expenditure responsibilities. Furthermore, after some countries have experienced episodes of macroeconomic instability following unsustainable subnational borrowing, as was the case in Latin America in the 1980s and 1990s, many countries have also concentrated borrowing powers at the national level.

Pursuing efficiency: fiscal equalization to address horizontal imbalances. Horizontal imbalances occur when the spatial distribution of local revenue sources and fiscal capacity do not match the spatial distribution of local government expenditures and expenditure needs. National governments generally attempt to mitigate these horizontal imbalances both on the grounds of social solidarity, such as equal access to some basic services independently of the place of residence, and economic efficiency, such as preventing fiscally induced migration and misallocation of economic resources. In relation to expenditure needs, economic efficiency concerns emerge in the situation where benefits from local services vary across different population strata rather than being uniform for all local residents. In this case, it has been suggested, for example, that an efficiency-inducing grant formula should take into account the differences in the proportion of entitled population (e.g., school-age children) in various localities.

Compensation for the presence of spillovers or "externalities" between jurisdictions. When local governments are left to make their own decisions, they may under-spend on certain services which may report substantial additional benefits to third parties, such as neighboring local governments. For example, sewage treatment by an upstream municipality benefits residents of downstream municipalities sharing the same river basin. Economic theory suggests that local governments should receive a unit (Pigovian) subsidy equal to the marginal value of the inter-jurisdictional spillovers created in the provision of one unit of local public services. Based on this rationale one would expect such subsidies to increase with the magnitude of external benefits but not with the local costs required to produce these benefits. On the contrary, under reciprocal externalities per unit subsidies should be inversely related to the unit costs in the recipient locality so that the national government could induce maximum externalities per unit of national grants.

Funding national priorities or "merit goods." The concept of merit (or demerit) good is mostly related to the situation when societal values override personal choice even though no spillover of benefits occurs. In particular, this includes paternalism in distribution, when society cares more about the distribution of certain goods, such as basic necessities of life, health, and citizenship rights than about income distribution in general. Similar to the case of externalities, economic theory suggests that conditional grants could stimulate local spending on such goods or services. For merit goods involving equal access or an assured universal minimum, such conditional grants should take into account differences in the local costs and might also require determining the adequate level of funding in order to secure this assured minimum.

The relative importance of these competing policy objectives defines the nature of a particular grant scheme. Therefore, the actual practice of intergovernmental transfers, further explored at the end of this chapter, might show various degrees of mitigation of infrastructure disparities when some of these other objectives override government action.

A simple theoretical framework for the optimal level of capital inputs. In order to be able to superimpose inter-jurisdictional disparities in infrastructure over the aforementioned set of policy objectives, let us assume for a moment that the balance of these policy objectives implies a certain level S of public service outcome in a given jurisdiction. Then, under standard cost-minimization, this fixed level of service outcome will translate into different optimal levels of capital inputs, depending on local service load factors (level of service output required to achieve a given level of outcome), and the relative costs of capital and non-capital inputs in a jurisdiction. Thus for a Cobb-Douglas technology, Wang *et al.* (2011) derive the following functional form for the optimal level of capital inputs:

$$K^* = \left(\frac{\beta}{1-\beta} \frac{P_O}{\beta P_K} \right)^{1-\beta} \alpha^{\frac{1}{\tau}} (bSN^{\alpha} Z^{\varphi})^{\frac{1}{\gamma\tau}} \qquad (1)$$

where
a and b are constant parameters;
τ captures returns to scale in production (increasing when $\tau > 1$)
β represents the cost share of capital;
P_K is the cost of capital inputs;
P_O is the cost of non-capital (operational) inputs;
γ is the elasticity capturing differences between technical economies of scale and economies of quality scale;
α and φ are elasticities measuring the impact of population size N and service load factors Z (e.g., proportion of disadvantage students) on the service outcome.

From equation (1) it is obvious that the optimal level of capital inputs is inversely related to the cost of capital P_K but positively related to the cost of non-capital inputs P_O. As expected, the optimal level of capital inputs is increasing with the targeted service outcome level S, population size N, and service load factors Z. It can be shown that these relationships are not specific to the Cobb–Douglas technology but also hold for a more general Constant Elasticity of Substitution (CES) production function.

Making the case for addressing disparities in capital infrastructure

Disparities in infrastructure costs. Overall, the theory of fiscal equalization presents a rather limited case for compensating subnational governments through grants for the presence of higher costs of producing subnational public services, as opposed to making the case of compensating for differences in service needs. However, this theoretical position contrasts markedly with the actual practice of intergovernmental grants, where adjustments for cost differences are very common outside North America.[4] But, such gaps between theory and practice are not unprecedented in public finance, as illustrated by decades of neglecting the VAT in the theory of public finance until long after it had been introduced in practice. In the case of intergovernmental grants, this gap is partially explained by the fact that the discussion in the economic theory of equalization has focused on the efficiency objective while in the practice of grant design cost disparities would appear to be addressed for reasons having to do with the objectives of social solidarity and merit goods.

Thus, if for example the merit goods objective were to require a uniform service outcome in all localities, then according to optimal production theory in equation (1), this would translate into lower levels of infrastructure in jurisdictions with higher costs of infrastructure. However, even this lower level of infrastructure might require higher levels of capital outlays if the elasticity of substitution of non-capital inputs for capital inputs is not high enough to offset a higher unit cost of capital. For example, for a Cobb–Douglas technology, which has a unitary elasticity of factor substitution, Wang *et al.* (2011) derive the following functional form for the optimal level of capital expenditures:

$$KE^* = P_K^{\beta}\left(\frac{\beta}{1-\beta}P_O\right)^{1-\beta}\alpha^{\frac{1}{\tau}}(bSN^{\propto}Z^{\varphi})^{\frac{1}{\gamma\tau}} \tag{2}$$

From this equation it is clear that, with a unitary elasticity of factor substitution, the optimal capital outlays increase with the costs of capital despite using fewer capital inputs. Thus, in order to assure a targeted outcome level of services under the Cobb–Douglas technology, intergovernmental grants have to accommodate higher capital outlays in localities with higher costs of capital. However, this is not necessarily the case for other technologies. In particular, for a more general CES production function, capital outlays can be decreasing in capital costs when the elasticity of substitution as well as the relative price and share of capital are sufficiently high: $P_K/P_O>(1-\beta)$.

One has to note that for any CES technology, optimal capital outlays have to increase with the service <u>need</u> parameters (Z) if we want to achieve a given outcome target of S. Furthermore, for this given outcome target S, capital outlays have to increase with the overall level of input costs (as opposed to the relative cost of capital). However, if the objective of intergovernmental policies is the efficient location of mobile resources, then the service target S might be set lower in jurisdictions with high costs, including higher costs of infrastructure. In this sense, Boadway (2004, p. 238) points out that, for a benevolent social planner, addressing cost differences across decentralized jurisdictions should be approached the same way as inter-local cost differences in a unitary country:

> To the extent that some regions have higher costs of provision than others, difficult problems arise for equalization. In a unitary state, if different regions have different costs, different levels of public services will generally be provided. The equity advantages of more equal provision will have to be

> set against the efficiency costs. Thus, the level of public services is typically lower in remote and scarcely populated areas than in urban areas, but how much lower involves a policy judgment.

While this argument appears reasonable, to our knowledge no formal model has been developed to feature such a trade-off between economic efficiency and fiscal equity. One would expect that analytically it should be no less feasible than modeling the trade-off between equity and efficiency in taxation.

The limited case for cost equalization ever developed in fiscal equalization models is entirely based on the existence of inter-jurisdictional externalities (Albouy, 2012). Concerning the externalities induced from the mobility of population, equalization grants should compensate for the loss of economies of scale from a marginal out-migrant only to the extent that such economies of scale are present in the production of local government services (that is, based on the "publicness" of local government services). This is because private benefits from local services are already fully internalized in the individual's migration decision. However, most empirical estimates of the congestion (or crowding) parameter for local government services imply the majority of these services are highly congestible and therefore they are more like private goods than pure public good (Albouy, 2012). Therefore, given the empirical findings related to the "privateness" of most local government services, there is little need from that perspective for intergovernmental grants to take into account differences in local costs.

Only very recently, Albouy (2012) has formally modeled differences in the unit costs of a public service provision in addition to differences in the levels of its congestion. In his model, Albouy (2012) allows the unit cost of the public good provision to vary among regions due to differences in their productivity. Thus, per capita costs of the public service provision are equal to pG/N, where p is the marginal rate of transformation of the private good (a numeraire) into a public good. At the same time per capita benefit S from the public good output G is a function of population size N: $S=G/N^{\alpha}$, where α is the extent of congestion as in the previous literature. The derived difference in the equalization grant due to the differences in expenditure needs looks like $(1-\alpha)*(p_1G_1/N_1-p_2G_2/N_2)$. Thus, it appears that efficiency-enhancing grants should take into account differences in the local costs of producing the public good.

However, this compensation term disappears in the case of complete congestability (lack of publicness) of the public service with $\alpha=1$. Furthermore, the derived equalization grant takes into account per capita costs of the local public goods provided at the levels which are *optimal* from the social planner's perspective. As Boadway (2004) conjectures that it would be optimal to have a lower level of public service provision in a high-cost region, then assessed expenditure needs p_iG_i/N_i can be higher or lower in a high-cost region depending on the interplay of p_i and G_i. Albouy (2012, p. 827) makes the following general interpretation of the formula for efficiency-inducing grants derived from his model:

> The transfer formula implies that it is inefficient to subsidize a household's location based on the cost of private or public goods. Neither [of these prices appear in the grant formula] independently of total expenditures p_iG_i which matters only for the public-good externality. Thus variation in these prices due either to factor costs or production efficiency are to be ignored. When prices are set efficiently, they represent the opportunity cost of scarce factors for producing tradable output. Subsidizing households to live in areas where providing local services costs more ignores these opportunity costs and leads to inefficient use of scarce factors.

Apart from economies of scale, the only theoretically conjectured case for efficiency-inducing equalization grants to be positively related to local infrastructure needs is due to differences in the composition of population in terms of entitlement to various capital-intensive services. However, this conjecture articulated by Boadway (2004) has not been formally derived in the theoretical literature. In this sense, it needs to be pointed out that taking into account the different segments of the population eligible for government services has been one of the key features in the design of intergovernmental grants throughout the world, mainly in the pursuit of social solidarity and merit goods, as we mentioned before.

All in all, even with a uniform standard of service, economic efficiency appears to generally require lower level of infrastructure in localities with higher costs of capital. However, even with this lower level of infrastructure, high-cost localities are likely to have higher capital expenditure needs unless the elasticity of substitution of non-capital for capital inputs is sufficiently high. For services where a uniform outcome standard is not an absolute government objective, efficiency considerations might require lower levels of service in high-cost localities in addition to producing those services with less capital.

Disparities in borrowing costs. Up to this point, in our discussion we have assumed that once a local government has determined the optimal level of capital inputs required to produce a given service standard with least costs, it can procure (i.e., lease) those assets (e.g., classrooms) from the market at a rate P_K. As discussed in Chapter 5 of this collection, in some sectors this is becoming increasingly feasible through various forms of private-public partnership. However, as of today, we can generally say that for most countries and most sectors, the bulk of capital infrastructure cannot be leased from the private sector. This is due to the usual risks associated with dealing with a single buyer and the high specificity of capital assets that have little alternative use. Therefore, the government typically has to assume all the risks and costs of creating these capital assets. Sometimes, these assets are built by one government agency, such as a government building authority, and leased to another government agency, such as the department of education. However, even these arrangements do not change the overall situation with the risks and costs, other than pooling the risks and spreading the fixed costs of managing the associated portfolios of capital assets and liabilities to entire government as opposed to a single agency unit.[5]

While public finance experts agree that government spending on recurrent (local) goods and services should be met by revenues from taxes and other recurrent revenue sources, the "golden rule" for (local) government borrowing states that it is proper for (local) governments to borrow for capital projects (Musgrave, 1939). As discussed in Box 6.1, the ability of local governments to borrow as part of an efficient system of intergovernmental fiscal relations is important on normative grounds.

Box 6.1 The efficiency gains from borrowing for local capital infrastructure

To a large extent, the efficiency of decentralized government finance rests on the benefit principle, which requires that the costs of public services be covered with taxes paid by those who benefit from these services. However, if current tax receipts were spent toward some capital project that brings fruits for many years ahead, such as a new road or a water treatment plant, the benefit principle would be violated in an inter-temporal sense across time periods. Unless corrected, this "inter-temporal spillover" of benefits would lead to the under-provision of local public capital goods. This is because current residents might not be willing to pay the full cost of the project while receiving only a fraction of its benefits.

Debt financing has the potential to rectify this situation by spreading the costs of building a facility over the entire period during which the benefits from this investment are received, and with future taxes being used to repay the loan taken in the earlier period.

Borrowing can also help address other issues such as the lumpiness of investments. For instance, while funding a piped water scheme from recurrent local resources may prove prohibitive, borrowing could help put in place a sustainable, fee-based public water scheme.

It is important to realize that within any country, with its own peculiar financing institutions, the ability to borrow is likely to differ markedly across subnational governments. Local government borrowing from competitive capital markets—either through private financial institutions or directly from the bond markets—requires the local authority to be creditworthy by demonstrating its financial ability to repay its loan over time and technical capacity to manage its debt. As such, the very nature of capital markets assures that local government borrowing is likely to exacerbate horizontal imbalances: credit markets provide larger and wealthier regional and local governments with access to capital funding, while smaller and poorer local governments are typically excluded altogether from access to capital.

However, the issue of inadequate fiscal capacity of poorer jurisdictions is not specific to debt financing. Without being addressed with effective remedies, insufficient fiscal capacity affects the ability of local governments to finance their operating costs just the same way it does affect their ability to borrow and repay their debt. In fact, debt financing is only a tool for managing the flow of income and expenditures across time periods. If the flow of income is overall inadequate to finance the flow of expenditures rather than there being a mismatch of these two flows across time, then debt financing by itself cannot improve this situation. However, when a decentralized fiscal system is able to effectively address fiscal disparities by equalizing fiscal capacity and expenditure needs, including infrastructure needs, this equalization should allow local governments to generate the necessary surpluses to cover amortization and interest on their debt in addition to maintenance of the associated capital assets. Stable and predictable intergovernmental equalization and other grants contribute significantly to building the creditworthiness of local governments, if not just the same way as stable revenues from their own sources. Other arrangements can facilitate the access to credit by poorer jurisdictions. An example may be the creation of a financial intermediary that borrows at lower costs in the markets and on-lends to smaller jurisdictions. Another example is provided by the practice of intercepting subnational government sources of revenues; the ability to intercept intergovernmental transfers can be seen by creditors as the most secure collateral.[6]

According to the theory of fiscal equalization, efficiency-inducing grants should take into account disparities in source-based taxes and local rents. Concerning disparities in residence-based taxes, the disparities that should be equalized are only those determined by the differences in the composition of residents in those jurisdictions in terms of their income-earning abilities, but not those based on their actual income, as for example determined by local income-generating opportunities. These normative prescriptions for fiscal equalization have been derived using a single-period model. Conceptually these arguments could be extended to a multi-period setting so that a migration decision by a local resident is determined by the present value of future revenues and costs. However, this introduces one additional aspect of disparities, namely the costs of inter-temporal smoothing or borrowing costs (Herrero-Alcalde *et al.*, 2011). Thus, for two jurisdictions with identical streams of future revenues, the one with higher borrowing costs will have a lower present value of its revenues.

Alternatively, one can look at disparities in borrowing capacities from the cost side. The normative framework above assumes that the use of infrastructure brings on the local government a cost of P_K for each unit of capital inputs. This cost is either explicit in the case of leasing this infrastructure from a private supplier or implicit if it is built and maintained by the local government itself. Regardless of the arrangements, the cost of infrastructure P_K is essentially made of the same elements: cost of financing (or opportunity cost) i, depreciation of the asset (equal to the amortization of the loan principal) d, and maintenance required to preserve existing assets in the serviceable form m. Depreciation and maintenances cost $(d+m)$ can vary with local conditions but should not depend on who supplies these capital assets.[7] By contrast, for a given provider, the cost of financing should not vary across different localities within the same capital market but can vary among suppliers, in particular among local governments. Therefore, depreciation and maintenances $(d+m)$ should be treated by equalization policies the same way as other costs of public services. However, the financing/opportunity costs of capital are special in a sense that the cost and availability of financing can be different for the central government than for a local government. Standard tools of bridging such misalignments include earmarked subsidies and on-lending with adjusted interest rates.[8]

Even when being able to generate revenue surpluses from their own sources and stable intergovernmental transfers, smaller jurisdictions might not be served by private markets because of the small size of their financial needs and relatively higher associated transactions costs. This suggests that policy makers need to consider alternative means of funding capital infrastructure in local authorities that lack access to capital markets. However, capital grants are only one of several alternatives to private sector borrowing for financing local capital development in smaller jurisdictions, as we discuss immediately below.

As already advanced above, intermediary financial institutions specializing in local governments can help break the vicious circle in which smaller less-developed localities are restricted in funding infrastructure investments because of lack in capacity to manage borrowing at reasonable costs. Although international practices vary substantially between countries, an intermediary institution can borrow in its own name at lower costs, sometimes with the backing of the central government, and use the proceeds to purchase debt instruments of local governments; this type of intermediary is known as a bond bank. Alternatively, financial intermediaries that serve local governments might assemble and repackage municipal debt instruments and make them available to the market (e.g., create local bond pools). Such intermediaries can provide access to capital markets for smaller governments that otherwise would not get credit or allow them to obtain credit at lower costs. In particular, financial intermediation brings savings on the fixed costs of debt issuance thanks to standardized borrowing procedures and documentation, and technical assistance to local governments with capital planning, cash flow projections, and pre-structuring of loan packages (Freire and Petersen, 2004). While this intermediation is provided for a fee, the costs associated with such intermediation for small-scale projects are generally less than the costs of bond issuance.[9]

In practice, financial intermediation, especially when run by the national government, can have its own problems. Besides creating moral hazards, if the "soft" financial assistance from the center is institutionalized, it can also create a culture of long-term dependency and impede capital market development. Therefore, as a practical compromise, complementing borrowing with equalizing capital grants would allow the grants component to be means tested, thus representing an upfront payment of future gaps between debt service costs and revenue collections at some reasonable rates. Such upfront grants can be superior to subsidized interest rates and operating subsidies as they bring transparency and eliminate the need for future surveillance and administration (Varley, 2001). The allocation of grants can be based on affordability analyses, targeting those projects that would become affordable only if subsidized with a partial grant.

Petchey and MacDonald (2007) argue that capital grants can be used as a "short-term option" in transition and developing countries until subnational governments get access to capital markets, tax handles, or predictable intergovernmental revenue. Furthermore, they argue that under the aforementioned constrains, capital grants can be used as a short-cut for ensuring equal access to public services that have capital as the main input (e.g., transport). While this might be a valid point in some specific settings, it is not uncommon in developing countries to see local governments not having cash to provide access to education even at a "school under a tree" at the backdrop of aborted government construction sites and idle pieces of infrastructure, which were found to be of little use upon completion. For a broad range of public services, allowing some degree of substitution between capital and non-capital inputs, the flexibility of, for example a sectoral block grant, could significantly enhance the chances of local governments to provide a larger access to these services than conditional grants earmarked to capital use or specific infrastructure projects. Indeed, regardless of central government objectives for financing subnational infrastructure, these objectives should apply to both construction and maintenance of such assets. This point was eloquently made by Hulten and Schwab (1997, p. 150):

> We can increase that flow [of services from the stock of public capital] by either adding to the stock through investment or by improving the stock through maintenance. If the federal government is interested in providing the proper incentives to lower levels of government, it is hard to see why it should encourage state and local governments to invest in new capital but not encourage them to maintain that capital once it has been put in place.

Disparities in capital endowments. Up to this point, we have assumed that local governments start with a clean slate when determining the optimal level of capital inputs and then lease or build this optimal infrastructure required to achieve a given service outcome level. In practice, localities already own some stock of infrastructure, which can be above or below the optimally required level. One of the open conceptual questions in the design of grant mechanisms is whether intergovernmental policies should address disparities in the accumulated stock of physical capital (sometimes referred to as "capital backlog" or "capital infrastructure gap") relative to some target level.

If the existing local infrastructure throughout the national territory is considered a true local good that has been built under optimal arrangements (so that those who currently enjoy the benefits also contribute to paying off the accumulated debt), there is no need to address this disparity with intergovernmental grants. Indeed, fiscally induced migration—a well-accepted justification for the introduction of equalization grants to avoid this type of migration—will not arise here because the incentives to migrate into infrastructure-rich jurisdictions will be offset by the disincentives of higher taxation necessary to pay off the associated debt incurred onto in the past to finance the infrastructure.

However, if the disparity in infrastructure resulted from some exogenous decision, e.g., discriminatory policies of the Apartheid regime in South Africa, this type of disparity is not equitable and indeed can cause fiscally driven migration and therefore the misallocation of population across the national territory. In the case of income-generating assets,[10] this would lead to disparities among localities in capital revenues accruing to different jurisdictions, which will need to be addressed with equalization grants according to the existing principles of fiscal equalization theory (Boadway, 2004). In the case of assets that do not generate income, under accrual accounting, the income from these assets would have to be imputed and accounted as part of own-source revenues.[11] Thus, at least conceptually, this form of disparity could be addressed by taking into account these imputed revenues and expenditures in the assessment of revenue capacity and expenditure needs as part of a conventional fiscal equalization grant. Of course, from a practical angle, there would remain questions of timing; for example, should all the past imputed revenues and expenditures be dealt with in a single period or multiple periods and how should be delays in the intervention be compensated for over time? Again the answer to this question is likely to be different depending on the policy objectives. Past inequities are likely to be irrelevant for efficient location of mobile resources but quite relevant for social solidarity.

When the infrastructure under consideration contributes to a redistributive government function (such as basic education or primary health care), then central government intervention might also be warranted. Thus, the decades of litigation on equity and adequacy of education finance in the US have included inequalities in school facilities in more than two-thirds of the states (Duncombe and Wang, 2009). Furthermore, in at least six states, suits have been brought solely on the grounds of school infrastructure inequality, starting with the Arizona case of *Roosevelt Elementary School District* v. *Bishop* (1994). According to Duncombe and Wang (2009, p. 327), the "Wyoming court saw no reason to separate facilities from other financing programs, regarding school infrastructure as a part of the total educational package."

However, the exact form of this intervention is not necessarily clear. Thus, when state-level litigation in the USA found school financing systems not meeting the "thorough and efficient" or "general and uniform" education clauses of states' constitutions, the improvements mandated by the trial courts sometimes included specific requirements in terms of physical facilities for each area of the curriculum. Thus, the 1979 West Virginia case (*Pauley* v. *Kelly*) resulted in a mandated master plan for educational improvements, among other things requiring an art room for each 350–500 pupils with at least 50 square feet per student (Crampton and Thompson, 2004). In *DeRolph* v. *State* (2000), the Ohio court included "sound buildings that are in compliance with state building and fire codes" in its definition of the meaning of an efficient system of schools.

Some scholars suggest that, when regional disparities are exogenously given, as in the case of the Apartheid regime in South Africa, the central government can also externally determine a fair or equitable distribution of physical infrastructure and introduce a series of earmarked grants to bring about the desired allocation of capital stock after a certain number of years (e.g., Levtchenkova and Petchey, 2007). However, this approach is not without problems, especially if the target level is not adjusted for differences in service needs or service costs according to the cost-minimization optimum captured by equation (1). For example, if some locality has redundant infrastructure, this doesn't mean we should replicate this redundancy everywhere else. The main rationale for decentralization is allowing local players to make efficient decisions based on their better knowledge of local conditions. The right mix of capital and non-capital inputs to the production of public services is one of the most important economic decisions that decentralized systems entrust to subnational officials. Even for the uniform standard of service outcome, the right level of capital inputs will vary with local costs, as was shown earlier in this chapter. Therefore, externally imposing the level of capital infrastructure has the potential of leading to inefficient modes of service production and delivery.

In general, the acquisition of assets through separate budgeting procedures can lead agencies to treat assets—once won in the struggle for a share of the government's capital budget—as a free good. This can lead to inefficient utilization of the assets due to the disregarding of the opportunity costs represented by the assets and also due to inefficiency in evaluating programs that utilize these facilities without accounting for the cost of capital. If one decides to address historical bias in the distribution of physical infrastructure, an alternative approach could be accounting for the impact of infrastructure availability on the recurrent costs of service provision when equalizing expenditure needs with unconditional grants. Thus, under accrual budgeting, as for example implemented in the New Zealand model of "new public management," a capital charge is levied on the net worth (as shown on its balance sheet) of each department to internalize the amortization of public assets in the production of public services (Laking, 1999). Applying this approach to the allocation of grants would impute potential capital income as part of the fiscal capacity of the asset-rich jurisdictions or alternatively assess the costs of leasing missing infrastructure as part of expenditure needs of those less fortunate.[12] This may not still deal in an appropriate way with the lumpiness of capital infrastructure; as we have argued earlier, having the necessary funds for leasing the infrastructure does not mean that such infrastructure will be available for leasing. However, this issue is not specific to unequal capital endowments and can be addressed with an array of instruments including credit enhancement and borrowing intermediaries as discussed earlier.

While it is an open question whether separate capital grants are required to address infrastructure gaps, when used for this or other reasons, capital grants do affect disparities in capital endowments.[13] As was demonstrated earlier with equation (1), even under the most egalitarian objective of a merit good with a uniform outcome standard, it would be optimal to have different levels of infrastructure if local conditions differ. Other policy objectives would likely require even more unequal distribution of capital assets among localities.

When these policy objectives are supported with effective policy tools, including grants, then we would observe an unequal stock of infrastructure accumulated over time, which nevertheless would be optimal for the given government policy objective.

In particular, unequal infrastructure allocation can be optimally pursued with capital grants under the following two kinds of circumstances: (1) because of the existence/compensation for spillover of benefits from capital infrastructure across jurisdictions and (2) due to delegation of the construction of national infrastructure projects to the localities where this infrastructure would be located. In fact, these two justifications are related because a spillover of benefits occurs when a local government undertakes a capital project which actually should be undertaken by a higher-level government whose jurisdiction encompasses the entire area where the project benefits accrue. In practice, the spillover of externalities is inevitable due to less than perfect correspondence between the varying benefit areas of the numerous types of public infrastructure and a limited number of scales of local government to assign them to. As Hulten and Schwab (1997, p. 141) again put it: "…if each of these goods offers benefits to different subsets of the population, then logically we would need hundreds of overlapping levels of governments."

The externality justification for capital grants is exemplified by the construction of the interstate highway system in the US, which is federally planned and financed but implemented by the state governments. These special cases call for earmarking of national financing not for general capital purposes but for specific capital projects that produce those externalities. Indeed, the central government would not want local officials to reprioritize these funds based on local needs, which by definition would disregard the spillovers of benefits. Thus, there is clearly a normative justification for project-based earmarking of capital grants in the case of externalities.[14]

The presence of these spillovers calls for intergovernmental financing in providing such infrastructure. However, under certain guidelines the administration of these infrastructure projects can be delegated to local authorities in order to achieve efficiency gains from utilizing their superior knowledge of local conditions. However, when the spillover of benefits occurs, conceptually it requires intergovernmental financing of both construction and maintenance of such assets. Following the logic in Hulten and Schwab (1997) cited earlier, "spillovers are generated by the flow of services from the stock of public capital," which is determined both by new investments and by preserving existing assets in the serviceable form. Therefore, conceptually, the spillover of benefits can justify earmarking of grants to infrastructure, which should include both the construction and maintenance costs.[15]

Crucially for our topic of equity, if the extent of spillovers varies across localities, then the matching rates of the Pigouvian subsidies should be inversely related to local costs and directly related to the extent of the benefit spillovers. The intuition is to signal the recipient government that these benefits can be produced more cheaply elsewhere and, given the reciprocal externalities, also enjoyed by the less cost-effective jurisdiction through the spillover of benefits from the more cost-efficient jurisdiction. This will further discourage the less cost-efficient local government from providing this service as, in addition to having higher per unit costs, it will also receive a lower per unit subsidy. For example if it costs less to achieve one ton reduction in carbon dioxide emissions by upgrading local utilities in one jurisdiction than in the other, not only will the second jurisdiction have higher costs per one ton reduction, they will also receive less in national subsidies per ton in the reduction of emissions. This will steer the second jurisdiction to use its resources for some more cost-effective expenditures while the national emissions reduction quota can be achieved where it is more cost effective. To the extent that there is a local impact from carbon dioxide emissions, the high-cost local government might still spend some of its own resources on emission reduction.

In practice, the estimation of the extent of externalities is not a trivial matter. For example, no evidence of quantitatively important spillovers from state highways on private output is found at the regional level in the United States (Holtz-Eakin and Schwartz, 1995). Furthermore, Boarnet (1998) finds evidence of negative spillovers in California as changes in county output are negatively associated with changes in street-and-highway capital infrastructure in other counties, while being positively associated with changes in street-and-highway capital within the same county.

By contrast, Pereira and Roca-Sagales (2003) find that the aggregate effects on private output from public capital built in each Spanish region are due in almost equal parts to direct and spillover effects. Cantos *et al.* (2005) also find very substantial spillover effects on regional growth associated with the capital stock of transport infrastructures in Spanish regions. In addition to belonging to different countries and different types of infrastructure, the difference in results could be also due to capturing dynamic feedbacks in the VAR approach used by Pereira and Roca-Sagales (2003), unlike in the production function approach used by Holtz-Eakin and Schwartz (1995) and Boarnet (1998).

In addition, given that external benefits of local infrastructure are spread over time, just like its direct benefits to local residents, the costs of subsidizing these external benefits should be spread across the generations of national taxpayers accordingly (to achieve inter-generational efficiency in the spirit of the Golden Rule). However, it would be more practical to provide a one-time subsidy for the construction of these assets to avoid administrative costs of continuing subsidizing these external benefits as they occur in the future. Under accrual accounting, this upfront subsidy can be amortized in the national budget over the years. In general, capital grants subsidizing construction of local assets can be used as a practical way of subsidizing future services produced with these assets on the basis of externalities or national policy objectives (Varley, 2001). However, this will not completely eliminate the costs of future surveillance that would be necessary to make sure that these assets are used as intended; for example ensuring that social housing is allocated by local authorities according to the criteria envisioned by the national government. To make these national conditions enforceable, it could be more practical to provide national funding as a loan that will have to be paid back if local governments do not adhere to the conditions in the future.

The discussion in the above paragraphs on how spillover effects and other government policies can justify the earmarking of capital grants illustrates the very significant point that disparities in the stock of infrastructure are to be accepted within a wider scope of equity. That is, it is not inequitable for two subnational governments to have different levels of capital infrastructure if for example these jurisdictions have different local costs and generate different levels of benefit spillovers.

How are capital disparities addressed in practice? Three country cases

The normative considerations above suggest that, if a government pursues fiscal equity, it has to address disparity in the needs for capital infrastructure. It can also account for differences in the endowment of capital assets in the computation of revenue capacity and expenditure needs. When a government pursues policies other than fiscal equity, such as compensation for externalities, then the flow of intergovernmental grants does not have to be directed at asset-poor regions. In this section we examine several country cases to look for evidence of inter-regional disparities in public infrastructure endowment and how they link to actual practice of intergovernmental grants. In particular, we focus on the experiences of Peru, Russia, and Spain to see how well they are aligned with the normative prescriptions. While the choice of the countries is determined by data availability and thus somewhat ad hoc, it is well suited for our research question. On the one hand, by representing different groups of countries (OECD member, middle-income commodity and energy exporter, middle-income raw mineral exporter) the selection of countries makes our finding somewhat more general. On the other hand, these countries have some common issue in their intergovernmental policy setup and that is historic and economic differences between regions within those countries. Furthermore, we can build on previous comparative studies of these countries, for example Jarocinska (2006) juxtaposing Russia and Spain.

For each of the three countries, we examine the grant elasticity with respect to regional service needs, service costs, revenue base, and infrastructure endowments. This is motivated by our discussion above on normative issues, which suggests that grants should take into account disparities in infrastructure needs and in some circumstances also disparities in infrastructure endowments. Given the complementary between capital and operational inputs, which is present in all forms of CES production technology with finite elasticity of factor substitution, infrastructure needs are modeled with the same indicators of service needs (school-age population, sickness rate, etc.) as those traditionally used in the case of the recurrent (equalization and other) grants. For example, for Cobb-Douglas technology, the impact of population size N and service load factors Z affects operational expenditure needs (OE) in exactly the same functional form as for capital expenditure needs captured in equation (2):

$$OE^* = P_O^{1-\beta}\left(\frac{1-\beta}{\beta}P_K\right)^{\beta} \alpha^{\frac{1}{\tau}}(bSN^{\propto}Z^{\varphi})^{\frac{1}{\gamma\tau}} \tag{3}$$

where
a and b are constant parameters;
τ captures returns to scale in production (increasing when $\tau > 1$)
β represents the cost share of capital;
P_K is the cost of capital inputs;
P_O is the cost of non-capital (operational) inputs;
γ is the elasticity capturing differences between technical economies of scale and economies of quality scale;
α and φ are elasticities measuring the impact of population size N and service load factors Z (e.g., proportion of disadvantage students) on the service outcome.

The only difference between equations (2) and (3) is the impact of factor prices P_K and P_O.

In fact, traditionally the fiscal equalization literature has been focusing on total expenditure needs, inclusive of both capital and operational inputs.[16] Thus, for any form of the CES production technology, the total expenditure needs (TE) are affected by population size N and service load factors Z in exactly the same way as the needs for operational or capital expenditures individually:

$$TE^* = c(P_K, P_O)\alpha^{\frac{1}{\tau}}(bSN^{\propto}Z^{\varphi})^{\frac{1}{\gamma\tau}} \tag{4}$$

where $c(P_K, P_O)$ is the unit cost function determined by the overall price level and the relative factor prices. Thus, for an efficient system of grants, we should expect the same service needs elasticity for capital grants as for general purpose grants or the sum of capital and operational grants.

Our estimates of the impact of grants on capital expenditures should further shed some light on the effectiveness of transfers in closing capital gaps.

The incidence of grants and public investments is modeled with cross-sectional and panel-data regressions, while controlling for other covariates.

We use two alternative empirical strategies: the between estimation explores the incidence of grants and public investments in a cross-region analysis while the within estimation analyzes changes over time. Conceptually we cannot favor one specification over the other. On the one hand, the within estimation procedure discards information on cross-region variation by region-demeaning (differencing from the region average over time) all variables. On the other hand, without demeaning, we cannot control for some unobservable factors specific to each region. If these factors are correlated with some of the included regressors, then we are likely to obtain biased estimates using the between estimator.[17]

Another econometric issue is a possible bias from the endogeneity of transfers. Indeed, regions with lower propensity to invest in public infrastructure might receive more grants. The best response to this problem is a set of valid instruments—that is, variables that affect regional outcomes only through their effect on grants. Unfortunately, it is hard to identify variables that would be good instruments for grant allocations. It is our hope that this potential endogeneity is partially mitigated in our panel data by including fixed region effects.

The case of Russia

The Russian Federation has a population of 142 million, out of which 73 percent reside in urban areas. Before the recent wave of regional amalgamations, the Federation was comprised of 89 subjects: ethnic republics, *krais*, *okrugs*, *oblasts*, and autonomous areas—hereafter referred to as "regions." Below the regional level, there are two levels of local government (before 2006 many regions had only one subregional tier).

Since 1994, rates for derivation-based sharing of tax revenue between the federal government and regional governments have been uniform across regions (while varying by tax).[18] The implication was that all regions, be they rich or poor, from that year on had to be treated the same when it comes to revenue sharing at source. Therefore, the attainment of more predictable and transparent revenue assignments brought about potentially larger fiscal disparities in the country. The federal government had to rely on a new system of equalization grants to offset the potential increase in disparities in the distribution of fiscal resources.[19] In addition, the federal government maintained an ad hoc mechanism of "mutual settlements," which were mostly non-explicitly budgeted transfers granted to some regions during the process of budget execution.[20]

The total amount of federal transfers to Russia's regions is distributed under four major categories: equalization grants, subventions, subsidies, and mutual settlements. The most dominant federal-regional grant modality is the equalization grant (the Federal Fund for the Financial Support of the Regions). The size of the federal equalization grant pool is set prior to the beginning of the fiscal year in the annual federal budget law. Although the shares of individual regions in the equalization fund are drafted based on the need/capacity formula, the legislated amounts may end up considerably different as a result of political bargaining in Parliament, in particular over specific weights to be used in the formula.[21]

Moreover, actual shares of regions in the equalization fund may differ from the legislated ones if the total size of the fund falls below the planned amount, and the Ministry of Finance adjusts the planned allocation unevenly across regions. The share of equalization grants in total federal transfers increased from 50 percent in 1995 to 70 percent in 2000, dropped again under 50 percent by 2005 due to earmarked funding for federal mandates, and more recently slipped under 30 percent after having been diluted with federal stimulus funds. In 1995, the other half of grants was comprised of "mutual settlements," which were typically not budgeted ex ante, but rather result ex post from emergency situations and political lobbying.

The relative decline of mutual settlements over time is an indication of improvements in the objectivity, stability, and predictability of the federal-regional transfer system. In addition, regional governments have been provided with intergovernmental loans for liquidity purposes. These loans can be considered additional grants because they are often rescheduled and eventually offset or written off.

Since 2001, equalization grants, which are unconditional, have been complemented with earmarked transfers to reimburse subnational governments for the two major federal mandates: payment of monthly child benefits and subsidies for payment on various goods and services by persons with disabilities. These earmarked grants work as partial replacement of the pre-2000 equalization funds, as the latter used to account for the mandates' burden in the assessment of regions' need. At the same time as these two large conditional grant programs were introduced, the regional derivation-based share of VAT collections was entirely centralized to the federal budget for subsequent redistribution across regions via the earmarked grants.

In Russia, less than 10 percent of the amount of federal grants to regions is earmarked for capital investments.[22] This is below the average for the upper-middle-income group, where the share of capital grants has reached 20 percent over the last two decades. As we mentioned earlier, in transition countries capital grants have played a smaller role in the financing of local infrastructure than general purpose revenues of subnational governments, from own and intergovernmental sources. This often resulted from the ad hoc delineation of responsibilities and resources during the first years of transition. Because central governments were sensitive to political costs of wage arrears in schools and hospitals, they wanted local authorities to pay salaries first under the pretext that resources for capital expenses would be coming separately. Such designation of operational expenses as core ("protected") items is believed to have caused underinvestment in some of those countries.

Estimation results

Pairwise correlations suggest that wealthier regions in Russia tend to have more hospital beds, lower road density (due to vast areas of oil-reach regions), and no relationship to the bus fleet size. In multivariate regressions, we try to parse out these relationships by controlling for land area and other covariates.

First, we report the estimates of grant elasticity with respect to subnational service needs, service costs, revenue base, and infrastructure endowments.[23] In the first column of Table 6.1 we report the results of the "between estimation," based on the time averages of the longitudinal observations for different regions. All monetary variables are normalized by the GDP deflator and by regional population. The included variables jointly explain about three-fourths of cross-region variation in per capita grants.

In the last column of Table 6.1 we report the results of the fixed effects estimation based on the deviation from time averages for different regions. The included variables jointly explain only 16 percent of the within variation in per capita grants.[24]

Table 6.1 Determinants of intergovernmental grants

	Between estimation	*Fixed region effects*
Road density	0.1405 (0.1778)	0.2358 (0.1869)
Buses, per 10,000 population	–0.0817 (0.1274)	–0.0222 (0.0708)
Hospital beds, per 10,000 population	1.0597*** (0.3801)	–1.1091* (0.5632)
First time diagnosis, per 1000 population	0.0809 (0.3329)	–0.1309 (0.3698)
Infant mortality rate	–0.0461 (0.3656)	–0.2548** (0.1258)
Population below working age, share	–0.0585 (1.0954)	1.4485** (0.7095)
Population over working age, share	–1.2443 (0.7700)	2.7413*** (0.8759)
Land area per capita	0.2648* (0.1396)	0.2174 (1.7728)
Real subsistence level	1.3772** (0.5577)	0.0576 (0.2547)
Real GRP, per capita	–1.1953*** (0.1996)	0.6948*** (0.2200)
Constant	–6.5467 (8.7454)	–8.1883* (4.4312)
N [regions]	498 [76]	498 [76]
R^2	0.76	0.16

Notes
* statistically significant at 10 percent.
** statistically significant at 5 percent.
*** statistically significant at 1 percent.

From the between estimation, one can see that on average more grants are flowing to regions with lower revenue base (measured by Gross Regional Product, GRP), higher service needs (measured by population of non-working age), and higher costs (measured with the regional subsistence level and land area). However, the grants do not seem to address disparities in transport infrastructure and in fact appear to counter-equalize disparities in social infrastructure, measured by hospital beds per person. Comparisons over time by means of the fixed effects estimation still show positive relationship to growing service needs captured with demographic changes. However, now we have a positive and weakly statically significant relationship between grants and road density. This might reflect a reverse causality capturing more roads in regions that saw a larger increase in grants. Another plausible explanation is that more grants are given for road maintenance and rehabilitation. At the same time, the intertemporal relationship between grants and hospital beds appears to be negative. As the negative sign rules out reverse causality, the only explanation that comes to mind is the denominator effect: with increasing population size, the per capita stock of existing infrastructure goes down at the same time larger grants are flowing in to address the growing need. This is also corroborated by the evidence that regions with a drop in infant mortality saw an increase in grants.

Tables 6.2 and 6.3 show the determinants of public investments (regardless of the ownership of assets, public or private), and acquisition of public assets (regardless of the source of financing, public or private). Both tables suggest more investments in regions with higher revenue, either from own base or grants, better outcomes, and a smaller population of elderly. There appears to be a positive relationship between investments and road density.

Thus, overall we can conclude that in the case of Russia grants and transfers are only partially designed to address regional differences in the endowments of capital infrastructure. They do however take mitigate disparities in revenues base and service needs and costs, which can potentially bridge expenditure needs in terms of both recurrent and capital inputs.

Table 6.2 Determinants of public investments

	Between estimation	*Fixed region effects*
Road density	0.2205 (0.1367)	0.3052* (0.1771)
Buses, per 10,000 population	0.0415 (0.0977)	–0.0284 (0.0965)
Hospital beds, per 10,000 population	–0.1589 (0.3073)	–0.0640 (0.7108)
First time diagnosis, per 1,000 population	–0.5842** (0.2547)	0.3897 (0.4286)
Infant mortality rate	–0.6146** (0.2796)	–0.4119*** (0.1388)
Population below working age, share	0.0129 (0.8364)	–2.4491*** (0.9096)
Population over working age, share	–1.1868 (0.5962)	–0.8059 (2.1430)
Land area per capita	0.0307 (0.1096)	0.9481 (2.3908)
Real subsistence level	–0.0886 (0.4504)	1.0752*** (0.3008)
Real GRP, per capita	0.8138*** (0.1893)	0.5801*** (0.2027)
Real transfers, per capita	0.4584*** (0.0949)	0.1559** (0.0762)
Constant	11.0220 (6.7173)	4.7798 (7.4090)
N [regions]	497 [76]	497 [76]
R^2	0.68	0.45

Notes
* statistically significant at 10 percent.
** statistically significant at 5 percent.
*** statistically significant at 1 percent.

Table 6.3 Determinants of acquisition of public assets

	Between estimation	*Fixed region effects*
Road density	0.3935** (0.1424)	0.1266 (0.1435)
Buses, per 10,000 population	0.0373 (0.1016)	0.0320 (0.0575)
Hospital beds, per 10,000 population	–0.2187 (0.3242)	0.1356 (0.5351)
First time diagnosis, per 1,000 population	–0.5173* (0.2654)	–0.1001 (0.3497)
Infant mortality rate	–0.0663 (0.2966)	–0.2485** (0.0950)
Population below working age, share	0.0554 (0.8946)	–0.5130 (0.7220)
Population over working age, share	–0.2807 (0.6432)	–0.2677 (1.1849)
Land area per capita	0.2810** (0.1143)	2.9229 (2.2206)
Real subsistence level	0.8690* (0.4566)	0.6646*** (0.2445)
Real GRP, per capita	0.9045*** (0.1998)	0.8497*** (0.1917)
Real transfers, per capita	0.2414** (0.0987)	0.0927** (0.0479)
Constant	0.2281 (7.1536)	7.8798 (6.6962)
N [regions]	491 [76]	491 [76]
R^2	0.70	0.38

Notes
* statistically significant at 10 percent.
** statistically significant at 5 percent.
*** statistically significant at 1 percent.

The case of Spain

Spain has three subnational tiers of governments: 17 regions (called "autonomous communities"), 50 provinces, and 8,000 municipalities.[25] While being a unitary and centralized state before adoption of the 1978 Constitution, over the last three decades the country has undergone deep transformations in terms of the role and organization of subnational governments. Currently, Spain is a highly decentralized country, having devolved a large share of public services to the 17 autonomous communities (AC) (or Comunidades Autónomas in Spanish). Although constitutionally Spain remains a unitary country, its system of intergovernmental fiscal relations has many features of a federal system.[26] These ACs have their own regional parliaments and executive bodies and enjoy considerable budgetary discretion in expenditure decisions and their own financing. The ACs play a limited liaison role between the central and local levels, but in large part the municipalities are fiscally disengaged from the ACs and receive direct transfers from the central government. In 2010, only 30 percent of transfers to municipalities came from regional budgets. Among these regions (autonomous communities), 15 have common intergovernmental fiscal arrangement and two (Basque Country and Navarre) are ruled by special laws. The two special charter regions are not receiving transfers from the central governments but instead collect most of the national taxes in their territories and then transfer an agreed fraction (the annual quota or "cupo" in Spanish) to the central government at the end of each fiscal year.

Over the last 30 years, Spain has decentralized many aspects of the formerly centralized public administration system to the 17 ACs. Regional governments account for 8 percent of public investments but for 31 percent of public spending excluding pensions (Sole-Olle, 2010). Subregional governments account for 27 percent of public investments but for only 18 percent of public spending excluding pensions.[27] Capital grants account for 30 percent of local government investments. The national government accounts for 57 percent of recurrent grants to subregional governments but only for 12 percent of capital grants. By contrast regional governments account for 26 percent of recurrent grants to subregional governments but for 52 percent of capital grants. While most of the recurrent grants from the central governments are not earmarked, most of the recurrent grants from regions are. All in all, about one-fifth of grants received by subregional governments were earmarked for capital use, in fact specific capital projects. Thus in Spain capital earmarking is higher than the OECD average (13 percent) but close to the sample average including non-OECD countries.

After the 1978 decentralization reform, the central government established a system of grants that provide funding for education, health, and transport. In addition, Inter-Territorial Compensation Funds (ICF hereafter) were established to achieve greater financial equity between wealthy and impoverished regions. Over these years the system of grants was reformed several times (1991, 1997, 2001, 2009). With the most recent reform of 2009, the former Sufficiency Fund—a revenue-sharing pool that had been allocated to the ACs since the mid-1980s—was replaced with two new main Funds, with the objectives of closing the vertical gap and regional horizontal imbalances. The first of the two funds, the Essential Public Services Fund (EPSF) is aimed at closing horizontal disparities by essentially redistributing resources from regions with above-average (adjusted) fiscal capacity per capita to those regions with a fiscal capacity below the average. The second large fund, the Global Sufficiency Fund (GSF) closes the remaining regional vertical gaps, measured as the difference between expenditure needs,[28] and the sum of aggregate regional fiscal capacity and the received EPSF funds.[29]

Although the general purpose grants from the two funds can be (and have always been) used to finance capital expenditure, their allocation does not take into account differences in the costs of construction and financing of fixed assets. Besides the general purpose grants, regional capital expenditures are also financed with revenues coming from a number of other sources: the Interterritorial Compensation Fund, funds coming from the European Union (EU), other matching capital transfers that finance part of bilaterally (center-region) agreed investment projects, and regional borrowing (subject to the strong restrictions that apply under the current legislation on budget stability based on the EU Maastricht Treaty). The first two instruments, ICF and EU funds, only apply to ACs with a per capita income below 75 percent of the European average.

Pairwise correlations suggest that wealthier regions tend to have more hospital beds and higher density of roads and highways. Similar to the Russia case, we employ multivariate regressions to parse out these relationships by controlling for other covariates. However, given the smaller number of regions, we are restricted in degrees of freedom available to analyze the between-region variation. All monetary variables are normalized by the GDP deflator and by regional population.

First, we report the estimates of elasticity of recurrent grants with respect to regional service needs, service costs, revenue base, and infrastructure endowments, paralleling the case of Russia. In the first column of Table 6.4 we report the results of the "between estimation," based on the time averages of the longitudinal observations for different regions. The covariates jointly explain half of the between-region variation but with the exception of regional GDP, none of the individual regressors play a statistically significant role. With only 17 regions, it is easy to run out of degrees of freedom in a multivariate regression. However, the indicators of capital endowment do not have a statistically significant impact when added one at a time to the GDP regressor. Thus, we can conclude that in Spain recurrent grants do not mitigate capital disparities beyond what is captured by differences in GDP.

Similar to the Russia case, comparisons over time (2002–2008) by means of the fixed effects model also show a positive relationship to growing service needs captured with demographic changes (first column of Table 6.5). Another similarity is a positive relationship between recurrent grants and additional highways, albeit with a weak statistical significance. Again we can explain it with either reverse causality or increased outlays on road maintenance. For the

Table 6.4 Between-region regression of grants in Spain

	General purpose grants	*Capital grants*
Road density	–0.0799 (1.6688)	–0.0845 (0.4936)
Highway density	0.1727 (0.9947)	0.0309 (0.2877)
Hospital beds, per 10,000 population	1.1496 (2.1025)	0.3614 (0.6298)
Population below working age, share	0.9545 (5.8295)	–3.9258** (1.7280)
Population over working age, share	2.6022 (5.2576)	–2.6816 (1.5573)
Land area per capita	–0.3476 (0.7808)	0.4935* (0.2289)
Regional GDP per capita	–3.4772* (1.7087)	–2.2940*** (0.5086)
Constant	10.5664 (15.2587	–6.4527 (4.5241)
N [regions]	118 [17]	119 [17]
R^2	0.41	0.90

Notes
* statistically significant at 10 percent.
** statistically significant at 5 percent.
*** statistically significant at 1 percent.

between-region incidence of capital grants, the same independent variables have much higher explanatory powers than for recurrent grants (second column of Table 6.5). It appears that on average more capital grants are flowing to regions with lower revenue base (measured by GRP) and higher service costs (measures by land area per capita) but surprisingly lower service needs (measured by population of non-working age). However, the between estimation does not yield a statistically significant relationship between the capital grants and disparities in infrastructure; not even when the latter are added one at a time. In the panel analysis we find a positive relationship of capital grants to additional highways.

Given the fungibility of funds, we also look at the incidence of the sum of capital and recurrent grants. However, the total does not seem to be any more

Table 6.5 Fixed-effects regression of grants in Spain

	General purpose grants	*Capital grants*
Road density	0.4465 (0.4165)	1.2326 (1.3368)
Highway density	0.1423 (0.1149)	0.7389** (0.3171)
Hospital beds, per 10,000 population	–0.1083 (0.2463)	0.4955 (0.8152)
Population below working age, share	0.5479 (0.5825)	–1.7246 (1.9323)
Population over working age, share	1.2933* (0.6467)	2.7396 (2.5571)
Land area per capita	–0.4699 (0.5255)	2.1259 (1.3326)
Regional GDP per capita	0.3891 (0.2526)	–0.6567 (1.1257)
Constant	–2.6214 (5.3222)	–0.3471 (12.4380)
N [regions]	118 [17]	119 [17]
R^2	0.19	0.16

Notes
* statistically significant at 10 percent.
** statistically significant at 5 percent.

responsive to the explanatory variables than capital and recurrent grants alone. Thus, the observed pattern (or lack of thereof) in grants incidence is not about some random splitting into capital and recurrent components.

Finally, in Table 6.6 we regress subnational capital expenditures on the recurrent and capital grants in addition to the same set of covariates as in Tables 6.4 and 6.5. These variables explain over 70 percent of the between-region variation in per capita capital expenditures. However, no regressor is statistically significant, suggesting multicolinearity. After trying different combinations of regressors, it appears that all between-region variation in capital expenditures is driven by road density, land area, and economic product (all having a positive association). Neither recurrent or capital grants have a statistically significant impact on capital expenditures (second column of Table 6.6).

Across time periods, capital expenditures appear to have a statistically significant association with capital grants (positive), regional GDP (positive), land area per capita (negative), and roads (positive).

In summary, for the case of Spain, the only common determinant for both recurrent and capital grants, is regional GDP. When summed up across years, the amounts of grants, capital or recurrent, do not seem to be related to the infrastructure stock other than what is already captured by differences in regional GDP. There are some peculiar co-movements across time, for example a positive association between capital grants and highway density. Thus, overall we can conclude that in the case of Spain grants and transfers are only partially designed to address regional differences in the endowments of capital infrastructure, with the disparities in endowments being more clearly addressed in the case of capital grants. Also, as in the case of Russia, general grants and transfers do appear to mitigate disparities in revenues base and service needs and costs, which can also help address expenditure needs in terms of both recurrent and capital inputs.

The case of Peru

The territorial composition of Peru includes, at the intermediate level, 24 regions (or departments) plus the Constitutional Province of Callao; and at the local level, 1,834 municipalities, of which 195 are provincial municipalities and the rest district municipalities. All regional and local governments approve their own budgets. The dual coexistence at the same local level of provincial and district municipalities is a peculiarity of Peru's vertical government structure. Regional governments vary significantly in area size, from 4,657 to 370,000, with the median at approximately 36,000 square kilometers. With the exception of the Metropolitan Municipality of Lima, the differences in population size are less pronounced, but nevertheless are still quite large, ranging from 92,000 to 1.6 million, with a median of 670,000.

Seven years after the decentralization was prompted by the deposition of President Fujimori, in 2009 subnational governments accounted for 40 percent public expenditure, equally split between the regional and local tiers. At the same time subnational share in public investments increased from under 45 percent in 2001 to

Table 6.6 Determinants of subnational investments in Spain

	Between estimation		*Fixed region effects*
	(1)	*(2)*	
Road density	0.5081 (0.3809)	0.4786* (0.2464)	1.5055* (0.8044)
Highway density	0.1760 (0.2270)		–0.0784 (0.1669)
Hospital beds, per 10,000 population	0.2576 (0.4895)		0.3362 (0.5494)
Population below working age, share	0.5319 (1.8589)		–0.0346 (0.4078)
Population over working age, share	–0.0262 (1.5702)		0.6150 (1.0623)
Land area per capita	0.3275 (0.2515)	0.2644** (0.1081)	–1.9982** (0.9420)
Regional GDP per capita	0.8255 (0.7112)	0.7235 (0.4180)	1.5182*** (0.4808)
Recurrent grants per capita	–0.0147 (0.0945)	–0.0028 (0.0685)	0.0151 (0.1329)
Capital grants per capita	0.2265 (0.3179)	0.1239 (0.1860)	0.1792*** (0.0393)
Constant	–4.6000 (4.4377)	–4.1400*** (1.1691)	–22.6768 (7.6953)
N [regions]	118 [17]	118 [17]	118 [17]
R^2	0.73	0.69	0.47

Notes
* statistically significant at 10 percent.
** statistically significant at 5 percent.
*** statistically significant at 1 percent.

almost 70 percent in 2008. However, fiscal disparities pre-date the recent wave of decentralization reforms and can be traced back to the introduction of revenue-sharing arrangements of rents from the exploitation of natural resources among the central government, local governments, and, to a lesser extent, the intermediate level of government, the departments ("oil canon" in 1973 and "mineral canon" in 1993).[30] The upward spiral in the world prices of natural resources in the second half of the 2000s led to a virtual explosion in fiscal disparities across local and regional governments. Because the canon funds are earmarked for capital infrastructure projects, this directly translates into infrastructure disparities.

The recent reform of the Regional Compensation Fund (Fondo de Compensación Regional, FONCOR) attempted to include in its formula an explicit measure of fiscal capacity thus depriving regional governments now relatively much richer because of the canon funds from receiving FONCOR funds. However, inter-regional fiscal disparities will not be resolved until similar modifications are made to the Municipal Compensation Fund (Fondo de Compensación Municipal, FONCOMUN) equalization transfers, which is the main tool to counterbalance the canon resources.

In 2009, through Ministerial Resolution No. 322–2009-EF-15, the General Directorate of Economic and Social Affairs introduced a new methodology to compute the FONCOR transfers, which should significantly improve its equalizing power. Under the new methodology, the aforementioned factors are used to compute the capital expenditure needs of each regional government, and then the net capital expenditure needs are obtained by subtracting from this amount the revenues received from canon, sobrecanon, royalties, and custom duties. Finally, the transfer is distributed proportionally among those regional governments with positive net capital expenditure needs. As a result, those governments for which the revenues from extractive industries exceed their capital expenditure needs receive no transfers from the FONCOR, and the available resources can be concentrated exclusively on the regions where there is not enough funding for capital expenditures.

In our empirical analysis we focus on the incidence of grants after the FONCOR reform (2009–2011). Because this gives us only three longitudinal observations per region, we are only able to perform a between-region estimation by regressing on the lagged cross-section of covariates. All monetary variables are normalized by the GDP deflator and by regional population. In columns of Table 6.7 we report the incidence of three groups of transfers: (1) canon; (2) capital grants; and (3) all other transfers. The estimates suggest that none of the three groups of grants compensate for infrastructure gaps. In fact, non-canon grants have a positive association in the three-year period, which is statistically significant for roads. Even after the 2009 reforms, all grants are positively related to regional economic product, and this association is statistically significant for canon transfers. Non-canon grants have a positive and statistically significant association with underage population, which is a proxy for the future need of infrastructure due to population growth. Finally, canon and capital grants have a positive association with land area per capita, which is a proxy for the costs of infrastructure.

Table 6.7 Between-region regression of grants in Peru

	Canon	*Capital grants*	*Other grants*	*Total grants*
Road density	0.1408 (0.3134)	0.2885*** (0.0959)	0.0432 (0.0330)	0.2112** (0.0793)
Hospital beds, per 10,000 population	–1.0335 (1.5270)	0.7131 (0.5790)	0.0524 (0.1920)	0.0284 (0.3201)
Infant mortality rate	0.7355 (1.3788)	–0.4090 (0.2692)	0.0019 (0.1326)	–0.0632 (0.2812)
Population below working age, share	3.7614 (6.6767)	4.2147* (2.0596)	2.4275*** (0.6319)	2.3511 (1.5766)
Population over working age, share	3.0369 (2.4331)	–0.8305 (0.6345)	–0.0266 (0.2372)	0.2863 (0.5409)
Land area per capita	0.3287* (0.1697)	0.1570 (0.1113)	–0.0218 (0.0757)	0.2228* (0.1109)
Regional GDP per capita	3.1201* (1.7651)	0.4763 (0.5242)	0.2730 (0.2068)	0.8978* (0.4073)
Constant	3.4365 (4.6655)	0.5553 (1.3271)	0.9679* (0.4444)	1.6875* (0.9711)
N [regions]	75 [25]	75 [25]	75 [25]	75 [25]
R^2	0.36	0.49	0.40	0.41

Notes
* statistically significant at 10 percent.
** statistically significant at 5 percent.
*** statistically significant at 1 percent.

Policy implications

This chapter makes a strong case that disparities in the availability of and need for capital infrastructure matters very significantly for fiscal equity. But, as we have also remarked, the objectives pursued with all intergovernmental policies largely condition what is the appropriate treatment of infrastructure disparities. Thus, for example, emphasis on the objective of fiscal equity in service provision here and now can lead to capital transfers policies that are different from those needed to address longer-term regional disparities in economic development. In this sense, an equitable distribution of infrastructure at the subnational level needs to be interpreted in the light of other government policy objectives, which no doubt have separate independent results in the spatial distribution of the stock of infrastructure.

At the same time, we have argued that the proper framing of infrastructure and fiscal equity should be in terms of the incidence of outputs and outcomes of public services produced with this infrastructure and the financing ability to get there. From that perspective, infrastructure projects alone should not be assigned any type of priority that is independent of the programs and public services that utilize these capital assets as inputs. Therefore, the question that matters from a policy viewpoint is: What is the best form of intervention? Should disparities in infrastructure be addressed in an earmarked fashion—in the line of project-based conditional capital grants still used in many countries or possibly separate capital equalization grants earmarked for capital use but not for specific projects? Or, should policy makers incorporate capital infrastructure disparities into a general-purpose equalization grant?

The answer to these questions is likely to depend on the type of infrastructure and it may also vary with country-specific parameters such as the availability of credit financing, technical capacity to manage loans, and so on. As a first approximation to an answer, it can be useful to distinguish between three different types of infrastructure: (i) infrastructure that has associated very large operation and maintenance costs, as is the case of many public schools and health centers; (ii) infrastructure, which is largely fee recoverable for the principal and also for maintenance and operation costs, such as is the case for many utilities (water, sewerage systems, incinerators); and (iii) infrastructure that is largely non-fee-recoverable, with sizable maintenance costs, such as public parks, no toll roads, and so on.

In the first category, given the large importance of operation and maintenance costs, and their recurrent nature, the best form of intervention to address disparities in infrastructure may be through the inclusion of these expenditure needs in the general purpose equalization grant. This is because, by removing the life-time costing of facilities from making investment decisions, capital earmarking would make the errors of omission and commission particularly grave for local finances. As sectors like education are highly labor intensive,[31] allowing separated capital funding decision would commit local governments to disproportionately larger life-time operational costs, which is like allowing the "tail to wag the dog."

In the case of the second category, the opportunity of using fees to cover the full cost plus maintenance and operation of the facilities would call for using credit markets and borrowing to facilitate those investments and fully abstain from any form of transfers. This is because the stream of future use fee receipts can be more easily pledged as a collateral for debt financing than general tax revenues vulnerable to the uncertainties of the political climate.

In the third category, given the importance of the infrastructure construction and maintenance costs in relation to the recurrent costs in operation, the best form of intervention may be conditional grants for construction and maintenance (but not operation) of infrastructure. This is because, for example, by disallowing road maintenance, separation of construction funds will prompt local managers to defer maintenance and convert these costs into an earlier or more extensive capital rehabilitation. By contrast the costs of road operation, such as powering traffic lights or manning intersections, are minor and do not pose a threat of deferred maintenance.

A good example of this third type of grant can be found in many transitional countries in the form of road funds. Fuel excises are collected nationally for administrative expediency but redistributed—ideally based on a formula, as for example in Latvia— among localities and earmarked for local roads (both construction and maintenance). In this case, intergovernmental redistribution is normatively justified by inter-jurisdictional externalities and tax efficiency while excise-financing brings elements of benefit taxation by creating a link to local road use. In Macedonia such a local road fund (0.08 percent of GDP in 2010) is apportioned among municipalities based on population and land area as well as length of municipal roads and the number of registered vehicles. As a precondition, municipalities have to submit to the Road Fund administration an annual work plan for road construction and maintenance; however, the disbursement and use of these funds is not earmarked for any specific projects.

Thus, from a normative point of view, disparities in the stock of capital infrastructure may be addressed as part of the general revenue equalization, through credit enhancement, and, in some cases, through earmarked capital grants depending on the type of infrastructure. In addition, the exact form of policy intervention will depend also on the relative importance of competing policy objectives, and it is logical to expect that those objectives will differ from country to country. In particular, intergovernmental grants can pursue a broad range of objectives:

- improving the vertical fiscal balance of the system of intergovernmental relations;
- funding national priorities or "merit goods";
- compensating for the presence of spillovers or "externalities" between jurisdictions in the provision of local public services;
- improving the horizontal fiscal balance between local governments (in other words, equalization);

- creating a level-playing field for evaluating performance of appointed heads of deconcentrated government units;
- promoting a positive change in some aspects of the performance of local governments (i.e., performance-based grants).

Canavire-Bacarreza *et al.* (2015) summarize the existing normative guidance and policy wisdom on the design approaches that are most suitable for each of the aforementioned objectives of a grant system. A key point of this discussion is that grants pursuing different objectives might require different designs of the allocation mechanism including measures of capital expenditure needs. Even in the case of the merit good objective aiming at a uniform level of service outcome, we need to be reminded that the optimal level of capital inputs will vary depending on local costs and other local conditions, and that in the case of spillover of benefits, the optimal level of infrastructure is more likely to be unequal than not. Table 6.8 summarizes the normative implications of capital disparities for various policy objectives.

This summary of normative guidance provides no room for earmarking grants for capital use other than under centralized borrowing and onlending/ongranting to municipalities. This is not surprising as capital earmarking is inherently against all principles of modern public finance as allocation of funds by economic item (i.e., investment) shifts the focus of budgeting away from prioritizing policy goals to merely funding inputs. However, as we mentioned earlier, the inefficiencies of capital earmarking (deferred maintenance, lack of life-time costing, etc.) might be overridden by non-economic reasons, such as moral hazard, liquidity constraints, etc. As these non-economic rationales are not specific to the issue of equity—on the contrary, we show that equity considerations equally apply to capital and non-capital inputs—we do not explore it any further in this chapter.

Most of this normative guidance was developed with models featuring social infrastructure; that is, infrastructure serving as capital inputs to the production of public services. For public inputs to the production of private goods (i.e., economic infrastructure) the working of the model is not the same.[32] Thus, while better social infrastructure translates into lower wages (workers accepting lower wages in order to have access to better local amenities), economic infrastructure is likely to increase wages due to higher productivity. However, the normative guidance for equalization remains the same: we should not equalize higher wages and higher capital returns stemming from better infrastructure but only the differences capitalized as the rent on local immobile factors. While not being easy to implement in practice, the theory calls for compensating for differences in the composition of residents in terms of their income-earning abilities, but not the differences in their actual income, as for example determined by local income-generating opportunities.

The normative basis provided in the above discussion would seem to justify a rather sparse use of capital transfers within the desired architecture of intergovernmental fiscal relations. Furthermore, normative considerations suggest that the allocation of capital grants should be determined by the same indicators of service need as those driving the allocation of general-purpose grants (e.g., demographics). The only difference in the allocation of capital grants should be due to relative costs of capital and the level of infrastructure stock. However, in reality many countries regularly implement capital transfer programs, in many cases quite considerable in size by comparison to other transfers, which do not always conform to the normative prescriptions, as illustrated by our three country cases (see Box 6.2).

Box 6.2 International cases and best practice in the design of capital transfers

International experience with the design of capital transfers shows that a large variety of approaches are used. Most countries use some form of capital transfers in support of subnational governments for specific sectoral expenditure areas such as roads, water and sewerage treatment plants, transportation, housing, education, health, and so on. Regarding the mechanism used to allocate capital transfers, country experiences vary from ad hoc allocation decisions to formalized approaches using pre-established formulae. Similarly, country experiences vary in flexibility from the least flexible "project-based grants" to unconstrained funds provided as part of a general revenue transfer. Often the amount of capital grants has to be matched with locally raised resources and the matching rate is sometimes inversely related to the local income (e.g., Finland).

The lack of information and the variety of approaches observed make it particularly difficult to generalize and extract lessons useful for just any country trying to establish or reform a system of capital transfers. At the risk of oversimplification, one can say that the typical country has a variety of capital transfers which are closed-funded in the national budget, have earmarked funds with n specific capital expenditure categories, require some level of matching funds from subnational governments, and whose funds are allocated either by an objective formula or on a specific project basis. The variety of specific details in the design of capital transfers is a reflection of the many institutional features associated with capital transfers and the multitude of objectives that may be pursued by governments in this area. The range of objectives for capital transfers include: closing disparities in local infrastructure stocks, subsidizing capital projects with cross-jurisdictional spillovers of benefits, addressing vertical imbalance in the assignment of revenue sources, addressing lack of credit availability, and others.

Source: authors' based on Martínez-Vázquez (2000).

How does this actual practice fit into the theoretical normative framework and policy recommendations we have described? According to the IMF GFS data, on average, 20 percent of intergovernmental grants in the sample are earmarked for capital use (Figure 6.3). This earmarked share is the lowest in OECD countries (13 percent) and the highest in upper-middle-income countries (40 percent). From juxtaposing Figures 6.1 and 6.3, it is interesting to note that OECD countries are the most decentralized in terms of the subnational share of capital expenditures but

Table 6.8 How policy objectives shape the form of addressing subnational disparities in infrastructure

Objective *Grant design choice*	*Revenue sharing/Adequacy*	*"Merit goods"/solidarity*	*Efficiency-enhancing equalization*	*Spillovers or "externalities"*
General purpose vs. capital grants	Infrastructure needs taken into account in determining the pool of general purpose grants; capital earmarking under the centralization of borrowing capacity	Earmarked for the merit goods	Capital inputs taken into account in the determination of local expenditure needs (top-down)	Earmarked for the externality-generating activities
Global vs. sector-earmarked	Global	Sector-earmarked	Global use but in determination of expenditure needs there is a trade-off between formula simplicity (perception of fairness) and accuracy of capturing disparities	Project-earmarked
Needs-based adjustment	Need for economic infrastructure can be addressed through differentiated retention rates since local economic infrastructure produces vertical externalities by increasing the yield of national/shared taxes in the locality	Differences in the proportion of population groups entitled to merit goods	Differences in the proportion of population groups entitled to capital-intensive local services; in case of inequitable distribution of existing infrastructure, imputed net capital income is subtracted from expenditure needs	Only needs of the neighboring jurisdictions

Cost-based adjustment	Only proportional to the extent of vertical fiscal externalities. As with other Pigouvian grants, the optimal matching rate can be inversely related to the local cost level	Full funding of capital needs which are optimal given local capital costs	Only if local services are not fully congestible (not fully private)	Inverse relation to the costs
Means-based adjustment	None	Subtracting of revenue capacity is equivalent to a matching rate: EN-RC=EN*(1-RC/EN). Thus, no need for means-testing if revenue capacity is equalized with the general purpose grant. If capital disparities are of higher concern for equity, than means-testing for investments can bring out extra equalization.	Only for source-based taxes and local rents; for residence-based taxes, grants should equalize potential earning (human capital) but not actual taxable income	Pigouvian subsidies should be derived from compensated demand functions, thus accounting for income
Asset-based adjustment	None	No need for asset-based adjustment if net capital income is equalized with the general purpose grants	Net capital income is equalized away like any other source of local rent	None

Source: Canavire-Bacarreza *et al.* (2015), further modified by the authors.

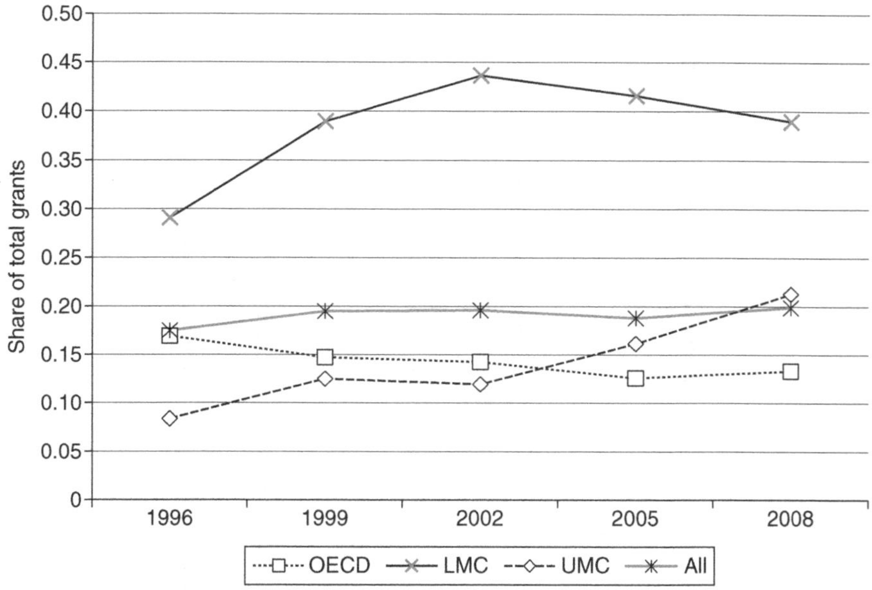

Figure 6.3 Capital grants as a share of total grants, 1993–2008 (source: author's computations based on Martínez-Vázquez and Timofeev, 2012).

Note
The sample includes 44 countries, out of which 1 is low-income, 9 are lower-middle-income, 9 upper-middle-income, 3 non-OECD high-income, and 22 OECD countries.

at the same time they use the least earmarking of intergovernmental grants for capital use. Similarly, a qualitative survey of governments revealed that three in five developed countries earmark transfers for capital use as opposed to four in in five transitional countries; this last point can be explained by the legacy of central planning (OECD/World Bank, 2003). In transition countries, capital transfers are often channeled through a plethora of extra-budgetary funds created within various line ministries (e.g., Romania until 2004).[33]

In practice, central governments implement capital grants for a variety of stated reasons including the need to address externalities across local governments, assist subnational governments in financing "lumpy" capital investments, offset significantly different infrastructure endowments (when these are not the result of voluntary decisions), and pursue sectoral policy objectives (Martínez-Vázquez, 2000). In other cases, capital transfers are implemented in the pursuit of regional economic development objectives toward economically lagged territories, as opposed to those pursuing more equal access to public services (Josie *et al.*, 2008). Guaranteeing minimum standards of services across a country is often seen as a main reason for creating specific capital transfers (Levtchenkova and Petchey, 2007; Petchey and MacDonald, 2007; Herrero- Alcalde *et al.*, 2011). Other times practical considerations regarding budgeting issues can come into play; for example, Ahmad and Searle (2006) view capital transfers as appropriate in tight financing environments where the pressure to fund immediate current needs may displace longer-term investment needs.

Conclusion

In this chapter we have argued that the equity of fiscal outcomes is affected by disparities in infrastructure endowments and infrastructure needs. Therefore, we conclude that equalization grants should take into account these disparities. However, the exact treatment of these disparities will depend on the policy objectives underlying equalization: efficient allocation of mobile resources, social solidarity, or merit goods. Furthermore, political and institutional considerations might require earmarking some of these grants for capital use.[34] Given the general complementarity between capital and operational inputs, the assessment of infrastructure needs should take into account the same indicators of service needs (school-age population, sickness rate, etc.) as for recurrent grants, in addition to the additional indicators assessing capital costs.

While the country cases do not provide a clear evidence of equalization of capital disparities, surprisingly there are quite a few similarities between these very different country cases. In none of these three countries is the incidence of grants related to disparities in capital endowments when the grants are summed up over the entire time period. Given the lumpiness of capital grants and capital projects, these between-region estimates are the key piece of evidence for our research question. To further understand what produces this outcome, some insights can be gained from looking at the inter-temporal statistical associations, which might also represent reverse causality, confounding, and other statistical artifacts. In both Russian and Spain, improvements in road density over time are associated with increases in grants.

The experiences of three countries, even as diverse as Peru, Russia, and Spain, are far from being representative of the vast array of developed and developing countries that have undergone considerable decentralization in the past. However, the practices in these three countries quite likely are pointing at a common policy deficiency in many other countries: the failure of transfers systems to specifically address territorial differences in capital infrastructure endowments that are not necessarily the product of self-made decisions. To be sure, there are many countries that use some form or other of earmarked capital grants and as many more use different forms of recurrent equalization grants. But it is rarely the case that these grants and transfers attempt to incorporate needs differences related to disparities in the endowments of infrastructure; to the extent that differences in expenditure needs capture some of those disparities, then equalization transfers that are expenditure need-based may partially address the problem. All this means that there appears to be a generalized need to develop new policy tools and/or reconvert existing ones within the conventional array of grants and transfers that can better address regional equity objectives in public infrastructure.[35]

Notes

1 As we explain further in our chapter, the appropriate treatment of infrastructure disparities depends on the exact objectives of intergovernmental policies. In particular, one has to distinguish the fiscal equity objective from that of balanced economic development. While the former objective aims at achieving equitable service provision in the presence of fiscal disparities, the latter objective attempts to narrow the economic disparities that are likely behind the fiscal disparities. Thus, by its nature, the first objective plays more of a short-term, mitigating role, while the second objective pursues long-term outcomes often with little immediate impact. However, given that education accounts for the bulk of local government expenditures in many countries, immediate mitigation of fiscal disparities is likely to translate into more equitable development patterns. Further, the association between school facilities and student achievements, frequently reported by education scholars, seems to represent causality as suggested by more rigorous economic studies using sophisticated controls for covariates (e.g., Cellini *et al.*, 2010).

2 For example, New York's Building Aid program does not fund routine maintenance while major renovations are eligible for state grants, covering on average half of the project costs. Curiously, 93 percent of projects approved in 1984–2002 were renovations of existing school buildings (Wang *et al.*, 2011).

3 In countries where subnational governments are required to finance investments with past savings instead of borrowing against future revenues (e.g., Denmark), a capital grant could be interpreted to represent essentially a bailout to a municipality that has failed to save in the past.

4 While most of the 38 US states that have aid grants for education facilities make adjustments for fiscal capacity of local jurisdictions, only a few states make adjustments for differences in needs and costs using such factors as enrollment growth, special need students, local costs, etc. (Wang *et al.*, 20π 21311).

5 An inter-agency building authority can be instrumental in dealing with lumpiness of capital outlays by annuitizing capital costs through inter-departmental (accrued) amortization charges. This is because in any given year only a fraction of many capital assets in various sectors undergo capital rehabilitation, which can be covered by pooling amortization charges from all sectors. However, when local jurisdictions are so small that that the lumpiness of capital outlays makes investments unfeasible without central government assistance, this suggests a problem with the jurisdiction size in general not just in relation to capital projects. If a municipality has only one school, it is hard to justify the operational costs of the additional layer of local bureaucracy (school inspectors, etc.) running a single school.

6 At the same time the right to intercept intergovernmental transfers can discourage lenders' effort to monitor local government finances, and in some cases could be interpreted by these lenders as a promise of central government bailout. For example, Mexico has recently abandoned the practice of the intercept for these same reasons.

7 Depreciation and maintenance should be considered in isolation from each other as a chosen schedule of maintenance determines the useful life and hence amortization of the asset.

8 While compensating for higher borrowing costs unrelated to local government actions, the central government would not want to undo the disciplining effect of a higher risk premium charged by capital markets as the volume of outstanding debt becomes too large relative to the expected future revenue stream (Capeci, 1994).

9 For example, in the United States bond banks have been quite successful in leveraging "economies of scale on behalf of the small borrowers" since 1960s (Government Finance Group, 1997, p. 29).

10 Here we should consider net capital income defined as revenues from sales less outlays for operation, maintenance, and depreciation of assets (equal to amortization

of the loan principal). Obviously, if the central government built a museum with negligible admission receipts but tremendous operation and maintenance costs, it would not increase local revenue capacity. Furthermore, the estimates of user fee revenues should take into account reduced tariffs mandated by the national governments for certain categories of local residents.

11 We have to acknowledge that our conceptual framework mostly applies to public service infrastructure. As to economic infrastructure (public inputs to the private economy), our framework suggests that we should not equalize higher wages and capital returns stemming from better infrastructure but only the differences capitalized as the rent on local immobile factors.

12 The potential capital income is quite real as exemplified by the fact that the fortunate half of Macedonia's municipalities that inherited high schools buildings finance two-thirds of non-labor costs in secondary education through facility-generated income, such as renting out school gyms for fitness classes (Feruglio *et al.*, 2008).

13 In addition to the intrinsic inequity in the conceptual nature of some conditional grants discussed in this subsection, lopsided levels of capital stock can result from peculiar administrative arrangements, where, for example, a disproportionate share of capital grants flows to subnational governments with better grantmanship skills or ability to come up with matching resources.

14 A normative case for a formula-based funding earmarked for the general purpose of capital expenditures would stem from the central government role in economic stabilization. In this case, the central government would want these funds to be used for absorbing unemployed labor in public works while allowing local governments to identify projects according to local infrastructure needs. For example, to recover from the economic recession of the early 1990s, the Canadian federal government was contributing one-third of the total cost of local infrastructure projects broadly defined. The money was allocated among provinces on the basis of population and the rate of unemployment.

15 Similarly, earlier we argued that maintenance outlays cannot be conceptually separated from amortization of the capital assets as, by being close substitutes, one determines the other.

16 Thus, the Representative Expenditure System (RES) proposed for the United States by Robert Rafuse, then Deputy Assistant Secretary of the Treasury for Intergovernmental Fiscal Relations, utilized the estimation of a translog cost function performed by Ladd and Yinger (1989) for a sample 86 largest cities.

17 We do not use the random effects model because the Hausman test rejects the absence of systematic differences from the fixed-effects model. While in the absence of consistency problems, the random effects model is expected to provide more accurate statistical inferences, in our cases it results in inconsistent estimates, which cannot be relied on.

18 Whereas revenue-sharing arrangements had been relatively stable from 1994 through 1997, several substantial changes were made in revenue-sharing arrangements before and after the economic crisis of August 1998 in the direction of recentralizing tax revenues. Changes in the assignment of revenues, especially periodic centralization of the share of PIT collections, reflected a tug of war over resources between the federal and regional governments. In the 2000s, fiscal policy reforms were aimed at reassigning tax revenues away from subnational governments and toward the federal government. Thus, the reassignment of the VAT to the central government most significantly contributed to the centralization of public-sector resources since 2000. The federal government's share in overall tax collections reached 60 percent by 2001 from a low of 42.5 percent in 1997. In 2002, it further increased to 65.1 percent as a result of the reform in the taxation of mineral resources, in which revenue sharing in these taxes was eliminated for local governments and reduced for regional governments. The centralizing impact of this latter reform became even more pronounced in the environment of higher oil prices after 2004.

19 Apparently, unification of sharing rates across regions was associated with reduced between-region variation in per-capita pre-transfer revenues. At the same time, the variation in per-capita expenditures increased. We can attribute this evidence to greater bargaining power of wealthier regions with respect to differentiated sharing rates. When the sharing rates were standardized, this bargaining power appears to have been redirected toward the distribution of intergovernmental grants.

20 The size of the equalization pool was initially set at 15 percent of the federal government's internal revenue. However, the fixed percentage was reduced to 13 percent by 1999 and eventually fixed as the previous year nominal amount annually adjusted for inflation.

21 The transfer formula undergoes some changes every year. Thus, for the 2005 transfers, the Index of Budget Expenditures was computed for the composite subnational expenditures rather than 15 separate expenditure categories as in previous years. However, the set of factors used in the formula is quite stable and traditionally has included variables accounting for differences in wage costs, price level, utility costs, accessibility of the region's localities by transport, and demographic composition of the population.

22 And even that small amount of capital grants is not explicitly classified as such in reporting of regional budget revenues. Thus precludes us from analyzing the incidence of capital grants in Russia.

23 In all three country cases, our unit of analysis is a consolidated region, which is the sum of the regional budget and budgets of all constituent local governments.

24 While the random effects model could yield potentially more efficient estimates, in our case it is not consistent according to the Hausman test.

25 The provinces and municipalities are often grouped as a single—the local—tier. The role of the provinces is quite limited mostly to support or provide basic services in small municipalities lacking capacity and to the coordination of certain services across municipalities.

26 For a review of the institutional framework, see Lopez Laborda *et al.* (2007).

27 However, according to the GFS data, subnational governments accounted for about 70 percent of public acquisitions of fixed assets, which is about the OECD average.

28 Expenditure needs are measured as the regional share in population (with a weight of 30%), the size of the jurisdiction (1.8%), scattered population (0.6%), insularity (0.6%), equivalent (adjusted per age) population covered by the National Health System (38%), population over 65 (8.5%), and population below 16 (20.5%).

29 The new system introduced in January 2009 is analyzed in De la Fuente (2009), Ruiz-Huerta and García (2010), and Lago Peñas and Martínez-Vázquez (2011).

30 The canon, sobrecanon, and royalties are the major natural resource sources of transfer. We will follow the convention of abbreviating all those sources under the name of canon.

31 There are estimates showing that in education capital costs account for only 10 percent of total costs after the costs of facilities are spread over their lifespan.

32 In fiscal federalism literature, economic infrastructure was mostly studied from the positive perspective as a strategic tool for local governments to attract mobile capital, with the causal links similar to those in tax competition (Keen and Marchand, 1997). In this literature, the role of equalization is preventing overinvestment ("arms race" analogous to the "race to the bottom" in tax competition) by redistributing some of the gains in this zero-sum game.

33 One significant exception is Vietnam, where capital expenditure needs are allowed for in the general equalization grant formula by using a gross up factor to the estimate of recurrent expenditure needs for each year, with the factor fixed for all provinces. See Gomez Reino and Martínez-Vázquez (2005).

34 Higher visibility of infrastructure construction can bias intergovernmental grants towards capital earmarking as for a legislative representative it would be easier to

claim credit for new infrastructure built in his electoral district (Lee *et al.* 2003). While most of the normative rationales for capital grants require project specific allocation as opposed to block grants, in practice such mechanism of grant allocation is also more susceptible to "log-rolling" than a formula-based allocation.

35 As a possible example of a first step in this direction, see the recent paper by Herrero-Alcalde *et al.* (2011).

References

Ahmad, Ehtisham and Bob Searle. 2006. "On the Implementation of Transfers to Subnational Governments," in E. Ahmad and G. Brosio (eds.), *Handbook of Fiscal Federalism*. Cheltenham, UK: Edward Elgar, pp. 381–404.

Albouy, David. 2012. "Evaluating the Efficiency and Equity of Federal Fiscal Equalization," *Journal of Public Economics*, 96(9–10): 824–839.

Boadway, Robin. 2004. "The Theory and Practice of Equalization," *CESifo Economic Studies*, 50(1): 211–254.

Boarnet, Marlon G. 1998. "Spillovers and the Locational Effects of Public Infrastructure," *Journal of Regional Science*, 38(3): 381–400.

Boothe, Paul. 2007. "Accrual Accounting in the Public Sector: Lessons for Developing Countries," in Anwar Shah (ed.), *Budgeting and Budgetary Institutions*. Public Sector Governance and Accountability Series. Washington, D.C.: World Bank, pp. 179–201.

Canavire-Bacarreza, Gustavo, Jorge Martínez-Vázquez, and Andrey Timofeev. 2015. "Fiscal Federalism and the Measurement of Expenditure Needs: Theory and International Practice," International Studies Program Working Paper. International Studies Program, Andrew Young School of Policy Studies, Georgia State University.

Cantos, P., M. Gumbau-Albert, and J. Maudos. 2005. "Transport Infrastructures, Spillover Effects and Regional Growth: Evidence of the Spanish Case," *Transport Reviews*, 25(1): 25–50.

Capeci, John. 1994. "Local Fiscal Policies, Default Risk, and Municipal Borrowing Costs," *Journal of Public Economics*, 53(1): 73–89.

Crampton, Faith E. and David C. Thompson. 2004. "When the Legislative Process Fails: The Politics of Litigation in School Infrastructure Funding Equity," in Karen DeMoss and Kenneth K. Wong (eds.), *Money, Politics, and Law: Intersections and Conflicts in the Provision of Educational Opportunity*, American Education Finance Association 2004 Yearbook. Larchmont, NY: Eye on Education.

Cellini, Stephanie R., Fernando Ferreira, and Jesse Rothstein, 2010. "The Value of School Facilities: Evidence from a Dynamic Regression Discontinuity Design," *Quarterly Journal of Economics*, 125(1): 215–261.

De La Fuente, Ángel. 2009. "El Nuevo Acuerdo de Financiación Regional: Un Análisis de Urgencia," FEDEA, *Colección Estudios Económicos*, nº 08/09.

Duncombe, William and Wen Wang. 2009. "School Facilities Funding and Capital-Outlay Distribution in the States," *Journal of Education Finance*, 34(3): 324–350.

Feruglio, Nicoletta, Jorge Martínez-Vázquez, and Andrey Timofeev. 2008. "Assessment of Fiscal Decentralization in Macedonia," ISP Working Paper Number 08–14. International Studies Program, Andrew Young School of Policy Studies, Georgia State University.

Freire, Mila and John Petersen, eds. 2004. *Subnational Capital Markets in Developing Countries: From Theory to Practice*. Washington, D.C., New York, and Oxford: World Bank, Oxford University Press.

Gomez Reino, Juan Luis, and Jorge Martínez-Vázquez. 2005. "Effective Fiscal Decentralization in Vietnam," in *Proceedings of the National Tax Association*. 98th Annual Conference on Taxation, Miami, FL, November 17–19.

Government Finance Group, Inc. 1997. "An Analysis of State Bond Banks," Council of Infrastructure. Financing Authorities Monograph N° 9, Washington, D.C.

Herrero-Alcalde, Ana, Jorge Martínez-Vázquez, and Encarnación Murillo. 2011. "The Challenge of Designing Capital Equalization Transfers: An Application to Spanish Regions," *Publius: The Journal of Federalism*, 42(2): 260–288.

Holtz-Eakin, Douglas and Amy Ellen Schwartz. 1995. "Infrastructure in a Structural Model of Economic Growth," *Regional Science and Urban Economics*, 25(2): 131–151.

Hulten, Charles R. and Robert M. Schwab. 1997. "A Fiscal Federalism Approach to Infrastructure Policy," *Regional Science and Urban Economics*, 27(2): 139–159.

Jarocinska, Elena. 2006. "Political Economy of Intergovernmental Grants." Doctoral thesis. Universitat Pompeu Fabra (http://hdl.handle.net/10803/7343).

Josie, Jaya, Garry MacDonald, and Jeffrey Petchey. 2008. "A Dynamic Equalisation Model for Economic and Social Capital Grants with a South African Example," *Journal of Development Studies*, 44(8): 1169–1189.

Keen, M. and M. Marchand. 1997. "Fiscal Competition and the Pattern of Public Spending," *Journal of Public Economics*, 66(1): 33–53.

Ladd, Helen F. and John Yinger. 1989. *America's Ailing Cities: Fiscal Health and the Design of Urban Policy*. Baltimore and London: Johns Hopkins University Press.

Lago Peñas, Santiago and Jorge Martínez-Vázquez. 2011. *Las Transferencias Intergubernamentales en España: Análisis y Propuestas de Reforma*. Madrid: Instituto de Estudios Fiscales.

Laking, Rob. 1999. "Don't Try This at Home? A New Zealand Approach to Public Management Reform in Mongolia," *International Public Management Journal*, 2(2): 217–235.

Lee, Robert D., Ronald Wayne Johnson, and Philip G. Joyce. 2003. *Public Budgeting Systems*. Boston, MA: Jones and Bartlett Publishers.

Levtchenkova, Sofia and Jeff Petchey. 2007. "A Model for Public Infrastructure Equalization in Transitional Economies," in J. Martínez-Vázquez and B. Searle (eds.), *Fiscal Equalization: Challenges in the Design of Intergovernmental Transfers*. New York: Springer, pp. 345–362.

Lopez Laborda, Julio, Jorge Martínez-Vázquez, and Carlos Monasterio. 2007. "The Practice of Fiscal Federalism in Spain," in A. Shah (ed.), *The Practice of Fiscal Federalism: Comparative Perspectives*. The Forum of Federations. London: McGill-Queen's University Press.

Martínez-Vázquez, Jorge. 2000. "An Introduction to International Practices and Best Principles in the Design of Capital Transfers," report prepared for the Center for Fiscal Policy, Moscow under USAID funding with Deloitte, Touche, Tomatsu.

Martínez-Vázquez, Jorge and Andrey Timofeev. 2012. "Propensity to Invest and the Additionality of Capital Transfers: A Country Panel Perspective," International Studies Program Working Paper 12–16. International Studies Program, Andrew Young School of Policy Studies, Georgia State University.

Moak, Lennox L. and Albert Miller Hillhouse. 1975. *Concepts and Practices in Local Government Finance*. Chicago: Municipal Finance Officers Association of the United States and Canada.

Musgrave, Richard Abel. 1939. "The Nature of Budgetary Balance and the Case for the Capital Budget," *The American Economic Review*, 29(2): 260–271.

OECD/World Bank. 2003. *Survey of Current Budgetary Practices for 30 OECD Countries and 30 Non-OECD Countries*. Database available at www.oecd.org/gov/budget/database.

Pagano, Michael A. 1993. "Balancing Cities' Books in 1992: An Assessment of City Fiscal Conditions," *Public Budgeting and Finance*, 13(1): 19–39.

Pereira, A.M. and O. Roca-Sagales. 2003. "Spillover Effects of Public Capital Formation: Evidence from the Spanish Regions," *Journal of Urban Economics*, 53(2): 238–256.

Petchey, Jeffrey and Garry MacDonald. 2007. "Financing Capital Expenditure Through Grants," in R. Boadway and A. Shah (eds.), *Intergovernmental Fiscal Transfers: Principles and Practice*. Washington, D.C: The World Bank, pp. 425–452.

Ruiz-Huerta, Jesús and Miguel Á. García. 2010. "La reforma del modelo de financiación autonómica de 2001. Una valoración del acuerdo de julio de 2009," in Nuria Bosch and Albert Solé (eds.), *Informe sobre Federalismo Fiscal en España*. Barcelona: IEB.

Sole-Olle, Albert. 2010. "Intergovernmental Transfers to Local Governments in Spain: An Assessment of Their Virtues and Perils," in J. Kim, J. Lotz, and N.J. Man, *General Grants Versus Earmarked Grants, Theory and Practice*; Workshop 2009, The Korea Institute of Public Finance and the Danish Ministry of Interior and Health.

Swianiewicz, P. 2004. "Comparing International Experiences: Emerging Markets of Local Borrowing?" in P. Swianiewicz (ed.), *Local Government Borrowing: Risks and Rewards: A Report on Central and Eastern Europe*, Budapest: OSI/LGI, pp. 385–424.

Varley, Robert C.G. 2001. *Indonesia: Financing Small Scale Urban Infrastructure in the Era of Decentralization*. Manila: Asian Development Bank.

Wallich, Christine I. ed. 1994. *Russia and the Challenge of Fiscal Federalism*. Washington, D.C.: The World Bank.

Wang, Wen, William D. Duncombe, and John M. Yinger 2011. "School District Responses to Matching Aid Programs for Capital Facilities: A Case Study of New York's Building Aid Program," *National Tax Journal*, 64(3): 759–794.

Wurzel, E. 1999. "Towards More Efficient Government: Reforming Federal Fiscal Relations in Germany," OECD Economics Department Working Papers, No. 209.

Part III

Sectoral perspectives

7 Investing in health infrastructure

How decentralization matters[1]

Bernard Dafflon and François Vaillancourt

Introduction

This chapter examines the infrastructure–decentralization nexus in the production of health services with a particular emphasis on the issue of health infrastructure.

The first part of the chapter presents evidence on spending on health services and infrastructure spending both in general and in health for various countries or groups of countries showing the importance of infrastructure spending in the provision of health services. The second part of the chapter examines how some of the characteristics of health services affect the decentralization of such services and thus the decentralization of health infrastructure. The third examines case studies and policy choices.

Health spending and health infrastructure spending; what is the evidence

This first part of the chapter pulls together what evidence we were able to gather on health spending, infrastructure spending, and health infrastructure spending, total and decentralized. Unfortunately, as the reader will see, the more relevant to us the data, the lesser its availability. We begin with a table (7.1) on health spending for groups of countries covering the world, followed by a set of tables (7.2a and 7.2b) examining some evidence on health spending for subsets of countries (low income in Africa; low and middle income in South/Central America) of potential interest to the reader before turning to a last set of tables (7.3 and 7.4) on health infrastructure spending for both the OECD countries and other countries for which data could be found.

Before proceeding to the tables, one should be aware of possible measurement issues that make international and inter-temporal comparisons difficult. We illustrate this with an example. Eurostat[2] classifies hospitals that obtain more than 50 percent of their revenues from billing their patients as market enterprises and not as part of the public sector even if they are publicly owned, see their deficits paid for by the government while their patients' bills are covered by insurance schemes mandated by the government. Hence in 2009 and 2010, public hospitals of five Swiss cantons (Basel-Stadt, Basel-Land, Fribourg, Glarus, and

Table 7.1 Importance of health and public health expenditures by country group, 2010

World bank group of countries	*Health expenditures per capita—2010 (current US$)*	*Health expenditures as percent GDP—2010*	*Public health expenditures as percent total health expenditures—2010*
Arab World	251.8	4.34	60.95
Caribbean small states	501.56	6.1	56.98
East Asia and Pacific (all income levels)	500.18	6.89	69.51
East Asia and Pacific (developing only)	182.82	4.75	53.38
Euro area	3,969.01	10.84	76.15
Europe and Central Asia (all income levels)	2,203.84	9.76	75.89
Europe and Central Asia (developing only)	438.68	5.81	64.98
European Union	3,368.31	10.41	77.37
Heavily indebted poor countries (HIPC)	39.1	5.96	43.12
High income	4,876.79	12.55	65.1
High income: non-OECD	–	–	–
High income: OECD	5,093.26	12.85	65.1
Latin America and Caribbean (all income levels)	671.46	7.68	50.22
Latin America and Caribbean (developing only)	670.24	7.69	50.18
Least developed countries: UN classification	34.39	5.13	42.84
Low and middle income	198.95	5.69	51.81
Low income	26.91	5.34	38.78
Lower middle income	70.93	4.28	39.54
Middle East and North Africa (all income levels)	322.23	4.64	57.8
Middle East and North Africa (developing only)	203.18	5.28	50.15
Middle income	225.13	5.7	52.04
North America	8,049.79	17.24	54.18
Not classified	–	–	–
OECD members	4,364.71	12.57	64.94
Other small states	264.57	6.14	63.57
Pacific island small states	175.83	6.6	78.23
Small states	314.81	6.15	61.78
South Asia	47.46	3.88	30.01
Sub-Saharan Africa (all income levels)	85.01	6.47	45.35
Sub-Saharan Africa (developing only)	84.32	6.5	45.07
Upper middle income	379.71	6.1	54.38
World	950.38	10.39	62.76

Source: Data from World Bank World Development Indicators Database (http://databank.worldbank.org/ddp/home.do.

Table 7.2a Health related information, public expenditure reviews 2000–2010, Latin America

	Expenditure on health/GDP	*Year for column 1*	*Public expenditure on health/GDP*	*Year for column 3*	*Health expenditure in public spending*	*Year for column 5*
	1	*2*	*3*	*4*	*5*	*6*
Belize	5.2	2001–2002	X	X	X	X
Dominica	6.0	2001–2002	4.3	2001–2002	X	X
Haiti	7.5	2003–2004	2.75	2003–2004	5.7	2002–2007
Nicaragua	X	X	3.1	2006–2007	14	2006–2007
Paraguay	X	X	2.3	2003–2004	9–10%	Recent years
El Salvador	8	2001–2002	3.7	2001–2002	X	X

Source: Authors using World Bank Public Expenditure Reviews.

Table 7.2b Health related information, public expenditure reviews 2005–2010, Africa

	Public expenditure on health/GDP	*Year for column 1*	*Health expenditure/ public spending*	*Year for column 3*	*Capital spending/health budget*	*Year for column 5*
	1	*2*	*3*	*4*	*5*	*6*
Burundi	n.a.		8.5	2008		
Guinée-Bissau	3.5	2007				
Liberia	2.3	2007	7.8	2009	6.0	2010
Mali			7.4	2007	36.1	2006
Uganda	1.7	2009	9.8	2006		
RDC-Congo			4.1	2007	22.0	2006
Tanzania	2.4	2009	3.7	2008	9.3	2010
Sierra Leone	1.3	2008	7.5	2007		
Chad	1.0	2007–2009			21–22	2005–2006

Source: Authors using World Bank Public Expenditure Reviews.

Zürich) were classified as belonging to the private sector;[3] but from 2012, since a new financing scheme will impose a maximum of 45 percent of revenues from billing patients they are again classified as public.

We present in Table 7.1 data on health expenditures (share of GDP and in US$ per capita) and public health spending for 2010 using 32 World Bank groupings of countries. It shows extremely large variations in per capita health spending with North American spending 200 times higher than the lowest spending region while the share of GDP spent on health varies from 4 percent to 17 percent and that of public health spending from 30 percent to almost 80 percent of total spending on health.

Table 7.3 Privately and publicly financed gross capital formation in the health sector for OECD countries: 2010 or earlier (*) as percent of total health expenditure and GDP

	Publicly financed gross capital formation in health sector, 2010		*Privately financed gross capital formation in health sector, 2010*	
	As % GDP	*as % total health expenditure*	*As % GDP*	*As % total health expenditure*
Australia*	0.2	2.42	0.27	3.21
Austria	0.35	3.16	0.24	2.14
Canada	0.53	4.63	0.09	0.77
Chile*	0.12	1.79	–	–
Czech Republic	0.19	2.56	–	–
Denmark	0.41	3.67	–	–
Estonia	0.01	0.15	0	0
Finland	0.36	3.98	0.08	0.89
France	0.25	2.18	0.15	1.33
Germany	0.26	2.21	0.15	1.28
Greece*	0.08	0.82	0.3	3.08
Hungary	0.19	2.38	0.04	0.51
Ireland	0.28	3.04	0.04	0.45
Israel*	0.1	1.34	0.15	–
Italy	0.21	2.24	0.14	1.52
Korea	0.12	1.7	0.24	3.41
Mexico*	0.15	2.57	–	–
Norway	0.3	3.16	0.05	0.55
Poland	0.31	4.4	0.13	1.86
Portugal	0.23	2.11	0.34	3.21
Slovak Republic	0.04	0.49	0.47	5.16
Slovenia	0.32	3.51	0.06	0.65
Spain	0.21	2.24	0.03	0.29
Sweden	0.4	4.21	0.1	1.02
Turkey*	0.22	4.05	0.1	–
United States	0.16	0.93	0.53	2.99

Source: Authors using "OECD Health Data: Health expenditure and financing," OECD Health Statistics Database

In addition to this data from the World Bank, we also examined a total of 30 World Bank Public Expenditure Reviews. We report the relevant information in Tables 7.2a–7.2b for the period 2000/5–2010.

Latin America

We found information for six countries; it is presented in Table 7.2a. We also found some information on decentralized provision of health services. In the case of Honduras, some municipalities provide health services through groupings of municipalities (known as mancomunidades). Also some of the municipalities provide financial or operational support (such as ambulances or security services) to Ministry of Health facilities. Mancomunidades depend mostly on municipal financing (74 percent), with user charges (12 percent) and international sources (14 percent) accounting for the rest for current spending. A sample of municipalities reported spending 6 percent of the municipal budget on health with 55 percent going to construction or repair of health centers. But only 20 percent of this spending came from their own resources, with the rest funded from various central transfers.

Table 7.4 Spending on capital formation of health care providers in 21 non-OECD countries, 2005–2010 (as percent total health care expenditure)

Country	*2005*	*2006*	*2007*	*2008*	*2009*	*2010*
Afghanistan	–	–	–	1.8		–
Armenia	9*	–	–	–	–	–
Bangladesh	7.3	8.6	6.3	–	–	–
Bhutan	–	–	–	–	20	
Burkina Faso	6.3	5.6	7.9*	9.3*	11.3*	–
Democratic Republic of the Congo	–	–	–	3	–	–
Ethiopia	–	–	6		–	–
Georgia	3.7	6.6	6.5	2.7	3.4	–
Kenya	1.3		–	–	3.6	
Liberia	–	–	7		–	–
Micronesia	3.4	6.8	4.9	1.9	–	–
Mozambique	6	9.02	–	–	–	–
Myanmar	3.1		–	–	–	
Qatar	–	–	–	–	18	15
Rwanda	–	7	–	–	–	–
Seychelles	–	–	–	–	8*	–
Sri Lanka	10.6	10.9	–	–	–	–
Tanzania	5.7		–	–	–	–
Vanuatu	5.2	–	–	–	–	–
Zambia	2.2	2.65	–	–	–	–

Sources: Authors using various National Health Accounts for the relevant country World Health Organization.

Note
We included all countries that had the relevant information available. Data are from reports such as for Kenya: www.who.int/entity/nha/country/ken/kenya_nha_2009–2010.pdf.

Turning to Nicaragua one finds that in 2006, the current health budget was financed mainly by the Treasury (83 percent), but capital expenditures remain heavily dependent on foreign aid with 68 percent thus funded in 2006.

Africa

We found some information for nine countries which we present in Table 7.2b. We also have some information on decentralization of health spending. In Mali deconcentrated (regional) health spending accounts for about 10 percent of central government health spending in 2007–2008, a small share. In Sierra Leone, transfers for health to local councils have been steadily increasing in recent years, now accounting for 30 percent of the central health budget. In Tanzania, in 2009–2010, health spending is split 50–50 between the central and local government for both recurrent and development (capital) spending.

Table 7.3 presents information on gross capital formation in the health sector for OECD countries.

Table 7.3 shows that gross capital formation (public + private) for health purposes is usually of the order of 0.3–0.5 percent of GDP. The USA with 0.7 or Canada (0.63) are high and Italy (0.35), France (0.40), or Germany (0.41) are in that range. The breakdown between public and private reflects the organization of health services in each country. For example, the private share is thrice the public share in the USA while the public share is six times the private share in Canada reflecting how hospitals, clinics, and other health facilities in both countries are owned and financed. As a share of health spending, gross capital formation in health is usually in the 3–6 percent range in OECD countries. This is a bit lower than the figures reported in Table 7.4 for a sample of non-OECD countries which are more in the 5–8 percent range, reflecting perhaps both a greater unmet need or catch-up phase and a population growing faster.

The main conclusions one can draw from this part of the chapter are:

- significant differences in the importance of health expenditures between groups of countries reflecting mainly their relative income level but also the organization of health services within each country;
- the fact that spending on health infrastructure is more important as a share of health spending in emerging countries than in OECD countries. Overall, one expects that it accounts worldwide for about 5–7 percent of health spending and 0.3–0.5 percent of GDP on a yearly basis.

The intergovernmental assignment of health services/infrastructure: what principles should apply?

In this part of the chapter, we first briefly recall the principles of decentralization and review a few empirical studies linking decentralization and health outcomes. We then examine issues linked to the decentralization of health services and finally discuss characteristics of health infrastructure with regards to decentralization. We attempt to assess if the characteristics of health services/infrastructure makes them different from other publicly provided services in terms of:

- the desirable degree of decentralization;
- the intergovernmental coordination arrangements both vertical and horizontal once a degree of decentralization has been settled.

Decentralization principles and empirical work on decentralization and health

Governments have two main ways to carry out their responsibilities to ensure the provision of a specific activity or service: spending, including tax expenditures, and regulation. These powers should be clearly assigned to appropriate levels of government. The two classic contributions to the literature on decentralization are those of Musgrave (1959) and Oates (1972). Musgrave (1959) suggests that, for conceptual purposes, the activities of government should be separated into three functions or branches: macroeconomic stabilization, redistribution, and resource allocation. Thus, health activities belong to both the allocation branch for the supply and production of health services and in the redistribution branch for access to services for the population who has not the capacity to pay—leaving aside at this point the political principle of "right to health for everyone." Oates (1972) puts forward three criteria to assign specific roles to specific levels of government as follows:

- Economies of scale. The existence of significant economies of scale constitutes an argument for a higher level of government to provide a particular good or service. In the area of health services, the personalized nature of many services makes health services a poor candidate for gains from scale.
- Heterogeneity of preferences also matters. Groups living in different parts of a country may display strong heterogeneity of preferences. Decentralization is an appropriate response to these different preferences if these groups are separated by political (devolved) borders that match those of areas with groups with differentiated preferences or circumstances. By extension, heterogeneity of circumstances also matter with different environments in terms of climate or topography. On this point Derycke and Gilbert (1988, p. 8) add the dimension of distance to service in the definition of local public service. So the inbound distance—the case for hospital—from the residence (or the place of accident) of the potential user to the place of service delivery or the outbound distance from the place where inputs (labor, capital) are assembled into a service provision mechanism and the place where the service is delivered—the case of the fire extinction brigade from the fire station to the location of the fire (or the cat in the tree).[4]
- The presence of externalities, negative or positive, has an impact. If some of the activities of one government at a given level have important external effects on the individuals or businesses located in other jurisdictions or on other

> governments at the same or a different level, then these activities should be more centralized, or at a minimum the actions of lower-level authorities should be well coordinated.

Finally one should note that emulation, also referred to as competition, which helps increase or introduce best practices in government, requires at least two, and probably more, units involved in a given activity. This is an argument for decentralizing government activities.

Before going further into the analysis, it seems relevant to inquire if there is evidence that varying levels of decentralization may matter to health outcomes. If the answer is no, then the above discussion is moot.

There are at least two strands of literature of potential interest in answering this question. The first can be characterized as analytical/descriptive with the work of Saltman *et al.* (2007) a good example. In it, one finds discussions of issues such as what is meant by decentralization in health (Chapter 1) or the difficulty of measuring decentralization (Chapter 3). Chapter 4 concludes by reminding us that: "most decentralization initiatives will be driven by a combination of functional performance-related concerns, legitimacy issues and self-interest" (p. 74). Interesting to note is that nowhere do Saltman *et al.* examine issues linked explicitly to infrastructure.

The second strand of literature is of an empirical nature. Using data on a sample of countries (Robalino *et al.*, 2001; Jiménez-Rubio, 2010) or on subnational units within a specific country, various authors examine the impact of decentralization on either health spending, health outcomes, or both. Examples of country specific work include that of Uchimura and Jütting (2007) who examine for China the impact on infant mortality using data for 26 provinces over seven years of within province decentralization (county level data). They find that "more decentralised provinces perform better with respect to health outcomes if two conditions are met: first, if a functioning transfer system is established between the province and county levels, and second, if county governments' own fiscal capacity is strengthened" (p. 21). Or Asfaw *et al.* (2004, p. 26) examine for India the impact on rural infant mortality rate for 14 states over the 1990–1997 period. They conclude that "Generally, the results of the study indicate that fiscal decentralization can help to reduce infant mortality rates and political decentralization can be one important factor that affects its effectiveness." Or finally Simatupang (2009) examines the case of Indonesian municipalities for 2006, noting that:

> decentralization brings mixed changes to measured health outcomes. The results show improvement of mortality rates with significant declines in infant under 5 mortality rates as well as longer life expectancy. But some decentralized health services seem to be less available, as percentage of labor assisted by medical workers, vaccination coverage, and number of active contraceptive users show declining trends.
>
> (p. 73)

Each study uses a specific measure of decentralization but none takes into account explicitly the decentralization of health infrastructure.

Overall, the literature supports the view that decentralization in the provision of health services can lead to better outcomes; but health infrastructure expenditures as such are not separately examined.

Decentralizing health; a functional analysis

How should one thus apply the criteria noted above to the field of health? One must first clarify that production of health involves numerous activities that may be assigned to one or another level of government. In what follows we will assume a three level country with a central, regional, and local governments. These are devolved entities that have some budgetary and regulatory autonomy and that have their own elected or coopted autonomous decision makers.

Categories of health services

Assume a fully public health system with no private provisions of health services. Such a system must provide three kinds of health services: population health, universal access on demand, and individual health. Population health, or public health as it is also called, offers services that are often preventive in nature, that do not target a specific individual but that benefit the population in general. These may be informational such as advice on hand washing or nutrition or health enhancing by vaccinating individuals against diseases. Individual health is comprised of both universal access on demand and curative services. "On demand access" means that potential users know that there is a network of (public) hospitals/clinics always available to them and ready to provide curative services in case of accidental or emergency need. It is a pure public good: everyone benefits from the same quality and quantity of potential access to health (usually hospital) care.[5] Both population health and universal access on demand are *public goods* (non-rival and non-excludable). Curative individual health services are offered to specific sick individuals with the aim to restore or maintain the health of individuals through drugs, surgery, and other interventions (speech therapy…). They are private or individual services (i.e., *private goods* rival and excludable). Decisions must be made on the quantity and quality of services provided including their accessibility (age, location…), on the quantity and quality of the human and physical capital inputs used to provide them and thus on their remuneration and on the financing of these services. Tables 7.5 and 7.6 present some answers to the various questions raised above; Table 7.5 addresses who should do what and Table 7.6 how should institutional governance be organized.

In both tables we assume a three tier system: primary care centers, that is, basic health units or clinics staffed by GPs and nurses or at least nurse practitioners and available at the municipal/village level; secondary health centers staffed by specialists MDs and specialized staff (speech therapists…) at the

Table 7.5 Provision of health services by level of government and type of service

Choice type	*Specific issue*	*Considerations*	*Decision maker*	*Implementation*
Population health	Who should set standards for vaccination, communicable diseases/cattle disease control, food quality	Spillovers within or beyond national borders (international treaties)	Supranational body (EC); Central government or for food importing government (USA FDA rules)	National regulations or financial incentives/penalties
Population health	Who should implement public health measures (vaccination, . . .)	Heterogeneity such as cultural sensitivity varying on a geographical basis	National for some inputs (vaccines) Level in charge of primary health center (regional/local?) for distribution	Primary health center & special teams
Hospital/clinic network	Territorial (geographical) distribution of hospital centers	Economies of scale, horizontal and vertical coordination of services, specialities and equipment	Central and regional government in partnership	Regional and local depending on the nature of the service; central or inter-regional for high-tech specialities
Individual health	Who should set standards for individual health care (delineation between standards and private health services, administrative prices of medical and hospital service, waiting lists, procedures covered. . .?	No spillovers (services are rival and excludable); redistributive consideration (user's capacity to pay)	Government that is main payer—higher individual territorial mobility for medical service calls for centralization	Issues to be addressed: cooperation agreements: border areas, specialized services
Individual health	How is access to health centers determined: free or boundary restricted	No spillovers Economies of scale Minimum size for excellence		

Source: Authors.

Table 7.6 Issues in the institutional governance of the health sector

General question	*Specific questions*
Who decides where to build/maintain/operate health facilities?	Assuming that who decides which health and hospital services are attributed to primary, secondary, and tertiary health centers. Issues then are: First, how is vertical coordination secured? Second, appropriate distances to service centers must be set in order to optimize the network. Finally if private clinics and hospitals are considered part of the health network, under what conditions?
How is health infrastructure financed?	There are two issues here. One is the funding mechanism used which can range from spending from general revenues to various forms of public borrowing to PPPs. Second is what government mobilizes this funding for public facilities. Is this based solely on the location and type of infrastructure or are interactions accounted for in the capital funding as such rather than solely in the current funding (with some compensation for the access to facilities)?
Who trains (sets quotas/provides facilities) health staff?	How much (inter)national mobility exists in trained health staff? Are diplomas delivered in one region (country) recognized in another? How is the limit set, by whom, between in-house doctors and independent doctors, specialists, and nurses?
Who sets the pay of health staff? Their pension arrangements?	Consideration of mobility and competition between public health facilities operated by different level of governments. Also consideration of mobility public—private; mobility in-house—independent doctors
Who hires/fires health staff?	How much room for maneuver do hospital/clinic boards have? Are employees covered by public law or by private labor market law?
Who decides on the structure (fees, taxes…) of financing of health services (given the amounts offered)?	One must first distinguish between the three types of services. Population health is usually paid out of general revenues. It is universal access and curative services that tend to have a fee based funding component. In those cases, who sets the shares of the various sources and the specific fees? If user-pay is implemented, how much is paid through health and accident insurances and how much is charged directly to the beneficiaries? In hospital stays, is there a difference between medical services and accommodation pricing?
Who supervises the quality of practice?	Competition and emulation between service units might not suffice.

Source: Authors.

regional level; tertiary health centers in a few locations in the country offering specialized care for the more complex problems.[6]

Aside from infrastructure, how does health compare to other commonly decentralized public services? One can only answer this by distinguishing between population and individual curative health and comparing this with for example education and roads; this is done in Table 7.7. Population health is the best candidate for centralized production while individual health is better suited for decentralization; yet both can be, and often are, provided by the same institutions such as local health centers. This is different from the education system where the provision of compulsory and higher education is usually carried out by separate institutions in different locations (although some facilities may be rented out by one body to another). Or from the provision of roads which are distinct in their spatial nature even if interconnected. So jointness of production appears to matter more for the two types (population and individual) of health services at the primary health center level than for other types of public services. This is much less of an issue at the secondary and tertiary level since these institutions specialize in individual health care.

The main conclusions one can draw from Tables 7.5, 7.6, and 7.7 are first that the provision of health services is more akin to a joint production decision than the provision of other publicly provided services, due to the overlapping of public and private services offered by a specialized personnel. The general consequence of this for health infrastructure is the need for substantial vertical and horizontal integration/coordination. Second, the joint nature of health services, that is on the one hand universal access, emergency services, and hospital network (collective) and on the other hand individual curative services (private), calls for nuances in financing health infrastructure. When both categories of services are offered, one cannot ask that user charges billed to individual patients cover the total infrastructure costs; there must be a public funding. Inversely, if (private) clinics do not offer services that are collective by nature, they should not receive public financing.

Characteristics of health infrastructures and decentralization

One can address the question of the decentralization of health infrastructures in a different way by noting that health infrastructures:

- have for various reasons increasing units costs per meter^2, as they become both more specialized, bigger, and less numerous, as shown in Table 7.8. First, primary facilities will for example have exam rooms but not operating rooms found in secondary and tertiary facilities. Such surgery rooms are more expensive to build and maintain. Second, the absolute size of secondary/tertiary facilities will require connecting spaces, isolation mechanisms (to avoid the spread of diseases), and so on. Third, they will have more developed ancillary services such as cafeterias for their staff. This last item if fully self–financing will have no impact on costs but this requires charging

Table 7.7 Comparative impact of determinants of decentralization: education, health, and roads

	Population health	*Individual health*	*Compulsory primary/ secondary education*	*Higher education*	*Local (market) roads*	*National roads*
Economies of scale	High (vaccine production, information)	Low (labor serves one patient at a time although some on the capital side)	Low-medium	Medium	Low	High
Heterogeneity of preferences	Low	Medium (as revealed by choices)	Medium (language, pedagogy, protection of territorial minorities)	High (variety of trainings)	Low	Low
Externalities	High	Nil-low	Medium (required for private employment but some social benefits: raising children, participation in society)	Medium (spillovers between jurisdictions with labor mobility	Low	Medium
Redistribution	Low	High (low fees; capacity to pay with a user-pays tariff)	Low (free access to compulsory school)	Medium	Low	Low (even with toll roads, generally no redistributive consideration

Source: Authors.

Table 7.8 Construction cost per meter^2, three types of health centers, seven selected countries, 2011, US$

Country	*Day centre (1)*	*Regional hospital (2)*	*General hospital (3)*	*Ratio (3)/(1)*
Australia	3,014	3,400	5,337	1.77
Canada	3,748	5,774	6,888	1.84
China	679	823	920	1.35
Germany	1,960	3,130	3,410	1.74
Malaysia	589	786	884	1.50
South Africa	845	1,056	1,267	1.50
Vietnam	676	1,302	1,302	1.93

Source: International construction cost survey (Turner and Townsend, 2012): Australia, p. 8; Canada, p. 10; China, p. 12; Germany, p. 14; Malaysia, p. 22; South Africa, p. 28; Vietnam, p. 38.

a proper rent to these services or imputing depreciation and so on. Is there a trade-off between local control and the availability of technologically differentiated care? For example, locally provided simple maternity services with slightly higher death rates than more sophisticated services with slightly better outcomes but further away from the place of residence of the expecting mother either because of better equipment or better skilled specialized MDs. Can distance spanning technology (tele-medicine) correct for this? Who decides what bundle of services to offer?

- are (should be) meshed in spatial and specialized units network operated by various levels of governments making coordination between autonomous governments at a given level and between levels of autonomous governments an issue. Spatial coordination is horizontal between service precincts that deliver the same baskets of services. Vertical coordination is needed not only from the territorial point of view, but also for the assignment of specialities to each governmental layer. One may be faced with deconcentrated entities of devolved governments interacting together. Thus one can ask if the coordination between levels of governments and governments at a given level is consensual or top down? Is it between local units producing services together? Through what means is coordination achieved? Through financial (ranging from soft, signalling devices like earmarking of funds … to hard, conditional, matching grants) financing; top down planning; or institutional [appointments to director positions, coordinating/dialog councils, etc.]). Or put differently, the assignment of services responsibilities (primary health; secondary health, etc.) and the assignment for infrastructure provision may differ. The latter might change constantly as projects go through several stages of the planning building cycle. The planning cycle for a new secondary health facility may be initiated by a local group of potential users who are tired of incurring high private costs (time and money) to use facilities away from their residence in a growing urban center. It may be taken up by a local politician or central deconcentrated bureaucrat who champions it, and then be formally accepted by the health planners. It is not always the case that the entity that plans, appraises, provides the budget, etc., is also the one that implements or later also operates the facility. Indeed, changing ownership of infrastructure over time is often required under private sector financial arrangements.

- are subject like all public projects to costs overruns. We were unable to find a systematic comparisons of the extent of cost overruns by type of infrastructure—education, health, roads—or by type of health facility (hospital, clinic). There is however evidence for transportation projects that costs overrun are more important for technologically complex projects at 45 percent for trains, 34 percent for fixed links (bridges), and 20 percent for roads (Flyvbjerg *et al.*, 2002, table 1, p. 283). The authors conclude that (p. 290):

    - *Cost underestimation exists across 20 nations and five continents; it appears to be a global phenomenon.*
    - *Cost underestimation appears to be more pronounced in developing nations than in North America and Europe (data for rail projects only).*
    - *Cost underestimation has not decreased over the past 70 years. No learning that would improve cost estimate accuracy seems to take place.*
    - *Cost underestimation cannot be explained by error and seems to be best explained by strategic misrepresentation, i.e., lying.*
    - *Transportation infrastructure projects do not appear to be more prone to cost underestimation than are other types of large projects.*

- have both characteristics of a stand-alone service and of a network. Going further than the stand-alone network dimension, one must note the jointness of the services. They are both private and public in nature. Private in that both rivalry and exclusion apply: when patient A is hooked up to a given machine, patient B is not. And one can exclude A or B using the pricing mechanism (should one do so it is another issue). Public in that the health network is available to all when an accident occurs; indeed access to emergency services is a priority in health institutions with triage giving more immediate access to more urgent cases.
- are more often in competition with private providers than roads or primary schools infrastructures. There is not only competition between private and public hospitals/clinics in a given territory/jurisdiction but also potential competition across jurisdictions between public hospitals. The normative reference here is that of FOCJs (for Functional Overlapping Competing Jurisdictions) put forward by Frey and Eichenberger (1999). Thus health zone borders and the rules that govern their setting and crossing will matter to infrastructure decisions. Do patients decide (if they have a choice and there are payment agreements)? Or are hospitals built independent of consideration of demand? Can private facilities offer only a subset of profitable activities or are they required to offer full coverage? With or without full

payment by the public providers or private insurers and using what price list? And what about the micro-locational choice of building a hospital within a given territory?

- are affected by a combination of roads and ambulances in two ways. First, this links the three tiers of institutions. An improvement in this network (lower travelling time, less jarring travel) facilitates the coordinated provision of services. It may also facilitate regrouping specialized activities in a smaller number of facilities. The resulting improvement in quality may well more than compensate for the additional cash and time costs to access them. Second, the same improvement may, depending on the existing spatial distribution, reduce the required number of primary care units since it may reduce the travel time of users of such facilities. Note that this matters the most for emergencies and unplanned health consumption.[7] However, better roads by facilitating the growth of private transportation options such as buses or moto-taxis may modify the supply of available services.

Let us return to the FOCJ issue. Assume two hospitals A and B located in two adjacent jurisdictions JA and JB; they are monopolies. Since the population of JA is larger than JB (but not too large so as to avoid the upward sloping part of the cost curve), A has lower operating costs than B due to economies of scale along the same cost function. If the rules stipulate that residents of JA are treated in hospital A and the same for JB except in case of emergencies, then the only issue is how both hospitals are compensated in that case: using their price/cost structure which is higher in B than A or the price structure of the place of residence of the patient.

But what happens if patients are allowed to access health services where they wish if they reside within 50 km of the JA–JB border? Or if the monopoly clause is abandoned?[8] Then if they must contribute a copayment (deductible) to the cost of their health care, residents of JB may prefer to use hospital A. Note that the lower cost in A is not due to greater efficiency or better procedures but simply to the size of JA relative to JB. This means than when planning its supply of services hospital A will plan on a share of JB residents, Bm (m for mobile) as users and thus will adjust its infrastructure size upwards accordingly. It could even pursue a proactive competition to attract more Bm users (beyond 50 km) and gain further economies of scale (going further in the upward sloping part of the cost curve). How will hospital B react? It could give up Bm users and thus plan on JB–Bm users with the required adjustment in services offered and thus the necessary infrastructure along with higher costs. Or it could ramp up its offerings targeting Am users; this would require it to invest more in infrastructure so as to lower its costs to the level of A. In this second case, it may well be able to retain the Bm users. Overall, however, both hospitals may have planned for too large a clientele in the absence of coordination. In hospital investment planning, as for other public services which are capital intensive, a pure FOCJ approach clearly leads to non-cooperative outcomes and, thus, allocative inefficiencies.

The main conclusions one can draw from this second part of the chapter are:

- health services include both public and private (as defined by economists) services;
- the delivery of both types of services is often carried out by the same agent even though their impact and financing are different;
- there are important benefits (economies of scales, expertise, better outcomes) to a tiered system with specialized care provided in specialized institutions that are less numerous and thus further away from users than basic health services centers;
- tiered systems require substantial horizontal and vertical coordination due to geographic spillovers as well as vigilance against over-provision;
- infrastructure costs increase per patient served with specialization of the health facility; thus intergovernmental finance arrangements for both operating and infrastructure provision matter;
- leaving hospital units competing for patient beyond their "natural" jurisdiction may lead to non-cooperative options and thus inefficiencies.

Case studies and policy choices

A key issue of this chapter is how health facilities in general and hospitals in particular are or should be financed in a decentralized setting. One way to answer this question is to examine how it is done in various countries in the world. Another way is to examine the debate between proponents and opponents of Private Public Partnership (PPP). That done we can turn to plausible policy recommendations.

Financing health facilities; country evidence

We examine information for three countries which are the United States, Canada, and Switzerland with more attention on the latter as it has since 1990 undergone changes in the provision and financing of health of particular interest in the context of this chapter.

United States

We begin with the United States where financing for hospitals is mainly from financial markets but not always, as we shall see. In the USA, access to markets by hospitals is a key factor in the financing of health infrastructure. Sussman and Jordahl (2010) examine the situation following the upheaval in the bond market of 2008. They argue that (p. 7):

> Health care is a very capital-intensive business and access to debt financing keeps hospitals in business. Few hospitals today can generate enough cash flow from their operations and reserves to fund short and long-term strategic investments in people, programs, facilities, and technology. Most hospitals

> must access external debt on a periodic basis to assure the provision of continued health care services in their communities. The ability to issue and support debt is not a "nice-to-have" capability; it is essential to the viability of nearly all US hospitals and health systems.

Hospitals often finance themselves by issuing municipal bonds and were thus quite affected by the collapse of the insurers in that market in 2007–2008. Hospitals bonds are about ten times more risky than standard municipal bonds (*WSJ*, August 9, 2012).[9] Thus Sussman and Jordahl (2010, p. 11) identify eight financing options: *municipal bonds, direct bank loans, FHA Section 242 credit enhancement, leasing, USDA Rural Development Program, New Market Tax Credit Program, debt restructuring, and asset sales.* Some are standard access to private markets (*municipal bonds [issued by municipalities on behalf of hospitals to take advantage of their established credit rating], direct bank loans, leasing)* while others use a mortgage guaranty from the federal government to reduce borrowing costs (*Federal Housing Administration Section 242*) or a mortgage guaranty or direct loans from the USDA Rural Development Community Facilities Program for health facilities in rural areas and towns with populations of up to 20,000.[10] For the direct loans, there are three levels of interest rates set according to the median household income and the type of project: poverty rate, market rate (set by US Treasury Department), and the intermediate rate is set halfway between these two. The rate used depends on the median household income (MHI) of the area and the type of project being financed. Finally the *New Market Tax Credit Program* allows individual and corporate investors to receive a tax credit against their federal income tax payable in exchange for investing in Community Development Entities (CDEs).[11] The credit totals 39 percent of the original investment amount and is claimed over a period of seven years.

The use of bond financing is likely to result in more autonomous investment choices by hospitals than the use of grants financing presented below for Canada and Switzerland. Thus bond financing results in less vertical and horizontal coordination since it is not the result of centralized decisions but of market choices

Canada

Before WWII the provision of private health services was funded by private payments either from the pocket of the patients or from their insurance with in some cases subsidies to the poor by provinces. It is after WWII that there is involvement of the governments in the provision of health services. With respect to intergovernmental relations four items should be noted.[12]

1 National Health Grants were introduced in 1948 by the federal government mainly for capital expenditures.
2 The federal Hospital and Diagnostics Services Act came into effect in 1958; it uses a 50–50 cost-sharing formula for covering hospital costs.

3 The federal Medical Care Insurance Act came in force in 1996; it also uses a 50–50 cost-sharing formula covering the cost of services by MDs in hospitals and their private offices.
4 A series of health accords in the early 2000s leading to increased federal funding.

This broadening financing by the federal government occurred often because "provincial push led to federal pull in convening the provinces and in drawing them into an intergovernmental arrangement" (Maioni, 2002, p. 3). So provinces introduced hospital insurance and then encouraged federal financing, knowing that there was interest at that level of government for doing this given past policy statements. One interesting point for us is that while infrastructure spending was the entry point,[13] it quickly became insufficient as a policy tool. Now in Canada there is no federal program funding hospital infrastructure. Hospital capital funding is usually a mix of (i) public funds provided by the province which borrows it or finances it out of general revenues and transfers it as grants to hospitals and (ii) privately raised funds by the foundation of the hospital carrying out a capital project. For example, in Montreal, the main children's hospital (Sainte-Justine) just launched a capital campaign to raise C$150 million with the support of Céline Dion. The previous campaign raised C$125 million used for new buildings.[14]

Federal capital grants were made between 1948 and 1969 and then anew as of 2000. The first type of grants was mainly for buildings while the second was for medical equipment. In both cases, grants are to provinces which pass them on to hospitals. There is no direct federal payment to hospitals as in the USA. That said, federal grants finance provincial priorities rather than determining them. Provincial priorities are set mainly by their respective ministries of health with inputs from intra-provincial bodies such as health districts.

Public capital in hospital was in the range of 3–4 percent of GDP in Canada in the 1961–2001 period (Mackenzie, 2004, Chart 5, p. 10); it declined slightly between 1981 and 2001 while health spending increased, yielding a lower output/capital ratio.

Day to day operations are under the control of autonomous hospitals who decide within the constraints of collective agreements that can be more or less uniform across hospitals such things as staffing levels, MDs accreditation, type of services offered, and so on. Surpluses or deficits may result from day to day operations. Deficits are quite common in Canadian hospitals;[15] while usually not allowed by regulations or laws, provinces cover them as provincial subsidies account for a substantial amount of hospital financing.[16] One explanation for this behavior is that at least in some provinces hospital deficits are not part of provincial deficits and thus the underfunding of hospitals that results in these deficits appear as cost cutting measures. Of interest to us is how surpluses are used; this is addressed by McKillop (2002). In the case of Canada, he finds (Table 5, p. 18) that in some provinces it is recommended that they be used for capital equipment (Alberta, British Columbia, Ontario) in others part (Manitoba) or all (PEI) goes back to provinces.

Switzerland

Up to the 1990s, the Swiss hospital system was comprised of three levels. Level 1 was small and regional hospitals, mainly operated by local governments (communes) organized except for large ones in multi-communal hospital districts.[17] Most of these establishments had religious or private charity origins. At level 2 one finds cantonal hospitals with more developed services while there are a few level 3 highly specialized university/cantonal hospitals (Genève, Lausanne, Berne, Zurich, Basel-Town), carrying out research activities and using cutting edge technologies. Level 3 hospitals are not federal; they are operated by the canton where they are located with horizontal access and cost sharing agreements (concordats) with neighboring cantons.

In the 1990s, centralization began when the cantons started promulgating technical norms and minimum standard requirements in order to limit inefficiencies: this was the case when new technology appeared (scanning instead of X-rays for example) so as to avoid each district hospital acquiring its own equipment that could serve more that the residents of the hospital district; or to improve quality with a minimum number of acts (obstetric departments are good examples).

In the 2000s, centralization accelerated. In most cantons, vertical coordination was obtained through the merging of district hospitals (level 1) into the cantonal level 2 in order to organize a larger cantonal hospital network.[18] This meant that—not without heated political debates in cantonal parliaments and opposition in the rural areas—several district hospitals were closed. Between 2000 and 2010, more than 35 percent of Swiss hospitals were closed.[19] This centralization was eased also by the improvement of mobile medical technologies found in ambulances and the development of helicopter rescue and inter-hospital link.

Two points are of interest in this move towards centralization: the arguments that are proposed for centralization at the cantonal level and the public finance solution.

In most cases, the arguments for the cantonalization of hospitals can be summarized as follows:[20]

- this stops a race between district hospitals leading to over-equipment overall at that level;
- this stops encroachment by district hospitals in the areas of competencies of cantonal hospitals, preventing the consequent vertical inefficiencies;
- this allows better organization in the purchase of medical products and equipment (no local overstocking yet more cantonal power in price negotiation);
- this facilitates harmonization of the management, computer program, billing, and other bureaucratic measures;
- this creates scale economies in infrastructures and equipment;
- this increases the quality of medical and surgery service delivered with a higher number carried out in each now larger hospital (practice makes perfect argument).

Financing the re-assignment of hospital care and thus investments from the communes to the cantons was done by modifying the taxation of various bases (mainly taxes on personal income and wealth, and on corporate profit and capital) levied by both communes and cantons. As one knows, re-assigning functions in a federal or decentralized system always creates budgetary problems. One way to render this shift acceptable is to group bottom-up and top-down re-assignments so as to obtain a zero-sum change. This has proved to be both difficult and hazardous not only at the moment of the re-assignment, but also because the rates of growth of the re-assigned functions can take unexpected paths—with the result that losers in a given round are reluctant to take on a second re-assignment round. This pitfall was avoided using an innovative technique (innovative in Switzerland at least): the vertical compensation of the tax coefficient on direct taxation. Each canton calculated how much the communes paid, in this case for hospital care, infrastructures, and equipment in the last three (sometimes five) years preceding the shift. Then the ratio (total past communal hospital expenditure)/(the tax base) is used to calculate the relevant communal tax coefficient. In counterpart, the communes have the obligation to reduce their own tax coefficient (piggyback taxation) in proportion.[21]

Let us now turn to the magnitude of decentralized health expenditures in general and for investments. Table 7.9 summarizes the situation for the period 1990–2010.[22] Investment expenditures at the cantonal and communal level have varied from 9.3 percent of total hospital and retirement home expenditures in 1990, decreasing to 7.7 percent in 2000 and going back to over 10 percent from 2008 onwards. The 2005–2007 figures are lower: they concerns the years where cantonalization took place in many cantons, thus limiting new investments in that period of institutional re-organization. The cantons' shares of investment expenditures have regularly increased over time, compared to the communes' share, from 64/36 percent in 1990 to 85/15 percent in 2010, and this will certainly continue in the near future up to a near 100 percent in the cantons' hands. The Confederation does not operate hospitals; it only legislates in that area.

From 2012 onwards, hospital financing has changed radically. Following years of political debate, the federal government imposed on the cantons and hospitals a funding system based on federally set unit costs for each medical act. Hospital expenditures will no longer be covered through lump-sum amounts and contracts with private health insurances. Thus the federal government sets the value of each medical act; the hospitals are reimbursed according to this fee schedule, which applies to all hospitals throughout the country. It benefits the hospital to be as efficient (cost minimizing) as possible given the fee schedule. Also new is that, at least on paper, the patient can chose which hospital to use—cantonal and district hospitals have lost their territorial monopoly. The objective is to increase competition between establishments and, through competition, to increase efficiency and lower hospital recurrent costs per medical act and thus per patient. Finally, according to the new law, the cantons will have to cover at least 55 percent of the hospital costs, current and capital. After one year of implementation, some problems already appear: (i) the implicit hypothesis of the

Table 7.9 Public health expenditure, Switzerland, 1990–2010, in 1,000 CHF

	1990	*1995*	*2000*	*2005*	*2006*	*2007*	*2008*	*2009*	*2010*
Total hospital and retirement home	**9,914,075**	**13,140,682**	**14,319,763**	**18,242,477**	**18,435,598**	**19,300,901**	**8,258,495**	**8,788,580**	**8,815,252**
Health expenditure: total	**10,769,188**	**14,251,061**	**15,579,322**	**19,751,925**	**19,974,506**	**21,072,410**	**10,634,149**	**11,270,274**	**11,328,790**
Public expenditures: total	**105,118,888**	**139,873,305**	**151,836,715**	**176,235,767**	**176,973,488**	**183,706,306**	**187,890,993**	**185,536,151**	**189,407,520**
Total hospital and retirement home/total health spending %	92	92	92	92	92	92	78	78	78
Health spending/total public expenditures %	10	10	10	11	11	11	6*	6*	6*
Cantons' share in total hospital and retirement home 41	60	56	56	58	59	59	91	91	92
Communes' share in total hospital and retirement home 41	40	44	44	42	41	41	9	9	8
Investment share in total hospital and retirement home	9.3	8.8	7.7	5.3	4.6	5.7	10.6	10.2	10.3
Cantons' share in health investment %	64	74	72	67	73	79	78	80	85
Communes' share in health investment %	36	26	28	33	27	21	22	20	15

Sources: Authors' computations based on Federal Department of Finance, Berne, www.efv.admin.ch/ Documentation > Statistique financière > Rapport > Modèle SF > sous-secteur et agrégats. Authors' report and calculation from various tables: F11.7, F40.7.5, F23.7 F70.7.5, F80.7.5 (all refreshed January 31, 2013). PIB: SECO, September 25, 2012. Information about the investment share in 41 and the cantons' and communes respective shares in percent have been obtained directly from the Federal Department of Finance, February 1, 2013.

Note

* This drop is the result of a statistical artifact noted above.

single fee schedule is that all hospitals are on the same position in the U-shape cost curve right from the beginning; this does not rely on empirical evidence and is unlikely to hold given the existing territory/clientele served by each hospital; (ii) since savings are not easily made in terms of spending on investment, equipment or medical products, pressure to save occurs mainly on human resources. Medical staff and nurses are complaining that priority is given to medical acts rather than to the relationship between staff and hospitalized patients; this relationship may matter more for their well-being but is not taken into account by the fee schedule. Thus some health experts are arguing that the system should return to cooperative rather than competitive federalism since hospital functions are first collective goods and not market services. It is too early to say if patient mobility and the capacity to choose one's hospital anywhere in Switzerland will enhance quality and efficiency. If it does, then this shift towards a more competitive (private) type of provision of hospital services may have been for the best; otherwise, it is most likely for the worse.

The discussion above only examines the public hospital health sector and says nothing about the private sector or PPP. Unfortunately, actual statistical data blur the debate on public/private hospitals so that the issue becomes uncontrollable. Consider the following situation (2010). The left column gives the number of establishments in the functional classification; the middle one the nature of the unit.

[function 411] 121 hospitals	30 university and cantonal 91 regional and small	84 public or private and subsidized 37 private and not subsidized
[function 412] 1,523 home for elderly people		465 public 467 private and subsidized 455 private and not subsidized 136 not precisely identified
[function 413] 179 clinics	88 selected hospital care and specialties 50 psychiatric 41 physical disability re-adaptation	72 public or private and subsidized 107 private and not subsidized

Source: «Statistiques de la santé 2010», vol. 14, pp. 71–76, Federal Statistical Office, Neuchâtel www.bfs.admin.ch/portal/fr/index/news/publications. Consulted February 1, 2013.

The interest of these figures is in the right-hand-side column. According to the normative view developed in the earlier section, only hospital units that deliver a collective good in terms of hospital health care, mainly with open access and day-night emergency services, should be (partly) funded out of public budget. But one can no longer cross-cut public/private ownership with collective service/individual care when public finance statistical data are organized according to the SEC95.[23] In there, the concept of "economically significant prices"[24] and a system of pricing which is applied to both public and private hospitals have eliminated from the "public" statistics into the "private" sector a substantial number of publicly owned hospitals. Hospital health expenditures have not been reduced, nor have they disappeared. They are simply recorded in the private sector and not accessible. This is more than unfortunate since hospital policy remains essentially in public hands.

A complement to a more market oriented provision of health services is a more market oriented financing of health investments as embodied in PPP. We thus turn to a discussion of this financing system now.

PPP

Montagu and Harding (2012) examine the role of the private sector in the provision of health services and health infrastructure. They first note a fair amount of confusion in the terminology and propose four definitions.

> **Services: Operating contract**: A private organization is brought in to operate and deliver publicly funded health services within a public facility.
>
> **Facility/finance: PFI**: A public agency contracts a private entity to finance, design, build, and operate a hospital facility. Health services within the facility are provided by government.
>
> **Combined BOT+PPIP**: A private organization establishes capacity (through new construction or expansion of existing facility) to provide health services under sustained public or social insurance reimbursement.
>
> **Co-location**: A public agency allocates a portion of a public hospital's land and/or premises for sustained use by a private organization in exchange for payment and specified benefits to the public agency.

McKee *et al.* (2006) review various PPP health facilities and note several issues both financial (Box 7.10) and in terms of quality of the facilities. Their abstract summarizes the issues well:

> Although experience is still very limited and rigorous evaluations lacking, four issues have emerged: cost, quality, flexibility and complexity. New facilities have, in general, been more expensive than they would have been if procured using traditional methods. Compared with the traditional system, new facilities are more likely to be built on time and within budget, but this seems often to be at the expense of compromises on quality. The need to minimize the risk to the parties means that it is very difficult to "future-proof" facilities in a rapidly changing world. Finally, such projects are extremely, and in some cases prohibitively, complex. While it is premature to say whether the problems experienced relate to the underlying model or to their implementation, it does seem that a public–private partnership further complicates the already difficult task of building and operating a hospital.

A presentation by Loening[25] shows that while the major spending item of hospitals is on delivery of care (54 percent), the second largest item at 15 percent is construction.

Table 7.10 The role of the private sector in the provision of health services and health infrastructure

	Infrastructure PPPs	*Hospital PPPs*	*Implications*
Government vs. private purchaser of output	Private buyers/payers • Government does not enter into long-term service purchasing relationship as part of transaction	Government (or social health insurers) buy all or most services • Government enters into long-term service purchasing relationship as part of transaction	Substantial risks to government payer as a result of long-term funding "lock in" obligation • Substantial political risks to private partners in hospital PPP
Business risk vs. political risk	Borrowing costs reflect estimated risk of demand for infrastructure services by total market of potential payers	Borrowing costs reflect risks associated with single (or multiple) government payer agencies	Cost of finance (and therefore capital) higher for hospital facility investment
Measurability	Comparators for benchmarking cost of facility availability services are somewhat limited	Comparators for benchmarking cost of services often extremely limited	Probability that payment contract will set excessive rates is higher for hospitals
Variability of outputs over time	Products stable over time	Products highly variable due to volatility in demographics and disease	• Risk to private partners necessitating either higher return contingencies, or flexibility in contract modification • Risk to government due to "locked in" commitment to hospitals/configuration that may not be needed in the future
Variability of technology over time	Service delivery technology and organizational models change slowly	Service delivery technology and organizational models change rapidly	Risks to government and private partners as a result of lost flexibility to adapt service organization; or cost of unpredictable adjustments to technology, systems, and staffing
Ratio of investment to operating capital	High ratio of capital to operating costs	Low ratio of capital to operating costs	Efficiency gains from private finance/design/construction and operation of hospital PPPs lower than for infrastructure PPPs

Source: Table 2 as such: Montagu and Harding (2012).

The main conclusions one can draw from this part of the chapter are that:

- there are various models commonly used to finance health infrastructure, relying more or less on debt and more or less on private funds;
- as shown for Switzerland it is possible to modify the role of various levels of governments in the provision of health services through more centralization for example but this needs to be accompanied by well thought out changes in financial arrangements;
- one model often put forward as the modern way, the PPP, should be considered with great caution.

Conclusion

Investment in health infrastructure is carried out to provide health services. These are among the commonly provided public services those that use more specialized manpower. Thus the complementarity of human and physical capital is an important factor in designing a proper health infrastructure funding arrangement. One must also note that the availability of medications is a key part of successful health outcomes. A second important factor is the need for quick universal access in case of emergency since not all health needs are predictable; this requires taking into account networks interactions between roads, ambulances, and facilities. Third, one must balance the benefits and costs of concentrating care in specialized care centers.

One difficult issue is that there are three inputs in health and particularly curative health services: labor, structures, and technology. The last one changes faster than the technology in education or road maintenance and trends higher cost wise. In a decentralized health system, how should one fund technology? As an ongoing cost or as a depreciable (at what rate) infrastructure? Does this have an impact on horizontal cooperation? For example one equips hospital A with technology T1, then B with T2, then A with T3 and so on in some kind of leapfrogging approach? With patients in the catchment area A sent to B when T2 benefits them and vice versa for T3. Or does one give T1 to A and B, skip T2 and go for T3 with a period when T2 which is useful is not available thus reducing the quality of health care for a while for all.

These various factors combined with the fact that one often finds decentralized (devolved) provision of health care with a link between less specialized care and smaller governments has consequences for the funding of infrastructure. In general, it will make sense to have a funding and standards role for the national government or at least large SNGs to internalize externalities and optimize the network while avoiding a medical arms race.[26]

Finally, it is common to end a chapter for a plea for more research. Here we believe this would not be useful given the lack of data. So we end with a plea for more data comparable over time and space. This is necessary not only for research but also to guide policy.

Notes

1 We thank Matthieu Strub and Ryan Leenhouts for their excellent research assistance.

2 *Manual of Government Deficit and Debt, Implementation of ESA95*, Eurostat Methodologies and Working Papers, European Commission, Luxembourg, 2012, 4th edition, pp. 14–16.

3 Source: *Statistique financières 2010 de la Suisse*, Rapport Annuel, Administration fédérale des Finances, OFS, Neuchâtel 2012, Série 18, pp. 17–19. www.bfs.admin.choffice fédéral de la statistique>thèmes>18>finances publiques>publications. Despite the fact that all cantons have hospital networks, some publicly owned hospitals are taken out of the public sector statistical data, in compliance with the SEC95 statistical system.

4 $Sai = Sa\, N^{-\alpha}$ where Sa is the supply of collective good "a" and N the total number of "i" potential consumers. $-\alpha$ gives the characteristic of the local versus central publicness: if $\alpha = 0$, then $N = 1$ and characterizes a pure collective good since the quantity offered to the "i" user is available for all others; $\alpha = 1$ correspond to a pure market good and consumer "i" receives $1/N$ of the total supply. With $0 < \alpha < 1$, the good supply is more or less divisible, that is local or a club service. α can have various specificities.

5 Note that the quality of the network (design, output...) will affect the health outcomes but a network of a given quality gives the same level universal access to potential beneficiaries.

6 If one adds a parallel set of private providers of health services then one must also address issues of coordination between the public and private services and of the regulation of private providers. Private hospital and clinic centers offer mainly curative or individual health services, which are private services. The questions are whether and how they contribute to population health and, more important, how they accommodate the constraints (in terms of organization, infrastructure, and medical staff) of acting as part of the health network that offers universal access (mainly by offering minor emergency services and non-discriminatory tariffs).

7 The exact relationship between health facilities and transport is not clear; see Toloo *et al.* (2011).

8 This is the very precise sense of FOCJs: Functional because the two service precincts supply the same function, here hospital health care; Overlapping since with C for Competing, the functional area for hospital A is not only JA but also JB (or part of it in the 50km deep border example), and inversely for hospital B. Thus the institutional and functional territories are not identical: for hospital A the functional territory is JA and JB whereas the institutional limit is the political governmental unit JA in charge of the public hospital A; and the reciprocal for hospital B.

9 Hospitals' Debt Gets a Checkup: http://online.wsj.com/article/SB1000087239639044 4900304577579360896916848.html.

10 For more details see www.rurdev.usda.gov/HAD-CF_Loans.html.

11 For more details see www.cdfifund.gov/what_we_do/programs_id.asp?programID=5.

12 We draw this information from the *Appendix: Key Events in Health Insurance Legislation in Canada* in Maioni (2002).

13 The grants offering financial support for planning and organization, public health, and hospital construction," in *Health Policy in Canada*, prepared by Nancy Miller Chenier, Political and Social Affairs Division. Revised 4 December 2002 http://publications.gc.ca/Collection-R/LoPBdP/CIR/934-e.htm.

14 http://fr.canoe.ca/divertissement/celebrites/nouvelles/2012/12/12/20426166-qmi.html.

15 For Ontario see "More than one-third of Ontario hospitals didn't balance books" (Maria Babbage, Toronto—*The Globe and Mail*), August 23, 2012 http://m.theglobeandmail.com/news/politics/more-than-one-third-of-ontario-hospitals-didnt-balance-books/article1320892/?service=mobile. For Québec see "Quebec to appoint financial monitor at MUHC McGill hospital centre's deficit could hit $115M" (CBC News), December 18, 2012 www.cbc.ca/news/canada/montreal/story/2012/12/18/muhc-cuts-patient-care.html.

16 Ninety percent in 2010—Figure 14, p.19, National Health Expenditure Trends, 1975–2011, Canadian Institute for Health Information https://secure.cihi.ca/free_products/nhex_trends_report_2011_en.pdf.

17 In several places, the functional limits of the hospital service jurisdiction overlap over two cantons. This is not uncommon and shows how federalism can organize adaptable and creative solutions in order to gain efficiency and economies of scale, taking into consideration distance and cantonal frontiers. These special jurisdictions sometimes have been given as illustrative examples of FOCJs. But the analogy is not correct. They were functional jurisdictions, but neither overlapping (their position was monopolistic in the territory of the members communes) nor competing (hospitals of first and second level were attributed their own political boundaries and hospitalized persons could not "choose" other establishments).

18 For example, in the cantons of Valais in 2004, Neuchâtel 2006, Vaud and Fribourg 2007

19 Statisques de la santé 2010, vol. 14, pp. 71–76, Federal Office of Statistics, Neuchâtel www.bfs.admin.ch/portal/fr/index/news/publications.

20 Message 251, March 13, 2006 for the executive government of canton Fribourg to the Parliament explaining the draft law on the cantonal hospital network (Message in French): pages 1 and 2. The arguments developed in this Message are illustrative of the arguments previously forwarded in other cantons (see footnote 17).

21 In the canton of Neuchâtel, the cantonal coefficient was increased with 0.30 from 1.00 to 1.30 and the communes' tax coefficients were globally reduced by 0.30 points. [Note: in the tax system $T=t\times B\times k$ where t is the tax rate schedule, B the tax base and k the annual coefficient; $k=1$ gives $T=t\times B$ which is the basic tax schedule written in the law, k serves to balance the budget. The calculation was (∑hospital expenditures in the communes divided per B the total cantonal tax base $=\Delta k$).] This global negative move was strongly criticized thereafter by individual communes because it did not correspond to their own hospital expenditures.
In the canton of Fribourg, the cantonal tax coefficient on direct taxation (personal income and wealth, corporate profit and capital) was increased from 1.00 to 1.089 points. The communes had to reduce accordingly their own coefficient. The decrease was calculated for each commune. In the author's commune, this corresponded to a decrease in the tax coefficient from 0.85 to 0.77 points.

22 In the nomenclature of Swiss public accounting, health expenditures are regrouped under Function 4, and several sub-functions. In Table 7.9, hospital infrastructures concern subgroup 411 Hospitals, 412 Homes for elderly people, and 413 Psychatric Hospitals and Clinics, which all give in-patient health care, grouped in sub-function 41.

23 See *Manual of Government Deficit and Debt, Implementation of ESA95*, Eurostat Methodologies and Working Papers, European Commission, Luxembourg, 2012, 4th edition, pp. 14–16. Also www.imf.org/external/pubs/ft/gfs/manual/fra/index.htm; http://epp.eurostat.ec.europa.eu/portal/page/portal/product_details/publication Déficit et dette, epp.eurostat.ec.europa.eu>governmentfinance statistics>manuel.

24 This is the 50 percent criterion: if half or more of the relevant total costs (to be defined?) are financed through user charges and bills to patient, then the producing unit is classified in the private merchant sector of the economy. Note that this methodology is adopted by the big five: EU, IMF, WB, UN, and OCDE. In consequence, the discussion in this paragraph goes much further than the simple "Swiss" case that is described.

25 2007 World Bank Workshop on Public Private Collaboration in Health Care Provision, Montenegro: http://web.worldbank.org/WBSITE/EXTERNAL/COUNTRIES/ECAEXT/EXTECAREGTOPHEANUT/0,,contentMDK:21494453~isCURL:Y~menuPK:3256336~pagePK:34004173~piPK:34003707~theSitePK:511545,00.html.

26 A term commonly used in health policy research. For example see Changes in Hospital Competitive Strategy: A New Medical Arms Race? *Health Services Research*. 2003 February; 38(1 Pt 2): 447–469 www.ncbi.nlm.nih.gov/pmc/articles/PMC1360894/.

References

Asfaw, Abay, Klaus Frohberg, K.S. James, and Johannes Jütting (2004) "Modeling the Impact of Fiscal Decentralization on Health Outcomes: Empirical Evidence from India," ZEF—Discussion Papers on Development Policy 87.

Derycke, P.H. and G. Gilbert (1988) *Economie publique locale*, Economica, Paris.

Flyvbjerg, Bent, Mette Skamris Holm, and Soren Buhl (2002) "Underestimating Costs in Public Works Projects: Error or Lie?," *Journal of the American Planning Association*, 68(3): 279–295.

Frey, B.S. and R. Eichenberger (1999) *The New Democratic Federalism for Europe: Functional, Overlapping and Competing Jurisdictions*, Studies in Fiscal Federalism and State-Local Finance, Edward Elgar, Cheltenham, UK.

Jiménez-Rubio, Dolores (2010) "Is Fiscal Decentralization Good for your Health? Evidence from a Panel of OECD Countries," HEDG Working Paper 10/30, York University.

Mackenzie, Hugh (2004) "Financing Canada's Hospitals: Public Alternatives to P3s," www.web.net/ohc/P3economistreportfinal.PDF.

Maioni, Antonia (2002) "Roles and Responsibilities in Health Care Policy," Discussion Paper 34, Commission on the Future of Health Care in Canada.

McKee, Martin, Nigel Edwards, and Rifat Atun (2006) "Public–Private Partnerships for Hospitals," *Bulletin of the World Health Organization*, 84(11), www.who.int/bulletin/volumes/84/11/06-030015.pdf.

McKillop, Ian (2002) "Financial Rules as a Catalyst for Change in the Canadian Health Care System," Discussion Paper 19, Commission on the Future of Health Care in Canada.

Montagu, Dominic and April Harding (2012) "A Zebra or a Painted Horse? Are Hospital PPPs Infrastructure Partnerships with Stripes or a Separate Species?," *World Hospital and Health Services*, 48(2): 15–19, www.globalhealthsciences.ucfc.edu and www.ihf-fih.org.

Musgrave, R.A. (1959) *The Theory of Public Finance*, McGraw-Hill, New York.

Oates, W. (1972) *Fiscal Federalism*, Harcourt Brace Jovanovich, New York.

Robalino, David A., Oscar F. Picazo, and Albertus Voetberg (2001) "Does Fiscal Decentralization Improve Health Outcomes? Evidence from a Cross-Country Analysis," World Bank.

Saltman, Richard, Vaida Bankauskaite, and Karsten Vrangbaek (2007) *Decentralization in Health Care Strategies and Outcomes*, Open University Press European Observatory on Health Systems and Policy Series, UK.

Simatupang, Rentanida Renata (2009) "Evaluation of Decentralization Outcomes in Indonesia: Analysis of Health and Education Sectors," Economics Dissertations. Paper 58. Georgia State University.

Sussman, Jason H. and Eric A. Jordahl (2010) *A Guide to Financing Strategies for Hospitals with Special Consideration for Smaller Hospitals*, Kaufman, Hall & Associates, Inc., www.hret.org/financial-strategies/resources/capital_financing_report.pdf.

Toloo, Sam, Gerard FitzGerald, Peter Aitken, Joseph Ting, Vivienne Tippett, and Kevin Chu (2011) *Emergency Health Services: Demand and Service Delivery Models*. Monograph 1: Literature Review and Activity Trends. Queensland University of Technology.

Turner & Townsend (2012) "International Construction Cost Survey 2012," www.turnerandtownsend.com/publications.html.

Uchimura, Hiroko and Johannes Jütting (2007) "Fiscal Decentralisation, Chinese Style: Good For Health Outcomes?," OECD Development Centre Working Paper 264.

8 Educational infrastructure, school construction, and decentralization in developing countries*

Key issues for an understudied area

Alec Gershberg

This chapter first discusses why the topic is interesting and worth considering; next we lay out the issues and considerations specific to educational infrastructure decentralization; we then connect the discussion to the broader infrastructure discussions in the other chapters as well as to the education decentralization literature. We examine an illustrative case study in Egypt exemplifying both the typical centralization of a national school construction authority, and the reasons for countries to consider certain kinds of decentralization. The case also highlights that school construction reforms involving potential decentralization are a long slog dominated and driven by politics. We provide a framework for unpackaging and considering key components of the processes involved in service provision and some promising strategies relating to decentralization. We conclude with some insights for practitioners and others interested in advancing knowledge of the topic.

Introduction: the potential importance of decentralization, accountability, and educational infrastructure

Poor and insufficient school infrastructure negatively impacts student learning and schooling outcomes. Myriad factors have contributed to an infrastructure gap in the education sector in many countries—rapid increases in enrolments, poor maintenance and aging capital stocks, rural to urban migration, and inefficient government planning and school construction to name a few. By some estimates, as many as 10 million classrooms and $100 billion in infrastructure investment are needed just to support the achievement of the Millennium Development Goals (MDGs);[1] which means the overall global challenges are far bigger.[2] Meeting the challenges may require increased funding, but it will also require improved efficiency of infrastructure provision. Various forms of decentralization are likely to be involved both to improve governance and accountability and to foster innovation and cost saving in the school construction industry and investment and project cycle.

Over the past three decades plus, a great deal has been written about infrastructure decentralization, and nearly as much about educational decentralization. Very little, however, has been written on decentralization issues pertaining specifically to educational infrastructure and school construction—and even less in developing country contexts. This chapter first discusses why the topic is interesting and worth considering; next we lay out the issues and considerations specific to educational infrastructure decentralization; we then connect the discussion to the broader infrastructure discussions in the other chapters as well as to the education decentralization literature. We examine an illustrative case study in Egypt exemplifying both the typical centralization of a national school construction authority, and the reasons for countries to consider certain kinds of decentralization. The case also highlights that school construction reforms involving potential decentralization are a long slog dominated and driven by politics. We review and highlight the results of a rare, detailed study in Sub-Saharan Africa. We conclude with some insights for practitioners and others interested in advancing knowledge of the topic.

We are not able to conclude under what circumstances and conditions infrastructure responsibilities should be assigned to different levels of governance. We argue that this critical question should be on the research agenda of the development community and we discuss how educational infrastructure decentralization might be different from recurrent expenditures. In addition, the very significant role of education (and school construction specifically) in subnational budgets in the US and Europe suggests considerable scope for expansion in the developing world. We suggest some key areas where the interactions between recurrent and capital expenditures are likely to be important. Most infrastructure decisions are a mix of central, regional, local, community, and/or private actors. That makes any categorization even more complicated, and one objective of the chapter is to provide a framework for unpackaging and considering key components of the processes involved in service provision and some promising strategies relating to decentralization.

The sparse literature on educational infrastructure decentralization is surprising given the magnitude of the needs, the clearly distinctive issues involved in educational infrastructure compared to other sectors, and the extent of centralization found in many countries. The financial scope is bigger than implied by capital expenditure figures because, like much "point" infrastructure associated with service provision, there is strong interplay between current service provision, on the one hand, and capital investment and school construction, on the other. As but one example, once built, schools must have teachers whose salaries are the most significant recurrent expenditures in many government budgets.

In addition, while it may seem obvious, it is worth stating explicitly that there are many reasons why, and modes through which, school infrastructure is related to student outcomes and performance. To highlight just a few:

- School proximity to home impacts attendance—travel and safety.
- The quality of infrastructure impacts enrolment and completion rates, learning outcomes as well as teacher absenteeism (this is particularly true for water and sanitation facilities).
- It is also very important to parental perception of and satisfaction with school quality, and therefore is (or should be) an important feature of politicians' calculus.

In addition, while investment expenditures represent a small share of the total (for instance when compared to health sector expenditures), there are several factors that compound the fiscal impact of educational infrastructure investments. Perhaps the most important factor is that infrastructure investments have an impact over teacher and payroll costs, which make up by far the lion's share of education expenditures. In addition to the impact on teacher effectiveness mentioned above, every school construction project implies an allocation of teachers to school buildings.

Thus, the topic of educational infrastructure and decentralization is an important one to the extent there is promise for cost reduction and other improvements in efficiency. In addition, during the so-called "massification" of educational access—periods in which a country is pushing to vastly expand enrolment quickly, centralization may indeed be successful. As reforms become more complicated, more about effectiveness, efficiency, and quality, the need to decentralize is likely to increase. Urbanization has also contributed to these needs. Indeed, many if not most countries now find at least part of their education system at such relatively more "advanced" stages of development, making the topic even more timely.

Educational capital investment, sources and uses of funds, and locus of decision-making

Before developing and then applying a decentralization typology specifically to school construction issues and the stakeholders most often connected to it, it is instructive to consider the level of capital spending in the education sector across and within countries. There are wide variations between countries in capital expenditure. Figure 8.1 shows capital expenditures in basic education as a proportion of the total education budget for a selection of countries for 2009. Clearly the expenditure effort is greatly varied across countries. The OECD average (not shown) is approximately 9 percent.

There are no clearly discernable patterns, and an additional analysis that ordered the countries by various broad measures of decentralization, yielded no relationship.[3] One surprising observation is the rather low level of educational capital investment from the large federal states in Latin America: Brazil, Mexico, and Argentina. Whereas some of the more recently decentralized countries like Peru are quite high, perhaps because of new investments being channeled through subnational governments, which often happens during early stages of decentralization.

Figure 8.2 shows that in some cases expenditures vary a great deal from year to year. But appear steady over time in others, and that this is true both in countries where spending is high and those where it is lower.[4]

Of course, these figures tell us nothing about the level of government (or school) responsible for different components of the capital investment. Very little information exists to allow legitimate comparisons across countries. However, we were able to use the locus of decision-making framework in OECD's *Education at a Glance* to examine the range of centralization and

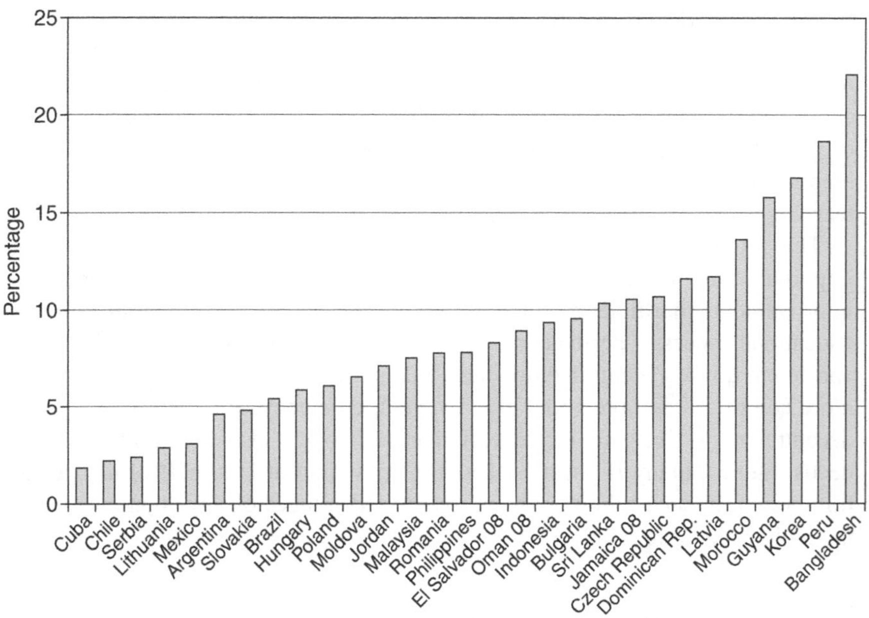

Figure 8.1 Primary and secondary educational capital expenditure, % of total public educational expenditure, selected countries, 2009 (source: Author's calculations from EdStats [2009, except where indicated by 08]. ISCED 1, 2, 3, & 4).

decentralization in a sample of countries—some of which are considered emerging or developing—albeit that the survey only covers a small part of the universe of decisions relevant to educational capital investment (see the Annex).

Mexico, for example, appears highly centralized with respect to capital expenditures, despite significant decentralization in the provision of education services over the past three decades. The central government alone allocated school-level capital expenditures and decides how they are spent. On the other hand, Mexican states do have autonomy over the decision to create or close a school. The high level of decentralization regarding these three decisions in Chile is consistent with the educational reforms there over the past three decades. With the exception of the Slovak Republic, the ECA countries all appear decentralized with some like Hungary even requiring school-level consultation on capital spending decisions.

Connecting educational infrastructure and school construction to the decentralization and accountability literature

While the traditional education decentralization literature focuses, almost exclusively, on service provision (recurrent expenditure), the typologies of decentralization and accountability developed in this literature are largely relevant to the

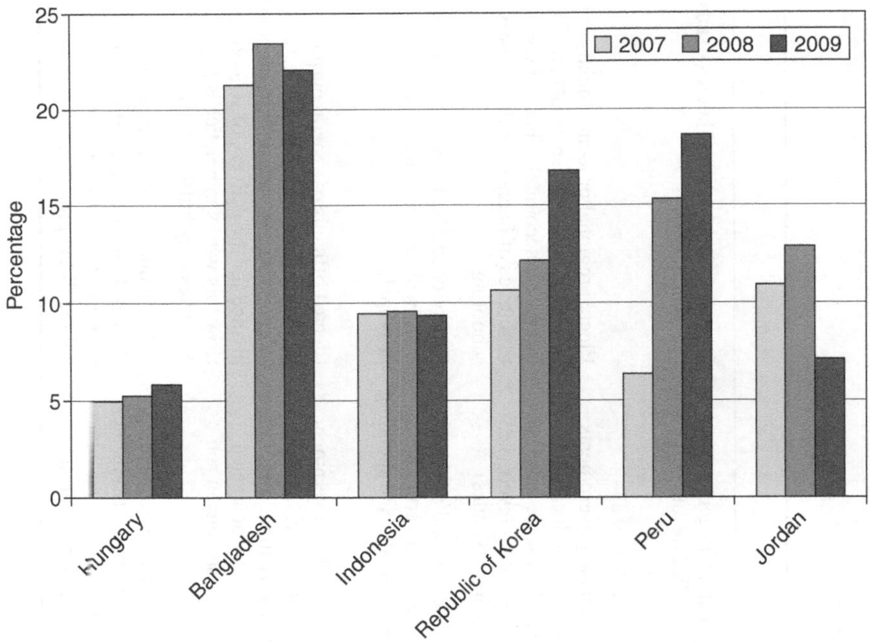

Figure 8.2 Primary and secondary educational capital expenditure, % of total public educational expenditure, selected countries, 2007–2009 (source: Theunynck, 2009).

discussion of infrastructure provision. For instance, we should distinguish between "Decentralization to Sub-national Governments" and "Decentralization to Schools" (most commonly School Based Management [SBM], school autonomy, community and parental involvement, school choice, client power, etc.).

While distinct, the two forms of educational decentralization are not mutually exclusive and are often intertwined in reform processes. Rondinelli's classic framework is clearly relevant regarding Deconcentration, Delegation, Devolution, Privatization.[5]

Gershberg and Winkler (2004) adapted this typology to education, and we present it here in Table 8.1, with slight adaptations to highlight the relevance for infrastructure provision. Naturally, this is a gross oversimplification. For instance, each "cell" of the table could be further subdivided into at least four cells to delineate school design, school location, school construction, and school maintenance, as we discuss later.[6] In addition, it is not particularly useful (or even correct) to try to attach any one of these decentralization "types" to any given reform. Rather, it is important to understand how performance accountability works, or is intended to work, and these concepts are likely to be useful in identifying how accountability flows through the system. Any given reform will indeed be a complex combination of each of these "types."

Table 8.1 Education infrastructure decentralization matrix

Education	*Administrative*	*Fiscal*	*Political*
Deconcentration to Regional Government Offices and Regional MOE Offices	Move managerial decisions and managerial accountability to regional offices of central government and MOE	Give regional managers greater authority to allocate and reallocate budgets	Create regional, elected bodies to advise regional managers
Devolution to regional or local governments	Education sector managers are appointed by elected officials at local or regional level	Give subnational governments power to allocate education spending and, in some cases, to determine spending levels (i.e., through raising revenues)	Elected regional or local officials of general purpose governments are ultimately accountable both to voters and to sources of finance for the delivery of schooling
Delegation (and/or Devolution) to schools and/or school councils	School principals and/or school councils empowered to make personnel, curriculum, and some spending decisions	School principals and/or school councils receive government funding and can allocate spending and raise revenues	School councils are elected or appointed, often with power to name school principals
Delegation to NGOs, Contract Management Agencies (CMAs), and/or Social Funds	Government responsible for provision, but delegates operational autonomy to implement large-scale small construction programs, to be carried out by small contractors with local labor	Funds provided by government (central, regional local, perhaps with community input) but handled largely by delegated agencies. Cost savings in some cases.	Elected officials of general purpose governments are, ideally, ultimately accountable to voters and to sources of finance for the delivery of schooling. How this works in practice is key. Agencies may buffer officials.
Implicit delegation to community schools and community based approaches	School principals and/or community school councils make key decisions	Some self-financing or local inputs with some government subsidies, especially in remote areas where public schools are not present	School councils are often popularly elected. Government is still usually responsible for service provision, though not the direct provider.

Of course, the regulations and laws relating to any particular aspect usually differ in important ways from the rules of the game in practice. For instance, with administrative deconcentration, while there may be some managerial decision-making transferred to local offices of central agencies, this is often coupled with ex-post accountability upwards, at least for results.[7]

Before proceeding to consider capital expenditures and school construction explicitly, it is worth reviewing the potential (theoretical) gains and drawbacks of decentralization, as well as what Gershberg and Jacobs (1998) aptly called *recentralization* because of the need to consider the interplay and changing nature of the role of the center during so-called decentralization:

> [D]isaggregating the different aspects of accountability … makes clear that, in many respects, the expected improvement [from decentralization] requires both greater autonomy for the local service provider, and also strengthened performance of some central functions. We refer to this necessary strengthening of central functions as recentralization.
>
> (Gershberg and Jacobs 1998)

Table 8.2 summarizes the arguments for and the attributes of decentralization and recentralization.

Key stakeholders and institutional actors in school construction

Many, and probably most developing countries, have a central School Construction Authority (SCA) of some kind. In developed countries, each local school district (especially in large cities) may have its own local SCA. The other stakeholders and institutional actors are similar to those of interest in any discussion of decentralization of service provision.

- Central School Construction Authority (SCA).
    - The SCA may or may not be part of MOE (e.g., may be located in the Ministry of Planning or Public Works).
    - The SCA may or may not be semi-autonomous even within MOE (i.e., it may have its own administrative structure and the Minister may not have full authority over it.
- Other ministries (planning, local development, finance, transport/roads, etc.): for instance, in many countries the ministry responsible for civil works takes on the actual construction of schools.
- Sub-national governments.
- Quasi-public authorities, Social Funds, Contract Management Agencies, etc.
- Community and School level stakeholders.
- Intermediary and other NGOs.

Table 8.2 Arguments for and against decentralization and recentralization

Efficiency & Fiscal Resources Arguments for Decentralization & Recentralization		
Production Efficiency	1. Sub-national governments may choose input mixes and/or develop programs and policies more effectively than national governments. 2. Sub-national governments may manage resources more efficiently than national governments by: a) Reducing bureaucratic red tape; b) Implementing more appropriate/effective personnel management; c) Accounting more to stakeholders regarding how funds are spent.	3. National governments must account for externalities and spillovers related to national goals. 4. National governments may have more expertise, particularly for evaluation and institution building in weak sub-national jurisdictions, and greater capacity for disseminating good practice. In addition, evaluation mechanisms must be comparable across jurisdictions and the national government must rely on comprehensive evaluation measures both for national planning and to hold sub-national jurisdictions accountable for use of national funds.
Allocative Efficiency	5. Sub-national governments know their constituents better than national governments and therefore provide services that more closely match citizen preferences. There may also be improved equity through more effective targeting of the poor populations. 6. If reforms improve services for disadvantaged groups, equity may improve despite regional disparities.	7. Central government has greater capacity for inter-regional and inter-personal redistributive policies. 8. Centralized allocation may be less vulnerable to capture by local elites and interest groups.
Fiscal Efficiency and Fiscal Resources	9. National governments can use leverage from fiscal transfers to stimulate economically efficient and/or socially beneficial behavior by sub-national governments. 10. As with #5 above, sub-national governments can set some limited number of taxes and/or user fees in a more efficient and responsive manner with respect to the regional/local economy, households, and other stakeholders. This *may* augment the public resource base.	11. Many important taxes (e.g., consumption [value added] taxes and income taxes) may be handled most efficiently and equitably at the national level. 12. Sub-national governments can run deficits that in extreme cases can threaten macro stability. 13. Importantly, greater sub-national fiscal responsibility may throw regions more to the mercy of their own endowments, thus increasing inequity nationally.
Democracy/Power Sharing Arguments for Decentralization & Recentralization		
	Decentralization	Recentralization
NGO	14. If reforms allow true power sharing, then democratic political participation and/or political stability could be improved. Political equity may also improve.	15. Improved power sharing assumes functioning sub-national democratic institutions, which are notoriously weak in many countries in the region. (See #8 above.)

Source: Adapted from Gershberg and Jacobs (1998).

- Private Sector (construction companies, Public Private Partnerships [PPPs], bond and other capital markets.

Each of these stakeholders will be discussed in the following sections about phases and taxonomies for educational infrastructure. It is instructive to note that there are many potential institutions and stakeholders (most likely well over ten in any given country context) and that sub-national governments—often the focus of decentralization reforms—are only one among many others.

Components of educational infrastructure provision that may be decentralized, or not

While there is considerable heterogeneity, school construction generally has key components, each of which may or may not be undertaken or managed in a centralized or decentralized manner. Note that while these components are in some sense sequential "phases" conceptually, there is often considerable overlap and iteration between them in practice.

1 School design. Usually at the very least, there are minimum design and construction standards that are set at the central government level.[8] These involve a range of issues of central concern: safety, equity, efficiency, and may also be connected to pedagogy (for instance if the MOE is transitioning to an open classroom setting for constructivist teaching methods). However, it is not uncommon for many if not most aspects of school design to be controlled centrally—including building and floor plans, construction methods and materials. It is, thus, not uncommon to find school design nearly uniform throughout even very geographically diverse countries.[9]

2 School location. Whatever level of government is responsible for access to schooling is likely to play a strong role in the decision about where new schools will be located or existing schools expanded. This is true even if that level of government does not actually provide schooling services. Thus, school location, school expansion, school creation, and school closure decisions tend to be more centralized than other aspects of a system. Where increasing enrolment is a chief concern (e.g., in countries seeking to achieve the education MDGs), the central government has an interest in how to maximize national enrollments (often resulting in a rural bias). Equity is also a key concern as are efficiency, scale economies, and cost containment—all of which, at least in theory, have aspects that benefit from centralized provision. On the other hand, these valid concerns for some degree of centralism could also be addressed in a more decentralized system via funding formulas and grants, thus leaving more of the key decisions to the more local body[10]—namely, creating incentives by weighting central funding formula, regional targeting policy and priorities to favor provinces or regions with significant disadvantaged populations (e.g., out of school children, or over-crowding, etc.).

Land acquisition is also a major issue, since the "ideal" location for a school from a planning perspective may not contain land owned by the government for the purpose. Land acquisition issues are particularly challenging in urban areas where vacant land is scarce and it is difficult to procure plots large enough to fulfill centralized design and construction standards. Governments are often reticent, or bureaucratically challenged, to make heavy use of rental and other non-traditional space in urban areas. In fact, increased urbanization has likely enhanced the need to explore and achieve various kinds of decentralization. Finally, school consolidation is a major concern in the ECA countries, thus involving surplus infrastructure and school closure more than school construction.

School staffing, student allocation, and opening the school are also important considerations. It may seem almost tautological, but at some point, the school needs to open and teachers, administrators, and other non-teaching staff will need to be assigned to the new school; students need to be assigned to the school, and the school has to function. While this may not typically be considered a phase of school construction per se, it is clear that the capital investments and recurrent costs mutually affect each other. Thus, infrastructure investments must be coordinated with personnel policies and vice versa, and capital investments directly impact the recurrent budget going forward. In practice, the decision to approve a major school infrastructure project is usually preconditioned on the determination of need, based on how many students will be served. This student count determines staffing, and thus the overall level of personnel costs would be built into the recurrent budget either before or while the project is being proposed and appraised. Finally, the deployment of teachers and other staff would follow normal personnel procedures and needs to be timed so that they are in place when the school opens.

3 School construction (including new schools and expansions of existing schools). The entity that actually takes on the school construction project and oversees construction can range from the central SCA to the local school district. And as discussed later, the various components of the process can be broken down and taken on by different levels of government. There may be some economies of scale from centralization (e.g., in the purchase of inputs like cement), but there is also plenty of experience to indicate that centralized procurement may foster corruption (Theunynck 2002, 2009). Nor has prefabricated construction generally succeeded. There may be advantages to leveraging local labor, knowledge, materials, and other inputs. Therefore, a priori, it is not possible to determine the "correct" level of government for each component of school construction.

4 Provision of non-infrastructure durable goods. These include furniture, equipment, and other capital costs associated with school construction. In addition, school staffing formulas and other standardized costs have significant recurrent cost implications for the education system, and because it is highly likely that different levels of government will be responsible for each, this complicates any decentralization reform efforts compared to network infrastructure (such as roads, water, etc.). And, even if these costs

are, like staffing costs, determined according to norms or formulas, the provision of these goods need not be done by the same level of government as the construction project. For instance, a municipality could build a school but furniture could be centrally procured for cost savings.

5 <u>Maintenance (both routine and major rehabilitation)</u>. All infrastructure and school construction has associated implications for on-going maintenance. Maintenance costs and expenditures are often more decentralized than construction. For instance, local governments may be charged with paying for and carrying out maintenance; school grants may be used to allow school-level maintenance, and contributions may be sought or required from community members and/or parents. Unfortunately, it is common practice to decentralize responsibility for maintenance to local governments without the corresponding funds or potential sources of local revenue. This is of course true for other types of expenditure, but maintenance is the one that most impacts the value of school construction and the accumulated capital assets. In addition, maintenance falls under both recurrent and capital expenditure. Major maintenance is generally a capital expenditure while minor maintenance is a recurrent expense albeit with direct impact on the capital asset.

6 <u>Ex-post evaluation</u>. This would include both a variety of audits to verify fiscal comity and structural integrity, as well as evaluations that determine if schools are properly designed to support educational goals, construction is of high quality and standing the test of time, and school location procedures accurately reflect actual demand for schools.

It is instructive to consider how one might relate the above six "phases" with the "usual" eight steps of any investment cycle developed considerably throughout this book (Figure 8.3). The clearest conclusion is that they do not "align" in any straightforward manner. For instance school location decisions are made to a varying degree across the first four cycle steps. In fact, even maintenance, which is primarily performed as part of the Service Delivery, must be factored in during the first four steps of project development and design. This means that planners and policymakers must consider the relationship of each phase with each cycle step. One could imagine, for instance, a 6×8 matrix with 48 cells each detailing the role of a particular educational infrastructure phase to a key cycle step, and that there could be considerable variation across countries and individual projects. Add to this the need to consider the nature and extent of decentralization for each phase and cycle step, and this underscores the complexity of the decision-making process and the different entities involved!

As we discuss further below, it is particularly in the second, third, and fourth steps where many governments exhibit high degrees of centralization and where consideration of some additional form of decentralization is likely warranted. There are multiple agencies involved in a complex investment cycle—this complicates considerably fostering accountability. The next section explores some of the main organizational arrangements for infrastructure provision under a range of different kinds of decentralized governance and accountability arrangements.

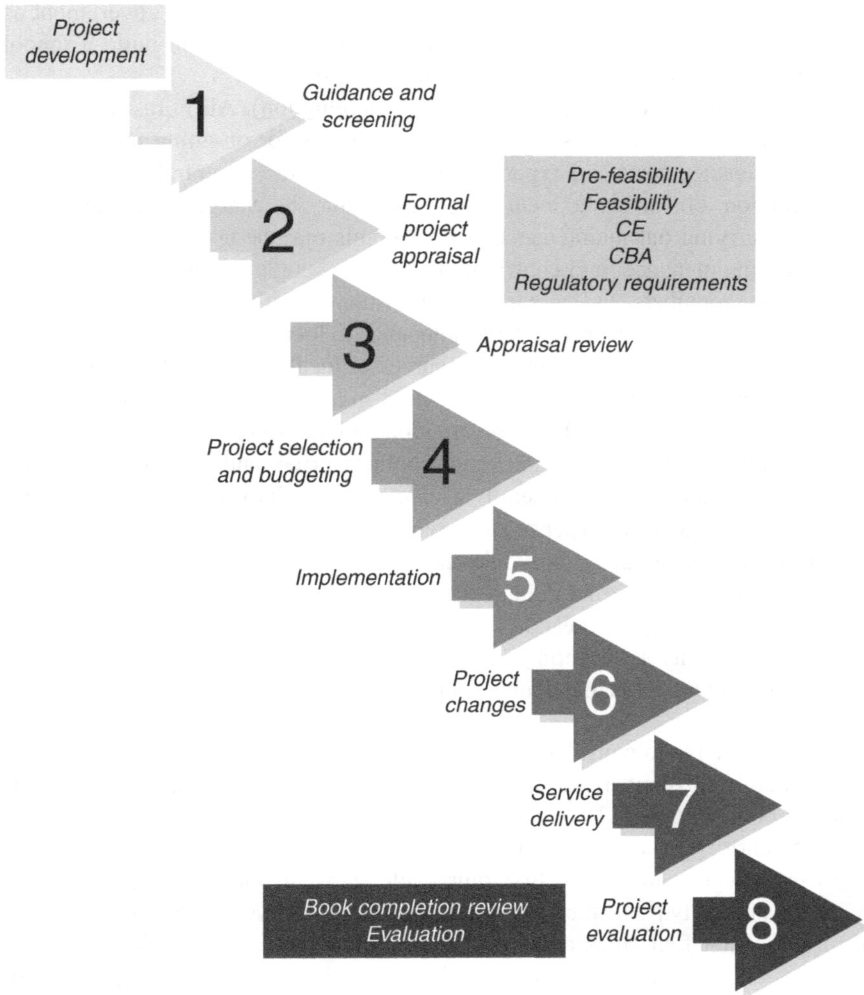

Figure 8.3 Public investment cycle: eight key steps (source: Rajaram *et al.* 2010; World Bank, 2010).

A taxonomy of school construction and decentralization[11]

As discussed above, historically in most countries the central government controlled and implemented virtually the entire school design, location, construction, and provision of non-infrastructure durable goods processes—particularly during periods of rapid expansion—and there is considerable international evidence that this resulted in poor quality and high costs. (Regional government provision fared little better.) In particular, the problems were: (i) inadequate classroom allocation, (ii) weak monitoring capacity of the implementation agency, and (iii) low construction quality. More decentralized arrangements (especially with municipalities) have been more common for routine maintenance but also need for major rehabilitation. The past two decades have seen considerable experimentation with various forms of decentralization in the school infrastructure sector beyond basic maintenance, with some positive results. The most common decentralization experiences have experimented with various forms of institutional arrangements—both devolution and delegation from both the central and sub-national governments to various quasi-governmental and non-governmental organizations (as detailed below). Of course, delegation in and of itself will only have positive impacts if there is accountability; that is, that the principal-agent relationships are built upon proper incentives, good information, and transparency (among other key factors).[12] Here we outline the most common and/or promising institutional relationships associated with education infrastructure decentralization.[13]

- *Devolution to local governments*, which was expected to improve "site monitoring by local government engineers" as well as "(i) closer monitoring leading to better work quality, (ii) local bidding, with increased use of local labor, lower costs and heightened community ownership leading to a greater commitment to maintenance, [and] (iii) better integration of municipal investment between sectors." Few cost savings or other gains were realized in Africa, Asia, and Latin America—with the exception of Mexico's 1994 major decentralization effort where substantial unit costs savings came rapidly.
- *Community-based approaches* have also taken many different forms and so it is not possible to say that they have worked or not without contextualizing the particular reform approach for any given country in any given time period. For instance, when coupled with centralized procurement—justified because of economies of scale and/or prefabricated design—results have been poor due to the complexity of supply chain and construction arrangements, failure to make best use of local knowledge and labor, etc. More positive results accrued to demand-driven approaches in Mauritania, Mali, Malawi, Uganda,[14] India, and Mexico. These successful community-based construction strategies shared key characteristics:

  > (i) only locally available materials are used, (ii) only construction techniques familiar to villagers and local craftsmen and contractors are used, (iii) design improvements are limited to those necessary to ensure standard durability and safety, (iv) duties and responsibilities of partners are well defined. Regular technical supervision will help in ensuring that quality standards of construction are met, but does not substitute to close monitoring by communities.... Community pride in ownership of a well-built school, combined with appropriate technical advice to local builder is the main factor of quality construction.[15]

- *Delegation to NGOs* has sought to leverage the closer connections and trust some organizations have developed with disadvantaged populations. It has taken many forms and yielded some positive, if mixed, results. Some build their own schools, which are often lower cost—in some cases because they have fewer requirements for non-classroom facilities than government schools, or they may have looser construction standards or more flexibility in bidding out to contractors. It may also be that the schools are lower quality in some cases, but there is not systematic evidence to that effect. (See example of CARE schools in the Egypt case study.) The challenge has generally been scalability.

- *Delegation to Contract Management Agencies* (CMAs) has proven successful both in terms of unit costs and project completion, particularly in Africa. CMAs are

> given operation autonomy to implement large-scale small construction programs, to be carried out by small contractors with local labor. They are staffed with skilled professionals recruited from the private sector. They select, pay and supervise contractors and architectural/engineering services for site supervision. Their mandate is to promote small and medium enterprises (SME) by allowing them to bid for contracts. These agencies have changed the "rules of the game" and have contributed to the growth of the construction industry.

The initial experiments with CMAs focused on urban areas, spreading to rural areas after they had established their value. Nevertheless, there are to date still more successful urban examples.[16]

The use of *Public Private Partnerships (PPP)* for school construction is an analogous policy to the delegations to CMAs.

- *Social funds* have played an important role in decentralized school construction often delivering lower unit costs and higher rates of project completion. Originally a strategy for short-term employment in times of crises, social investment funds have gradually become more permanent fixtures, often acting as CMAs for their own school construction projects. While most are not community-based they do always call for some significant level of community participation and/or involvement of sub-national governments.

Figures 8.4 and 8.5 show the relationships between two spectrums of centralized and decentralized actors as well as public and private actors for two of these categories of institutional arrangements: a typical local government delegation and social fund or CMA arrangement, respectively.

It is important to emphasize that these figures only highlight one of many potential examples of the institutional arrangements for only two of the categories in the taxonomy above. The possible combinations are myriad and many more are explored in greater detail in Theunynck (2009).

Table 8.3 provides some comparisons of cost differences of the different approaches from Sub-Saharan Africa. Though care should be taken in the comparisons given the caveat that quality cannot be compared or assumed constant, the various delegation models from the above taxonomy do appear to provide significant cost savings.

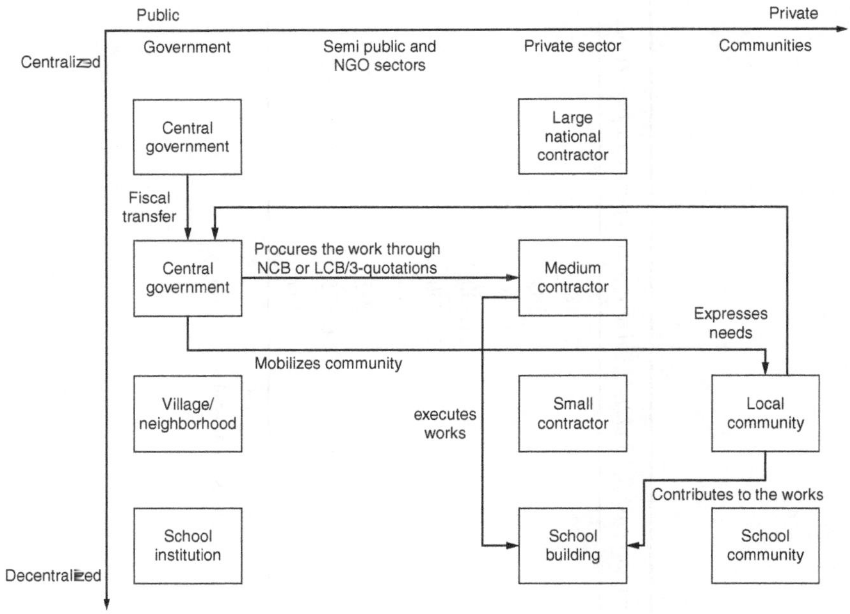

Figure 8.4 Devolution to local government (source: Theunynck, 2009).

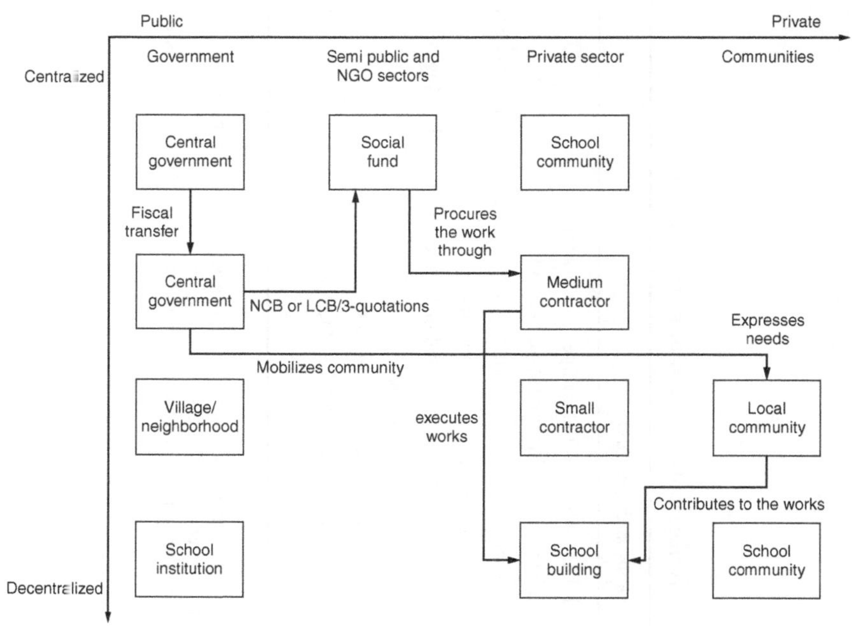

Figure 8.5 Delegation to CMA using a social fund, after delegation to local government (source: Theunynck, 2009).

Table 8.3 Average unit costs per procurement method

Type of procurement method	*Average unit cost (US$/m2)*	*Average cost per classroom (US$)*
Central ministry international competitive bidding	269	17,485
Central ministry national competitive bidding	189	12,285
Delegation of project implementation unit/contract Management agency	190	12,350
Delegation to NGOs acting as contractors	180	11,700
Ministry decentralized office national or local competitive bidding	180	11,700
Local government national or local competitive bidding	172	11,180
Delegation to communities from ministry	103	6,695
Delegation to communities from local government	95	6,175
Delegation to communities from NGOs	80	5,200

Notes

1 All costs in this table are taken from Theunynck (2009) and are based on a comparative study of 215 projects in Sub-Saharan Africa.

2 All costs adjusted to 2006 prices.

3 Average cost per classroom assumes a 65 m^2 gross classroom area in all cases.

Case study of a large, centralized school construction operation: Egypt's General Authority for Educational Buildings (GAEB)[17]

Few would deny that Egypt's achievements in school construction have been impressive, even historic. Between 1992 and 2006 the government built about 14,000 schools, most by the General Authority for Educational Buildings (GAEB), thus greatly expanding access to and enrollment in basic education especially for the poorest half of the income distribution. By some accounts, more schools were built in this period than in the preceding 110 years.[18] Thus, the centralized approach made sense at these earlier stages of educational development especially after a severe earthquake required swift rebuilding of infrastructure and inspired highly restrictive building codes.

Yet there is a wide-spread impression that school construction in Egypt is also too expensive for the quality of service provided—inefficient both in the cost of construction and in the match between the structures built and the needs of stakeholders—and that these inefficiencies are in no small part due to centralization of the design, planning, and construction processes in GAEB. In particular, this case sheds light on the issue of school location, community involvement, and decentralization.

There are lower cost models of school construction, most interestingly from the arm of the government providing religious schools (Al-Azhar), which are about 33 percent less expensive on a per classroom basis.[19] While officially part of the central government, these schools are not run by the Ministry of Education nor are the schools built by GAEB. For its part, GAEB claims that the Al-Azhar schools are of lower quality, particularly with respect to earthquake risk, an assertion that is hard to refute in the absence of major earthquakes.

The NGO-built CARE schools also have lower unit costs (about 22 percent less costly), in part through focusing more tightly on classroom rather than on non-classroom construction. Additional inefficiencies stem from several pervasive problems with the incentive environment for educational infrastructure provision.

The agency in charge of school construction and contracting (GAEB) also plans, proposes, and decides the type and quantity of schools needed.

- This creates a conflict of interest—the larger the investment amount, the greater the contracting function).
- Despite claims of high-tech mapping and school location and demand models, GAEB has shown poor population forecasting, in part because
  - The agency in charge of school construction and contracting also forecasts population growth to determine needs.
  - The same agency decides the type, quantity, and locations of schools required.
  - This creates a conflict of interest—the greater the estimated needs, the larger the contracting function.

While never a singular solution, decentralization of some form would likely mitigate some of GAEB's biggest challenges. For instance, one of the major issues included building schools where they were not needed but where the price of land was low (or could be acquired for free), which led to providing schools where existing crowding did not demand it, and leaving crowded schools just as crowded. This is a function of an accountability that emphasizes the number of schools built, and not the satisfaction of parents and communities with the schools. Historically this might have not been so problematic, as low-population-density areas tended to be those with lower enrollment rates. But as enrollment became nearly universal, the problems of overcrowding became more significant than the problems of non-coverage, and the areas with overcrowding tended to be those with the more expensive land. Almost by definition, jurisdictions with cheaper land tended to be those where schools were less overcrowded.

So not only was the system centralized, but it did not allocate resources in a rational way. If the system was somewhat decentralized, and had to allocate construction according to some transparent criteria, the strangeness of allocating funding to areas with cheap land would become clearer, and the system would find itself pressured to allocate more money to areas with overcrowding.

In part driven by the exposure of inefficiencies in GAEB, the Egyptian Government undertook a highly public program to bring the private sector into the school construction game through Public Private Partnerships (PPP). In theory PPPs can leverage private sector access to capital markets where bond markets are less robust. Unfortunately PPP has not been successful in Egypt for several reasons, chief among them that the private sector needs even larger scale contracts to make bids worthwhile, and these have proven untenable given the risk involved with having to trust in 10–15 year relationships with the Egyptian Government. The events of the Arab Spring have perhaps borne out those risks. The end result is that GAEB ended up being the contractor for most of the PPP bidders!

Still, decentralizing GAEB in other ways has been part of the government's reform rhetoric for nearly a decade. Yet progress has been very slow. In part, the lack of reform stems from a political economy that generates strong incentives to remain centralized. GAEB has operated as a nearly autonomous unit run by military generals allocating vast sums of resources. Decentralization signifies a major loss of power for these stakeholders. On the other hand, the case shows that under most conditions educational infrastructure decentralization is likely to be a long, complex, hard slog. A few capital investment and maintenance responsibilities have indeed been transferred to the regional (governorate) level of the MOE and/or GAEB—known as the "muderiyas." A couple of examples are the purchase and installation of educational technology in new buildings along with major maintenance funding at technical schools. Schools now receive control over some minor maintenance funds. Whether such developments are stepping stones towards more significant reform is hard to tell. Since the transition to the government led by Mohammed Morsi after the fall of Hosni Mubarek, the GAEB has its first civilian director.

In 2010, a major consultancy through USAID argued to the Egyptian government that national conditions…

> … call for a system where infrastructural needs are identified locally at the Idara [district] level, vetted and approved for funding at the Markaz [regional] level by Local Popular Councils (LPCs) via ear-marked decentralized fiscal transfers, and coordinated sub-nationally at the governorate level as part of the governor's portfolio where he ensures that MoE's strategy and directions are followed and implemented, and where tradeoffs between idaras are assessed and decided (following nationally-set criteria). To induce local entities to choose efficiently within the construction envelope, the Idara must keep its own formula-given money if it can carry out savings. The idara (perhaps as mediated by the mudiriya) should also act as a client and commission the services of the local GAEB governorate office to act as a project manager for the Idara as a client. Distribution of funds may, at least in the beginning, be based on a formula or formula-like mechanism that takes specific local access needs into account, perhaps along with the human development index (HDI) of an Idara. This combination may allow for the use of valid indicators that can be specific enough for MoE to gauge infrastructure earmarking.
>
> RTI (2010)

This is similar to proposals in a 2007 strategic plan and a 2005 World Bank Public Expenditure Review. The point is not that there is not change, but that it is slow and highly political.

Table 8.4 revisits the decentralization matrix presented above (Table 8.1) and explores the potential application to our Egyptian school construction case study. We explain the manner in which each aspect of decentralization is (*or more importantly could or <u>should</u> be*) present in reform efforts.[20]

Perhaps the most important point to highlight is that most of the aspects are present de facto to some extent and all are relevant. That is, *it is not fruitful to provide a single label for the decentralization reforms of Egyptian school construction and the reality is that it is a complex mix of many components*— some weakly decentralized and other less so. The analysis also indicates the absence of the "stronger," more "bottom up," more "local" decentralization that many analysts have hypothesized are more likely to improve accountability. Below we present briefly the results of qualitative analysis with local stakeholders that puts some meat on the bone of this framework and the inefficiencies that remain, at least in part, due to the continued strong centralization of the institutions and the fact that the most prominent decentralization components are what we labeled "vertical," which we argued are less likely to yield positive outcomes and foster accountability than more "horizontal" decentralization.

In addition to high unit costs for school construction, there are several other "typical" inefficiencies evident in the Egyptian case study of GAEB relating to

Table 8.4 Potential application of decentralization matrix to Egyptian school construction case

Decentralization component	*Issues and likely application to GAEB and Egyptian case*
Deconcentration to Regional Government Offices and Regional MOE Offices	At the governorate level, GAEB has offices that have traditionally been involved as implementers of central plans under tight control. Some increase in autonomy has been announced by GAEB and will certainly be needed.
Devolution to regional or local governments	Governorates are supposed to provide input into plans, fiscal allocations, and project implementation. Pilot projects have shown promise (especially regarding maintenance, ICT, and some vocational classrooms) but also the difficulty of GAEB ceding real control. Recognition of need to involve local governments but very little (and/or very problematic) in practice.
Delegation (and/or devolution) to schools and/or school councils	School councils (Boards of Trustees) established at many schools officially, many do not operate in practice or have significant power. In any case, even in de jure terms, the powers and duties of the Boards of Trustees were not always clear (they were not fully specified and yet non-overlapping with the powers and duties of other bodies) though the regulations on this aspect did improve in the late 2000s. Some control over some maintenance projects, none over major renovation.
Delegation to NGOs, Contract Management Agencies (CMAs) and/or social funds	In theory, this practice could prove fruitful, but has not been tried in a strict sense. Public Private Partnerships (PPP) garnered much attention in the early 2000s but was largely unsuccessful for many reasons.
Implicit delegation to community schools and community-based approaches	Virtually no input from communities on crucial issue of new school location and construction. Very much needed in future.

school design and school location that appear to imply potential reasons for some decentralization. For instance, there is often no differentiation in design between urban and rural areas, high population density or remote areas, between high-risk earthquake zones and lower risk, etc.

Not surprisingly, thus, many schools have inappropriate designs for local conditions and local people.

In short, there is simply no way that a central bureaucracy—even armed with remote sensing, GIS, and the best population projections available—can collect, in a cost-effective manner, the data necessary to make the best decisions regarding school location to avoid such hazards. A few excerpts from interviews of stakeholders exemplify the concerns of school administrators and community members alike (see Box 8.1). Clearly local knowledge of parents and school staff should be solicited and given serious consideration in school location decisions. The same is likely true for other aspects of school construction.

Box 8.1 Stakeholder insights on school location in Egypt

Gershberg and Gohary (2007) examined issues with school location for the Population Council and USAID. They used qualitative interview and focus group methods to gather the impressions and insights of local actors (parents, school directors, and teachers) regarding school location. Here is a selection of direct quotations from the interview and focus group data. Allowing the voices of the stakeholders to emerge lends power and substance to many of the key arguments developed through our case study.

"If the land is government-owned, they build wherever they like; if the inhabitants donated the land, they build on it."

"No-one consulted us. The land is owned by the government, and they decided to build a school there."

"They don't ask anyone's opinion. If the Ministry cared enough to ask, some problems would be avoided, such as the unsavory social environment around the school."

"The students come a long way, and they have to walk on the main road, where there are vehicles driven by young kids, many of whom don't have a driver's license. The girls leave school in the evening shift at 5 or 6 p.m., and they walk a long way in the fields alone."

"Some students walk five or six kilometers to get to school."

"It's completely inappropriate that we're directly on the road; it's the Agricultural Highway. Most of the kids come from the same three or four villages, which causes a drop out problem because the school is far away from where the kids live."

"There are three or four road accidents annually.... In the fields there are kidnappers, because the school is far away from the pupils' homes. Last year a student was kidnapped.... The kids also walk across the canals by balancing on drainage pipes, so naturally there's a risk of falling in."

"It's very hard to get to school. We walk five routes, all of which are very dangerous."

Concluding remarks

Perhaps the simplest but very important point is that while a typology of school construction decentralization is useful for identifying the components of a reform and exploring which components are more (or less) likely to enhance accountability, classifying or labeling a complex decentralization reform into a "type" is not particularly fruitful. In fact most country contexts will exhibit some degree of decentralization along most if not all of the potential components of a reform.

One important point to take from the Egypt case, that we argue may generalize to other cases, is that when the main issue is massive out-of-school numbers, governments can put a school anywhere, even with overly centralized and standard design, and, assuming that out-of-school problems are mostly supply-side issues, then students will fill the new schools. But as countries have progressed, at least three things have happened.

i First, in some areas schools are overcrowded, and then the decision to add more spaces by adding to schools, by buying expensive but close-by land to build new ones, etc. requires more subtle, localized information and interaction; therefore such progress appears to strengthen the case for some decentralization.

ii Second, as countries put most of the children into school, the ones that remain out of school are increasingly special, harder to reach, and serve populations—the extreme poor and disenfranchised, the disabled, nomadic families, populations with different cultures (ethnic or linguistic minorities)—whose needs are often best met with special-purpose infrastructure.

iii Third, the more infrastructure has been built in the past, the more there is a need for the recurrent cost of maintenance, by definition, and maintenance is often best done locally, since a central entity has a hard time deciding in which local school to fix broken windows and in which local schools to paint the walls, or fix the bathrooms. This is to argue that, as countries have advanced, the arguments favoring some form of decentralization, as outlined in Table 8.2 above, increase. However, this leaves each country with a very important and very difficult set of institutional incentives and arrangements to ensure accountability: namely, when school construction is centralized and school operations and maintenance decentralized, what are the right institutional arrangements for giving decentralized governments the right incentives to keep building maintenance at the right level?

In addition, our discussion highlights important factors for policymakers to consider when contemplating decentralization and intergovernmental relations in educational infrastructure provision.

- While sub-national governments are often the focus of infrastructure decentralization reforms, they are only one among a long list of other entities and stakeholders involved. On the one hand, this means at least very carefully thinking through the inter-institutional relationships and environment within which sub-national governments operate. On the other hand, it could mean that under some conditions sub-national government need not be the central focus of any given reform in any given country context.

- Our discussion also illustrates clearly how imperative it is to consider and explore how conditions and opportunities change over time, and that it is a very different task to provide for infrastructure where the out-of-school population is 30 percent versus 3 percent—the latter case often favoring decentralization for various reasons explored above. The mix of conditions and effective components of a school infrastructure decentralization strategy is obviously quite different in Egypt compared to Niger, and in Egypt in 1990 compared to Egypt in 2010. This latter evolution presents a challenge for decentralization policies in that institutions (especially strong centralized, school construction authorities) almost by definition resist change and are slow to decentralize (at best).
- Planning and appraisal, especially location and design features, are two areas where the role of local government and communities may be particularly important and particularly difficult to achieve.
- Financing and procurement: while there is no generalizable formula for successful improvement, it is clear that:
  - this area offers big potential costs and cost savings: various decentralized strategies appear to lower costs and foster accountability, efficiency, and effectiveness (and provide likely political gains, too);
  - "earmarking" and other fixed or formula-driven costs (recurrent and capital) associated with construction are strategies worth considering;
  - equalization transfers or other redistributive fiscal transfers are key to enhancing equity. And, it is important to consider how to include maintenance and infrastructure expenditures into these transfers.
- Community-based approaches, intermediary NGOs, social funds, and Contract Management Agencies (CMAs) all hold promise for accountability and performance enhancement across many of the key phases of the infrastructure planning and school construction—as does the use of medium and sometimes small scale contractors.
- There is likely a need for a continued strong role at the central level in school design and standards, even while there are many reasons why in reality this may foster inefficiencies. As in any decentralization effort, it is crucial that the center sets the "rules of the game" clearly and enforces them consistently and transparently.
- There is not nearly enough attention to evaluating the potential and actual impact of decentralization reforms on cost and other key aspects of construction programs. And there is hardly any ex-post evaluation of the actual performance of school buildings as an input to either attendance or learning.

Table 8.5 Level of government at which decisions are taken, public lower secondary education

OECD	*Capital expenditure, allocation of resources to the schools*	*Capital expenditure, use of resources in the school*	*Creation or closure of school*
Australia	**State** In full autonomy	**State** After consultation with school level	**State** After consultation w/state & local level
Canada	**State** After consultation with school level	**Local** Within framework set by state level	**State** In full autonomy
Chile	**Local** Within framework set by central level	**Local** In full autonomy	**Local** Within framework set by central level
Czech Republic	**Local** In full autonomy	**Local** In full autonomy	**Local** Within framework set by regional level
England	**Local** In full autonomy	**School** In full autonomy	**Local** In full autonomy
Estonia	**Local** In full autonomy	**Local** In full autonomy	**Local** Within framework set by central level
Finland	**Local** In full autonomy	**Local** After consultation with school level	**Local** In full autonomy
France	**Sub-regional** Other	**Sub-regional** In full autonomy	**Sub-regional** Other
Germany	**Local** Within framework set by state level	**Local** In full autonomy	**Local** After consultation with state level
Greece	**Central** Other	**Central** Other	**Central** After consultation with state level
Hungary	**Local** Within framework set by central level	**Local** After consultation with school level	**Local** After consultation w/sub-regional level

Ireland	**Central** In full autonomy	**School** Within framework set by central level	**Central** After consultation w/sub-regional level
Japan	**Local** In full autonomy	**Local** In full autonomy	**Local** In full autonomy
Korea	**Regional** In full autonomy	**Regional** In full autonomy	**Regional** In full autonomy
Mexico	**Central** In full autonomy	**Central** In full autonomy	**State** In full autonomy
Netherlands	**School** In full autonomy	**School** In full autonomy	**Central** In full autonomy
Poland	**Local** In full autonomy	**Local** In full autonomy	**Local** Within framework
Slovak Republic	**Central** After consultation with local level	**School** After consultation with local level	**Central** After consultation with local level
Slovenia	**Local** After consultation with local level	**Local** After consultation with local level	**Local** Within framework set by central level
Turkey	**Central** In full autonomy	**Regional** Within framework set by central level	**Regional** Within framework set by central level
United States	**Local** In full autonomy	**Local** After consultation with school level	**Local** Within framework set by state level
Other G20			
Indonesia	**Sub-regional** Other	**School** In full autonomy	**Sub-regional** After consultation with central level

Source: Author adaptation of OECD, *Education at a Glance* (2012).

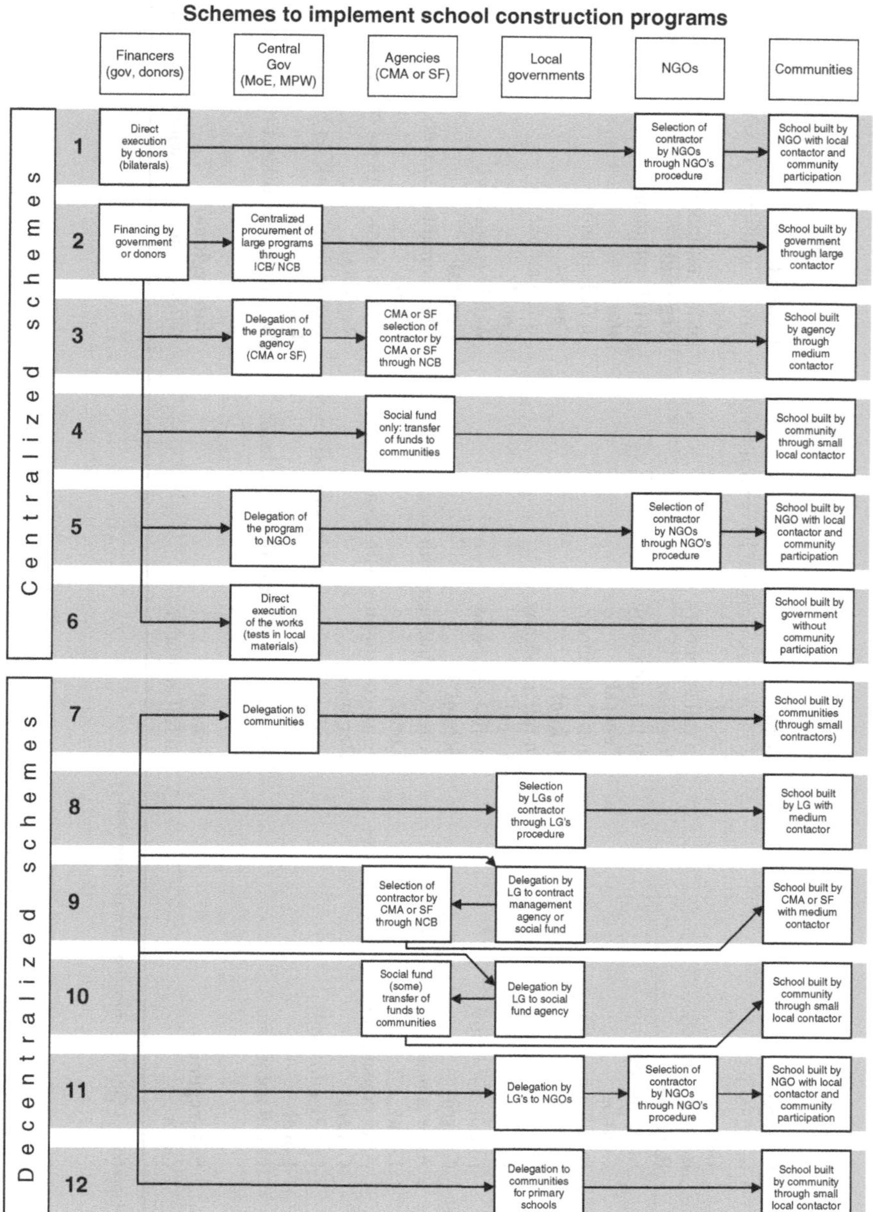

Figure 8.6 Schemes to implement school construction programs (source: Theunyck (2009)).

We believe the discussion in this chapter has made clear that various fiscal levers and institutional arrangements can often be applied to achieve better implementation. However, without equal attention to the critical issues of school design and location also highlighted in this chapter, the dilemma is the risk that a country better implements poorly designed schools. To avoid this paradox some parallel application of organizational models we have explored is justified and is warranted. This type of organizational asymmetry holds promise for improved efficiency for decentralized education infrastructure.

Annex: Application of OECD's locus of decision-making framework to examine the range of centralization and decentralization in a sample of countries

Table 8.5 shows the level of governmental authority responsible for three relevant decisions: (i) the allocation of capital expenditure resources to schools, (ii) the decision over how schools use those resources, and (iii) the decision to create or close a school, which impacts school construction and location.[21] The table also shows the relative autonomy that governmental authority has over the decision (in full autonomy versus being required to consult with another governmental level to make the decision[22]). Figure 8.6 shows some schemes for implementing school construction programs.

Notes

* The author thanks Luis Crouch and Emet Mohr for several conversations that significantly improved this chapter. The usual caveat regarding errors and interpretations applies.

1 Source: TI-UP.org *Delivering Cost Effective and Sustainable School Infrastructure.* (Bonner *et al.*, n.d.)

2 And the infrastructure issues extend well beyond classroom construction. In fact, classroom construction may only be about 60 percent of investment costs; the non-classroom infrastructure associated with school construction includes water and sanitation, furniture, ICT, and office space for administration (Theunynck, 2009).

3 We used data on sub-national government expenditures as a proportion of total government expenditures for 2009 or the most recent year available (cash or accrual basis) as an index for fiscal decentralization. We lose five countries from the sample in the figure, and we observe no pattern. There are very few countries reporting sub-national educational expenditure as a proportion of total educational expenditure so we are unable to use an education-specific fiscal decentralization index. The results are available upon request from the author. The data for the index was taken from the World Bank's fiscal decentralization web page: www.worldbank.org/publicfinance/decentralization.

4 One reviewer questioned the credibility of the data on Bangladesh, given that the capital expenditure appears so high. Given that these data come directly from EdStats, and that it is beyond the scope of this study to verify the accuracy of such broadly used data sources, it will suffice to note that spending levels in Bangladesh are likely high and steady, even if the precise numbers must be used with caution.

5 Rondinelli (1981, 1989) and Rondinelli and Nellis (1986) created the original basic vocabulary for describing the various ways in which governments may be expected to pursue administrative decentralization. It is important to note that very rarely can any

given reform be given one single label. That is, any reform is likely to be a complex combination of each of these sets of arrangements. Accountability for the results of decisions remains largely bureaucratic, vertical, and internal to the executive branch, but sub-national entities can make decisions and report ex-post on the decision or the results of the decisions. (1) *Deconcentration* involves the central or federal government granting greater authority to its own sub-national authorities under its direct control. It is the weakest form of decentralization for it does not transfer any significant authority to sub-national governments. (2) *Delegation* involves creating semi-autonomous agencies, such as state-owned enterprises or public corporations. (3) *Devolution* entails the transfer of service delivery responsibility to independent sub-national levels of government, regions, provinces, municipalities, etc. Accountability is now horizontal and takes place, to some degree, between the local executive and the local representative branches of government. (4) *Privatization* is often considered the most far-reaching form of decentralization. Early studies focused on *fiscal decentralization*; that is, the decentralization of functions related to public finance and public financial management. Fiscal decentralization can be further divided into two broad categories: (i) revenue-side fiscal decentralization, which involves granting sub-national levels of government greater control over tax and other revenue sources, and (ii) expenditure-side fiscal decentralization, which involves greater expenditure responsibility on the part of sub-national governments. Revenue-side fiscal decentralization almost always includes expenditure-side fiscal decentralization; however, the latter may take place without the former, with the central government usually transferring financial resources to sub-national governments via grants or revenue sharing schemes. Again, nearly all reforms exhibits aspects of several of these trends.

6 Policymakers involved in such reform processes would benefit from such an effort specific to their country and regional contexts.

7 An example might be when a district manager can decide what type of automobiles to buy for the district office, but if he is found to have broken rules, or the cars turn out to be poor quality or poor choices, the district managers are accountable upwards back to the home office. Another way to categorize reforms within this typology is the extent to which different components of decentralization may be conceived as horizontal or vertical. In the case of administrative devolution or the political aspects of delegation to schools, the accountability becomes horizontal. To me this is the key issue: whether accountability becomes more horizontal (devolution) or stays vertical (deconcentration).

8 There are examples where such standards are set at the local or regional level, but in the developing world they appear to be rare. In addition, donor projects may be exempt from these standards and have their own.

9 This author first experienced the homogeneity of rural school design resulting from centralization, despite tremendous geographic heterogeneity in Mexico in the early 1990s—where school materials and design were the same whether in the high sierra or the coastal plains.

10 Below we discuss the connection of infrastructure provision with school staffing. Here, it is worth noting that any compensatory funding formula policy is likely to have some impact on teacher-student ratios—either indirectly or even directly if class size is used as a weight or criteria for funding allocation.

11 This section draws heavily upon Serge Theunynck (2002). Unless otherwise indicated, all citations in this section are to this source. Readers interested in project by project detail will benefit greatly from reviewing the original source.

12 There is a large literature on accountability, in particular stemming from the WDR 2004. See Gershberg *et al.* (2012) for a detailed exploration of the myriad potential relationships between principals, agents, and clients.

13 We cannot provide details on the specific accountability relationships in the many projects considered in the development of this taxonomy, but it stands to reason that the instances that were successful effectively created incentives by which the "delegates"

were answerable to the stakeholders responsible for service provision. While beyond the scope of this discussion, see the Annex for a detailed summary of all potential elements.

14 Theunynck (2009) calls Uganda's community-driven development (CDD) approach "the most important single construction program ever executed in an African country for primary classroom and sanitation in schools," having built in four years 21,000 classrooms, 20,000 latrines, 325,000 desks, and 556 teacher houses.

15 In our Egypt case study below we will also explore the potential for community-based approaches in school design and location.

16 And delegation to CMAs is fraught with challenges of its own. If they are, for instance, under-capitalized when given contracts, without sufficient allowance for advances and cash flow management (partly out of fear for providing too many advances ahead of results), then there is a danger that they could fail and abandon the projects anyway. Balancing the need for cash flow advances with the need for payment-for-results, with under-capitalized builders, is a factor not sufficiently considered in many cases.

17 This case study is based upon a study the author did for the Population Council and USAID (Gershberg and Gohary, 2007). This study used qualitative interview and focus group methods to gather the interview data presented here.

18 MOE, National Strategic Education Plan 2007/08–2011/12. This figure may also include schools built by donors and NGOs whose construction was overseen by and coordinated with the MOE and GAEB.

19 These figures come from the World Bank Public Expenditure Review.

20 Note that we do not attempt to disentangle the de facto reality of actual practice, which is quite often weaker than *de jure*. De facto practice is, of course, more important with respect to fostering the actual accountability gains reforms hope to accrue from decentralization, but uncovering that is beyond the scope of this case study.

21 Unfortunately, the first two relate only to capital investment at already constructed schools and the third is only the broadest decision related to the issue of school location for new construction and the potential re-use of existing infrastructure. It would be very useful in future if OECD could expand the questions on capital investment in their survey to cover school design, location, and construction.

22 "Other" means the authority over decision-making cannot be categorized by either of these two descriptions.

References

Bonner R., P.K. Das, R. Kalra, B. Leathes, and N. Wakeham (n.d.) "Delivering Cost Effective and Sustainable School Infrastructure." TI-UP.org.

Gershberg, A. and H. Gohary (2007). "Building the Schools Egyptians Need and Want: A Qualitative Evaluation of the Policy and Practice of School Location, Design, Construction and Maintenance," The Population Council, May.

Gershberg, A. and M. Jacobs (1998). "Decentralization and Recentralization: Lessons from the Social Sectors in Mexico and Nicaragua," OCE Working Paper Series, WP-379. Inter-American Development Bank, Washington, DC. August.

Gershberg, A. and D. Winkler (2004). "Education Decentralization in Africa," in Brian Levy and Sahr Kpundeh (eds.), *Building State Capacity in Africa: New Approaches, Emerging Lessons*, World Bank, World Bank Institute, Washington, DC.

Gershberg, A., P. Gonzalez, and B. Meade (2012). "Understanding and Improving Accountability in Education: A Conceptual Framework and Guideposts from Three Decentralization Reform Experiences in Latin America," *World Development*, 40(5): 1024–1041.

Rajaram, Anand, Tuan Minh Le, Nataliya Biletska, and Jim Brumby (2010). "Framework for Reviewing Public Investment Efficiency," World Bank Policy Working Paper, No. 5397, Washington, DC.

Rondinelli, Dennis A. (1981). "Government Decentralization in Comparative Theory and Practice in Developing Countries," *International Review of Administrative Science*, 47(2): 133–147.

Rondinelli, D. (1989). "Decentralizing Public Services in Developing Countries: Issues and Opportunities," *Journal of Social, Political and Economic Studies*, 14(1): 77–98.

Rondinelli, Dennis A. and John R. Nellis (1986). "Assessing Decentralization Policies in Developing Countries: The Case for Cautious Optimism," *Development Policy Review*, 4: 3–23.

RTI (2010). "Planning the Decentralization of School Infrastructure," Discussion Document, September 2.

Theunynck, S. (2002). *School Construction in Developing Countries—What Do We Know?* World Bank, Washington, DC.

Theunynck, S. (2009). *School Construction Strategies for Universal Primary Education in Africa: Should Communities Be Empowered to Build Their Own Schools*? World Bank, Washington, DC.

9 Rural roads

The challenge of decentralized implementation

Simon D. Ellis and Aurelio Menendez

Introduction

The benefits from investments in rural roads are well understood both by the communities who demand them for improved access to essential economic and social facilities and the policy makers who see their impact on poverty reduction and economic growth. However, rural roads pose particular challenges in terms of their effective management and sustainable use. Rural roads usually make up the majority of the road network in any country but only carry a fraction of the traffic. The extent and physical isolation of the network poses problems for managing construction and long term maintenance and the local authorities tasked with management of the network very often don't have the expertise, financial resources, or incentive structure to effectively carry out their responsibilities. It is therefore important to have close coordination between the various stakeholders involved in rural roads provision from the national government to the beneficiary communities.

Particular emphasis has to be given to effective mechanisms for managing and financing long term maintenance. The sustainability of many rural roads programs have been compromised through inadequate maintenance. Maintenance requires an appropriate incentive framework, a steady and sufficient flow of funds, and effective management systems but crucially the involvement and engagement of the community. For this reason some of the most successful rural roads maintenance schemes have involved community based contractors working in parallel with public works departments.

This chapter will review the key elements required for effective decentralized implementation of rural roads programs. It will review the range of options available and the evidence for successful implementation where it exists. The first section makes the case for the importance of rural roads and sets out the evidence for the socio-economic benefits. The following section addresses the responsibilities for implementation and critical importance of having clarity over network ownership. The section after that highlights the difficulties of finance, particularly for longer term maintenance, and sets out options for improving allocations and the reliability of receipt for those allocations. The next section sets out the project cycle from planning, design, implementation, maintenance, and subsequent evaluation. The final section summarizes the key issues and highlights the main policy considerations.

The objectives and nature of rural road infrastructure and transport services

Transport accessibility represents a key factor that influences livelihood conditions and opportunities. The time distance to reach social services or markets affects the possibilities of receiving adequate health care or education and of bringing products to markets or opting to a range of labor prospects. The literature on transport access as a necessary element (though not sufficient) for the reduction of poverty and the induction of productive development is varied and extensive, and it encompasses situations in both urban and rural settings. This chapter focuses on rural settings and discusses the dimensions that are necessary for the appropriate provision of transport access to and from rural communities and the division of responsibilities between national and sub-national (local) entities.[1] The importance of rural accessibility in the reduction of poverty and access to essential social and economic services is reflected by one of the International Development Association's (IDA) core indicators which is the percentage of the rural population who live within 2 km of an all-season road. Figure 9.1 shows a transformed map indicating the extent of the rural inaccessibility is particularly acute in Africa and South Asia.

Rural transport consists of the rural roads—the infrastructure—and the services provided to transport people and products between rural communities and market facilities. The definition of "rural transport" or "rural roads" is not the same across countries. The term can be defined as the set of infrastructure or services that are provided to facilitate the access to and from rural communities, usually on roads of reduced standards, of widths of up to six meters that allow traffic in both directions but at moderate speeds of less than 50 km/hr.

These roads usually represent the last link of a network of roads categorized by the type and level of service they can provide and the size of the communities or cities they connect. Primary or national roads are the backbone of the road network, linking the major urban centers and generally paved to support traffic that includes trucks of all sizes and weights (up to the maximum allowed by the law) and of high volumes (requiring in some cases roads with two or more lanes in each direction). The so-called secondary roads flow into the primary network and connect medium-sized communities or the last links of the tertiary or rural networks. The secondary roads have the standards for traffic of medium weight and, depending on the stage of development of the country, can be to a greater or lesser extent paved. Most countries also have a network of district roads (sometimes combined with rural roads) which link the secondary roads to district centers. The rural roads are the last links that connect the more distant rural communities to the medium-sized cities, secondary and district roads. These roads carry low volumes of traffic and are often unpaved or sealed with a thin bituminous surface. As indicated before each country has a slightly different categorization of the roads; all represent the capillary channels through which people and products move around and facilitate the social interconnections and economic interchanges. Table 9.1 shows a classification in a selected number of

Figure 9.1 Transformed map indicating areas most affected by rural inaccessibility (source: World Bank, 2007).

Table 9.1 Road classification and length in kilometers of selected number of countries

Country	*National highways*		*State/provincial highways*		*District roads*		*Rural roads*		*Total*
	Km	*% total*	*Km*	*% total*	*Km*	*% total*	*Km*	*% total*	*Km*
India	70,934	2	163,898	4	1,005,327	25	2,749,805	69	3,989,964
Vietnam	17,295	8	21,841	10	45,250	22	124,994	60	209,380
Rwanda	2,860	20	–	–	1,840	13	9,300	67	14,000
Honduras	3,284	22	2,771	19	–	–	8,685	59	14,740
Peru	24,092	19	24,953	19	–	–	80,244	62	129,289
Argentina	39,000	8	195,000	38	–	–	285,000	55	519,000
Colombia	17,382	9	38,315	20	–	–	135,679	71	191,376

countries and highlights the challenge for managing the rural road network which often represents over 60 percent of the network but typically carries less than 20 percent of the traffic.

Enhancements to rural accessibility often take place in the form of improvements to the infrastructure through the upgrading of road conditions, improvements to surface conditions, and reconstruction of structures such as bridges and draining systems. These enhancements are then expected to encourage users to provide more, better, and safer transport services, through the incorporation of vehicles of higher standards and more frequent scheduling of those services. The upgrading can also help in facilitating the use of non-motorized transport (bicycles or rickshaws) or motorcycles, which are cheaper to acquire and can provide the level of accessibility for certain activities in rural areas. The basic premise is that improved roads will encourage lower transport costs through the use of more efficient vehicles (e.g., head loading to bicycles, pick-up trucks to trucks, or just the more efficient use of existing vehicles). These lower transport costs then promote more competitive and productive rural economies and improved access to essential social services.

The number of studies that have demonstrated the benefits from improved road conditions and enhanced accessibility has expanded over the years as it was seen that reduction in poverty and, particularly, extreme poverty and the achievement of the Millennium Development Goals (MDG) required access to health and education facilities. Much of the initial work on rural roads and poverty reduction was carried out in the 1980s and 1990s with work that focused on the impacts of improved roads on household incomes, agricultural production, and wage rates (Howe and Richards, 1984; Gannon and Liu, 1997). More recently the International Food Policy Research Institute has looked at the most effective use of scarce public expenditures on reducing poverty in rural areas and they have found that in projects of agricultural extension, the construction of rural roads is also the most effective way of reducing poverty in many countries, including China, India, Vietnam, and Uganda (Fan *et al.*, 2007). Increasingly, however, there has been a focus on the broader poverty impacts of improved rural roads including on access to health and education facilities and how they affect education and health outcomes (Mu and van de Walle, 2007; Bell and van Dillen, 2011).

Box 9.1 Socio-economic impacts from improved rural access

Public investments in rural roads provide some of the best returns in terms of reducing poverty and promoting agricultural and non-agricultural growth. A paper by Mu and van de Walle (2007) which analyzed the impacts of a rural roads project in Vietnam found the following:

> There are indications of significant impacts on the development of markets and commercialization. Some outcomes, such as food goods availability, responded rapidly to the new and improved roads. Others, such as the presence and frequency of markets and non-food goods and services availability, took two

> years more on average to emerge. The project resulted in households switching from agriculture to non-agricultural, mostly service-based, activities. Perhaps most notable, the project had significant, sustained and robust, impacts on primary school completion rates. Yet there are many indicators of local area development for which we find little significant impact attributable to better roads.
>
> A paper by Bell and van Dillen (2011) analyzed the effects of providing all-weather roads to some villages in a poor, drought-prone region of India. The paper looked at effects in three domains: "commercial" (output and trade), education, and health. The following were the main results:
>
> (i) an all-weather connection measurably reduced unit transport costs; (ii) pupils in all three levels of the school system lost substantially fewer days of schooling due to bad weather, in large part because their teachers had fewer such absences; (iii) the acutely sick received more timely treatment and were more likely to be treated in a hospital than in the nearest primary health clinic; and (iv) the respondents ranked the ensuing benefits in the domains of health and education at least as highly as those in the "commercial" domain.

These studies have shown that improvements to rural accessibility, when properly designed (as explained later in this chapter), can lead to substantial reduction in poverty rates (and of extreme poverty, which is more prevalent in rural areas). In projects and studies carried out in Chile and Peru, among others, it was also seen that coordinating investments in rural roads along with those in other infrastructure sectors (water and sanitation, telecommunications, and electrification) in tandem with the potential productive activities in a defined rural territory has a robust potential for jumpstarting the local economy and multiply several times over the impact of the rural roads investments (Escobal and Torero, 2005). Institutional coordination represents the biggest challenge in these investment efforts. Studies have also shown that in some areas the building of a road doesn't necessarily attract improved transport services and policy makers need to consider the mobility needs of the communities concerned (Starkey *et al.*, 2002).

In all cases, it is seen that benefits do not come all at once but rather they start with enhancements to transport indicators and then expand later to increased prices to agricultural and local product and eventually to increased local incomes. In this vein, the causality of benefits takes place starting with the reduction in transport operating costs and travel times, lower freight and passenger tariffs and hence the ability of the producer to keep a higher proportion of the final market price, i.e., farm-gate prices increase. The reductions in tariffs are also allowed through the reduction in the spoilage of rural products (generated by lower transit times, more reliable service, and smoother rides) and in accidents (as a consequence of safer riding conditions—though this requires the appropriate road safety features and enforcement as speeds normally increase as a consequence of improved road conditions).

Ensuing economic benefits are realized by a greater competitive edge of the rural territory, greater interpersonal connections, and an enhanced setting for innovation and access of productive extension services, particularly for agricultural products. In the longer term, the safer and shorter travel times lead to higher attendance to school by children and a faster access to health facilities by people in need of medical attention (particularly pregnant women and infants—with a reduction in death of expecting mothers and in infant mortality rates) and a more sustained presence of teachers and medical personnel and school and hospital administrators, all leading to medium term improvements to health and educational indicators and achievements. In a broad analysis carried out in China, the additional benefit was an opportunity to expand the relationships among populations and the opportunities for marrying.

The above benefits include also another very important one: the improvement to the living conditions and generally livelihoods of women. As explained earlier, rural accessibility brings education and health benefits that accrue to a greater extent to women given their childbearing and often child caretaking responsibilities. Improved access can further facilitate women's opportunities to undertake activities related to local economic endeavors, from participation in agriculture, livestock, fisheries, or local artifacts, to the actual participation in road maintenance and rehabilitation works.

Higher accessibility however has also led to higher migration rates and the depopulation of rural areas or secondary cities, though this can be seen as a natural consequence of the lack of competitive edge of specific rural economies and a natural process of transfer of economic activity to areas with higher productive potential. It is also related to deforestation and generally the destruction of the natural habitat, though this is more a question of properly addressing the potential negative impacts on the environment through incorporation early on (starting at the planning stage through the design of strategic environmental plans, for instance) of appropriate environmental management practices and sustaining those practices when civil works or maintenance activities are carried out. In fact, the adequate consideration of environmental management practices in rural roads can help enhance environmental conditions and the mitigation of natural disasters that can happen in the event of extreme weather events.

Responsibilities

Along with the classification of roads along three levels (principal or national, secondary or feeder, and tertiary or rural), legislations across countries tend to assign responsibilities to a similar three tier levels of government, with the national/central government in charge of the primary network, departments or regional governments in charge of the secondary network, and rural communities or provincial governments in charge of rural networks. This is the natural consequence of a perspective that assigns responsibilities to that level of government elected by the population that benefits from the services provided by the different types of roads. For rural roads, it is understood that the benefits provided by those last links of the network accrue largely or solely to the inhabitants of the rural communities they serve. From that perspective, countries like Bolivia or Colombia assign the entire responsibility for the upkeep, upgrading, or expansion of the rural roads networks, and the financing required by any of these interventions, to the lower tier of the government.

There are however several shortcomings to that perspective given that the ultimate benefits to the country as a whole go beyond the boundaries of the rural communities, territories, or populations. As discussed earlier, rural roads can lead to enhanced livelihood conditions in rural areas, leading to reduced poverty rates and a more equal prosperity in the country, a benefit that has been demonstrated reverberates in more sustained growth rates for the country as a whole. The increased levels of educational achievement and health indicators are an added benefit that expands beyond the rural boundaries and produces positive effects in national wellbeing. When seen from the perspective of these benefits the involvement of national governments in ensuring adequate rural access becomes justified and necessary.

This involvement is required as the third tier of government will tend to underprovide the required level of rural road infrastructure as a consequence of three key factors: (1) limited planning and technical capacity to define investments and technological solutions, at least at an early stage of a rural roads development program; (2) limited financial capacity to address the needs, at least as far as local revenue raising capacity is not well developed; and (3) governance structures that may affect the definition of proper plans when both (1) and (2) are not well structured. These factors however may not be necessarily adequately addressed by involvement of national entities as they themselves may also face issues of lack of capacity and the existence of weak governance structures (that can lead to political patronage and poor investment decisions). Nonetheless, it is likely more feasible to produce a core professional cadre of specialists and a supporting management and financial framework from a national entity that can then gradually help strengthen the capacities and procedures at the local level. Figure 9.2 provides an institutional framework for rural roads development in India. As discussed above the Government of India has decided that there should be a role for national government both in the finance and planning of the rural roads network but at the same time is trying to strengthen its local level institutions to implement and manage maintenance over the long term.

The coalescence of the two tiers of government—national and local—however should not diminish the need to entrust responsibilities to local/sub-national levels of government taking into account the closer relationship between the location and function of the infrastructure and the major beneficiaries from that infrastructure. This is particularly relevant and appropriate in engaging local communities and governments in defining priorities and designing investments that are appropriate for the needs, resources, and potential of the communities. There is also a need to establish the ownership of those communities and governments in the management and maintenance of rural networks. This collaboration and coordination should help in defining a set of common objectives for the achievement of benefits that intersect at both the realms of local and national authorities.

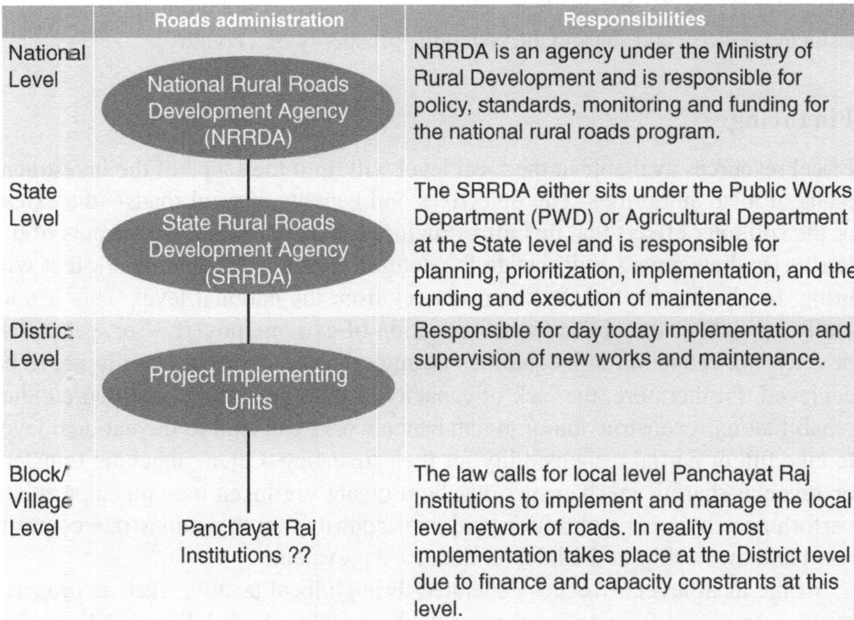

Figure 9.2 Institutional arrangements for the decentralized implementation of rural roads in India (source: adapted from International Labor Office, 2005).

This discussion helps establish the key dimensions that need to be considered when discussing the allocation of responsibilities for a program of rural roads, as follows:

- Capacities: how structured/ready are the local governments to plan, design, manage, finance, and maintain the rural road infrastructure?
- Needs: what are the expected short, medium, and long term needs of the rural territory and the extent to which improvements to the rural roads can address those needs? What are the size and characteristics of the population that will receive the benefits and the level of spillover effects beyond the rural territory? This dimension requires careful definition of the territorial unit of analysis as depending on how that unit is defined the extent and scope of the needs can vary substantially.
- Impacts: What are the potential environmental, social, institutional, and financial impacts of meeting the identified needs and what are the alternative mechanisms to address them?

The location of a country along that set of dimensions will help dictate the level and form of engagement of the various tiers of government (the depth and scope of the decentralization) and the set of collaborative interventions towards establishing a path for enhancing rural accessibility and strengthening the methodological and institutional process that can help achieve that objective (and ultimately the goal of reducing poverty and sharing the economic prosperity of a country).

Financing

Fiscal resources available at the local level will limit the scope of the investment plans of local authorities. The objectives and benefits of rural roads—the extent of the spillover effects that this infrastructure can have beyond the borders of the territories they serve—will dictate the definition of a fiscal framework that will bring the sharing (or transfer) of resources from the national level. This is normally required if the objectives of reduction of extreme poverty—or, generally, poverty—or reduction in inequalities through the sharing of prosperity are to be achieved. Furthermore, the lack of capacity to plan, prioritize, or procure either rehabilitation/reconstruction or maintenance works can lead to the national level to take full or partial responsibility for their financing. Often, matching transfers or revenue sharing mechanisms that help create the incentives for appropriate performance by local authorities (and their contribution to demonstrate commitment and ownership of the interventions) are prevalent.

At the local level, revenues generated through local taxation such as property taxes or transfers from national taxes such as Value Added Tax (VAT) or fuel levies are used for the purpose of financing activities in rural roads, as they are understood to have a relationship with or benefit from good access. Other revenue raising alternatives include tolls or charges for the use of infrastructure or taxes raised from the licensing or registration of vehicles or the issuance of driving licenses. In the context of rural communities and low volume roads however these revenues tend to be rather small (or non-existent when the administrative costs of their collection surpass or are closer to the amount of revenues that can be potentially raised). The revenues from property taxes tend also to be very limited due to deficient property cadaster and low taxation rates. Transfers from national taxation on the other hand have a stronger base but since they are also charged nationally the portion that comes back to the local level is often insufficient. As such an agreed formula should be developed such that local authorities get a fair share and also have some certainty over future revenue streams. In Peru, for instance, by law, a portion of the national value-added tax (a revenue source selected because it is correlated—albeit imperfectly—to the same formula used for the allocation) is transferred to local authorities for the purpose of maintaining rural roads in good condition. Table 9.2 sets out the main sources of revenue at the local level.

In many cases, contributions from the national governments have tended to focus on support to capital investments while local entities have been responsible for the recurrent costs of maintenance. This assignment of financing responsibilities reflects the interest at the national level on ensuring the proper allocation for investments that contribute to national goals of growth and equity, and the importance of commitments of local authorities to the recurrent activity

Table 9.2 Sources of local revenue for building and maintaining rural roads

Revenue from national transfers		*Local revenue sources*	
Transfers from general taxation (income taxes, VAT, etc.)	In most countries the majority of local funds come from national level transfers in the form of block grants	Property taxes	Limited revenues due to cadaster issues
Transfers from road funds (fuel levies)	Some countries have dedicated road funds and transfer generally a small share for local roads	Local income taxes	Limited due to limited tax base
Transfers from vehicle license fees/registrations, etc.	Limited transfers as share of revenues	Levies on agricultural marketing	Some countries, particularly where there are marketing boards, will levy charges for upkeep of roads
		Community contributions (in-kind or cash)	This can be a substantial source of revenue where countries have this tradition
		Toll revenues	Very limited due to difficulty of tolling rural roads and administrative costs of collection compared to revenue potential

of maintaining the assets. However, this model can cause problems where there is not full ownership at the local level or where local entities simply do not have the capacity to fulfill their responsibilities. There can be a tendency to over-design roads as national government is paying which may reduce short term maintenance burdens but can make longer term maintenance unaffordable particularly at the time of renewals. A better approach is to share costs of both capital and recurrent costs between national and local authorities with a plan to phase out national level funding over time. In parallel to this there has to be a policy of shifting revenues to the control of local entities so they have resources commensurate with their responsibilities.

The challenge however in the sharing of resources for rural roads is how to define the distribution of the potential national resources to cover a larger or smaller part of either capital or maintenance costs. The distribution should be established on the basis of the ultimate goals to be achieved though also considering the efforts local authorities are ready to take on to upgrade and maintain their rural roads networks. In some instances, such as in Peru, where for the initial phases of a rural roads program supported by the national government, the sharing formula included population and size of geographic area (as a proxy of the overall needs of the territory for rural roads) and key socio-economic indicators (such as those related to the human-development index—a composite statistic of life expectancy, education, and income, the latter as a proxy for poverty levels) complemented by the level of fiscal resources collected for the provision of municipal services as a whole or those allocated to rural roads.[2] In India national level grants have been provided to States based on the length of their rural road networks. However, the grants are only paid if the States have demonstrated that they have already committed their own resources to maintenance budget lines. In a few cases, the productive potential of that territory can also enter the criteria if it can be measured with a good level of reliability (when, for instance, there is information about GDP or GDP per capita of that territorial unit). Allocations for maintenance tend to be based on existing needs and the fiscal contributions the rural government is ready to bring to cover the costs of that maintenance.

The project cycle

Planning and priority setting

From a bird's view of a particular rural territory, one would expect to see a very large number of needs in effectively enhancing local access. As indicated earlier, the number of kilometers of rural roads is several times that of the other networks, given the sheer size of reaching the most remote areas of the territory. The project cycle then starts with the selection of priorities and the identification of how those priorities will help achieve the economic and social needs of the territory's population. The definition of the broader development plans for the territory must then be the first step as the basis for identifying the accessibility needs.

The definition of those broader development plans can take the form of sophisticated models for larger geographic areas with multiple productive options or that include a large number of rural inhabitants or simple approaches in the case of more contained territories with a smaller, well defined population. In both cases this step requires adequate participatory processes that ensure that the views of the population are incorporated into the identification of potential productive endeavors and impacts that are not desired by that population. Box 9.2 describes the approaches followed in Chile and Peru in the definition of the plans.

Box 9.2 Territorial planning for rural infrastructure in Chile and Peru

For instance, in Chile, in the context of the development of a national rural infrastructure program, the mechanism used for the definition of the development plan was developed along with the then Ministry of Planning as the so-called Territorial Development Master Plans. These plans sought to identify the potential future uses of "rural communes" and from that the needs in terms of infrastructure (including roads) and productive alliances (seeking to attract funds in support of productive activities), with consideration of potential environmental impacts. In another example, in Peru, the Rural Transport Program seeks to improve accessibility of territories in the mountainous Rural Sierra, some of which due to geographic constraints include a limited number of people and productive activities. The program works through the provincial governments and with the direct participation of the communities to identify further productive opportunities and from there the specific needs for accessibility enhancements.

The participatory process is required given that resources are limited and, depending on the network structure, addressing development plans may lead to competing investments in roads that can contribute equally to specific requirements of that plan. The participatory process should help elucidate priorities. Also, since the road infrastructure may not be enough to reach out to the majority of the (often dispersed) population, the participatory process should help identify the requirements for lower-standards infrastructure (including those such as foot or bike paths) to facilitate the access to the major arteries of the road infrastructure and ensure that rural roads connect to critical facilities of other sectors (markets, hospitals, or schools). It can also help identify the particular needs of specific segments of the population (e.g., women, indigenous groups), ensuring the benefits, economic and otherwise, from the rural roads are adequately and effectively internalized by the communities. Participatory processes and communications with the communities can further help define appropriately the environmental and social development impacts and the management actions that need to be implemented to address those impacts.

Environmental practices are important as this infrastructure is located in areas relatively untouched by human activity (and potentially having a greater impact on biodiversity or forests) but also because of the need to manage environmental factors for the proper upkeep of the infrastructure. It is important to ensure that mechanisms are in place to ensure adequate environmental practices and adequate monitoring. For example, in Honduras, an innovative approach of payment to landowners in exchange for conservation of natural habitats has been implemented to protect an endangered species (Box 9.3).

Box 9.3 Compensation for environmental protection: Honduras San Lorenzo–Olanchito Rehabilitation Project

In Honduras, a thorn forest area of approximately 2,000 hectares has been placed under a legally binding, financially sustainable, and operationally effective system for long term conservation to preserve an endangered and endemic hummingbird species in the area of influence of a road rehabilitation project (partly financed by the World Bank). This area includes some 1,400 hectares of privately owned lands, which have been placed under conservation through the signing of long term (ten years), renewable, Environmental Service Payments Agreements (PSA is its name in Spanish) to ensure adequate protection of the hummingbird habitat. Under said agreements, the landowners must ensure the conservation of the thorn forest and refrain from certain specified activities that could degrade the habitat, receiving a monetary compensation for any loss of income that this restraining measure may impose on them. The framework is characterized by: (1) a legal basis for the PSA contracts; (2) clear institutional responsibilities and a functional mechanism for verifying compliance and adequate disbursement of PSA payments; (3) a sustainable source of financing (for making current and expected future PSA payments; and (4) a protected area overlay (or other land use zoning) that would prohibit those types of future public investments (and help discourage those private investments) that could undermine thorn forest conservation by raising the opportunity cost.

The identification of priorities should be complemented with a more rigorous assessment of the economic worth of the proposed investments. Given the low traffic volumes on rural roads, the standard methodologies for cost-benefit analysis are not normally applicable and other methods must be used, such as cost-effectiveness (accepting those priorities for whom the cost per kilometer is below a predefined threshold that reflects that the cost of the investments is commensurate with the expected overall benefits) or the producer's surplus approach, through which the expected incremental value of production as a consequence of the investment is compared against the cost of the rehabilitation/construction and the annual maintenance outlays during a defined period of time (normally 15–20 years).

The planning and priority setting should be led by the local institutions responsible for the defined rural territory, but in the context of reduced capacities the national government has a key role to play to ensure the priorities reflect a well defined set of interventions in line with the expected development plans.

The broader development perspective however requires the involvement of national entities that do not have a stake in a particular sector but rather on the broader development of rural areas. In the case of Chile, for instance, the entity in charge of advancing the rural infrastructure program was located in the Ministry of Interior with the accountability of enhancing development and capacities at the decentralized levels of government. In Peru, a new entity—the Rural Roads Program—was initially created with autonomy and reporting to both the Ministries of Transport and Economy. The experience of these cases shows that a national entity with a comprehensive perspective of rural development can be more effective in achieving a more integrated support to local entities and, when applicable, an effective gradual transfer of responsibilities as capacities are built up at the local level.

Project design and technology

The analysis described in the previous sections should inform the decision about the type of pavement or geometric standards of the various links for the rural roads. With low volumes of traffic (around 150 vehicles per day or fewer) and limited number of heavy traffic, gravel pavements can yield the expected level of benefits and, if well maintained, sustained over long periods of time. In various countries in Latin America, gravel rural roads have sustained year-round access when upkeep has been provided on a continuous basis. Every three to five years these roads require re-graveling but in all they can provide the expected level of service for a fraction of the cost of paved roads. In a few countries, cobblestones have been used very successfully, as is the case of Nicaragua (with a far reaching program of the so-called *adoquines*, or concrete slabs that are interlocked together manually—see Box 9.4). Topography and climate conditions also are important elements of the design. Mountainous topography coupled with frequent and heavy rains might dictate paving even in the context of medium traffic volumes, with paving often being asphalt double treatment and, in those cases with heavier traffic, concrete (as it can be observed in rural roads in mountainous areas of China, for instance). As in the previous section, the national authorities can play an important role in sharing information and knowledge about the experience in the application of one or another technology and in measuring the effects in their application in one context of another.

Box 9.4 Decentralized nature of the MCA *adoquines* model in Nicaragua

The Nicaragua "MCA *adoquines* (concrete blocks) model" is an interesting decentralized development experience that involves the central government Ministry of Transport & Infrastructure (MTI) collaborating with the local authorities (municipal government) and target beneficiaries to deliver rural road public infrastructure. First, the local authorities in consultation with MTI agree on the roads that get evaluated at the national level for priority intervention. Once roads to be intervened have been approved, a legally binding agreement is signed between the MTI and the local mayor describing the works to be undertaken and the modality to be followed in executing the works. The municipal authorities then organize a meeting to call on community members that meet the qualifications for particular posts to present themselves for constitution into community development modules (MCAs). MCAs are local entities staffed by a board of five directors (with the president of each MCA as the legal representative) to perform a specific road upgrading task. Each MCA has responsibility for a specific stretch of road (limited to 3 km and a ceiling of US$500,000 per MCA due to administrative and fiduciary concerns). The MCA personnel receive technical support and training from the centralized MTI from inception, and have an MTI supervisor and promoter accompanying them throughout the implementation process. The contract awarded to each MCA is signed jointly by the MTI (as the contracting party); and the Mayor and President of the MCA on the other hand (as the contracted party). Individually, each MCA hires its own local labor in order to construct a specified stretch of road. MCAs join together and use economies of scale to contract an earthworks contractor and an *adoquines* supplier. For these "group MCA contracts," the Mayor and Presidents of all the contracting MCAs are the "contracting party" and the earthworks contractor and *adoquines* supplier is the "contracted party." This contracting follows national competitive bidding procedures to ensure transparency and competition. Quality control is outsourced to a supervision firm. Rural road infrastructure delivery under this decentralized model has been successful with roads built on time, at reasonable cost, and with the required quality. In addition to creating short term employment opportunities, and building technical and entrepreneurial capabilities, the involvement of the local population in the infrastructure delivery process has also engendered a sense of ownership in the roads.

Based on Muzira and Hernandez de Diaz (2013).

But local context is critical and the choice of paving technology must be further considered the universe of potential firms that can compete for the procurement of the civil works and the possibilities of using local labor for the rehabilitation or reconstruction tasks. The examples of Nicaragua or Peru show that local labor can play an important role and reduce the overall costs of the investments when the paving technology is tailored for labor intensive activities. Similarly the ultimate capacity for the maintenance of the rehabilitated roads (and the accompanying infrastructure of bridges, drainage, or culverts) and generally their management (with attention to vegetation and the environment at large) represent factors that must inform the final decision for the selection of paving technology. In this respect, as indicated earlier, the need to create resilience to ensure that extreme weather events do not affect substantially the condition of the rural roads should be built into the design and maintenance strategy. The role national entities can play in establishing technical standards (for instance, in light of more frequent extreme weather events) is paramount, as it is, as stated earlier, in promoting and facilitating the sharing of knowledge, with the aim of helping local entities to optimize their investments and ensure their upkeep. By requiring the application of planning methodologies and technical standards (including environmental impact assessments) as prerequisite to access national resources and technical assistance, the national governments can ensure that decentralized entities adhere to appropriate engineering practices and investments in line with the expected benefits and the needs of the local populations.

On environmental issues, the basic challenge is ensuring the upgraded infrastructure does not lead to negative and irreversible effects on the area of influence of the road, such as erosion or deforestation. Overall one of the most important environmental mitigations to avoid problems is just the application of good engineering design, coupled with good planning and an environmental consciousness (Keller and Shrar, 2003). Sustainable practices involve application of good long term planning (that include strategic environmental planning that evaluates the potential environmental impacts of increasing agricultural/economic activities and the actions to prevent negative impacts—such as deforestation); adequate engineering design, such as drainage structures that are designed to last their design life (25–100 years) and that help protect water quality; the use of local materials and labor pools whenever possible; and inspection and quality control. Control of drainage and slope stabilization are two key actions that can be implemented through proper use of vegetation, and particularly deep-rooted vegetation. Attention to greener construction practices yields important economic benefits as they can help reduce the ultimate deterioration of the rehabilitated roads and the impact on the surrounding areas. National governments have an important role to play in defining the environmentally friendly planning and engineering practices and creating the incentives for their effective application through co-financing mechanisms and technical assistance support.

Management and maintenance of road assets

One of the greatest challenges in the rural roads sector is the effective long term maintenance of the network. This requires not only a sufficient and reliable stream of resources but also systems to prioritize expenditures and mechanisms for the effective implementation of maintenance. Experience suggests that sustainability is more likely when there is a good partnership between the community beneficiaries and local public works department. The communities are the "owners" and have the "desire" for good roads, they can often provide labor (paid or unpaid), sometimes funding but also the eyes on the ground to identify problems when they arise. The public works department provides the technical expertise and equipment when this is required. Table 9.3 provides a summary of implementation mechanisms used around the world, all have their place.

Successful approaches at the local level for the maintenance of rural roads have been put in place in countries as varied as Peru, Chile, Nicaragua, Vietnam, and Nepal. These successful approaches have often relied on use of local labor and local entrepreneurship to sustain year-round access and longer useful life for the rehabilitated infrastructure. These decentralized mechanisms consist usually in the formation of small enterprises of local labor (called microenterprises in many countries) that are contracted (initially on a sole source basis but later can

Table 9.3 Summary of implementation mechanisms for maintenance

Mechanism for maintenance	*Main characteristics*	*Advantages*	*Disadvantages*	*Countries where system is used*
Length-man system	A local person is paid to undertake routine maintenance of a set length of road	Simple to organize, uses local labor and minimal equipment requirements	Difficult to maintain consistent standards. There is a limit to the work an individual can do.	Used globally on lower volume roads
Community—voluntary labor	Some countries have traditions where communities provide time and/or money for the maintenance of common infrastructure assets	Community ownership, less influenced by external financial/political issues	Difficult to enforce and maintain consistent standards	Some countries in East Asia such as China and Vietnam, some Scandinavian countries such as Sweden and Finland
Micro-enterprises	Group of local people forming a company to undertake routine maintenance activities	Increases professionalism of activity, groups tend to work more efficiently than individuals	Some countries have contractual problems in appointing on a sole source basis	Many Latin American countries but variations have also been used in China and Eastern Europe
Force account	Unit with staff paid by the local authority to undertake maintenance activities	Can take longer term ownership of an asset, no procurement necessary, and can be more responsive in emergency	Can suffer from public sector inefficiencies with large percentage of costs going to overheads	All countries use some form of force account
Private contract—short or long term	Through procurement a private contractor is appointed to undertake various maintenance functions either as a one off activity or over a set period	Benefit from private sector efficiencies, reduce need for equipment/staff in public agencies, good for larger maintenance activities	Tend to have short term horizon, slower to appoint private contractors	Most countries are now moving to some form of private sector contracting
Area wide contracts	As above a private contractor is appointed to maintain a number of geographically close road segments as part of an area wide contract. These contracts will tend to be for longer time periods and include performance criteria.	Outsources road agency functions to benefit from private sector efficiencies	Require strong contract management. Over time public monopoly can be replaced by private monopoly.	Increasingly common in high income and middle income countries

Table 9.4 List of countries with microenterprises (include activities in national and rural roads)

Country	*Name*	*Start*	*#ME*	*km*	*Surface*
Bolivia	Adminisradora Boliviana de Carreteras—ABC	2003	302	8,228	Paved
Colombia	Instituto Nacional de Vías—INVIAS	1984	318	14,157	Paved
Ecuador	Unidad de Caminos Vecinales—UCV	2001	36	420	Unpaved
	Ministerio de Obras Públicas—MOP	2003	84	2,259	Paved
	Municipalidad de Azuay	1998	20		Unpaved
Guatemala	Unidad Ejecutora de Conservación Vial—COVIAL	1997	130	4,200	Paved
Honduras	Fondo Vial	2000	70	2,762	Paved
Nicaragua	Programa de Mantenimiento Rutinario por Microempresas	1997	37	2,140	Paved
	Programa de Apoyo al Sector de Transporte	1999			Unpaved
Paraguay	Programa Nacional de Caminos Rurales—PNCR	2000			Unpaved
Peru	PROVIAS Rural	1996	600	14,251	Unpaved
	PROVIAS Nacional	2003	127	7,256	Paved
Uruguay	Dirección Nacional de Vialidad—DNV	1996	10	1,613	Paved

Source: Cartier van Dissel (2008).

be subject to competition) for a period of time (normally a year, renewable as pertinent) and paid on the basis of performance standards. These microenterprises cover a length of road that varies from 10 to 30 kilometers depending on topographic and weather conditions. The contract often includes resources for the acquisition of simple tools and their reposition when they have reached their useful life. In a few cases, the contract also includes acquisition of mechanized equipment. The microenterprise approach has been generally successful because it establishes a virtuous circle by means of the incentives built into the contract and by the fact that the members of the microenterprises are also members of the communities served by the rural roads, communities that rely on the availability of the access to achieve its development plans. Microenterprises have increasingly included women, both as administrators or as labor. Their participation has been highlighted as an opportunity for women to earn income and assert themselves as full members of the communities they live in.

The planning of maintenance is normally a local responsibility with road entities at the local level taking charge and held accountable for the procurement and supervision of the maintenance contracts and the planning of maintenance activities (that become part of the contracts). In the initial stages of rural roads development, the national government plays a critical role of building up capacities at the local level. This has been the case in Peru where over the course of about ten years the national entity was initially responsible for the upkeep of rural roads and gradually transferred that responsibility to local road entities (the so-called Provincial Road Institute or IVP for its Spanish acronym) with currently 193 local entities (one per almost every province of Peru) being responsible for the maintenance of about 17,000 km of maintainable rural roads.

Transport services

In some countries the building of rural roads will provide sufficient incentives for the private sector to provide transport services. In other countries, particularly where there is a low density of demand, the market may not respond and communities are as isolated as before they had a new road. Transport services (passenger buses or trucking) on the rural roads are ultimately the means by which the majority of people and cargo are transported to their destinations. In rural areas, the number of individual private modes of transport is very limited and very often non-motorized modes of transport are used for shorter distances. While those transport services are self-financing, the regulatory framework (and the oversight of its application) can play an important role to ensure that the benefits from improved roads are transferred to the end users in the form of greater availability of transport services and lower passenger and freight tariffs. The regulatory framework includes legislation or procedures that seek to encourage a competitive environment while requiring safe driving and operating practices. The definition of the regulatory framework corresponds to the national level, while the oversight of its application usually relies on local authorities (or local entities to whom a national delegation has been established).

Ex-post evaluation

The project cycle closes with the evaluation of the impacts of rural roads over a period of a few years after the upgrade of the infrastructure. The results of these evaluations represent a critical input to inform the next round of investments.

These evaluations however present important methodological challenges, given that proper scientific evaluation requires counterfactual cases that help identify the net impact of a with-project situation compared to a similar case of a without-project situation—that is, the changes in the values of various economic and social indicators in a rural community subject to the upgrade of its rural roads compared to another area with overall similar social and economic conditions but not subject to improvements in its rural network. Since there may be other intervening factors, the search for a comparable situation can pose important challenges. Alternatively, though not as precise but more practical to identify trends, the changes in the conditions of the rural area can be compared to average changes for rural areas as a whole in the country to identify whether or not the interventions have yielded changes significantly different from the average values for the whole set of rural areas. Improvements in geographic information systems and in data collection (through such instruments as living standards surveys or poverty assessments) can help in facilitating the ex-post evaluations. National entities have a critical role to play in advancing them.

In sum, the project cycle encompasses a set of analyses with an objective at taking into account the best use of the limited resources to achieve the goal of enhancing rural access and with it underpinning improvements to rural economies and livelihood conditions. While most of the activities should be undertaken by entities at the local level, national entities have a critical role to play in building up local capacities in planning, priority settings, technical design, and the dissemination of knowledge and experiences in the application of alternative options.

Conclusions

To summarize the discussion above there are a number of dimensions that should be considered when designing a rural roads program or developing policy in support of rural roads development:

Rural roads and development: There is a significant body of research which demonstrates the positive impact of rural roads development in reducing poverty, improving access to essential social services, and providing access for rural communities to participate is the wider economy. However, there are significant challenges in successfully implementing rural roads programs where networks are often large, lightly trafficked, and in remote areas. Often local level capacity is inadequate both in terms of its financial and human resources which poses challenges for the long term management and maintenance of the network. Any interventions in the rural roads sector have to give sufficient consideration to the long term management of the network.

Institutional responsibilities: It is important that there is clarity on who will plan, design, manage, finance, and maintain the networks even if responsibilities shift through the project cycle. A major issue in many countries is that there is insufficient clarity over who owns the network and by extension who has subsequent responsibility for maintenance and management. This is particularly a problem where roads are built under a national program without sufficient consultation with local communities and thought over subsequent management responsibilities. If any of these functions will be undertaken by local government a capacity assessment should be undertaken to ensure that they have the necessary human and financial resources to undertake the work. In all cases the ultimate beneficiaries need to be consulted and where possible involved in each step of the project cycle.

Financing: In many countries the financial resources are not available at the local level for both capital and maintenance works. Very often there is some form of national level financing at least for capital works that also helps to signal priorities to local levels. However, alignment is required so that national transfers or grants, and their equity or equalization objectives, create the right incentives for adequate planning (including environmental planning), engineering designs, and maintenance practices. Where possible some form of local level contribution is required to ensure the necessary ownership and incentive structure for subsequent maintenance. It is common that roads are handed on to the local authority following construction without a sufficient funding mechanism for their long term maintenance. This can be a particular problem where funds come from central government as a block grant and maintenance activities usually take second place to new construction activities.

The project cycle: The project cycle includes planning and priority setting, project design and implementation, the management and maintenance of the assets created, consideration for the supply of transport services, and the subsequent evaluation of outcomes. All are essential for the provision of long term sustainable access and mobility for rural communities. Experience suggests that one of the greatest challenges is in the long term maintenance of assets as insufficient attention has been given to this part of the project cycle. Successful approaches to maintenance have tended to include a strong partnership between the community and public works departments where both have been involved throughout the project cycle. The community monitors road condition and ensures routine maintenance is undertaken and the public works department provides technical support and resources for heavier maintenance activities.

Notes

1 This chapter focuses on road infrastructure and not on urban streets of local towns or secondary cities where the responsibilities tend to be well defined and entirely in the hands of the local municipalities/governments.

2 More recently the Rural Transport Program was expanded to all the 193 provinces of the country and maintenance grants are provided against confirmation of compliance with a framework that includes development, technical, administrative, and financial management criteria.

References

Bell, C. and S. van Dillen (2011), "How Does India's Rural Roads Programme Affect the Grassroots? Findings from a Survey in Upland Orissa." University of Heidelberg.

Escobal, Javier and Máximo Torero (2005), "Measuring the Impact of Asset Complementarities: The Case of Rural Perú." *Cuadernos de economía*, 42(125): 137–164.

Fan, S., J. Brzeska, and G. Shields (2007), "Investment Priorities for Economic Growth and Poverty Reduction, 2020 Focus Brief on the World's Poor and Hungry People." International Food Policy Research Institute, Washington, DC.

Gannon C. and Z. Liu (1997), "Poverty and Transport." TWU-30, World Bank, Washington, DC.

Howe, J. and P. Richards (1984), *Rural Roads and Poverty Alleviation.* Intermediate Technology Publications Ltd, London.

International Labor Office (2005), *Situation Analysis of Rural Road Maintenance in Madhya Pradesh. Volume 1: Strategy Elements and Options for Reforms.* ILO, Geneva.

Keller, Gordon and James Shrar (2003), *Low Volume Roads Engineering—Best Management Practices Field Guide*, USAID in cooperation with US Forest Service and Conservation Management Institute of Virginia Polytechnic Institute and State University.

Mu, R. and D. van de Walle (2007), "Rural Roads and Poor Area Development in Vietnam." World Bank Policy Research Working Paper 4340.

Muzira, Stephen and Damaris Hernandez de Diaz (2013) "Rethinking Infrastructure Delivery: Case Study of a Green Inclusive and Cost Effective Road Program in Nicaragua." Transport Sector Paper, World Bank, Washington, DC.

Starkey, Paul, Simon Ellis, John Hine, and Anna Ternell (2002), "Improving Rural Mobility: Options for Developing Motorised and Non-Motorised Transport in Rural Areas." World Bank Technical Paper No. 525.

World Bank (2007), http://siteresources.worldbank.org/EXTTRANSPORT/Resources/337115-1214499672078/5154009-1214508441379/5155078-1214576942487/map.html.

Part IV

Investing into the invisible

Management and coordination of decentralized public investment

10 The challenge of operating and maintaining infrastructure

William F. Fox and Matthew Murray

Introduction

Infrastructure is a key ingredient both to economic growth and quality of life. Infrastructure is "an umbrella term for many activities referred to as social overhead capital," and includes public utilities, such as power, piped water supply and sanitation and sewerage, public works, such as roads and dams, and other transport sectors, such as railways, urban transport, and airports (World Bank, 1994, p. 2). This chapter focuses on an essential component of an effective infrastructure network—the ability to operate and maintain the infrastructure properly. The tendency in much of the earlier infrastructure literature was to focus on infrastructure as capital investments and thus the core of the capital project cycle rather than to think of a series of infrastructure *services* that are produced using a set of inputs that includes physical capital.[1] In the production function context, operations and maintenance are another group of inputs that are essential to reaping the value of the services. Viewing operations and maintenance expenditures in this fashion highlights their role in service provision but also heightens the importance of political economy considerations and service assignment responsibilities in financing effective services.

The remainder of the chapter is divided into six sections. The next section places operations and maintenance in the context of infrastructure service delivery. The second section examines the impact of operations and maintenance on production and welfare. The third section describes organizational options for operations and maintenance including decentralization and privatization. The following section evaluates decision making and efficiency of operations and maintenance in a social efficiency and political economy context. The fifth section identifies some options for improved operations and maintenance policy. The chapter finishes with a conclusion.

Understanding the role of operations and maintenance in infrastructure services

The contribution of infrastructure to production and economic growth has often been analyzed as if it is a series of capital investments[2] though more importantly users have a derived demand for the services that are produced using a combination of capital, labor, and other inputs. The tendency to emphasize capital in infrastructure research likely stems from the easier capacity to quantify public sector capital expenditures combined with their sheer size as opposed to the difficulties of measuring some service flows and their quality. Also, the focus on capital may be because infrastructure services are often delivered as congestible public goods that operate as capital-intensive networks (Hulten, 1996).

The non-capital inputs in the production of infrastructure services are what we refer to as operations and maintenance. These inputs include labor, replacement parts and materials (potentially including some replacement capital), electricity (which is itself an infrastructure service), and many other infrastructure-specific factors. Straub (2008) is a recent example recognizing that infrastructure services are produced through a production process where the services cannot be defined simply by the public capital. Straub notes that empirical infrastructure research has increasingly moved from an emphasis on the capital stock to the use of physical indictors as the proxy for infrastructure. Nonetheless, these proxies are often difficult to use because the data are frequently not systematically available across time and countries, the indicators are often poor proxies for the services (e.g., miles of paved road), and the indicators fail to account for quality of infrastructure services.

Efficient delivery of infrastructure services relies on understanding that services are being produced using multiple inputs with the goal of optimally meeting users' demands. Operations and maintenance inputs and physical infrastructure investments work together both as substitutes and complements through the service production function. They are complements because greater capital investments generally require greater operations and maintenance. But, they are substitutes because altering the type of investment, such as building more expensive cement rather than asphalt roads, can sometimes reduce the necessary maintenance—that is, they are not simply components of a fixed proportions production function. Also, better maintenance can reduce future capital investments.

Good operations and maintenance practices when combined with appropriate capital investments affect the value of infrastructure services through several avenues. First, operations and maintenance is essential to allowing use of many types of infrastructure services—users obtain no benefits from a water system or electric network that does not operate. Thus, infrastructure investments that are otherwise adequate may be made inaccessible simply because of poor operations and maintenance. As a result, good operations and maintenance makes infrastructure capital investments more productive and expands the value of infrastructure investments. The World Bank *World Development Report* (1994) concluded that only 60 percent of electric generating capacity in developing countries is available, versus a best practice of 80 percent. The relationships are similar for improved water, where 70 percent of capacity is used in developing countries versus best practice of 85 percent. Operations and maintenance that expands the share of productive capacity can entail up-front costs but may reduce the need for additional investments as they make previous investments more productive. Second, the life cycle costs of infrastructure investments can often be lowered through good maintenance. Roads, for example, last much longer, and the total costs of providing roads can be lower, if proper maintenance occurs.

Finally, efficiently operating infrastructure lowers the private costs for users and makes it easier to access the infrastructure. This happens either because users may develop or identify alternative capacity to replace poorly functioning infrastructure services or because use of the infrastructure directly becomes more costly to users. For example, Clarke (2013) concludes that users regard reliability as the key attribute of some infrastructure, such as power, and they often must provide costly backup to ensure reliability. Similarly, people often must seek out alternative water supply because piped water is insufficient or unreliable even though the system appears to have sufficient capacity. Also, poorly maintained roads can damage vehicles and raise the fuel costs associated with travel. Nonetheless, some users may prefer bearing the private sector costs, even if this means higher society costs, if significant fees or charges would raise their share of public costs.

Several authors have concluded that the returns to maintenance are much higher than the returns to new infrastructure. For example, the *World Development Report* (World Bank, 1994) concluded that the rate of return to maintenance is often twice the return to new infrastructure investments. Hulten finds a significant effect of infrastructure on per capita country GDP, using measures such as faults per 100 telephone calls, electricity generation losses, and percent of paved roads in good condition, and observes the marginal benefits of better operations and maintenance are seven times greater than making additional infrastructure capital investments. Indeed, he concludes that new infrastructure investments can have a perverse effect on national growth if they shift resources away from operations and maintenance of the existing capital stock. The relative magnitude of returns to operations and maintenance is not surprising given Clarke's finding that users are often more concerned with the quality than with the quantity of infrastructure—and quality of services is often determined by the extent of operations and maintenance. Clarke (2013) found that firm managers are much more concerned about service quality and reliability than access to electricity.

Conceptualizing operations and maintenance

The conceptual literature on operations and maintenance, like the empirical literature, is relatively small but analyzes the impact of operations and maintenance on production, and welfare more broadly, through three avenues. This section describes the three channels and then briefly reviews how the literature has examined each. Again, these channels may be better thought of as how infrastructure services affect welfare, where operations and maintenance are inputs in the production of the services. First, operations and maintenance are inputs in the production of infrastructure services, such as electricity and water. Sufficient capital investments and appropriate operations and maintenance can ensure that services are of high quality and delivered to where users want them. The quality of services delivered across the network to the desired location will not consistently occur without good operations and maintenance, though earlier empirical literature has often effectively presumed that operations and maintenance will take place if capital investments are made.

The next two channels indicate that inadequate maintenance increases the operating and capital costs for both public and private investments and many ongoing forms of economic activity. Second, operations and maintenance increase the life of *public* capital, as evidenced by good maintenance expanding the life of roads. This is the sense in which public capital investments and operations and maintenance are substitutes.

Third, operations and maintenance expand the durability of private capital, as seen in good road maintenance enhancing the life of vehicles and consistent electric flow extending the life and usefulness of computers.[3] Effectively, this means that good infrastructure services can extend the life of *private* capital investment. Note that this channel applies both to infrastructure that users go to for the benefits, such as roads, and infrastructure that is delivered to the user, such as electricity and water.

The relationship between infrastructure and private capital is broader than is seen in some of the conceptual literature since not only is the life of private capital extended, but the amount of private investment can actually be lowered by good infrastructure services. Poor quality operations and maintenance and/or infrastructure may require private firms to self-produce infrastructure services, thereby requiring additional private investment and potentially expanding private operating costs. Reinikka and Svensson (2002) discuss how some firms must make private capital investments in electric generators as a backup to unreliable service capacity. The problem often is not that physical capacity of public infrastructure is inadequate, but that the quality of services flowing from the capital stock is too low or unreliable. The solution may be better operations and maintenance of the infrastructure, not more capital investments, but the best use of resources depends on the specific situation. Some have argued that good infrastructure services allow firms to shift investment to expanding productive capacity rather than providing backup for infrastructure, which simply means self-produced infrastructure services and expansion of productive capacity are often substitutes (see Agenor and Moreno-Dodson, 2006, for example). The scarcity of investment capital in developing countries should normally make alternative uses substitutes. Thus, better infrastructure services can increase overall production in the economy if the returns to productive capacity exceed those to self-production of infrastructure services. Still, as we note below, there may be instances where it is socially efficient to allow some self-production.

Straub (2008) identifies a series of other channels through which infrastructure affects production and welfare including impacts on labor productivity, human development, and ability for the private sector to reap economies of scale and scope. Good operations and maintenance can influence welfare through these other avenues as well, but these have not been addressed in detail in the literature despite the fact that spillover benefits are known to exist. Considering these issues will allow a more comprehensive assessment of the returns to both capital investments and operations and maintenance.

Relatively little rigorous empirical work has taken place on operations and maintenance, and specifically on the trade-off between more infrastructure capital investment and more operations and maintenance (or more broadly between operations and maintenance of infrastructure and other public services). Data are the major challenge in studying operations and maintenance, at least in part because much of the maintenance occurs outside of traditional markets, and inside individual enterprises that do not report on specific operations and maintenance activities (see McGrattan and Schmitz, 1999). Part of this is a reflection of budgeting and accounting practices that may show initial capital investments in a capital account and subsequent maintenance and operations embedded in a current expenditure account. Thus, recent work on operations and maintenance generally remains conceptual rather than econometric.

Theoretical research

Several authors including Rioja (2003), Kalaitzidakis and Kaluvitis (2004), and Agenor (2009) have theoretically modeled operations and maintenance in the macro economy of developing countries. This section briefly summarizes these papers. Among the conclusions are that higher donor finance for public capital reduces the optimal maintenance, optimal expenditures on infrastructure occur where the last dollar spent on maintenance yields the same value to the public capital stock as the last dollar of investment, and optimal maintenance is greater than seen in traditional growth models because maintenance of public capital reduces depreciation of private capital. For example, Rioja identifies the optimal level of maintenance, defined as to maximize social welfare. He models output as a function of public and private capital and labor. Government imposes an output tax and uses the funds to finance operations and maintenance of public capital. Maintenance is presumed to lower the depreciation of public capital (thus maintenance and private capital are substitutes in production of infrastructure services). Donors are assumed to fully finance public capital, though the World Bank (1994) notes that donor spending accounts for a little less than one-half of infrastructure investment. He finds that optimal maintenance depends on the amount of public capital, private capital, and donor funding and concludes that the higher donor funding relative to public capital, the lower the optimal level of maintenance. In other words, countries will lessen domestic resources to maintain existing infrastructure as they receive more free public capital from outside.

Kalaitzidakis and Kaluvitis (2004) extend Rioja's model by creating an environment where the public sector finances both maintenance and new public capital. Government reduces the marginal product of private capital through taxation and raises it through infrastructure. The durability of public capital depends positively on the extent of maintenance and negatively on production in the economy. Optimal government occurs where the marginal cost of government (infrastructure) exactly equals the marginal benefits. The steady state growth rate of the economy is shown to increase with maintenance, if maintenance is relatively low, and fall with maintenance if maintenance is relatively high, evidencing the benefits of choosing the optimal level of maintenance. An inverse relationship between maintenance and new public capital investment is evidenced, since the net increase in public capital for any particular expenditure rises with more maintenance. Kalaitzidakis and Kaluvitis demonstrate that optimal public investment occurs when the last dollar spent on maintenance has the same contribution to the public capital stock as the last dollar of public investment, which is consistent with infrastructure services (as measured by capital) being maximized for any level of expenditures. An important conclusion is that further maintenance can be productive in cases where additional public capital would not be. Indeed, simulations by Rioja (2003) evidence significant welfare gains from shifting resources from new projects to maintenance of existing projects.

The amount of investment and maintenance in the Kalaitzidakis and Kaluvitis model depends on the current tax rate. The optimal tax rate in the standard endogenous growth model equals the elasticity of public capital in the production function, but in this model the optimal tax rate is higher because of the positive effects of maintenance on the amount of public capital. The analysis assumes that these taxes can be levied and collected, which may be difficult in practice.

Agenor (2009) extends the basic framework by bringing in the effects of maintenance on the durability of private capital. He concludes that the growth maximizing share of public expenditures on maintenance rises with the marginal effect that maintenance has on the depreciation of private capital. The chapter focuses on how maintenance affects depreciation of private capital, but does not address how poor quality infrastructure can require additional private investment for self-production. Taken together, these papers argue for greater public investment (and therefore a higher tax rate) than in the standard growth model because of the impact of maintenance on the amount of public and private capital.

Organizing operations and maintenance

Designing and executing appropriate operations and maintenance should be a key consideration at every step of the project cycle. Indeed, decisions on public capital investments and operations and maintenance should be made simultaneously in the planning phase to achieve the best output for given life cycle costs. Such decisions should recognize the ability and willingness of different levels of government to generate resources for operations and maintenance and the capacity to execute operations and maintenance, and should not be made based on engineering designs and expectations alone. Similarly, consideration of operations and maintenance should carry through the entire project cycle and be part of the ex-post evaluation.

Several organizational structures can be selected for undertaking operations and maintenance and the choice between them should depend on the ability to motivate efficient and optimal service provision and to properly price services.

The options include private, public, and community-based operations and maintenance. Community-based operations and maintenance is normally linked to small systems where limited expertise is necessary (though appropriate expertise may be available in the private sector or through central ministry staff) and where the user-base is well defined. Community-based systems by their very nature are decentralized, though they can be operated in either the public, private, or not-for-profit sectors. The investments in infrastructure capital and operations and maintenance can be separated from the investments constructed or financed by central government entities (such as the Local Government Engineering Division in Bangladesh) or donors while the community-based organization is responsible for operations and maintenance. Ideally, community-provided services should be priced to fund operations and maintenance activities (and where possible infrastructure investments) and ration use of the service.

Private operations and maintenance can be linked with either public or private infrastructure ownership. Private sector operations and maintenance can help to introduce competition into infrastructure delivery, though public regulation may be necessary and can limit the ability to mimic the private market especially in the face of political influences on service contracting. Also, first mover advantages can be afforded to those private firms that get the initial contract to deliver infrastructure services and could yield some rents associated with specific knowledge learned from operating the network. Public sector operations and maintenance could be consistent with either public or private (through a leaseback) ownership of the capital. As discussed more below, public sector activities could be sited at the national, regional, or local level depending on the type of infrastructure and the ability to coordinate decisions across governments.

Two interconnected issues arise: Is public or private sector operations and maintenance preferred and is it desirable to decentralize service delivery if public sector production is selected? The decision whether to decentralize operations and maintenance is related to but not precisely the same as the choice of whether to privatize since infrastructure functions can be privatized regardless of whether the responsibilities have been decentralized.

Decentralization of government, which is taking place around the world, may improve infrastructure service delivery. Incentives for efficiently operating and maintaining infrastructure would appear to be higher if the responsibilities are more localized because the decisions will be closer to those who benefit more from service quality, and for many services the geographic spillovers will be modest. This is consistent with the subsidiary rule to which many public sector economists subscribe. At the same time there must be sufficient resources and/or willingness to pay to support operations and maintenance, and a political climate that can support effective service delivery.

Decisions of whether to decentralize are not all or nothing choices. Infrastructure services, like other public services, can be unbundled into a series of activities that can be delivered by different levels of government. For example, the national government may have responsibility for broad control over the national watershed and water supply and quality standards in the country. The national government may also set standards on water quality delivered to users. The regional government may regulate and oversee actual water service delivery. Finally, the operation of water systems may be more localized. Also, national roads may be planned by the Ministry of Transportation and provided by national or cooperating regional authorities. Local roads can be planned and provided by city authorities. Unbundling can permit infrastructure activities with interregional spillovers to remain at the regional or national level while other components can be decentralized to where market and political incentives for good operations and maintenance are greater and lead to less cost shifting. Such unbundling has worked well with secondary and tertiary roads in Peru, and can be helpful in other cases as well. But problems of the tragedy of the commons can remain and require good leadership at the local level to ensure good maintenance occurs whether responsibilities fall on the public or private sector.

At least four factors should enter the decision of whether to decentralize operations and maintenance if public sector delivery is selected, including:[4]

- the desire for equalization and tolerance for cross-subsidies;
- variation in preferences for services;
- the potential for interregional spillovers;
- the potential for economies of scale.

The judgment on whether to decentralize will likely differ by infrastructure service since these four factors may point in different directions. First, decentralization is a better option if interregional cross-subsidies in the country are undesirable, though grants can achieve cross-subsidies and financial equalization even in a decentralized structure. Cross-subsidies are not an important concern if user fees finance the infrastructure, but cross-subsidies could be more likely and important for roads, dams, and other infrastructure where exclusion is more difficult and for public health services where there may be geographic externalities.

Second, variation in service demands makes decentralized service delivery a better option. Decentralization is a strong option in countries with differing regional or localized infrastructure demands because of topological diversity or varying consumer demands. Third, significant interregional spillover of public service benefits makes decentralized decision making less efficient as non-resident demands are likely to be ignored in service delivery decisions and full cost recovery may not be possible. This suggests that services such as large dams and national roads should be controlled at the national or regional level.[5] But, interregional spillovers will be less important for many infrastructure services including electricity, water, and local roads. These are broad conclusions whereas in practice the answer will depend on how localized operations and maintenance interacts with the infrastructure itself.

Finally, the potential for economies of scale or size in infrastructure service delivery/operations and maintenance is a key issue. Decentralized delivery is less effective as economies from larger size expand. Technological changes continue to allow more localized service delivery but, some services such as electricity probably cannot be decentralized to the extent of others. Water provides an example, where research (see Fox and Gurley, 2006) suggests there are economies of size to providing services across wider geographic areas. However, the extent of economies for any place depends on population density and other factors because water must be gathered and cleaned, which may benefit from economies, but the purified water must be distributed via pipes, which may not benefit from economies depending on the location and density of users. Analysis in countries around the world has tended to focus on determining whether there are benefits to consolidation of infrastructure services, and the research suggests that economies will often not result from merging areas together. This is suggestive that any diseconomies from decentralizing will not be large if responsibilities are properly unbundled, but important transition costs may result from decentralization. Reorganization of supervisory responsibilities and staff is an example of transition costs that might arise from decentralization (or centralization) of services.

Diseconomies of delivering water (or electricity) through decentralized providers may be linked mostly to investments in collecting and cleaning water and may have little to do with operations and maintenance of the distribution systems. So, at least large local governments could purchase electricity or purified water from regional companies and distribute the services to constituents. Economies may exist for technical operations and maintenance staff, such as for engineering and information systems, but these can potentially be offset if technical skills can be obtained from regional offices of the appropriate ministry or purchased through the private sector.

Unbundling of services offers the potential for placing components of service delivery at the appropriate level and offers the opportunity to focus on assignment of services rather than the engineering project cycle. But, assigning components of infrastructure to different levels of government raises the potential for conflicts in decisions or policies because the incentives of national and local decision makers will often not align. For example, the national government may expand water and sewer systems in places that have low tastes for the services, or that feel they are unable to adequately operate and maintain the facilities. Separation of the decision makers on capital investments and operations and maintenance increases the likelihood of significant deviation of operations and maintenance from the efficient level from an engineering perspective because local governments (and private sector entities) may not have the technical or engineering resources or may not have the user demand and willingness to pay to support the required operations and maintenance. Thus, decentralization requires coordination and cooperation across levels of government.

Simply, centralized decisions on capital investments may not allow for variation in local preferences. Preference variation across a country likely will surface if local governments have control over operations and maintenance, and the operations and maintenance may be less related to engineering outcomes and more to local service taxes. Thus, the advantages of assigning different services to different levels of government must be balanced with the costs of inconsistencies in the decisions made by different levels of government. Thus, the desirability of decentralizing operations and maintenance depends heavily on the capacity of different levels of government to work together and coordinate decisions on every aspect of the planning and execution process and this could vary across regions and countries. This suggests that good operations and maintenance depends on changing processes throughout the project cycle, including the process through which decisions are made on what projects and where they are to be if operations and maintenance are to ensure the best life cycle cost use of resources. Below, we investigate the political economy of these issues in more detail.

Social efficiency and political economy considerations

Operations and maintenance levels are often deemed insufficient for a variety of reasons including (i) the infrequency of actual infrastructure breakdowns which may lead to the view that maintenance can be postponed, (ii) much of the repair is in areas not visible to politicians and service consumers and (iii) decision making for capital investments and operations and maintenance is often separated (Pagano, 2011). As discussed here, it may not be socially efficient (given tastes and revenue capacity) to spend more on operations and maintenance. Even in cases where social efficiency could in principle be supported, there may be political economy factors that drive a wedge between actual policy decisions and socially efficient outcomes.

Consider Straub (2008) who argues that maintenance of infrastructure networks is probably better analyzed with economic-engineering models than with traditional econometric analysis. He notes that surveys of actual practice could be undertaken to determine the appropriate amounts of maintenance that should take place over time as new investments are made. The survey approach provides an engineering answer to appropriate operations and maintenance, but the political economy environment likely determines the amounts that are actually undertaken. Moreover, there may be insufficient resources and revenue capacity to support engineering solutions. The engineering perspective does not take into account the opportunity cost of resource use in either the public or private sectors. If the capacity for revenue mobilization is low, there will be high private opportunity costs associated with funding infrastructure operations and considerable competition for resource use within the public sector where other services are funded at low levels.

Here we consider the social planner and political economy views that place the operations and maintenance question in a broader social context. Each view has consequences for how one might evaluate the efficiency of operations and maintenance expenditures and points to different opportunities and bottlenecks for improving expenditure patterns and infrastructure service flow performance. The points raised below are not unique to developing countries—they could conceivably apply to any country. But the developing country context is arguably more challenging for a number of reasons, including extraordinarily depressed revenue capacity and weak institutional and governance structures.

Social efficiency

The social planner perspective recognizes the multiple forms and heterogeneity of infrastructure capital and thus the uses to which operations and maintenance expenditures might be applied. The uses include capital that provides private service flows (in principle subject to exclusion and congestion), production processes characterized by economies of scale, as well as pure and impure public goods. Pure public goods raise the specter of the free rider problem while the introduction of impure public goods increases attention to the costs and practicality of exclusion and determination of the optimal number of users. These are not trivial considerations anywhere but they may be especially important in developing countries. Recognizing these classic problems would likely change optimality conditions and highlight differences across types of infrastructure and levels of operations and maintenance expenditure. The social planner must also balance the use of resources in support of infrastructure against their potential alternative uses in individual consumption and in public service supply (e.g., public safety) funded by taxes and fees and at the expense of private consumption. In other words, infrastructure choices cannot be made in a vacuum that ignores other uses of resources.

A second-best perspective recognizes the political and technical/cost constraints associated with attempts to impose exclusion on access to infrastructure service flows, including services like electricity even if they are provided by private sector entities. The inability to exclude can lead to overuse and more rapid depreciation of the capital stock as a tragedy of the commons unfolds, necessitating ever-higher operations and maintenance expenditures to maintain system integrity. Rationing may arise as a consequence of use and overuse, through congestion, queuing and interrupted service flows. Even if exclusion is feasible from a cost perspective, there may be political constraints that limit the capacity for revenue mobilization from users whether services are privately or publicly provided. For example, there may be political pressures or threats of political instability if the population is denied access to services and it may prove impossible to charge marginal cost; even if charges are in place there may be difficulties with the collection of user fees and arrears. The end result may be a stressed infrastructure network with little revenue to support operations and maintenance. These problems are pervasive in developing countries and often render simple, classical solutions to the operations and maintenance problem unworkable. What in practice may appear to be an inefficient allocation of resources from an engineering perspective may instead simply reflect the practical constraints within the developing world.

A question arises whether resources should be devoted to operating and maintaining poorly selected infrastructure investments. Should roads that were not built in the optimal location be well maintained, should investments that differ from local tastes still be operated and maintained, and so forth? One would likely observe operations and maintenance spending that might be deemed "too low" in such situations. The response depends on the alternative uses of the funds, how poor the investments are, and so forth. The investments should generally be seen as sunk costs (at least for their expected life) so the issue is whether the marginal benefits of operating and maintaining the capital offer a good return to the resources necessary. Capital costs would only enter the decision when replacement issues arise.

There are important lessons here. First, operations and maintenance expenditures cannot be considered in isolation, but must be evaluated against alternative uses of resources in both the private and public sectors. While it is likely that too little is spent on infrastructure maintenance, there are also likely cases where low levels of observed spending are consistent with the efficient use of resources especially in places with very low capacity for revenue mobilization where opportunity cost for funds in the public sector may be high. The other side of the problem may simply be too much capital demanding too much operations and maintenance spending, reflecting the generosity but also paternalism of outside donors. Second, because of the challenges associated with exclusion—whether related to technological or political considerations—operations and maintenance expenditures often must be evaluated in a second-best setting where standard engineering rules for best-practice maintenance may not be applicable.

It is also important to recognize that the demand for infrastructure services is derived from their use in market and home production processes where they can serve as either substitutes or complements to other inputs. Water and electricity are two examples of services that might be provided by private or public enterprises but also lend themselves to substitution and private provision. Observing private substitution is a necessary but not sufficient condition that social inefficiency exists. Poor quality electricity service, characterized by voltage irregularities and service interruptions, may induce some firms to self-supply electricity and thus directly incur operations and maintenance expenditures for maintenance of a private capital stock. This will be costly to the firm and will in turn hamper competitiveness, particularly for firms engaged in the production of tradable goods and commodities. Greater operations and maintenance expenditures could reduce these costs, but these expenditures should be weighed against the private costs that would otherwise arise from individual action.

Households may also substitute and self-supply inputs to home production like water and electricity through the use of small-scale storage facilities and generators or may simply ration supplied use depending on service availability. Home production in developing countries will generally rely on time and labor intensive processes because of the low opportunity cost of labor relative to the cost of market-purchased inputs to production; consumption will also tend to be time rather than goods intensive. The nature of household production does not always necessitate the same high quality and continuous service flows that may be required of firms producing for market. For example, a firm may require continuity of electricity service throughout the day to maintain production while households may be able to change the timing of home production that relies on electricity to accommodate daily service interruptions.

These considerations suggest a mixed approach to service delivery that may yield different quality service flows and different levels of operations and maintenance expenditure for different consumer groups (or lower total operations and maintenance expenditures). For example, it may be best in certain circumstances to maintain high quality electricity service for business and industrial districts while offering poorer quality services to households, particularly when constraints limit the potential for local resource mobilization.

Efficiency in the use of operations and maintenance expenditures must be carefully balanced against opportunities and costs associated with private substitution (and complementary) possibilities. The goal of operations and maintenance expenditures should not be to minimize private sector costs per se, but to balance these cost reductions against the use of resources in supporting infrastructure, ongoing public services, and private consumption. In other words, there are many margins to balance in practice.

Electricity and transportation services are examples of infrastructure outputs that can be complements to market and home production. Private costs will generally be lower when the quality of infrastructure services is higher. For example, a high quality road may greatly facilitate the transportation of goods thereby yielding substantial reductions in time costs and vehicle wear and tear. Private agents thus incur lower out-of-pocket and time opportunity costs from operations and maintenance expenditures. This is a margin that should be considered when determining the socially optimal level of operations and maintenance expenditures. The practical importance will depend on the type of infrastructure and the type of user. For example, it may be appropriate to have lower operations and maintenance expenditures if complementary production processes are labor intensive and labor has a low opportunity cost. However, operations and maintenance spending should be higher, all else the same, the greater is the wear and tear on private capital.

Some political economy considerations

It is well understood that a political process can only yield a socially efficient level of output under the most unique circumstances and the same would apply to operations and maintenance expenditures. In practice, political processes in developing countries may be a significant impediment to efficiency. In many developing countries there is no viable public choice process so that decisions reflect the preferences of elites or sub-groups of the population. In countries with some form of democratic process, public sector choices will have some chance of capturing the preferences of those who vote, but the situation is greatly complicated by the fiscal hierarchy of government finance. Regardless of the institutions and processes that yield public sector outcomes, choices will reflect self-interest and the tastes and costs of decision makers. There is no reason to think that these outcomes will align with what is required from a social efficiency perspective.

Political gains, economic impacts, and distributional consequences associated with infrastructure spending can easily interfere with optimal operations and maintenance spending. For example, political leaders may happily accept donor-financed infrastructure projects for the prestige and private economic gains (including private sector contracting) that are associated with facility construction, even if there is little social value placed on services or there is inadequate fiscal capacity to provide warranted operations and maintenance expenditures. So consistent with Rioja (2003), there may in some sense be too much infrastructure, the source of which is well-intentioned but paternalistic donor finance.

In a stylized public choice setting, agents must allocate income across own-consumption and the provision of public services, including infrastructure services, based on private sector prices and the public sector tax/fee structure. This will require equating the marginal benefits and costs of operations and maintenance expenditures, but also a more general equilibrium calculus across all forms of public and private consumption. The structure of tastes, prices, and taxes may not be consistent with engineering notions of efficiency in operations and maintenance expenditures especially if there is too much capital. Efficient input *combinations* are still required but potentially at low operations and maintenance levels that would be socially inefficient. In other words, even if engineering standards are not pursued, operations and maintenance should be undertaken efficiently.

In general, one would expect less support for operations and maintenance expenditures where there is less citizen engagement in the processes that determined the initial capital investments. This outcome might reflect the decision of a benign but non-representative government, a despot, a benevolent but paternalistic leader or an international donor; in a country with a well-functioning democracy, the same outcome may occur if there is heterogeneity in tastes across places and regions. In all of these cases, preferences may compromise application of the optimal level of operations and maintenance expenditures from both an engineering and social planner perspective.

Even if infrastructure choices are made with the full consent of the population, myopia and high discount rates associated with the essential nature of current consumption in developing countries may hamper efforts to mobilize operations and maintenance resources. Of course the same problem arises to varying degrees in developed countries. The benefits of operations and maintenance expenditures may not be obvious especially if existing service flows are of acceptable quality. So it will prove difficult to generate funding streams and allocate revenues, while earmarked fund balances might easily be diverted to competing uses.

Finally, it should be recognized that operations and maintenance expenditures represent an opportunity for rent extraction. Political and personal gain may accrue from the diversion of operations and maintenance expenditures to other uses. Even if operations and maintenance expenditures are incurred in support of infrastructure, there may be waste and inefficiencies through the contracting process and granting of contracts to friends, family, and political supporters. This could lead to the wrong quality and mix of operations and maintenance inputs.

Improving operations and maintenance policy

Decisions regarding infrastructure investments and operations and maintenance expenditures are generally made or influenced by the political process. Hence the first step to ensuring sound decision making is to allow for preference revelation through citizen engagement. Improving local resource mobilization so that preferences can be financed is an important aspect of getting preferences reflected in operations and maintenance and service flows. Once investment decisions are made, accountability in operations and maintenance spending can be promoted by providing information on service reliability and transparency in budgeting processes and resource allocation.

Infrastructure service decisions need to be made with a clear understanding of the life-cycle costs, including initial investments and on-going operations and maintenance, and in the context of overall public and private sector welfare maximization. This can only occur if operations and maintenance are part of the project cycle from the appraisal to the ex-post evaluation stages. Still, practical mechanisms may be appropriate to ensure that annual resources are consistent with longer-term plans. Several options could be considered for enhancing how operations and maintenance are to operate, particularly in the public sector.

Legislating an operations and maintenance fund

Earmarking revenues can to some extent separate operations and maintenance from the vagaries of the annual appropriation process. A number of questions have been raised about the usefulness of earmarking including whether it actually influences decisions at the margin, whether it is good to separate some expenditures from annual appropriation decisions, particularly during times when general revenues are declining, and so forth. But, operations and maintenance decisions should be determined to a significant extent as part of the life-cycle choice for infrastructure services and this may call for protecting or highlighting the expenditures to some extent.

Earmarking user fees can provide an effective funding source if there is sufficient demand and fiscal accountability and helps ensure efficient consumption of infrastructure services. Earmarking is also possible when user fees are not the funding source. For example, the US state of Utah requires a five-year capital plan that includes proposed projects, details about the projects and costs, and approaches to funding operations and maintenance (Pagano, 2011). Further, state law requires that 1.1 percent of the replacement value for existing state buildings be appropriated to a capital maintenance fund before any new capital projects are built. The required fund grows with the replacement cost of capital, which depends both on construction costs and the amount of buildings. Utah restricts the approach to state buildings, but broader application can be envisioned so that the fund covers all fixed assets and in principle operating costs in addition to maintenance. The fixed percentage allocated to the fund is somewhat arbitrary, but an engineering analysis of requirements could be developed and used in project cycle planning.

The creation of the earmarked maintenance fund and articulation of the mechanism for depositing funds is an important signal, even if the fund cannot be enforced effectively through legislation. The requirement/existence of a maintenance fund can signify the importance placed on maintenance by government and demonstrates the intent to focus on good maintenance. It can also promote fiscal accountability if appropriately managed.

Assign components of infrastructure to appropriate delivery units

Decisions should be made on the extent to which each broad infrastructure category should be unbundled and the services should be assigned to the appropriate entity. The decisions involve determining both appropriate service decentralization and the extent of privatization. Such decisions must be nuanced and based on subjective information because precise, quantitative information does not exist for some of the factors in the decisions. These decisions should consider the benefits and costs from allowing for local preferences in service choices, reaping efficiency in delivery of the functions, and experiencing losses from non-aligned decision making across multiple entities. The net effect of these factors must be weighed and balanced.

Pricing infrastructure services

Many infrastructure services, including electricity and water, are excludable private goods (potentially subject to congestion) and the resulting services can be priced. Economic efficiency will be maximized by setting marginal cost prices, even if two-part tariffs are necessary to accommodate the declining part of the average cost curve or to finance the distribution network. Pricing plays a key rationing role to ensure the optimal level of services is produced. User fees also provide a financing mechanism for operations and maintenance so the revenues must be earmarked for service delivery so that consumers link marginal benefits and marginal costs on well-functioning infrastructure.

User fee revenues are not always earmarked or spent for the priced service, particularly if the service is provided publicly, and this can distort the rationing function for infrastructure services and result in poor service levels. Palestinian municipalities, particularly in the West Bank, are reputed to divert electric and water revenues for general fund purposes (though this may not be true in many municipalities). Limitations on alternative general fund revenues may be a key reason because essentially all local revenues operate mostly as transfers. Further, it may be politically less costly to divert user fees and underprovide services than to levy and collect a set of small fees and taxes.

The price needs to be set regularly to ensure that all costs, including capital and operations and maintenance, are properly reflected in the pricing decision. Pagano (2011) notes that the public sector is often unwilling to price services properly because of a disconnect between capital and operations and maintenance budgets, the lack of visibility to users of the capital stock, and a common pool resource problem. He observes that private sector providers are often better able to price services and will also be better at earmarking the revenues for service delivery, both of which create a significant advantage to privatization.

Pricing is complicated for infrastructure where exclusion is difficult, such as roads.[6] Second-best financing mechanisms can often be found even when marginal prices cannot be set, such as fees imposed on all property owners along a road. The fees are lump sum and do not offer rationing benefits since they are unrelated to usage but they provide a revenue source for operations and maintenance of the assets. In many such cases, general revenues and/or transfers may be required/used to finance operations and maintenance. Good operations and maintenance has less implication for linking marginal benefits and marginal costs when general revenues are used since consumers are not confronted with the true marginal costs (except through means such as congestion). But, the broader value of infrastructure services to welfare and production is not compromised.

Operations and maintenance funding is determined through the political process in competition with other service options when general fund revenues are used.[7] Resources to operate and maintain infrastructure will be allocated on an annual basis and would be consistent with user demand if the political system efficiently makes allocation choices. However, the inconsistent incentives in investment and operations and maintenance decisions and low capacity and resource constraints imposed on local governments may result in inappropriate funding of operations and maintenance (and other public services).

Conclusion

Infrastructure services are essential to promoting economic growth and well-being in developing countries. Recent academic work has finally come to recognize what many practitioners already knew: operations and maintenance expenditures are key to meeting the demands of households and businesses and ensuring accessibility and viable service flows from the stock of infrastructure capital. Adequate operations and maintenance also reduces pressures on the capital stock itself and can provide cost savings for users, as with a good quality road that does not impose excess wear and tear on vehicles.

Recent theoretical contributions have greatly improved our understanding of the possible effects of operations and maintenance spending. Noteworthy is the finding that greater donor finance optimally means lower operations and maintenance spending. There is also formal recognition that poor operations and maintenance can reduce the durability of private capital. It is somewhat surprising that such findings are just now appearing in the literature.

Operations and maintenance activities could conceivably be undertaken by a higher level of government, a local government, or the private sector. We believe that private sector options should be pursued to the extent possible as should decentralization of operations and maintenance. Competitive bidding and private sector competition offer the hope of lower costs and improved quality service. The proposed private sector solution is not a panacea. The private sector can be inefficient absent sufficient competition and private sector agents are prone to corruption and bribery as are many public sector officials. Moreover, private enterprises are not entirely free of pressures from the state in developing countries. But private sector entities may have greater motivation to price and charge (as feasible) for services and better ensure cost recovery and the ability to sustain service flows than the public sector.

We also ask for a broader perspective on the puzzle that considers the social efficiency of operations and maintenance expenditures that have typically been viewed in isolation of other public sector choices. Observed levels of operations and maintenance can easily be criticized as being too low. At the same time it is entirely possible that developing countries have too much of some forms of infrastructure relative to tastes, private sector consumption opportunities, and the ability to support operations and maintenance.

Finally, we recognize the potential political economy problems that arise in setting operations and maintenance spending. These problems are nothing less than daunting and raise the specter of ongoing and potentially unavoidable compromises to proper funding of operations and maintenance. The private sector solution noted above offers the best hope of ensuring infrastructure service delivery.

Notes

1 See Aschauer (1989) for an earlier example of the technical literature on infrastructure and the economy.

2 The investments have often been termed public capital (though the services are generally congestible), which refers to publicly available infrastructure whether provided by the public or private sector. Private capital refers to investments like buildings and equipment that yield private benefits. Private agents may make more efficient operations and maintenance decisions because the benefits of these investments are internalized to the firm. We will follow this terminology.

3 Though, Straub observes that the simple access to infrastructure, such as electricity or roads, may be necessary for private investment to occur.

4 See Fox and Wallich (1998).

5 Intergovernmental transfers can be used to create incentives for local governments to account for the spillover of service benefits.

6 Tolls and other marginal cost mechanisms can be imposed in some cases.

7 Of course, earmarking of revenues for excludable infrastructure does not strictly prevent government from reconsidering the expenditure uses during the budget process since the earmarking can often be changed by statute.

References

Agenor, P. 2009. "Infrastructure Investment and Maintenance Expenditure: Optimal Allocation Rules in a Growing Economy," *Journal of Public Economic Theory*, 11(2), 233–250.

Agenor, P. and B. Moreno-Dodson. 2006. "Public Infrastructure and Growth: New Channels and Policy Implications," *World Bank Policy Research Working Paper* 4064.

Aschauer, D. 1989. "Is Public Expenditure Productive," *Journal of Monetary Economics*, 23, 177–200.

Clarke, George D. 2013. "How and Why Does the Quality of Infrastructure Service Delivery Vary?" in Gregory K. Ingram and Karin L. Brandt (eds.), *Infrastructure and Land Policies*, Lincoln Institute of Land Policy, Cambridge, 370–407.

Fox, W and T. Gurley. 2006. "Will Consolidation Improve Sub-National Governments," *World Bank Policy Research Working Paper* 3913, May.

Fox, W. and C. Wallich. 1998. "Bosnia-Herzegovina: Fiscal Federalism—the Dayton Challenge," in Richard M. Bird and Francois Vaillancourt (eds.), *Fiscal Decentralization in Developing Countries*, Cambridge University Press, Cambridge.

Hulten, C. R. 1996. "Infrastructure Capital and Economic Growth: How Well You Use It May Be More Important Than How Much You Have," *NBER Working Paper* 5847.

Kalaitzidakis, P. and S. Kaluvitis. 2004. "On the Macroeconomic Implications of Maintenance in Public Capital," *Journal of Public Economics*, 88, 695–712.

McGrattan, E. and J. Schmitz. 1999. "Maintenance and Repair: Too Big to Ignore," *Federal Reserve Bank of Minneapolis Quarterly Review*, 23, 2–13.

Pagano, Michael. 2011. "Funding and Investing in Infrastructure," Urban Institute, December.

Reinikka, E. and J. Svensson. 2002. "Coping with Poor Public Capital," *Journal of Development Economics*, 69(1), 51–69.

Rioja, F. 2003. "Filling Potholes: Macroeconomic Effects of Maintenance vs. New Investment in Public Infrastructure," *Journal of Public Economics*, 87, 2281–2304.

Straub, S. 2008. "Infrastructure and Growth in Developing Countries: Recent Advances and Research Challenges," *World Bank Policy Research Working Paper* 4460, January.

World Bank. 1994. *World Development Report 1994: Infrastructure for Development*, World Bank, Washington, D.C.

11 Multi-tier monitoring of infrastructure: top down and bottom up

Ha T. T. Vu and Robert D. Ebel

Introduction

There is a robust literature on how a nation's infrastructure can promote economic growth, further the goal of poverty reduction, facilitate movement of people and goods, provide energy where it is needed, and improve a nation's health.[1] The literature also attests that although due to their varying starting points of their systems of public financial management that different countries go about the infrastructure process differently, there is also a common feature among countries in that the delivery of infrastructure services is inherently intergovernmental or "multi-tier." These twin messages fit the topic of this chapter: the monitoring of (decentralized) infrastructure assets that provide a range of services designed to meet basic, but at the same time, varied and social and economic needs in a manner that addresses a multiplicity of stakeholder interests (Bird, 1994; NRC, 1995).

Richard M. Bird frames decentralizing infrastructure theme by posing several questions: Which type of organization will design, build, finance, and eventually own an infrastructure project? Will that organization be a general or special purpose government, a regional public entity, a state enterprise or other agency reporting to government(s), a privately regulated instrumentality, or a donor? And, once those questions are addressed, who will then be accountable for monitoring the capital asset and who will the monitoring agent be accountable to? Once the monitoring accountability links are established, how is that monitoring to be documented or measured? Is infrastructure monitoring about tracking facilities maintenance (inputs)? Measuring a flow of services (outputs)? Or an assessment of a project's social and economic benefits and costs (outcomes) (Bird, 1994)? Or all of these? And, are decentralized agents capable of carrying out the monitoring task? If not all, then which monitoring task(s) are they capable of undertaking and what is the practice?

The focus of this chapter is on the last set of these questions—that of the capacity and the practice of decentralized infrastructure monitoring. The experience and practice of low, middle, and high income countries alike is considered. The chapter is organized as follows: the next section defines how infrastructure is defined for purposes here, and then proceeds to discuss how the monitoring of infrastructure fits into the broader activity of decentralized infrastructure management. The third section then lays out some of the "pre-conditions" for effective decentralized monitoring of infrastructure, leading to the conclusion that for many developing countries these pre-conditions are not satisfied and, thus, why in order to make useful statements about decentralized monitoring of infrastructure one turns to specific case studies for lessons learned from current practice. Accordingly, the fourth section focuses on a mix of illustrative country practices on governmental monitoring of infrastructure that serve to reinforce the conventional view that though there are core lessons common to all intergovernmental societies, there is no single "best" approach since each country faces different starting and end points to which they aspire (Thomas, 2006: 3). The fifth section reviews selected non-governmental and civil society role in what the chapter labels as decentralized "bottom up" monitoring. Concluding comments are provided in the final section

Multi-tier infrastructure management

Definition and scope

The term "infrastructure" has been used in different ways by different authors in different contexts. In this chapter infrastructure is defined as an expenditure that directs economic resources away from current consumption in the form of tangible capital assets (structures and equipment) toward publicly provided physical assets—capital spending—that provide a platform for future consumption.[2] But even with that definition, what counts as "core" infrastructure varies across countries and sectors. Thus, for rural areas, local roads, irrigation networks, community water boreholes are core. For urban systems facilities such as interconnector roads and highways, tram systems, power and telecom, supply-to-point-of-distribution water systems, wastewater (sewerage and storm water), and street lighting dominate. Complementing the focus of the physical infrastructure as discussed here is the social overhead capital of schools, health clinics, general government office buildings, post offices, sports and entertainment facilities, fire and police stations, and prisons.

The infrastructure management process can be depicted has having two stages: *creation* of the physical infrastructure (planning and implementation of infrastructure investment) and *utilization* of a physical asset: operation and maintenance of infrastructure. The monitoring activity partially overlaps the first stage (investment and implementation) and the entirety of the utilization stage (Figure 11.1).[3] The monitoring function overlays three activities: planning, implementation, and operation and maintenance (O&M). In multi-tier government systems, different types of governments may be responsible for different functions. Some aspects of infrastructure management may also be taken on by non-governmental institutions; accordingly, both governmental and non-governmental monitoring will be discussed below.

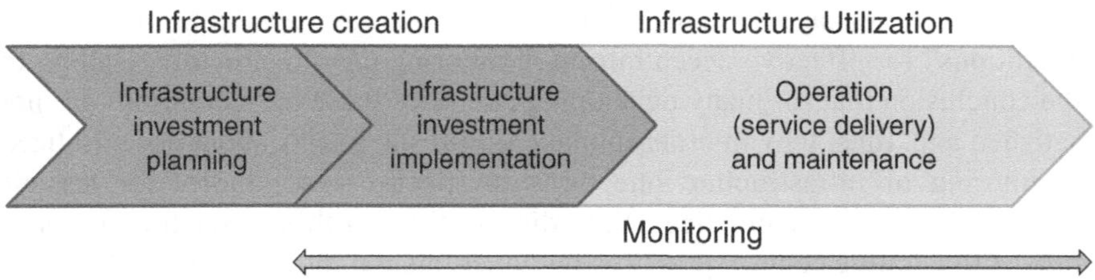

Figure 11.1 The infrastructure management sequence.

Four models

For a start in setting the intergovernmental (decentralized) monitoring context, four arrangements can be identified (Table 11.1).

1 *National planning and implementation, subnational maintenance.* Infrastructure can be created by the national government and then transferred to subnational governments for operation and maintenance. Water infrastructure in Albania is an example of this type of arrangement.
2 *National planning, subnational implementation.* Infrastructure can be planned by the national government and implemented by subnational governments. In Vietnam, for example, the central government sets investment priorities for most infrastructure projects while provincial and local governments act as the central government's agents to implement the central decisions. As an agent the role of the province is to prepare investment proposals for central government approval.
3 *National goal setting, subnational planning and implementation.* Infrastructure can be created by the subnational governments according to the goals and plans of national governments. In the People's Republic of China the central government sets investment priorities across and within sectors, including the setting of targets and timetables for infrastructure coverage in different classes of cities. Subnational governments implement the centrally established policies and standards, but may have authority to plan where and how the local infrastructure is implemented and maintained.
4 *Devolution.* Subnational governments can make their own choice of infrastructure investment priorities and manage throughout infrastructure creation and utilization. However, the central government may have a role in planning and finance. The classic case is that of the United States with its 50 unitary "state" governments and its nearly 90,000 local governments. Nearly three out of five of those local governments are special (rather than general) purpose governments, and of those, a fourth are organized as special districts for the sole purpose of the delivery infrastructure services as defined above (US Census Bureau, 2012).

Table 11.1 Stylized governmental arrangements in subnational infrastructure

Option	*Infrastructure creation*		*Infrastructure utilization*	*Example*
	Planning	*Implementation*	*O&M*	
1	N	N	S	Albania
2	N	S	S	Sierra Leone Vietnam
3	N, S	S	S	China
4	S	S	S	United States

Note
N: National government, S: Subnational government.

The monitoring phase

As depicted in Figure 11.1, the monitoring task begins once the planning and investment steps are completed. There are two aspects of the monitoring phase.

- *Monitoring implementation of infrastructure investment* aims to ensure infrastructure projects are implemented on time, within budget, and with the intended output goals met. Implementation monitoring thus focuses on cost, timeline, and quality of infrastructure construction and, at its most basic level, requires comparisons of project progress against project plan. Accordingly, an effective monitoring process should be able to detect project construction cost overruns and delays in a manner that allows for timely corrective actions.[4]
- *Monitoring operation and maintenance* of infrastructure is to ensure that created assets achieve desired outputs and outcomes over their useful life, and that the assets are properly maintained over their life cycle. Monitoring infrastructure operation and maintenance focuses on output and outcomes of operation and cost of operation and maintenance, and at its most basic level, requires comparison of operation outputs and outcomes against the infrastructure design. Accordingly, an effective monitoring process should be able to detect any underperformances and their causes so that relevant solutions can be made timely to restore adequate performance.

Infrastructure can be monitored by those who plan, finance, manage, own, and/or use the infrastructure, a division of roles that will vary by country and by sector. In principle, the manner in how these tasks are arranged in a multi-tier system of government begins with the sorting out of expenditure and revenue assignment arrangements as discussed by Bird, DeMello and Sutherland in this volume. Though there are generally accepted "assignment rules" for a well-designed multi-tier system, such sorting out will vary due to the political and fiscal architecture that is unique to each country case (Wallace,

2003). Thus, in some cases, the parties that plan and finance infrastructure may also take on the monitoring role as in Vietnam whereby the central government not only plans infrastructure projects, but then also assumes the monitoring role that in other countries may be carried out by a regional (e.g., in Vietnam, provincial) or local government. There are also countries such as Sierra Leone where the central government plans infrastructure, but then does not monitor local implementation of the plan. And, in Albania only localities that receive central subsidies for water infrastructure operation and maintenance report to the central government about their financial needs, though with this arrangement it is often the result that the center does not receive full information it seeks.

In a devolved system like the United States (US), where federal government directly accounts for only about 15 percent of total infrastructure investment, (Petersen and Vu, 2012: 2) the federal role is largely limited to that of monitoring environmental outcomes, a role that often leads to the federal government's promulgation of national environmental standards and regulatory practices for projects that in the center's judgment (which can be challenged in court) create negative externalities across state borders (US CBO, 2008: 4–5).[5]

And, in many countries the monitoring process can be heavily influenced by civil society organizations through mechanisms such as citizen "report cards" or other forms of citizen feedback activities (e.g., public hearings, establishment of government established advisory groups). In Germany citizens can go directly to a readily accessible website to add their voice to the infrastructure monitoring process.[6] This citizen/civil society role is further discussed below.

Pre-conditions for effective decentralized monitoring

The "Gaps to Solutions" theme of this book well fits the practice of decentralized monitoring of infrastructure. But, in the context of decentralized governance, the gaps are not just that of the monitoring process per se; rather, the problem is that in many countries the infrastructure practice never even gets to a stage that permits a subnational monitoring role. To paraphrase Kornai, a *precondition* for effective decentralized monitoring of infrastructure is that there is a well-designed, functioning of political and fiscal decentralized authority of infrastructure to begin with. And, for that "well-functioning" system to be a reality, central and subnational governments alike must have developed the capacity to be intergovernmental (Kornai, 1992). However, due to the reality that at present much of the world, particularly the developing world, is still at the early stages of becoming intergovernmental, there is little evidence of effective decentralized monitoring other than the episodic.

If one looks at a conventional textbook expenditure assignment matrix that links broad categories (e.g., water supply vs. distribution) on a vertical axis with generalized economic and engineering criteria for "which type of government does what," the assignment of the monitoring responsibility seems to be straightforward. For example, in the case of water supply and distribution, national (or maybe even supra-national) entities have the intergovernmental responsibility for water supply and subnational (e.g., local) governments take on the local pipeline/water distribution role. That is the broad first cut at the question of "which government" should then take on the monitoring function.

But, as Table 11.2 reveals (and even here there is heroic simplification of the complexity of the nature of all the decisions that require monitoring by some entity or entities), when one gets in the "small stuff" there is no often bright-line between supply and distribution.[7] Thus, in the case of water management the conventional assignment exercise would assign the monitoring of the source-to-distribution point of a water flow to a central or regional authority, with the local government then taking on the monitoring of pipeline distribution to households and businesses. But, a closer look takes into account net negative externalities. It may turn out that the central authority has a high monitoring interest in the occurrence of, say, local management of pipeline leakage, reservoir/storage capacity, and water pressure. Similarly, the central authority has a high interest in monitoring water quality in order to be able to assess willingness to pay and, thus, the structure of general vs. user financing (Table 11.2).[8] None of this is to say that these monitoring issues cannot be sorted out among governments, but rather to stress the point that to get it "right" will require both central and subnational governments (and not just general purpose governments) to be intergovernmentally capable as a pre-condition to how monitoring will work in multi-tier systems.[9]

An illustration for the lack of decentralized monitoring of infrastructure is found in the decentralization of the water sector in Eastern Europe and Central Asia. While some aspects of infrastructure management have been decentralized, monitoring responsibilities have not been decentralized accordingly. Based on the World Bank's recent study of the institutional arrangements in water infrastructure in Eastern Europe and Central Asia, out of 19 countries surveyed, 17 countries have some aspects of decentralized infrastructure management (Table 11.3).[10] However, there is a disconnect between the type of government (typically subnational) authority that creates and utilizes the water infrastructure services (Table 11.3, Columns 2 and 3) and the authority, typically national, that monitors (Table 11.3, Column 4). Moreover, only four countries, Albania, Belarus, the Czech Republic, and Turkey report that monitoring of infrastructure is part of the overall strategic planning process. This lack of decentralized monitoring of infrastructure well fits the argument that if there are no pre-conditions for decentralization, one cannot expect to find a decentralized role for multi-tier infrastructure monitoring.

Organizational capacity

The matter of becoming intergovernmentally capable enough to have a discussion about infrastructure monitoring in multi-tier systems is not only about whether individuals in subnational governments are adequately trained for the task; rather, it is the failure of having in place the *organizational and institutional*

Table 11.2 An illustration of a conceptual framework checklist: decentralization of the infrastructure monitoring function

Framework and system inventory for monitoring		*Who monitors?*	*Monitoring measures*	
Generic goals	*Decentralization: determinant of scale and jurisdictional coverage*	*Institutional considerations*	*Output*	*Outcomes*
• Economic productivity • Economic health • Environmental quality • Poverty reduction (distribution of flow of services) • Employment stimulus	• System size • System cost • Degree of cost recovery • Technology • Area of extent • Distribution of general population • Distribution of poverty population	• Formal vs. informal institutions • Conventional vs. traditional governance • Collectivity: governmental or CSO/CDD? • Political "level" of government having a benefits stake in the goals • Political: general or special purpose?	• Availability per unit of time (per unit of time such per hours; on demand? peak?) • Technical productivity (output/unit input) • User satisfaction (and, thus, willingness to pay) • Safety • Environmental externalities	• Willingness to pay • User "report card" (formal and/or informal) satisfaction • Public health and safety • Environmental considerations • Equity (distribution of costs, benefits, consequences)
Water supply & distribution goals	*Decentralization: determinants of scale and jurisdictional coverage*	*Institutional considerations*	*Output*	*Outcomes*
• Provide adequate, reliable source of water • Ensure general public health • User safety • Access to employment and schooling (and gender economics) • Access to poor	• Meters and capacity protocols of main supply system (e.g., pipeline) • Meters and capacity protocols of local distribution systems • Treatment plants • Storage capacity • Reservoirs (natural and constructed) • Pipe leakage	• By system ownership (by whole or parts; public vs. private? • By agent that financed the project plan and implementation • Service area users • General or special purpose government • Intergovernmental cooperative • Major users (e.g., industrial)	• Gallons delivered • Pipeline pressure (main supply and local distribution) • Storage rate (e.g., % of capacity to store) • Leakage/loss rates • Consumption per unit user • Financing: user charges vs. general finance • Lifeline user payment arrangements • Water pressure	• Public health/disease incidents • Maintenance tracking/disruption of service rates • Poverty reduction service and catchment areas • Poverty reduction access to water (to the home?) • Willingness to pay • Economic growth and employment stimulus

Note
This presentation is not designed for a bullet-to-bullet cross table reading. Thus, for example, the Column 1 generic of employment stimulus may relate to one or more of the bulleted entries in columns 2–4. Source: Adapted from U.S. National Research Council (1995).

Table 11.3 Institutional arrangement in water sector management, Eastern Europe and Central Asia, 2012

Country	*Infrastructure creation authority*	*Infrastructure utilization (O&M) authority*	*Infrastructure utilization monitoring authority*	*Use of monitoring in strategic planning*
Albania	Regional	Regional	National	Yes
Armenia	National	National/Regional	None	NA
Azerbaijan	National	National	None	NA
Belarus	Municipal	Municipal	None	Yes
Bulgaria	Regional	Regional	National	No
Croatia	Municipal	Municipal	National	No
Czech Republic	Municipal	Regional	National	Yes
Georgia	Regional	Regional	None	NA
Hungary	Municipal	Municipal	National	No
Kazakhstan	Municipal	Municipal	None	NA
Lithuania	Municipal	Municipal	National	No
Moldova	Municipal	Municipal	National	No
Poland	Municipal	Municipal	National	No
Romania	Municipal	Regional	National	No
Serbia	Regional	Regional	National	No
Slovak Republic	Regional	Regional	National	No
Turkey	Municipal	Municipal	National	Yes
Ukraine	Municipal	Municipal	None	No
Uzbekistan	Municipal	Municipal	National	No

Source: World Bank, Urban Water Notes, 2012 (unpublished).

Note
NA: Information not available.

capacity for the system as a whole. The World Bank's Independent Evaluation Group's (IEG) report on the evaluation of the Bank's support or capacity building found that "individuals are often trained for specific tasks before the organizational framework has been reformed to allow them to use the training effectively" (Thomas, 2006: 1; World Bank, 2005b). In short, if a country is not broadly organized to be intergovernmental—that is, if its system of political and fiscal decentralization is flawed from the start in that the fundamental questions of "which government does what" has not been sorted out, well, then, so much for a decentralized monitoring (Muwonge and Ebel, 2014). As Frank and Martínez-Vázquez note in their summary chapter to this volume, such organization capacity is a "first aspect of the decentralization and infrastructure at hand." Yes, there can be a deconcentrated dispersion of responsibilities to monitor within a central bureaucracy, and central-to-local agency delegation is also an option; but, from a conceptual as well as empirical perspective, this is not *multi-tier* or *decentralized* governance.[11]

But, that said, for this discussion of infrastructure monitoring it is useful to set aside the conceptual argument regarding the degree of organizational capacity required for a country to be "decentralized" and accept the proposition that if there is a degree of deconcentration and/or delegation *with authority*—that is, regional/local branches of central offices are created with an ability to make decisions independent of the center—there is, therefore, some degree of a *de facto* decentralization system.[12]

Institutional capacity

Regardless of the degree of organizational capacity, the capacity to be decentralized—and, therefore, carrying out a decentralized task as key as monitoring of infrastructure—is incomplete unless there is an *institutional* capacity to be multi-tier. By institutional capacity, one is referring to whether "the rules of the game" (e.g., relating to the assignment of the monitoring function) are linked with sustained performance of both entities responsible for service delivery (such as ministries and their agents, local governments) and individuals responsible for delivering results (Thomas, 2006: 2). Now a question is: What is the incentive structure of the local staff to effectively monitor local infrastructure to meet the interests and needs of their communities? If in the end the final reporting procedures and rules that the local-in-the-field staff are those that satisfy the goals of the central ministry or department, then for effective decentralized infrastructure monitoring to work there must be the happy case that the goals and incentives of central ministry or department staff happen to coincide with the desired outcomes of the end users of infrastructure services. However, the history of centralized governance leads one to conclude that there will likely not be such a happy coincidence. A good illustration is that of the pre-1990s socialist systems in Eastern Europe and Central Asia whereby the policy of the central authority, the supra-national Soviet Union that planned infrastructure for its nation-states, was to build–but-then-ignore local infrastructure, with the result that the pay and promotion incentive of the "decentralized' (e.g., county) local field staff was to go along with the same incentives that their central managers responded to (Alm and Buckley, 1994; Bird *et al.*, 1995).

But, one not need reach back to Soviet socialism to note this problem of a breakdown in the institutional capacity for effective decentralization of infrastructure monitoring. The Independent Evaluation Group (IEG) of the World Bank reports that "only about one third of the projects reviewed in Africa were clear about the relationships among organizational, institutional, and individual capacity" (World Bank, 2005b). In its work the IEG found that though a "lot of effort was devoted to fixing weaknesses in organizational capacity, the main problem was poor incentives for staff" and, furthermore, that "individuals were too often trained for specific tasks without reforming the [institutional] framework to let them use the training effectively" (Thomas, 2006: 4). Thus, if one makes what for many places is the heroic assumption that the organizational capacity for decentralization—and therefore decentralized monitoring—is in place, one still runs into the problem of failure of the institutional capacity to be effective.

The water sector in Albania provides a good example of the lack of an institutional capacity to monitor locally.[13] Albania initiated a process to decentralize the water sector in 2000 when the *Organic Law* defined water sector service as a function of local government units.[14] The principal mode of decentralization was the transfer of ownership of water utilities from the central government to local government units (LGUs). This was accomplished either by detaching rural independent systems from existing utilities and transferring them to the communes, or through direct investments in stand-alone systems in communes, financed by the central budget or by foreign donor organizations. Then the new systems were passed onto LGUs. By 2007, the decentralization was considered largely complete with 83 percent of the total number of utilities having been transferred, involving 76 percent of municipalities and 88 percent of communes, and serving 53 percent of the population.[15] But, even though these organizational arrangements were effected, performance of water sector did not improve after the decentralization. Continuity of water service remains low, at only 11 hours per day, compared with the Western European Benchmark of 24 hours per day. Utility staff per 1,000 connections is about ten while the benchmark is only two. Monitoring of water infrastructure has not improved. It was weak with the central government before decentralization and continues to be weak under the ownership of LGUs due to the lack of intergovernmental capability and institutional capacity to monitor. Two failures of institutional capacity are particularly evident. First, a five-year business plan is considered as a benchmarking tool that would facilitate LGUs to monitor performance of water companies. However, per the *de facto* "rules of the game" there is no legal obligation for water companies to prepare and submit such a plan to the central government or to the LGUs. Second, LGUs can monitor the performance of water companies against a performance agreement between an LGU and a water company; but, again, the *de facto* "rules" are such that none of the transferred water companies has concluded such an agreement with their LGUs because most LGUs do not have sufficient revenue to fund the operating and maintenance of water infrastructure (World Bank, 2011b). In sum, though the Albanians got the organizational framework "right," there was no follow-up to make the intergovernmental institutional arrangement capable of carrying out its monitoring task.

Individual capacity

Even if both the organizational and institutional capacity is in place, there remains the matter of the capacity of individuals—the staff—to be able to be decentralized. In Nigeria the Lagos State government has attached high importance to monitoring and evaluation of infrastructure projects. Monitoring is primarily undertaken by the Monitoring and Evaluation Directorate in the state Ministry of Economic Planning and Budget (MEPB), and supported by the Project Implementation Monitoring Unit (PIMU) in the Governor's Office and an Independent Consultants Monitoring Team.

Implementing ministries, departments, and agencies submit quarterly reports to the MEPB and PIMU and explanation is required for cost variances. MEPB and PIMU review project costs and benefits and make quarterly monitoring and evaluation reports. These reviews are, however, not as detailed as expected because of inadequate technical skills. Projects are to be stopped if irregularities are discovered by the MEPB or PIMU, but this rarely happens.

Despite Lagos government's stated effort in improving monitoring, it is still weak as characterized by a low quality of monitoring reports. To compensate there has been a Personal Assistant to the Governor in infrastructure project monitoring and evaluation. Moreover, the Governor's Office has collaborated with the World Bank mission in Nigeria to build the capacity of monitoring and evaluation of state Ministry of Economic Planning and Budget, and the Project Implementation Monitoring Unit (PIMU) in the Governor's Office. However, low individual capacity still constrains quality of monitoring.

Case studies

As the forgoing discussion reveals, it makes little sense to talk of "decentralized monitoring of infrastructure" in a country if the pre-condition solutions involving organizational, institutional, and individual capacity is not in place. Nevertheless, there are lessons to be learned from both "top-down" and "bottom-up" case examples—practices that the IEG notes that when it comes to the practice of project monitoring and evaluation, "can be more art than science" (Thomas, 2006: 3). And, taking that cue, there are several case studies that give guidance of how one can move from gaps to solutions. It is also true that in closing these gaps, there is opportunity for developed and developing to learn from each other. Though there are good examples of a well-designed intergovernmental systems of subnational monitoring of infrastructure projects, there is also ample evidence of monitoring failures—or, at least of the failure of policymakers to use the monitoring information presented to them—in "advanced" decentralized countries (ASCE, 2013).

Adopting the same stylized format as above (Table 11.1) for presentation of multi-tier infrastructure and utilization arrangements, one can link the phases of creation and utilization to that of monitoring (Table 11.4). Thus, for example, in central officials coordinate on infrastructure implementation and O&M, but then make monitoring a wholly central function (Table 11.4). In the Republic of Korea (South Korea) the role of which government finances is determinate whereby the central government monitors only the projects that receive large amount of central subsidy. In China, the central government is part of the planning process but then does not generally monitor locally implemented and operated infrastructure. The US provides the classic devolution case—four "Ss" in a row.

Chile has a strong top-down monitoring of infrastructure projects (Arancibia, 2013) Chile. Project implementation is systematically reported and carefully reviewed as part of the budgeting process and project costs are controlled with performance an effective use of performance budgeting. This is accomplished by combining a mature appraisal system for project design with a strong National Investment System (SNI) that facilitates the monitoring of project implementation. The Ministry of Planning and Ministry of Finance jointly monitor project implementation through reports submitted by the financial unit in regional governments to the ministries and through the SNI. Implementing agencies in the subnational governments then report to the financial unit in regional governments about project implementation. All information relating to investment initiatives and projects from formulation to appraisal and implementation is recorded in the SNI and posted in the Integrated Projects Bank (BIP). This information includes a listing of contracts and the expenses with each expense item being paid out and the contracting company receiving (i) the payment; (ii) *ex ante* cost estimates; (iii) the requested resources by item; and (iv) the assigned resources.

For sectoral monitoring and evaluation, a deconcentrated regional agency supervises and monitors the project implementation and the reports to relevant line ministry. For example, a regional Health Authority monitors the implementation of infrastructure for health and reports to the Ministry of Health. For education, it is the Superintendent for Education that supervises project implementation and reports to the Ministry of Education.

Table 11.4 Stylized governmental arrangements of monitoring implementation of infrastructure investment

Infrastructure creation		*Infrastructure utilization*	*Monitoring of implementation*	*Example*
Planning	*Implementation*	*O&M*		
N	S	S	N	Chile
N, S	S	S	N, S	South Korea
N, S	S	S	S	China
S	S	S	S	U.S.

Note
N: National government, S: Subnational government.

Regarding cost monitoring during project implementation, investment initiatives must be reassessed whenever the tendering process yields costs in excess of 10 percent of the estimate. In this case, the institution formulating the project or the institution financially responsible must provide the analysis with all of the technical and economic information required to justify the cost increase. The project will then be re-appraised using the new information. Once the re-appraisal is done and resources earmarked, the goal is for no further change in project costs.[16]

In the **Republic of Korea**, the central government monitors local infrastructure projects that receive more than 30 billion Won (about US$30 million) from the central government subsidy. Local governments as implementing agencies annually report to the Total Project Cost Management System in the Ministry of Finance. The Ministry of Finance then compares the project implementation status with the project planning for a given project and decides on the merits of further funding of the project. For projects that receive less than 30 billion Won the role of monitoring is assigned to local governments. The *Local Finance Law* provides the legal framework for the local government monitoring of these projects (Kim, 2013).

In the **People's Republic of China**, growing reliance on extra-budgetary funds has reduced government's control over spending units and, thus, local accountability to the center (Wong, 2012). Thus by default, China provides a case where there has been decentralization of infrastructure (including monitoring), but a decentralization that can be characterized as having insufficient funding and little oversight.[17] China does have a National Key Construction Projects Monitoring Office with special agents assigned to each province to monitor selected projects for policy and legal compliance, disbursement of funds, project progress, tendering, and construction quality. However, their role is limited because oversight is confined to only budget funded projects which are only a small portion of infrastructure projects in China.

Local investment corporations (LICs)[18] have been established to provide funds for local infrastructure and have come to play a key role in financing infrastructure in many localities.[19] However, there is no systematic oversight, monitoring, and evaluation of infrastructure investment by LICs. According to Wong,

> [a]t the national level no agency has been assigned the responsibility for oversight of their activities—not the Ministry of Finance (MoF), nor the National Development and Reform Commission (NDRC), the Ministry of Construction (MoC) or the China Banking Regulatory Commission (CBRC). In the absence of national guidelines, management and supervision of LICs by local governments varies greatly across localities.
>
> (Wong, 2014: 23)

In the **US**, a highly decentralized country, subnational governments typically manage local infrastructure investment from planning to implementation. Most of the states in the US have an effective process for monitoring infrastructure construction. A recent assessment on infrastructure performance in all 50 states finds that ten states have high performance on monitoring infrastructure construction, 38 at middle level and only two states at low ranking (Pew, 2008). The practice of infrastructure monitoring in the US states reported during 1999–2008 suggests that effective monitoring can be achieved when there is a comprehensive, frequent, and systematic collection of performance data and effective use of the data collected in budgeting and intervening in project implementation (Pew, 2008).

Some US states improved their infrastructure monitoring between 2005 and 2008 by making more frequent reports and shortening time for corrective action. For example, project monitoring was much better in Wyoming state in 2008 compared to 2005 because its Department of Transportation effectively reduced the average time to correct problems from months to weeks since workers must now immediately notify project managers of problems or concerns. In Ohio state meetings are regularly held between project managers and contractors on the progress of capital projects who review reports on cost overruns, delays, and safety compliance. The result is that the state architect is able to respond more quickly to solve problems, such as providing solutions relating to inefficiencies, quality issues, and cost overruns. The Ohio solution response time ranges from one to two weeks for (typically civil-engineer) identified efficiency and quality matters and to up to two months to address costs issues identified by financial analysts. Alabama state improved its monitoring by focusing on collection of data on performance that allows quarterly adjustment for its performance budget reports. In New Mexico state officials instituted a bottom-up performance review process that includes weekly reports from project managers that allows the state to respond within a week for most cost overruns, delays, inefficiencies, and quality concerns, and, often within one day, for safety issues (Pew, 2008).

A recent survey of OECD member states finds that all national and regional governments answering the survey reportedly monitor implementation of infrastructure investment in one form or another (OECD, 2012; Charbit and Gamper, this volume). The majority of countries report (15 of 19 respondents to the survey) that some forms of performance monitoring of public investment projects are conducted at central government level (Figure 11.2).[20] This includes the use of performance indicators as well as the formulation of objectives defined in the form of target values. An example is the Urban Solid Waste Management project in **Galicia (Spain)**, which is one of the European Union's (EU) pilot regions using outputs and outcomes indicators as a central mechanism for management infrastructure investment funded by the EU (Hulbert, 2012). It is an example of a project subject to strong external constraints that have influenced its design and development.[21] Monitoring requirements established for the two major EU Structural Funds, the European Regional Development Fund and Cohesion Fund, often include reporting requirements, requirements related to the spending timeframe, the prioritization of policy areas, co-financing requirements, additional requirements, the use of *ex ante* economic evaluation tools as well as the use of environmental impact analysis (European Commission, 2012b). EU practice is summarized in Box 11.1.

Box 11.1 Multi-tier monitoring in European Union structural funds

The European Union Structural Funds are intended to reduce fiscal disparities among the member states. These funds make up one of the largest items of the budget of the European Union (€278 billion in 2013, which is about 28 percent of the committed Community Budget, and of that about a third is earmarked for infrastructure, largely for air, water, rail, and road transport). To monitor these funds, the European Council and Parliament define the priorities, tasks, and organization of the funds, and make regulations through the ordinary legislative procedures. Monitoring of the EU structural funds is implemented in the context of multilevel governance and is based on output and result indicators.[1] *Monitoring of outputs* means to observe whether intended services or products are delivered and whether implementation is on track with respect to a set of common output indicators. *Result indicators* are variables that provide information on some specific aspects of results that lend themselves to be measured.[2] As a national policy, each EU Member State establishes a committee to monitor implementation of each funded program in coordination with the European Commission (the Executive body of the Council).[3] At the subnational level monitoring procedures are program-specific and dependent on organizational and institutional settings of each member country. Galicia (Spain) provides an example of a region that is applying outputs and outcomes indicators as a central mechanism for managing public investment funded by EU funds. Compared to national or local funds for public investment, the use of EU funds involves more extensive conditionality and monitoring, as well as a performance assessment report. Requirements attached to EU funds include reporting requirements related to the spending timeframe, the prioritization of policy areas, co-financing requirements, and the use of *ex ante* economic evaluation tools as well as the use of environmental impact analysis. This focus on conditionalities and the related monitoring procedures were judged as excessive by some Spanish authorities although there is agreement that EU conditionality, monitoring, and performance evaluation has contributed to a stronger focus on results, particularly with respect to the main objectives of the closure of illegal landfills and the provision of a more environmentally sustainable waste management system in compliance with EU and Spanish national directives. The introduction of performance budgeting indicators in Galicia is further interpreted by many as a pre-emptive policy from the regional government that anticipates further EU requirements.

Sources: CSIL (2012), European Commission (2012a, 2012b), Hulbert (2012), OECD (2012), and Sartori and Catalano (2013).

Notes

1 European Commission (2012a).
2 European Commission (2012b).
3 European Commission (2012b).

Monitoring of regional infrastructure in non-OECD countries is less well established, which implies that the potential for indicators to inform policy and improve outcomes over time is often not being realized in many developing countries. Indeed, the evidence shows that maintenance in the transport sector in developing countries often suffered from underfunding and, thus in part by

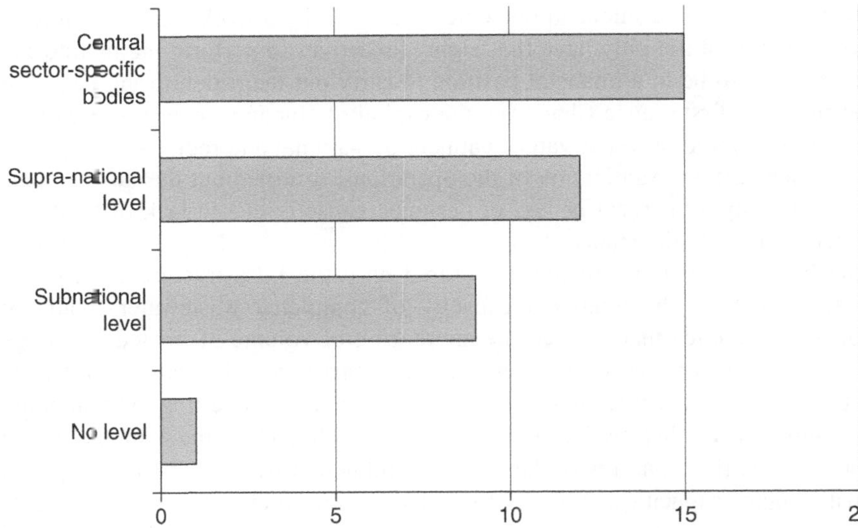

Figure 11.2 Level at which monitoring is performed in OECD countries (source: OECD, 2012; OECD national questionnaire: multi-level governance of public investment in sectoral context, 2012. "No level" refers to lack of response to the survey).

default, neglect (World Bank, 2003). The evidence further shows that many countries in East Asia lack standardized performance monitoring. China, Vietnam, the Philippines, Indonesia, and Cambodia are cited as countries that have not as yet established central institutions for routine monitoring and reporting of infrastructure systems (Peterson and Muzzini, 2003: 215).

Measurement

As countries develop the capacity to be intergovernmental and thereby make progress to toward multi-tier infrastructure monitoring, a task to be managed will be that reaching of an intergovernmental agreement on appropriate national and subnational guidelines, standards, indicators on progress, intended outputs and outcomes.

Monitoring can be done according to *mandatory standards*, either absolute levels or as measure of improvement from a base line. In principle, mandatory standards can be used as a condition of capital grants; however, in practice such conditionality may not be applied. For example, Indonesia's DAK (Dana Alokasi Khusus), a special purpose grant providing funds to subnational governments that carried with it a requirement for performance measurement, nevertheless failed to incorporate standards in account in the funding process (Peterson and Muzzini, 2003: 214).

The selection of *indicators and targets* to monitor is the next important step if one is to capture intended outcomes; but for this to work, subnational governments must not only have the "right" incentives to perform the monitoring role, but also be in a financial position to carry out their monitoring task. For example, at first glance Changsha, the capital of Hunan province, scored well when monitored on wastewater treatment by national and regional authorities, but upon further examination of the operations, it turned out that it was operating at only 50 percent or less of designed capacity due to lack of funds for operation and maintenance (Peterson and Muzzini, 2003: 217). This is because the higher level governments monitored only the infrastructure targets that were based on the treatment capacity of completed wastewater treatment plants, a practice that omitted the monitoring of volume of treated discharge or the quality of receiving water bodies. In this case, Changsha operated its current wastewater treatment plants at half capacity by diverting the remaining incoming flows directly into the Xiang River (a branch of the Yangtze River) at the same time that it was planning to build new wastewater treatment plants with higher capacities. A similar problem arises when infrastructure targets such as cost targets specific to a locality are imposed by a "higher" level of government on a local government, but then some of the costs turn out to not be under control of localities.

Performance agreements can be arranged between central government and subnational governments, between governments and service providing companies. For example, in Sierra Leone, the Strategic Policy Unit in the President's Office has performance agreements with ministries, departments, and agencies. In Albania, local government units are supposed to have performance agreements with local-government-owned water companies so that they can monitor the operation and maintenance of water infrastructure performed by these companies. However, due to the lack of funding from the local governments to these companies, there has been no commitment from these companies to the local governments to report on the performance of these companies.

Monitoring tools

Good practice suggests that the *project planning and design* should build in the monitoring criteria. Weak planning without requirements on monitorable outcome indicators, progress indicators, and implementation beyond financing make it difficult for the government to monitor progress towards clearly defined objectives. In many countries, however, the inclusion of monitoring in planning is not common. For example, in the set of the 19 Eastern Europe and Central Asia countries surveyed by the World Bank, only four have monitoring incorporated in strategic planning for water infrastructure (see Table 11.3). In a similar manner in Sierra Leone, the general lack of documented project objectives, projected timelines, and appraisal analysis makes it almost impossible to assess whether a completed project has achieved its intended objectives and whether the objectives were met on time at the approved cost (Foday *et al.*, 2012).

Project reporting is another monitoring tool. It has been a good practice at subnational governments to have reports on the project implementation progress submitted frequently (e.g., quarterly) to a mayor, governor, or other representative body in an understandable format accompanied by an explanation of delays, cost overruns, funding and construction problems, and proposed corrective actions (Kaganova, 2011: 44–45). Yet, in some donor dependent countries, it is hard for the government to monitor donor-financed projects because different donors impose their own reporting format and the often-weak-capacity government is not capable of issuing and/or enforcing a standardized reporting template. For example, in Sierra Leone, there are no national or sectoral project implementation manuals nor standardized reporting templates with the result of a monitoring system that is described as very weak (Foday *et al.*, 2012).

Progress meetings between project managers and monitoring agencies have also been shown to increase the effectiveness of decentralized monitoring. In a study on public investment management that included Arlington County, Virginia in the US, Petersen and Vu (2012) found that weekly progress meetings held between infrastructure project managers and the county finance officers resulted in an institutional ability to address implementation problems in infrastructure project in a timely and effectively manner.

The site visit is a useful monitoring tool in verifying visible effectiveness of an infrastructure project and project reports. At the minimum, site visits would help detect such obvious problems as ghost schools and ghost hospitals in a number of developing countries.[22]

Information system management provides another monitoring tool whereby all (or, at least some the core set) of information about infrastructure from planning to implementation and operation and maintenance is recorded. A "good" information system report for project construction includes project title, responsible department(s), and start date, estimated completion date, key contact people, percentage of completion, funding, and budgeted vs. actual costs (Kaganova, 2011: 44–45). In Chile, all information relating to investment initiatives and projects from formulation to appraisal and implementation is recorded in the National Investments System (SNI) and posted in the Integrated Projects Bank (BIP). Many institutions interact within this system and take part in the process of public investment management. The Ministry of Public Works also uses the information recorded in the system to carry out its monitoring role.

Performance management systems for monitoring combine the audit function with statistical reporting. These have proved to be a useful monitoring tool, but can be difficult to establish at subnational government level due to capacity constraints. Thus in China, although the National Audit Office has achieved remarkable success in pushing for performance management reform over the past 15 years at the national level, the progress in subnational government is limited due to a lack in many local governments of a staff that is adequately trained in performance evaluation. As a result, monitoring and auditing is constrained to financial compliance rather than economic assessments, performance, and value for money (Wong, 2013).[23]

Bottom-up monitoring: the role of civil society

Developing economies

Infrastructure management and monitoring may also be undertaken by citizens and civil society community organizations. In community-driven development (CDD) projects, much (sometimes all) of the management of the project from planning, implementing, operation and maintenance is done by citizen organizations. Such infrastructure projects are often of small scale and may receive support from international organizations such as the World Bank, the Asian Development Bank, and the United Nations Development Programme along with support from bilaterals and the central or local government. And there can be a demonstrable efficiency gain.

For example, Gross *et al.* (2001) in their study on water infrastructure projects in 15 countries[24] found that access to community households to services was higher and the services are more sustained when women participated in monitoring project implementation. Local people including women have good local knowledge about what works and what can be sustained. The knowledge can be utilized when the agencies of water infrastructure projects "consult and listen to them, and give them some responsibility for and influence on the quality of project implementation" (Gross *et al.*, 2001: 20).

In **Indonesia** the World Bank's Kecamatan Development Program introduced a process for citizen choice relating to small infrastructure projects for Indonesian sub-districts and as part of that process explicitly includes support for building the capacity for community monitoring of the "quality and effectiveness of infrastructure projects" (Wong, 2003).[25] Moreover, there some evidence that the cost of monitoring is less than that of similar construction projects run through a Ministry of Public Works contracts (Peterson and Muzzini, 2003: 215).

In **Bangladesh** a World Bank Social Investment Program Project (SIPP) was launched (2003) that supported community monitoring through a citizens participatory process whereby information was collected regarding on spending projects ranging from rural roads to tube wells. This information is publicly displayed in most villages and then communities graded the performance of their Village Development Committees (VDCs) using a report card mechanism. A social accountability framework was established to allow community members to directly demand accountability from their leaders and service providers on infrastructure and to participate in monitoring their performance (Box 11.2).[26]

Box 11.2 Community Assessment Process in Bangladesh villages

A number of villages in Bangladesh have been applying a Community Assessment Process (CAP) to assess the quality of public services including those of infrastructure. CAP is a process through which village people participate in assessing the performance of public services provided by their village committees and assuring the public services meet their needs. In the process, the village council (*Gram*

Parisad) identifies the services to be evaluated, the service provider's responsibilities, the planned and used resources, the outputs, and the indicators of performed service. Service providers and service recipients separately assess the performance and quality of public services through score cards in which they give scores to each of the identified public services, justification for the scores, and recommendations for future improvement of the service. Service providers include Village Committee (*Gram Samiti*) and other committees such as Procurement Committee, Finance Committee, and Sub-project Committee. Service providers and service recipients (village people) present their score card results in a joint meeting with Village Council, discuss, and agree on the final assessment. Then, service providers and recipients jointly prepare an action plan to improve the services. Social Audit Committee monitors the implementation of the action plan and Village Council arranges CAP every six months.

Source: World Bank, *Social Investment Program Project in Bangladesh* (2009, 2011a).

OECD countries

Non-governmental "watchdog" organizations may also play an important role in monitoring infrastructure that is managed by subnational governments. For example, in the United States, a well-funded non-partisan research foundation (Pew Foundation) conducts research and analysis to develop a dialogue on issues of state infrastructure management (Box 11.3).[27]

Box 11.3 The Pew Performance Matrix, United States

The Pew Center of the Study of the States periodically issues infrastructure "report cards" on all 50 US states. Based on an explicit set of performance criteria, the grading has been done four times in 1999, 2002, 2005, and 2008 in four management areas—Information, Infrastructure, Money, and People. Each of the four management areas received a score ranging from A to D (including the ten possible grades of A, A–, B+, B, B–, C+, C, C–, D+, and D). The Pew studies assessed state infrastructure project monitoring to determine whether a state has an effective process for monitoring infrastructure projects throughout their design and construction. The criteria included that of whether a state (i) adequately monitors, evaluates, and detects project-cost overruns, delays, and safety compliance; and (ii) effectively intervenes to take corrective action, as necessary, in managing the construction of capital projects. Pew's state-by-state surveys are carried out by journalists and academics and involve interviews of elected and appointed officials, questionnaires, and document reviews. The evaluations are based on data collected from more than 12,000 different sources—including surveys, written documents, and interviews with over 1,000 persons in all 50 states.

Source: Pew (2008).

Also in the US every four years the American Society of Civil Engineers (ASCE) releases an on-line *Report Card for America's Infrastructure*, which presents data by state and assigns letter grades to each major type of physical infrastructure.[28] The *Report Card* is based on information for each of the infrastructure categories—including reports, studies, articles, surveys, and other research materials—from professional societies, non-profit associations, and local, state, and federal agencies. Civil engineers from across a given state then use these materials to develop a detailed picture for the state, examining the condition of the state infrastructure, its performance, funding, and service capacity versus a measure of the capacity "need."[29] Based on an explicit set of engineering criteria, grades are then assigned to each category.

The *Report Card* provides grades and details of the state of infrastructure in a given locality and, *inter alia*, estimates the costs to improve it for each category. Infrastructure categories examined include transportation (roads, bridges, dams, levees, and ports), waste, water (drinking water, storm water, waste water) navigable waterways, parks and recreation, rail, school, and transit. The ASCE has archives of report cards so infrastructure states for a given locality can be compared over time.

A report card on infrastructure in a given state includes:

- a summary of state of infrastructure and its need for renewal;
- a mini report card, a summary of grades given in each infrastructure category;
- a summary of justification for grades given in each infrastructure category;
- a Citizen's Guide, a detailed report of facts and analyses for each infrastructure category and a guide for citizens' understanding of infrastructure state of their locality and what can be done to improve it.

Similar "watchdog" activities are occurring elsewhere. In 2012 in Canada a consortium of professional engineering associations and the Federation of Canadian Municipalities recently initiated the *Canadian Infrastructure Report Card* project that surveyed municipal road systems and water systems (drinking, waste, and storm water) in 123 municipalities in ten of Canada's 13 provinces. The Canadian report is instructive for other countries contemplating such "report card" monitoring in that because it was a first of its kind exercise for Canada's municipalities, it provides in addition to its main report and analysis a concluding section on "Lessons Learned" regarding data requirements, data collection techniques, and how a survey process may have to be adjusted to survey communities of different size and degree of development (Canadian Infrastructure Report Card, 2012).

Two other countries that have developed community-based monitoring include Germany and South Korea. In Germany, as noted above, there is a government-issued website whereby citizens can provide their feedback on road construction across the country. South Korea provides project information upon request according to the Information Disclosure Act (a process which often involves a long response time lag).

Concluding comments

Countries commit millions ... billions ... of capital investment monies on infrastructure. The reasons are well documented: physical infrastructure is about a society's foregoing of current consumption in order for future consumption. The societies that do this will become developed societies. Those who do it poorly are.... poor. Thus launches the infrastructure management sequence: planning, implementation, operation and maintenance. Once one is past the planning stage, the need to integrate monitoring into the next three steps of implementation, operation and maintenance is crucial to making it all work.

Next the question arises: Who monitors? As adequately documented elsewhere in this book, spatial considerations reveal that except in a very few cases physical infrastructure has a multi-jurisdictional character. Within a country (which is the frame of reference for this book and chapter), that means that the monitoring task is inherently intergovernmental or "multi-tier." Moreover, as again reported elsewhere in this book but also referenced in several places in this chapter, the decentralization and monitoring of infrastructure has two types of payoffs. The first is political: decentralization provides a political vehicle for citizens to engage with and hold accountable their government representatives. Indeed, in some cases—post-conflict Cambodia is an example—decentralizing infrastructure can be a strategy to recreate people's trust in the very notion of "their government" (Smoke and Taliercio, 2007).

The second is economic: decentralization of infrastructure can have high efficiency payoffs in terms of not only the metrics of economic growth and poverty reduction, but also in the overall "well-being" of a people. But, for this result to be realized, that infrastructure must be technically well monitored throughout the infrastructure management sequence. Here it should be clearly noted that while decentralization of the infrastructure monitoring task has been shown to have payoffs in terms of sustainability and efficiency, decentralization is not the *sine qua non* for infrastructure generated development and poverty alleviation. It's just that, as noted, it has been demonstrated that when a country is intergovernmentally capable, there are economic gains from decentralized monitoring of infrastructure.

But, one of the clear findings of this chapter is that many countries are not ready for decentralized monitoring. That is, they have not met the "preconditions" of a well-designed (or, in many cases, even a partially well-designed) intergovernmental system: there is a gap to be addressed in terms of organizational, institutional, or individual (or all three) types of capacity development. This is the case for many countries. And, even when a country might be judged intergovernmentally capable, it does not necessarily follow that it is getting its component of decentralized monitoring of infrastructure "right." Indeed, as pointed out in the above text, project monitoring can be more art than science. It can also be more opportunistic than "well designed." And with those lessons one can draw some conclusions regarding decentralized monitoring of fiscal infrastructure. There are at least five.

The first, which repeats the comments above, is that decentralized monitoring matters. There are, or can be, measurable political and economic efficiency gains.

Second, there should be clear guidance and standards for infrastructure monitoring at all government levels. When there is a national or regional interest in how an infrastructure system will work, national/regional standards and targets should be discussed with the subnational governments to insure that if monitoring is to be decentralized that the decentralized monitoring unit can meet those standards and carry out its monitoring task in an autonomous manner. In this context an example to avoid is that as cited in the text of a "local" staff that responds to central government incentives for salary and promotion.

Third, decentralized infrastructure monitoring should be imbedded in the full project management cycle so that there is a multi-tier agreement on infrastructure service modalities (e.g., timelines, funding, monitoring measures and tools, and outputs and outcomes).

Fourth, recognizing that every decentralized infrastructure project or system is different in some manner than from all others, there are also many technical, political, financial, and economic similarities for knowledge sharing from place to place. Different jurisdictions that have the same type of infrastructure investment may nevertheless have different monitoring strategies, measures, and tools— and, that's knowledge to be shared.

And fifth, community monitoring of multi-tier infrastructure can play an important role in the monitoring, and thus, the delivery, of infrastructure services and should be encouraged. If governments and civil society agencies cooperate in providing reliable information and feedback, the case for decentralized monitoring will be enhanced.

Notes

1 Yilmaz *et al.* (2012), Ch. 4 review the general case. Martínez-Vázquez and Frank (this volume) and Aschauer (1989) and World Bank (1994) examine the case of infrastructure.

2 Thus excluded from the discussion here is both the fully privately provided and the public-private partnership, also important topics, but that are adequately discussed elsewhere; e.g., World Bank (1994) and Dannin and Cokorinos (2012).

3 The questions of functional assignment and finance are discussed by Bahl and Bird and by de Mello and Sutherland elsewhere in this volume.

4 Nonetheless, in even the most technically and administratively advanced of countries some timelines will not be met and cost overruns will occur. A cross-country study by the Construction Sector Transparency Initiative shows that more advanced countries like the UK have much lower cost and time overruns than developing countries like Ethiopia and Malawi (CoST 2011). However, the evidence is not confined specifically to subnational projects.

5 See Viñuela (this volume) for cross-country data on governmental infrastructure spending.

6 For the German practice see www.bmvbs.de/DE/Service/Baustellenmelder/baustellenmelder_node.html.

7 Gershberg (2006) provides a country illustration of this complexity for allocation K-12 education tasks among different types of governmental authorities.

8 The topic of financing infrastructure is addressed in this volume by de Mello and Sutherland.

9 And add to this the reality of the asymmetric capacity to govern, let alone be intergovernmental, in many developing countries. See Congleton (2006: 131–154) and Dafflon (2006: 271–305).

10 World Bank, Urban and Sector, Country Sector Notes, 2012. Unpublished as of this writing.

11 Not all analysts are willing to so readily formally rule out deconcentration or delegation as viable forms of decentralization. E.g. see Amin and Ebel (2006).

12 Smoke and Taliercio (2007: 70) address the nature of "deconcentration" vs. "decentralization" for Cambodia.

13 This section draws on World Bank (2011b).

14 Article 10 of the Organic Law of Albania.

15 However, the transfer of two of the largest water companies, Tirana and Durres, serving 37 percent of the population, has not been completed as yet. Mayors of Tirana and Durres have refused to accept the utilities' transfer without guarantees of ongoing financial support from the central government. World Bank (2011b).

16 Chile, in which the entire infrastructure process is highly centralized, can be judged as having an advanced public investment management system. A recent study of a sample of 387 regional investment projects (8 percent of total regional projects) before 2007 showed that only 28 percent of regional projects had time overruns and actual costs at completion were 5 percent lower than estimated at appraisal (Arancibia, 2013).

17 Subnational government share of total budgetary investment has increased over the past three decades (up to 88.8 percent in 2007) (Wong, 2013a: 9).

18

> By design, LICs are complex hybrid financial organizations that mix public (fiscal) and private (financial) funding to engage in both public and private (profit-making) activities. As such, they bear similarities to public-private partnership arrangements in other countries. In China, though, the government is the only participant and decision-maker.
>
> (Wong, 2014: 17)

19

> The China Banking Regulatory Commission (CBRC) estimated that LICs accounted for about two-thirds of local government debt in 2009. More recent estimates, based on findings by the National Audit Office and the central bank, is that the total debt of LICs is likely to have reached CNY 10–14 trillion by year-end 2010—as much as 45 per cent of current GDP.
>
> (Wong, 2014: 17–18)

20 The survey question is "Do central levels or supra-national authorities monitor the use of public investment funding in your sector that goes to sub-national governments over the course of implementation?" One country may report more than one monitoring level.

21 The project consists of the construction of a set of facilities operated by the private-public company, Sogama, in the municipality of Cereda, Galicia for the separation of recyclable materials and the incarnation of mixed waste with energy recovery. With a project financing period of 1997–2010, the total investment costs were €274 million (in €2011), 36 percent of which was EU financed through the Cohesion Fund with the remainder funded by Sogama. Sogama's financing comes from its shareholders (which include the government of Galicia) and through private loans (CSIL, 2012; Sartori and Catalano, 2013).

22 There have been ghost schools and ghost hospitals in developing countries where school and hospital building projects are reportedly completed without the real construction of any school or hospital (see Shah in this volume).

23 A Kecamatan is a sub-district of a city or regency, which are in turn local government units of local government "below" the provincial level.
24 The study looks at a random sample of communities chosen from 18 projects in 15 countries, funded by a range of donors, NGOs, and governments. The sample comprises 88 communities that had managed and sustained water supply systems for three or more years. Fifteen countries are from five regions: Bolivia, Colombia, Ecuador, and Peru in Latin America; Kenya, Malawi, South Africa, and Zambia in East and Southern Africa; Cameroon and Ghana in West Africa; Indonesia and the Philippines in East Asia, and India, Nepal, and Sri Lanka in South Asia.
25 The Kecamatan Development Project's objectives are to raise rural incomes, strengthen kecamatan and village government and community institutions, and to build public infrastructure through labor intensive methods. There are four components (i) block grants; (ii) technical assistance for implementation; (iii) monitoring; and (iv) policy studies. www.worldbank.org/Kecamatan Development Project, May 13, 2013. Also see Wong (2003).
26 Roughly two million people have benefited from community infrastructure activities ranging from rural roads to schools and tube-wells.
27 There are other assessments on infrastructure status and needs such as the American Society of Civil Engineers' Infrastructure Report Card, and annual reports on infrastructure needs and surveys of major projects by the Urban Land Institute and Ernst & Young.
28 ASCE Report Card, www.ascecareportcard.org.
29 A word of caution: The engineer's measure of infrastructure capacity "need" (typically workload × average unit cost) may not be the same as the economists' concept of quantity demanded for a flow of infrastructure services (which accounts for change in relative prices).

Bibliography

Alabama Department of Finance website. www.smart.alabama.gov/.

Alm, James and Robert Buckley (1994). "Decentralization, Privatization and Solvency of Local Governments in Reforming Economies: The Case of Budapest," *Environment and Planning, C: Government and Policy* 12(3): 337–347.

American Society of Civil Engineers (2013), *Report Card on America's Infrastructure 2013*. www.infrastructurereportcard.org/.

Amin, Khaled and Robert Ebel (2006). *Egyptian Decentralization and Intergovernmental Relations: An Agenda for Reform, World Bank Egypt Public Expenditure Review*. Washington, DC: World Bank.

Andersen, Henry (2004). *Cambodia's Seila Program: A Decentralized Approach to Rural Development and Poverty Reduction*. A World Bank Conference on Scaling Up Poverty Reduction: A Global Learning Process and Conference, Shanghai, 19pp.

Arancibia, Hugo (2013). "Public Investment Efficiency: The Case of Chile," The World Bank, *Investing to Invest: Building the Foundation for Effective Public Investment Management*, Washington, DC.

Aschauer, David (1989). "Is Public Expenditure Productive?" *Journal of Monetary Economics* 23: 177–200.

Bird, Richard M. (1994). "Decentralizing Infrastructure: For Good or For Ill?" Policy Research Working Paper Series 1258, World Bank.

Bird, Richard M., Robert D. Ebel, and Christine I. Wallich (1995). *Decentralization of the Socialist State*. Washington, DC: World Bank.

Canadian Infrastructure Report Card (2012). A Joint Report by the Canadian Construction Association, Canadian Public Works Association, Canadian Society for Civil Engineering, and the Federation of Canadian Municipalities. www.canadianinfrastructure.ca.

Chanthaphone, Soutsakhone and Santanu Lahiri (2003). "Looking Backward to See Forward." In N. Mukherjee and C. van Wijk (eds.), *Sustainability Planning and Monitoring in Community Water Supply and Sanitation.* Washington, DC: World Bank.

Congleton, Roger D. (2006). "Asymmetric Federalism and the Political Economy of Decentralization." In Ehtisham Ahmad and Giorgio Brosio (eds.), *Handbook of Fiscal Federalism.* Cheltenham, UK and Northampton, MA: Edward Elgar, 131–153.

CoST (2011). "Briefing Note 5: Baseline Studies," Washington, DC: Report of the CoST International Advisory Group, December, 2pp. www.constructiontransparency.org/TechnicalFinancialAssistance/CoSTBriefingNotes/.

CSIL, Centre of Industrial Studies (2012). *Urban Solid Waste Management in Galicia: Ex Post Evaluation of Investment Projects Co-Financed by the European Regional Development Fund or Cohesion Fund.* Milan: CSIL, 167pp. www.csilmilano.com.

Dafflon, Bernard (2006). "The Assignment of Functions to Decentralized Government: From Theory to Practice." In Ehtisham Ahmad and Giorgio Brosio (eds.), *Handbook of Fiscal Federalism.* Cheltenham, UK and Northampton, MA: Edward Elgar, 271–305.

Dannin, Ellen and Lee Cokorinos (2012). "Infrastructure and Privatization in the New Millennium." In Robert D. Ebel and John E. Petersen (eds.), *The Oxford Handbook of State and Local Government Finance.* Oxford and New York: Oxford University Press, 727–757.

de Mello, L. (2010). "Fiscal Decentralisation and Public Investment: The Experience of Latin America," *OECD Economics Department Working Papers*, No. 824, OECD Publishing, http://dx.doi.org/10.1787/5km347r2hhbp-en.

Engineers Australia (2010). Infrastructure *Report Card 2010, Australia.* Barton Act: Engineers Australia. www.engineersaustralia.org.au.

European Commission (2012a). "Guidance Document on Monitoring and Evaluation—European Regional Development Fund and Cohesion Fund: Concepts and Recommendations."

European Commission (2012b). *Common Provisions of the European Regional Development Fund, the European Social Fund, the Cohesion Fund, the European Agricultural Fund for Rural Development and the European Maritime and Fisheries Fund.* Brussels: The Commission.

Foday, Yusuf, Douglas Addison and Murray Petrie (2012). "Sierra Leone – PIM in a Donor-Dependent Post-Conflict Economy." In Anand Rajaram, Tuan Minh Le, Kai Kaiser, Jay-Hyung Kim and Jonas Frank (2014). *The Power of Public Investment Management*, Washington, DC.

Gershberg, Alec (2006). "Making Egyptian Education More Effective." Decentralizing Education in Egypt. Egypt Public Expenditure Review, Policy Note 2 Washington, DC: World Bank.

Gross, Bruce (2003). "Do Project Rules Promote Sustainability and Equity?" In N. Mukherjee and C. van Wijk (eds.), *Sustainability Planning and Monitoring in Community Water Supply and Sanitation.* Washington, DC: World Bank, International Water and Sanitation Centre.

Gross, Bruce, Christine van Wijk, and Nilanjana Mukherjee (2001). "Linking Sustainability with Demand, Gender, and Poverty: A Study in Community-Managed Water Supply Projects in 15 Countries." Delft, Netherlands: Water and Sanitation Program and IRC International Water and Sanitation Centre.

Hughes, Caroline and Kim Sedara (2004). "The Evolution of Democratic Process and Conflict Management in Cambodia." Working Paper 30. Phnom Penh: Cambodia Development Resource Institute.

Hulbert, Claudia (2012). "Public Investment Across Levels of Government: The Case of Galicia, Spain," OECD 28th Territorial Development Policy Committee.

Kaganova, Olga (2011). "Guidebook on Capital Investment Planning for Local Governments," Urban Development Series, Knowledge Papers, Washington, DC: World Bank.

Kim, Jay-Hyung (2012). "The Republic of Korea: PIM Reform after the Financial Crisis." In Anand Rajaram, Tuan Minh Le, Kai Kaiser, Jay-Hyung Kim and Jonas Frank (2014). *The Power of Public Investment Management*, Washington, DC.

Knight, Joshua (2007). "SMART Governing: Alabama's Performance Management Initiative," GFOA Annual Meeting, March 2. www.gfoaa.org/SMART.pdf.

Kornai, Janos (1992). *The Socialist System: The Political Economy of Communism*: Princeton, NJ: Princeton University Press.

McKay, Keith (2006). "Institutionalization of Monitoring and Evaluation Systems to Improve Public Sector Management," World Bank ECD Working Paper Series No. 15.

Muwonge, Abdu and Robert D. Ebel (2014). "Intergovernmental Finances in a Decentralized World." In Catherine Farvacque-Vitkovic and Mihaly Kopanyi (eds.), *Municipal Finance: A Handbook for Local Governments*. Washington, DC: World Bank, 1–40.

National Council on Public Works Improvement (1998). *Fragile Foundations: A Report on America's Public Works*. Washington, DC: US Government Printing Office.

National Research Council (1995). *Measuring and Improving Infrastructure Performance*. Washington, DC: National Academy Press, 122pp.

OECD (2012). "Investing Together: Meeting the Co-ordination and Capacity Challenges across Levels of Government," document submitted to Delegates of the Territorial Development Policy Committee for discussion and approval at the 28th session.

Petersen, John, and Ha Vu (2012). "United States Infrastructure Investments by State Governments: Grading the Decision Process." In Anand Rajaram, Tuan Minh Le, Kai Kaiser, Jay-Hyung Kim and Jonas Frank (2014). *The Power of Public Investment Management*, Washington, DC.

Peterson, George E. and Elisa Muzzini (2003). "Decentralizing Basic Infrastructure Services," The World Bank, *East Asia Decentralizes*, Washington, DC.

Pew Center for the Study of the States (2008). "Grading the States 2008 Report." www.pewcenteronthestates.org/initiatives_detail.aspx?initiativeID=36072.

PREM Notes, Special Series on Government Monitoring and Evaluation.

Rajaram, Anand, Tuan Minh Le, Nataliya Biletska, and Jim Brumby (2010). "Framework for Reviewing Public Investment Efficiency," Washington, DC: World Bank Policy Working Paper, No. 5397.

Sartori, Avide and Gelsomina Catalano (2013). "Infrastructure Investment Long Term Contribution: Economic Development and Wellbeing," Milan: Centre for Industrial Studies, Working Paper No. 01.2013 (January).

Smoke, Paul and Robert T. Taliercio, Jr. (2007). "Aid, Public Finance and Accountability: Cambodian Dilemmas." In James K. Boyce and Madalene O'Donnell (eds.), *Peace and the Public Purse: Economic Policies for Postwar State Building*. London: Lynne Rienner Publishers, 55–84.

Thomas, Vinod (2006). "Linking Individual, Organizational and Institutional Capacity Building To Results," World Bank Institute *Capacity Development Brief Number 19*, December.

Treichel, Volker and Olubgenga Ebenerze Oyewol (2011). "Lagos State, Nigeria – PIM in Infrastructure for a Modern Megacity." In Anand Rajaram, Tuan Minh Le, Kai Kaiser, Jay-Hyung Kim and Jonas Frank (2014). *The Power of Public Investment Management*, Washington, DC.

US Census Bureau (2012). *Census of Governments: Government Organization*. www.census.gov/govs/go/index.html.

US Congressional Budget Office (CBO) (2008). *Issues and Options in Infrastructure Investment*, Washington, DC.

Wallace, Sally (2003). "Changing Times: Demographic and Economic Changes in State and Local Finance." In David L. Sjoquist (ed.), *State and Local Finance at the Beginning of the 21st Century*. Northampton, MA: Edward Elgar, 30–39.

Wong, Christine (2012). "Toward Building Performance-Oriented Management in China: the Critical Role of M&E and the Long Road Ahead," Independent Evaluation Group, World Bank, ECD Working Paper Series, No. 27.

Wong, Christine (2013). *Performance, Monitoring, and Evaluation in China*, PREM Notes Special Series on the Nuts and Bolts of M&E Systems, No. 23.

Wong, Christine (2014). "China – PIM under reform and decentralization." In Anand Rajaram, Tuan Minh Le, Kai Kaiser, Jay-Hyung Kim and Jonas Frank (2014). *The Power of Public Investment Management*, Washington, DC.

Wong, Susan (2003). Indonesia Kecamatan Development Program: *Building and Monitoring and Evaluation System for a Large-Scale Community-Driven Development Program*. Environmental and Social Development Unit, East Asia and Pacific Region. Washington, DC: World Bank, 62pp.

World Bank (1994). *World Development Report: Infrastructure and Development*. New York: Oxford University Press.

World Bank (2002). *Selling Sanitation in Vietnam: What Works?* Vietnam Country Report, WSP-EAP. Washington, DC: World Bank, Water and Sanitation Programme.

World Bank (2003). *Indonesia: Selected Fiscal Issues in a New Era*, Report 25437-IND, Washington, DC: World Bank.

World Bank (2005a). *China: Deepening Public Service Unit Reform to Improve Service Delivery*. Washington, DC: World Bank.

World Bank (2005b). Independent Evaluation Group, *Capacity Building in Africa: An OED Evaluation of World Bank Support*. OED, Washington, DC.

World Bank (2009). *Social Investment Program Project Report*. www.worldbank.org/bangladesh/sipp.

World Bank (2011a). *Implementation Completion and Results Report on a Credit for a Social Investment Program Project (SIPP) in Bangladesh*. www.worldbank.org/bangladesh/sipp.

World Bank (2011b). "Decentralization and Service Delivery in Albania: Governance in the Water Sector." A World Bank Issue Brief. Washington, DC.

Yilmaz, Serdar, Francois Vaillancourt, and Bernard Dafflon (2012). "State and Local Government Finance: Why it Matters." In Robert D. Ebel and John E. Petersen, (eds.), *The Oxford Handbook of State and Local Government Finance*. New York: Oxford University Press, 105–137.

12 Coordination of infrastructure investment across levels of government[1]

Claire Charbit and Cathérine Gamper

Motivation

Decentralization trends in OECD countries have generally led to increased investment spending at subnational government level. A number of indicators show an average increasing trend over the last 10–15 years, such as the share of total public investment spending[2] at the subnational level[3] that has been rising very slowly but steadily since 1995. Central government transfers to subnational governments have similarly steadily increased since 1995, by an average of 0.7 percent (Blöchliger and Vammalle, 2009). Sixty percent of total public spending on education, 40 percent on health, 30 percent on economic affairs, and 20 percent on social protection is spent at the subnational level across OECD countries (Charbit, 2011; OECD, 2011a). These averages hide not only considerable variations with generally bigger shares for subnational governments in federal countries, but can also not provide a full picture of changes in actual autonomy of governments at subnational levels. Generally speaking though, the crisis has led to the share of public investment to decline significantly in some federal countries (e.g., Austria and Switzerland), while increasing in some unitary ones (e.g., Norway) (Figure 12.1).

Yet, independent of the institutional context, infrastructure investment entails intensive engagement across levels of government. Hardly any subnational infrastructure investment is carried out isolated at one level of government. Partial funding often flows from national or supra-national authorities into projects managed by subnational governments. Lower tiers of authority often help shape infrastructure priorities, and contribute to the financing.

As a result, complex situations have been formed that require coordination across levels of government. Not only do the vertical interactions for infrastructure decisions, financing, and implementation have to be managed carefully to ensure all levels of government aim at convergent objectives and play by compatible rules. The management of infrastructure investment frequently also requires horizontal interaction, with other subnational jurisdictions, as projects may require a certain scale efficiency and may have positive (or sometimes negative) external spillovers which require joint design, financing, or implementation. Where policy makers seek to realize potential complementarities across sectors, it will also involve a second form of horizontal engagement—collaboration among actors and institutions responsible for different sectoral policies at different government levels.

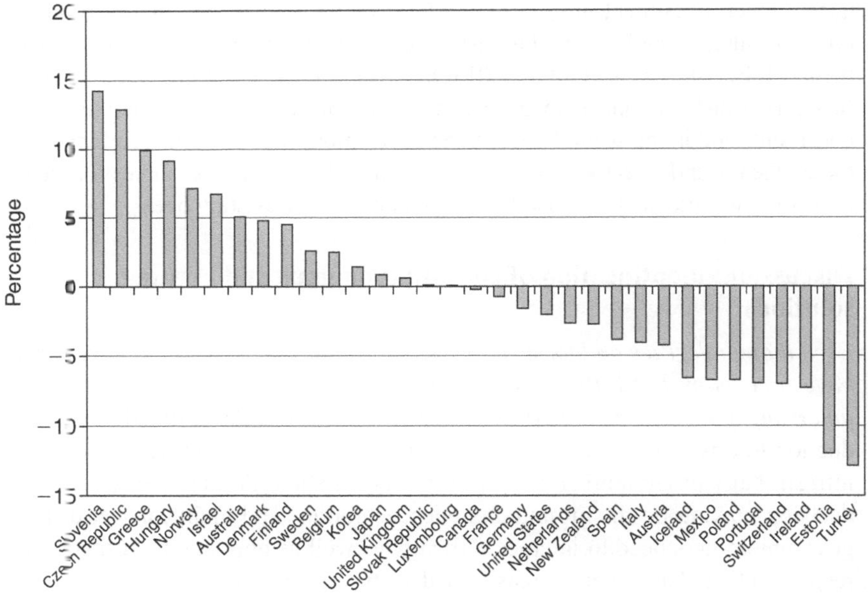

Figure 12.1 Changes in the share of subnational governments in total public investment in OECD countries (2007–2011) (source: OECD National Accounts, 2012).

Various drivers explain the complexity and the gaps that have arisen in intergovernmental coordination. Policy making authority, especially also for infrastructure investments, has been progressively more distributed across levels of government, both downwards to subnational governments and upwards to supranational authorities, in the case of European countries. Moreover the private sector's role has grown as a result of deregulation of past state-owned monopolies, and the move to joint projects with the private sector characterizes many public investment choices at the local level. Past OECD work on multi-level governance points to gaps and potential risks associated with weak coordination mechanisms and weak capacity at subnational level that will be addressed later in this chapter (Allain-Dupré, 2011; Charbit 2011; Mizell and Allain-Dupré, 2013).

Improving infrastructure governance, especially the coordination mechanisms across levels of government and line ministries, has become a key to increasing investment efficiency and effectiveness. In the aftermath of the financial crisis that caused a scissors effect on public finances, i.e., the combined impact of lower tax revenues and increased demand for social services (Vammalle and Hulbert, 2013), the initial policy response of many OECD countries was to invest in large-scale stimulus packages, leading to a significant increase in public infrastructure projects at the subnational level. Following this most OECD governments have moved to consolidation measures, negatively affecting not only overall public investment spending, but also private investment spending (Figure 12.2), and threatening the deterioration of existing capital through lack of funding for operations and maintenance. Direct investment in the EU was reduced by 6.6 percent, and even more in countries already hit hard by the crisis, such as in Spain where total public investment fell by 30 percent (OECD, 2013c). This has created the imperative to in the first phase disburse and manage investments rapidly under given administrative constraints and in the second phase to achieve "more with less," thereby increasing the efficiency and effectiveness of the available infrastructure resources for the creation of new structures, but also for the maintenance of existing ones.

Discussion: identification of coordination gaps and existing solutions

Even though degrees and forms of decentralization vary widely, all governments have a common need, that is to mobilize authorities with different degrees of autonomy along shared infrastructure policy objectives. As outlined in the introduction to this chapter, no level of government works isolated when it comes to infrastructure programming or project implementation. From objective setting to decision-making on the ground and even operations and maintenance, different government tiers need to interact vertically as well as horizontally, especially as responsibilities have been increasingly distributed across all tiers of government. To make the most of infrastructure investments, governments need to coordinate accordingly to avoid a fragmented approach to investment spending, leading to inefficiency (more could be achieved with the same level of resources), but also allocative ineffectiveness, failing to maximize citizens' preferences.

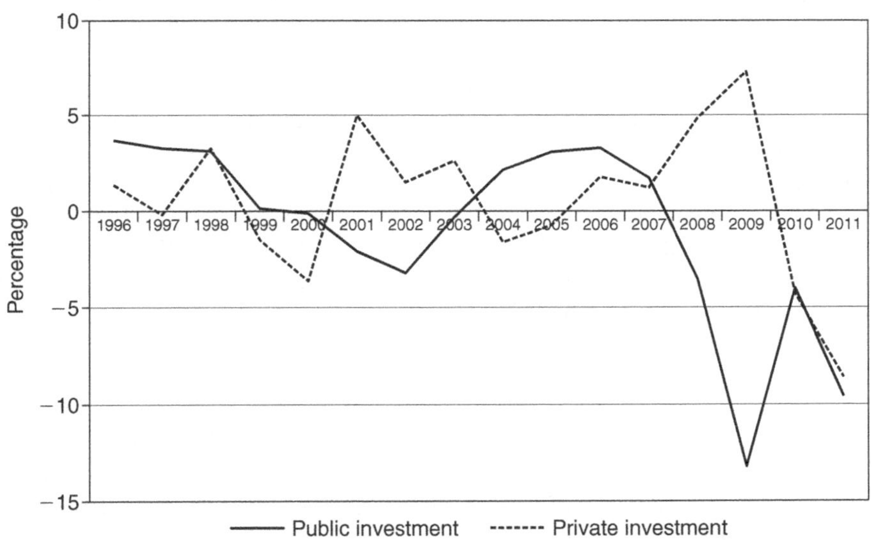

Figure 12.2 Annual changes (in %) of public and private investment in OECD countries (source: Vammalle and Hulbert, 2013, based on OECD National Accounts, 2012).

Political economy constraints often lie at the heart of coordination failures. First and above all information asymmetries may exist concerning infrastructure policy objectives of the center at subnational levels, but also the other way around. Second, disincentives may exist on lower levels of government to engage horizontally. This could be because resources from the center are allocated in a way that each jurisdiction seeks to obtain the highest share. Third, the objective of achieving scale efficiency may be dwarfed by subnational governments seeking political rents from the electorate of their jurisdiction only. Fourth, in a complex structure of multiple principal-agent relationships between the center and the subnational entities, accountability may often be blurred, which renders coordination challenging (e.g., as is the case when citizens do not know who is responsible for which task). Finally, from a center's perspective there may be several disincentives to make coordination work. The center may be reluctant to give away full control over resources and infrastructure policy planning, or may prefer giving it to subnational governments of their party affiliation, which can act as an impeding factor. In addition, the center may have an incentive to work with the most capable subnational governments only as coordination is easier to organize, but leaves other subnational governments subject to distorted incentives for intergovernmental coordination. To make effective coordination happen requires developing adequate incentives, politically and financially, to both share information and collaborate across levels of government for public infrastructure provision.

Experiences with mechanisms that facilitate a shared policy agenda and a coordinated approach to infrastructure investment reveal challenges across OECD countries. Past OECD work and a recently conducted OECD survey show that OECD countries have used a wide range of mechanisms to align incentives and policy agendas, sharing of information, and increasing accountability across levels of government. However, their functionality is seen by most actors as not fully effective.

Gaps in intergovernmental coordination can exist on a programmatic and on a project level. From a programming perspective, gaps in intergovernmental coordination can arise in aligning policy objectives across different tiers of the government, or in establishing joint financing mechanisms and budgeting attached to that. However, it can also arise in failing to ensure the right scale for infrastructure investments that often reaches beyond established administrative boundaries. This could result in gaps in horizontal coordination that should facilitate cross-jurisdictional collaboration (Table 12.1). In addition to potential gaps arising during the programming period, infrastructure coordination is of course also required for actual investment projects' implementation (Table 12.2). Here coordination gaps can arise practically during each step of the project management cycle from ex-ante appraisal to ex-post evaluation, but also in the regulatory framework governing this process.

This chapter will focus mainly on intergovernmental coordination with regard to infrastructure programming. While coordination mechanisms for actual project implementation (Table 12.2) are equally relevant, other contributions in

Table 12.1 Coordination gaps in intergovernmental relations on a *programmatic* level

Coordination gap	*Description → potential remedy*	
Overall planning and investment strategies	Exists when different rationales among national and subnational policy makers create obstacles for adopting convergent targets. Can lead to policy coherence problems and contradictory objectives across investment strategies. → Need for instruments to align objectives; need to align both appraisal as well as selection criteria for public investment programs.	**Information** Asymmetries of information (quantity, quality, type) to guide decision makers about the economic, environmental, social, and financial implications of investment; limited central knowledge of local assets and needs; limited local knowledge of central government programs; limited data; unclear or over-local perception of investment gap and service delivery problem to be addressed → Need for instruments for revealing and sharing information; need to address "optimism bias" of public investment.
Multi-sector relevant planning and policies	Results when line ministries do not align their policies (i) in a cross-sectoral fashion, or (ii) vertically, when they need to be territorially implemented → Need for mechanisms to create multi-dimensional/systemic approaches and to make these engagements credible through national political leadership and commitment.	

Funding	Unstable, no multi-annual or insufficient funding, or misaligned conditionalities attached to transfers undermining effective execution of responsibilities at subnational level or for shared competencies → Need effective incentives for partnership approach when establishing cross-governmental financing mechanisms, including conditionalities; determining the balance of co-finance with autonomous finance; allowing a forward looking perspective through multi-annual budgeting.
Administrative and public services	Occurs when the administrative boundaries for infrastructure decisions do not correspond to the socio-economic geographic area sharing the infrastructure and its externalities → Need for instruments to encourage collaboration between jurisdictions and assignment of responsibilities for reaching "effective size" (coordination tools among subnational units, reassignment of responsibilities at a higher level of government, potential mergers of administrations, etc.).
Capacity	Arises when there is limited human, knowledge or institutional resources available to carry out tasks → Need for instruments to build local capacity (top-down; or peer-to-peer); earmarking co-financing as a way to induce capacity while avoiding micro management, performance assessment.

Source: Adapted from Charbit and Michalun (2009); Charbit (2011).

Table 12.2 Coordination gaps in intergovernmental relations on a *project* level

Coordination gap	*Description → potential remedy*
Regulation: public-private	Reflects difficulties in clear selection and appraisal criteria to involve private sector in a determined investment project, in different stages of the project cycle → develop a "unified framework" for evaluation of public and private involvement; assess risk and possibility to cope with financial risk and contingent liabilities; introduce "independent review" to weed out poor projects early in the project cycle.
Responsibilities over the project cycle	Reflects difficulties in ensuring separate or sufficient accountability over specific steps in the project cycle (pre-appraisal, appraisal, procurement, monitoring of implementation; operation of facility, ex-post evaluation, among others), which can lead to transparency integrity challenges for policy makers involved in the management of investment → Need for institutional quality instruments; need for instruments to strengthen the integrity framework at the local level (focus on public procurement); need for continuity in subnational public administration; need for instruments to enhance citizens' involvement.
Capacity	Arises when there is limited human, knowledge, or institutional resources available to carry out tasks → Need for instruments to build local capacity (top-down; or peer-to-peer); earmarking co-financing as a way to induce capacity while avoiding micro management, performance assessment.

Source: Adapted from Charbit and Michalun (2009); Charbit (2011).

this volume focus on these aspects. The dividing line is not always perfect, as several of the coordination instruments used in practice have multiple functionalities, serving programming and project implementation periods, and are applied in diverse intergovernmental frameworks in different political contexts. It also bears noting that the recent emphasis of the development community on results and outcomes, which is adopted with quickening pace in the subnational and intergovernmental area, blurs many of the traditional divisions for tools related to planning, funding, and budgeting and underlines the powerful role of evaluation information in the design of investment policies.

The objective of this chapter is to explore the range of vertical and horizontal coordination mechanisms applied to intergovernmental coordination for public investment across OECD and selected non-OECD countries. The goal of this assessment is to discuss their achievements as well as persisting challenges. To this end, it attempts to relate existing mechanisms to the areas of potential gaps identified in Table 12.1, namely policy misalignments, failures to coordinate cross-sectorally, gaps in joint financing mechanisms, failure to achieve efficient scale, and gaps especially in subnational capacity. Two common complementary devices for improving horizontal and vertical interactions among different levels of government for infrastructure provision will be looked at, namely conditionality and contracts. This will be followed by a discussion of the political economy risks if actors choose to opt out of coordination. The final section will provide some conclusions about how coordination mechanisms need to be developed and tailored to specific contexts.

Evidence presented in the following part of the chapter is based on three main sources. The first one encompasses a national level OECD questionnaire[4] exploring the existing mechanisms and challenges as well as best practices with regard to coordination and subnational capacity of public investment in general, and infrastructure in particular. This is complemented by results from in-depth qualitative information from seven subnational/regional case studies carried out across OECD countries, and selected choosing a balance between EU and non-EU member countries, as well as economically strong and less strong regions across those countries.[5] Finally, other country examples will be selected from past OECD work that includes mostly OECD countries, but also some selected non-members (such as Brazil or Peru).

Vertical coordination mechanisms

Vertical alignment of infrastructure policy

Central and subnational governments are interdependent actors, who need to establish mechanisms for coordinating their shared tasks of overall and sectoral planning, funding, and administering infrastructure provision. Aligning policy and implementation across levels of government requires coordination during a number of steps, not just co-financing. It requires actors to align their policy objectives, which in turn requires exchanging information about regional realities and their respective policy preferences. If governments fail to coordinate this may result in a highly fragmented approach to infrastructure policy, potentially reinforcing inequalities and failing to make the most of available resources.

Central level actors acknowledge that they know very little about subnational needs and policy preferences, while their subnational counterparts would like to be better informed about central level policy priorities. The results presented in Figures 12.3 and 12.4 point to a significant information gap between the central and subnational levels of government in terms of policy agendas. Regional case studies provide a more differentiated interpretation of these results: in countries where subnational governments need to secure central government financial or implementation support for the investment project they would like to carry out (such as in Sweden or in Germany for financial support), for example, subnational authorities seem well aware of the need to keep informed about central policy makers' agendas. In other countries, such as Peru, an absence of a mutual understanding of policy preferences between central and subnational levels has led to infrastructure planning and priority setting to be conducted on a bottom-up basis, without considering national top-down criteria in, for example, budgeting and regional development planning procedures. This has resulted in significant fragmentation of policy and program practices across subnational levels (Guerra-Garcia and Frank, 2013).

To respond to those reciprocal needs, OECD countries have created different platforms that facilitate communication and the alignment of interests around common investment policy objectives. National bodies in charge of subnational

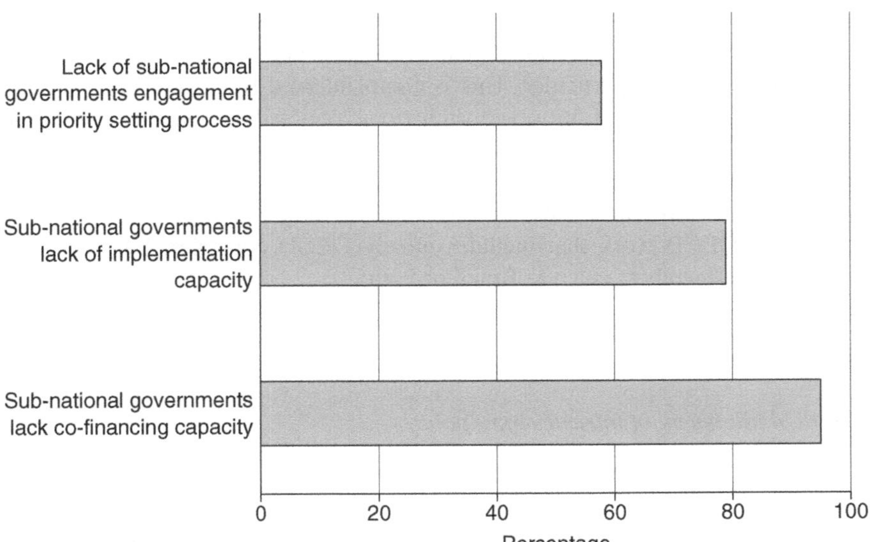

Figure 12.3 Vertical coordination challenges of public investment, as seen from the center (source: OECD national questionnaire, 2012).

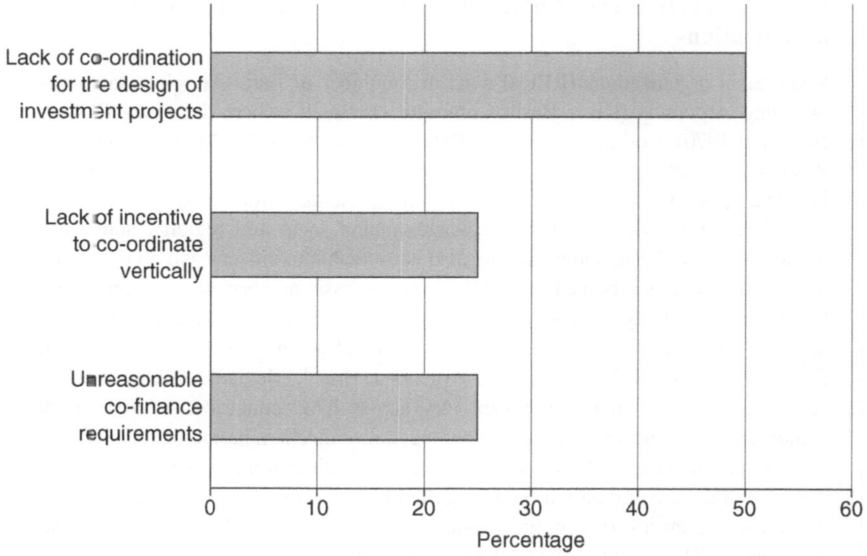

Figure 12.4 Vertical coordination challenges, as seen from the subnational level (source: OECD regional questionnaire, 2012).

coordination and fora in which subnational representatives gather are the most frequent types of platforms. Most federal countries have created such platforms to exchange information on policy objectives between the different levels of government. In Germany or Spain, for example, there are so-called "conferences," or in the German case also the "Joint Tasks," in specific sectors, like science or regional development, in which different levels of government regularly gather to determine policy priorities. Even though the German *Länder* still rely on approval and implementation of specific infrastructure projects by the federal government, through the existing platforms, they can better prepare and align their preferences with the federal government ones.

In a number of federal OECD countries platforms that facilitate the federal-state dialogue have long been established. In Canada the provinces, through their own platform, deliberate among themselves to determine investment priorities, while federal arms of the government are located in the provinces (e.g., the Regional Federal Councils or the Regional Development Agencies) to ensure the central government's priorities are represented, and to communicate the provinces' priorities to the federal authorities. The federal-state dialogue in Australia is organized through the Council of Australian Governments. In Italy, political dialogue is ensured through the State-Regions Conference, a permanent negotiation body. Another example are the vertical coordination bodies established in many Latin American countries to organize water policies across levels of government (see Box 12.1).

Box 12.1 Vertical coordination in Latin America's river basin organizations

River basin organizations (RBOs) exist in a number of Latin American countries, including Argentina (River Basin Committees), Brazil (where the first RBO was created in 1970), Costa Rica (where RBOs are regulated by the 2000 Law on Water Resources), Nicaragua (Regional Organizations for River Basins), and others in Panama, Mexico, and Peru. In most cases, the principal actors in RBOs are central government ministries and public agencies and/or local and regional authorities. Sometimes, river basin authorities are also accountable to citizens and NGOs. In the sample of countries surveyed in the OECD study, basin authorities are financed both by autonomous budgets (e.g., collection of water revenues) and grants from the central government, and in some cases, subnational governments also contribute to river basin authorities' funding (e.g., Argentina, Brazil, Mexico). RBOs' missions, constituencies, and financing modes vary across LAC countries. All river basin authorities have functions related to planning, data collection, harmonization of water polices, and monitoring. However, their role in the allocation of water uses, prevention of pollution, coordination, financing, and regulation is not systematic, and none of the LAC countries' river basin organizations (contrary to OECD ones) has regulatory powers. The maturity of river basin organizations also varies across LAC countries, especially in coordinating competing uses, which requires equitable approaches to resolving conflicts in the political and legal arenas. Argentina and Brazil are pioneers in setting up river basin agencies, while other LAC countries, such as Peru, have only recently adopted such arrangements areas.

Source: OECD (2012a).

Some of the more centralized countries have more informal platforms for consultation. In Norway, for example, the Ministry of Local Government and Regional Development gathers with all regional administrations and other relevant regional stakeholders to inform them about central policies for regional development and to discuss issues important to the regions. In Sweden, subnational administrations take central information platforms as opportunities to lobby for infrastructure investments at the center that will ultimately decide upon, finance, and implement them.

Cross-sectoral coordination

The effectiveness of intergovernmental policy coordination also depends on the extent to which infrastructure policy is coordinated and aligned across line ministries. Policy complementarities matter to mutually reinforce the impact of different sectoral actions on an infrastructure policy outcome in specific places. Despite this, even highly decentralized federal systems have been shown to work in a deeply sectorally entrenched way (OECD, 2011b). Entrenched sectoral approaches at the national level hamper the necessary coordination of infrastructure implementation at the subnational level. Central levels of governments need to commit resources to align policies and their implementation at the subnational level.

In many places, subnational governments have worked to make up for gaps in sectoral coordination at the central level. In Poland, for example, information on infrastructure investment decisions and their locations rests within various sectors and does not get communicated consistently to subnational governments which are aiming to execute their spatial planning role. Subnational actors need to engage in an effort to find and collect the information necessary, thereby collaborating with each of the sectoral ministries separately to draw up spatial plans at the subnational level. This process generates transaction costs and makes it harder to realize potential synergies among a wide range of infrastructure policies, such as transport, the environment, and housing, for example. In Spain bilateral agreements are made between regions and the center (*convenios de collaboración*) that cover much of their cooperation. The *convenios* (see also the section on contracts) tend to be sectoral and are distributed across the central ministries. To overcome potential entrenchments, the region of Galicia has developed a multi-annual strategic plan that brings together several regional-level sectoral plans, including those for road infrastructures, transport, water, and innovation, with the aim of avoiding conflicting objectives and improving outcomes. In Germany, *Land* Brandenburg has engaged in an effort to bundle the different sources of funding (such as from the Joint Task, EU funds, etc.) that make up the roughly 10 percent of its budget over which it has real spending discretion, as opposed to other resources that are pre-committed to centrally decided spending targets. This bundling of resources ensures maximum coherence between different policies at the state level. In addition, it has inter-ministerial working groups involving *Land* ministries. One challenge the *Land* faces at the moment is that the funding instruments of the Joint Task and the EU have different programming periods. This is contrasted by the central level approach to coordinating between the center and the *Länder* that remains very sectorally driven, with few cross-sectoral coordination mechanisms that are as firmly institutionalized as the vertical ones.

In the absence of national cross-sectoral coordination, however, regional efforts to realize policy complementarities can be undermined. Region Skåne in Sweden has both sectoral (e.g., transport, innovation) and cross-sectoral regional development strategies. They are the outcome of an important effort to define a regional development policy. However, it has had only limited impact, as the region lacks the resources to finance it and the plan is not tied to resource commitments from local or central sectoral budgets. As long as the regional strategy is not linked to a concrete implementation plan supported by financial commitments, it is unlikely to leverage the expected policy complementarities.

Horizontal coordination mechanisms

There are two main drivers that necessitate horizontal coordination across subnational jurisdictions. First, positive (and negative) spillover effects of infrastructure projects may challenge the traditional management of public investment within administrative boundaries, creating incentives for other jurisdictions to free-ride on infrastructure provided by others. This may eventually lead to an under-provision of infrastructure. Second, it may not always be effective to implement infrastructure projects along jurisdictional borders. Limited in size, jurisdictions could largely benefit from investing together with other jurisdictions in terms of economies of scale. A more function- instead of administrative boundary-oriented approach to decentralized infrastructure provision may also be useful to allow for local synergies in infrastructure policy making (Frey and Eichenberger, 1996, 1999; OECD, 2013b).

Significant engagement can be observed across countries to encourage horizontal coordination

The great majority of OECD countries have mechanisms in place to encourage coordination across subnational governments. Two-thirds of the countries responding to the OECD questionnaire report having mechanisms in place to encourage subnational coordination across jurisdictions, both at local and intermediate levels of government. Federal or quasi-federal countries all report to have such mechanisms in place. A recent survey in the water sector revealed that a majority of Latin American countries has also put in place horizontal coordination mechanisms, including Argentina, Costa Rica, Dominican Republic, Honduras, Nicaragua, and Panama (OECD, 2012a). In certain countries a collaborative culture has to be created, especially in those where forced mergers have not nourished such a culture at the onset. Strengthening such collaboration where it has historically been weak involves certain risks, as there may be a lack of or limited inter-institutional trust on the subnational level, stemming from a planning tradition oriented towards the center, such as is the case for Poland.

Coordination across medium tiers of government

The mechanisms employed to foster inter-jurisdictional coordination vary widely. They can range from the legal requirement to collaborate across states, such as enshrined in Mexico's planning law, to the creation of special purpose cross-border platforms like the Pacific Northwest Economic Region (incorporating both Canadian provinces and US states). In countries like Italy and Switzerland, collaboration between regions is financially incentivized. In Switzerland, one-third of subnational funding from the central government is reserved for inter-cantonal investment projects. In addition, some 800 inter-cantonal agreements have been created that focus on collaboration in specific fields, such as fishing, healthcare services, inter-cantonal roads, and police networks. The fiscal decentralization reform of 2008 further reinforced these agreements, allowing the central government to forbid cantons from opting out of specific agreements.

Coordination across local government tiers

Local horizontal coordination has been encouraged through "soft" mechanisms, like policy-exchange fora, as well as "harder" financial incentives. A number of countries (e.g., Canada, Sweden) have established fora to facilitate policy dialogue among municipalities. More formal mechanisms include the provision of financial preferences at the national level for joint subnational public investment proposals; Estonia, Spain, and Norway all use such measures. In Portugal, grants were provided under the National Strategic Reference Framework for the 2007–2013 European Union programming period to establish and implement territorial development plans among collaborating municipalities. In some countries, there have been efforts to reduce the need for such special arrangements by "scaling up" municipalities or regions, in an effort to strengthen their capacities and/or reduce fragmentation and administration costs. Denmark, for example, reduced the number of municipalities from 271 to 98 and the number of regions from 16 to 5 in a reform that took effect in 2007. Most other countries have preferred to encourage voluntary mergers, albeit with limited impact in most cases (e.g., Finland and others). Sweden has been trying to encourage a bottom-up consolidation of its 22 counties, but the outcome of this effort remains unclear (OECD, 2010). France is the OECD country with the greatest fragmentation at municipal level, but it has made extensive use of agreement mechanisms to foster cooperation among its 36,000 municipalities (Box 12.2).

Box 12.2 Using incentives to promote municipal cooperation: the case of France

France has more than 36,000 communes (the basic unit of local governance). Nevertheless, France has long resisted municipal mergers. Though many are too small to be fully efficient, municipalities are considered as an essential component of the French democracy. For more than two decades, the central government has been encouraging cooperation among municipalities, both to allow small rural communes to surpass minimal thresholds necessary to provide public services, and to allow urban areas, which are often fragmented into several municipalities, to be managed coherently. There are approximately 19,000 inter-communal structures aimed specifically at facilitating horizontal cooperation, and almost all municipalities are involved in them. There are three main types of supra-communal structures: communities of communes (groupings of small rural communes), "agglomeration" communities (groups of 50,000 inhabitants subject to a single business tax), and the urban communities (groupings of 500,000 inhabitants or more). Each grouping of communes constitutes a "public establishment for inter-communal cooperation" (EPCI). The EPCIs assume limited, specialized, and exclusive powers transferred to them by member communes. Unlike the communes themselves, the EPCI is not governed by elected officials, but by delegates of municipal councils. Although the EPCI are created by the communes directly, there are two notable roles for the central government. First, EPCIs must be approved by the state in order to exist legally. Second, to encourage municipalities to form an EPCI, the central government provides an "inter-communality grant" to those communes that accept a single business tax. This is to preclude competition on tax rates among participating municipalities. EPCIs draw on budgetary contributions from member communes (for the syndicates) and/or their own tax revenues (for the EPCIs).This inter-municipal level has become the key actor for big infrastructure investment or environment-related investments (such as for water infrastructure). Reforms are currently discussed for making this inter-municipal approach more effective and for developing new governance schemes for metropolitan areas.

Source: OECD (2006); Charbit and Vammalle (2010).

Demographic change has been an important driver for efforts to encourage scale efficiency at local level, particularly in low-density regions where population ageing and out-migration are making it increasingly difficult to sustain service provision. After a wave of top-down enforced municipal mergers to downsize local administrations following unification, Germany has had to respond to demographic change in the last years by trying to streamline public service provision at the local level. Demographic change has left some municipalities shrinking, with the per capita costs of infrastructure investment and service provision increasing. Therefore some *Länder*, such as Brandenburg, implemented a directive[6] on the financial support for voluntary municipal mergers, with the aim of increasing the efficiency and quality of service provision at the municipal level. In 2012, €10 million have been allocated to support municipal mergers, whereby €50,000 are offered for municipalities where some administrative functions are merged, and up to €500,000 for entire mergers of municipalities' administrations. Among the first ones to take up this initiative one finds cities and their adjacent municipalities.

Another incentive for horizontal collaboration may lie in strengthening subnational governments in their dealings with the central government. For example, Region Skåne in Sweden has had an incentive to cooperate with its much smaller neighbors across the larger South Sweden Region in pursuit of shared priorities. Their joint weight shapes the negotiations at national level. One such sector where this plays a role is transport infrastructure and specifically projects that increase the connectivity between southern Sweden and its capital. The extension of the railway lines to Stockholm is one recent example.

In Canada a culture of inter-jurisdictional collaboration has given rise to many forms of encouraging joint infrastructure management. In a more top-down fashion, the Province of British Columbia (BC) can create inter-municipal institutions, oblige municipalities to adhere to them, and review their mandates when it deems this necessary. BC has created a number of institutions in an effort to facilitate coordination between municipalities and reach efficient scale for service provision and public investment (regional districts, Trans Link, British Columbia Rail Company, etc.), as well as authorities that run specific public services for the municipalities. Once created, they are administered independently of the province, directed by a board that represents the relevant interests given their mandate (municipalities, regional districts, civil society, etc.). They are funded by specific taxes and fees and are not allowed to run budget deficits, but they may borrow for capital investment. By providing services to a pool of municipalities, they allow for economies of scale and lower prices. The Municipal Finance Authority (MFA) is one such example, financing most of regional districts' and municipalities' long-term debt, and encompassing all local governments in British Columbia except the City of Vancouver. Regarding public transportation, the province decided in 1999 to create Trans Link, an independent regional authority to which it gave the mandate of designing, building, financing, and managing the public transit system in the regional district of Vancouver.

Persistent challenges though exist

Horizontal collaboration nevertheless faces significant challenges. In Mexico, for example, states have autonomy in their designated fields of competence, which makes it difficult to coordinate agendas, priorities, and fiscal resources with other states. A number of governments point to a perceived lack of capacity for horizontal collaboration at subnational level (e.g., Sweden). In other cases, competition between subnational tiers of government for central level funding often undermines collaboration incentives (e.g., Germany and Switzerland). Supranational institutions (such as the EU) have not yet adapted all their structural/cohesion fund rules that would allow regions using obtained funds for cross-jurisdictional projects.

Inter-jurisdictional competition and regulatory impediments also complicate efforts to foster horizontal collaboration at local level in many places. In Estonia, for example, municipalities compete to obtain funding from higher levels of government. A lack of strategic planning capabilities at the local level may impede inter-municipal collaboration as well (e.g., Slovenia or Canada). Regulatory impediments may also arise. National legislation may raise the costs associated with organizing joint undertakings among municipalities (OECD, 2011c, 2012b).

Differences in size, wealth, and priorities can make it difficult for neighboring municipalities to reconcile investment decisions together, particularly where very large agglomerations are engaged with much smaller municipalities. Cooperation can also be difficult where there are significant differences in income levels between adjacent jurisdictions. Yet competitive pressures arise even in a partnership of equals. For example, in low-density places like Slovenia (OECD, 2011c) or southeastern Sweden, municipalities can readily see the scale economies to be realized by collaborating in fields like education and health care, but each may fear that its own long-term viability depends in part on ensuring that the key facilities (and related employment) are located within its jurisdiction.

Encompassing instruments to structure vertical or horizontal coordination: the case of conditionalities and intergovernmental contracts

Conditionality and intergovernmental contracts[7] *are encompassing, crosscutting mechanisms for coordination.* They can help actors across levels of government to address a number of existing coordination challenges simultaneously and can employ different coordination devices together. Conditionality can be used to address the lack of horizontal collaboration, for example, by making it a requirement in earmarked transfers for infrastructure investment. Mutually designed and agreed upon contracts across levels of government can improve the basis of information on common policy priorities, make objectives clear and transparent, as well as commit all levels to generate and use information on infrastructure performance outcomes. The two instruments can, of course, be employed as complements rather than substitutes: conditionality can be part of a contract design, and in fact, very often is. Contracts simply take the discussion a step further, creating credible partnership arrangements between levels of government that allow for mutual accountability as well as alignment of responsibilities and resources to generate a well-coordinated approach and joint commitment to infrastructure policy. A very powerful dimension of the contractual approach may lie in the fact that it includes information about the enforcement mechanism that guarantees the credibility of both parties' commitments (OECD, 2007).

Box 12.3 From program to project contracting – relational versus transactional contracts

The typology of contracts identified in earlier OECD work lends itself to distinguishing contracts according to their program or project nature (as identified in Table 12.1 above). "Transactional" contracting involves an ex-ante determination of the complete set of binding and enforceable rights and duties of the parties. This includes the coordination arrangements. The key challenge concerns the incentives needed to encourage the parties to make good on their obligations. The resulting contracts are contingent, complete (in theory, at least), often complemented by an incentive mechanism and ultimately enforced by third parties, such as the judiciary. By contrast, "relational" contracting involves parties committing to cooperate ex-post (after the signing of the agreement) and supervision of compliance with the agreement tends to be bilateral, relying on a cooperative spirit. In other words, their primary purpose is not to fix the parties into a complete set of binding and enforceable commitments but rather to serve as a mechanism for collective decision-making which generates trust and facilitates cooperation, information sharing, and capacity building. In practice, most contracts are characterized by both transactional and relational elements and fall somewhere on a continuum from being pure transactional to pure relational contracts.

Source: OECD (2007).

A partnership approach to conditionality is likely to reinforce its effectiveness

Nearly all OECD countries use some type of conditionality attached to central government transfers to ensure infrastructure provision across levels of government. Out of the 22 OECD countries responding to the questionnaire 17 report that intergovernmental transfers come with certain conditionalities defined by the central government and, in EU countries, they are often subject to requirements defined by the supra-national level—the European Commission. The most frequent conditions attached to central funding include matching (co-financing) and reporting requirements, as well as predetermined timeframes for spending investment funds. In most of the respondent countries, earmarking, environmental assessments, and additionality requirements are also frequently applied (Figure 12.5).

Conditionality can be an effective tool to align objectives across levels of government and strengthen mutual accountability, but in OECD countries a partnership approach is key to making them an effective instrument of coordination. Several countries report having found conditionality, including the timeframe of spending, earmarking, and matching requirements, as well as ex-ante assessments, effective tools for framing policies and strategic planning across levels of government. They find that conditionality has contributed to a better understanding of local conditions at the central level (e.g., Slovak Republic, Estonia, and Italy). In Estonia and Canada, conditionality has helped to enhance systematic assessments of likely and actual impacts of investments, thereby reducing the incidence of "bad" investments. In Norway and Italy, conditionality has successfully encouraged the concentration of resources, thereby making it easier to promote and anticipate crucial infrastructure investments. Even though only just over half of the respondent countries report that conditionality poses an additional administrative burden, it is not perceived as being very effective in increasing the quality of investment projects. This may point to the fact that conditionality is still largely applied as a control instrument, rather than an

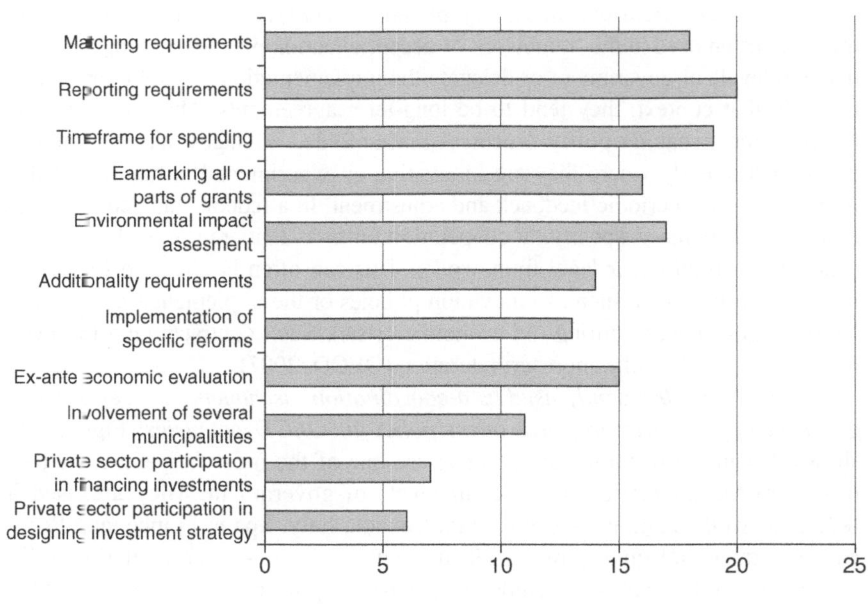

Figure 12.5 Types of conditionalities attached to public investment funds (source: OECD national questionnaire, 2012).

outcome-oriented tool that decreases inefficiencies that may arise in lengthy and unorganized coordination. Also, ill-defined, exhaustive top-down developed conditionality can render itself ineffective because there may not be sufficient ownership at the subnational levels to implement its prescriptions. Generally speaking, the effects of reputation attached to results seem to be more powerful tools than sanctions with regard to positively influencing subnational entities.

Intergovernmental contracts encourage processes and outcomes

Contracts are a more ambitious mechanism that allow for a tailor-made approach to arranging responsibilities across governments. They are distinguished by the fact that they are formal devices to enable governments across levels to arrange joint action or to delegate action, as independent entities, and to clarify the complexity of processes and responsibilities for subnational infrastructure investment. This can be useful not only because of the inherent interdependencies among levels of government involved in the design and execution of infrastructure projects, but also because the assignment of responsibilities among levels of government can be "imperfect." There may be overlaps leading to shared responsibilities, or policy domains not specifically assigned to any level of government, which all give rise to the need for cooperation and clarification of roles arises. Contractual arrangements present the advantage of avoiding a one-size-fits-all approach and leaving scope for adapting policies to specific subnational infrastructure needs and opportunities. They thereby help to address asymmetries of information and potential differences in capacity.

Contracts can be useful in unitary or federal contexts. In unitary states, contracts are often used in the framework of decentralization policies, to empower subnational levels of government or delegate the implementation of public investment tasks. In that context, they tend to be long-term agreements. These can be quite effective for managing policy processes that unfolded in stages over an extended period, particularly where they are innovative or experimental in nature and thus imply a need for periodic feedback and adjustment. In a federal state, contracts are more complementary, specifying cooperation on tasks that are not well defined by existing constitutions or legal frameworks. This can often be the case for new or intermittent measures, such as innovation policies or the implementation of stimulus packages (as seen during the economic crisis). Such contracts tend to have a narrow focus and be of a short-term duration (OECD, 2007).

Contracts are frequently used as a coordination instrument between levels of government for governing investment policy in OECD countries. Figure 12.6 shows that intergovernmental contracts are one of the most frequent tools used to govern the interaction of different levels of government. They are used in federal as well as unitary systems (e.g., Canada, Italy, Spain, France, and Portugal). Contracts are quite powerful instruments for cross-governmental coordination: they are frequently concluded by high-level political actors, and they often include both dedicated budgets to ensure implementation and clearly defined mechanisms to resolve any conflicts that arise (Box 12.4 and 12.5).

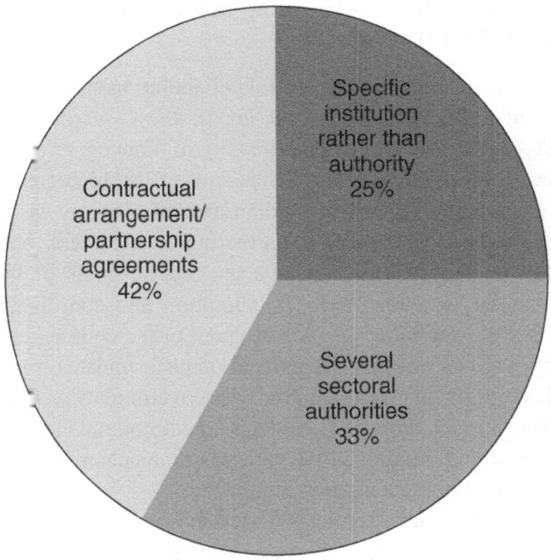

Figure 12.6 Mechanisms used for cross-governmental coordination (source: OECD national questionnaire, 2012).

Box 12.4 Intergovernmental contracts in Poland

The initial regional contracts in Poland served as a learning device preparing the regional authorities for the management of the EU Structural Funds in a multi-level setting The contracts created a stable and multi-annual framework for cross-level coordination, allowing regional authorities to complete long-term investment plans. Nonetheless, it has been argued that the contracts remained stuck in what was previously a centralized framework, rather than putting the regions at the center of regional development policy-making. Instead of introducing a coordinated, place-based approach, the contracts served as a tool for the local implementation of national programs, the need for which arose because fiscal decentralization did not match the regions' assigned responsibilities. This reinforced their financial dependence on the central government. The center's approach to managing EU Structural Funds further undermined the regions' role, making the regional contracts simply an instrument part of the EU funded programs instead of regional policy planning and coordination instruments. The National Regional Development Strategy for 2010–2020, which replaces the existing contracts, aims at introducing a more integrated and place-based approach to create synergies between all regional policy instruments having a territorial dimension across levels of government, especially by specifying the sources of funding for the strategy's envisioned interventions.

Source: Ferry (2003); OECD (2008); Regulski *et al.* (2012).

Box 12.5 The Vancouver Agreement—bringing actors across levels together through successful contracts

The Vancouver Agreement is an example for successful collaboration and coordination between the Government of Canada (federal level), the Government of British Columbia (province, intermediate tier), and the City of Vancouver (municipal level) to establish horizontal governance mechanisms to tackle economic, social, and health policy challenges in the metropolitan area of Vancouver. The agreement was characterized by an open, flexible partnering arrangement, based on equality of all partners that do not know ex-ante the precise goals of their cooperation, but wish to engage in a long-term collaboration and coordination process (a "relational contract"). Credibility and enforcement of the contract commitments was fostered by various means. Negotiated annual updates to the schedule of initiatives and commitments were required. All governments were directed to work within their own jurisdictions and mandates, and accountable to their electorate. In addition, political and administrative supervision mechanisms were established that supported contract implementation monitoring.

In an evaluation carried out ten years after the VA's establishment, participants were unanimously positive in their response, acknowledging that the prior existence of jurisdictional fragmentation was successfully addressed through the VA. The VA was found to have strengthened relationships, especially also with the local community and the private sector, achieved through a constant collaboration and coordination of resources to ensure effective and efficient investment. The generalizable conclusions from the VA experience seem to be twofold: first of all successful contracts need a clear description of the roles of each participating level of government. In addition, each participant needs to be accountable; therefore accountability mechanisms have to be equally designed at the contractual development stage.

Source: OECD (2007); Western Economic Diversification Canada (2010).

From existing intergovernmental contracts important lessons can be drawn out:

- First, contracts seem to be an effective instrument to introduce a coordinated approach to local, integrated development policies. They seem to succeed in bringing actors together to form a joint policy strategy.
- Second, however, the contracts remain largely unsuccessful in changing existing fragmented and compartmentalized structures, because the relevant competences that go along with the strategies often remain unchanged.
- Third, while contractual arrangements can be employed as a capacity-building device, they run the risk of creating "parallel" structures to existing administrative processes, which increase the administrative burden at the local and higher levels to engage in these new structures.

Therefore, it is crucial to make sure contractual arrangements are as much as possible aligned with existing ways of "doing business," and go along with a training for all levels of government in knowing how to implement the agreed arrangements.

The need for information to make coordination work

Information lies at the core of making coordination work. Information is essential to the alignment of objectives and assessment of projects, as well as mutual accountability and transparency. Information collected through monitoring and evaluating public investment also lies at the heart of efforts to increase the efficiency and effectiveness of subnational infrastructure provision.

Monitoring has become a standard for ensuring the success of an investment project; all national and regional governments answering the project questionnaire report that monitoring is carried out in one form or another. In their responses to the survey, the great majority of countries reported that some form of performance monitoring of public investment projects is conducted at central government level (Figure 12.7). This includes the use of performance indicators as well as the formulation of objectives defined in form of target values (OECD, 2009). Strikingly, the exceptions to this rule include both very decentralized federations, in which federal-level monitoring might transgress on the rights of the federal units, and highly centralized countries, in which the sums available to the regional level for regional development are typically very small (even if larger sums go to local governments, which are monitored).

Robust ex-post evaluations are picking up gradually as over half of the regions surveyed report that they conduct ex-post evaluations. Generally speaking, monitoring and evaluation will only become effective coordination tools if the information generated facilitates learning, and makes actors become accountable to their citizens as well as their partners in government. This means that results of evaluations have to be used for shaping future policies and inscribed in long-term partnerships where evaluation results should inform consecutive program phases (encouraging engagement for results through "repeated games" settings).

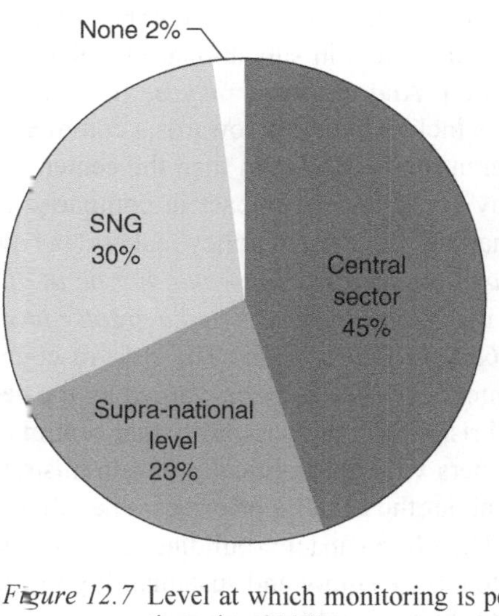

Figure 12.7 Level at which monitoring is performed (source: OECD national questionnaire, 2012).

The political economy risks of actors "opting out"

Coordination is not a self-fulfilling goal—it is as rational to refuse to coordinate as it is to collaborate vertically and horizontally. Coordination instruments such as conditionalities or contracts cannot per se guarantee the implementation of agreed decisions. Political or economic incentives may persist for actors to not comply or opt out of coordinating with other levels of government or jurisdictions at the same level. This may lead to administrative inefficiency, redundancy of infrastructure provision, and misalignment of development policies across levels of government. As a result a central government may be confronted with a highly fragmented territory in practice where it will eventually face difficulties in implementing country-wide policies.

A key political economy risk in intergovernmental coordination lies in the multiple principal-agent relationships that may lead to blurred accountability and disincentives to coordinate. If interpreted in a simplified way through principal-agent theory, subnational governments are subject to two principals—the central (or supra-national) governments and their electorate. On the one hand, it may bring higher political/electoral rewards for subnational governments to engage in infrastructure investments that serves their jurisdiction only than one in which such rewards are either fully or partly attributed to other subnational governments, even if the jurisdiction can share the utilization of the infrastructure. On the other hand, subnational governments are, to different extents, dependent on the central governments to provide them with grants and transfers as well as autonomy to implement their infrastructure priorities. If well designed, the central government can use this lever to increase incentives in a way that maximizes infrastructure efficiency and effectiveness.

The "principal-agent" relationship between central and subnational governments may be further undermined by political party affiliation. On the one hand central level governments may, as has been shown in a number of political economy works, exercise preferential treatment in subnational jurisdictions that share the government's party affiliation. And the same may be true for subnational governments. They may be less inclined to work towards a common infrastructure policy, if they have a different party affiliation than the center. On the other hand, the party belonging may be of limited impact in comparison with local re-elections perspectives for shaping subnational policy makers' behavior.

When it comes to vertical coordination, as a rule, it would not be at all surprising that the level of government with fewer resources had a greater incentive to understand the priorities of the better-resourced tier. The risk, of course, is that the subnational levels' development priorities may be warped by the need to align with central agendas. A related risk lies in the possibility that central actors will focus on those subnational partners who are politically or administratively more adept at responding to signals about the center's priorities—i.e., those who know best how to "play the game." Therefore capacity-building is needed across administrative places and localities to ensure equity and sustainability in vertical engagements of subnational tiers with their central governments.

Central governments therefore need to set the right incentives to overcome political economy challenges. In the above we have seen that central governments have successfully encouraged collaboration across subnational levels of government, when financial incentives were provided. Vertical coordination has worked in federal as well as unitary countries, when lower levels of government could gain necessary information on central level priorities, based on which they framed their local level preferences. Conditionalities per se may also not be effectively enforced, unless they were developed in an inclusive, top-down manner. Contracts can, and should have, built-in enforcement mechanisms, such as performance indicators. In addition, the reputational and capacity-building effects of such mechanisms may often be effective enforcement instruments, even more than pure sanction devices that are difficult to implement across levels of government and may incite narrow instead of "complete" engagement by implicated actors.

Lessons learned

Gaps in coordination have widely been recognized, however they still exist. This chapter has shown that, to different extents, in the majority of OECD and the selected subset of non-OECD countries recognizing the potential costs to failures in coordination has led to the introduction of several instruments to facilitate intergovernmental coordination. However, challenges are still widespread. Vertical coordination is hampered by asymmetric information. Gaps in information sharing, impeding the development of a shared policy vision, exist both from the center to the subnational levels of government and vice versa. Capacity issues, especially in terms of co-financing infrastructure investments, hamper subnational governments to carry out their assigned roles properly. Instead of encouraging horizontal coordination, central governments sometimes set incentives for subnational jurisdictions to compete with each other to obtain funding (such as in Germany). Multiple principal-agent relationships may undermine the incentives of lower levels of government to engage horizontally with other actors. Finally, encompassing instruments such as conditionality or intergovernmental contracts have proven their usefulness, but they have also shown to reinforce skewed incentives, if political economy risks (such as asymmetric information, externalities, and accountability) are not considered in their design.

Challenges to intergovernmental infrastructure coordination in OECD countries also exist in different nuances in developing countries. In OECD countries, central governments may face bigger challenges in overcoming very strong identities formed by traditional administrative boundaries at the subnational level that may pose significant obstacles in making horizontal coordination work. In more developing country contexts, the risk of capture may loom larger, and the central government may develop a tendency to collaborate vertically more with the actors that are already comparatively stronger than others. A more in-depth investigation into a subset of developing countries in the future could greatly enrich the debate on global challenges with intergovernmental coordination.

The need for intergovernmental coordination has reinforced the importance of accountability. Actors engaged in horizontal or vertical collaboration with different levels of government may have to engage in an ever greater effort to ensure accountability towards their own electorate, while at the same time the higher governmental tier. Subnational governments may find themselves in often contradictory incentive mechanisms, where important trade-offs have to be made. Central governments have an important responsibility to ensure that subnational governments are subject to the right incentives, and can be accountable for their engagement in intergovernmental coordination of infrastructure policy.

No matter how well designed coordination mechanisms are, they remain ineffective if they are not enforceable. There are a number of instruments central governments can use to enforce intergovernmental coordination for infrastructure investments. Financial incentives have proven effective when it comes to encouraging horizontal collaboration. A center-focused decision making of infrastructure investments has made subnational actors adapt their policy options, aligning them more with the center. Conditionality and contracts can be effective instruments for defining potential punishments if actors do not comply to previously agreed upon collaboration. It can be observed, however, that the instruments are undermined if subnational actors are not integrated in the development and negotiation of the framing conditions.

To make coordination happen and to make it work effectively requires collecting and sharing information. The essence of making coordination work lies in the collection and availability of information; hence any coordination mechanism implemented has to be coupled to a strategy for information collection and sharing, including with civil society.

Notes

1 The opinions expressed and arguments employed herein do not necessarily reflect the official views of the OECD or of the governments of its member countries. This chapter is based on OECD (2013a). This chapter was drafted in 2013. Since then, to promote good practices in the area of multi-level governance of public investment, the OECD has developed a Recommendation on Effective public investment across levels of government, adopted by the OECD Council in March 2014 as an official instrument (OECD, 2014).

2 Public investment is generally understood as the public expenditure that serves to accumulate physical capital (such as roads, government buildings, etc.) and human capital (capital expenditures linked to education, innovation, and research and development). Exact definitions vary greatly by country.

3 Subnational here and in the remainder of this chapter refers to both the intermediate and the local tiers of government.

4 The questionnaire was carried out as part of a wider project on systematically assessing coordination and subnational capacity challenges across OECD countries. See project website: www.oecd.org/regional/effectivenessofpublicinvestmentatsubnationallevelintimesoffiscalconstraints.htm.

5 Case studies were carried out in Basilicata (Italy), Brandenburg (Germany), British Columbia (Canada), Galicia (Spain), Skane (Sweden), Victoria (Australia), Wielkopolskie (Poland). Reports of each of the case studies can be found at: www.oecd.org/regional/effectivenessofpublicinvestmentatsubnationallevelintimesoffiscalconstraints.htm.

6 See website link for the directive's content: www.mi.brandenburg.de/cms/detail.php/bb1.c.253080.de.

7 A contract is a set of mutual promises by which the parties commit themselves either to take actions or to follow the prescription of a decision mechanism that has been mutually agreed upon. In the latter case, the contract is an agreement by which decision-making rights are transferred among parties. In the case of contracts among levels of government, contracts allow the reorganization of the rights and duties of governments other than by changes to the constitution (OECD, 2007).

References

Allain-Dupré, D. (2011). "Multi-level Governance of Public Investment: Lessons from the Crisis," *OECD Regional Development Working Papers*, 2011/05, OECD Publishing, Paris. http://dx.doi.org/10.1787/5kg87n3bp6jb-en.

Blöchliger, H.J. and C. Vammalle (2009). "Intergovernmental Grants in OECD Countries: Trends and Some Policy Issues." In: Junghun Kim, Jørgen Lotz, and Niels Jørgen Mau (eds.), *General Grants versus Earmarked Grants: Theory and Practice*. Korea Institute of Public Finance and the Danish Ministry of Interior and Health, Seoul and Copenhagen.

Charbit, C. (2011). "Governance of Public Policies in Decentralised Contexts: The Multi-level Approach," *OECD Regional Development Working Papers*, 2011/04, OECD Publishing, Paris. http:/dx.doi.org/10.1787/kg883pkxkhc-en.

Charbit, C. and M. Michalun (2009). "Mind the Gaps: Managing Mutual Dependence in Relations among Levels of Government," *OECD Working Papers on Public Governance*, No. 14, OECD Publishing, Paris. doi: 10.1787/221253707200.

Charbit, C. and C. Vammalle (2010), "Modernising Government." In: OECD, *Making Reform Happen: Lessons for the Future*, OECD Publishing, Paris.

Ferry, M. (2003). "The EU and Recent Regional Reform in Poland," *Europe–Asia Studies*, 55: 1097–1116.

Frey, B.S. and R. Eichenberger (1996). "FOCJ: Competitive Governments for Europe," *International Review of Law and Economics*, 16(3): 315–327.

Frey, B.S. and R. Eichenberger (1999). *The New Democratic Federalism for Europe—Functional, Overlapping and Competing Jurisdictions.* Edward Elgar, Cheltenham, UK.

Guerra-Garcia, G. and J. Frank (2013). "Public Investment in Peru." World Bank, *Investing to Invest.*

Mizell, L. and D. Allain-Dupré (2013). "Creating Conditions for Effective Public Investment: Sub-National Capacities in a Multi-Level Governance Context," *OECD Regional Development Working Papers*, No. 2013/04, OECD Publishing, Paris. doi: 10.1787/5k49j2cjv5mq-en.

OECD (2006). *OECD Territorial Reviews: France 2006*, OECD Publishing, Paris. doi: 10.1787/9789264022669-en.

OECD (2007). *Linking Regions and Central Governments: Contracts for Regional Development*, OECD Publishing, Paris. doi: 10.1787/9789264008755-en.

OECD (2008). *OECD Territorial Reviews: Poland, 2008*, OECD Publishing, Paris. doi: 10.1787/9789264049529-en.

OECD (2009). *Governing Regional Development Policy: The Use of Performance Indicators*, OECD Publishing, Paris. doi: 10.1787/9789264056299-en.

OECD (2010). *OECD Territorial Reviews: Sweden 2010*, OECD Publishing, Paris. 10.1787/9789264081888-en.

OECD (2011a). *Making the Most of Public Investment in a Tight Fiscal Environment: Multilevel Governance Lessons from the Crisis*, OECD Publishing, Paris. http://dx.doi.org/10.1787/9789264114470-en.

OECD (2011b). *OECD Regional Outlook 2011: Building Resilient Regions for Stronger Economies*, OECD Publishing, Paris. doi: 10.1787/9789264120983-en.

OECD (2011c). *OECD Territorial Reviews: Slovenia 2011*, OECD Publishing, Paris. doi: 10.1787/9789264120587-en.

OECD (2012a). *Water Governance in Latin America and the Caribbean: A Multi-level Approach*, OECD Studies on Water, OECD Publishing, Paris. http://dx.doi.org/10.1787/9789264174542-en.

OECD (2012b). *OECD Territorial Reviews: Småland-Blekinge (Sweden)*, OECD Publishing, Paris. doi: 10.1787/9789264169517-en.

OECD (2013a). *Investing Together: Working Effectively Across Levels of Government.* OECD Publishing, Paris. doi: 10.1787/9789264197022-en.

OECD (2013b). *Rural-Urban Partnership: An Integrated Approach to Economic Development.* OECD Publishing, Paris. doi: 10.1787/9789264204812-en.

OECD (2013c). *Subnational Governments in OECD Countries: Key Data.* OECD Publishing, Paris.

OECD (2014). *Recommendation of the Council on Effective Public Investment across Levels of Government*, March 12, 2014 – C(2014)32- C/M(2014)3/REV1.

Regulski, A., J. Zawistowski, and A. Żurawski (2012). *Kontrakty terytorialne jako instrument polityki rozwoju. Optymalizacja kontraktów terytorialnych w kontekście wdrażania Krajowej Strategii Rozwoju Regionalnego 2010–2020.* Instytut Badań Strukturalnych, Warsaw.

Vammalle, C. and C. Hulbert (2013). "Sub-National Finances and Fiscal Consolidation: Walking on Thin Ice," *OECD Regional Development Working Papers*, No. 2013/02, OECD Publishing, Paris. doi: 10.1787/5k49m8cqkcf3-en.

Western Economic Diversification Canada (2010). *Evaluation of the Vancouver Agreement*, Audit & Evaluation Branch, May.

Part V

The political economy and corruption challenges

13 The political economy of local infrastructure planning

Leonardo Romeo and Paul Smoke

Introduction

Developing countries often have complex, multi-level infrastructure planning systems that not uncommonly underperform relative to needs and expectations.[1] These systems have undergone numerous transformations as development thinking and practice have evolved. Many countries, however, continue to face great challenges in making local infrastructure planning and delivery more effective. Political economy forces are a critical factor in how local infrastructure planning systems have developed and perform.

Planning, both in general with respect to infrastructure, covers a vast landscape. It can involve multiple levels of government and administration, from central to grassroots, and relationships among levels can be complex and poorly defined in law and/or in practice. Sub-tiers within levels may play a role in infrastructure. At each level, there is an array of interested and/or influential actors—elected bodies, government bureaucrats, and diverse nongovernmental entities ranging from business to civil society groups. In aid dependent countries, international agencies can play a major role, and particularly in large urban areas, private sector firms may be engaged as infrastructure service delivery partners. Each actor faces incentives that may support or undermine infrastructure delivery.

Infrastructure itself is diverse because of variations in its inherent characteristics, such as the extent to which it is "public" in nature, the scale at which it must be provided, and the types of skills required to deliver it, among others. Land and natural resources, often subject to complex legal frameworks and contested control and use, are involved in creating and operating infrastructure, adding further complexity. The various levels, actors, and characteristics of infrastructure shape the political economy environment in which it must be delivered.

Some challenges of infrastructure planning have been at least partly created or exacerbated by the pursuit of the very reforms intended to improve public sector performance in developing countries. Decentralization, which has been an influential trend for more than two decades, typically augments existing local infrastructure responsibilities and introduces important new actors, processes, funding sources, and accountability channels into development planning. Existing actors, however, do not simply disappear, and political economy dynamics set in motion by decentralization can affect how local planning and the overall intergovernmental reforms in general perform.

Beyond decentralization, reforms in service delivery and financing mechanisms pursued through sectoral line ministries, finance ministries, and community driven development initiatives can further affect the development planning landscape. Such reforms may be undertaken in response to perceived threats from or independently of decentralization. Whichever the case, gaps and redundancies in service responsibilities and conflicts over power and resources can easily arise as the multiple—typically uncoordinated—reform processes unfold. These in turn can have consequential effects on the delivery of infrastructure and citizen confidence in and satisfaction with government.

Other evolving dynamics can significantly affect local infrastructure planning. The demand for more and better infrastructure increases with greater economic development, higher citizen awareness/expectations, and the influence of external trends and global agreements (e.g., the Millennium Development Goals). The 2008 global financial crisis affected resource availability for infrastructure and placed subnational governments in many countries under pressure to replace funds they could no longer get from national budgets.[2] Spatial factors may also evolve in consequential ways. Commercial and residential developments in legally separate jurisdictions, for example, may grow physically closer over time, making administratively independent jurisdictions more interdependent and potentially complicating infrastructure planning.

Finally, local political dynamics can be very important. These are related to interactions among different types of subnational institutions (e.g., cooperation or lack thereof among neighboring jurisdictions in providing network infrastructure) and relationships between local governments and their constituents (e.g., the degree of political competition, the extent of elite capture and patronage, and the nature of citizen interactions with locally elected officials). These dynamics can affect the success of decentralized planning systems in using securable resources for the right infrastructure in the right places.

Given the vast scope of local infrastructure planning systems, approaches, and influences, this chapter is selective in coverage. A broad overview of the political economy landscape of infrastructure planning is provided in the first few sections, but the core of the chapter focuses on the development of planning systems under decentralization, particularly in least developed countries. The next section briefly summarizes the evolution of thinking about development planning with a focus on the role of decentralization reforms that have emerged under varying political economy conditions. The third section provides a brief overview of infrastructure planning related roles played by key actors, and the fourth section reviews how a range of public sector reforms beyond decentralization—with their own political economy dynamics—affect local infrastructure planning. The fifth section summarizes a country case that illustrates common challenges to local infrastructure planning and their political economy underpinnings. The sixth and seventh sections provide a more detailed treatment of local infrastructure planning with a focus on least developed countries, respectively outlining relationships between decentralization and planning systems and considering the role of planning systems in infrastructure development. Finally, the last section provides some concluding comments.

The basic structure and changing context of planning systems

Public sector development planning systems for infrastructure and beyond have historically been structured in diverse ways.[3] In the post-World War II era of industrialized country support for developing countries, planning systems were based on a development model predicated on a large government role in the economy, and infrastructure planning was built around macroeconomic development needs. Such planning was centralized and technocratic, although interactions among government levels allowed modest local input. Traditional urban spatial and land use planning was often conducted separately, sometimes through dedicated subnational systems and sometimes through central agencies. This general approach persisted in the era of rolling back the state that began in the 1980s, although there was more emphasis on public-private partnerships to deliver roads, water, and other major infrastructure.

Planning systems

Local planning—in the sense that it focused on local infrastructure and involved local actors—was, of course, occurring even in the era of heavy centralization. National governments set up ministries, subnational administrations, and various bodies at one or more levels to play some role in planning. Local infrastructure could be provided for in national, sectoral, or subnational plans, and various mechanisms bridged certain aspects of one or more types of plan and involved different combinations of actors (Table 13.1).

A range of planning relationships existed, but in relatively centralized systems there was usually some hierarchical orientation, such that any one actor needed approval from a higher level. A wide variety of mechanisms, some in the national budget and some off budget, were used to finance infrastructure. The planning process could be top-down (lower levels awaited plans or instructions for preparing local plans from the center), bottom-up (central plans and budgets for local services were not prepared until requests from lower levels had been passed up and reviewed), or something in between. The locus of accountability and control of resources, however, was dominantly upward.

In some countries with local government traditions, semi-autonomous local planning could exist in parallel with the main planning system. Local governments might produce—sometimes independently from the national multi-level planning system—urban or rural development plans, which commonly focused on infrastructure. These typically had dedicated but insufficient funding sources—transfers or project funding mechanisms—attached to them. Separate legal status and more independence in infrastructure planning and finance were

Table 13.1 Relationships in multi-level planning

	National planning	*Sectoral planning*	*Regional planning*	*Local planning*
National level	National plans	Inter-sectoral plans	Inter-regional plans	(May be local inputs to national level planning)
Sectoral level	Inter-sectoral plans	Sectoral plans	Regional sectoral plans	(Sub-regional, multi-sectoral, area-based plans, among others)
Regional level	Inter-regional plans	Regional sectoral plans	Regional plans	
Local level	(May be national directives for local level planning)	Sub-regional, multi-sectoral, area-based plans, among others)		Local (municipal, village, etc.) plans

more likely in metropolitan and larger urban areas, although would still typically be subject to a national legal, administrative, and financial framework.[4] These bodies may or may not be linked to elected councils, and there may or may not have been interjurisdictional planning or coordination in metropolitan areas.

The emergence of decentralization

As institutional and governance concerns became prominent and global political and economic conditions evolved, a wave of public sector restructuring, democratization, and civic engagement reforms took center stage. This included a growing decentralization trend.[5] As decentralization became more common in developing countries, an appropriate role for subnational governments in infrastructure had to be considered. The approach has varied considerably across countries due to differences in political and economic factors driving reform, variations in the relative priority of decentralization, and diversity in the institutional structures and systems operating when decentralization was initiated.[6]

With respect to initial goals, it is well established that countries decentralize for various essentially political reasons.[7] In some cases, transition from a military/authoritarian regime to a more democratic society, as in Argentina and Brazil, included moves to decentralize. At the same time, some weakly democratic countries, such as Cambodia, decentralized modestly to reinforce the power of a dominant ruling party. A number of post-conflict, post-crisis, or fragile nations, such as South Africa and Uganda, pursued decentralization to build political credibility and national identity. In some crisis cases, such as Ethiopia and Indonesia, the main objective was to offset perceived subnational pressures for state disintegration. The forces driving reform create incentives for system design and implementation, including planning, in varying ways and at different paces.

Whatever the dominant political motive(s) for decentralization, complete restructuring of subnational institutions is uncommon. Existing jurisdictions rarely disappear, although political forces may allow asymmetric empowerment (deconcentration versus devolution). Even with genuinely transformative reform ambitions, the challenges of what happens to standing systems and processes can be daunting. Agencies that lose power from a stronger subnational government role in infrastructure, for example, are likely to resist scaling back or eliminating deconcentrated planning systems. Thus, the original (more centralized) planning systems may continue to operate to various degrees in ways that are inconsistent with their role under decentralization. Moreover, sectoral ministries may adopt dedicated planning and financing mechanisms for specific services, sometimes in direct response to decentralization, further complicating coherent planning.

The implications of decentralization for city planning have also varied considerably. In general, urban jurisdictions, at least larger metropolitan areas, are granted more freedom and resources, and there have been efforts to promote urban development by improving local infrastructure planning in broader context.[8] Steps to increase discretion and access to finance (e.g., through municipal development banks and facilitation of access to credit markets) are often accompanied by accountability and fiscal responsibility reforms. Urban local authorities, however, remain subject to varying degrees of oversight and control by national agencies, some of which can be onerous and counteract the forces that decentralization is supposed to unleash.

In addition to formal public sector planning systems, there has also been a strong trend to develop community-based planning for small-scale infrastructure in many developing countries. Initially these were mostly created as parallel systems that bypassed local governments, often where decentralization had not yet been adopted or was weak or where crisis situations created a need to get resources to impacted communities quickly. In some countries these community mechanisms have been more integrated with local government systems as decentralization reforms evolved, but in other cases they continue to function as separate systems that plan local infrastructure independently.[9]

A core practical challenge for infrastructure planning in developing countries has been that institutional reforms have encountered and generated political and bureaucratic incentives that allow formal adoption of new systems but hinder their implementation and fail to motivate adequate modification of existing structures. In addition, planning reforms have tended to be technical, commonly placing more emphasis on creating formal systems than on developing the means, incentives, and capacity for the political connection to constituents that is considered essential for successful decentralization.

Overview of actors, institutions, and planning roles under decentralization

A wide range of central actors has a role in designing and implementing the legal and/or constitutional parameters of decentralization[10] that are relevant for infrastructure. National legislatures can face incentives to promote or inhibit decentralization, and how this plays out can depend on the degree of political competition. Various government agencies may have different opinions regarding how far decentralization should go and what their roles should be relative to local actors. In some cases, central agencies may face incentives to overtly or covertly obstruct decentralization of major functions, including infrastructure planning, when this undermines their powers and control over the often-substantial resources at stake. These agencies may also directly compete for control of infrastructure provision, and they may pursue policies that are consequentially inconsistent with the formal intergovernmental framework.

A first step in understanding these bureaucratic incentives is to determine which actors are involved in the process and what role(s) they play, formally and informally. Whether local planning systems are independent or integrated, they invariably face national guidelines and/or oversight. Most countries have an agency dedicated to developing and supporting local government/administration, such as a Ministry of Local Government, Home Affairs, or Interior. Other agencies manage overall national processes, such as a Ministry of Finance, Planning, or Public Service. Given the overarching nature of their functions, they usually have some control over agencies at all levels (except local governments in federal systems), and they have tendencies towards standardization and control. The framework and oversight are sometimes managed by the planning ministry and sometimes by the local government ministry. In cases where more than one system exists, deconcentrated planning may be managed under the former and local government (devolved) planning under the latter.

Sectoral ministries also have important responsibilities for infrastructure—roads, water, etc. Separate sectoral bodies that cross multiple jurisdictions, such as a roads or water authority, may also be created. In some countries, portions of the infrastructure portfolios may be coordinated under national agencies with specific mandates, such as a Ministry of Regional, Rural, or Urban Development, or regional development bodies. Sectoral and territorial agencies are typically oriented towards service delivery, so they are more concerned about technical inputs and outcomes than about building local institutions and governance, There are, of course, cases in which central ministries promote decentralization and local capacity building.

Although the loss of central agency power and inter-agency competition to play prominent roles provide strong incentives for overtly or covertly obstructive behavior or careful institutional positioning, less obvious dynamics can also be at work. Especially in least developed countries with weak institutions, informal mechanisms for raising and allocating resources may dominate formal systems. These mechanisms are often clientelistic or patrimonial in nature, and it is difficult for reformers to change long-established rules of behavior.[11] This is particularly prevalent in certain environments, e.g., if transparency is limited, if informal rules are derivative of or validated by traditional norms or cultural allegiances, or if low civil service salaries create incentives for staff to extract resources by whatever means feasible. Even where it is possible to pursue reform under such circumstances, it is likely to take a long time.

Subnational politics and institutional arrangements

Beyond the behavior of the central government, local institutions and relationships matter. The most obvious concern is the extent to which elected councils represent their constituents versus get captured by local elites or higher-level politics. Bureaucratic dynamics can also matter, for example where decentralization involved assignment of former central employees to new local governments. In such cases, these employees may continue to look to national ministries for direction on infrastructure planning rather than to locally elected councils to which they now formally report. National standards and some upward accountability remain justifiable and important even in decentralized systems, but downward and horizontal accountability must also be developed and respected for decentralized planning to create appropriate incentives and realize its intended benefits.[12]

Some types of devolved or delegated infrastructure services may be more efficiently delivered across multiple local jurisdictions, so provisions for inter-jurisdictional cooperation, such as special districts for specific services or metropolitan planning commissions that include several contiguous autonomous jurisdictions, can be essential. Such mechanisms may be mandatory (imposed by the central government) or voluntary (formed at the discretion of the jurisdictions involved). In either case, political dynamics and embedded incentives affect how the mechanism will operate and perform. For example, the imposition of a special district may be resisted, and where cooperation is voluntary there are often issues with how the agreement will be governed by the multiple jurisdictions (with separately elected councils and separately appointed staff) involved, and this will have consequences for how it performs in delivering infrastructure.

A few examples can help to illustrate the diversity and importance of metropolitan governance arrangements (Table 13.2).[13] One model is unified metropolitan administration, as is practiced in Cape Town, a metropolitan municipality composed of several formerly distinct local governments. Cape Town prepares, as per national requirements, an Integrated Development Plan that is partly financed with resources from the central government and partly with city resources.[14] The Cape Town Partnership (CTP), an independent non-profit organization linked to the city's development planning, has been influential in pushing infrastructure development to promote private investment. The CTP Board of Directors includes private and public sector. Some critics charge that the CTP and the city in general focus on the central business district and do not sufficiently take into account other parts of the city, but the integrated political structure and administration of the city and the broad involvement of key stakeholders seem to lead to a more effective planning process than occurs in many other metropolitan areas.

In the Philippines, the central government created the Metropolitan Manila Development Authority (MMDA) to coordinate metropolitan planning and service delivery among the 16 cities and one municipality located in the greater Manila metropolitan region. The MMDA is not considered very effective—there is a

Table 13.2 Metropolitan planning

Model	*Planning coordination*	*Example*
Single multi-purpose, area-wide jurisdiction	Jurisdiction has extensive authority; also works with other entities/levels	Cape Town Metropolitan Municipality
Several multi-purpose jurisdictions of one or more type in metropolitan areas	• May or may not be formal/strong • May be voluntary or mandatory • May be locally or centrally driven • May have considerable fiscal resources or depend on the center • May or may not be incentives to work together	Metropolitan Manila Development Authority (16 cities and one municipality); centrally created/ financed
Single multi-purpose jurisdiction and one or more special purpose jurisdictions in metropolitan area		Nairobi (City Council & service authorities); Ministry of Nairobi Metropolitan Development extended beyond City Council until abolished
Multi-purpose government jurisdictions and special development jurisdictions in metropolitan area		Cairo (five governorates and eight "new cities"); separate governance structures and limited cooperation

metropolitan plan, but each city tends to focus on its own needs. Part of the problem is that MMDA is widely seen as a national agency with roots in the authoritarian Marcos era. Another major problem is the financial dependence of MMDA on the center. Resources are limited and institutional arrangements create few incentives or accountability mechanisms to induce individual city mayors to work beyond their own constituencies for the larger metropolitan good.[15]

Nairobi has long been government by an elected city council that plans for the territory under its jurisdiction. Over the years, a number of special service authorities have also been set up. In 2008 the central government created the Ministry of Nairobi Metropolitan Development (see below), which was intended to coordinate across all local authorities (including the city council) in the greater metropolitan area. This Ministry, however, was abolished after the 2010 constitution.

A very different situation prevails in the greater Cairo region, which incorporates five contiguous governorates (intermediate tier of Egyptian administration) and eight new cities.[16] Governorates are part of a highly centralized system and have limited authority unless the governor is politically powerful. New cities were created to attract people from the Nile Delta to Cairo and have no formal relationship with local administration. They are overseen by the Ministry of Housing, Utilities, and Urban Development (MHUUD). Governorates have limited authority and face fragmented planning and budgeting behavior of central agencies. Prior to the 2011 revolution, governors and new city managers in the Cairo region began an effort to create a strategic plan for greater Cairo with support from the MHUUD and donors. What will happen in the evolving environment remains to be seen, but the lack of a comprehensive plan for the Cairo region and poor incentives for coordination among component entities creates great challenges for infrastructure planning and invites political maneuvering.

These cases illustrate great variation in how metropolitan planning is managed. The degree of institutional fragmentation, the role of higher level mandates in specific political environments, the incentives for politicians in separate jurisdictions to work together (whether from national policies or organic political forces), the existence and nature of alternative institutions or mechanisms for managing area-wide functions, and the role of multi-stakeholder partnerships of interested parties, among others, are all important factors. These arise from specific political economy incentives and can create further dynamics that can support or undermine coordinated infrastructure planning.

External actors

The role of international development agencies can obviously be important in the developing world, particularly in aid dependent countries. On the one hand, these agencies play a vital role. At the same time, they may behave in competitive and uncoordinated ways that reinforce problematic incentives and behaviors of government institutions. One agency, for example, may support devolved infrastructure planning through a Ministry of Planning or Ministry of Local Government, while others promote more centralized infrastructure planning through individual sectoral ministries (see below). Such inconsistencies must ultimately be recognized and dealt with if a coherent and effective infrastructure planning system is to be developed and institutionalized.

Broader public sector and governance reforms and their impact on local planning

As already suggested, other major public sector reforms, such as public financial management, civil service, service delivery, and community driven development, are also highly relevant for decentralization. The way these reforms are designed and unfold can have a major impact on the performance of local infrastructure planning.[17] The basic problem stems from the competitive relationships among national agencies involved in public sector operations that have incentives to protect their own divergent interests, as outlined in various ways above. These agencies are often poorly coordinated, and they are thus relatively free to pursue reforms that are inconsistent with each other. The situation is exacerbated by the power imbalances among them, and it is reinforced by international development agencies that too often competitively approach the programming of their support for public sector and governance reforms.

Friction is common, for example, between the Ministry of Local Government (MoLG) or its equivalent and the Ministry of Finance (MoF). The former commonly (if not always) seeks to expand the role of local governments and enhance its own relationship to them, while the latter is often reluctant to relinquish fiscal powers to local governments or oversight of them to MoLG. In some cases, conflicts stem from MoLG reforms that fail to meet sound Public Financial Management (PFM) principles that the MoF has a legitimate interest in enforcing for all public entities. It is, however, often a result of MoF desire to excessively control local government fiscal behavior. Since the MoLG or equivalent is typically weaker than the MoF (because of stronger political connections and the power inherent in wielding legal control over the national budget), the latter often has the upper hand.

The consequences of such a situation can be considerable. If MoF wishes, for example, to adopt PFM reforms that limit local government access to autonomously programmable development resources, then local infrastructure planning can be greatly weakened. Similar dynamics may emerge with other broad-based central agencies, such as a Ministry of Planning that is developing an unnecessarily centralized planning system or a Ministry of Public Service that decides to adopt reforms that unduly constrain the ability of local governments to make sufficiently autonomous staffing decisions.

Other major players in decentralization and in infrastructure specifically are sectoral ministries, such as a Ministry of Roads and Transport or a Ministry of Water. The dual impact of their common reluctance to relinquish control over resources and their focus on service delivery with less concern for local governance and institution building is often considerable. Sectoral ministries may exert a powerful centralizing tendency either through heavy management of resources officially devolved to local governments or through continued planning and delivery of services after their legal devolution. Formal Sector Wide Approaches (SWAps) promoted by donors often reinforce the incentives of sectoral ministries to pursue centralizing reforms for service delivery, commonly in conjunction with national poverty reduction or Millennium Development Goal strategies.

The centralist tendencies of sectoral agencies and their reform programs coincide conveniently with those of finance and planning agencies, overpowering relatively weak local government ministries and nascent local governments. Thus, a centralizing MoF PFM reform that reduces local government fiscal autonomy and simultaneous adoption of centralizing SWAps in key sectors can effectively neutralize local government infrastructure planning processes or reduce them to the limited role of providing an optional input to resource programming decisions controlled by higher levels.

In some cases, however, there can be clashes among the various central actors that impact local infrastructure planning. Sectoral ministries, for example, may pursue SWAps that create sector specific systems and procedures for managing services—mechanisms for channeling resources, special districts distinct from local governments, etc.—that are at odds with decentralization reforms and formal intergovernmental PFM, development planning, or civil service systems promoted by other cross-cutting ministries. Even though relevant overarching ministries should be able to discipline such behavior by virtue of their legal powers, they may be unable to do so if sectoral ministers have strong political connections or international development partners, which provide considerable sectoral resources in aid dependent countries, prefer particular modalities. The result can be a system of local infrastructure planning and finance with muddled incentives.

Community driven development (CDD)—the umbrella for Social Investment Funds and other community-based mechanisms discussed below—is another common element of the governance reform agenda, and it is heavily promoted and supported by donors. CDD is qualitatively different than other activities discussed here because it is not primarily a component of public sector reform. Although a centrally based government or quasi-government agency is normally the national administrator of CDD planning and financing mechanisms, the resources typically target nongovernmental or community-based organizations with diverse decision-making and accountability mechanisms rather than popularly elected local governments. CDD is relevant for local infrastructure planning precisely because it finances small-scale local investments, many of which are or could be the responsibility of local governments.

In countries where local governments are weak and CDD proponents are more concerned about community empowerment than public sector reform, CDD—and its dedicated planning and financing mechanisms—may undermine development of nascent local government systems. Citizens may come to view local infrastructure as the role of CDD mechanisms rather than elected local governments. In addition, CDD bodies, unlike local governments, do not have access to regularized revenue sources.

Together these realities raise concern about the effect of CDD on local accountability, the linkages between CDD and public investment (particularly for network infrastructure), and the source of funds required to operate and maintain CDD-financed infrastructure. All of these could be dealt with by appropriate design features, which might evolve as local governments become stronger. In many countries, however, CDD continues to use independent planning and financing systems long after the need for a separate identity has passed, and this may have nontrivial consequences for local infrastructure planning.

This brief treatment of how various public sector and governance reform efforts may affect local infrastructure planning cannot do justice to the range of issues involved or the complexity of the political economy landscape that surround them. The overarching point, however, is clear. Local infrastructure planning cannot be effectively reformed independently of other public sector and governance reform initiatives that could either support or undermine it. The existing and potential relationships among these various reforms need to be documented, and the incentives of various actors to cooperate or obstruct improved local development planning needs to be understood.

An illustrative cautionary case

The evolution of development planning in Kenya illustrates the challenges created by political economy forces in the type of complex intergovernmental and multi-actor environment outlined above.[18] The country has produced medium-term national plans and subnational land use plans since the colonial era, although they evolved in purpose and form as international conventions and local conditions changed. Until recent constitutional reforms, there was a bifurcated system of planning and budgeting that reflected a dichotomy between the deconcentrated and hierarchical provincial-district system and the semi-autonomous elected local authority system. The former was strengthened and the latter weakened after independence.[19] The post-colonial favoring of deconcentration was officially justified as means to build national unity in the ethnically diverse nation with competing visions of the role of central government, but critics saw an effort by the dominant tribal group and its political party to build a unitary state that was under their control.

National development planning conducted under the authority of the Ministry of Planning and National Development (MPND) went down to administrative units at provincial and district level, which were under the Office of the President. Provincial and District Development Plans were prepared under MPND field staff. The subnational process occurred concurrently with the national process, such that it neither flowed directly from nor truly influenced the national plan. The politically motivated creation of many new districts diluted infrastructure funds and staff in individual districts and compromised planning.

Although a major share of line ministry resources flowed through provincial and district budgets, some ministries maintained separate sectoral planning activities and/or set up dedicated regions/mechanisms (e.g., in water and roads) for public services under their jurisdiction. These may support better investments (this has not been well studied), but there was often inadequate coordination with districts and local governments that were active in the sector. This can be a problem if these local actors faced no incentives to assume the burden of operating and maintaining infrastructure not planned by them.

The linkage of the planning to the annual budgeting process in the deconcentrated system is weak, and involvement of citizens or their elected representatives was limited. Decisions are made by District Development Committees (DDCs) chaired by a presidential appointee. District staff of national ministries dominated DDCs, with only a few members from local governments and NGOs. This system emerged under the District Focus for Rural Development Strategy (DFRD) of 1983, a reform framed as returning "power to the people" in response to a 1982 *coup d'état* attempt. Critics saw DFRD as reinforcing ruling party control and further weakening local government performance incentives.

The local government planning system was fully separate. The Ministry of Local Govenent (MLG) initiated Local Authority Development Plans (LADPs) in the 1980s to program donor funds for local investments, and they were often poorly linked to physical development plans (mostly prepared by the Ministry of Lands, Housing, and Physical Planning). As with DDPs, LADPs were poorly linked to local budgets, and popular participation mechanisms were weak. A Local Authority Service Delivery Action Plan (LASDAP) initiated in 2000 to allocate resources from a new transfer fund provided a partial linkage to the local budget and mandated participatory planning. This process essentially replaced the LADP. As with districts, many new local authorities were created for political reasons, further compromising infrastructure planning and provision.

In addition to resources provided through the provincial-district and local government systems, the government operated (under MPND, the same ministry responsible for provincial and district planning) a mechanism for planning and financing community driven development at levels below district administration and local governments through the Community Development Trust Fund (CDTF). Substantial small-scale rural infrastructure has been provided through CDTF. Coordination with district planning and local government planning has been ad hoc and varied greatly across jurisdictions.

Finally, the Kenyan Parliament created a Constituency Development Fund (CDF) in 2003 with the stated purpose of fighting poverty by improving basic services.[20] Rather than try to fix existing systems, the Members of Parliament opted to find another way to channel resources for local service delivery—one that served their political interests. A planning process was developed for CDF funds, but its link to other planning processes was ad hoc and generally weak. In recent budgets, increasing proportions of resources under other programs have also been allocated on a constituency basis.[21]

In larger urban areas, the role of the district planning system was limited, but the process for coordinating infrastructure was also relatively ad hoc. There was however, one move to respond to the problems of fragmented urban planning. In 2008 the government created the Ministry of Nairobi Metropolitan Development (MNMD) as part of the process of implementing Vision 2030, Kenya's latest development strategy. The mission of the now defunct MNMD was to ensure that the various jurisdictions work together so as "to manage the Nairobi Metropolis by providing sustainable infrastructural services and high quality of life to all its residents, visitors and investors".

Figure 13.1 summarizes the former development planning systems in Kenya. All five of the existing planning/finance channels—sectoral, provincial/district, local government, constituency, and community—had some role in local infrastructure provision. While this situation was not necessarily undesirable, a number of consequential problems were evident. First, there was extensive territorial overlap among the jurisdictions covered by these various systems, and this was exacerbated by the above-noted creation of new districts and local governments. Second, there was considerable lack of clarity about specific infrastructure responsibilities across them. Third, each of the planning systems was financed by different sources. Fourth, each system had its own political economy incentives and dynamics, and these inevitably came into conflict. Finally, given these concerns, the various plans and finance mechanisms were largely uncoordinated, and any coordination that occurs was ad hoc rather than systematic. Other public sector reform efforts—public financial management, civil service and sectoral—had largely ignored or constrained all but the deconcentrated system.

Collectively, these structural and procedural issues had major consequences. First, they generated redundancies and gaps in infrastructure provision. Second, accountability was compromised since citizens were unclear about which actor was responsible for specific infrastructure. Third, lack of functional clarity,

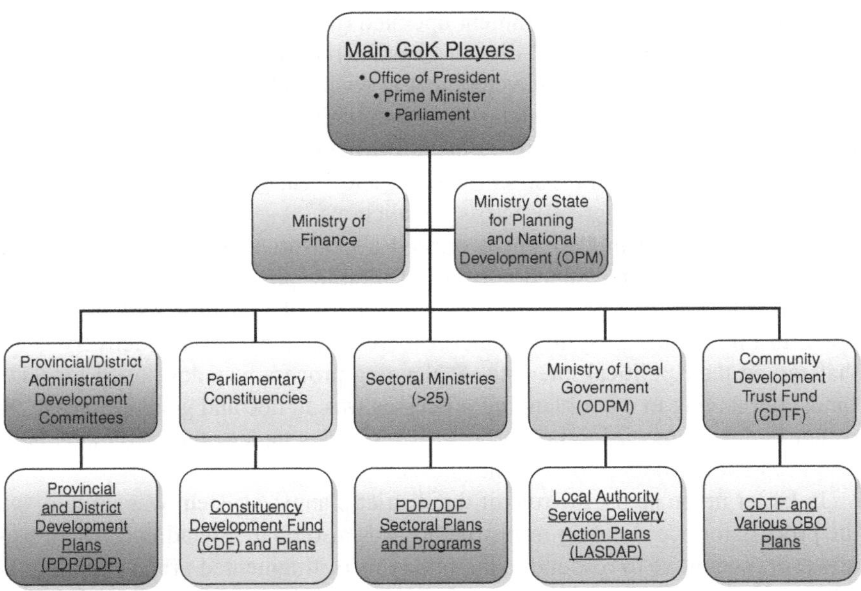

Figure 13.1 The pre-2010 constitution planning system in Kenya.

fragmentation of resources, and muddled accountability create incentives and opportunities for political dynamics and bureaucratic behavior that undermine efficient use of public resources. Although Kenya's former system was a relatively extreme case, such problems are not uncommon in developing countries.

Recent political developments and deterioration of government performance created conditions for a new constitution (2010) that is dramatically altering the intergovernmental system. Mandated reforms consolidate hundreds of districts and local authorities into 47 newly empowered county governments. This should allow the eventual creation of a more integrated infrastructure planning and finance system, although to date there is limited clarity on how the fragmented planning systems will be integrated in the new institutional landscape.

Many lessons can be derived from the Kenya case, but the principal point for current purposes is the importance of documenting the larger institutional context in which infrastructure planning is taking place. This context is in great part created by political economy dynamics. Once the various institutions and associated planning systems are created, they are each subject to their own internal political economy influences and the political economy interrelationships that exist and develop among them. Without an understanding of this context and the underlying and evolving political economy dynamics, efforts to improve local infrastructure planning are unlikely to succeed.

How decentralization reforms shape subnational planning

The previous sections have outlined the larger context of local infrastructure planning. This section and the next one focus more specifically on how decentralization reforms shape subnational planning systems and then on how such systems may affect local infrastructure outcomes. The logic of the argument is summarized in Figure 13.2. The main context of our discussion is that of aid dependent least developed countries (LDC), where decentralization reforms involve major efforts to get the very basic systems in place and international development partners may play a significant role in supporting such efforts.

The extent to which decentralization reforms institute an effective subnational development planning system depends on the design of the reforms and ultimately on the political rationale and bureaucratic incentives behind their implementation. We have already stressed the centrality of domestic politics for initiating and sustaining decentralization reforms and the role of bureaucratic incentives in explaining their incomplete and fragile implementation. But it is also important to stress is that this is an inherently contested and dynamic process which continues to open (and close) space for action by domestic reformers and for supportive engagement by their international development partners.[22] Moreover, as argued elsewhere,[23] understanding the dynamic nature of the process is only the first step; it must then be followed by an analytical shift that places less emphasis on the contribution decentralization may make to a global democratization and good governance agenda and more on understanding decentralization reforms as part of a domestic "developmental state-building"

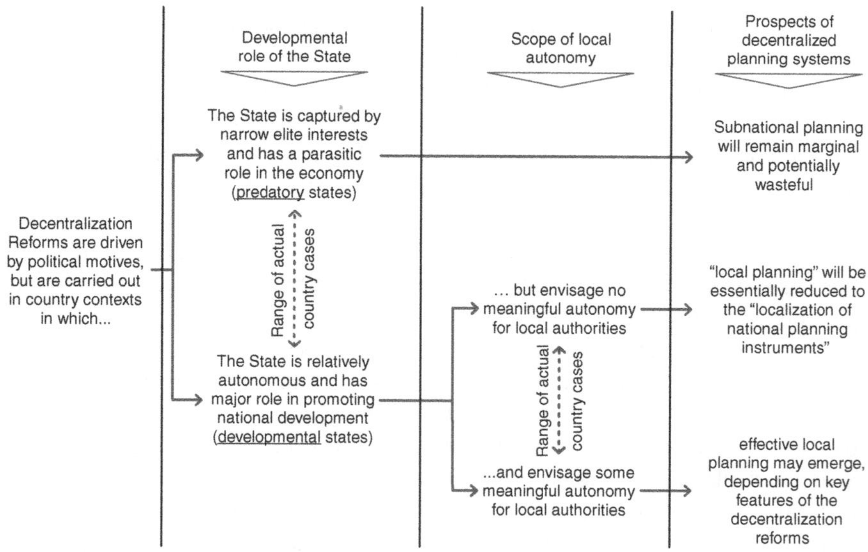

Figure 13.2 From decentralization reforms to decentralized development planning.

agenda.[24] Such an approach goes beyond recognizing that decentralization is driven by politics and asks the critical question of whether it coexists with, or relates to, a developmental state-building project, an understanding of the potential of local development within it, and a related commitment to effective subnational planning. This raises two general observations on the potential for decentralization to develop effective local planning.

First, the weaker the link between the immediate political objectives of reform and a larger project of developmental statebuilding, the less likely that effective subnational development planning will ever emerge. Without a developmental underpinning in the very nature of the state, the formal addition of subnational planning to the national system of public resource management is bound to remain cosmetic, and a genuine transition from a centralized (hierarchical) to a decentralized (multi-level/negotiated) national planning system is likely to be blocked. Second, even where decentralization reforms are linked to developmental statebuilding,[25] an effective subnational planning system ultimately depends on a proper understanding of the nature and role of local development within national development efforts and therefore on the scope and degree of autonomy enjoyed by subnational authorities. We return below to common misconceptions regarding local development and local autonomy as key obstacles for genuinely decentralized development planning. Figure 13.3 summarizes these key relationships between decentralization reforms and effective subnational planning.

Beyond such generalizations, a more detailed assessment of how the design and implementation of politics-driven decentralization reforms affect the practice of decentralized development planning requires looking at four basic dimensions

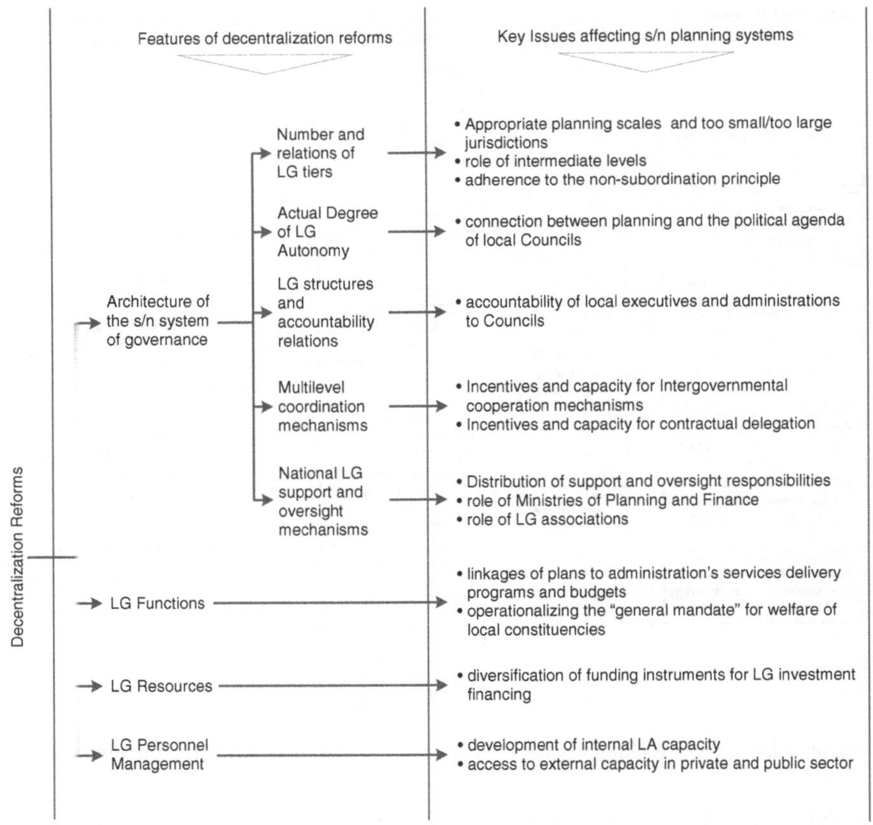

Figure 13.3 Dimensions of decentralization reform subnational planning systems.

of a national decentralization policy. These include (i) changes in the architecture of the governance and public administration system, (ii) reassignment of functions across the system, (iii) reassignment of fiscal powers and financial resources and associated changes in public finance management, and (iv) changes in human resource management responsibilities among levels. Together these four dimensions provide a framework for assessing the transition from centralized to decentralized development planning and understanding actual arrangements occurring in diverse country contexts. Figure 13.4 summarizes these dimensions and some of the issues they raise for subnational planning.

Architecture of subnational governance and decentralized development planning

Decentralization reforms introduce changes in the architecture of the subnational governance and public administration system, including in (i) tiers of local

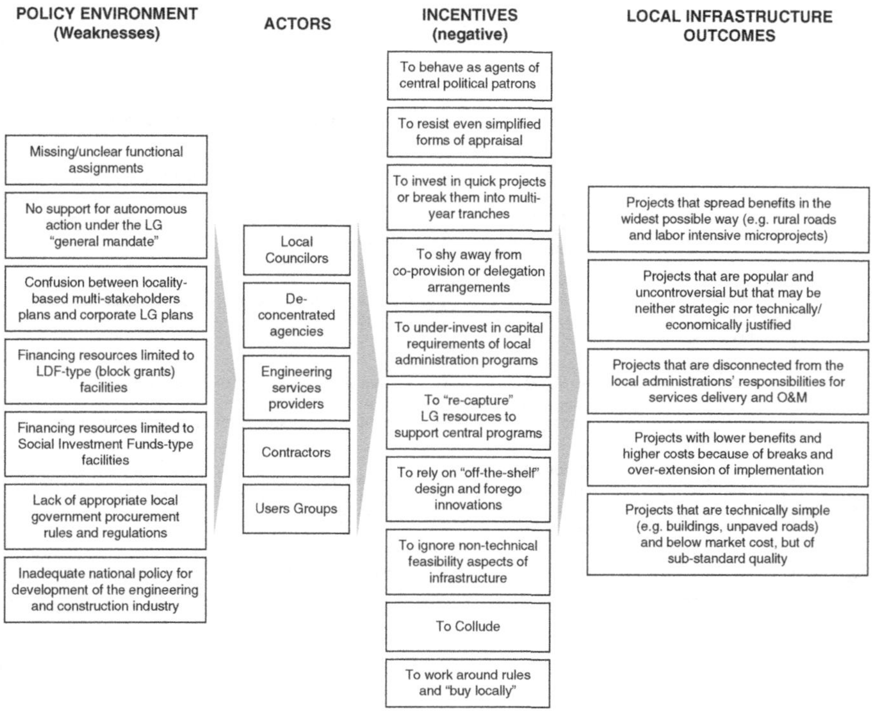

Figure 13.4 Policy weaknesses, negative incentives, and local infrastructure outcomes.

authorities and their mutual relationships, (ii) the degree of autonomy, (iii) internal structures and accountability relations, (iv) mechanisms for joint action, and (v) the national system for support and supervision. Issues with any of these elements impact the performance of subnational planning systems. Definitive analysis must be country specific, but there are typical problems, some of which have been the subject of extensive literature.

The first issue is that of the "right size" of a local authority. Smaller jurisdictions, often established as first-tier units, may lack the functional and fiscal capacity to be viable planning units. On the other hand, larger (provincial/regional) jurisdictions are inadequate as units of "local" development planning, if "local" is properly understood as leveraging a territorial identity and mobilizing community resources, including social capital. Assigning local planning responsibilities to units whose functions and capacities are severely constrained by their size, or assigning them to large units that lack the comparative advantage to promote territory-specific solutions and to mobilize community resources, may lead to costly inefficiencies (more below).

The multiplication of subnational government tiers can also be problematic. For example, intermediate authorities can be critical for an effective public sector and they are core actors in federal systems. In unitary systems with weak capacity and governance, however, they may receive autonomy prematurely or inappropriately. Stronger regional levels of administration may facilitate coordination of central and local government plans and action, but their political empowerment in emerging systems may complicate cooperation between elected national and local governments as well as constrain or undermine the role of the latter.[26] In many cases, autonomous local government planning and stronger central-local government partnerships could be better supported by deconcentrating the state than by creating intermediate political authorities.[27]

The most critical issue for establishing genuine decentralized planning is the degree of autonomy assigned to emerging local authorities. Whether the goal is to improve national programs efficiency or to develop local policies and mobilize resources, it is ultimately the extent of their autonomy, understood as powers of initiative and immunity from higher levels controls (Clark, 1984) that may generate locally "added value" to centralized development efforts. Yet a quarter of a century into the latest wave of decentralization, local autonomy remains highly contested in theory and highly constrained in practice in many LDCs. Politics-driven decentralization reforms may create new subnational political bodies but mostly rearrange administrative and fiscal powers within the central administration rather than support local autonomy in making and implementing local plans, programs, and budgets. This reduces subnational planning to a marginally valuable technical exercise with weak or no linkage with the political agenda of local councils.

The disconnect between the political activity of the local elective councils and the preparation of local development plans, programs, and budgets is compounded by the structural problems of weak accountability of local executives and administrations often created by politics-driven decentralization reforms. As already suggested, the prime objective of such reforms is to legitimize national government action at the periphery and/or to consolidate and diffuse the networks of political patronage of the party in power, and not necessarily to share development and service delivery responsibilities with autonomous subnational actors. As a result, the reforms stop short of establishing genuine local authorities with their own executive and administrative structures. To the extent that newly created councils cannot develop and implement their own plans, their role is reduced to approving subnational plans prepared and implemented by centrally controlled administrative agents, which at best "localize" national policies.

Another concern is that political disincentives and technical complexities make multi-level intergovernmental cooperation difficult. Once a multi-level governance and administration system is set up, formerly hierarchical relations among layers of a centralized administration should be replaced by "negotiated" arrangements between relatively autonomous public entities, as well as between them and community and private sector actors. Yet central-local cooperation remains elusive in decentralizing LDCs. In particular, contractual delegation arrangements,[28] which can facilitate gradual and selective decentralization of service responsibilities, have proven difficult to devise. And, contrary to common perceptions, the problem has often been as much or more one of bureaucratic disincentives and weak capacity of central agencies to structure and manage such contracts than lack of capacity of local authorities to implement them.

Finally subnational planning systems are affected by confusion and conflicts about whom in central government should regulate, support, and supervise their operation. As noted above, various key national ministries have dissimilar attitudes towards decentralization, and often opposing views on the scope and modalities of subnational planning. The consequences are multiple requirements and confusing guidelines that overwhelm rather than build the limited capacity of local government planning units.

Functional assignments and decentralized development planning

The scope and outcomes of subnational planning are obviously affected by what functions are devolved or delegated to local authorities. Lack of clarity makes it difficult for local governments to structure administration around specific responsibilities and link local development plans to the operations and budgets of their departments. As a result, subnational planning ends up being disconnected not only from the local political process, but also from the organization and daily work of the local administration.

Beyond the effects of inadequate functional assignments, the quality of subnational plans and operations are also negatively affected by the inability of local authorities to fully espouse and operationalize their own "general mandate" for local development, which may be provided for in decentralization legal frameworks.[29] Where decentralization reforms *neither* reassign specific services delivery functions *nor* support the adoption of a service delivery agenda under a general mandate, subnational planning ends up focusing on stand-alone, small-scale infrastructure projects. These projects are seen as the easiest, least controversial, highest political return options, as need not be aligned with mandated functions and do not require potentially controversial, political deliberations about which service delivery operations local authorities should engage in by their own initiative.

Subnational finances and decentralized development planning

Ultimately, local planning systems are shaped by how local authorities are financed and local finances are managed. All too often politics-driven reforms create subnational authorities but fall short of empowering them with the full range of fiscal and financial instruments needed to perform developmental functions. The situation differs from country to country, and, within countries, between larger urban areas and less endowed rural jurisdictions, but most local authorities in LDCs typically suffer from: limited scope or capacity for own source revenue raising; legal or de facto exclusion from credit financing; lack of specialized national institutions supporting subnational capital spending; and inadequate mechanisms for contractual financing of delegated functions.

The primary source of financing for local development plans (and only incentive to pursue subnational planning), has often been grants from central government. These have been provided as more or less discretionary resources, either as part of a regular transfer system, or from more ad hoc and externally financed facilities.[30] The bulk of these grants has been spent on *small-scale infrastructure*, either because funds have been earmarked for that purpose by central governments or donors, or because infrastructure spending has been the default option for local authorities for the reasons suggested above.

Thus, in many decentralizing LDCs, subnational planning systems have been largely shaped by various central grant mechanisms. Importantly, where these grants have been introduced as regular transfers for local budgets support, this has facilitated the adoption of statutory procedures for local planning programming and budgeting. By contrast, where grants have come from specific project-financing facilities, this has often been associated with the introduction of ad hoc, rather demanding,[31] and less sustainable planning exercises essentially meant to allocate the resources of the financing facility.

National mechanisms to transfer resources for subnational development spending and the donor-supported facilities (i.e., Local Development Funds–LDFs—and similar programs) that have often piloted or complemented them, have played important roles in the emergence of sustainable subnational planning systems in LDCs. By providing a minimum of locally programmable resources to emerging local authorities they have helped break the vicious circle of "no capacity-no responsibilities-no resources," put local authorities on a "learning-by-doing" path of institutional development, and facilitated the local adoption of statutory and participatory development planning processes.[32]

Yet if decentralization reforms remain incomplete and do not proceed to functional reassignments and diversification of financing instruments, the LDF-type regular (and necessarily modest) annual transfers end up being stretched much beyond their original function of creating incentives for local planning and management capacity-building, and they become the primary or only source for local infrastructure financing. We elaborate below on how this affects the type and quality of local infrastructure. Here we simply note that this modality has another effect on local planning: it often involves less rigorous investment appraisal procedures than those used by an independent financing facility.

Local authority human resources and decentralized development planning

Effective local development planning requires capabilities that are typically scarce in developing countries. Necessary skills, particularly for strategic and participatory planning, are difficult to embed in bureaucratic routines and are not easy to develop in the first place since they depend more on experience than on specialized training. In other words, effective subnational planning requires not only technical skills that people can be trained in, but also learning how to think strategically through experience. Similarly, participatory planning training will neither make local governments participatory nor turn their constituents into active citizens, which require learning from working together.

Incomplete decentralization reforms often hamper development of subnational planning capacity, as they do not effectively address the need for local planning professionals or develop regulations to allow local authorities to flexibly source planning skills in the professional services market. But even with fuller reforms, complete reliance of local authorities on private consultants would neither be desirable nor feasible because their effective use requires local authority capacity to manage their services and link them to both the political work of local councils and the organization of local administration.

Returning to the core rationale of subnational planning: local development

The above review of how politics-driven, incomplete decentralization impacts local planning systems underscores a basic point. Effective development planning depends on the extent to which decentralization reforms, beyond their potential to foster good *local governance*, support *local development* and its role in a developmental state agenda.

As we argue elsewhere[33] the adjective "local" in "local development" refers not only to the *where*, but also and most importantly to the *who* and *how* of development promotion. Development is local if it is endogenous, open, and incremental, that is: if it makes use of locality-specific resources, combines them with national/global resources, and brings them to bear on national development as *additional* benefits in a positive sum game.

Understood in this more specific sense, local development could be an integral part of the developmental state agenda and the object of a supportive national policy with a status similar to that of more conventional macroeconomic and industrial policies. The principal instrument for its implementation would be a subnational planning system in which local authorities mobilize local resources and negotiate their joint use with state and civil society resources. Unfortunately, generic views of local development (as development that happens locally) continue to prevail, missing comparative advantages of local government and the developmental rationale of decentralization. This is seen in common "*decentralization without autonomy*" reforms, which set up subnational planning systems that "localize" national plans, but fail to generate genuine local plans or mobilize additional resources from civil society and private sector.

Subnational planning and infrastructure development outcomes

We now turn to the question of how subnational planning systems set up by politics-driven and incomplete decentralization reforms affect infrastructure outcomes. It is important to note that, no matter what drives decentralization and how far it proceeds, the scope for decentralizing *infrastructure provision* remains limited not just by technical and economic factors, but also and more importantly, by core political economy issues.

The scope for decentralizing infrastructure

As noted above, local authorities in many decentralizing LDCs end up spending most of their (limited) discretionary resources on stand-alone small-scale infrastructure projects. This is the default option when incomplete reforms and political disincentives for local councilors prevent broader responsibilities for service delivery from being assigned to or claimed by emerging local authorities. The relative surge in local infrastructure spending at the early stages of decentralization is, therefore, more of a necessary corollary (a sort of price to pay) than an intended policy objective. It occurs as larger-scale infrastructure remains centralized and no responsibilities for any infrastructure are formally devolved. The "pooling" of smaller infrastructure projects (for water, rural roads, rural electrification) into larger centrally managed programs also continues to be widespread.

Central management of larger-scale infrastructure programs that "pool" smaller-scale ones is often justified on technical-economic grounds (network integrity, high capital requirements, economies of scale, interjurisdictional benefits). Powerful political economy realities, however, are often equally or more important. In fact, the management of infrastructure is a notoriously "'wet' area of government," offering great opportunities for illicit generation of funds that are critical to political parties in power (Booth and Golooba-Mutebi, 2009). These funds are used to extend patronage networks and effect the intra-elite distribution of rents, which are essential for managing risks of violent conflicts between elite factions and maintaining political stability, a common need in "limited access" political systems prevailing in less developed countries (North *et al.*, 2006). The extraction of funds, in turn, requires "well-oiled machines" (Booth and Golooba-Mutebi, 2009) that may be easier to control as units of central agencies than as multiple local administration departments. Unless the center can extract rents through local authorities while controlling their distribution and containing the risk of "runaway local elites," more decentralization of infrastructure responsibility is unlikely. Within these constraints, the situation differs across countries, depending on whether decentralization also has a *developmental* rationale and if a role is seen for *local* development, as well as on political forces and dynamics that launching reforms unleashes.

If accelerated economic growth is critical to sustain creating and distributing rents, decentralizing regimes may go beyond purely predatory logic to combine a *political* rationale for reform with a *developmental* one. If the potential of *local* development is recognized, there may be a shift of resources to local authorities and more decentralized provision of infrastructure. Reforms may also open space for emerging political actors (within and outside dominant coalitions) to champion local development as an integral part of a developmental state agenda and eventually push for greater local autonomy in managing infrastructure. Thus, political and institutional environments may evolve and redefine roles of the multiple actors involved in local infrastructure, creating mechanisms for their interaction and shaping the political and personal incentives they face.

These environments can be distinguished by how they institutionalize and regulate the main stages of the infrastructure project cycle, namely (i) planning, (ii) financing, and (iii) implementation. Actors whose incentives are shaped by these environments include national politicians from the locality, local councilors, local executives and staff, state agents operating locally, technical service providers, construction firms, community-based contractors, materials and equipment suppliers, laborers, and infrastructure users. We selectively review their positioning and incentives in response to the regulatory and institutional framework for local infrastructure set by decentralization reforms.

Planning local infrastructure

Where decentralization reforms are driven by politics and fail to define local authority developmental responsibilities and autonomy, local politicians (councilors) essentially serve as agents of national political forces and are under pressure to pursue the goals of their patrons: legitimizing the party in power and extending its influence at the periphery. They therefore seek to both maximize the transfers they spend (as this is linked to their status with the party), and make the best political use of resources from the perspective of their central patrons. They have little incentive to link infrastructure spending to locally owned policies or service delivery agendas. Local planning exercises then result in a list of infrastructure investments that are neither derived from locally owned development strategies nor support independent work programs of local administration departments.

Such lists typically give preference to projects that are not politically controversial and spread benefits in the widest possible way. Rural roads construction in Cambodia is a typical example. Another example from Bangladesh is the fragmentation of limited investable local authority funds into multiple micro-projects under "one community, one project" schemes, primarily conceived as labor-intensive local employment programs. The selected infrastructure projects may or may not respond to real local priorities, and may or may not represent value for money. While there are few systematic ex-post evaluations, most donor accounts and rapid surveys of beneficiaries tend to be positive.[34] Thus, local communities seem to appreciate such projects, and they generally cost less than estimated, even if issues of quality and implementation often arise (see below).

Although these projects are not necessarily wasteful, it is hard to imagine they represent the best use of scarce local resources. Credible ex-ante appraisal is typically missing from subnational planning processes, not only because of local capacity limitations, but also, because local politicians have few incentives to let independent appraisal potentially constrain their political decision-making. Thus, local infrastructure investments are often selected through a subnational planning process that is not informed by technical or financial analysis, and investment decisions are ultimately driven by the urgency to spend immediately available resources on popular projects with widespread benefits.

More generally, subnational planning processes introduced by politics-driven, incomplete, decentralization reforms, do not provide local politicians with incentives to align local capital programming and infrastructure investment decisions with either strategic planning or operational budgeting. As a result they may overlook *larger*, more complex projects that support a local strategic development vision but require greater efforts over a multi-year horizon to build partnerships and mobilize additional resources. They may also overlook *smaller* investments that build the capacity of their own administration to deliver certain services (and possibly realize contributions from users).

Beyond shaping incentives of local politicians, how subnational planning is framed also determines how deconcentrated agents based in the locality will participate in local planning and contribute to shape infrastructure outcomes. In many LDCs, local authorities remain embryonic, and deconcentrated agents are expected to help them carry out their functions. However, even when overseen by a strong governor (or similar state agent), who should coordinate and clear actions with elected councils, deconcentrated agents remain weakly accountable to these councils and have little incentive to transfer responsibilities to them or build their capacity. Instead they are often keen to recapture decentralized functions and resources for the center. In fact local planning may play an instrumental role in this respect if no distinction is made between multi-stakeholder *jurisdiction-wide* strategic planning[35] and local authority corporate strategic planning.[36]

When this is the case, deconcentrated agencies may heavily influence or formulate plans of emerging local authorities. After the creation of district local authorities in Cambodia, for example, these agencies came to see local planning as a way to capture resources of new district authorities to finance investments they could not afford with their own budgets. State-appointed governors, who act as chief executives of local councils, also have incentives to support this view of local planning, which strengthens their role vis-à-vis local councils both as local development managers and policy makers. This scenario is common in countries experiencing the "*decentralization without autonomy*" discussed above. It results in *localized* national plans[37] that local elected councils are pushed to endorse as part of a wider effort to legitimize the central government in the periphery.

The infrastructure investments generated by this type of subnational planning system may be more service delivery oriented and less "free-standing" than those selected by councilors operating as political party agents in the locality, and they do often have a stronger link to sectoral agendas. But the technicians who formulate these projects may not face incentives to seek input from beneficiaries or to conduct proper technical and financial appraisal. The risk of costly technical error is low for "off-the-shelf" projects with standard designs (e.g., education, health care, administrative facilities), but it may rise for projects requiring site-specific assessment and careful management (e.g., irrigation, water supply, flood control). In addition, local agents of technical ministries tend to give less attention to non-engineering aspects of projects, including institutional, social, financial, or economic feasibility and risks, which are critical for sustainability.

Subnational planning systems designed to localize national plans may also lead to a sub-optimal use of local authority resources, as pressures to give each sector a share of the programmable funds may reinforce the loss of a strategic territorial perspective. Overall, such planning systems do not take advantage of the potential efficiency gains expected when autonomous local governments formulate their own development strategies and negotiate their financing and implementation with users and the local private sector.

Financing local infrastructure

Local infrastructure planning is driven by financing, and, as noted above, the structure and outcomes of local planning systems depends on available financing instruments.[38] In many LDCs, where the local authorities' ability to raise own source revenue or access credit are limited, infrastructure spending depends on intergovernmental transfers, often piloted and/or supplemented by externally funded LDF-type facilities. Through formula-based annual block grants, often with access conditions and performance criteria attached, these provide programmable resources that support a local development planning process. There may be a list of allowable or prohibited uses, but generally the transfer criteria are not meant to assess the developmental relevance of the infrastructure investments. This is left to how local councils strike a balance between advancing the interests of their local constituencies and serving the political objectives of their national patrons. This in turn depends on whether local authorities, both individually (through strong local leadership) and collectively (through independent national associations) eventually emerge as relatively autonomous political actors on the national scene.

Resources transferred annually through LDF-type facilities are relatively small and may have to go back to the national treasury if unspent during the fiscal year, so they can only finance infrastructure projects that are very small, simple, and quick. This reinforces the local political bias towards fragmented use of resources to maximize the number of beneficiary communities. If the fragmentation bias is resisted and attempts are made to invest in a large project that costs more than the annual LDF allocation (e.g., road link or water reservoir), the resulting implementation delay may reduce efficiency of resources allocated to the project by immobilizing capital, increasing costs, and delaying benefits.

Political and bureaucratic obstacles also work against the decentralized planning and financing of larger, more strategic infrastructure projects and the leveraging of LDF resources through co-financing arrangements with central agencies. Local politicians may be unable to effectively interact with the central administration or are reluctant to lose control of the project. More commonly, central agents, in the absence of national instructions and guidance, may resist venturing into the new and somewhat more complex arrangements necessary for co-providing infrastructure with local authorities.

Other limitations also affect the degree to which LDF resources can be leveraged by mobilizing private and community resources for co-provision of services and related infrastructure (e.g., pre-school/primary education, water supply, sanitation, transport). This critically depends on the quality of local leaders and the actual (and perceived) degree of their autonomy.[39] The emergence of proactive, development-minded local leaders is often hindered by the politics-driven decentralization reforms discussed above.

In general, where "pay-as-you-go" through LDF-style annual transfers is the only option available to local authorities for infrastructure finance, larger, more efficient investments are rejected in favor of smaller and/or less viable projects. Alternatively, their implementation may be split over several years, increasing costs and delaying benefits.[40]

In principle, the limitations of annual general-purpose block grants could be overcome by establishing dedicated facilities that provide *project-specific* grants or loans for larger and more strategic investments. The main examples include Municipal Development Funds (MDF), many of which have been established with substantial external aid. Social Investment Funds (SIF) and to some extent Community Driven Development (CDD) programs, could be counted among such facilities if they can be used to support local authority investment programs. The design of these facilities has been heavily influenced by donors and has created specific and often problematic incentives and disincentives for local actors.

Conceived as specialized domestic financial institutions to extend concessional credit to local authorities, MDFs have run into difficulties and the original expectations of their proponents had to be scaled down.[41] Many MDFs could only assist a limited number of creditworthy urban/metropolitan authorities. Smaller urban and rural authorities could not generate revenue streams to service debts for non-revenue-generating infrastructure. Many local authorities, hamstrung by national regulations and low internal capacity, have been reluctant or unable to borrow even for revenue-generating infrastructure. The use of intergovernmental transfer intercept mechanisms for MDF loans created a moral hazard and disincentive for proper financial appraisal of investments. Opportunities arose for local politicians to shift resources from future service delivery and operation and maintenance spending to the immediately visible bricks-and-mortar projects they prefer without transparent justification of welfare enhancement or poverty targeting.

By using capital grants SIFs avoid some difficulties of MDFs and can be key vehicles for financing subnational investment. In contrast to MDFs, SIFs were not born to finance *local authority* investment, but to support *national* pro-poor policies through delivering community-level social infrastructure (schools, clinics, and water and sanitation). SIFs were also intended to disburse large amounts of external aid rapidly. As the types and quantities of

SIF-eligible investments could not be generated quickly enough through existing local authority systems, SIFs introduced parallel planning processes. Initially these simply involved eliciting direct requests from communities informed of SIF resources ("first come first served"), but they were later replaced by participatory planning processes carried out in communities targeted by the SIF.

Given their different nature, SIF-driven and local authority planning systems may generate *different* investment priorities even if they both finance schools, clinics, and water systems.[42] This is because the SIF offers local authorities an opportunity to shape the local content of a *national* infrastructure program, not necessarily to finance their own local priorities. The SIF also does not provide local authorities with incentives to assume greater responsibilities or to reflect them in local budgets, as the management of most of the SIF-financed facilities remains under the concerned sectoral ministries.

Political economy analyses of SIF operations in Latin America[43] have shown that the allocation of SIF resources to specific localities is often driven by political/electoral calculations and that the bulk of SIF resources were spent on technically simple infrastructure, often with off-the-shelf designs, which could be quickly delivered. This was justified by the original emergency response mandate of the SIF, but the bias for the quick and simple persisted because of the preferences of both local politicians and international aid agencies. As a consequence, the diversification of SIF investments has been slow and halfhearted, and spending on projects less amenable to standardized designs (e.g., water supply and sanitation) has remained relatively minor in SIF portfolios.

Beyond dedicated mechanisms for budget or project support from treasury or specific central agencies and programs, issuing bonds remains a potentially appropriate option for local authorities. Experience, however, suggests that the development of a sub-sovereign bond market depends on conditions that require relatively advanced levels of national development and local autonomy and must be sustained by a national policy recognizing the role of local development for national growth. These generally include a supporting regulatory environment, a diversified financial sector, and an increased capacity for debt support and management by local authorities.[44] Such conditions exist widely only in advanced developing and transition countries,[45] and most bonds in developing countries have been issued by subnational states and major cities.

Attempts however have been made to overcome the capacity limitations of smaller and less endowed jurisdictions, by developing pooled financing mechanisms.[46] In the last decade, international agencies have been active in assisting central and local authorities in developing countries to access domestic and international capital markets for financing infrastructure, particularly in certain sectors, such as water supply and sanitation.

Since issuing bonds requires a rating of local authority creditworthiness, the prospect of such financing for local infrastructure may pressure local politicians to exercise fiscal discipline and improve financial management. Unfortunately, such incentives are diluted where access to bond financing is made possible by credit enhancement mechanisms that are poorly designed and transfer all or most default risk to the national treasury.

Implementing local infrastructure

The legal framework regulating local infrastructure procurement also shapes the behavior of actors involved in local planning. A common problem is insufficient national attention to developing *appropriate* local authority procurement systems and capacity. Standard legal provisions and guidelines often largely reproduce the central procurement process. Local authorities, however, require flexibility to realize the benefits of decentralization, and central regulations may invite rule violation, abuse of exceptions, and fiduciary risks, which can be great without strong enforcement systems and actions.

Local authorities often encounter difficulties because of legal rigidities or inadequate central guidance on implementing infrastructure projects through community contracting or innovative service delivery programs that use community co-provision and co-production arrangements. In addition, rules intended to minimize the influence of private contractors on local procurement, if not well formulated and explained, may impede efforts to leverage local social capital, strengthen local public-private cooperation, and help develop the local construction industry. Standardized and inappropriate procurement rules may create incentives to avoid them. An example is the practice of artificially breaking procurement of larger projects into smaller contracts, or worse, to choose certain projects over potentially better ones because their small size allows avoidance of competitive bidding requirements for contracts above a certain amount.[47]

Beyond the effects of the legal framework for local procurement, the efficient implementation of locally planned infrastructure depends critically on the capacities of the stakeholders. These include the capacity of the local administration to manage the procurement process, the capacity of local engineers and contractors to deliver quality services and works, and the capacity of local communities to oversee implementation.

The capacity to manage infrastructure procurement is generally a function of the size of a jurisdiction and of a country's overall development. It is particularly weak for small rural local authorities in LDCs. Efforts to build capacity may appear disproportionately costly. In some infrastructure programs in aid dependent countries, infrastructure spending is overshadowed by capacity building, forcing consideration of alternative arrangements for interjurisdictional cooperation and delegation of the procurement function.

Different capacity constraints plague the engineering function. Local authorities could use private services, but national policies are often required to support the emergence of an engineering consulting industry that could sustainably serve local infrastructure development needs and make transparent the operation of the market for engineering services to local authorities. In many LDCs, local authorities source engineering services from deconcentrated agencies and accountability issues may arise. Deconcentrated technicians may assume the functions of both client and engineer, reducing transparency and compromising the monitoring role of local councils and user committees.

Similar considerations apply to the local contracting industry, the development of which is constrained by the low volume of work available annually in a single jurisdiction. In this respect, the strong political preference of local authorities for "buying locally" may work against the interests of the most capable local construction firms, which are not helped by an extreme segmenting of the market. Much as in the engineering services industry, the construction industry could be effectively helped by the development of supra-local (regional) markets in which they could compete annually for multiple contracts until their level of capacity launches them onto the national market.

Finally, community oversight may have a positive impact on the quality, timeliness, and cost-effectiveness of local infrastructure implementation. This, however, requires the definition of clear rules of engagement of the concerned communities in the construction administration process. When this is not the case the consequences may be either an ineffective and cosmetic role for community monitoring, or, at the other extreme, the possibility for community groups to illicitly extract concessions from contractors (in the forms of materials leakages and/or undocumented extra work) that may eventually be recouped through quality reduction or cost increases paid by the local authority.

Figure 13.4 summarizes key points from the preceding discussion, highlighting the type of incentives that weak decentralization policies and institutional environments can create for the range of actors involved in local infrastructure development and outcomes. Some of these incentives are at least partly inherent to the nature of the particular aspects of the process under consideration, but they can be exacerbated or worsened by the way in which national governments, or in the case of aid dependent countries, international development agencies, structure the local infrastructure development systems they promote and support.

Looking forward

Developing countries face considerable challenges in the design and operation of local infrastructure planning systems in decentralized or decentralizing systems. Many of these challenges are driven or influenced by diverse political economy dynamics that differ in importance and degree across countries. From the beginning, the political economy motivations underlying decentralization and other public sector reforms shape how the planning system is developed and lay the foundations for how it functions and performs.

In practice, local infrastructure planning may involve a diverse range of actors at multiple levels in various ways. These actors are differentially powerful depending on the context in a particular country, and each typically has incentives to pursue some specific agenda. In many countries, traditional centralist tendencies that are supposed to have been lessened can remain influential during implementation. Even if political economy incentives at higher levels allow genuine subnational government empowerment, complex dynamics internal to local governments and their interactions with other local governments, with higher levels of government and with nongovernmental actors can be consequential. These dynamics can support authentic local infrastructure planning or undermine it, with potentially considerable impact on the results.

This chapter has only selectively covered the complex terrain involved, and much of the more detailed treatment focused primarily on the development of decentralized planning systems in least developed countries. More work is clearly needed to better understand the political and bureaucratic dynamics of local infrastructure planning and their impact on infrastructure provision. In specific countries, it is necessary to determine the mix of actors involved and their incentives to support, alter, or capture the local planning process. With such knowledge, it should be possible in many countries to redesign local infrastructure planning systems in ways that would help to improve their performance.

Notes

1 There is diverse literature on infrastructure in developing countries, including the effects of infrastructure on development (e.g., Straub, 2011), infrastructure policy (e.g., Estache, 2004), outcomes (e.g., Briceno-Garmendia *et al.*, 2004), finance (e.g., Kehew *et al.*, 2005; Estache, 2010; Helm, 2010), and private participation. (e.g., Harris, 2003). The literature on infrastructure planning is primarily technical and sector specific. Work on the political economy of local infrastructure planning in developing countries is limited, but the general political economy of decentralization literature discussed below is relevant.

2 See United Cities and Local Governments (2010).

3 See, for example, Agarwala (1983), Conyers and Hills (1984), Healey (1997), Sundaram (1997), Rodwin and Sanyal (2000), Sanyal (2005), Hall and Tewdwr-Jones (2010), and Healey (2012) for overviews from various perspectives on development planning and urban and regional planning.

4 Smoke (2013) reviews the literature on intergovernmental frameworks and provides some comparative information on a number of developing countries.

5 There is much literature on this trend. A few general synthetic sources include: Litvack *et al.* (1998), World Bank (2000), Bardhan and Mookerjee (2006), Cheema and Rondinelli (2007), Connerley *et al.* (2010), and Martínez-Vázquez and Vaillancourt (2011).

6 See, for example, Atinc *et al.* (2004) and Beard *et al.* (2008).

7 A range of literature on this topic is reviewed in Connerley *et al.* (2010) and Eaton *et al.* (2011).

8 New and more integrated approaches to thinking about urban infrastructure planning as part of broad-based, multi-actor city development strategies are discussed in World Bank (2009) and Frank (2011).

9 A synthetic review of the evolution of community driven development and various operational models is provided in Binswanger-Mkhize *et al.* (2009).

10 Much of the relevant literature is synthesized in Connerley *et al.* (2010) and Eaton *et al.* (2011).

11 See for example, discussions of public financial management reform in Malawi (Rakner *et al.*, 2004) and public sector revenue reform in Uganda (Fjeldstad, 2006).

12 Much of the synthetic literature on this topic is reviewed in Eaton *et al.* (2011), and Yilmaz *et al.* (2010) provide a thorough overview of subnational accountability.

13 See, for example, Slack (2007, 2010), and Slack and Chattopadhyay (2009).
14 See Darch and Emezi (2012) for more details on Cape Town.
15 See Nasehi and Rangwala (2011) for more detail on Manila.
16 See Algoso and Magee (2011) for more detail on Cairo.
17 These issues are discussed and more examples are provided in Smoke (2010) and Eaton *et al.* (2011).
18 The country case is discussed more fully in Smoke (2003, 2008) and Smoke and Whimp (2011).
19 The system is summarized in Cohen and Peterson (1999) and Government of Kenya (2005).
20 Constituency Development Fund Act, Government of Kenya Law No. 10 of 2003.
21 For example, a percentage of funding for rural roads earmarked through the Road Maintenance Levy Fund is allocated by constituency.
22 The case for more strategic and diversified engagement of external aid in support of decentralization reforms, in a variety of developing countries contexts, is made in Romeo (2003, 2013), Weimer (2009), Ojendal (2010), and Romeo and El Mensi (2011).
23 Romeo (2013).
24 The need for a more realistic "good-enough" governance agenda in international development is elaborated in Grindle (2004) and its relation to the developmental state building agenda is highlighted in Fritz and Menochal (2006, 2007).
25 Evans (1995) and Leftwich (1995) contrast the "developmental state" model (whether democratic or authoritarian) with the "predatory" state model. The most general distinction is not the role of the state in the appropriation and intra-elite distribution of rents (as this is common to both models to secure political stability and prevent intra-elite conflicts) but rather the priority given by the developmental state to the *expansion* of the economic base from which rents can then be extracted and its relative or "embedded" autonomy (Evans, 1995) from internal and external interests, in fostering such expansion.
26 This is particularly the case in decentralizing unitary states where the basic principle of "non-subordination" of one local authority to another is systematically violated and lower council decisions (plans and budgets) are subject to approval by higher levels. True local plans are relatively independent and realize synergies and complementarities through negotiation among multiple autonomous entities (local authorities at different levels and national and deconcentrated agencies). If higher-level approval is required, local plans remain components of hierarchically organized regional plans, ultimately to be integrated into a single plan and budget, as would occur in any unreformed, centralized planning system.
27 Yet experience shows that it is easier for the initiators of politics-driven decentralization reforms to create a new provincial/regional council than to deconcentrate the state administration at those levels and direct it to support and cooperate with lower-level local authorities.
28 These differ from either deconcentration or outright devolution arrangements and require contractual agreements by which local authorities make use of meaningful discretion to improve the delivery efficiency of central services for which the "contracting" central agency retains primary responsibility.
29 This point is often missed in the fiscal decentralization literature, where functional assignment is understood as the offloading to local governments of functions formerly provided by higher levels.
30 Donors-supported facilities of the first type include Local Development Funds (LDF) and similar local budget-supporting mechanisms, while examples of the second type include the Social Funds and numerous other subnational project-financing facilities.
31 This is particularly true in terms of mechanisms for popular participation in local government decision-making.

32 See UNCDF (1996). An early discussion of the role of LDFs as tools for local capacity building and initial steps in support of decentralized planning and financing is in Romeo (1999).

33 For a more extensive discussion of the role of local development as driver of decentralization reforms and the limits of "decentralization without autonomy" processes see Romeo (2013).

34 Romeo and Spyckerelle (2004) and Abrams (2008) assess local infrastructure investments funded by the Commune/Sangkat Fund (CSF) and Commune Infrastructure Development Fund (CIDF) of Cambodia.

35 Jurisdiction-wide strategic planning aims at developing a shared vision among multiple actors (public, private, and community) operating in the locality, providing the basis for negotiations among them and guiding the preparation of each of their planning, programming, and budgeting instruments.

36 For a review of the difference between community or *jurisdiction-wide* strategic planning facilitated by local governments and the statutory instruments of their *corporate* planning, see Cities Alliance (2006).

37 Genuinely local plans reflect the agenda of a local authority and mobilize the resources of a local polity.

38 The main instruments include: (i) own source revenue; (ii) discretionary and conditional development transfers; (iii) specialized development finance windows (Municipal Development Funds, Social Funds); (iv) access to the capital market (municipal bonds, bank loans); and (v) direct access to international aid.

39 Many factors contribute to the emergence of effective local leaders. A most important one however is whether or not the local electoral system allows voters to express individual preferences.

40 Unfinished infrastructure projects and long implementation delays that retard benefits and inflate costs can occur for multiple reasons, but they are likely to be more pervasive and problematic where full funding of the investments cannot be secured upfront and the only available funding is from annual (typically modest and often volatile) central transfers. The authors observed the effects of this scenario almost two decades ago in Vietnam, where there were many unfinished district-level rural infrastructure projects with substantial "sunk costs" that could rarely be "rescued" by additional investments.

41 See, for example, Peterson (2000) and Friere and Petersen (2004).

42 For an assessment of the different priorities revealed by the community-level microplanning process introduced by the Social Fund and the municipal planning exercises in Nicaragua, see Romeo (2000).

43 See Schady (2000) and Penfold-Becerra (2006).

44 See Platz (2009).

45 These include India, the Philippines, South Africa, Mexico, Brazil and some other South American countries, Russia, and several European transition countries.

46 Interesting pilot projects have been launched in Tanzania and Uganda under the UNCDF Local Finance Initiative (LFI). The conceptual approach is documented in Bond *et al.* (2012).

47 A recent report on Bangladesh by Abrams *et al.* (2010) provides a good example.

References

Abrams, J. 2008. *Assessment on the Implementation of the Commune Infrastructure Development Fund*, IFAD report (unpublished).

Abrams, J., B. Hafiz, and H. Sung Kim. 2010. *Review of Procurement Practice in the Bangladesh Local Government Support Programme—Learning and Innovation Component*. New York: United Nations Capital Development Fund.

Agarwala, Ramgopal. 1983. "Planning in Developing Countries: Lessons of Experience," Staff Working Paper No. 576. Washington, DC: World Bank.

Algoso, D. and J. Magee. 2011. *Structures of Metropolitan Governance and Finance: A Case Study of Cairo*. Cambridge, MA: Lincoln Institute of Land Policy.

Atinc, Tamar Manuelyan, Stephen Ndegwa, Robert Taliercio, Tilla Sewe MacAntony, and Taranaki Mailei. 2004. *Poverty Reduction Strategies in Decentralized Contexts: Comparative Lessons in Local Planning and Fiscal Dimensions*. Washington, DC: World Bank.

Bardhan, Pranab and Dilip Mookherjee, eds. 2006. *Decentralization and Local Governance in Developing Countries: A Comparative Perspective*. Cambridge, MA: MIT Press.

Beard, Victoria, Faranak Miraftab, and Christopher Silver. 2008. *Planning and Decentralization*. London: Routledge.

Binswanger-Mkhize, H., J. de Regt, and S. Spector. 2009. *Scaling Up Local and Community Development*. Washington, DC: World Bank.

Bond, D., D. Platz, and M. Magnusson. 2012. "Financing Small-scale Infrastructure Investments in Developing Countries," UN DESA Working Paper No. 144. New York: United Nations Department for Economic and Social Affairs.

Booth, D. and F. Golooba-Mutebi. 2009. "The Political Economy of Roads Reform in Uganda," ODI Working Paper No. 307. London: Overseas Development Institute.

Briceno-Garmendia, Cecilia, Antonio Estache, and Nemat Shafik. 2004. "Infrastructure Services in Developing Countries: Access, Quality, Costs and Policy Reform," Policy Research Working Paper Series 3468, Washington, DC: World Bank.

Cheema, G. Shabbir and Dennis Rondinelli, eds. 2007. *Decentralized Governance: Emerging Concepts and Practices*. Washington, DC: The Brookings Institution.

Cities Alliance. 2006. *Guide to City Development Strategies: Improving Urban Performance*. Washington, DC: Cities Alliance.

Clark, Gordon L. 1984. "A Theory of Local Autonomy," *Annals of the Association of American Geographers*, 74(2), pp. 195–208.

Cohen, John M. and Stephen Peterson. 1999. *Administrative Decentralization in Developing Countries*. Boulder, CO: Lynne Rienner Publishing.

Connerley, Ed, Kent Eaton, and Paul Smoke, eds. 2010. *Making Decentralization Work: Democracy, Development and Security*. Boulder, CO: Lynne Rienner Publishers.

Conyers, Diana and Peter Hills. 1984. *An Introduction to Development Planning in the Third World*. Oxford, UK: John Wiley and Sons.

Darch, Emma and Emezi, Akwaeke. 2012. *Structures of Metropolitan Governance and Finance: A Case Study of Cape Town*. Cambridge, MA: Lincoln Institute of Land Policy.

Eaton, Kent, Kai Kaiser, and Paul Smoke. 2011. *The Political Economy of Decentralization: Implications for Aid Effectiveness*. Washington, DC: World Bank.

Estache, Antonio. 2004. *Emerging Infrastructure Policy Issues in Developing Countries: A Survey of the Recent Economic Literature*. Washington, DC: World Bank.

Estache, Antonio. 2010. "Infrastructure Finance in Developing Countries: An Overview," EIB Papers 8/2010, Brussels: European Investment Bank, Economics Department.

Evans. P. 1995. *Embedded Autonomy: States and Industrial Transformation*. Princeton, NJ: Princeton University Press.

Fjeldstad, Odd-Helge. 2006. "Corruption in Tax Administration: Lessons from Institutional Reforms in Uganda," in Susan Rose-Ackerman (ed.), *International Handbook on the Economics of Corruption*. Cheltenham, UK: Edward Elgar, pp. 484–511.

Frank, D. 2011. "City Development Strategy: A Conceptual Framework," Cities Alliance Discussion Paper No. 1. Washington, DC: World Bank.

Friere, Mila and John Peterson, eds. 2004. *Subnational Capital Markets in Developing Countries: From Theory to Practice*. Oxford, UK: Oxford University Press.

Fritz, V. and A. Rocha Menocal. 2006. *(Re)building Developmental States: From Theory to Practice*. London: Overseas Development Institute.

Fritz, V. and A. Rocha Menocal. 2007. "Developmental States in the New Millennium: Concepts and Challenges for a New Aid Agenda," *Development Policy Review*, 25(5), pp. 531–552.

Government of Kenya. 2005. *Guidelines for Preparation, Implementation and Monitoring of the Local Authority Service Delivery Action Plan*. Nairobi.

Grindle, M.S. 2004. "Good Enough Governance: Poverty Reduction and Reform in Developing Countries," *Governance*, 17(4), pp. 525–548.

Hall, Peter and Mark Tewdwr-Jones. 2010. *Urban and Regional Planning*. London: Taylor & Francis.

Harris, Clive. 2003. *Private Participation in Infrastructure in Developing Countries*. Washington, DC: World Bank.

Healey, Patsy. 1997. *Collaborative Planning*. Vancouver: University of British Columbia Press

Healey, Patsy. 2012. "The Universal and the Contingent: Some Reflections on the Transnational Flow of Planning Ideas and Practices," *Planning Theory*, 11, pp. 188–207.

Helm, Dieter. 2010. "Infrastructure and Infrastructure Finance: The Role of the Government and the Private Sector in the Current World," EIB Papers 5/2010, Brussels: European Investment Bank, Economics Department.

Kehew, Robert, Tomoko Matsukawa, and John Petersen. 2005. *Local Financing for Sub-sovereign Infrastructure in Developing Countries*. Washington, DC: World Bank.

Leftwich, Adrian. 1996. *Democracy and Development: Theory and Practice*. New York: Wiley.

Litvack, J., J. Ahmad, and R. Bird. 1998. *Rethinking Decentralization in Developing Countries*. Washington, DC: World Bank.

Martínez-Vázquez, J. and F. Vaillancourt, eds. 2011. *Decentralization in Difficult Environments*. Cheltenham, UK: Edward Elgar.

Nasehi, C. and R. Rangwala. 2011. *Structures of Metropolitan Governance and Finance: A Case Study on Manila*. Cambridge, MA: Lincoln Institute of Land Policy.

North, D., J. Wallis, S. Webb, and B. Weingast. 2006. "Limited Access Orders in the Developing World: A New Approach to the Problems of Development," Policy Research Working Paper 4359. Washington, DC: World Bank.

Ojendal, J. 2010. *Risk Analysis of Cambodian Decentralisation*. Stockholm: Swedish International Development Agency.

Penfold-Becerra, M. 2006. *Clientelism and Social Funds: Empirical Evidence from Chávez's "Misiones" Programs in Venezuela*. Caracas, Venezuela: Instituto de Estudios Superiores de Administración (IESA).

Peterson, George. 2000. "Building Local Credit Institutions," Urban and Local Government Background Paper No. 3. Washington, DC: World Bank.

Platz, D. 2009. "Infrastructure Finance in Developing Countries—the Potential of Sub-sovereign Bonds," UN DESA Working Paper No. 76. New York: United Nations Department for Economic and Social Affairs.

Rakner, Lise, Luke Mukubvu, Naomi Ngwira *et al.* 2004. *The Budget as Theatre: The Formal and Informal Institutional Makings of the Budget Process in Malawi*. London: UK Department for International Development.

Rodwin, Lloyd and Bish Sanyal, eds. 2000. *The Profession of City Planning: Changes, Images and Challenges*. New Brunswick, NJ: Rutgers Center for Urban Policy Research.

Romeo, L. 1999. "Systems Experimentation in Support of Decentralization Reforms," *Regional Development Dialogue*, 20(2).

Romeo, L. 2000. "Towards an Improved Municipal Planning Process," a report of the Second Rural Municipalities Development Program (Protierra-II), INIFOM-World Bank, Managua (mimeo).

Romeo, L. 2003. "The Role of External Assistance in Supporting Decentralization Reforms," *Public Administration and Development*, 23(1).

Romeo, L. 2013. "Decentralizing for Development: The Developmental Potential of Local Autonomy and the Limits of Politics-driven Decentralization Reforms," in J. Ojendal and A. Dellnas (eds.), *The Imperative of Good Local Governance: Challenges for the Next Decade of Decentralization.* Tokyo: United Nations University Press.

Romeo, L. and M. El Mensi. 2011. "The Difficult Road to Local Autonomy in Yemen: Decentralization Reforms between Political Rationale and Bureaucratic Resistances in a Multi-party Democracy of the Arabian Peninsula," in J. Martínez-Vázquez and F. Vaillancourt (eds.), *Decentralization in Difficult Environments.* Cheltenham, UK: Edward Elgar.

Romeo, L. and L. Spyckerelle. 2004. "Decentralization Reforms and Commune-level Services Delivery in Cambodia." Presented at the ADB-ADBI-UNCDF Workshop on "Local Government Pro-Poor Service Delivery," Manila, February. www.uncdf.org/english/local_development/documents_and_reports/thematic_papers/adb/UNCDF_Cambodia.pdf.

Sanyal, Bish, ed. 2005. *Comparative Planning Cultures.* London: Routledge.

Schady, N. 2000. "The Political Economy of Expenditures by the Peruvian Social Fund, 1991–1995," *American Political Science Review*, 94(2), pp. 289–304.

Slack, E. 2007. "Managing the Coordination of Service Delivery in Metropolitan Cities: The Role of Metropolitan Governance," Policy Research Working Paper 4317, Washington, DC: World Bank.

Slack, E. 2010. *Financing Large Cities and Metropolitan Areas.* Toronto: Institute on Municipal Finance and Governance, Munk School, University of Toronto.

Slack, E. and R. Chattopadhyay. 2009. *Finance and Governance of Capital Cities in Federal Systems.* Montreal: McGill-Queens University Press.

Smoke, Paul. 2003. "Erosion and Reform from the Center in Kenya," in James Wunsch and Dele Olowu (eds.), *Local Governance in Africa: The Challenges of Democratic Decentralization.* Boulder, CO: Lynne Rienner Publishers.

Smoke, Paul. 2008. "Local Revenues under Fiscal Decentralization in Developing Countries: Linking Policy Reform, Governance and Capacity," in Gregory Ingram and Yu-Hung Hong (eds.), *Fiscal Decentralization and Land Policies.* Cambridge, MA: Lincoln Institute Press, pp. 38–69.

Smoke, Paul. 2010. "Implementing Decentralization: Meeting Neglected Challenges," in Ed Connerley, Kent Eaton, and Paul Smoke (eds.), *Making Decentralization Work.* Boulder, CO: Lynne Rienner Publishers, pp. 191–217.

Smoke, Paul. 2013. "Metropolitan Cities in the National Fiscal Structure," in Roy Bahl, Johannes Linn, and Debbie Wetzel (eds.), *Metropolitan Government Finances in Developing Countries.* Cambridge, MA: Lincoln Institute, pp. 57–84.

Smoke, Paul and Kathy Whimp. 2011. "The Evolution of Fiscal Decentralization under Kenya's New Constitution: Opportunities and Challenges," *National Tax Association Proceedings*, pp. 109–115.

Straub, Stephane. 2011. "Infrastructure and Development: A Critical Appraisal of the Macro-level Literature," *The Journal of Development Studies*, 47(5), pp. 683–708.

Sundaram, K.V. 1997. *Decentralized Multilevel Planning Principles and Practices (Asian and African Experiences)*. New Delhi: Concept Publishing Co.

UN Capital Development Fund. 1996. *Local Development Funds: Promoting Decentralized Participatory Planning and Financing*. New York: UNCDF.

United Cities and Local Governments. 2010. *Local Government Finance: The Challenges of the 21st Century*. Cheltenham, UK: Edward Elgar.

Weimer, B. 2009. *Decentralization of the African State—or State Building Through Local Governance—a Paradox? Challenges to Governance and Decentralization in Mozambique*. Report on the Conference on "Bringing the State Back In: The New Roles and Responsibilities of the 21st Century State," The Association of Development Researchers in Denmark, Copenhagen, May 12–13.

World Bank. 2000. *World Development Report: Entering the 21st Century*. Washington, DC: World Bank.

World Bank. 2009. *Systems of Cities: Harnessing Urbanization for Growth and Poverty Alleviation* (World Bank Urban Strategy). Washington, DC: World Bank.

Yilmaz, Serdar, Yakup Beris, and Rodrigo Serrano-Berthet. 2010. "Linking Local Government Discretion and Accountability in Decentralization," *Development Policy Review*, 28(3), pp. 259–293.

14 Decentralized provision of public infrastructure and corruption[1]

Anwar Shah

Introduction

During the past two decades a silent revolution has swept the globe and a large number of industrial and developing countries have pursued decentralization reforms that attempt to move public decision making closer to people. The reform agenda has been pursued through varying combinations of political, administrative, and fiscal decentralization initiatives that aim to shift some traditional central government functions to intermediate or lower orders of government. These reforms have proven to be controversial. This is because decentralization is perceived as a solution to some problems such as a dysfunctional public sector with lack of voice and exit as well as a source of new problems such as capture by local elite, aggravation of macroeconomic management due to a lack of fiscal discipline, race to the bottom, and potentially greater barriers to common economic and social union through beggar-thy-neighbor policies. The impact of decentralization on corruption (defined as the abuse of public office for private gain or exercise of official powers against public interest) is an area of growing interest inviting much controversy and debate. While this debate has largely centered on the overall impact of decentralization, the focus of the current chapter is to examine various arguments in this debate in the specific case of decentralized provision of infrastructure—a yet largely unexplored area of research.

What is special about decentralized provision of infrastructure?

Infrastructure projects are typically lumpy, have long gestational periods, and are long lived. This implies that a local government must have assured financing of capital and maintenance costs and a plan for recovering capital costs and recurring costs over the life of the project. Infrastructure projects are typically costly and since in most countries local governments have constrained tax autonomy and even more constrained access to capital market finance, higher level financing and assistance for capital market access assumes critical importance for initiation of projects. Even if local governments may enjoy significant tax autonomy, poorer local jurisdictions would not have the revenue capacity to finance infrastructure provision from own revenue surpluses and would have typically no access to capital market finance due to a lack of credit worthiness even in the absence of prohibitions usually practiced against local bond finance. Higher level capital grant financing without local matching funds creates incentives for softer budget constraints as local governments do not have to justify these expenses to the electorate to have buy in for additional taxation. Infrastructure projects may entail inter-jurisdictional externalities as the optimal size to reap economies of scale may be larger than required by one jurisdiction such as water purification and waste disposal plants or in the absence of user fees free ridership may be possible by residents of other jurisdictions such as for roads, bridges, mass transit, sports and recreation centers, and libraries. Therefore inter-municipal partnerships for cost sharing or higher level transfers to compensate for benefit spill-outs may be required.

Why is it important to examine the implications of decentralized provision of infrastructure for the incidence of corruption?

Decentralized provision of infrastructure is advocated for better matching of infrastructure services with local preferences and needs and for enhancing efficiency and equity of public provision. But if decentralized provision is seen to lead to a higher incidence of corruption especially with higher order grant financing then these advantages may be undermined. Corrupt practices in infrastructure affect the whole project investment and operations cycle and result in projects with roads and bridges to nowhere and creation of white elephants while a median voter is denied access to basic services such as clean water and sanitation. Potential of such corrupt practices is enhanced when these projects are mostly financed by higher order governments which is often a necessity with decentralized provision of infrastructure or external donors. Since infrastructure projects are typically lumpy and have long gestational periods, corrupt strategic behavior of current regimes can tie hands of future regimes to the priorities set by the initiating regime. The times of fiscal stress offer even greater opportunities for corruption as projects must be approved, financed, and implemented on an accelerated schedule. In view of the potential negative impact of corruption on good governance, it is important to analyze the implications of decentralized provision of infrastructure for good government both in theory and in practice with a view to examining options for limiting opportunities for corruption while enhancing possibilities of detection and punishment. This chapter takes an important first step in this direction by providing a synthesis of conceptual and empirical literature on this subject and highlighting the limits of our knowledge in this area especially the void in the area of empirical underpinnings of lessons in combating corruption.

The chapter is organized as follows. The second section provides an introductory review of fundamental concepts and concerns relating to corruption, its many facets, and its drivers. The third section highlights corruption concerns with decentralized infrastructure provision. The fourth section presents counter arguments and discusses the promise of decentralized provision of infrastructure for improved service delivery and reduced corruption. The fifth section synthesizes available evidence on the relationship between decentralized infrastructure provision and corruption. The sixth section draws overall tentative conclusions on the susceptibility of decentralized provision to corruption. The seventh section draws lessons for a strategy to combat corruption when infrastructure provision is decentralized. A final section provides concluding remarks.

Corruption and its drivers: fundamental concepts and concerns

Corruption is defined as exercise of official powers against public interest or the abuse of public office for private gains. Public sector corruption is a symptom of failed governance. Here, we define "governance" as the norms, traditions, and institutions by which power and authority in a country is exercised—including the institutions of participation and accountability in governance and mechanisms of citizens' voice and exit and norms and networks of civic engagement; the constitutional-legal framework and the nature of accountability relationships among citizens and governments; the process by which governments are selected, monitored, held accountable, and renewed or replaced; and the legitimacy, credibility, and efficacy of the institutions that govern political, economic, cultural, and social interactions among citizens themselves and their governments.

Concern about corruption—the abuse of public office for private gain—is as old as the history of government. In the fourth century BCE, Kautaliya who served as an advisor responded to the Indian King's concerns about corruption by arguing that corruption is inevitable. He wrote that: "Just as it is not possible to not taste honey placed on the surface of the tongue, even so it is not possible for one dealing with the money of the king not to taste the money in however a small quantity." He further advised the king that corruption would be difficult to detect. He stated: "Just as fish moving under water cannot possibly be found out either as drinking or not drinking water, so government servants employed in the government work cannot be found out [while] taking money [for themselves]." In 350 BCE, Aristotle suggested in *The Politics* that "… to protect the treasury from being defrauded, let all money be issued openly in front of the whole city, and let copies of the accounts be deposited in various wards."

In recent years, concerns about corruption have mounted in tandem with growing evidence of its detrimental impact on growth and development (see World Bank, 2004). Figure 14.1 highlights the negative consequences of corruption for affordable housing for the poor in Indonesia. As a result of this growing concern, there has been universal condemnation of corrupt practices, leading to the removal of some country leaders. Moreover, many governments and development agencies have devoted substantial resources and energies to fighting corruption in recent years. Even so, it is not yet clear that the incidence of corruption has declined perceptibly, especially in highly corrupt countries. The lack of significant progress can be attributed to the fact that many programs are simply folk remedies or "one size fits all" approaches and offer little chance of success. For programs to work, they must identify the type of corruption they are targeting and tackle the underlying, country-specific causes, or "drivers," of dysfunctional governance. This calls for examination of structure of government among other factors.

The many forms of corruption in infrastructure

Corruption is not manifested in one single form; indeed it typically takes at least four broad forms.

Petty, administrative, or bureaucratic corruption. Many corrupt acts are isolated transactions by individual public officials who abuse their office, for example, by demanding bribes and kickbacks, diverting public funds, or awarding favors in return for personal considerations. Such acts are often referred to as petty corruption even though, in the aggregate, a substantial amount of public resources may be involved. For infrastructure provision, petty corruption is often observed for "greasing the wheels" in public-private interface in proposals, registration, procurement, and access to public services.

Grand corruption. The theft or misuse of vast amounts of public resources by state officials—usually members of, or associated with, the political or

Figure 14.1 Impact of corruption on housing for the poor. Slums built on swamp land near a garbage dump in East Cipinang, Jakarta, Indonesia (source: Wikimedia Commons [photo taken by Jonathan Macintosh, 2004]).

administrative elite—constitutes grand corruption. For infrastructure provision, grand corruption occurs in the selection process for public procurement and in procurement itself and in public-private partnerships and interface. In developing countries, foreign private sector participation is considered a major source of such corruption.

State or regulatory capture and influence peddling. Collusion by private actors with public officials or politicians for their mutual, private benefit is referred to as state capture. That is, the private sector "captures" the state legislative, executive, and judicial apparatus for its own purposes. State capture coexists with the conventional (and opposite) view of corruption, in which public officials extort or otherwise exploit the private sector for private ends. This form of corruption is prevalent in both industrial and developing countries.

Patronage/paternalism and being a "team player." Using official position to provide assistance to clients having the same geographic, ethnic, and cultural origin so that they receive preferential treatment in their dealings with the public sector including public sector employment. Also providing the same assistance on a quid pro quo basis to colleagues belonging to an informal network of friends and allies. Geographic, ethnic, and culture based patronage is commonplace in developing countries and "team player" form of corruption is a fact of everyday life in industrial countries.

It is also known that corruption is country-specific; thus, approaches that apply common policies and tools (that is, one-size-fits-all approaches) to countries in which acts of corruption and the quality of governance vary widely are likely to fail. One needs to understand the local circumstances that encourage or permit public and private actors to be corrupt. Finally, we know that if corruption is about governance and governance is about the exercise of state power, then efforts to combat corruption demand strong local leadership and ownership if they are to be successful and sustainable.

Many facets of corruption in the provision of infrastructure

An important distinguishing aspect of infrastructure corruption is that mostly it comes in the form of grand corruption which is commonplace in both industrial and developing countries. OECD estimates that in OECD countries the bribe rate in procurement for construction projects ranges from 5 to 25 percent of contract value (Ehlermann-Cache, 2007). In developing countries guesstimates place these much higher. Industrial countries have largely been successful in eliminating petty corruption through higher wages which remains widespread and adversely affects billions of people in developing countries. Table 14.1 highlights the incidence of corruption in infrastructure provision at various decision points in the legislative-executive-private sector interface in provision of public infrastructure.

Vulnerability to corruption is significant regardless of centralization or decentralization of provision as described in Table 14.2. With decentralization, however, the probability of detection of corruption is significantly enhanced.

What drives corruption?

Public sector corruption, as a symptom of failed governance, depends on a multitude of factors such as the quality of public sector management, the nature of accountability relations between the government and citizens, the legal framework, and the degree to which public sector processes are accompanied by transparency and dissemination of information. Efforts to address corruption that fail to adequately account for these underlying "drivers" are unlikely to generate profound and sustainable results. To understand these drivers, a conceptual and empirical perspective is needed to understand why corruption persists and what can be a useful antidote. At the conceptual level, a number of interesting ideas have been put forward. These ideas can be broadly grouped together in three categories: (i) principal-agent or agency models; (ii) new public management perspectives; and (iii) neo-institutional economics frameworks.

Conceptual perspectives on drivers of corruption

Principal-agent models

This is the most widely used modeling strategy. A common thread in these models is that the government is led by a benevolent dictator, the principal, who aims to motivate government officials (agents) to act with integrity in the use of public resources (see Becker, 1968, 1983; Becker and Stigler, 1974; Banfield 1975; Rose-Ackerman, 1975, 1978; Klitgaard, 1988, 1991). One such view, the so-called crime and punishment model by Gary Becker (1968), states that self-interested public officials seek out or accept bribes so long as the expected gains from corruption exceed the expected costs (detection and punishment) associated with corrupt acts. Thus, according to this view, corruption could be mitigated by (a) reducing the number of transactions over which public officials have discretion; (b) reducing the scope of gains from each transaction; (c) increasing the probability for detection; and (d) increasing the penalty for corrupt activities. Moreover, since it is costly to increase detection, but not to increase penalties (at least assuming detection is accurate), the most efficient way to eliminate corruption is to impose very high penalties with a relatively low probability of detection. Klitgaard (1988) restates this model to emphasize the unrestrained monopoly power and discretionary authority of government officials. According to him, corruption equals monopoly plus discretion minus accountability. To curtail corruption under this framework, one has to have a rules-driven government with strong internal controls and with little discretion to public officials. This model gained wide acceptance in public policy circles and served as a foundation for empirical research and policy design to combat administrative, bureaucratic, or petty corruption. Experience in highly corrupt countries, however, contradicts the effectiveness of such an approach as the rules enforcers themselves add an extra burden of corruption and lack of discretion is also thwarted by collusive behavior of corruptors. In fact, lack of discretion is often

Table 14.1 Many facets of corruption in the provision of infrastructure—decentralized or not

Decision point	*Incidence of corruption*	*Type of corruption*
AT APPRAISAL/PLANNING STAGE		
Legislative framework	Lobbying legislators for pet projects, log rolling, political campaign financing, perks and privileges in exchange for legislative favors, preparation of draft legislation by lobbyists	Grand corruption, State capture (universal phenomenon)
Policy making	Policy framework to suit special interest groups and bribe payers	Executive capture, grand corruption, most countries
Regulation	Zoning and regulatory framework tailored to favor special interest groups. Extortion over licensing.	Executive capture, grand corruption, most countries
Planning and budgeting	Rezoning and selection of projects based upon bribes received	Executive capture, grand corruption, most countries
AT PROJECT FINANCING STAGE		
External financing	Higher costs of externally financed projects, donors favor PPPs especially with foreign participation. Kickbacks in return for favorable terms.	Executive capture, grand corruption, most developing countries
Bond financing	Higher costs for floating bonds	Grand corruption, some developing countries
Grant financing	Pork barrel grants as quid pro quo for political finance	Grand corruption by financing pork projects such as "The Bridge to Nowhere in Alaska," most countries
Tax financing	Elite capture	Grand corruption through tax expenditures and financing of projects preferred by elites

AT IMPLEMENTATION STAGE		
Public-private partnerships	Collusion among public managers and private providers to give favorable terms to private participants in return for a bribe commonly practiced in energy and road projects, re-negotiation of contracts during and after execution	Grand corruption, most countries
Program and project management	Ghost projects, ghost employees, phantom expenditures	Mostly grand corruption, most developing countries
Public procurement	Kickbacks, rigged bidding and tendering. Mechanisms: intermediary collusion, consulting fees, false services, overpayment, payment to a front company, Swiss and Cayman Island bank accounts, collusion among competitors. Procurement cycle: registration, manipulating specifications, insider info, quality reduction, clearance from inspectors, expediting payments.	Mostly grand corruption, most countries
Construction	Use of low quality materials, theft of materials, false prices	Mostly grand corruption, most developing countries
AT OPERATIONS STAGE		
Operations and maintenance	False reporting, ghost workers	Mostly grand corruption, most developing countries
User charges	Theft and free ridership	Petty corruption, most developing countries
Public access	Delay or denial of access	Petty corruption, most developing countries
AT EX-POST EVALUATION STAGE		
Evaluation	Project financing and selection of evaluators leads to lack of independence and biased evaluations	Patronage, most countries

Source: Author's perspectives.

Table 14.2 Vulnerability to corruption observed in decentralized or not provision of infrastructure in various sectors

Water and sanitation	Land acquisition, selection of contractors, bid rigging, compromising quality, bribes for connections, meter tampering, conflict of interest with officials involved in private provision, collusion with companies offering bottled water or tanker provision
Roads	Land acquisition at above market prices, rehabilitation, selection of contractors, false procurement and maintenance expenditures, certification of quality of construction
Electricity	Public utilities: land acquisition, rights of way, rehabilitation, equipment purchase and repair mark-ups, patronage appointments, defective meters, meter tampering, theft of electricity by tapping distribution lines with side payments, connections delays, false billing, response to non-payment of bills, false subsidy payments, public sector guarantees for assured demand for supply at above market rates Private utilities: selection, regulatory regime, price hikes, regulators turning blind eye to capital deterioration
Hospitals	Ghost hospitals, bribes for admissions and drugs, false procurement and construction
Schools	Ghost schools, bribes for admissions, ghost enrollments, false procurement and corruption
Fitness and recreation centers	Padding up cost of construction and purchase of equipment

Source: Author's perspectives.

cited as a defense by corrupt officials who partake in corruption as part of a vertically well-knit network enjoying immunity from prosecution.

Another variant of principal-agent models integrates the role of legislators and elected officials in the analysis. In this variant, high level government officials—represented by legislators or elected public officials—institute or manipulate existing policy and legislation in favor of particular interest groups—representing private sector interests and entities or individual units of public bureaucracy competing for higher budgets—in exchange of rents or side payments. In this framework, legislators weigh the personal monetary gains from corrupt practices and improved chances of re-election against the chance of being caught, punished, and losing an election with a tarnished reputation. Factors affecting this decision include campaign financing mechanisms, information access by voters, the ability of citizens to vote out corrupt legislators, the degree of political contestability, electoral systems, democratic institutions, and traditions and institutions of accountability in governance. Examples of such analyses include: Rose-Ackerman (1978); Advig and Moene (1990); Grossman and Helpman (1994); Flatters and Macleod (1995); Chand and Moene (1997); Van Rijckeghem and Weder (2001); Acconcia *et al.* (2003). This conceptual framework is useful in analyzing political corruption or state capture.

There is a fine line dividing theoretical models that focus on the effects of localization on corruption and those that analyze the decentralization of corruption within a multi-tier hierarchy from an "industrial organization of corruption" type of framework. In the latter group a distinction is made between "top-down corruption"—where corrupt high levels buy lower levels by sharing a portion of gains—and "bottom-up corruption"—where low level officials share their own collected bribes with superior levels to avoid detection or punishment. The former phenomenon is more likely to exist in a federal system of governance where powers may be shared among various orders of government and the alternate is more likely to prevail under unitary or centralized forms of governance or dictatorial regimes. The impact of governance on the corruption networks is an interesting yet unresearched topic. Tirole (1986) analyzed one aspect of this network by means of a three-tier principal-supervisor-agent model (see also Guriev, 1999). This extension of a conventional principal-agent model assists in drawing inferences regarding the type of corrupt relations that could evolve under a three-tier unitary government structure. These inferences are highly sensitive to underlying assumptions regarding principal-agent relationships under a multi-tiered system of governance (four-tier hierarchies are modeled by Bac and Bag, 1998; Carillo, 2000). In Guriev's three-tier hierarchy model the mid level bureaucrat supervises the agent and reports to the principal. In comparing the characteristics of equilibria with top-bottom and all level corruption Guriev concludes that top-level corruption "is not efficient, as it redistribute rents in favor of agents, and therefore makes it more attractive for potential entrants" (p. 2) thereby leading to higher total corruption.

Shleifer and Vishny (1993) utilize conventional industrial organization theory model and conclude that decentralization is likely to increase corruption. In this model, government bureaucracies and agencies act as monopolists selling complimentary government-produced goods which are legally required for private sector activity. The main idea behind the model is that under centralized corruption bureaucracies act like a joint monopoly, whereas under decentralized corruption bureaucracies behave as independent monopolies. When bureaucracies act as independent monopolies, they ignore the effects of higher prices on the overall demand for a good and hence drive up the cumulative bribe burden.

Waller *et al.* (2002) define decentralized corruption as a system in which higher level officials collect a fixed amount of bribe income from each of the bureaucrats that take bribes, without mandating on the bribe size that the bureaucrats charge. In a centralized system, on the contrary, bribe size is determined by the higher level of government which collects them from bureaucrats and redistributes it among them after keeping a share. Waller *et al.* posit that decentralized corruption leads to lower levels of total corruption in the economy (lower spread), higher levels of bribe per entrepreneur (higher depth), and a smaller formal sector vis-à-vis a centralized corruption equilibrium. Yet, these results vary widely for specific "regimes" in the model—when given parameters satisfy key conditions—for instance, for high-enough wages and monitoring systems, centralized corruption may reduce total corruption and expand the formal economy.

While previously discussed studies centered on the organizational structure of corruption, Ahlin (2001) differs by concentrating on the effects of bureaucratic decentralization. Under the assumption of no interregional mobility, corruption increases with the degree of bureaucratic decentralization but is independent of the degree of regional decentralization, whereas for perfect interregional mobility corruption decreases with regional decentralization and is independent of bureaucratic decentralization. A key intuition of the model is that corrupt bureaucrats fail to internalize the costs of increases in bribe-charges imposed on other bureaucrats. Arikan (2004) uses a tax competition framework to examine localization-corruption links and finds that higher degree of decentralization is expected to lead to lower levels of corruption. Bardhan and Mookherjee (2000) shed light upon the determinants of the capture of the democratic process. Not surprisingly, they conclude that the extent of relative capture is ambiguous and context specific.

In conclusion, no definitive conclusions can be drawn regarding corruption and the centralization-decentralization nexus from the agency type conceptual models. These models simply reaffirm that the incidence of corruption is context dependent and therefore cannot be uncovered by generalized models.

New public management frameworks

The new public management (NPM) literature, on the other hand, points to a more fundamental discordance among the public sector mandate, its authorizing environment, and the operational culture and capacity. According to NPM, this discordance contributes to government acting like a runaway train and government officials indulging in rent-seeking behaviors with little opportunity for citizens to constrain government behavior. This viewpoint calls for fundamental civil service and political reforms to create a government under contract and accountable for results. Public officials will no longer have permanent rotating appointments but instead they could keep their jobs as long as they fulfilled their contractual obligations (see Shah, 1999, 2005).

The new public management (NPM) paradigms have clear implications for the study of localization and corruption as they argue for contractual arrangements in provision of public services. Such a contractual framework may encourage competitive service delivery through outsourcing, purchaser-provider split under a decentralized structure of governance. The NPM goals are harmonious with decentralization as greater accountability for results reinforces government accountability to citizens through voice and exit mechanisms. Conceptually, therefore, the NPM is expected to reduce opportunities for corruption (see Shah, 1999, 2005). Andrews and Shah (2005) integrate these two ideas in a common framework of citizen-centered governance. They argue that citizen empowerment holds the key to enhanced accountability and reduced opportunities for corruption.

Others disagree with such conclusions and argue that the NPM could lead to higher corruption as opposed to greater accountability. This may happen because the tendering for service delivery and separation of purchasers from providers may lead to increased rent seeking behavior and enhanced possibilities for corruption (Batley, 1999; Von Maravic, 2003). Further, some argue that decentralized management leads to weaker vertical supervision from higher levels and the inadequacy of mechanisms to exert controls over decentralized agencies (Scharpf, 1997). This loss in vertical accountability is seen as a source of enhanced opportunities for corruption. Of course, this viewpoint simply neglects potential gains from higher horizontal accountability.

Neo-institutional economics (NIE) frameworks

Finally, Shah (2006) has utilized the transactions costs approach of the neo-institutional economics (NIE) to present a newer perspective on the causes and cures of corruption. Shah argues that corruption results from opportunistic behavior of public officials (agents) given that citizens (as governors and principals) are either not empowered or face high transaction costs to hold public officials accountable for their corrupt acts. The principals have bounded rationality—they act rationally based upon the incomplete information they have. In order to have a more informed perspective on public sector operations, they face high transaction costs in acquiring and processing the information. On the other hand, agents (public officials) are better informed. This asymmetry of information allows agents to indulge in opportunistic behavior which goes unchecked due to high *transactions costs* faced by the principals and a lack of or inadequacy of countervailing institutions to enforce accountable governance. Thus corrupt countries have inadequate mechanisms for contract enforcement, weak judicial systems, and inadequate provision for public safety. This raises the transactions costs in the economy further raising the cost of private capital as well as the cost of public service provision. The problem is further compounded by path dependency (i.e., a major break with the past is difficult to achieve as any major reforms are likely to be blocked by influential interest groups), cultural and historical factors and mental models where those who are victimized by corruption feel that attempts to deal with corruption will lead to further victimization, with little hope of corrupt actors being brought to justice. These considerations lead principals to the conclusion that any attempt on their part to constrain corrupt behaviors will invite strong retaliation from powerful interests. Therefore, citizen empowerment (e.g., through decentralization, citizens' charter, bill of rights, elections, and other forms of civic engagement) assumes critical importance in combating corruption because it may have a significant impact on the incentives faced by public officials to be responsive to public interest.

The perils of decentralized provision of infrastructure in breeding corruption

A number of arguments have been advanced to support the notion that corruption increases with localization. A few of these are summarized below.

a **_Personalism._** Vito Tanzi (1995) argued that localization brings officials in close contact with citizens. This promotes personalism and reduces professionalism and arms length relationships. Personalism in his view breeds corruption as officials pay greater attention to individual citizen needs and disregard public interest. Further, a higher degree of discretion at the local level and long tenure of local officials make it easier to establish unethical relationships (Prud'homme, 1994).

b **_Weak monitoring and vertical controls._** Impediments to corrupt practices also decrease as local politicians and bureaucrats collude to advance narrow self-interests while the effectiveness of auditing agencies and monitoring from the central level wanes (Prud'homme, 1994). Localization may increase the motivation for corruption among public officials by creating an impression that they are subject to lower monitoring, control, and supervision.

c **_Fiscal decentralization and overgrazing._** Treisman argues that decentralized federal systems tend to have higher corruption ratings due to (a) their larger size; (b) they are more likely to have separate police forces at both central and sub-national levels (which increases corruption due to overgrazing) and their greater propensity to have a regionally elected upper house of parliament with veto power (which also may increase corruption as regional governments may buy off these veto-players or have greater leverage to protect their ill-gotten gains). Using cross-country regression analysis Treisman (1999, 2000; Treisman and Shleifer, 2002) presents empirical evidence that supports the existence of this negative relationship. Treisman's empirical results, however, are sensitive to the inclusion of other variables in the equation and may have omitted variables bias in view of a lack of underlying framework for corruption.

A recent study by Fan *et al.* (2007) provides a more nuanced view of the impact of fiscal decentralization. Combining cross-sectional secondary data for 80 countries with a survey of 9,000 business owners, it finds that

> in countries with large number of government or administrative tiers and (given local revenues) a larger number of local public employees, reported bribery was more frequent. When local or central governments received a larger share of GDP in revenue, bribery was less frequent.
>
> (p. 1)

> These results suggest that while decentralization in general opens up possibilities for rent seeking by a larger number of individuals, tax decentralization limits such opportunities by bringing greater citizen oversight of local government operations.

d ***Political decentralization and lack of discipline.*** Political decentralization is seen as a cascading system of bribes by Shleifer and Vishny (1993). They note that

> to invest in a Russian company, a foreigner must bribe every agency involved in foreign investment including the foreign investment office, the relevant industrial ministry, the finance ministry, the executive branch of the local government, the legislative branch, the central bank, the state property bureau, and so on.
>
> (p. 615)

In the same vein, Bardhan (1997) and Blanchard and Shleifer (2000) [B&S] have argued that political centralization leads to lower levels of corruption. B&S sustain that political decentralization is seen as a source of corruption in Russia but not China. This conclusion emerges from the contrasting role of local governments in their relations with local enterprises observed in China and Russia. In China, local governments have provided a supporting role whereas in Russia, local governments have stymied the growth of new firms through taxation, regulation, and corruption. The authors note that the behavior of Russian local governments can be explained by (a) state capture by old firms, leading local governments to protect them from competition and (b) rent seeking behavior of local officials discouraging new firms to enter. The authors attribute this contrasting experience to the presence of political decentralization in Russia and its absence in China. They argue that political centralization in China contributes to party discipline which in turn reduces the risk of local capture and corruption. However, the B&S analysis does not pay sufficient attention to local-enterprise relations in the two countries. Local enterprises in China are owned and run by local governments and even deliver local services such as education, health, and transportation in addition to their economic functions. Thus local enterprises are part and parcel of the local government. In Russia, on the other hand, a mixed pattern of these relationships has begun to emerge. Therefore, the contrasting experience of the local governments may better be explained by agency problems rather than by political decentralization. In fact the weakening of party discipline through the emergence of powerful local leaders may be contributing to growth of local industry as the strong arm of central planning is held at bay by these leaders.

e ***Interest group capture.*** Opportunities for corruption increase due to a greater influence of interest groups at the local level (Prud'homme, 1994). In this regard, Bardhan and Mookherjee (2000) argue that the probability of capture by local interest groups could be greater at the local level if, for example, interest group cohesiveness (fraction of the richest class that contribute to lobby) is higher, or the proportion of informed voters is lower at the local level. Lower levels of political awareness at the local level and less coverage of local elections by media may also impair local democracy and lead to higher capture. The notion of capture at the local levels due to weaknesses of the democratic system has also been raised by Shah (1998). Concerns about risks of local capture are also expressed in a recent World Bank Study (World Bank, 2004). The study argues that decentralization may increase opportunities for corruption in some developing countries where interference in public administration is the norm, merit culture and management systems in the civil service are weak, and institutions of participation and accountability are ineffective. The issue is significant, for example, in Pakistan and the Philippines and also relevant to Guatemala and Tanzania where more limited decentralization has been carried out. Pakistan has recently carried out a strong program of devolution to the provinces (Shah, 2012). Given systemic politicization of public services in Pakistan, decentralization to the provinces may intensify rather than reduce pressures for political/bureaucratic collusion, although this may be further mitigated by further administrative decentralization, giving elected local officials the power to, hire, fire, and set terms of employment of civil servants in their jurisdiction. Note that administration decentralization in areas under feudal influence is likely to exacerbate the corruption concerns. Identical concerns are pertinent in the Philippines, where legislation in 1991 devolved to regions and localities powers to provide services and raise revenues. In the Philippines, there is a long tradition of elected local public offices rotating among family members. The World Bank study is concerned with the effect of decentralization on corruption when there is a local capture by political and bureaucratic elites. There is little disagreement in the literature that in such a situation, localization without fundamental electoral and land reforms is likely to increase corruption. On the contrary, the perception of localization as a breeding ground for corruption in the presence of democratic participation and accountability, is neither grounded in theory nor in evidence.

f ***Lack of competition fosters collusive practices.*** It has been argued that in environments with weak or less developed private sectors, as found in many developing countries, lack of competition at the local level fosters corruption in public-private sector interface as third party oversight is missing in such an environment. A national database on benchmarking could limit such opportunities for corruption as local residents would be better informed about costs of comparable operations in other jurisdictions.

Table 14.3 attempts to capture the impact of the multitude of negative influences of decentralization on the incidence of corruption at various decision points. These negative influences dominate in the absence of representative democracy and competitive market pressures typically found in rural feudal dominated local governments. They are typically found also in urban areas when a few dominant developers build special patronage relationships with local council members.

Table 14.4 attempts to draw the implications of these negative influences for corruption in individual sectors. Patron-client relationships immune from public scrutiny are the major sources of various forms of corruption.

The promise of decentralized provision of infrastructure in limiting opportunities for corruption

Decentralization's ability to curtail corruption opportunities has been commonly based on the potential for greater accountability when the decision making is closer to the people. This line of thought is supported from the following perspectives:

a ***Competition among local governments*** for mobile factors of production reinforces the accountability culture. Such enhanced accountability has the potential to reduce corruption (Weingast, 1995; Arikan, 2004).

b ***Exit and voice mechanisms at the local level.*** There is a general agreement in the literature that localization can open up greater opportunities for voice and choice thereby making the public sector more responsive and accountable to citizens-voters. Furthermore, due to regional heterogeneity of political preferences localization may reduce the range of potential capture by a unique nationally dominant party.

c ***Higher levels of information.*** Seabright (1996) argues that accountability is always better at the local level, since local citizens who are better informed about government performance can vote these governments out of office. Under centralization people vote for parties or candidates partly on the basis of performance in other regions and partly on issues of national interest. As a result accountability is defused and potential for corruption increases. Bardhan and Mookherjee (2001) also argue that decentralization in developing countries promotes cost-effectiveness and reduces corruption, owing to the superior access of local governments to information on local costs and needs.

d ***Lower expected gains from corruption but greater probability of detection and punishment.*** Administrative decentralization causes a loss in control to

Table 14.3 Perils of decentralized provision of infrastructure at various decision points

Decision point	*Impact of decentralization on the incidence of corruption*	*Impact by type of corruption*
AT APPRAISAL/PLANNING STAGE		
Legislative framework	In rural areas where feudal or industrial elites may dominate local councils local government may serve the interests of elite to the neglect of its services to rural residents at large	Enhanced opportunities for grand corruption through state capture
Policy making	Rural councils dominated by elites can impose policy framework to suit special interest groups and bribe payers	Enhanced executive capture, grand corruption
Regulation	Greater possibility of having zoning to favor developer interests in exchange for political finance and bribes and regulatory framework tailored to favor special interest groups	Enhanced executive capture, grand corruption
Planning and budgeting	Greater opportunities for rezoning and selection of projects based upon bribes and other benefits received	Enhanced executive capture, grand corruption
AT PROJECT FINANCING STAGE		
External financing	Higher costs of externally financed projects. Donors favor PPPs especially with foreign participation. Kickbacks in return for favorable terms.	Enhanced executive capture, grand corruption, most developing countries
Bond financing	No impact	Negligible incidence of corruption
Grant financing	Some pork barrel grants as quid pro quo for political finance still possible	Some grand corruption by financing pork projects as bridge to nowhere in Alaska, most countries
Tax financing	Little impact	

AT IMPLEMENTATION STAGE		
Public-private partnerships	Collusion among public managers and private providers to give favorable terms to private participants in return for a bribe commonly practiced in energy and road projects, re-negotiation of contracts during and after execution	Grand corruption persists when transparency and competitive pressures are lacking
Program and project management	Little perverse impact	
Public procurement	Kickbacks, rigged bidding and tendering still possible. Mechanisms: intermediary collusion, consulting fees, false services, overpayment, payment to a front company, collusion among competitors. Procurement cycle: registration, manipulating specifications, insider info, quality reduction, clearance from inspectors, expediting payments.	Grand corruption could be enhanced in the short run
Construction	Use of low quality materials, theft of materials, false prices	Mostly grand corruption, most developing countries
AT OPERATION STAGE		
Operations and maintenance	False reporting still possible	Mostly grand corruption, most developing countries
User charges	Theft and free ridership feasible	Petty corruption could go up in the short run
Public access	Isolated incidences of delays or denial of access still possible	Some petty corruption
AT EX-POST EVALUATION STAGE		
Evaluation	Biased favorable evaluation	Patronage—most countries

Source: Author’s perspectives.

Table 14.4 Enhanced vulnerability to corruption introduced by decentralized provision of infrastructure in various sectors

Water and sanitation	Favoritism in selection of contractors, bid rigging, bribes for connections, meter tampering, conflict of interest with officials involved in private provision, collusion with companies offering bottled water or tanker provision
Roads, bridges and mass transit	Favoritism in selection of contractors, some false procurement and maintenance expenditures, and false certification of quality of construction still possible
Electricity	*Public utilities*: equipment purchase and repair mark ups, patronage appointments, defective meters, meter tampering, theft of electricity by tapping distribution lines with side payments, connections delays, false billing, response to non-payment of bills, false subsidy payments, public sector guarantees for assured demand for supply at above market rates. *Private utilities*: selection, regulatory regime, price hikes, regulators turning blind eye to capital deterioration
Hospitals	False procurement and padding up of construction costs, bribes for admissions and drugs
Schools	False procurement and padding up of construction costs, false enrollments, bribes for admissions
Fitness, sports, and recreation centers	Padding up cost of construction and purchase of equipment

Source: Author's perspectives.

higher levels, thus curbing their incentives to monitor and detect corrupt activities. However, it also lowers the expected gains from corruption as, following decentralization, the number of individuals who are in charge of a single decision is reduced. It is then more likely that corrupt agents are called to bear the consequences of their actions. This line of thought complements those put forward by Carbonara (1999), who concludes that decentralization, although creating agency problems inside an organization, can help in controlling corruption; and Wildasin (1995), who argues that local officials with limited powers have little scope to engage in grand corruption.

e ***Reduced corruption due to reduction in information asymmetry between politicians and bureaucrats.*** Ahlin (2000) has argued that deconcentration has the potential to increase corruption, whereas political decentralization has the potential to contain it due to interjurisdictional competition. This may result from a reduction in the information asymmetry between bureaucrats and the politicians that appoint them vis-à-vis a politically centralized systems. Crook and Manor (2000) examined the process of political decentralization in India (Karnatka state), Bangladesh, Côte d'Ivoire, and Ghana and find that such decentralization leads to enhanced transparency. With this enhanced transparency, ordinary citizens become better aware of government's successes and failures and they may perceive the government institutions more corrupt than the perception they had before. They observed that in Karnatka, India, political decentralization substantially reduced the amount of public funds diverted by powerful individuals. However, since citizens were not aware of these diversions, they concluded that corruption had increased. Crook and Manor, based upon evidence from Karnatka, conclude that political decentralization reduces grand theft but increases petty corruption in the short run but in the long run both may go down. Olowu (1993) also finds political centralization as a root cause of endemic corruption in Africa. Fiszbein (1997), based upon a review of political decentralization in Colombia, concludes that competition for political office opened the door for responsible and innovative leadership that in turn became the driving force behind capacity building, improved service delivery, and reduced corruption at the local level.

f *Improved local accountability with administrative decentralization reduces corruption.* A few studies show that administrative decentralization reduces corruption. Wade (1997) finds that over-centralized top-down management accompanied by weak communication and monitoring systems contributes to corruption and poor delivery performance for canal irrigation in India. Kuncoro (2000) finds that with administrative decentralization in Indonesia, firms relocated to areas with lower bribes.

g ***Local fiscal autonomy improves economic management and reduces corruption.*** Huther and Shah (1998) using international cross-section and time series data find that fiscal decentralization is associated with enhanced quality of governance as measured by citizen participation, political and bureaucratic accountability, social justice, improved economic management, and reduced corruption. Arikan (2004) reconfirms the same result. De Mello and Barenstein (2001), based upon cross-country data, conclude that tax decentralization is positively associated with improved quality of governance. Fisman and Gatti (2002) find a negative relation between fiscal decentralization and corruption. Gurgur and Shah (2002) is the only study providing a comprehensive theoretical and empirical framework on the root causes of corruption. They identify major drivers of corruption in order to isolate the effect of decentralization. In a sample of industrial and non-industrial countries, lack of service orientation in the public sector, weak democratic institutions, economic isolation (closed economy), colonial past, internal bureaucratic controls, and centralized decision making are identified as the major causes of corruption. For a non-industrial countries sample, drivers for corruption are lack of service orientation in the public sector, weak democratic institutions, and closed economy. Decentralization reduces corruption but has a greater negative impact on corruption in unitary countries than in federal countries. They conclude that decentralization is confirmed to support greater accountability in the public sector and reduced corruption.

h ***Lower transactions costs for citizens to hold the government to account.*** Decentralization brings greater clarity in division of responsibilities and services that are delivered locally; citizens' transactions costs to hold the government to account are significantly reduced as they have better information on service delivery performance and costs as well as redress opportunities and mechanisms.

i ***Greater transparency.*** Local government operations are by their nature more transparent due to greater local knowledge. In the USA, this transparency is further enhanced by output based budgeting and reporting adopted by most local governments voluntarily to build citizens' trust. In such an environment collusive practices are well recognized by citizens thereby curtailing corrupt practices.

Table 14.5 captures the combined impact of the confluence of factors mentioned above to limit opportunities for corruption while enhancing potential for detection and prosecution at various points in public decision making. The table shows that decentralization will have some positive influence on curtailing corruption at almost all decision points. However, decentralization offers some promising entry points for having a major impact on reducing corruption. The first major entry point is public hearings on zoning. This process offers residents an opportunity to learn the reasons behind rezoning and interest groups involved. The second and probably the most important entry point in curtailing corruption is the public procurement process. The transparency and integrity of this process will significantly curtail the incidence of corruption. The incidence of corruption also depends upon the nature and source of infrastructure finance available to local governments. If financing is no concern as in oil rich countries, incidence of corruption may be higher as the local governments no longer have to seek approval of additional financing or justify such expenses to the local electorate. The incidence of corruption is accentuated by having non-elected local governments as in the Middle East. Local governments that finance infrastructure projects from own sources are likely to have a greater integrity of the entire project cycle due to active involvement of the electorate in ensuring that their tax dollars are put to best use. Thus citizen activism and openness of the democratic processes plays a critical role in curtailing the impact of corruption.

Table 14.6 embodies the influence of decentralized institutions on combating corruption to develop an aggregate view of these influences at the sector level. The table highlights potential positive influences of government closeness to the people on the integrity of provision of infrastructure at the local level. The table shows that while decentralization limits opportunities for corruption especially grand corruption, the overall positive impact may be less observable for fitness, sports, and recreation centers. This is because the non-standard nature of these projects makes benchmarking of costs more difficult as compared to standard infrastructure projects such as roads and bridges.

In all, a small yet growing body of theoretical and empirical literature confirms that localization offers significant potential in bringing greater accountability and responsiveness to the public sector at the local level and reducing the incidence of grand corruption. While most of this literature is focused on decentralized provision of all services (aggregate local expenditures), their conclusion would apply in equal force to infrastructure as infrastructure provision dominates local government expenditures.

The evidence

While a growing number of empirical studies have examined the relationship between decentralization and corruption, only a handful of these studies have examined the specific impact of decentralized provision of infrastructure. De Sousa-Santos (1998) discovered that sectoral allocation of spending improved with participatory budgeting in Porto Alegre, Brazil. Isham and Kahkonen (1999) observed improvements in water services in Central Java, Indonesia with local community management. A World Bank study (2004) found improvement in a few local government areas in decentralized provision of water and sanitation services. A study of local government procurement in the Philippines revealed that (see Tapales, 2001, p. 21):

> contractors admit to paying mayors of the towns where they have projects, because, they say, the officials can delay the work by withholding necessary permits or harassing the workers. Municipal mayors get seven percent while the barangay [village] captain is given three percent. The heads of implementing agencies—usually the district, municipal or city engineer—get about 10 percent.

Table 14.5 Potential of decentralization in curtailing corruption at various decision points

Decision point	*Impact of decentralization on the incidence of corruption*	*Impact by the type of corruption*
AT APPRAISAL/PLANNING STAGE		
Legislative framework	In urban areas with greater citizens engagement, lobbying influences and perks and privileges in exchange for legislative favors are constrained	Opportunities for grand corruption are curtailed due to smaller projects and greater transparency. State capture rare in urban areas.
Policy making	Policy framework to suit special interest groups and bribe payers stunted due to adversarial citizen watch groups	Executive capture and grand corruption is reduced in most countries
Regulation	Extortion over licensing is eliminated	Executive capture and grand corruption is reduced in most countries
Planning and budgeting	Competitive providers limit rezoning and selection of projects based upon bribes received	Executive capture, grand corruption is reduced in most countries
AT PROJECT FINANCING STAGE		
External financing	No positive impact	Executive capture, grand corruption, most developing countries
Bond financing	Little opportunity for corruption in bond financing as it is only done for major metropolitan areas with central oversight	Incidence of corruption is minimal
Grant financing	Competitive inter-jurisdictional pressures typically result in transparent formula driven grant financing limiting funds for pork barrel grants as quid pro quo for political finance	Grand corruption opportunities are constrained
Tax financing	Greater transparency in local tax policy and administration limits elite capture	Grand corruption though tax expenditures and financing of projects preferred by elites is curtailed

AT IMPLEMENTATION STAGE		
Public-private partnerships	Little impact on public officials' and private managers' collusive practices due to complex contractual relationship not easily understood by residents/voters	Little impact on opportunities for grand corruption in most countries
Program and project management	Greater transparency in decentralized provision largely eliminates potential for ghost projects, ghost employees, phantom expenditures	Opportunities for grand corruption are greatly constrained
Public procurement	Potential for kickbacks, rigged bidding and tendering is greatly reduced.	Opportunities for grand corruption reduced in most countries
Construction	Benchmarking limits opportunities for padding costs	Grand corruption is curtailed
AT OPERATION STAGE		
Operations and maintenance	False reporting, ghost workers constrained due to citizen feedback loops	Opportunities for grand corruption curtailed in most developing countries
User charges	Little impact	Little impact on petty corruption
Public access	Some positive impact on delay or denial of access due to timely recourse and lower transactions costs for citizens to hold corrupt officials to account	Petty corruption reduced
AT EX-POST EVALUATION STAGE		
Evaluation	Independent evaluations and citizen-based monitoring and evaluation lead to fair evaluations	Patronage curtailed

Source: Author's perspectives.

Table 14.6 Promise of decentralization in reducing vulnerability to corruption observed in provision of infrastructure in various sectors

Water and sanitation	Diminished potential for land acquisition at above market rate due to wider local knowledge of land values, lower potential for compromising quality due to improved citizen feedback loops
Roads, bridges, and mass transit	Diminished potential for land acquisition at above market prices, diminished opportunities for false procurement and maintenance expenditures, constrained opportunities for false certification of quality of construction
Electricity	*Public utilities*: diminished potential land acquisition at above market rates and acquiring the rights of way, and false subsidy payments and public sector guarantees for assured demand for supply at above market rates *Private utilities:* reduced potential for corruption in the regulatory regime due to greater citizen oversight
Hospitals	Eliminates opportunity for ghost hospitals
Schools	Eliminates opportunities for ghost schools
Fitness, sports, and recreation centers	Little impact on padding up costs

Source: Author's perspectives.

A study of canal irrigation in India attributed corruption to centralization of management (Wade, 1997).

A World Bank study (World Development Report, 1994) compared results under centralized vs. decentralized maintenance of roads and found that countries with decentralized maintenance had better roads (Figure 14.2). This finding indirectly implies that with centralized provision there were greater leakage of public funds through mismanagement, inefficiency, waste, and corruption.

Empirical work on the impact of decentralization on the incidence of corruption is seriously hampered by a lack of reliable data especially on the incidence of corruption. The two most widely used sources are Transparency International's Corruption Perception Indexes (CPIs) and Worldwide Governance Indicators (WGIs) published by the World Bank. Both measures are seriously flawed and indefensible as they make false comparisons across countries for any year and over time and for tracking any country over time.[2] The underlying databases they use simply do not permit such rankings and comparisons as different sources of survey data and questions with weights that vary over time for each country and across countries are used (see Arndt, 2008a 2008b and Ivanyna and Shah, 2011b for a critique and illustration of this point using data sources and weights used by both CPI and WGI indicators and Ivanyna and Shah, 2011a for an illustration of an alternate methodology). Professor Joel Slemrod, University of Michigan, has aptly remarked in another context but his saying applies equally well here, "Whatever we have learned is false and whatever we know is half truth. We really do not know what we do know or do not know." Moreover, these measures are simply not

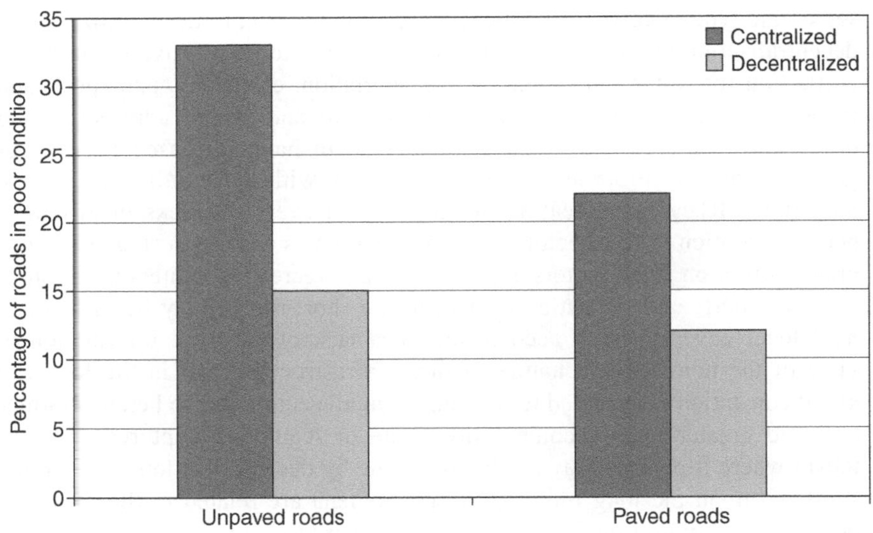

Figure 14.2 Countries with decentralized road maintenance have better roads (source: World Bank, 1994, p. 75).

available at subnational levels. What is needed is a worldwide survey using a uniform questionnaire and employing a stratified random sampling approach in each country to seek an aggregate view of local perceptions on the incidence of corruption. Ivanyna and Shah (2011a, 2011b, 2014) take a first small step in this direction as well as developing subnational indicators. There is also a need for a rigorous case study work in this area. In recent years, the University of Gotenburg and the World Bank has taken small steps to improve our knowledge on quality of governance at subnational levels.[3]

Overall impact of decentralized provision of infrastructure on corruption—by sector and by type of corruption: some tentative conclusions

An earlier section demonstrated that empirical work on the impact of decentralized provision of infrastructure is scant. A handful of studies available indicate the overall positive influence of decentralization on the integrity of public infrastructure provision. Given the paucity of evidence, one cannot, however, reach any conclusive view on this issue. Conceptual literature on the subject, is, however, vast and yet equally inconclusive. While the dominant theme in this literature again is the positive influence of decentralization in curtailing corruption, it cannot serve as the basis for reaching any definitive conclusions. In fact there is some wisdom in not reaching any conclusive view as the incidence is case dependent. Much depends upon the history, culture, organization, and public and private sector environment of each case study. Recognizing this important proviso, Table 14.7 presents a stylized conjectural view of the overall impact of decentralized provision of infrastructure on the sector and type of corruption. The short run (SR) impact of decentralization of decentralization on petty corruption is conjectured to be positive in curtailing corruption for water and sanitation, transportation, electricity, and sports and recreation centers but petty bribes for hospital and school admissions and drugs may continue and could be perceived to have increased in view of greater access to information and transparency with decentralization. In the long run (LR), greater local accountability and oversight kicks in to reduce petty corruption in all sectors. Decentralization is also expected to reduce grant corruption in all sectors except sports and recreation centers in the short run. For sports and recreation centers in the short run, it may be difficult to hold local government to account due to a lack of adequate information in view of the non-standard nature of these infrastructures but in the long run grand corruption is expected to be reduced in all sectors due to better information and greater local accountability. State or regulatory captures or clientelism where it persists may not be overcome by decentralization either in the short run or in the long run as these phenomena are related to the nature of political and cultural institutions and may be hard to overcome without fundamental political finance and land reforms. And the latter reforms may be blocked by powerful local elites.

Table 14.7 Overall impact of decentralization on curtailing corruption in infrastructure in developing countries

Sector	*Type of corruption*							
	Petty		*Grand*		*State or regulatory capture*		*Clientelism*	
	SR	*LR*	*SR*	*LR*	*SR*	*LR*	*SR*	*LR*
Water and sanitation	+	+	+	+	–	–	–	–
Roads, bridges, mass transit	+	+	+	+	–	–	–	–
Electricity—public	+	+	+	+	–	–	–	–
Electricity—private	+	+	+	+	–	–	–	–
Hospitals	–	+	+	+	–	–	–	–
Schools	–	+	+	+	–	–	–	–
Fitness, sports, and recreation centers	+	+	–	+	–	–	–	–
OVERALL	?	+	+	+	–	–	–	–

Source: Author's perspectives.

Ensuring integrity of decentralized provision of public infrastructure: the way forward

The decentralized provision of infrastructure holds the promise of curtailing corruption provided there is no elite capture, strong institutions of accountability in governance, results based governance culture, and an educated and empowered citizenry. These ideal conditions are absent to varying degrees in most countries. In view of this, one has to tailor institutional design for integrity to individual country and locality conditions. In the following, we provide a stylized view of such policies based on the initial state of public governance in the country.

As a starting point, one has to consider unbundling infrastructure services for market competition. By isolating first the natural monopoly segments of the sector, one can examine a range of market alternatives for unbundling the rest of infrastructure provision. This includes regulatory framework that encourages: (a) competition for substitutes; (b) competition for infrastructure markets; (c) competition for the right to supply the entire market through leases and concessions; (d) privatization of some monopolies to reap efficiency gains; and (e) having national and regional databases to provide a benchmark on similar operations.

Beyond that one has to apply a "corruption opportunity test" (Khan, 2008) to each case of government intervention by asking,

1 Is the culture of government organization and environment conducive to corruption?
2 What is the probability that applicable laws, rules, regulations, procedures, instructions, or practices could be misused or bypassed by corrupt intentions?
3 Are there controls in place that would forestall a corrupt person from indulging in corruption by abuse of authority or misuse of discretion or misinterpretation or disregard of rules?

Answers to the above questions will help in developing location specific safeguards in ensuring integrity of public financing or provision of infrastructure. In dealing with various forms of corruption in infrastructure provision, policy and institutional response will vary according to local circumstances. Table 14.8 provides a stylized view of such responses in two polar cases of countries and localities with good and poor governance. The table stresses the importance of more fundamental policy and institutional reforms in the case of poor governance and mostly direct focus on detection and punishment of corruption in the case of good governance.

Table 14.9 presents options for improving governance of individual sectors to ensure incorruptible governance. The table emphasizes creating an incentive cum accountability regime to ensure that all stakeholders advance public interest. This is best done by introducing a bottom line for government where no bottom line exists, introducing competition to improve voice and exit options for citizens, and strengthening citizens' oversight of all providers and sunshine provisions to ensure that government and private providers are subjected to continuous scrutiny. These practices are expected to improve management of infrastructure provisions and its responsiveness to citizens' needs and preferences as well accountability of providers to residents. Such incentives and accountability regime is expected to improve efficiency, equity, and integrity of public provision of infrastructure.

Having a broader local public finance management framework that is focused on incorruptible, responsible, and accountable governance at the local level can also help in safeguarding against malfeasance and corruption. This framework emphasizes fiscal transparency, a framework for fiscal discipline, output based central-local financing, output based budgeting and activity based costing, people empowerment, competitive financing and provision with voice and exit options, contractual rather than life-long local service appointments, output based performance contracts and external audits (see Shah and Shah, 2006 for details on the institutional framework for FAIR [fair, accountable, incorruptible and responsive] governance).

In short the success of decentralized provision of infrastructure with integrity strongly rests on having an open local government with a citizen based accountability framework that is reinforced by results based higher level financing. Once there is at least a fair level of institutional framework that supports such local governance, then there are some promising entry points such as open process of zoning or a framework for integrity in procurement and results based management that have the significant potential to curtail corruption at the local level.

Concluding remarks

During the past three decades, a large number of countries have introduced reforms to decentralize public decision making. Such reforms have proved controversial. Critics of these reforms argue that decentralized provision of

Table 14.8 Ensuring integrity of decentralized provision of public infrastructure: options

Type of corruption	*Existing state of governance in national and local jurisdictions*	
	Good	*Poor*
Legislative capture	Political finance reforms	Establish rule of law, strengthen institutions of accountability in governance, land reforms, citizen empowerment, media independence
Executive capture	Separation of legislative and executive powers, citizen empowerment	Transparency in governance, anti-monopoly and pro-competition legal framework, results based accountability
Grand corruption at various decision points	Transparency requirements; investigations and prosecution	Managing for results human resource framework. Transparency rules. Police, justice reforms. Output based budgeting and activity based accounting, benchmarking. Results based and competitive financing of all providers. Text messaging to a complaints bureau, prosecution, punitive sanctions on conviction.
Grand corruption in public procurement	Investigations and prosecution	PFM reforms, corruption opportunity test framework for procurement, transparency, competitive open bidding, independent tender evaluation, simplification of tender document, smaller size contracts, benchmarking requirements, severe sanctions for non-compliance
Grand corruption in public-private partnerships	Transparency provisions for contracts. Managerial accountability for safeguarding public interest. Prohibition on renegotiating contracts during or post implementation. Investigations and prosecution.	Facilitating private sector development and enhancement of competition to provide public services. Transparent and open contracts subject to legislative ratification, public scrutiny and examination, benchmarking requirements. Investigations and prosecution.
Administrative corruption and theft in public distribution	Investigations and prosecution	Rights based approach to public services. Greater voice and exit options. Transparency, open management information system, mopping operations.
Conflict of interest by employees	Oversight and sanctions by peers	Citizen complaints bureaus, peer based sanctions

Source: Author's perspectives.

Table 14.9 Ensuring integrity of decentralized provision of public infrastructure: options for sectoral reforms in developing countries

Sector	*Policies for incorruptible management*
Water and sanitation	Commercialized public authority, concessions and lease, local community, user group oversight, transparency requirements
Roads, bridges, and mass transit	Commercialized public authority, concession or lease with tolls, rural roads by community self-help or user groups, user group oversight, transparency of financial and service delivery reports
Electricity—public utilities	Commercialization of public utilities with explicit contractual mandates, and citizen oversight boards, transparency requirements
Electricity—private utilities	Regulatory oversight on capital and maintenance, price regulation, citizens' oversight board, transparency requirements
Hospitals	Competitive financing of public and private hospitals to foster competition. Commercialization of public hospitals with autonomous citizen management and oversight boards, transparency requirements.
Schools	Competitive financing of public and private schools to foster competition. Parents' committees oversight on all aspects of school operations, transparency requirements
Fitness, sports, and recreation centers	Citizens' oversight boards, referenda provisions for approving new projects, transparency requirements

Source: Author's perspectives.

infrastructure enhances vulnerability to corruption. Proponents of these reforms counter that corruption arises from lack of people empowerment and decentralization by bringing decision making closer to the people, shining sunlight on government operations, and empowering people to hold government to account. Thereby it offers the potential for combating corruption in the long run. They further state that decentralized provision of infrastructure holds a great promise in upgrading infrastructure to underserviced especially rural areas with local self-government. In theory such decentralization is also expected to improve integrity of such operations especially in the event of local financing. These debates, nevertheless, remain unsettled as empirical evidence on the impact of decentralization on infrastructure provision is scant or non-existent. Empirical work is hampered by a lack of reliable data on the incidence of corruption. This chapter has presented conceptual underpinnings of the impact of decentralized provision of infrastructure on the incidence of corruption and synthesized scant available empirical evidence to make a case for further empirical research to document the real world experiences to update our current state of knowledge on this subject. Much work lies ahead to limit our wide zone of ignorance in this area.

Notes

1 The author is grateful to Jonas Frank, Jorge Martínez, Timothy Goodspeed, François Vaillancourt, and conference participants for helpful comments on earlier drafts of this chapter presented at the Infrastructure and Decentralization Conferences organized by the Georgia State University and the World Bank at the Stone Mountain National Park, Atlanta, GA, September 25–27, 2012 and at the World Bank, Washington, DC, February 13–14, 2013.

2 The editors of this volume take strong exception to the author's view and state,

> While the first statement is correct—we have a gap of data on governance at the subnational level, the second statement would need to be re-considered since it seems to suggest that the authors of the indicators are suggesting to use the data to evaluate governance over time at the subnational level. The authors of the WGI have over and over warned researchers and practitioners about the limit of their data, meaning of a cross country/cross-year comparison and the objective of their data: to simply highlight that there is a governance issue in a country. The WGI also seem to be the only indicators that provide the margin of errors and the sources of the data. The authors also emphasize that the WGI are not actionable and cannot help to design a policy reform. They are simply a starting point to mobilize public opinion around this issue (as the CPI).
>
> (May 13, 2013 email to the author, p. 3)

See also Galtung (2006).

3 See University of Goteburg, www.qog.pol.gu.se/ and the 2012 Business Environment and Enterprise Performance Survey (BEEPS) focus on quality of governance at the subnational level. The BEEPS is a joint initiative of the European Bank for Reconstruction and Development (EBRD) and the World Bank Group. http://beeps.prognoz.com/beeps/Home.ashx and World Bank Governance Diagnostic Surveys (http://go.worldbank.org/Q7ZUV9AG).

Bibliography

Abed, George T. and Hamid Davoodi (2000). "Corruption, Structural Reforms, and Economic Performance in the Transition Economies." International Monetary Fund Working Paper 00/132.

Acconcia, Antonio, Marcello D'Amato, and Riccardo Martina (2003). "Corruption and Tax Evasion with Competitive Bribes." CSEF Working Papers 112 (University of Salerno, Italy: Centre for Studies in Economics and Finance).

Ades, Alberto and Rafael Di Tella (1997). "National Champions and Corruption: Some Unpleasant Interventionist Arithmetic." *The Economic Journal*, 107: 1023–1042.

Advig, Jens Chr. and Karl O. Moene (1990). "How Corruption May Corrupt." *Journal of Economic Behavior and Organization*, 13: 63–76.

Ahlin, Christian (2000). "Corruption, Aggregate Economic Activity and Political Organization." University of Chicago, unpublished.

Ahlin, Christian (2001). "Corruption: Political Determinants and Macroeconomic Effects." Working Paper 01-W26 (Vanderbilt University: Department of Economics).

Andrews, Matthew and Anwar Shah (2005). "Towards Citizen-centered Local Budgets in Developing Countries." In Anwar Shah, ed., *Public Expenditure Analysis*. Washington, DC: World Bank.

Arikan, Gulsun (2004). "Fiscal Decentralization: A Remedy for Corruption?" *International Tax and Public Finance*, 11: 175–1995.

Arndt, C. (2008a). "The Politics of Governance Ratings." *International Public Management Journal*, 11: 275–297.

Arndt, C. (2008b). "What Is Happening to the Level of Corruption in ECA and the World." PowerPoint presentation at the World Bank, Washington, DC (mimeo).

Bac, Mehmet and Parimal K. Bag (1998). "Corruption, Collusion and Implementation: A Hierarchial Design." Mimeo, University of Liverpool.

Banfield, Edward (1975). "Corruption as Feature of Government Organization." *Journal of Law and Economics*, 18: 587–695.

Bardhan, Pranab (1997). "Corruption and Development: A Review of Issues." *Journal of Economic Literature*, 35 (September): 1320–1346.

Bardhan, Pranab and Dilip Mookherjee (2000). "Decentralizing Anti-Poverty Program Delivery in Developing Countries." Working Paper (University of California, Berkeley).

Bardhan, Pranab and Dilip Mookherjee (2001). "Corruption and Decentralization of Infrastructure Delivery in Developing Countries." Working Paper (Boston University).

Batley, R. (1999). "The Role of Government in Adjusting Economies: An Overview of Findings." International Development Department, University of Birmingham, Birmingham, Alabama.

Becker, Gary Stanley (1968). "Crime and Punishment: An Economic Approach." *Journal of Political Economy*, 76(2): 169–217.

Becker, Gary Stanley (1983). "A Theory of Competition Among Pressure Groups for Political Influence." *Quarterly Journal of Economics*, XCVII(3): 371–400.

Becker, Gary Stanley and George Stigler (1974). "Law Enforcement, Malfeasance and the Compensation of Enforcers." *Journal of Legal Studies*, 3: 1–19.

Blanchard, Olivier and Andrei Shleifer (2000). "Federalism With and Without Political Centralization: China versus Russia." National Bureau of Economic Research Working Paper 7616 (March): 1–14.

Boadway, Robin and Anwar Shah (2009). *Fiscal Federalism: Principles and the Practice of Multiorder Governance*. New York and London: Cambridge University Press.

Carbonara, Emanuela (1999). "Bureaucracy, Corruption and Decentralization." University of Bologna, Italy, Department of Economics Working Paper 342/33.

Carillo, Juan D. (2000). "Corruption in Hierarchies." *Annales D'economie et de Statistique/Institut National de la Statistique et des Etudes Economiques* (France), 59: 37–61.

Chand, Sheetal K. and Karl O. Moene (1997). "Controlling Fiscal Corruption." International Monetary Fund Working Paper WP/97/100.

Crook, Richard and James Manor (2000). "Democratic Decentralization." OED Working Paper Series 11, Summer (Washington, DC: World Bank).

De Mello, Luis and Matias Barenstein (2001). "Fiscal Decentralization and Governance—A Cross-Country Analysis." IMF Working Paper 01/71.

De Sousa-Santos, B. (1998). "Participatory Budgeting in Porto Alegre: Toward a Redistributive Democracy," *Politics & Society*, 26(4): 461–510.

Ehlermann-Cache, Nicola (2007). *Bribery in Public Procurement: Methods, Actors and Counter-Measures*. Paris: OECD.

Fan, C., Lin, C., and Treisman, D. (2009). "Political Decentralization and Corruption: Evidence from Around the World."' *Journal of Public Economics*, 93: 14–34.

Fisman, Raymond and Roberta Gatti (2002). "Decentralization and Corruption: Evidence Across Countries." *Journal of Public Economics*, 83: 325–345.

Fiszbein Ariel (1997). "Emergence of Local Capacity: Lessons from Colombia." *World Development*, 25(7): 1029–1043.

Flatters, Frank and W. Bentley Macleod (1995). "Administrative Corruption and Taxation." *International Tax and Public Finance*, 2: 397–417.

Galtung, F. (2006). "Measuring the Immeasurable: Boundaries and Functions of (Macro) Corruption Indices." In C.A. Sampford, C.A. Shacklock, C. Connors, and F. Galtung, eds., *Measuring Corruption*. Hampshire, UK and Vermont, US: Ashgate, 101–130.

Grossman, Gene M. and Elhanan Helpman (1994). "Protection for Sale." *American Economic Review*, 84(4): 833–850.

Gulati, Mohinder and M.Y. Rao (2007). "Corruption in the Electricity Sector: A Pervasive Scourge." In J.E. Campos and S. Pradhan, eds. *The Many Facets of Corruption*. Washington, DC: World Bank, 115–158.

Gupta, Sanjeev, Hamid Davoodi, and Rosa Alosno-Terme (1998). "Does Corruption Affect Income Inequality and Poverty?" International Monetary Fund Working Paper 98/76.

Gupta, Sanjeev, Hamid Davoodi, and Erwin Tiongson (2000). "Corruption and the Provision of Health Care and Education Services." International Monetary Fund Working Paper 00/116.

Gurgur, Tugrul and Anwar Shah (2002). "Localization and Corruption: Panacea or Pandora's Box?" In Ehtisham Ahmad and Vito Tanzi, eds., *Managing Fiscal Decentralization*. London and New York: Routledge, 46–67.

Guriev, Sergei (1999). "A Theory of Informative Red Tape with an Application to Top-level Corruption." Unpublished paper from the Web.

Guriev, Sergei (2003). "Red Tape and Corruption." Discussion Paper, Centre for Economic Policy Research (UK) 3972: 1–27.

Huther, Jeff and Anwar Shah (1998). "Applying a Simple Measure of Good Governance to the Debate on Fiscal Decentralization." Policy Research Working Paper 1894 (Washington, DC: World Bank).

Huther, Jeff and Anwar Shah (2000). "Anti-corruption Policies and Programs: A Framework for Evaluation." Policy Research Working Paper 2501 (Washington, DC: World Bank).

Isham, Jonathan and Satu Kahkonen (1999). "What Determines the Effectiveness of Community-Based Water Projects? Evidence from Central Java, Indonesia on Demand Responsiveness, Service Rules, and Social Capital." Social Capital Initiative Working Paper Series 14 (Washington, DC: World Bank).

Ivanyna, Maksym and Anwar Shah (2011a). "Decentralization and Corruption: New Cross-country Evidence." *Environment and Planning C: Government and Policy*, 29(2): 344–362.

Ivanyna, Maksym and Anwar Shah (2011b). "Citizen-centric Governance Indicators: Measuring and Monitoring Governance by Listening to the People." *CESifo Forum*, 1/2011: 59–71.

Ivanyna, Maksym and Anwar Shah (2014). "How Close Is Your Government to Its People? Worldwide Indicators on Localization and Decentralization." *Economics: The Open-Access, Open-Assessment E-Journal*, 8(2014-3): 1–61. http://dx.doi.org/10.5018/economics-ejournal.ja.2014-3.

Khan, Akram (2008). "Auditing for Combatting Corruption in Procurement." World Bank Institute, unpublished.

Klitgaard, Robert E. (1988). *Controlling Corruption.* Berkeley: University of California Press.

Klitgaard, Robert E. (1991). "Gifts and Bribes." In Richard Zeckhauser, ed., *Strategy and Choice*. Cambridge, MA: MIT Press.

Kuncoro, Ari (2000). "The Impact of Licensing Decentralization on Firm Location Choice: The Case of Indonesia." Faculty of Economics, University of Indonesia, unpublished.

Lambsdorff, Johann (1999). "Corruption in Empirical Research—A Review." Transparency International, unpublished.

Mauro, Paolo (1995). "Corruption and Growth." *Quarterly Journal of Economics*, 110(3): 681–713.

Olowu, Dele (1993). "Roots and Remedies of Government Corruption in Africa." *Corruption and Reform*, 7(3): 227–236.

Paterson, William and Pinki Chaudhuri (2007). "Making Inroads on Corruption in the Transport Sector through Control and Prevention." In J.E. Campos and S. Pradha, eds., *The Many Facets of Corruption.* Washington, DC: World Bank, 159–190.

Plummer, Janelle and Piers Cross (2007). "Tackling Corruption in the Water and Sanitation Sector in Africa: Starting the Dialogue." In J.E. Campos and S. Pradhan, eds., *The Many Facets of Corruption.* Washington, DC: World Bank, 221–264.

Prud'homme, Remy (1994). "On the Dangers of Decentralization." World Bank Policy Research Working Paper 1252 (Washington, DC: World Bank).

Rose-Ackerman, S. (1975). "The Economics of Corruption." *Journal of Public Economics*, 4(February): 187–203.

Rose-Ackerman, S. (1978). *Corruption: A Study in Political Economy*. New York, San Francisco, London: Academic Press.

Scharpf, Fritz W. (1997). *Games Real Actors Play—Actor-Centered Institutionalism in Policy Research*. Boulder, CO: Westview.

Seabright, Paul (1996). "Accountability and Decentralization in Government: An Incomplete Contracts Model." *European Economic Review*, 40(1): 61–89.

Shah, Anwar (1998). "Balance, Accountability, and Responsiveness: Lessons about Decentralization." World Bank Policy Research Working Paper Series 2021, December.

Shah, Anwar (1999). "Governing for Results in a Globalized and Localized World." *The Pakistan Development Review*, 38(4), Part I: 385–431.

Shah, Anwar (2005). "On Getting the Giant to Kneel: Approaches to a Change in the Bureaucratic Culture." In Anwar Shah, ed., *Fiscal Management*. Public Sector Governance and Accountability Series. Washington, DC: World Bank, 211–229.

Shah, Anwar (2006). "Decentralized Governance and Corruption." In E. Ahmad and G. Brosio eds., *Handbook of Fiscal Federalism*. Cheltenham, UK: Edward Elgar, 478–498.

Shah, Anwar (2012). "The 18th Constitutional Amendment: Glue or Solvent for Nation Building and Citizenship in Pakistan." *The Lahore Journal of Economics*, 17(September): 387–424.

Shah, Anwar and Mark Schacter (2004). "Combating Corruption. Look Before You Leap." *Finance and Development*, 41(4, December): 40–43 (Washington, DC: IMF).

Shah, Anwar and Sana Shah (2006). "The New Vision of Local Governance and the Evolving Role of Local Governments." In Anwar Shah, ed., *Local Governance in Developing Countries*. Washington, DC: World Bank.

Shah, Anwar, Theresa Thompson, and Heng-fu Zou (2004). "The Impact of Decentralization on Service Delivery, Corruption, Fiscal Management and Growth in Developing and Emerging Market Economies: A Synthesis of Empirical Evidence." *CESifo Dice Report. A Quarterly Journal for Institutional Comparisons*, 2(Spring): 10–14.

Shleifer, Andrei and Robert W. Vishny (1993). "Corruption." *Quarterly Journal of Economics*, 108: 599–617.

Tanzi, Vito (1995). "Fiscal Federalism and Decentralization: A Review of Some Efficiency and Macroeconomic Aspects." *Annual World Bank Conference on Development Economics*, 295–316.

Tanzi, Vito and Hamid Davoodi (1997). "Corruption, Public Investment, and Growth." International Monetary Fund Working Paper 97/139.

Tapales, Prosperpina (2001). "An Evaluation of Anti-corruption Programs in Philippines." World Bank Operations Evaluation Department, Washington, DC.

Tirole, Jean (1986). "Hierarchies and Bureaucracies: On the Role of Collusion in Organizations." *Journal of Law Economics and Organization*, 2: 181–214.

Tirole, Jean and Jean-Jacques Laffont (1988). "Politics of Government Decision-making: A Theory of Regulatory Capture." Working Paper (Department of Economics, Massachusetts Institute of Technology) 506: 1–48.

Tomaszewska, Ewa and Anwar Shah (2000). "Phantom Hospitals, Ghost Schools and Roads to Nowhere: The Impact of Corruption on Public Service Delivery Performance in Developing Countries." Working Paper Operations Evaluation Department, World Bank.

Treisman, Daniel S. (1999). *After the Deluge: Regional Crises and Political Consolidation in Russia.* Ann Arbor, MI: University of Michigan Press.

Treisman, Daniel S. (2000). "The Causes of Corruption: A Cross National Study." *Journal of Public Economics*, 76(3): 399–457.

Treisman, Daniel S. and Andrei Shleifer (2002). "A Normal Country." National Bureau of Economic Research Working Paper 10057, October: 1–46.

Van Rijckeghem, Caroline and Beatrice Weder (2001). "Bureaucratic Corruption and the Rate of Temptation: Do Low Wages in Civil Service Cause Corruption?" *Journal of Development Economics*, 65: 307–331.

Von Maravic, Patrick (2003). "How to Analyse Corruption in the Context of Public Management Reform?" Paper presented at the first meeting of the Study Group on Ethics and Integrity of Governance EGPA Conference, September. Portugal.

Wade, Robert (1997). "How Infrastructure Agencies Motivate Staff: Canal Irrigation in India and the Republic of Korea." In Ashoka Mody, ed., *Infrastructure Strategies in East Asia*. Washington, DC: World Bank.

Waller, Christopher J., Thierry A. Verdier, and Roy Gardner (2002). "Corruption: Top-Down or Bottom-Up." *Economic Inquiry*, 40(4): 688–703.

Weingast, Barry (1995). "The Economic Role of Political Institutions: Market Preserving Federalism and Economic Growth." *Journal of Law, Economics, and Organization*, 11: 1–31.

Wildasin, David (1995). "Comment on 'Fiscal Federalism and Decentralization'." *Annual World Bank Conference on Development Economics*, 323–328.

World Bank (1994). *World Development Report, 1994*. Washington, DC: World Bank.

World Bank (2004). *Mainstreaming Anti-Corruption Activities in World Bank Assistance—A Review of Progress Since 1997*. Washington, DC: World Bank.

Index

Page numbers in *italics* denote tables, those in **bold** denote figures.